Exam 70-516: TS: Accessing Data with Microsoft .NET Framework 4

OBJECTIVE	CHAPTER	LESSON
MODELING DATA (20%)		
Map entities and relationships by using the Entity Data Model.	Chapter 6	Lesson 1
Map entities and relationships by using LINQ to SQL.	Chapter 4	Lesson 1
Create and customize entity objects.	Chapter 6	Lesson 1
Connect a POCO model to the entity Framework.	Chapter 6	Lesson 1
Create the database from the Entity Framework model.	Chapter 6	Lesson 1
Create model-defined functions.	Chapter 6	Lesson 1
MANAGING CONNECTIONS AND CONTEXT (18%)		
Configure connection strings and providers.	Chapter 2	Lesson 1
Create and manage a data connection.	Chapter 2	Lesson 1
Secure a connection.	Chapter 2	Lesson 1
Manage the DataContext and ObjectContext.	Chapter 4 Chapter 6	Lesson 1 Lesson 1
Implement eager loading.	Chapter 4 Chapter 6 Chapter 7	Lesson 1 Lesson 1 Lesson 1
Cache data.	Chapter 1 Chapter 4	Lesson 1 Lesson 3
Configure ADO.NET Data Services.	Chapter 7	Lesson 1, 2
QUERYING DATA (22%)		
Execute a SQL query.	Chapter 2	Lesson 2
Create a LINQ query.	Chapter 3 Chapter 4	Lesson 1, 2 Lesson 2
Create an Entity SQL (ESQL) query.	Chapter 3 Chapter 4 Chapter 6	Lesson 1, 2 Lesson 2 Lesson 2
Handle special data types.	Chapter 1 Chapter 2	Lesson 2 Lesson 2
Query XML.	Chapter 5	Lesson 1, 2, 3
Query data by using ADO.NET Data Services.	Chapter 7	Lesson 1
MANIPULATING DATA (22%)		
Create, update, or delete data by using SQL statements.		
Create, update, or delete data by using DataContext.		
Create, update, or delete data by using ObjectContext.		
Manage transactions.	Chapter 2 Chapter 6	Lesson 3 Lesson 2
Create disconnected objects.	Chapter 1	Lesson 1

Exam Objectives   The exam objectives listed here are current as of this book's publication date. Exam objectives are subject to change at any time without prior notice and at Microsoft's sole discretion. Please visit the Microsoft Learning Web site for the most current listing of exam objectives: http://www.microsoft.com/learning/en/us/Exam .aspx?ID=70-516.

MCTS Self-Paced Training Kit (Exam 70-516): Accessing Data with Microsoft® .NET Framework 4

Glenn Johnson

PUBLISHED BY
Microsoft Press
A Division of Microsoft Corporation
One Microsoft Way
Redmond, Washington 98052-6399

Library of Congress Control Number: 2011927329
ISBN: 978-0-7356-2739-0

Printed and bound in the United States of America.

Microsoft Press books are available through booksellers and distributors worldwide. If you need support related to this book, email Microsoft Press Book Support at mspinput@microsoft.com. Please tell us what you think of this book at http://www.microsoft.com/learning/booksurvey.

Acquisitions Editor: Martin Del Re
Developmental Editor: Karen Szall
Project Editor: Valerie Woolley
Editorial Production: nSight, Inc.
Technical Reviewer: Christophe Nasarre; Technical Review services provided by Content Master, a member of CM Group, Ltd.
Copyeditor: Kerin Forsyth
Indexer: Luci Haskins
Cover: Twist Creative • Seattle

Contents at a Glance

Contents

What do you think of this book? We want to hear from you!

Microsoft is interested in hearing your feedback so we can continually improve our
books and learning resources for you. To participate in a brief online survey, please visit:

      www.microsoft.com/learning/booksurvey/

What do you think of this book? We want to hear from you!

Microsoft is interested in hearing your feedback so we can continually improve our books and learning resources for you. To participate in a brief online survey, please visit:

www.microsoft.com/learning/booksurvey/

Introduction

This training kit is designed for developers who write or support applications that access data written in C# or Visual Basic using Visual Studio 2010 and the Microsoft .NET Framework 4.0 and who also plan to take the Microsoft Certified Technology Specialist (MCTS) exam 70-516. Before you begin using this kit, you must have a solid foundation-level understanding of Microsoft C# or Microsoft Visual Basic and be familiar with Visual Studio 2010.

The material covered in this training kit and on exam 70-516 relates to the data access technologies in ADO.NET 4.0 with Visual Studio 2010. The topics in this training kit cover what you need to know for the exam as described on the Skills Measured tab for the exam, which is available at *http://www.microsoft.com/learning/en/us/exam.aspx?ID=70-516&locale=en -us#tab2*.

By using this training kit, you will learn how to do the following:

- Work with the ADO.NET disconnected classes
- Work with the ADO.NET connection classes
- Write and execute LINQ queries
- Implement LINQ to SQL classes
- Implement LINQ to XML in your applications
- Implement the ADO.NET Entity Framework in your applications
- Create and Implement WCF Data Service applications
- Monitor and Collect ADO.NET performance data
- Synchronize offline data
- Deploy Data Access applications

Refer to the objective mapping page in the front of this book to see where in the book each exam objective is covered.

System Requirements

The following are the minimum system requirements your computer needs to meet to complete the practice exercises in this book and to run the companion CD. To minimize the time and expense of configuring a physical computer for this training kit, it's recommended, but not required, that you use a virtualized environment, which will allow you to work in a sandboxed environment. This will let you make changes without worrying about your day-to-day environment. Virtualization software is available from Microsoft (Virtual PC, Virtual Server, and Hyper-V) and other suppliers such as VMware (VMware Workstation) and Oracle (VirtualBox).

Hardware Requirements

Your computer should meet the following minimum hardware requirements:

- 2.0 GB of RAM (more is recommended)
- 80 GB of available hard disk space
- DVD-ROM drive
- Internet connectivity

Software Requirements

The following software is required to complete the practice exercises:

- Windows 7. You can download an Evaluation Edition of Windows 7 at the Microsoft Download Center at *http://technet.microsoft.com/en-us/evalcenter/cc442495*.
- SQL Server 2008 Developer Edition is recommended because some labs and sample code use this edition for permanently mounted databases. An Evaluation Edition is available from *http://msdn.microsoft.com/en-us/evalcenter/bb851668.aspx*.
- SQL Server 2008 Express Edition is recommended because some labs and sample code use this edition for User Instance mounted databases. A full release is available from *http://www.microsoft.com/express/Database*.

> **NOTE** **SQL SERVER INSTALLATION**
>
> If you are using a 64-bit OS, you should install 64-bit SQL Server before installing Visual Studio 2010. Visual Studio 2010 includes, and attempts to install, the 32-bit SQL Server 2008 Express Edition.
>
> If you install the 64-bit versions of SQL Server first, the Visual Studio 2010 installer will see that SQL Server Express Edition is already installed and will skip over installing the 32-bit SQL Server 2008 Express Edition.

- Visual Studio 2010. You can download an evaluation edition from *http://msdn.microsoft.com/en-us/evalcenter/default*. Although the labs and code samples were generated using Visual Studio 2010 Premium Edition, you can use the Express Edition of Visual Studio for many of the labs, which is available from *http://www.microsoft.com/express*.

Code Samples

The code samples are provided in Visual C# and Visual Basic. You will find a folder for each chapter that contains CS (C#) and VB (Visual Basic) code. In these folders, you will find the sample code solution and a folder for each lesson that contains the practice code. The Practice Code folder contains Begin and Completed folders, so you can choose to start at the beginning and work through the practice or you can run the completed solution.

Using the CD

A companion CD is included with this training kit. The companion CD contains the following:

- **Practice tests**   You can reinforce your understanding of the topics covered in this training kit by using electronic practice tests that you customize to meet your needs. You can run a practice test that is generated from the pool of Lesson Review questions in this book. Alternatively, you can practice for the 70-516 certification exam by using tests created from a pool of over 200 realistic exam questions, which give you many practice exams to ensure that you are prepared.

- **Code Samples**   All of the Visual Basic and C# code you see in the book you will also find on the CD.

- **An eBook**   An electronic version (eBook) of this book is included for when you do not want to carry the printed book with you.

> **Companion Content for Digital Book Readers:** If you bought a digital edition of this book, you can enjoy select content from the print edition's companion CD.
> Visit *http://go.microsoft.com/fwlink/?Linkid=216910* to get your downloadable content. This content is always up-to-date and available to all readers.

How to Install the Practice Tests

To install the practice test software from the companion CD to your hard disk, perform the following steps:

1. Insert the companion CD into your CD drive and accept the license agreement. A CD menu appears.

> **NOTE** **IF THE CD MENU DOES NOT APPEAR**
>
> If the CD menu or the license agreement does not appear, AutoRun might be disabled on your computer. Refer to the Readme.txt file on the CD for alternate installation instructions.

2. Click Practice Tests and follow the instructions on the screen.

How to Use the Practice Tests

To start the practice test software, follow these steps:

1. Click Start, All Programs, and then select Microsoft Press Training Kit Exam Prep.

   A window appears that shows all the Microsoft Press training kit exam prep suites installed on your computer.

2. Double-click the lesson review or practice test you want to use.

> **NOTE** **LESSON REVIEWS VS. PRACTICE TESTS**
>
> Select the (70-516): Accessing Data with Microsoft .NET Framework 4 lesson review to use the questions from the "Lesson Review" sections of this book. Select the (70-516): Accessing Data with Microsoft .NET Framework 4 practice test to use a pool of questions similar to those that appear on the 70-516 certification exam.

Lesson Review Options

When you start a lesson review, the Custom Mode dialog box appears so that you can configure your test. You can click OK to accept the defaults, or you can customize the number of questions you want, how the practice test software works, which exam objectives you want the questions to relate to, and whether you want your lesson review to be timed. If you are retaking a test, you can select whether you want to see all the questions again or only the questions you missed or did not answer.

After you click OK, your lesson review starts. The following list explains the main options you have for taking the test:

- To take the test, answer the questions and use the Next and Previous buttons to move from question to question.

- After you answer an individual question, if you want to see which answers are correct—along with an explanation of each correct answer—click Explanation.

- If you prefer to wait until the end of the test to see how you did, answer all the questions and then click Score Test. You will see a summary of the exam objectives you chose and the percentage of questions you got right overall and per objective. You can print a copy of your test, review your answers, or retake the test.

Practice Test Options

When you start a practice test, you choose whether to take the test in Certification Mode, Study Mode, or Custom Mode:

- **Certification Mode**   Closely resembles the experience of taking a certification exam. The test has a set number of questions. It is timed, and you cannot pause and restart the timer.
- **Study Mode**   Creates an untimed test during which you can review the correct answers and the explanations after you answer each question.
- **Custom Mode**   Gives you full control over the test options so that you can customize them as you like.

In all modes, the user interface when you are taking the test is basically the same but with different options enabled or disabled depending on the mode. The main options are discussed in the previous section, "Lesson Review Options."

When you review your answer to an individual practice test question, a "References" section is provided that lists where in the training kit you can find the information that relates to that question and provides links to other sources of information. After you click Test Results to score your entire practice test, you can click the Learning Plan tab to see a list of references for every objective.

How to Uninstall the Practice Tests

To uninstall the practice test software for a training kit, use the Program And Features option in Windows Control Panel.

Acknowledgments

The author's name appears on the cover of a book, but I am only one member of a much larger team. Thanks very much to Valerie Woolley, Christophe Nasarre, and Karen Szall for working with me, being patient with me, and making this a great book. Christophe Nasarre was my technical reviewer, and he was far more committed to the project than any reviewer I've worked with in the past. I certainly could not have completed this book without his help.

Each of these editors contributed significantly to this book and I hope to work with them all in the future.

And a special thanks to Kristy Saunders for writing all of the practice test questions for the practice test located on the CD.

Support & Feedback

The following sections provide information on errata, book support, feedback, and contact information.

Errata

We have made every effort to ensure the accuracy of this book and its companion content. If you do find an error, please report it on our Microsoft Press site at oreilly.com:

1. Go to *http://microsoftpress.oreilly.com*.

2. In the Search box, enter the book's ISBN or title.

3. Select your book from the search results.

4. On your book's catalog page, under the cover image, you will see a list of links.

5. Click View/Submit Errata.

You will find additional information and services for your book on its catalog page. If you need additional support, please send an email message to Microsoft Press Book Support at *mspinput@microsoft.com*.

Please note that product support for Microsoft software is not offered through the addresses above.

We Want to Hear from You

At Microsoft Press, your satisfaction is our top priority, and your feedback our most valuable asset. Please tell us what you think of this book at:

http://www.microsoft.com/learning/booksurvey

The survey is short, and we read every one of your comments and ideas. Thanks in advance for your input!

Stay in Touch

Let us keep the conversation going! We are on Twitter: *http://twitter.com/MicrosoftPress*.

Preparing for the Exam

Microsoft certification exams are a great way to build your resume and let the world know about your level of expertise. Certification exams validate your on-the-job experience and product knowledge. While there is no substitution for on-the-job experience, preparation through study and hands-on practice can help you prepare for the exam. We recommend that you round out your exam preparation plan by using a combination of available study materials and courses. For example, you might use the Training kit and another study guide for your "at home" preparation, and take a Microsoft Official Curriculum course for the class-room experience. Choose the combination that you think works best for you.

Note that this Training Kit is based on publicly available information about the exam and the author's experience. To safeguard the integrity of the exam, authors do not have access to the live exam.

Microsoft
CERTIFIED
Technology
Specialist

CHAPTER 1

ADO.NET Disconnected Classes

D ata access is an important factor in most applications, and ADO.NET provides the means of accessing data in your applications. This chapter describes the ADO.NET disconnected data classes; the next chapter describes the ADO.NET connected data classes.

This chapter is about foundation building. These classes have been in the Microsoft .NET Framework since its first release but are not obsolete. You should know the classes covered in this chapter to feel comfortable using many of the newer features covered in the chapters that follow.

> **IMPORTANT**
>
> ### Have you read page xix?
>
> It contains valuable information regarding the skills you need to pass the exam.

Exam objectives in this chapter:

- Create disconnected objects.
- Cache data.
- Handle special data types.

Lessons in this chapter:

Before You Begin

To complete this book, you must have some understanding of Microsoft C# or Microsoft Visual Basic. This chapter requires the hardware and software listed at the beginning of this book.

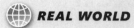 **REAL WORLD**

Glenn Johnson

When trying to solve a problem, my first goal is to find the solution. The solution is not always elegant or pretty, but the goal is to find a solution, right? After that, the next step is to refactor your code and look for better performance. This book covers some aspects of ADO.NET performance, but a good book that delivers more in-depth information regarding ADO.NET performance tuning is *Improving .NET Application Performance and Scalability*, and you can download it for free. Chapter 12, "Improving ADO.NET Performance," focuses on ADO.NET performance.

Many of the classes in the future chapters use the classes in this chapter. What do those higher-level classes offer that these classes don't offer? They offer ease of programming for you, the developer. Generally, adding layers to provide ease of programming can reduce performance, but the amount of performance degradation will vary based on the code you write. If your code runs fast enough, it makes sense to take advantage of the ease-of-programming benefit.

Obtaining the best performance in scenarios in which maximum performance is more important than ease of programming might mean using the classes covered in this chapter.

Lesson 1: Working with the *DataTable* and *DataSet* Classes

The ADO.NET class hierarchy can be split into two categories: connected and disconnected objects. Figure 1-1 shows the principal connected and disconnected classes. This lesson describes the two primary disconnected classes, *DataTable* and *DataSet*, as shown in the diagram, and many other classes of this category as well. The disconnected classes are covered in detail because these classes can be used without ever creating a connection to a data store.

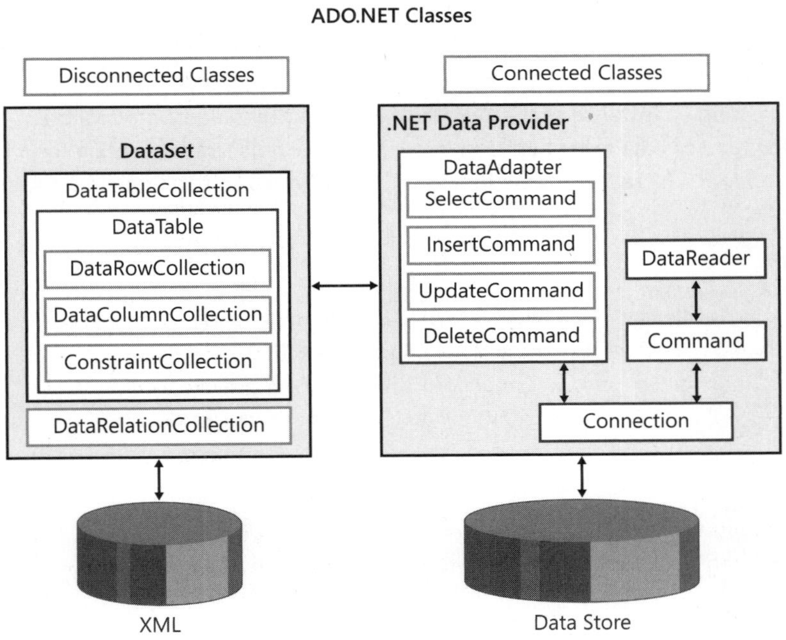

ADO.NET Classes

Disconnected Classes	Connected Classes

DataSet
- DataTableCollection
  - DataTable
    - DataRowCollection
    - DataColumnCollection
    - ConstraintCollection
- DataRelationCollection

.NET Data Provider
- DataAdapter
  - SelectCommand
  - InsertCommand
  - UpdateCommand
  - DeleteCommand
- DataReader
- Command
- Connection

XML   Data Store

FIGURE 1-1 The common ADO.NET classes are shown here.

The classes shown in Figure 1-1 are the primary ADO.NET classes and are important for successfully implementing an ADO.NET solution. With each new version of ADO.NET, changes have been made to these primary classes to improve functionality and performance.

The disconnected data access classes you instantiate in your applications are implemented in the System.Data.dll assembly from the .NET Framework. These classes are in the *System.Data* namespace. Because you must use the *DataTable* object when you're using disconnected classes, this chapter begins by covering the *DataTable* object and the objects with which the *DataTable* object works closely. The *DataSet* object is covered in detail later on.

> **After this lesson, you will be able to:**
> - Use a *DataTable* object to hold tabular rows of data.
> - Use a *DataSet* class to hold *DataTable* objects that are related.
> - Implement a *DataView* object to provide sorting and filtering of a data table.
>
> **Estimated lesson time: 45 minutes**

The *DataTable* Class

A *DataTable* object represents tabular data as an in-memory, tabular cache of rows, columns, and constraints. You typically use the *DataTable* class to perform any disconnected data access. You start by creating an instance of the *DataTable* class, and then add *DataColumn* objects that define the type of data to be held and insert *DataRow* objects that contain the data. The following code, which creates a table for storing cars information, demonstrates the creation of a data table:

Sample of Visual Basic Code

```
'Create the DataTable named "Cars"
Dim cars As New DataTable("Cars")
```

Sample of C# Code

```
//Create the DataTable named "Cars"
DataTable cars = new DataTable ("Cars");
```

> **NOTE   ON THE COMPANION MEDIA USING THE SAMPLE CODE**
> The sample code is included in the accompanying media. Many of these are small samples that couldn't run by themselves, so they have been joined to create a sample project that does run. Look for the projects that end with "SampleCode." For example, these samples are in the DisconnectedClassesSampleCode project of the DisconnectedClassesSampleCodeSolution solution.

This code creates an empty data table for which the *TableName* property is set to *Cars*. You can use the *TableName* property to access this data table when it is in a *DataTable* collection (as detailed later in this chapter in the section titled "Using a *DataSet* Object to Coordinate Work between Data Tables").

Adding *DataColumn* Objects to Create a Schema

The *DataTable* object is not useful until it has a schema, which is created by adding *DataColumn* objects and setting the constraints of each column. Constraints help maintain data integrity by limiting the data that can be placed in the column. The following code adds *DataColumn* objects to the *cars DataTable* object:

Sample of Visual Basic Code

```vb
'Add the DataColumn object using all properties
Dim vin As New DataColumn("Vin")
vin.DataType = GetType(String)
vin.MaxLength = 23
vin.Unique = True
vin.AllowDBNull = False
vin.Caption = "VIN"
cars.Columns.Add(vin)

'Add the DataColumn using defaults
Dim make As New DataColumn("Make") 'default is String
make.MaxLength = 35 'default is -1
make.AllowDBNull = False 'default is True
cars.Columns.Add(make)
Dim year As New DataColumn("Year",GetType(Integer))
year.AllowDBNull = False
cars.Columns.Add(year)

'Derived column using expression
Dim yearMake As New DataColumn("Year and Make")
yearMake.MaxLength = 70
yearMake.Expression = "Year + ' ' + Make"
cars.Columns.Add(yearMake)
```

Sample of C# Code

```csharp
//Add the DataColumn using all properties
DataColumn vin = new DataColumn("Vin");
vin.DataType = typeof(string);
vin.MaxLength = 23;
vin.Unique = true;
vin.AllowDBNull = false;
vin.Caption = "VIN";
cars.Columns.Add(vin);

//Add the DataColumn using defaults
DataColumn make = new DataColumn("Make");
make.MaxLength = 35;
make.AllowDBNull = false;
cars.Columns.Add(make);
DataColumn year = new DataColumn("Year", typeof(int));
year.AllowDBNull = false;
cars.Columns.Add(year);

//Derived column using expression
DataColumn yearMake = new DataColumn("Year and Make");
yearMake.DataType = typeof(string);
yearMake.MaxLength = 70;
yearMake.Expression = "Year + ' ' + Make";
cars.Columns.Add(yearMake);
```

The *DataColumn* object has several constructor overloads, so you can choose the overload that accepts the parameter values that fit best to your scenario. In this example, the constructor of each *DataColumn* object expects the column's name. The *DataType* property is set to *String* for all the *DataColumn* objects except the year, which is set to an *Integer* (int) that limits this column to be numeric data. The *MaxLength* property limits the length of the string data. Setting the *Unique* property to *true* creates an index to prevent duplication of entries. The *AllowDBNull* property is set to *false* to ensure that the column is populated with data. If *AllowDBNull* is set to *true*, you are not obligated to populate the column with data, and the column's default value is *DBNull*, which is stored to the database as a null value. The *Caption* property isn't really a constraint; it's a string that holds the column heading when this *DataTable* object is used with graphic data grid controls. The *yearMake DataColumn* object demonstrates the creation of a calculated column. In this particular case, the string expression defines a formula to concatenate the value of the Year column with a space and the value of the Make column to shape what this column contains. Adding a calculated column is especially beneficial when data is available but not in the correct format.

Some of the *DataColumn* objects were created without specifying values for all the properties. The default values for the common properties are shown in Table 1-1.

TABLE 1-1 *DataColumn* Defaults

DATACOLUMN PROPERTY	DEFAULT VALUE	
DataType	Default is the *string* type.	
MaxLength	Default is –1, which means that no check for maximum length is performed.	
Unique	Default is *false*, which allows the existence of duplicate values.	
AllowDBNull	Default is *true*, which means the data column does not need to have a value. If no value is provided, its value will be *DBNull*.	
Caption	Default is the *ColumnName* property value passed in the constructor.	

Creating Primary Key Columns

The primary key of a *DataTable* object consists of a column or columns that make up a unique identity for each data row. In the previous example, the vehicle identification number (VIN) is considered as a unique key from which data for a given car can be retrieved. In other situations, getting a unique key might require combining two or more fields. For example, a sales order might contain sales order details that comprise the items being purchased on the sales order. The primary key for each of the sales order detail rows might be the combination of the order number and the line number. The *PrimaryKey* property must be set to an array of *DataColumn* objects to accommodate composite (multiple) keys. The following code shows how to set the *PrimaryKey* property for the *cars DataTable* object:

Sample of Visual Basic Code

```
'Set the Primary Key
cars.PrimaryKey = new DataColumn(){vin}
```

Sample of C# Code

```
//Set the Primary Key
cars.PrimaryKey = new DataColumn[] {vin};
```

Using Automatic Numbering for the Primary Key Column

You can also designate a column in your table as an auto-increment column. This column will be automatically populated with a number that will be the primary key. To set up an auto-increment column, set the *AutoIncrement* property of your data column to *true*. After that, you set *AutoIncrementSeed* to the value of the first number you want and set *AutoIncrementStep* to the value you want to increment by each time a new row is added.

Auto incrementing is found in many database products, but how can it possibly work properly in your application? The connected classes haven't been covered yet, but you can imagine that at some point you might want to send your new data to a back-end database. If your application supplies the auto-increment values, what will the database do, especially if it receives duplicate values from different client applications?

The answer is that these auto-increment values are never sent to the database because the auto-increment column in the database table will provide a value when the new row is added. After each new row is added, the back-end database table generates a new auto-increment number, and then your application will query the database to get the newly created number. Your application will then update its primary key number to the values that came from the database. This means that all foreign key references will need to be updated as well.

So what happens if you add new rows in your application to generate auto-increment values of 1 to 100 and then send these rows back to the database table, and the table already has 10 rows? When the first row is sent from your application, it has an auto-increment value of 1. The new auto-increment number created in the database will be 11. Your application queries for the 11 and tries to change the 1 to an 11 but throws an exception because 11 is already in your data table.

To solve this problem, set *AutoIncrementSeed* to -1 and set *AutoIncrementStep* to -1. This will cause negative numbers to be generated; they won't conflict with the values coming from the database because the database doesn't generate negative numbers.

EXAM TIP

For the exam, don't forget that setting *AutoIncementStep* and *AutoIncrementSeed* to -1 will ensure that your numbers don't conflict with values retrieved from the database server, because you will be questioned on this.

Creating *DataRow* Objects to Hold Data

After the *DataTable* object is created and contains *DataColumn* objects, you can populate the *DataTable* object by adding *DataRow* objects. A *DataRow* object can be created only in the context of a data table because the data row must conform to constraints of the *DataTable* object's columns.

Adding Data to the Data Table

The *DataTable* object contains a *Rows* property of type *DataRowCollection* that stores *DataRow* objects. There are several ways to insert data into this collection.

DataRowCollection has an *Add* method that accepts a *DataRow* object. The *Add* method is also overloaded to accept an array of objects instead of a *DataRow* object. If an array of objects is passed to the *Add* method, the array object count must match the exact number of *DataColumn* objects the data table has.

The *Add* method works well when you are creating a new row of data. If you want to import *DataRow* objects that have been modified, you can use the *ImportDataRow* method, which will preserve the original state and all other settings. The *DataTable* class also provides several overloaded *Load* methods, which can be used to update existing *DataRow* objects or load new *DataRow* objects. The data table requires the *PrimaryKey* property to be set so the *DataTable* object can locate the rows to be updated. If you need to generate a data row, you can use the *LoadDataRow* method, which accepts an array of objects, and a *LoadOption* enumeration value. The possible values for the *LoadOption* enumeration are shown in Table 1-2.

TABLE 1-2 *LoadOption* Enumeration Members

LOADOPTION MEMBER	DESCRIPTION
OverwriteChanges	Overwrites the original data row version and the current data row version and changes the row state to *Unchanged*. New rows will have a row state of *Unchanged* as well.
PreserveChanges (default)	Overwrites the original data row version but does not modify the current data row version. New rows will have a row state of *Unchanged* as well.
Upsert	Overwrites the current data row version but does not modify the original data row version. New rows will have a row state of *Added*. Rows that had a row state of *Unchanged* will have a row state of *Unchanged* if the current data row version is the same as the original data row version, but if they are different, the row state will be *Modified*.

The following code sample demonstrates the methods of creating and adding data into the *cars DataTable* object:

Sample of Visual Basic Code

```vb
'Add new DataRow by creating the DataRow first
Dim newCar As DataRow = cars.NewRow()
newCar ("Vin") = "123456789ABCD "
newCar ("Make") = "Ford"
newCar ("Year") = 2002
cars.Rows.Add(newCar)

'Add new DataRow by simply passing the values
cars.Rows.Add("987654321XYZ", "Buick", 2001)

'Load DataRow, replacing existing contents, if existing
cars.LoadDataRow(new object() _
   { "987654321XYZ", "Jeep", 2002 },LoadOption.OverwriteChanges)
```

Sample of C# Code

```csharp
//Add New DataRow by creating the DataRow first
DataRow newCar = cars.NewRow();
newCar ["Vin"] = "123456789ABCD";
newCar ["Make"] = "Ford";
newCar ["Year"] = 2002;
cars.Rows.Add(newCar);

//Add New DataRow by simply adding the values
cars.Rows.Add("987654321XYZ", "Buick", 2001);

//Load DataRow, replacing existing contents, if existing
cars.LoadDataRow(new object[]
   { "987654321XYZ", "Jeep", 2002 },LoadOption.OverwriteChanges);
```

This code adds new *DataRow* objects to the *cars* data table. The first example explicitly creates a new data row, using the *NewRow* method on the *cars* data table. The next example adds a new data row by simply passing the values to the *cars.Rows.Add* method. Remember that nothing has been permanently stored to a database. Sending updates to a database will be covered in Chapter 2, "ADO.NET Connected Classes."

Viewing the State of the *DataRow* Object by Using *DataRowState*

DataRow goes through a series of states that can be viewed and filtered at any time. You can retrieve the current state of a data row from its *RowState* property, which returns a value from the *DataRowState* enumeration. The *DataRowState* values are described in Table 1-3.

TABLE 1-3 *RowState* Enumeration Members

ROWSTATE VALUE	DESCRIPTION
Detached	The data row has been created but not added to a data table.
Added	The data row has been created and added to the data table.

Unchanged	The data row has not changed since the last call to the *AcceptChanges* method. When the *AcceptChanges* method is called, the data row changes to this state.
Modified	The data row has been modified since the last time the *AcceptChanges* method was called. Adding a row and modifying the row will keep the row in the *Added* state. The row changes to the *Modified* state only if it was previously in the *Unchanged* state.
Deleted	An attached data row is deleted by using the *Delete* method of the *DataRow* object or when it is removed from its table by calling the *DataTable.DeleteRow* method.

You can read the *RowState* property of the data row at any time to determine the current state of the data row. Figure 1-2 shows the *RowState* transitions at different times in the *DataRow* object's life.

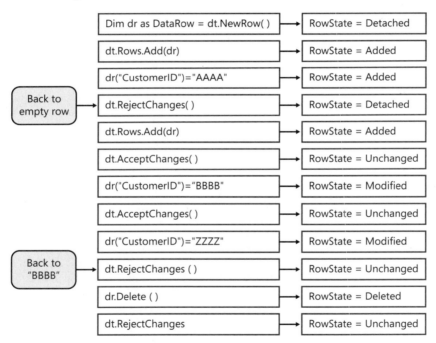

FIGURE 1-2 *RowState* is shown as it changes during the lifetime of a *DataRow* object.

After the CustomerID is assigned a value of "AAAA," the row state does not change to *Modified*. The row state is still *Added* because *RowState* is an indicator of an action required to send an update of this data to the database. The fact that "AAAA" was placed into the CustomerID is not as important as the fact that the data row needs to be added to the database.

Managing Multiple Copies of Data by Using *DataRowVersion*

The *DataTable* object can hold up to three versions of the data row data: *Original*, *Current*, and *Proposed*. When the data row is loaded, it contains a single copy of the data. At that time, only the *Current* version exists. You might be wondering why you have only the *Current* version and not the *Original* version: *Original* implies that the row has been modified. Executing the *BeginEdit* method will place the row into edit mode, and changes to the data are placed into a second instance of the data, called the *Proposed* version. When the *EndEdit* method is executed, the *Current* version becomes the *Original* version, the *Proposed* version becomes the *Current* version, and the *Proposed* version no longer exists. After *EndEdit* is called, there are two instances of the *DataRow* data, the *Original* and the *Current* versions. If the *BeginEdit* method is called again, the *Current* version of the data is copied to a third instance of the data, which is the *Proposed* version. Once again, calling the *EndEdit* method causes the *Proposed* version to become the *Current* version, and the *Proposed* version no longer exists. Notice that the *Original* version is not changed.

When you retrieve data from the data row on a per-column basis, the data row version can be specified as well. Table 1-4 describes the *DataRowVersion* enumeration members you can specify.

TABLE 1-4 *DataRowVersion* Enumeration Members

DATAROWVERSION VALUE	DESCRIPTION
Current	The current value of the data row, even after changes have been made. This version exists in all situations except when *DataRowState* is *Deleted*. If *DataRowState* is *Deleted*, an exception is thrown.
Default	If *DataRowState* is *Added* or *Modified*, the default version is *Current*. If *DataRowState* is *Deleted*, an exception is thrown. If the *BeginEdit* method has been executed, the version is *Proposed*.
Original	The value that was originally loaded into the data row or the value at the time the last *AcceptChanges* method was executed. This version is not populated until *DataRowState* becomes *Modified*, *Unchanged*, or *Deleted*. If *DataRowState* is *Deleted*, this information is retrievable. If *DataRowState* is *Added*, a *VersionNotFound* exception is thrown.
Proposed	The value at the time of editing the data row. If *DataRowState* is *Deleted*, an exception is thrown. If the *BeginEdit* method has not been explicitly executed, or if *BeginEdit* was implicitly executed by editing a detached data row (an orphaned *DataRow* object that has not been added to a *DataTable* object), a *VersionNotFound* exception is thrown.

DataRow contains the *HasVersion* method that can query for the existence of a particular data row version. Using the *HasVersion* method, you can check for the existence of a data row version before attempting to retrieve it. The following code sample demonstrates how to retrieve a string, using *RowState* and *DataRowVersion*. This sample uses the *HasVersion* method to figure out the data row version information without throwing an exception.

Sample of Visual Basic Code

```vb
Private Function GetDataRowInfo( _
ByVal row As DataRow, ByVal columnName As String) _
    As String

    Dim retVal As String = String.Format( _
        "RowState: {0}" + vbCrLf

    Dim versionString As String
    For Each versionString In [Enum].GetNames(GetType(DataRowVersion))
    Dim version As DataRowVersion = _
        CType([Enum].Parse(GetType(DataRowVersion), versionString), _
        DataRowVersion)

    If (row.HasVersion(version)) Then
        retVal += String.Format( _
            "Version: {0} Value: {1}" + vbCrLf, _
            version, row(columnName, version))
    Else
        retVal += String.Format( _
            "Version: {0} does not exist." + VbCrLf, _
            version)
    End If
    Next
    Return retVal
End Function
```

Sample of C# Code

```csharp
private string GetDataRowInfo(DataRow row, string columnName)
{
    string retVal=string.Format(
    "RowState: {0} \r\n",
    row.RowState);

    foreach (string versionString in Enum.GetNames(typeof (DataRowVersion)))
    {
        DataRowVersion version = (
            DataRowVersion)Enum.Parse(
            typeof(DataRowVersion),versionString);

        if (row.HasVersion(version))
        {
            retVal += string.Format(
                "Version: {0} Value: {1} \r\n",
                version, row[columnName, version]);
        }
        else
```

```
    {
        retVal += string.Format(
            "Version: {0} does not exist.\r\n",
            version);
    }
  }
  return retVal;
}
```

Resetting the State by Using the *AcceptChanges* and *RejectChanges* Methods

You can use the *AcceptChanges* method to reset the *DataRow* state to *Unchanged*. This method exists on the *DataRow*, *DataTable*, and *DataSet* objects. (This chapter covers the *DataSet* object later, in the section titled, "Using a *DataSet* Object to Coordinate Work between Data Tables.") In a typical data environment (after data has been loaded), the *DataRow* state of the loaded rows is set to *Added*. Calling *AcceptChanges* on the data table resets the row state of all the *DataRow* objects to *Unchanged*. Next, if you modify the *DataRow* objects, their row state changes to *Modified*. When it is time to save the data, you can easily query the *DataTable* object for its changes by using the *DataTable* object's *GetChanges* method. This method returns a *DataTable* object populated with only the *DataRow* objects that have changed since the last time *AcceptChanges* was executed. Only these changes need to be sent to the data store.

After the changes have been successfully sent to the data store, you must change the state of the *DataRow* objects to *Unchanged*, which essentially indicates that the *DataRow* objects are synchronized with the data store. You use the *AcceptChanges* method for this purpose. Note that executing the *AcceptChanges* method also causes the *DataRow* object's *Current* data row version to be copied to the *DataRow* object's *Original* version.

> **NOTE** **DON'T FORGET TO CALL ACCEPTCHANGES**
>
> Remember that it is important to call the *AcceptChanges* method after you have made a successful update to the database server because the *AcceptChanges* method marks all rows as *Unchanged*. Why? Because the rows are now synchronized with the rows at the database server.

The *RejectChanges* method rolls *DataTable* content back to what it was since its creation or before the last time *AcceptChanges* has been called. Note that both *AcceptChanges* and *RejectChanges* typically reset *RowState* to *Unchanged*, but *RejectChanges* also copies the *DataRow* object's *Original* data row version to the *DataRow* object's *Current* data row version.

Using *SetAdded* and *SetModified* to Change *RowState*

DataRow contains the *SetAdded* and *SetModified* methods, which enable a data row state to be set forcibly to *Added* or *Modified*, respectively. These operations are useful when you want to force a data row to be stored in a data store different from the data store from which the data row was originally loaded. For example, if you loaded a row from one data store, and you want to send that row to a different data store, you execute the *SetAdded* method to make the row look like a new row. In Chapter 2, you learn that the *DataAdapter* object sends changes to the data store. When you connect to the destination data store, the data adapter object sees that your row has an *Added* row state, so the data adapter object executes an insert statement to add the row to the destination data store.

These methods can be executed only on *DataRow* objects whose row state is *Unchanged*. An attempt to execute these methods on a *DataRow* object with a different row state throws the exception called *InvalidOperationException*.

If the *SetAdded* method is executed, the *DataRow* object discards its *Original* data row version because *DataRow* objects that have a row state of *Added* never contain an *Original* data row version.

If the *SetModified* method is executed, the *DataRow* object's *RowState* property is simply changed to *Modified* without modifying the *Original* or *Current* data row version.

Deleting the Data Row, and What About Undeleting?

DataRow contains a *Delete* method with which you can set the row state of the data row to *Deleted*. *DataRow* objects that have a row state of *Deleted* indicate rows that need to be deleted from the data store. When the *DataRow* object is deleted, the *Current* and *Proposed* data row versions are discarded, but the *Original* data row version remains.

Sometimes you need to recover a deleted data row. The *DataRow* object doesn't have an *Undelete* method. However, in some situations, you can use the *RejectChanges* method to roll back to a previous state when the deleted row was still there. Be aware that executing the *RejectChanges* method copies the *Original* data row version to the *Current* data row version. This effectively restores the *DataRow* object to its state at the time the last *AcceptChanges* method was executed, but any subsequent changes that were made to the data prior to deleting have been discarded.

Enumerating the Data Table

It is possible to loop through the rows and columns of the data table by using a *foreach* statement. The following code shows how the rows and columns of a data table can be enumerated.

Sample of Visual Basic Code

```vbnet
Public Sub EnumerateTable(ByVal cars As DataTable)
    'enumerate the data table
    Dim buffer As New System.Text.StringBuilder()
    For Each dc As DataColumn In cars.Columns
        buffer.AppendFormat("{0,15} ", dc.ColumnName)
    Next
    buffer.Append(vbCrLf)
    For Each dr As DataRow In dt.Rows
        If (dr.RowState = DataRowState.Deleted) Then
            buffer.Append("Deleted Row")
```

```
        Else
            For Each dc As DataColumn In cars.Columns
                buffer.AppendFormat("{0,15} ", dr(dc))
            Next
        End If
        buffer.Append(vbCrLf)
    Next
    TextBox1.Text = buffer.ToString()
End Sub
```

Sample of C# Code

```
public void EnumerateTable(DataTable cars)
{
    var buffer = new System.Text.StringBuilder();
    foreach (DataColumn dc in cars.Columns)
    {
        buffer.AppendFormat("{0,15} ", dc.ColumnName);
    }
    buffer.Append("\r\n");
    foreach (DataRow dr in cars.Rows)
    {
        if (dr.RowState == DataRowState.Deleted)
        {
            buffer.Append("Deleted Row");
        }
        else
        {
            foreach (DataColumn dc in cars.Columns)
            {
                buffer.AppendFormat("{0,15} ", dr[dc]);
            }
        }
        buffer.Append("\r\n");
    }
    textBox1.Text = buffer.ToString();
}
```

The code begins by simply collecting the column names to use as a header and places this information in the *StringBuilder* object, called *buffer*. Next, the table rows and columns are enumerated, and all values are placed into the buffer. Code such as this can be used to walk through the rows in a data table and perform an action on all the data. Figure 1-3 shows the output of this code. (The *TextBox* font is set to Courier New to get the columns to line up.)

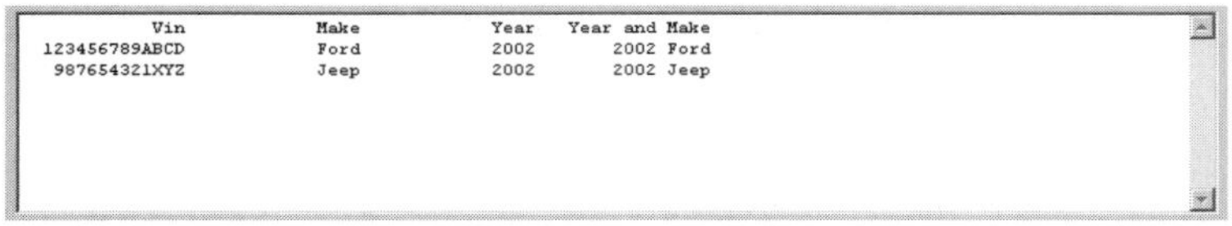

```
           Vin        Make       Year   Year and Make
123456789ABCD          Ford       2002      2002 Ford
987654321XYZ           Jeep       2002      2002 Jeep
```

FIGURE 1-3 Shown here is the output when enumerating the *DataTable* object's columns headers and rows.

Copying and Cloning the Data Table

Sometimes you want to create a full copy of a data table. You can do this by using the *DataTable* object's *Copy* method, which copies the *DataTable* object's schema and data. The following code sample shows how to invoke the *Copy* method.

Sample of Visual Basic Code

```
'copy the table and its data
Dim copy As DataTable = cars.Copy()
```

Sample of C# Code

```
//copy the table and its data
DataTable copy = cars.Copy( );
```

On some occasions, you might need a copy of the *DataTable* schema without data. To copy just the schema without data, you can invoke the *DataTable* object's *Clone* method. This method is commonly used when an empty copy of the data table is required; at a later time, *DataRow* objects can be added. The following code shows the *Clone* method.

Sample of Visual Basic Code

```
'only copy the table, not the data
Dim clone As DataTable = cars.Clone()
```

Sample of C# Code

```
//only copy the table, not the data
DataTable clone = cars.Clone( );
```

Importing *DataRow* Objects into a Data Table

After cloning a data table, you might need to copy certain *DataRow* objects from one data table to another. *DataTable* contains an *ImportRow* method, which you can use to copy a data row from a data table that has the same schema. The *ImportRow* method is useful when the *Current* and *Original* data row version must be maintained. For example, after editing a data table, you might want to copy the changed *DataRow* objects to a different data table but maintain the *Original* and *Current* data row version. The *ImportRow* method on the *DataTable* object will import the *DataRow* objects as long as a data row with the same primary key does not exist. (If a duplicate data row exists, a *ConstraintException* is thrown.) The following code sample shows the process for cloning the data table and then copying a single data row to the cloned copy.

Sample of Visual Basic Code

```
Dim clone as DataTable = cars.Clone( )
'import the row and include all row versions
clone.ImportRow(cars.Rows(0))
```

Sample of C# Code

```
DataTable clone = cars.Clone();
//import the row and include all row versions
clone.ImportRow(cars.Rows[0]);
```

Using *DataView* as a Window into a Data Table

The *DataView* object provides a window into a data table that can be sorted and filtered. A data table can have many *DataView* objects assigned to it, so the data can be viewed in many ways without requiring it to be reread from the database. The *Sort*, *RowFilter*, and *RowStateFilter* properties on the *DataView* object can be combined as needed. You can use the *DataView* object's *AllowDelete*, *AllowEdit*, and *AllowNew* properties to constrain user input.

Internally, the *DataView* object is essentially an index. You can provide a sort definition to sort the index in a certain order, and you can provide a filter to simply filter the index entries.

Ordering Data Using the *Sort* Property

The *Sort* property requires a sort expression. The default order for the sort is ascending, but you can specify ASC or DESC with a comma-separated list of columns to be sorted. The following code sample shows how a data view is created on the *cars* data table with a compound sort on the Make column in ascending order and on the Year column in descending order.

Sample of Visual Basic Code

```
Dim view as new DataView(cars)
view.Sort = "Make ASC, Year DESC"
```

Sample of C# Code

```
DataView view = new DataView(cars);
view.Sort = "Make ASC, Year DESC";
```

Narrowing the Search by Using the *RowFilter* and *RowStateFilter* Properties

A view exposes a *RowFilter* property and a *RowStateFilter* property. The *RowFilter* property is set to a SQL WHERE clause without the word "WHERE". The following code shows a filter on the Make column for cars beginning with the letter B and on the Year column for cars newer than 2003.

Sample of Visual Basic Code

```
Dim view as new DataView(cars)
view.RowFilter = "Make like 'B%' and Year > 2003"
```

Sample of C# Code

```
DataView view = new DataView(cars);
view.RowFilter = "Make like 'B%' and Year > 2003";
```

The *RowStateFilter* property provides a filter that applies on the *RowState* property or on each data row. This filter provides an easy method of retrieving specific versions of rows within the data table. The *RowStateFilter* property requires the use of *DataViewRowState* enumeration values, which are shown in Table 1-5. The *DataViewRowState* enumeration is a bit-flag enumeration, which means you can use the bitwise OR operator (that is, |) to build compound filters. For example, the default *RowState* filter value is set to display multiple states by using | to combine the *Unchanged*, *Added*, and *ModifiedCurrent* enumeration values. Note that this combination is so useful that a dedicated value has been defined in the enumeration: *CurrentRows*.

TABLE 1-5 *DataViewRowState* Enumeration Members

DATAVIEWROWSTATE VALUE	DESCRIPTION
Added	Retrieves the *Current* data row version of *DataRow* objects that have a row state of *Added*.
CurrentRows	Retrieves all *DataRow* objects that have a *Current* data row version. Equivalent to *Added*	*Unchanged*	*ModifiedCurrent*.
Deleted	Retrieves the *Original* data row version of *DataRow* objects that have a row state of *Deleted*.
ModifiedCurrent	Retrieves the *Current* data row version of *DataRow* objects that have a row state of *Modified*.
ModifiedOriginal	Retrieves the *Original* data row version of *DataRow* objects that have a row state of *Modified*.
None	Clears the *RowStateFilter* property, which means that there is no filter and you see all rows.
OriginalRows	Retrieves the *DataRow* objects that have an *Original* data row version.
Unchanged	Retrieves *DataRow* objects that have a row state of *Unchanged*.

The following code sample shows a *RowState* filter used to retrieve only the *DataRow* objects that have a row state of *Deleted*.

Sample of Visual Basic Code

```
Dim view as new DataView(cars)
view.RowFilter = "Make like 'B%' and Year > 2003"
view.RowStateFilter = DataViewRowState.Deleted
```

Sample of C# Code

```
DataView view = new DataView(cars);
view.RowFilter = "Make like 'B%' and Year > 2003";
view.RowStateFilter = DataViewRowState.Deleted;
```

Enumerating the Data View

The procedure for walking through the data view is similar to that for enumerating the data table except that the objects are different. The following code can be used to enumerate the rows and columns of a data view.

```vb
Public Sub EnumerateView(ByVal view As DataView)
    Dim buffer As New System.Text.StringBuilder()
    For Each dc As DataColumn In view.Table.Columns
        buffer.AppendFormat("{0,15} ", dc.ColumnName)
    Next
    buffer.Append(vbCrLf)
    For Each dr As DataRowView In view
        For Each dc As DataColumn In view.Table.Columns
            buffer.AppendFormat("{0,15} ", dr.Row(dc))
        Next
        buffer.Append(vbCrLf)
    Next
    TextBox1.Text = buffer.ToString()
End Sub
```

Sample of C# Code

```csharp
private void EnumerateView(DataView view)
{
    var buffer = new System.Text.StringBuilder();
    foreach (DataColumn dc in view.Table.Columns)
    {
        buffer.AppendFormat("{0,15} ", dc.ColumnName);
    }
    buffer.Append("\r\n");
    foreach (DataRowView dr in view)
    {
        foreach (DataColumn dc in view.Table.Columns)
        {
            buffer.AppendFormat("{0,15} ", dr.Row[dc]);
        }
        buffer.Append("\r\n");
    }
    textBox1.Text = buffer.ToString();
}
```

This code loops over the rows in the view. The data type for the row is *DataRowView* as opposed to *DataRow*, which *DataTable* has. Also, retrieving column information requires you to access the *Table* property that the view has. The results are rendered into a text box.

Exporting a *DataView* Object to a New Data Table

A *DataView* object can be used to export data from one *DataTable* object to another. This can be especially useful when a user-defined set of filters is applied and the user wants to convert the view that is seen into a new data table. Exporting to a new data table is done with the *DataView* object's *ToTable* method, as shown here.

Sample of Visual Basic Code

```vb
'here is the method signature that will be used
'Public Function ToTable(tableName as String, distinct as Boolean, _
'   ParamArray columnNames() as String) as System.Data.DataTable
    Dim export as DataTable = view.ToTable( _
        "MyCarTable", true, "Vin", "Make", "Year")
```

Sample of C# Code

```
//here is the method signature that will be used
//DataTable DataView.ToTable(string tableName,
//   bool distinct, params string[] columnNames)
   DataTable export = view.ToTable(
      "MyCarTable", true, "Vin", "Make", "Year");
```

This code sample exports the data seen through the data view called "view" to a new *DataTable* object named *export*. Note that the name of this table is "MyCarTable". Passing *true* for the *distinct* parameter indicates that only distinct values are kept (which filter out duplicate values). If *false* is used, all values should be shown. The names of the columns to include in the new table are then passed to the method.

Using a *DataSet* Object to Coordinate Work Between Data Tables

DataSet is a memory-based, tabular, relational representation of data and is the primary disconnected data object. Conceptually, think of *DataSet* as an in-memory relational database, but it's simply cached data and doesn't provide any of the transactional properties (atomicity, consistency, isolation, durability) that are essential to today's relational databases. *DataSet* contains a collection of *DataTable* and *DataRelation* objects, as shown in Figure 1-4. The *DataTable* objects can contain unique and foreign key constraints to enforce data integrity. *DataSet* also provides methods for cloning the *DataSet* schema, copying the data set, merging with other *DataSet* objects, and listing changes.

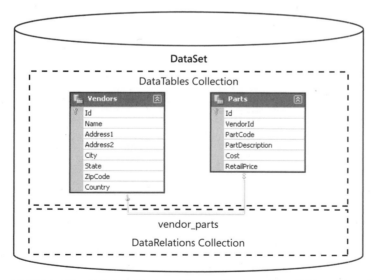

FIGURE 1-4 The *DataSet* object contains a collection of *DataTable* and *DataRelation* objects.

You can create the *DataSet* schema programmatically or by providing an XML schema definition. The following code demonstrates the creation of a simple data set containing a data table for vendors and a data table for parts. The two *DataTable* objects are joined using a *DataRelation* object named *vendors_parts*. (*DataRelation* is discussed in more detail in the next section.)

Sample of Visual Basic Code

```vb
'create vendor dataset
Dim vendorData as new DataSet("VendorData")

Dim vendor as DataTable = vendorData.Tables.Add("Vendors")
vendors.Columns.Add("Id", GetType(Guid))
vendors.Columns.Add("Name", GetType(string))
vendors.Columns.Add("Address1", GetType(string))
vendors.Columns.Add("Address2", GetType(string))
vendors.Columns.Add("City", GetType(string))
vendors.Columns.Add("State", GetType(string))
vendors.Columns.Add("ZipCode", GetType(string))
vendors.Columns.Add("Country", GetType(string))
vendors.PrimaryKey = new DataColumn() { vendors.Columns("Id") }

Dim parts as DataTable = vendorData.Tables.Add("Parts")
parts.Columns.Add("Id", GetType(Guid))
parts.Columns.Add("VendorId", GetType(Guid))
parts.Columns.Add("PartCode", GetType(string))
parts.Columns.Add("PartDescription", GetType(string))
parts.Columns.Add("Cost", GetType(decimal))
parts.Columns.Add("RetailPrice", GetType(decimal))
parts.PrimaryKey = new DataColumn() { parts.Columns("Id") }

vendorData.Relations.Add( _
    "vendors_parts", _
    vendors.Columns("Id"), _
    parts.Columns("VendorId"))
```

Sample of C# Code

```csharp
//create vendor dataset
DataSet vendorData = new DataSet("VendorData");

DataTable vendors = vendorData.Tables.Add("Vendors");
vendors.Columns.Add("Id", typeof(Guid));
vendors.Columns.Add("Name", typeof(string));
vendors.Columns.Add("Address1", typeof(string));
vendors.Columns.Add("Address2", typeof(string));
vendors.Columns.Add("City", typeof(string));
vendors.Columns.Add("State", typeof(string));
vendors.Columns.Add("ZipCode", typeof(string));
vendors.Columns.Add("Country", typeof(string));
vendors.PrimaryKey = new DataColumn[] { vendors.Columns["Id"] };

DataTable part = vendorData.Tables.Add("Parts");
parts.Columns.Add("Id", typeof(Guid));
parts.Columns.Add("VendorId", typeof(Guid));
parts.Columns.Add("PartCode", typeof(string));
parts.Columns.Add("PartDescription", typeof(string));
parts.Columns.Add("Cost", typeof(decimal));
```

```
parts.Columns.Add("RetailPrice", typeof(decimal));
parts.PrimaryKey = new DataColumn[] { parts.Columns["Id"] };

vendorData.Relations.Add(
    "vendors_parts",
    vendors.Columns["Id"],
    parts.Columns["VendorId"]);
```

Being More Specific with Typed *DataSet* Objects

The previous code created a schema for a data set. Accessing the data table corresponding to the vendors would require code like this:

Sample of Visual Basic Code

```
Dim vendorTable as DataTable = vendorData.Tables("Vendors")
```

Sample of C# Code

```
DataTable vendorTable = vendorData.Tables["Vendors"];
```

What happens if the table name is spelled incorrectly? An exception is thrown, but not until run time. A better approach is to create a new, specialized *DataSet* class that inherits from *DataSet*, adding a property for each of the tables. For example, a specialized *DataSet* class might contain a property called *Vendors* that can be accessed as follows:

Sample of Visual Basic Code

```
Dim vendorTable as DataTable = vendorData.Vendors
```

Sample of C# Code

```
DataTable vendorTable = vendorData.Vendors;
```

Using this syntax, a compile-time error is generated if *Vendor* is not spelled correctly. Also, the chances of incorrect spelling are significantly reduced because Visual Studio IntelliSense displays the *Vendors* property for quick selection when the line of code is being typed. The standard *DataSet* class is an *untyped data set*, whereas the specialized data set is a *typed data set*.

You can create a typed *DataSet* class manually, but it's usually better to provide an XML schema definition (XSD) file to generate the typed *DataSet* class. Visual Studio contains a tool called the DataSet Editor that you can use to create and modify an XSD file graphically, which, in turn, can generate the typed *DataSet* class. You can invoke the DataSet Editor by adding a *DataSet* file to a Visual Studio project: Right-click the project, choose Add, choose New Item, and select the DataSet template in the Data section. After you add the DataSet template to the project, the template will be open for you to edit by using the DataSet Editor. Figure 1-5 shows the files created when the DataSet template is added to a project. Notice that you might need to select the Show All Files button, located at the top of the Solution Explorer window, to see all these files. One of the files has a .cs extension, which is the extension for a C# source code file. A Visual Basic application would have a file with a .vb extension. The source code file contains the definition of a class that inherits from *DataSet* (that is, the typed data set) and is generated automatically by the DataSet Editor.

FIGURE 1-5 The DataSet template contains an XML schema definition and generates source code to create a typed data set.

Connecting the Tables with *DataRelation* Objects

The *DataRelation* objects join *DataTable* objects in the same data set. Joining *DataTable* objects creates a path from a column of one *DataTable* object to a column of another. This *DataRelation* object can be traversed programmatically from parent data table to child data table or from child data table to parent data table, which enables navigation between the *DataTable* objects. The following code example populates the *vendor* and *part DataTable* objects and then demonstrates *DataRelation* object navigation, first from parent to child and then from child to parent, using the *vendors_parts* data relation.

Sample of Visual Basic Code

```vb
'add vendors and parts
Dim vendorRow as DataRow = nothing
vendorRow = vendors.NewRow()
Dim vendorId as Guid = Guid.NewGuid()
vendorRow("Id") = vendorId
vendorRow("Name") = "Tailspin Toys"
vendors.Rows.Add(vendorRow)

Dim partRow as DataRow = nothing
partRow = parts.NewRow()
partRow("Id") = Guid.NewGuid()
partRow("VendorId") = vendorId
partRow("PartCode") = "WGT1"
partRow("PartDescription") = "Widget 1 Description"
partRow("Cost") = 10.00
partRow("RetailPrice") = 12.32
parts.Rows.Add(partRow)

partRow = parts.NewRow()
```

```vb
partRow("Id") = Guid.NewGuid()
partRow("VendorId") = vendorId
partRow("PartCode") = "WGT2"
partRow("PartDescription") = "Widget 2 Description"
partRow("Cost") = 9.00
partRow("RetailPrice") = 11.32
parts.Rows.Add(partRow)

'Navigate parent to children
textBox1.AppendText(vbCrLf + "Parent to Children" + vbCrLf)
Dim childParts As DataRow() = vendorRow.GetChildRows("vendors_parts")
For Each dr As DataRow In childParts
    textBox1.AppendText( _
        String.Format("Part: {0} from {1}" + vbCrLf, _
                        dr("PartCode"), vendorRow("Name")))
Next
textBox1.AppendText("-------------------------------" + vbCrLf)

'Navigate child to parent
textBox1.AppendText(vbCrLf + "Parent to Children" + vbCrLf)
Dim parentRow As DataRow = parts.Rows(1).GetParentRow("vendors_parts")
textBox1.AppendText( _
        String.Format("Vendor: {0} for {1}" + vbCrLf, _
            parentRow("Name"), parts.Rows(1)("PartCode")))
textBox1.AppendText("-----------------------------" + vbCrLf)
```

Sample of C# Code

```csharp
//add vendors and parts
DataRow vendorRow = null;
vendorRow = vendors.NewRow();
Guid vendorId = Guid.NewGuid();
vendorRow["Id"] = vendorId;
vendorRow["Name"] = "Tailspin Toys";
vendors.Rows.Add(vendorRow);

DataRow partRow = null;
partRow = parts.NewRow();
partRow["Id"] = Guid.NewGuid();
partRow["VendorId"] = vendorId;
partRow["PartCode"] = "WGT1";
partRow["PartDescription"] = "Widget 1 Description";
partRow["Cost"] = 10.00;
partRow["RetailPrice"] = 12.32;
parts.Rows.Add(partRow);

partRow = parts.NewRow();
partRow["Id"] = Guid.NewGuid();
partRow["VendorId"] = vendorId;
partRow["PartCode"] = "WGT2";
partRow["PartDescription"] = "Widget 2 Description";
partRow["Cost"] = 9.00;
partRow["RetailPrice"] = 11.32;
parts.Rows.Add(partRow);

//Navigate parent to children
```

```
textBox1.AppendText("\r\nParent to Children\r\n");
DataRow[] childParts = vendorRow.GetChildRows("vendors_parts");
foreach (DataRow dr in childParts)
{
    textBox1.AppendText(
        string.Format("Part: {0} from {1}\r\n",
            dr["PartCode"],vendorRow["Name"]));
}
textBox1.AppendText("-------------------------------\r\n");

//Navigate child to parent
textBox1.AppendText("\r\nChild to Parent\r\n");
DataRow parentRow = parts.Rows[1].GetParentRow("vendors_parts");
textBox1.AppendText(
    string.Format("Vendor: {0} for {1}\r\n",
        parentRow["Name"], parts.Rows[1]["PartCode"]));
textBox1.AppendText("-------------------------------\r\n");
```

Creating Primary and Foreign Key Constraints

You can create a *DataRelation* object with or without unique and foreign key constraints for the sole purpose of navigating between parent and child *DataTable* objects. The *DataRelation* class provides a constructor that enables the creation of a unique constraint on the parent *DataTable* object and a foreign key constraint on the child *DataTable* object. These constraints enforce data integrity by ensuring that a parent *DataRow* object exists for any child *DataRow* object. The following code demonstrates the creation of the *DataRelation* object named *vendor_part*, passing *true* to create constraints if they don't already exist.

> **NOTE FOREIGN KEYS AND NULL VALUES**
>
> If a foreign key constraint is set to a *DataColumn* object that allows nulls, this child data row can exist without having a parent *DataRow* object. In some situations, this might be desired or required, but in other situations, it might not. Be sure to verify the *AllowDBNull* property of the *DataColumn* objects being used as foreign keys.

Sample of Visual Basic Code

```
vendorData.Relations.Add( _
  "vendors_parts", _
  vendors.Columns("Id"), _
  parts.Columns("VendorId"), True)
```

Sample of C# Code

```
vendorData.Relations.Add(
  "vendors_parts",
  vendors.Columns["Id"],
  parts.Columns["VendorId"], true);
```

Cascading Deletes and Cascading Updates

A foreign key constraint ensures that a child *DataRow* object cannot be added unless a valid parent *DataRow* object exists. In some situations, it is desirable to force the deletion of the child *DataRow* objects when the parent *DataRow* object is deleted. You can do this by setting *DeleteRule* to *Cascade* on the *ForeignKeyConstraint* constraint of the child table corresponding to the relation. *Cascade* is the default setting. Table 1-6 describes the other members of the *Rule* enumeration.

As with deleting, on some occasions, you'll want to cascade changes to a unique key in the parent *DataRow* object to the child *DataRow* object's foreign key. You can set *ChangeRule* to a member of the *Rule* enumeration to get the appropriate behavior.

TABLE 1-6 *Rule* Enumeration Members

RULE VALUE	DESCRIPTION
Cascade	Default. Deletes or updates the child *DataRow* objects when the *DataRow* object is deleted or its unique key is changed. This is the default behavior.
None	Throws an *InvalidConstraintException* if the parent *DataRow* object is deleted or its unique key is changed.
SetDefault	Sets the foreign key column(s) value to the default value of the *DataColumn* object(s) if the parent *DataRow* object is deleted or its unique key is changed.
SetNull	Sets the foreign key column(s) value to *DBNull* if the parent *DataRow* object is deleted or its unique key is changed.

The default setting for a *ForeignKeyConstraint* object's *DeleteRule* property is *Rule.Cascade*. The following code sample shows how to force an *InvalidConstraintException* to be thrown when a parent that has children is deleted or when a child is being added that has no parent.

Sample of Visual Basic Code

```
'set delete rule
Dim fk as ForeignKeyConstraint = part.Constraints("vendors_parts")
fk.DeleteRule = Rule.None
```

Sample of C# Code

```
//set delete rule
ForeignKeyConstraint fk =
    (ForeignKeyConstraint)part.Constraints["vendors_parts"];
fk.DeleteRule = Rule.None;
```

Using Merge to Combine *DataSet* Data

On many occasions, data available in one data set must be combined with another data set. For example, a sales application might need to combine serialized *DataSet* objects received by email from a number of sales people. Even internally within an application, you might want to create a copy of *DataTable* objects the user can edit, and, based on the user clicking Update, the modified data can be merged back to the original data set.

The *DataSet* class contains a method called *Merge* that can be used to combine data from multiple *DataSet* objects. The *Merge* method has several overloads to merge data from *DataSet*, *DataTable,* or *DataRow* objects. The following code example demonstrates using the *Merge* method to combine changes from one data set into another data set.

Sample of Visual Basic Code

```vb
'Create an initial DataSet
Dim masterData As New DataSet("Sales")
Dim people As DataTable = masterData.Tables.Add("People")
people.Columns.Add("Id", GetType(Guid))
people.Columns.Add("Name", GetType(String))
people.PrimaryKey = New DataColumn() { people.Columns("Id")}
people.Rows.Add(Guid.NewGuid(), "Joe")

'Create a temp DataSet and make changes
Dim tempData As DataSet = masterData.Copy()

'get Joe's info
Dim tempPeople As DataTable = tempData.Tables("People")
Dim joe As DataRow = tempPeople.Select("Name='Joe'")(0)
Dim joeId As Guid = CType(joe("Id"), Guid)

'Modify joe's name
joe("Name") = "Joe in Sales"

'Create an Order table and add orders for Joe
Dim orders As DataTable = tempData.Tables.Add("Orders")
orders.Columns.Add("Id", GetType(Guid))
orders.Columns.Add("PersonId", GetType(Guid))
orders.Columns.Add("Amount", GetType(Decimal))
orders.PrimaryKey = New DataColumn() { orders.Columns("Id")}
orders.Rows.Add(Guid.NewGuid(), joeId, 100)

'Now merge back to master
masterData.Merge(tempData, False, MissingSchemaAction.AddWithKey)
```

Sample of C# Code

```csharp
//Create an initial DataSet
DataSet masterData = new DataSet("Sales");
DataTable people = masterData.Tables.Add("People");
people.Columns.Add("Id", typeof(Guid));
people.Columns.Add("Name", typeof(string));
people.PrimaryKey = new DataColumn[] { person.Columns["Id"] };
people.Rows.Add(Guid.NewGuid(), "Joe");

//Create a temp DataSet and make changes
```

```
DataSet tempData = masterData.Copy();

//get Joe's info
DataTable tempPeople = tempData.Tables["People"];
DataRow joe = tempPeople.Select("Name='Joe'")[0];
Guid joeId = (Guid)joe["Id"];

//Modify joe's name
joe["Name"] = "Joe in Sales";

//Create an Order table and add orders for Joe
DataTable orders = tempData.Tables.Add("Orders");
orders.Columns.Add("Id", typeof(Guid));
orders.Columns.Add("PersonId", typeof(Guid));
orders.Columns.Add("Amount", typeof(decimal));
orders.PrimaryKey = new DataColumn[] { orders.Columns["Id"] };
orders.Rows.Add(Guid.NewGuid(), joeId, 100);

//Now merge back to master
masterData.Merge(tempData, false, MissingSchemaAction.AddWithKey);
```

This code creates a data set that contains a single *DataTable* object, called *People*. A person named Joe was added to the *people DataTable* object. The data row state for Joe's data row is *Added*. Next, the code copies the *masterData DataSet* object to a *DataSet* object called *tempData*. The code modifies the *tempData DataSet* object by changing Joe's name to "Joe in Sales", and then it creates a new *DataTable* object called *Orders* and adds an order.

The *Merge* method on *masterData*, which takes three parameters, is then called. The first parameter is the *tempData* object. The second parameter is a Boolean called *preserveChanges*, which specifies whether updates from the *tempData* data set should overwrite changes made in the *masterData* object. For example, Joe's data row state in the *masterData* data set is not *Unchanged*, so if the *preserveChanges* setting is *true*, Joe's name change (to "Joe in Sales") will not be merged into *masterData*. The last parameter is a *MissingSchemaAction* enumeration member. The *AddWithKey* value is selected, which means the Sales data table and its data are added to *masterData*. Table 1-7 describes the enumeration members.

TABLE 1-7 *MissingSchemaAction* Enumeration Members

MISSINGSCHEMAACTION VALUE	DESCRIPTION
Add	Adds the necessary *DataTable* and *DataColumn* objects to complete the schema.
AddWithKey	Adds the necessary *DataTable*, *DataColumn*, and *PrimaryKey* objects to complete the schema.
Error	An exception is thrown if a data column does not exist in the data set being updated.
Ignore	Ignores data that resides in data columns that are not in the data set being updated.

When you use the *Merge* method, make sure the *DataTable* objects have a primary key. Failure to set the *PrimaryKey* property of the *DataTable* object results in *DataRow* objects being appended rather than existing *DataRow* objects being modified.

PRACTICE   Working with *DataTable* and *DataSet* Classes

In this practice, you create a small application that works with the disconnected data classes that have been defined in this lesson. The scenario is based on a person who owns several vehicles and wants to track all repairs for each vehicle.

When the application starts for the first time, a data set will be created and populated with a schema.

This practice is intended to focus on the classes that have been explained in this lesson, and at this time, there is no focus on the graphical user interface (GUI). The next lesson covers data binding to the GUI and will focus on the GUI.

If you encounter a problem completing an exercise, the completed projects can be installed from the Code folder on the companion CD.

EXERCISE   Create the Project and the *DataSet* Schema

In this exercise, you create a Windows application project and then add code to create a data set with a Vehicles data table and a Repairs data table. These data tables will be related through the Vin column in both data tables.

1. In Visual Studio .NET 2010, click File | New | Project.

2. Select your desired programming language and then select the Windows Forms Application template.

3. For the project name, enter **VehicleRepairLab**. Be sure to select a desired location for this project.

4. For the solution name, enter **VehicleRepairLabSolution**. Be sure that Create Directory for Solution is selected and then click OK.

   After Visual Studio .NET finishes creating the project, Form1 will be displayed using the Windows Forms Designer.

> **NOTE   DO YOU SEE A PROMPT FOR THE LOCATION?**
>
> If you don't see a prompt for the location, it's because your Visual Studio .NET settings are set up to enable you to abort the project and automatically remove all of the project files from your hard drive. To select a location, simply click File | Save All after the project has been created. To change this setting, click Tools | Options | Projects and Solutions | Save new projects when created. When this option is selected, you are prompted for a location when you create the project.

5. Double-click the title bar of the form. This adds a Form1_Load event handler method to the code, and the code editor for Form1 is displayed.

6. Add code to define a data set to use in this application. Your code should be added at the class level of Form1 and should look like the following:

Sample of Visual Basic Code

```vb
Private ds As DataSet
```

Sample of C# Code

```csharp
private DataSet ds;
```

7. Add code to the *Form1_Load* event handler method to call a method called *CreateSchema* that hasn't been created yet. This method will create the schema for the data set. Your code should look like the following:

Sample of Visual Basic Code

```vb
Private Sub Form1_Load(ByVal sender As System.Object, _
     ByVal e As System.EventArgs) _
     Handles MyBase.Load
   CreateSchema()
End Sub
```

Sample of C# Code

```csharp
private void Form1_Load(object sender, EventArgs e)
{
    CreateSchema();
}
```

8. Create the *CreateSchema* method to add the tables and columns for the Vehicles table and the Repairs table, add the relationship between the tables called *vehicles_repairs*, and then save the *DataSet* schema to a schema file. Your *CreateSchema* method should look like the following:

Sample of Visual Basic Code

```vb
Private Sub CreateSchema()
     ds = New DataSet("VehiclesRepairs")

     Dim vehicles = ds.Tables.Add("Vehicles")
     vehicles.Columns.Add("VIN", GetType(String))
     vehicles.Columns.Add("Make", GetType(String))
     vehicles.Columns.Add("Model", GetType(String))
     vehicles.Columns.Add("Year", GetType(Integer))
     vehicles.PrimaryKey = New DataColumn() {vehicles.Columns("VIN")}

     Dim repairs = ds.Tables.Add("Repairs")
     Dim pk = repairs.Columns.Add("ID", GetType(Integer))
     pk.AutoIncrement = True
     pk.AutoIncrementSeed = -1
     pk.AutoIncrementStep = -1
     repairs.Columns.Add("VIN", GetType(String))
     repairs.Columns.Add("Description", GetType(String))
```

```
    repairs.Columns.Add("Cost", GetType(Decimal))
    repairs.PrimaryKey = New DataColumn() {repairs.Columns("ID")}

    ds.Relations.Add( _
        "vehicles_repairs", _
        vehicles.Columns("VIN"), _
        repairs.Columns("VIN"))

    MessageBox.Show("Schema created!")
End Sub
```

Sample of C# Code

```csharp
private void CreateSchema()
{
    ds = new DataSet("VehiclesRepairs");

    var vehicles = ds.Tables.Add("Vehicles");
    vehicles.Columns.Add("VIN", typeof(string));
    vehicles.Columns.Add("Make", typeof(string));
    vehicles.Columns.Add("Model", typeof(string));
    vehicles.Columns.Add("Year", typeof(int));
    vehicles.PrimaryKey = new DataColumn[] { vehicles.Columns["VIN"] };

    var repairs = ds.Tables.Add("Repairs");
    var pk = repairs.Columns.Add("ID", typeof(int));
    pk.AutoIncrement = true;
    pk.AutoIncrementSeed = -1;
    pk.AutoIncrementStep = -1;
    repairs.Columns.Add("VIN", typeof(string));
    repairs.Columns.Add("Description", typeof(string));
    repairs.Columns.Add("Cost", typeof(decimal));
    repairs.PrimaryKey = new DataColumn[] { repairs.Columns["ID"] };

    ds.Relations.Add(
        "vehicles_repairs",
        vehicles.Columns["VIN"],
        repairs.Columns["VIN"]);

    MessageBox.Show("Schema created!");
}
```

9. Build the application. From the main menu, click Build | Build Solution to build. If you have errors, you can double-click the error to go to the invalid line in the code and correct it.

10. Run the application. From the main menu, click Debug | Start Debugging.

   When the application starts, a message box should pop up stating that the schema has been created. The application doesn't do much, but in the next lesson you learn how to save and load data as well as how to bind the data to the GUI.

Lesson Summary

This lesson provided a detailed overview of the *DataTable* and *DataSet* classes.

- When you work with disconnected data, a *DataTable* object is almost always a requirement.
- The *DataTable* object contains *DataColumn* objects, which define the schema, and *DataRow* objects, which contain the data.
- *DataRow* objects have *RowState* and *DataRowVersion* properties.
- The *RowState* property indicates whether the data row should be inserted, updated, or deleted from the data store if the data is ever persisted to a database or merged to another data set or data table.
- The *DataTable* object can contain up to three copies of *DataRow* data, based on the *DataRowVersion* property. This feature enables the data to be rolled back to its original state, and you can use it when you write code to handle conflict resolution.
- To create an auto-number primary key, set the *AutoIncrement* property to *true*, set the *AutoIncrementSeed* property to -1, and set the *AutoIncrementStep* property to -1.
- Use the *DataView* object to create a sorted, filtered window on a *DataTable* object.
- The *DataSet* object is an in-memory, relational data cache.
- The *DataSet* object contains a *DataTable* collection called *Tables* and a *DataRelation* collection called *Relations*.
- Data from other *DataSet*, *DataTable*, and *DataRow* objects can be merged into a *DataSet* object.

Lesson Review

You can use the following questions to test your knowledge of the information in Lesson 1, "Working with the *DataTable* and *DataSet* Classes." The questions are also available on the companion CD if you prefer to review them in electronic form.

> **NOTE ANSWERS**
>
> Answers to these questions and explanations of why each answer choice is correct or incorrect are located in the "Answers" section at the end of the book.

1. Which class should you use to manage multiple tables and relationships among them?

   A. *DataRow*

   B. *DataView*

   C. *DataTable*

   D. *DataSet*

2. You want to set up a primary key on a column. Which properties on the data column must be set? (Each correct answer presents part of a complete solution. Choose three.)

   A. *MappingType*

   B. *AutoIncrementSeed*

   C. *AutoIncrementStep*

   D. *AutoIncrement*

Lesson 2: Serialization, Specialized Types, and Data Binding

After you learn the basics of working with *DataTable* and *DataSet* classes, you'll probably want to save your data to a file or load a *DataTable* or *DataSet* object from a file. You might also be wondering whether a column value can contain custom objects. Finally, you're probably wondering how you can connect your data to GUI controls. This lesson explains these items.

> **After this lesson, you will be able to:**
> - Use the disconnected classes to create an application that can collect data from a user and store it to a binary or XML file.
> - Store specialized objects into a column value and retrieve these objects.
> - Connect ADO.NET classes to the GUI by using data-binding techniques.
>
> **Estimated lesson time: 30 minutes**

Serializing and Deserializing the Data Table with XML Data

The contents of a data table can be written to an XML file or stream, using the *DataTable* object's *WriteXml* method as shown in the following code:

Sample of Visual Basic Code

```
'helper method for creating desktop file names
Private Function desktopFileName(ByVal fileName As String) As String
    Return Path.Combine( _
        Environment.GetFolderPath(Environment.SpecialFolder.Desktop), _
        fileName)
End Function

'write to xml file using defaults
cars.WriteXml(desktopFileName("Cars.xml"))
```

Sample of C# Code

```
//helper method for creating desktop file names
private string desktopFileName(string fileName)
{
    return Path.Combine(
        Environment.GetFolderPath(Environment.SpecialFolder.Desktop),
        fileName);
}

//write to xml file using defaults
cars.WriteXml(desktopFileName("Cars.xml"));
```

If this code is executed on the *cars DataSet* defined in the previous lesson, the cars.xml file will look like this:

```
<?xml version="1.0" standalone="yes"?>
<DocumentElement>
  <Cars>
    <Vin>123456789ABCD </VIN>
    <Make>Ford</Make>
    <Year>2002</Year>
    <Year_x0020_and_x0020_Make>2002 Ford</Year_x0020_and_x0020_Make>
  </Cars>
  <Cars>
    <Vin>987654321XYZ</VIN>
    <Make>Jeep</Make>
    <Year>2002</Year>
    <Year_x0020_and_x0020_Make>2002 Jeep</Year_x0020_and_x0020_Make>
  </Cars>
</DocumentElement>
```

This example uses *DocumentElement* as the root element and repeating *Cars* elements for each data row. The data for each data row is nested as elements within each *Cars* element. An XML element name cannot contain space characters, so "Year and Make" was automatically converted to Year_x0020_and_x0020_Make.

You can tune the XML output by providing an XML schema or by setting properties on the data table and its columns. To change the name of the repeating element for the *DataRow* objects from *Car* to *Auto*, you can change the *DataTable* object's *TableName* property. To change the Vin, Make, and Year to XML attributes, you can set each *DataColumn* object's *ColumnMapping* property to *MappingType.Attribute*. The "Year and Make" column is a calculated column, so its data does not need to be stored. To prevent the "Year and Make" column from storing its data, set its *ColumnMapping* property to *MappingType.Hidden*. Table 1-8 describes the *MappingType* enumeration members, and the following samples show the necessary code and the resulting XML file contents.

Sample of Visual Basic Code

```
'set the table name and column mapping
cars.TableName = "Auto"
cars.Columns("Vin").ColumnMapping = MappingType.Attribute
cars.Columns("Make").ColumnMapping = MappingType.Attribute
cars.Columns("Year").ColumnMapping = MappingType.Attribute
cars.Columns("Year and Make").ColumnMapping = MappingType.Hidden
```

Sample of C# Code

```
//set the table name and column mapping
cars.TableName = "Auto";
cars.Columns["Vin"].ColumnMapping = MappingType.Attribute;
cars.Columns["Make"].ColumnMapping = MappingType.Attribute;
cars.Columns["Year"].ColumnMapping = MappingType.Attribute;
cars.Columns["Year and Make"].ColumnMapping = MappingType.Hidden;
```

XML File

```
<?xml version="1.0" standalone="yes"?>
<DocumentElement>
  <Auto Vin="123456789ABCD " Make="Ford" Year="2002" />
```

```
        <Auto Vin="987654321XYZ" Make="Jeep" Year="2002" />
</DocumentElement>
```

The resulting XML file is quite compact, but the data types aren't saved, so all data is considered to be string data. The solution is to store the XML schema with the data, which you can do by including the *XmlWriteMode.WriteSchema* enumeration when you are saving, as shown here:

Sample of Visual Basic Code

```
cars.WriteXml(desktopFileName("CarWithSchema.xml"), XmlWriteMode.WriteSchema)
```

Sample of C# Code

```
cars.WriteXml(desktopFileName("CarWithSchema.xml"), XmlWriteMode.WriteSchema);
```

XML File

```xml
<?xml version="1.0" standalone="yes"?>
<NewDataSet>
  <xs:schema id="NewDataSet" xmlns=""
    xmlns:xs="http://www.w3.org/2001/XMLSchema"
    xmlns:msdata="urn:schemas-microsoft-com:xml-msdata">
    <xs:element name="NewDataSet" msdata:IsDataSet="true"
      msdata:MainDataTable="Auto" msdata:UseCurrentLocale="true">
      <xs:complexType>
        <xs:choice minOccurs="0" maxOccurs="unbounded">
          <xs:element name="Auto">
            <xs:complexType>
              <xs:attribute name="Vin" msdata:Caption="VIN" use="required">
                <xs:simpleType>
                  <xs:restriction base="xs:string">
                    <xs:maxLength value="23" />
                  </xs:restriction>
                </xs:simpleType>
              </xs:attribute>
              <xs:attribute name="Make" use="required">
                <xs:simpleType>
                  <xs:restriction base="xs:string">
                    <xs:maxLength value="35" />
                  </xs:restriction>
                </xs:simpleType>
              </xs:attribute>
              <xs:attribute name="Year" type="xs:int" use="required" />
              <xs:attribute name="Year_x0020_and_x0020_Make"
                msdata:ReadOnly="true"
                msdata:Expression="Year + ' ' + Make" use="prohibited">
                <xs:simpleType>
                  <xs:restriction base="xs:string">
                    <xs:maxLength value="70" />
                  </xs:restriction>
                </xs:simpleType>
              </xs:attribute>
            </xs:complexType>
          </xs:element>
        </xs:choice>
```

```
    </xs:complexType>
    <xs:unique name="Constraint1" msdata:PrimaryKey="true">
      <xs:selector xpath=".//Auto" />
      <xs:field xpath="@Vin" />
    </xs:unique>
  </xs:element>
</xs:schema>
<Auto Vin="123456789ABCD " Make="Ford" Year="2002" />
<Auto Vin="987654321XYZ" Make="Jeep" Year="2002" />
</NewDataSet>
```

With the XML schema included in the file, the data types are defined. The XML schema also includes the maximum length settings for Vin and Make. A *DataTable* object can be loaded with this XML file, and the resulting *DataTable* object will be the same as the one that was saved to the file. The following code sample reads the XML file into a new *DataTable* object.

Sample of Visual Basic Code

```
Dim xmlTable as new DataTable()
xmlTable.ReadXml(desktopFileName("CarWithSchema.xml"))
```

Sample of C# Code

```
DataTable xmlTable = new DataTable();
xmlTable.ReadXml(desktopFileName("CarWithSchema.xml"));
```

Although the data for the "Year and Make" column was not saved, the column data is populated because this column is calculated, and the schema contains the expression to recreate this column data.

Serializing and Deserializing *DataSet* Objects

A populated *DataSet* object can be saved, or serialized, as XML or as binary data to a stream or file; it can also be loaded, or deserialized, with XML or binary data from a stream or file. The data stream can be transferred across a network by many protocols, including HTTP. This section examines the various methods of transferring data.

Serializing a *DataSet* Object as XML

You can easily serialize a populated *DataSet* object to an XML file by executing the *DataSet* object's *WriteXml* method. The following code sample uses the populated *vendorData* data set that was created earlier in this chapter and writes the contents to an XML file. The resulting XML file contents are also shown.

Sample of Visual Basic Code

```
vendorData.WriteXml(desktopFileName("Vendors.xml"), _
    XmlWriteMode.IgnoreSchema)
```

Sample of C# Code

```
vendorData.WriteXml(desktopFileName("Vendors.xml"),
    XmlWriteMode.IgnoreSchema);
```

XML File

```xml
<?xml version="1.0" standalone="yes"?>
<VendorData>
 <Vendor>
  <Id>d9625cfa-f176-4521-98f5-f577a8bc2c00</Id>
  <Name>Tailspin Toys</Name>
 </Vendor>
 <Part>
  <Id>df84fa52-5aa3-4c08-b5ba-54163eb1ea3a</Id>
  <VendorId>d9625cfa-f176-4521-98f5-f577a8bc2c00</VendorId>
  <PartCode>WGT1</PartCode>
  <PartDescription>Widget 1 Description</PartDescription>
  <Cost>10</Cost>
  <RetailPrice>12.32</RetailPrice>
 </Part>
 <Part>
  <Id>c411676a-ec53-496c-bdbd-04b4d58124d0</Id>
  <VendorId>d9625cfa-f176-4521-98f5-f577a8bc2c00</VendorId>
  <PartCode>WGT2</PartCode>
  <PartDescription>Widget 2 Description</PartDescription>
  <Cost>9</Cost>
  <RetailPrice>11.32</RetailPrice>
 </Part>
</VendorData>
```

The XML document is well formed, and its root node is called *VendorData*. You can set the name of the root node by changing the *DataSet* object's *DataSetName* property. This property can be changed at any time. Note that the code that created the data set earlier in this chapter implicitly set the *DataSetName* property by passing its value as the parameter of the *DataSet* object constructor.

The *DataRow* objects have been represented as repeating elements in the XML. For example, the unique vendor *DataRow* object is represented in the XML file by a single *Vendor* element, whereas the two-part *DataRow* objects are represented in the XML file by two *Part* elements. Also, each column is represented by an element within the data row element. You can change the format of the column data by assigning a new value to the *ColumnMapping* property of the *DataColumn* objects. Table 1-8 shows the available settings.

TABLE 1-8 *MappingType* Enumeration Members

MAPPINGTYPE VALUE	DESCRIPTION
Attribute	The column data is placed in an XML attribute.
Element	The default. The column data is placed in an XML element.
Hidden	The column data is not sent to the XML file.
SimpleContent	The column data is stored as text within the row element tags. In other words, the data is stored as text like the *Element* setting but without the additional element tag.

Another formatting option would be to nest the *Part* elements inside the *Vendor* element that owns the parts. You can do this by setting the *Nested* property of the *DataRelation* object to *true*. The following code sample shows how the XML format can be changed substantially, first by nesting the data and then by setting all the *DataColumn* objects except those with a data type of *Guid* (globally unique identifier) to *Attribute*. The resulting XML file is also shown.

Sample of Visual Basic Code

```
'nested data and xml attributes
vendorData.Relations("vendor_part").Nested = True
For Each dt As DataTable In vendorData.Tables
    For Each dc As DataColumn In dt.Columns
        If Not (dc.DataType.Equals(GetType(Guid))) Then
            dc.ColumnMapping = MappingType.Attribute
        End If
    Next
Next
vendorData.WriteXml(desktopFileName("Vendors1.xml"), _
    XmlWriteMode.IgnoreSchema)
```

Sample of C# Code

```
//nested data and xml attributes
vendorData.Relations["vendor_part"].Nested = true;
foreach (DataTable dt in vendorData.Tables)
{
    foreach (DataColumn dc in dt.Columns)
    {
        if (dc.DataType != typeof(Guid))
            dc.ColumnMapping = MappingType.Attribute;
    }
}
vendorData.WriteXml(desktopFileName("Vendors1.xml"),
    XmlWriteMode.IgnoreSchema);
```

XML File

```
<?xml version="1.0" standalone="yes"?>
<VendorData>
  <Vendor Name="Tailspin Toys">
    <Id>d012b54d-c855-4c1f-969e-74554d2cb0c7</Id>
    <Part PartCode="WGT1" PartDescription="Widget 1 Description"
        Cost="10" RetailPrice="12.32">
      <Id>167583e9-f4eb-4004-9efa-5477e0f55208</Id>
      <VendorId>d012b54d-c855-4c1f-969e-74554d2cb0c7</VendorId>
    </Part>
    <Part PartCode="WGT2" PartDescription="Widget 2 Description"
        Cost="9" RetailPrice="11.32">
```

```
        <Id>d3b42db7-b23f-4c33-9961-f7a325342167</Id>
        <VendorId>d012b54d-c855-4c1f-969e-74554d2cb0c7</VendorId>
      </Part>
    </Vendor>
</VendorData>
```

In the example, the XML file is being written, but it contains no information that describes the data types of each value. When not specified, the default type for all data is *string*. If the XML file is read into a new data set, all data, including *DateTime* data and numeric data, is loaded as a *string*. One fix is to store the data type information within the XML file by also storing the schema definition. The following code shows how passing *XmlWriteMode.WriteSchema* as the second parameter of the *WriteXml* method generates the schema definition within the XML file.

Sample of Visual Basic Code

```
vendorData.WriteXml(desktopFileName("Vendors2.xml"), _
   XmlWriteMode.WriteSchema)
```

Sample of C# Code

```
vendorData.WriteXml(desktopFileName("Vendors2.xml"),
   XmlWriteMode.WriteSchema);
```

XML File

```
<?xml version="1.0" standalone="yes"?>
<VendorData>
  <xs:schema id="VendorData" xmlns="" xmlns:xs="http://www.w3.org/2001/XMLSchema"
      xmlns:msdata="urn:schemas-microsoft-com:xml-msdata">
    <xs:element name="VendorData" msdata:IsDataSet="true"
        msdata:UseCurrentLocale="true">
      <xs:complexType>
        <xs:choice minOccurs="0" maxOccurs="unbounded">
          <xs:element name="Vendor">
            <xs:complexType>
              <xs:sequence>
                <xs:element name="Id" msdata:DataType="System.Guid, mscorlib,
                   Version=4.0.0.0, Culture=neutral, PublicKeyToken=b77a5c561934e089"
                    type="xs:string" msdata:Ordinal="0" />
                <xs:element name="Part" minOccurs="0" maxOccurs="unbounded">
                  <xs:complexType>
                    <xs:sequence>
                      <xs:element name="Id" msdata:DataType=
                         "System.Guid, mscorlib, Version=4.0.0.0, Culture=neutral,
                          PublicKeyToken=b77a5c561934e089"
                           type="xs:string" msdata:Ordinal="0" />
                      <xs:element name="VendorId" msdata:DataType=
                         "System.Guid, mscorlib, Version=4.0.0.0, Culture=neutral,
                            PublicKeyToken=b77a5c561934e089" type="xs:string"
                            minOccurs="0" msdata:Ordinal="1" />
                    </xs:sequence>
                    <xs:attribute name="PartCode" type="xs:string" />
                    <xs:attribute name="PartDescription" type="xs:string" />
                    <xs:attribute name="Cost" type="xs:decimal" />
```

```
                    <xs:attribute name="RetailPrice" type="xs:decimal" />
                </xs:complexType>
              </xs:element>
            </xs:sequence>
            <xs:attribute name="Name" type="xs:string" />
            <xs:attribute name="Address1" type="xs:string" />
            <xs:attribute name="Address2" type="xs:string" />
            <xs:attribute name="City" type="xs:string" />
            <xs:attribute name="State" type="xs:string" />
            <xs:attribute name="ZipCode" type="xs:string" />
            <xs:attribute name="Country" type="xs:string" />
          </xs:complexType>
        </xs:element>
      </xs:choice>
    </xs:complexType>
    <xs:unique name="Part_Constraint1" msdata:ConstraintName="Constraint1"
          msdata:PrimaryKey="true">
      <xs:selector xpath=".//Part" />
      <xs:field xpath="Id" />
    </xs:unique>
    <xs:unique name="Constraint1" msdata:PrimaryKey="true">
      <xs:selector xpath=".//Vendor" />
      <xs:field xpath="Id" />
    </xs:unique>
    <xs:keyref name="vendor_part" refer="Constraint1" msdata:IsNested="true"
          msdata:DeleteRule="None">
      <xs:selector xpath=".//Part" />
      <xs:field xpath="VendorId" />
    </xs:keyref>
  </xs:element>
</xs:schema>
<Vendor Name="Tailspin Toys">
  <Id>d012b54d-c855-4c1f-969e-74554d2cb0c7</Id>
  <Part PartCode="WGT1" PartDescription="Widget 1 Description" Cost="10"
        RetailPrice="12.32">
    <Id>167583e9-f4eb-4004-9efa-5477e0f55208</Id>
    <VendorId>d012b54d-c855-4c1f-969e-74554d2cb0c7</VendorId>
  </Part>
  <Part PartCode="WGT2" PartDescription="Widget 2 Description" Cost="9"
        RetailPrice="11.32">
    <Id>d3b42db7-b23f-4c33-9961-f7a325342167</Id>
    <VendorId>d012b54d-c855-4c1f-969e-74554d2cb0c7</VendorId>
  </Part>
</Vendor>
</VendorData>
```

When the *XmlWriteMode.WriteSchema* is used as parameter, the resulting XML file is substantially larger. When few files are being generated for this data, this approach is acceptable, but if many files are being created, it would be better to create a separate XSD file that can be loaded before the data. You can use the *DataSet* object's *WriteXmlSchema* method to extract the XML schema definition to a separate file, as shown here.

Sample of Visual Basic Code

```
vendorData.WriteXmlSchema(desktopFileName("VendorSchema.xsd"))
```

```
vendorData.WriteXmlSchema(desktopFileName("VendorSchema.xsd"));
```

Serializing a Changed *DataSet* Object as a DiffGram

A DiffGram is an XML document that contains all the data from your *DataSet* object, including the original *DataRow* object information. A *DataSet* object can be serialized as a DiffGram by simply passing *XmlWriteMode.DiffGram* to the method as shown in the following sample.

Sample of Visual Basic Code

```
vendorData.WriteXml(desktopFileName("Vendors3.xml"), XmlWriteMode.DiffGram)
```

Sample of C# Code

```
vendorData.WriteXml(desktopFileName("Vendors3.xml"), XmlWriteMode.DiffGram);
```

Where is the DiffGram useful? Picture this: You are writing an application that occasionally connects to a database to synchronize your disconnected *DataSet* object with the current information contained in the database. When you are not connected to the database, you will want your *DataSet* object to be stored locally. All the previous examples of serializing a *DataSet* object stored the current data but not the original data of each row. This means that when you deserialize the data, you will have lost the information needed to find the changed *DataRow* objects that should be sent back to the database.

The DiffGram contains all the *DataRowVersion* information, as shown in the following XML document. Part1 has been modified, and its status is indicated as such. Also, the bottom of the XML document contains the "before" information for *DataRow* objects that have been modified or deleted. This XML document also shows Part2 as being deleted because Part2 has "before" information but not current information.

Sample of a DiffGram XML File

```
<?xml version="1.0" standalone="yes"?>
<diffgr:diffgram xmlns:msdata="urn:schemas-microsoft-com:xml-msdata"
xmlns:diffgr="urn:schemas-microsoft-com:xml-diffgram-v1">
  <VendorData>
    <Vendor diffgr:id="Vendor1" msdata:rowOrder="0" Name="Tailspin Toys">
      <Id>9e3fe885-8ffd-4c58-9cbf-a486dcbc930e</Id>
      <Part diffgr:id="Part1" msdata:rowOrder="0" diffgr:hasChanges="modified"
          PartCode="WGT1" PartDescription="Widget 1 Description"
          Cost="12" RetailPrice="12.32">
        <Id>4e91d3ca-a4a0-416e-ad4d-cebf047afcf4</Id>
        <VendorId>9e3fe885-8ffd-4c58-9cbf-a486dcbc930e</VendorId>
      </Part>
    </Vendor>
  </VendorData>
  <diffgr:before>
    <Part diffgr:id="Part1" msdata:rowOrder="0" PartCode="WGT1"
        PartDescription="Widget 1 Description" Cost="10" RetailPrice="12.32">
    <Id>4e91d3ca-a4a0-416e-ad4d-cebf047afcf4</Id>
    <VendorId>9e3fe885-8ffd-4c58-9cbf-a486dcbc930e</VendorId>
    </Part>
    <Part diffgr:id="Part2" diffgr:parentId="Vendor1" msdata:rowOrder="1"
```

```
      PartCode="WGT2" PartDescription="Widget 2 Description" Cost="9"
      RetailPrice="11.32">
    <Id>75a54b24-f8bd-4bbd-8427-20a277a44908</Id>
    <VendorId>9e3fe885-8ffd-4c58-9cbf-a486dcbc930e</VendorId>
  </Part>
 </diffgr:before>
</diffgr:diffgram>
```

Deserializing a Data Set from XML

You can easily create a data set by deserializing an XML file or stream. Remember that when a schema is not provided, all XML data is treated as string data, so you should first load the schema if it is in a separate file. The following code can be used to read the schema file and then load the XML file.

Sample of Visual Basic Code

```
'read xml file into dataset
Dim vendorData as new DataSet()
vendorData.ReadXmlSchema(desktopFileName("VendorSchema.xsd"))
vendorData.ReadXml(desktopFileName("Vendors3.xml"), _
  XmlReadMode.IgnoreSchema)
```

Sample of C# Code

```
//read xml file into dataset
DataSet vendorData = new DataSet();
vendorData.ReadXmlSchema(desktopFileName("VendorSchema.xsd"));
vendorData.ReadXml(desktopFileName("Vendors3.xml"),
  XmlReadMode.IgnoreSchema);
```

In the preceding example, *XmlReadMode.IgnoreSchema* is used, so if the XML data file contains an XML schema definition, it is ignored. Table 1-9 lists the other options of the *XmlReadMode* enumeration.

TABLE 1-9 *XmlReadMode* Enumeration Members

XMLREADMODE VALUE	DESCRIPTION
Auto	The XML source is examined by the *ReadXml* method and the appropriate mode is selected.
DiffGram	If the XML file contains a DiffGram, the changes are applied to the data set using the same semantics that the *Merge* method uses.
Fragment	Reads the XML as a fragment. Fragments can contain multiple root elements. FOR XML in Microsoft SQL Server is an example of something that produces fragments.
IgnoreSchema	Ignores any schema that is defined within the XML data file.

InferSchema	The XML file is read, and the schema (*DataTable* objects and *DataColumn* objects) is created based on the data. If the data set currently has a schema, the existing schema is used and extended to accommodate tables and columns that exist in the XML document but don't exist in the *DataSet* object schema. All data types of all *DataColumn* objects are treated as a string.
InferTypedSchema	The XML file is read, and the schema is created based on the data. An attempt is made to identify the data type of each column, but if the data type cannot be identified, it will be a string.
ReadSchema	Reads the XML file and looks for an embedded schema. If the data set already has *DataTable* objects with the same name, an exception is thrown. All other existing tables will remain.

Inferring a schema simply means that the data set attempts to create a schema for the data by looking for patterns of XML elements and attributes.

Serializing the *DataSet* Object as Binary Data

Although the data set can be serialized as XML, in many situations, the size of the XML file causes problems with resources such as memory and drive space or bandwidth when you move this data across the network. If XML is not required, the data set can be serialized as a binary file. The following code sample writes to a binary file the contents of the *vendorData* data set you previously defined and populated.

Sample of Visual Basic Code

```vb
'Added the following Imports statements to the top of the file
Imports System.Runtime.Serialization.Formatters.Binary
Imports System.IO
...
Dim fs as new FileStream( _
    desktopFileName("VendorData.bin",FileMode.Create)
Dim fmt as new BinaryFormatter()
fmt.Serialize(fs, vendorData)
fs.Close( )
```

Sample of C# Code

```csharp
//Added the following using statements to the top of the file
using System.Runtime.Serialization.Formatters.Binary;
using System.IO;
...
FileStream fs = new FileStream(
    desktopFileName("VendorData.bin",FileMode.Create);
BinaryFormatter fmt = new BinaryFormatter();
fmt.Serialize(fs, vendorData);
fs.Close( );
```

```
00000000  00 01 00 00 00 FF FF FF  FF 01 00 00 00 00 00 00  ................
00000010  00 0C 02 00 00 00 51 53  79 73 74 65 6D 2E 44 61  ......QSystem.Da
00000020  74 61 2C 20 56 65 72 73  69 6F 6E 3D 32 2E 30 2E  ta, Version=2.0.
00000030  33 36 30 30 2E 30 2C 20  43 75 6C 74 75 72 65 3D  3600.0, Culture=
00000040  6E 65 75 74 72 61 6C 2C  20 50 75 62 6C 69 63 4B  neutral, PublicK
00000050  65 79 54 6F 6B 65 6E 3D  62 37 37 61 35 63 35 36  eyToken=b77a5c56
00000060  31 39 33 34 65 30 38 39  05 01 00 00 00 13 53 79  1934e089......Sy
00000070  73 74 65 6D 2E 44 61 74  61 2E 44 61 74 61 53 65  stem.Data.DataSe
00000080  74 03 00 00 00 17 44 61  74 61 53 65 74 2E 52 65  t.....DataSet.Re
00000090  6D 6F 74 69 6E 67 56 65  72 73 69 6F 6F 58 58 6D  motingVersion.Xm
000000a0  6C 53 63 68 65 6D 61 0B  58 6D 6C 44 69 66 66 47  lSchema.XmlDiffG
000000b0  72 61 6D 03 01 01 0E 53  79 73 74 65 6D 2E 56 65  ram....System.Ve
000000c0  72 73 69 6F 6E 02 00 00  00 09 03 00 00 00 06 04  rsion...........
000000d0  00 00 00 FF 16 3C 3F 78  6D 6C 20 76 65 72 73 69  .....<?xml versi
000000e0  6F 6E 3D 22 31 2E 30 22  20 65 6E 63 6F 64 69 6E  on="1.0" encodin
000000f0  67 3D 22 75 74 66 2D 31  36 22 3F 3E 0D 0A 3C 78  g="utf-16"?>..<x
00000100  73 3A 73 63 68 65 6D 61  20 69 64 3D 22 56 65 6E  s:schema id="Ven
00000110  64 6F 72 44 61 74 61 22  20 78 6D 6C 6E 73 3D 22  dorData" xmlns="
00000120  22 20 78 6D 6C 6E 73 3A  78 73 3D 22 68 74 74 70  " xmlns:xs="http
00000130  3A 2F 2F 77 77 77 2E 77  33 2E 6F 72 67 2F 32 30  ://www.w3.org/20
00000140  30 31 2F 58 4D 4C 53 63  68 65 6D 61 22 20 78 6D  01/XMLSchema" xm
00000150  6C 6E 73 3A 6D 73 64 61  74 61 3D 22 75 72 6E 3A  lns:msdata="urn:
00000160  73 63 68 65 6D 61 73 2D  6D 69 63 72 6F 73 6F 66  schemas-microsof
00000170  74 2D 63 6F 6D 3A 78 6D  6C 2D 6D 73 64 61 74 61  t-com:xml-msdata
00000180  22 3E 0D 0A 20 20 3C 78  73 3A 65 6C 65 6D 65 6E  ">.. <xs:elemen
00000190  74 20 6E 61 6D 65 3D 22  56 65 6E 64 6F 72 44 61  t name="VendorDa
000001a0  74 61 22 20 6D 73 64 61  74 61 3A 49 73 44 61 74  ta" msdata:IsDat
000001b0  61 53 65 74 3D 22 74 72  75 65 22 3E 0D 0A 20 20  aSet="true">..
000001c0  20 20 3C 78 73 3A 63 6F  6D 70 6C 65 78 54 79 70  <xs:complexTyp
000001d0  65 3E 0D 0A 20 20 20 20  20 20 3C 78 73 3A 63 68  e>.. <xs:ch
000001e0  6F 69 63 65 20 6D 69 6E  4F 63 63 75 72 73 3D 22  oice minOccurs="
000001f0  30 22 20 6D 61 78 4F 63  63 75 72 73 3D 22 75 6E  0" maxOccurs="un
00000200  62 6F 75 6E 64 65 64 22  3E 0D 0A 20 20 20 20 20  bounded">..
00000210  20 20 20 3C 78 73 3A 65  6C 65 6D 65 6E 74 20 6E  <xs:element n
00000220  61 6D 65 3D 22 56 65 6E  64 6F 72 22 3E 0D 0A 20  ame="Vendor">..
```

FIGURE 1-6 The data set is serialized to a binary file, but the binary file contains embedded XML.

In this example code, a *BinaryFormatter* object is created and is then used to create the binary file. Opening the binary file by using the Visual Studio hex editor would reveal that the binary file contains embedded XML, as shown in Figure 1-6. This file will be referenced as the BinaryXml file. The size of this small sample is 4186 bytes. Adding the following line to the beginning of the code sample will cause the file to be saved with true binary data.

Sample of Visual Basic Code

```
vendorData.RemotingFormat = SerializationFormat.Binary
```

Sample of C# Code

```
vendorData.RemotingFormat = SerializationFormat.Binary;
```

You can then run the code with the results shown in Figure 1-7. This file will be referenced as the TrueBinary file. Depending on what version of the .NET Framework you're using, the size of this small *DataSet* object is between 20,000 and 30,000 bytes. This file was supposed to get smaller, but the initial overhead to create the TrueBinary file was over 20,000 bytes, compared to about 3400 bytes of initial overhead for the BinaryXml file. With 10,000 vendors and 20,000 parts, the BinaryXml file size grows to 7,938,982 bytes, and the TrueBinary file grows to only 1,973,401 bytes. This means that small objects might not benefit from changing the *RemotingFormat* property to *Binary*, whereas large objects will be about one-fourth the size, or four times faster.

EXAM TIP

Remember for the exam that setting the *RemotingFormat* property to *SerializationFormat.Binary* is required to obtain true binary serialization.

> **NOTE BINARY SERIALIZATION OF TABLES**
>
> The data table also contains the *RemotingFormat* property, which can be used when only a single data table is to be saved as binary data.

```
00000000  00 01 00 00 00 FF FF FF  FF 01 00 00 00 00 00 00  .................
00000010  00 0C 02 00 00 00 51 53  79 73 74 65 6D 2E 44 61  ......QSystem.Da
00000020  74 61 2C 20 56 65 72 73  69 6F 6E 3D 32 2E 30 2E  ta, Version=2.0.
00000030  33 36 30 30 2E 30 2C 20  43 75 6C 74 75 72 65 3D  3600.0, Culture=
00000040  6E 65 75 74 72 61 6C 2C  20 50 75 62 6C 69 63 4B  neutral, PublicK
00000050  65 79 54 6F 6B 65 6E 3D  62 37 37 61 35 63 35 36  eyToken=b77a5c56
00000060  31 39 33 34 65 30 38 39  05 01 00 00 00 13 53 79  1934e089......Sy
00000070  73 74 65 6D 2E 44 61 74  61 2E 44 61 74 61 53 65  stem.Data.DataSe
00000080  74 2B 00 00 00 17 44 61  74 61 53 65 74 2E 52 65  t+....DataSet.Re
00000090  6D 6F 74 69 6E 67 56 65  72 73 69 6F 6E 16 44 61  motingVersion.Da
000000a0  74 61 53 65 74 2E 52 65  6D 6F 74 69 6E 67 46 6F  taSet.RemotingFo
000000b0  72 6D 61 74 13 44 61 74  61 53 65 74 2E 44 61 74  rmat.DataSet.Dat
000000c0  61 53 65 74 4E 61 6D 65  11 44 61 74 61 53 65 74  aSetName.DataSet
000000d0  2E 4E 61 6D 65 73 70 61  63 65 0E 44 61 74 61 53  .Namespace.DataS
000000e0  65 74 2E 50 72 65 66 69  78 15 44 61 74 61 53 65  et.Prefix.DataSe
000000f0  74 2E 43 61 73 65 53 65  6E 73 69 74 69 76 65 12  t.CaseSensitive.
00000100  44 61 74 61 53 65 74 2E  4C 6F 63 61 6C 65 4C 43  DataSet.LocaleLC
00000110  49 44 1A 44 61 74 61 53  65 74 2E 45 6E 66 6F 72  ID.DataSet.Enfor
00000120  63 65 43 6F 6E 73 74 72  61 69 6E 74 73 1A 44 61  ceConstraints.Da
00000130  74 61 53 65 74 2E 45 78  74 65 6E 64 65 64 50 72  taSet.ExtendedPr
00000140  6F 70 65 72 74 69 65 73  14 44 61 74 61 53 65 74  operties.DataSet
00000150  2E 54 61 62 6C 65 73 2E  43 6F 75 6E 74 10 44 61  .Tables.Count.Da
00000160  74 61 53 65 74 2E 54 61  62 6C 65 73 5F 30 10 44  taSet.Tables_0.D
00000170  61 74 61 53 65 74 2E 54  61 62 6C 65 73 5F 31 17  ataSet.Tables_1.
00000180  44 61 74 61 54 61 62 6C  65 5F 30 2E 43 6F 6E 73  DataTable_0.Cons
00000190  74 72 61 69 6E 74 73 17  44 61 74 61 54 61 62 6C  traints.DataTabl
000001a0  65 5F 31 2E 43 6F 6E 73  74 72 61 69 6E 74 73 11  e_1.Constraints.
000001b0  44 61 74 61 53 65 74 2E  52 65 6C 61 74 69 6F 6E  DataSet.Relation
000001c0  73 23 44 61 74 61 54 61  62 6C 65 5F 30 2E 44 61  s#DataTable_0.Da
000001d0  74 61 43 6F 6C 75 6D 6E  5F 30 2E 45 78 70 72 65  taColumn_0.Expre
000001e0  73 73 69 6F 6E 23 44 61  74 61 54 61 62 6C 65 5F  ssion#DataTable_
000001f0  30 2E 44 61 74 61 43 6F  6C 75 6D 6E 5F 31 2E 45  0.DataColumn_1.E
00000200  78 70 72 65 73 73 69 6F  6E 23 44 61 74 61 54 61  xpression#DataTa
```

FIGURE 1-7 After setting *RemotingFormat* to binary data, the binary file no longer contains embedded XML.

Deserializing a Data Set from Binary Data

The binary data file you saved in the previous example can easily be deserialized into a data set. The *BinaryFormatter* object stores the schema automatically, so there is no need to load a schema first. The *BinaryFormatter* object automatically identifies the file as having been saved as BinaryXml or TrueBinary. The following code can be used to load the binary file:

Sample of Visual Basic Code

```vb
'deserialize
Dim vendorData as DataSet
Dim fs as new FileStream( _
    desktopFileName("VendorData.bin"), FileMode.Open)
Dim fmt as new BinaryFormatter()
vendorData = CType(fmt.Deserialize(fs),DataSet)
fs.Close()
```

Sample of C# Code

```csharp
//deserialize
DataSet vendorData;
FileStream fs = new FileStream(
    desktopFileName("VendorData.bin"), FileMode.Open);
BinaryFormatter fmt = new BinaryFormatter();
vendorData = (DataSet)fmt.Deserialize(fs);
fs.Close();
```

Looping through Data with the *DataTableReader* Class

The *DataTableReader* class enables you to iterate through *DataRow* objects in one or more *DataTable* objects. *DataTableReader* provides a stable, forward-only, read-only means of looping over *DataRow* objects. For example, if you are using *DataTableReader* to iterate over the rows in a *DataTable* object, you will be able to add or remove rows while in your looping code. You can also use *DataTableReader* to populate many Web controls without having to write looping code because many of the list-type Web controls accept an object that implements the *IDataReader* interface.

If an underlying *DataRow* object is deleted or removed from its data table before *DataTableReader* gets to the *DataRow* object, no attempt is made to retrieve the *DataRow* object. If a *DataRow* object that has already been read is deleted or removed, the current position is maintained; there is no resulting shift in position.

If *DataRow* objects are added to the underlying *DataTable* object while *DataTableReader* is looping, these *DataRow* objects are included in the *DataTableReader* iterations only if the data row is added after the current position of the *DataTableReader* object. *DataRow* objects inserted before the current position of the *DataTableReader* class are not included in the iterations.

The *DataTableReader* class contains a method called *Read* that is executed to load *DataTableReader* with the data row at the current position, and then the position is advanced. If the end of data is reached, the *Read* method returns null. Any attempt to execute the *Read* method after the end of data is reached will always return null, even if more *DataRow* objects are added.

The *DataSet* class contains a method called *CreateDataReader* that returns an instance of the *DataTableReader* class. If the data set contains more than one table, the *DataTableReader* object reads rows from the first *DataTable* object, and you can use the *NextResult* method to continue looping through all data tables in the data set.

The following code example demonstrates the use of *DataTableReader* to loop over a data table and display the *Person* object's *Name* property, and then the *NextResult* method is executed to move to the *Part* data table and display the *PartName* property to a text box.

Sample of Visual Basic Code

```vbnet
'Create an initial DataSet
Dim masterData As New DataSet("Sales")
Dim person As DataTable = masterData.Tables.Add("Person")
person.Columns.Add("Id", GetType(Guid))
person.Columns.Add("Name", GetType(String))
person.PrimaryKey = New DataColumn() {person.Columns("Id")}
Dim part As DataTable = masterData.Tables.Add("Part")
part.Columns.Add("Id", GetType(Guid))
part.Columns.Add("PartName", GetType(String))
part.PrimaryKey = New DataColumn() {part.Columns("Id")}

For i As Integer = 0 To 100
    person.Rows.Add(Guid.NewGuid(), "Joe " + i.ToString())
    part.Rows.Add(Guid.NewGuid(), "Part " + i.ToString())
```

```
Next

'read the data in the DataTable
Dim rd As DataTableReader = masterData.CreateDataReader()
While (rd.Read())
    TextBox1.AppendText(rd("Name").ToString() + vbcrlf)
End While
rd.NextResult()
While (rd.Read())
    TextBox1.AppendText(rd("PartName").ToString() + vbcrlf)
End While
```

Sample of C# Code

```
//Create an initial DataSet
DataSet masterData = new DataSet("Sales");
DataTable person = masterData.Tables.Add("Person");
person.Columns.Add("Id", typeof(Guid));
person.Columns.Add("Name", typeof(string));
person.PrimaryKey = new DataColumn[] { person.Columns["Id"] };
DataTable part = masterData.Tables.Add("Part");
part.Columns.Add("Id", typeof(Guid));
part.Columns.Add("PartName", typeof(string));
part.PrimaryKey = new DataColumn[] { part.Columns["Id"] };

for (int i = 0; i < 100; i++)
{
    person.Rows.Add(Guid.NewGuid(), "Joe " + i);
    part.Rows.Add(Guid.NewGuid(), "Part " + i);
}

//read the data in the DataTable
DataTableReader rd = masterData.CreateDataReader();
while (rd.Read())
{
    textBox1.AppendText(rd["Name"].ToString() + "\r\n");
}
rd.NextResult();
while (rd.Read())
{
    textBox1.AppendText(rd["PartName"].ToString() + "\r\n");
}
```

The *DataTableReader* class inherits from the *DbDataReader* class. You'll find more information on the properties inherited from *DbDataReader* in Chapter 2.

Handling Specialized Types

The *DataTable* class enables you to have a column whose type is specialized, which allows for columns to contain XML data or even an instance of a custom class you created.

A column whose data type is a reference type—except string—requires special treatment in certain cases, because if a column's data type is a reference type and is used as a primary key or as a *Sort* or *RowFilter* key for a data view, any change to the column value must involve assigning a new object to the column as opposed to just changing properties on the column's existing object. This assignment is required to trigger the update of the internal indexes used by sorting, filtering, and primary key operations. The following code example shows how you can assign a custom *Car* object to a column value.

Sample of Visual Basic Code

```vb
<Serializable()> _
Public Class Car
    Public Property Make() As String
    Public Property Model() As String
    Public Property Year() As Integer
End Class

Private Sub specializedTypesToolStripMenuItem_Click( _
        ByVal sender As System.Object, ByVal e As System.EventArgs) _
        Handles specializedTypesToolStripMenuItem.Click
    Dim cars = CreateTableWithUDT()

    'Add New DataRow by creating the DataRow first
    Dim newAuto = cars.NewRow()
    newAuto("Vin") = "123456789ABCD"
    Dim c = New Car With {.Make = "Chevy", .Model = "Impala", .Year = 2003}
    newAuto("CarObject") = c
    cars.Rows.Add(newAuto)
    Dim theCar = CType(cars.Rows(0)("CarObject"), Car)
    textBox1.AppendText(String.Format("Car: {0} {1} {2}\r\n", _
            theCars.Year, theCars.Make, theCars.Model))
End Sub

Public Function CreateTableWithUDT() As DataTable
    'Create the DataTable named "Car"
    Dim cars = New DataTable("Car")

    'Add the DataColumn using all properties
    Dim vin = New DataColumn("Vin")
    vin.DataType = GetType(String)
    vin.MaxLength = 23
    vin.Unique = True
    vin.AllowDBNull = False
    vin.Caption = "VIN"
    cars.Columns.Add(vin)

    'UDT column
    Dim carColumn = New DataColumn("CarObject", GetType(Car))
    cars.Columns.Add(carColumn)

    'Set the Primary Key
    cars.PrimaryKey = New DataColumn() {vin}
    Return Car
End Function
```

Sample of C# Code

```csharp
[Serializable]
public class Car
```

```
{
    public int Year { get; set; }
    public string Make { get; set; }
    public string Model { get; set; }
}

private void specializedTypesToolStripMenuItem_Click(
    object sender, EventArgs e)
{
    DataTable cars = CreateTableWithUDT();

    //Add New DataRow by creating the DataRow first
    DataRow newAuto = cars.NewRow();
    newAuto["Vin"] = "123456789ABCD";
    Car c = new Car { Make = "Chevy", Model = "Impala", Year = 2003 };
    newAuto["CarObject"] = c;
    cars.Rows.Add(newAuto);
    Car theCar = (Car)cars.Rows[0]["CarObject"];
    textBox1.AppendText(string.Format("Car: {0} {1} {2}\r\n",
        theCars.Year, theCars.Make, theCars.Model));
}

public DataTable CreateTableWithUDT()
{
    //Create the DataTable named "Car"
    DataTable cars = new DataTable("Car");

    //Add the DataColumn using all properties
    DataColumn vin = new DataColumn("Vin");
    vin.DataType = typeof(string);
    vin.MaxLength = 23;
    vin.Unique = true;
    vin.AllowDBNull = false;
    vin.Caption = "VIN";
    cars.Columns.Add(vin);

    //UDT column
    DataColumn carColumn = new DataColumn("CarObject", typeof(Car));
    cars.Columns.Add(carColumn);

    //Set the Primary Key
    cars.PrimaryKey = new DataColumn[] { vin };

    return car;
}
```

In this code example, the *Car* class has the *Serializable* attribute on it, which is necessary if you will be serializing the data table that contains this value.

Data Binding Overview

Most of the controls you would use in Windows Forms, ASP.NET, or Windows Presentation Foundation (WPF) are bindable (connectable) to data. This section provides a small overview of data binding, using these technologies. As you browse through the sample code, you will see various examples of data binding.

Data Binding in Windows Forms Applications

When binding data to controls in a Windows Forms application, at a minimum, you must set the *DataSource* property of the control to an object that implements the *IList* interface. In addition, you might need to set other properties, depending on the type of control and the source of the data. Here is a list of the data-binding properties you might need to set.

- **DataSource**   This is the primary property to which you assign your data. You can assign anything that implements the *IList*, *IListSource*, *IBindingList*, or *IBindingListView* interface. Some examples of items that can be assigned to the *DataSource* property are arrays (*IList*), lists (*IList*), data tables (*IListSource*), and data sets (*IListSource*).

- **DataMember**   When assigning to the *DataSource* property, if your data source object contains more than one tabular set, you must specify which one to use. The *DataMember* property is assigned a string that specifies which tabular set to use. For example, a data set can contain Customers, Orders, Employees, and Products tables. If you assign the data set to the *DataSource* property, you must assign a value to the *DataMember* property to indicate to which of the tables you want to bind. Controls that work with a single value (non-list controls) typically use the *Binding* or *BindingSource* property instead of *DataSource* and *DataMember*.

- **DisplayMember**   This property is used on list controls, such as *ComboBox* and *ListBox*, to indicate which column of a data table or which property of the items in a collection will be displayed.

- **ValueMember**   This property is also used on list controls, such as *ComboBox* and *ListBox*, to indicate which column will be retrievable when a selection is made. Although not required, this is usually set to the primary key column of the table.

Data Binding in an ASP.NET Application

When binding data to controls in an ASP.NET Web Forms application, at a minimum, you must set the *DataSource* property to an object that implements the *IList* interface. In addition, you might need to set other properties, depending on the type of control and the source of the data. Here is a list of the data-binding properties you might need to set.

- **DataSource**   This is the primary property to which you assign your data. For ASP.NET application, you can assign anything that implements the *IEnumerable* interface.

- **DataMember**   When assigning to the *DataSource* property, if your data source object implements *IListSource* (for example, it contains more than one tabular set), you must specify which one to use. The *DataMember* property is assigned a string that specifies which tabular set to use. For example, a data set can contain Customers, Orders, Employees, and Products tables. If you assign the data set to the *DataSource* property, you must assign a value to the *DataMember* property to indicate to which of the tables you want to bind.

- **DisplayMember** This property is used on list controls such as *DropDownList* and *ListBox* to indicate which column will be displayed.

- **ValueMember** This property is also used on list controls, such as *DropDownList* and *ListBox*, to indicate which column will be retrievable when a selection is made. This usually is set to the primary key column of the table.

ASP.NET controls require you to execute the *DataBind* method on the control to indicate that the data is ready to be rendered. If you don't execute the *DataBind* method, the control won't render. When executing the *DataBind* method on a control, the control is obliged to call the *DataBind* method on its child controls. This means that you can execute the *DataBind* method on the Web form, and it will call the *DataBind* method on all its controls.

Data Binding in Windows Presentation Foundation (WPF) Applications

WPF applications require you to have a target and a source when data binding. The binding target can be any accessible property derived from *DependencyProperty*. The binding source can be any public property. This means that you can bind to data sets and data tables, and you can bind to common language runtime (CLR) objects, XAML elements. For list-bound controls, you can use the following *ItemsSource* property as the target. *ItemsSource* is the primary property to which you assign your data.

PRACTICE **Working with Disconnected Data Classes**

In this practice, you extend the application from Lesson 1 of this chapter. Remember that this scenario is based on a person who owns several vehicles and wants to track all repairs for each vehicle.

When the application starts for the first time, a data set is created and populated with a schema. The schema will be saved so that it can be used on subsequent startups of the application and can also be shared with others who want to use your data.

When you enter vehicles and repairs, they will be in the data set that is in memory, but they won't be persisted to the XML file until you close Form1, which will save the data set to the XML file and end the application.

This practice is intended to focus on the classes that have been defined in this lesson, so the GUI will be minimal.

If you encounter a problem completing an exercise, the completed projects can be installed from the Code folder on the companion CD.

EXERCISE   Create the Graphical User Interface

In this exercise, you open the Windows Forms application project from Lesson 1. You add controls to the main Windows form to create the graphical user interface.

1. In Visual Studio .NET 2010, click File | Open | Project.

2. You can select the project you created in Lesson 1, or you can open the Lesson 2 Begin project, which gives you the starting point for this practice.

3 Drag and drop two DataGridView controls from the toolbox to the form as shown in Figure 1-8.

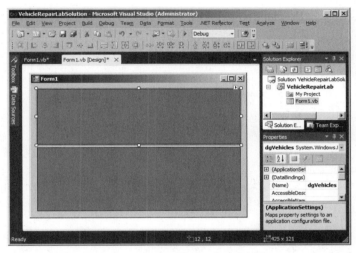

FIGURE 1-8 The GUI is shown here with two *DataGridView* controls added.

4. Name the top *DataGridView* control **dgVehicles** and the bottom *DataGridView* control **dgRepairs**. On dgVehicles, set the *Anchor* property to *Top*, *Left*, *Right*. On dgRepairs, set the *Anchor* property to *Top*, *Bottom*, *Left*, *Right*.

5. Right-click Form1 and click View Code. This displays the code window.

6. Add code to define the name of the schema definition file that will be used to hold the schema of the data set, and add code to define the name of the XML file that will hold the data. Your code should be added at the class level of Form1 and should now look like the following:

Sample of Visual Basic Code

```
Private ReadOnly xsdFile = Path.Combine(Environment.GetFolderPath( _
    Environment.SpecialFolder.ApplicationData), "VehiclesRepairs.xsd")
Private ReadOnly xmlFile = Path.Combine(Environment.GetFolderPath( _
    Environment.SpecialFolder.ApplicationData), "VehiclesRepairs.xml")
Private ds As DataSet
```

Sample of C# Code

```
private readonly string xsdFile = Path.Combine(Environment.GetFolderPath(
    Environment.SpecialFolder.ApplicationData),"VehiclesRepairs.xsd");
private readonly string xmlFile = Path.Combine(Environment.GetFolderPath(
    Environment.SpecialFolder.ApplicationData),"VehiclesRepairs.xml");
private DataSet ds;
```

The path is specified with the file names. Feel free to change the paths of both of these files to suit your needs.

7. Change the code in the *Form1_Load* event handler method to call a *PopulateDataSet* method that hasn't been created yet.

   This code will replace the existing call to the *CreateSchema* method that you added in the Lesson 1 practice. This method will populate the data set with a schema and data. Your code should look like the following:

Sample of Visual Basic Code

```
Private Sub Form1_Load(ByVal sender As System.Object, _
        ByVal e As System.EventArgs) _
        Handles MyBase.Load
    PopulateDataSet()
End Sub
```

Sample of C# Code

```
private void Form1_Load(object sender, EventArgs e)
{
    PopulateDataSet();
}
```

8. Add code to create the *PopulateDataSet* method. This method will check to see whether the schema file exists and, if it does exist, loads the schema into the data set. If the schema doesn't exist, add code to call the *CreateSchema* method that was created in the Lesson 1 practice. Also add code to load the XML file if it exists. You will also want to add *Imports System.IO* (C# using *System.IO;*) to the top of your code. Your *PopulateDataSet* method should look like the following:

Sample of Visual Basic Code

```
Private Sub PopulateDataSet()
    If File.Exists(xsdFile) Then
        ds = New DataSet()
        ds.ReadXmlSchema(xsdFile)
    Else
        CreateSchema()
    End If
    If File.Exists(xmlFile) Then
        ds.ReadXml(xmlFile, XmlReadMode.IgnoreSchema)
    End If
End Sub
```

Sample of C# Code

```csharp
private void PopulateDataSet()
{
    if(File.Exists(xsdFile))
    {
        ds = new DataSet();
        ds.ReadXmlSchema(xsdFile);
    }
    else
    {
        CreateSchema();
    }
    if(File.Exists(xmlFile))
    {
        ds.ReadXml(xmlFile, XmlReadMode.IgnoreSchema);
    }
}
```

9. At the bottom of the *CreateSchema* method, remove the call to *MessageBox.Show* and add a call to save the *DataSet* schema to a file. Your *CreateSchema* method should look like the following:

Sample of Visual Basic Code

```vb
Private Sub CreateSchema()
    ds = New DataSet("VehiclesRepairs")

    Dim vehicles = ds.Tables.Add("Vehicles")
    vehicles.Columns.Add("VIN", GetType(String))
    vehicles.Columns.Add("Make", GetType(String))
    vehicles.Columns.Add("Model", GetType(String))
    vehicles.Columns.Add("Year", GetType(Integer))
    vehicles.PrimaryKey = New DataColumn() {vehicles.Columns("VIN")}

    Dim repairs = ds.Tables.Add("Repairs")
    Dim pk = repairs.Columns.Add("ID", GetType(Integer))
    pk.AutoIncrement = True
    pk.AutoIncrementSeed = -1
    pk.AutoIncrementStep = -1
    repairs.Columns.Add("VIN", GetType(String))
    repairs.Columns.Add("Description", GetType(String))
    repairs.Columns.Add("Cost", GetType(Decimal))
    repairs.PrimaryKey = New DataColumn() {repairs.Columns("ID")}

    ds.Relations.Add( _
        "vehicles_repairs", _
        vehicles.Columns("VIN"), _
        repairs.Columns("VIN"))

    ds.WriteXmlSchema(xsdFile)
End Sub
```

Sample of C# Code

```csharp
private void CreateSchema()
{
```

```
        ds = new DataSet("VehiclesRepairs");

        var vehicles = ds.Tables.Add("Vehicles");
        vehicles.Columns.Add("VIN", typeof(string));
        vehicles.Columns.Add("Make", typeof(string));
        vehicles.Columns.Add("Model", typeof(string));
        vehicles.Columns.Add("Year", typeof(int));
        vehicles.PrimaryKey = new DataColumn[] { vehicles.Columns["VIN"] };

        var repairs = ds.Tables.Add("Repairs");
        var pk = repairs.Columns.Add("ID", typeof(int));
        pk.AutoIncrement = true;
        pk.AutoIncrementSeed = -1;
        pk.AutoIncrementStep = -1;
        repairs.Columns.Add("VIN", typeof(string));
        repairs.Columns.Add("Description", typeof(string));
        repairs.Columns.Add("Cost", typeof(decimal));
        repairs.PrimaryKey = new DataColumn[] { repairs.Columns["ID"] };

        ds.Relations.Add(
            "vehicles_repairs",
            vehicles.Columns["VIN"],
            repairs.Columns["VIN"]);

        ds.WriteXmlSchema(xsdFile);
    }
```

10. Add code to the *Form1_Load* method to bind (connect) the Vehicles data table to the *dgVehicles* control and add code to bind the vehicles_repairs relationship to the *dgRepairs* control as follows:

Sample of Visual Basic Code
```
Private Sub Form1_Load(ByVal sender As System.Object, _
            ByVal e As System.EventArgs) _
        Handles MyBase.Load
    PopulateDataSet()
    dgVehicles.DataSource = ds
    dgVehicles.DataMember = "Vehicles"
    dgRepairs.DataSource = ds
    dgRepairs.DataMember = "Vehicles.vehicles_repairs"
End Sub
```

Sample of C# Code
```
private void Form1_Load(object sender, EventArgs e)
{
    PopulateDataSet();
    dgVehicles.DataSource = ds;
    dgVehicles.DataMember = "Vehicles";
    dgRepairs.DataSource = ds;
    dgRepairs.DataMember = "Vehicles.vehicles_repairs";
}
```

11. Add code to save the data set to the XML file when Form1 is closing. To add a *Form1_Closing* event handler method, click the Form1 [Design] tab, click the title bar of

Form1 to select it, and then, in the Properties window, click the Event lightning bolt to view the available events for Form1.

12. In the Events window, double-click the FormClosing event to add the event handler method to your code. In this method, add code to save the XML file as follows:

Sample of Visual Basic Code

```
Private Sub Form1_FormClosing(ByVal sender As System.Object, _
                          ByVal e As FormClosingEventArgs) _
                    Handles MyBase.FormClosing
    ds.WriteXml(xmlFile, XmlWriteMode.DiffGram)
End Sub
```

Sample of C# Code

```
private void Form1_FormClosing(
      object sender, FormClosingEventArgs e)
{
    ds.WriteXml(xmlFile, XmlWriteMode.DiffGram);
}
```

13. Build the application. On the main menu, click Build | Build Solution to build. If you have errors, you can double-click the error to go to the error line and correct.

14. Run the application. On the main menu, click Debug | Debug Application to run. Add a couple of vehicles and then go back to the first vehicle and add some repairs. Figure 1-9 shows an example of what your screen should look like.

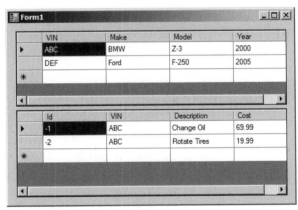

FIGURE 1-9 The complete application is shown here with two vehicles and the repairs for the selected vehicle.

Lesson Summary

This lesson provided detailed information about serialization and deserialization of the ADO.NET disconnected classes as well as about handling specialized data types in a data set or data table. Finally, this chapter provided an overview of data binding.

- *DataSet* and *DataTable* objects can be serialized and deserialized to and from a binary or XML file or stream.
- A column value can contain custom objects as well as instances of base .NET types.
- You can use *DataTableReader* to provide stable, forward-only, read-only looping over a data table. You can also use it to populate many Windows and Web controls.
- Data binding is the connecting of data to a GUI control.
- Most GUI controls have a *DataSource* property and a *DataMember* property, which are used for data binding.

Lesson Review

You can use the following questions to test your knowledge of the information in Lesson 2, "Serialization, Specialized Types, and Data Binding." The questions are also available on the companion CD if you prefer to review them in electronic form.

> **NOTE ANSWERS**
>
> Answers to these questions and explanations of why each answer choice is correct or incorrect are located in the "Answers" section at the end of the book.

1. If you want to assign a *Car* object to a column called CarObject, which attribute must be on the *Car* class to enable saving the data table to a file?

   A. *Bindable*

   B. *DataObject*

   C. *Serializable*

   D. *FileIOPermission*

2. You are storing custom *Car* objects in a data table whose *DataView* property displays a filtered list of *Car* objects, filtered on Make Of The Cars. If you change the make of one of the *Car* objects, you want to ensure that the filter will dynamically update. What must you do to be assured that the filter will detect the change made to your custom *Car* object?

   A. Create a new *Car* object and assign it to the column value.

   B. Nothing, because this scenario works by default.

3. You are storing custom *Car* objects in a data table that will be serialized to a file. After serializing to a binary file called cars.bin, you open the file with a binary editor and notice that XML is in the file. Which setting can you use to ensure that you will create a binary file without embedded XML?

   A. Set the *BatchUpdate* setting to *SerializationFormat.Binary*.

   B. Set the *RemotingFormat* property to *SerializationFormat.Binary*.

C. Set the *DefaultView* property to *SerializationFormat.Binary.*

D. Set the *Constraints* property to *SerializationFormat.Binary.*

4. When working with a data set that has data in it, you decide you want to store the schema, but not the data, of the data set to a file so you can share the schema with other users. Which method must you execute to store the schema?

   A. *InferXmlSchema*

   B. *ReadXmlSchema*

   C. *WriteXmlSchema*

   D. *WriteXml*

Case Scenarios

In the following case scenarios, you apply what you've learned about serialization and dese-rialization of the ADO.NET disconnected classes as well as about handling specialized data types in a data set or data table. You can find answers to these questions in the "Answers" section at the end of this book.

Case Scenario 1: The Traveling Sales Team

Your company has several traveling salespeople who are on the road most of the time, calling on customers and taking orders for new equipment. While they are on the road, they need to access information about existing customers, add new customers, and add new orders.

Answer the following questions regarding the application you might need to build to sup-port these salespeople.

1. How can you write code that enables the salesperson to hold customers' information and orders in your program? In other words, which classes will you use?

2. How can you save the data while the salesperson is traveling and load the same data when the program is started again?

3. When the salesperson is connected to the company network, which objects can be used to send the changes back to the company database?

Case Scenario 2: Sorting and Filtering Data

In your application, you are using a data set that contains several *DataTable* objects. The ap-plication is running fine, but the users want to see which rows have been modified, inserted, and deleted. They also want to sort the data being displayed.

1. How can you show rows that have been inserted, modified, or deleted?

2. How can you show the data in a sorted fashion?

Suggested Practices

To help you successfully master the exam objectives presented in this chapter, complete the following tasks. Create at least one application that uses the disconnected objects. This can be accomplished by performing the practice at the end of Lesson 1 or by completing the fol-lowing Practice 1.

- **Practice 1**   Create an application that requires you to collect data into at least two *DataTable* objects that are related. This could be about customers who place orders, employees who have performance reviews, vehicles that have repairs, or contacts that have phone numbers.

- **Practice 2**   Complete the preceding Practice 1 and then add code to save and load the data to an XML file.

Take a Practice Test

The practice tests on this book's companion CD offer many options. For example, you can test yourself on just the lesson review content, or you can test yourself on all the 70-516 certification exam objectives. You can set up the test so that it closely simulates the experience of taking a certification exam, or you can set it up in study mode so that you can look at the correct answers and explanations after you answer each question.

> **MORE INFO** **PRACTICE TESTS**
>
> For details about all the practice test options available, see the "How to Use the Practice Tests" section in this book's introduction.

CHAPTER 2

ADO.NET Connected Classes

In the previous chapter, the disconnected classes were covered in great detail, code samples were included, and the practice even created an application that could be used without ever making a connection to a database server. However, you must connect to a database server to load, modify, and save data that will be shared with other people and other applications. This is when you can use the connected classes.

To access data in a database, you must have a good understanding of the ADO.NET connected classes. These classes provide you with granular connectivity you can use directly to write data-centric applications. In later chapters, you will see that these classes provide the foundation for achieving connectivity when you want to write object-centric applications.

Exam objectives in this chapter:

- Configure connection strings and providers.
- Create and manage a data connection.
- Secure a connection.
- Execute a SQL query.
- Handle special data types.
- Create, update, or delete data by using SQL statements.
- Manage transactions.
- Synchronize data.

Lessons in this chapter:

Before You Begin

To complete the lessons in this chapter, you must have some understanding of Microsoft C# or Visual Basic 2010. You should have also completed Chapter 1, "ADO.NET Disconnected Classes." Note that although ADO.NET can connect to many data stores, the focus throughout this book will be on connectivity to Microsoft SQL Server.

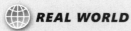 **REAL WORLD**

Glenn Johnson

One of the cool things about ADO.NET connectivity is that the classes are almost identical for each database manufacturer's product. I have found this to be very helpful because after you learn how to connect to and query one database product, it's easy to learn how to connect to other products. Usually, the hardest part is the actual connection string. After you come up with a connection string that works, the rest is a breeze.

Lesson 1: Connecting to the Data Store

The ADO.NET libraries contain classes (listed in the *System.Data* namespace) that you can use to transfer data between a data store and the client application. There are many kinds of data stores, so you need specialized code to provide the necessary bridge between the disconnected data access classes (discussed in Chapter 1) and a particular data store. This lesson focuses on these specialized classes, starting with the most essential classes, such as *DbConnection* and *DbCommand*. The lesson concludes with the more elaborate classes, such as *DbProviderFactory* and *DbProviderFactories*.

> **After this lesson, you will be able to:**
> - Identify the providers included in the .NET Framework.
> - Use the *SqlConnection* object to access SQL Server.
> - Encrypt and decrypt a connection string.
> - Store a connection string in a configuration file.
> - Configure connection pooling.
>
> **Estimated lesson time: 45 minutes**

Using Providers to Move Data

The classes responsible for the movement of data between the disconnected data classes in the client application and the data store are referred to as *connected classes* or *provider classes*. The Microsoft .NET Framework contains the following providers:

- **OleDb**   Contains classes that provide general-purpose data access to many data sources. You can use this provider to access SQL Server 6.5 and earlier, SyBase, DB2/400, and Microsoft Access.

- **Odbc**   Contains classes that provide general-purpose data access to many data sources. This provider is typically used when no newer provider is available.

- **SQL Server**   Contains classes that provide functionality similar to the generic *OleDb* provider. The difference is that these classes are tuned for SQL Server 7 and later data access. SQL Server 6.5 and earlier must use the *OleDb* provider.

> **NOTE   CONNECTING TO AN ORACLE DATABASE**
> The Oracle provider that existed in earlier versions of the .NET Framework has been deprecated in .NET Framework 4. If you need to connect to an Oracle database, you should download Oracle's provider from the Oracle website.

You can also use third-party providers, such as DB2 and MySql, which can be downloaded from the Web.

Table 2-1 lists the primary provider classes and interfaces. The classes are subclassed by the provider, which replaces the *Db* prefix with a provider prefix such as *Sql*, *Odbc*, or *OleDb*. You can use the base classes with factory classes to create client code that is provider agnostic. The following sections describe these classes in detail.

TABLE 2-1 Primary Provider Classes and Interfaces in ADO.NET

BASE CLASSES	SQLCLIENT CLASSES	GENERIC INTERFACE
DbConnection	*SqlConnection*	*IDbConnection*
DbCommand	*SqlCommand*	*IDbCommand*
DbDataReader	*SqlDataReader*	*IDataReader/IDataRecord*
DbTransaction	*SqlTransaction*	*IDbTransaction*
DbParameter	*SqlParameter*	*IDbDataParameter*
DbParameterCollection	*SqlParameterCollection*	*IDataParameterCollection*
DbDataAdapter	*SqlDataAdapter*	*IDbDataAdapter*
DbCommandBuilder	*SqlCommandBuilder*	
DbConnectionStringBuilder	*SqlConnectionStringBuilder*	
DbDataPermission	*SqlPermission*	

Getting Started with the *DbConnection* Object

You need a valid, open connection object to access a data store. The *DbConnection* class is an abstract class from which the provider inherits to create provider-specific classes. Figure 2-1 shows the connection class hierarchy.

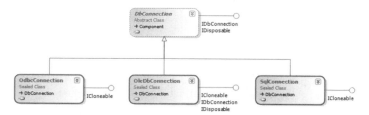

FIGURE 2-1 This is the *DbConnection* class hierarchy.

Opening and Closing the Connection

You need a valid connection string to create a connection. The following code sample shows how first to create the connection and then assign the connection string. With a valid connection string, you can open the connection and execute commands. When you are finished working with the connection object, you must close the connection to free up the resources being held. You need the Northwind sample database to use this connection. This sample database is available from the Microsoft download site and is included with the sample media.

Sample of Visual Basic Code

```
Dim connection = new SqlConnection()
connection.ConnectionString = _
    "Server=.;Database=northwind;Trusted_Connection=true"
connection.Open()
'Do lots of cool work here
connection.Close()
```

Sample of C# Code

```
var connection = new SqlConnection();
connection.ConnectionString =
    "Server=.;Database=Northwind;Trusted_Connection=true";
connection.Open();
    //Do lots of cool work here
connection.Close();
```

> **NOTE *CLOSE* METHOD VERSUS *USING* BLOCKS**
>
> IN ADO.NET, the connection classes also implement the *IDisposable* interface, so you can also define the connection in a *using* block and, when you exit the *using* block, the connection will automatically be disposed. The *Dispose* method on the connection calls the *Close* method on the connection. You can use either the *using* block or the explicit *Close* method. Generally, the *using* block is considered better because you don't have to call the *Close* method explicitly, and, if an exception is thrown while in the *using* block, the connection will still be closed. If a connection is left open across multiple method calls, you can't use the *using* block. In this chapter, you will see examples of both implementations. Decide which works for you, but make sure that you do close the connection when you are finished with it.

The *ConnectionString* property is initialized with a string that contains *key=value* pairs separated by a semicolon. The first part of the connection string ("Server=.") dictates the use of your local computer. The period can be replaced with an actual computer name or IP address. The second part of the connection string (Database=Northwind) indicates that you want to connect the Northwind database. The last part of the connection string (Trusted_Connection=true) indicates that you will use your Windows login account for authentication with SQL Server.

By creating an instance of the *SqlConnection* class, a *DbConnection* object is created because *SqlConnection* inherits from *DbConnection*. This is accomplished by the SQL Server .NET provider. The connection string is the same regardless of the programming language used. The following sections explain how to configure a connection string by using each of the .NET Framework providers.

Configuring an ODBC Connection String

The connection string can be the most difficult object to set up when you're working with a provider for the first time. Open Database Connectivity (ODBC) is one of the older technologies the .NET Framework supports, primarily because you still need the .NET Framework to connect to older database products that have ODBC drivers. Table 2-2 describes the most common ODBC connection string settings.

TABLE 2-2 ODBC Connection String Keywords

KEYWORD	DESCRIPTION
Driver	The ODBC driver to use for the connection
DSN	A data source name, which can be configured by navigating through Control Panel | Administrative Tools | Data Sources (ODBC)
Server	The name of the server to which to connect
Trusted_Connection	Specifies that security is based on using the domain account of the currently logged-on user
Database	The database to which to connect
DBQ	Typically refers to the physical path to a data source

Sample ODBC Connection Strings

The following connection string instructs the text driver to treat the files located in the C:\Test\MyFolder subdirectory as tables in a database.

```
Driver={Microsoft Text Driver (*.txt; *.csv)};
    DBQ=C:\\Test\\MyFolder;
```

The following connection string instructs the Access driver to open the Northwind database file located in the C:\Program Files\myApp folder.

```
Driver={Microsoft Access Driver (*.mdb)};
    DBQ=C:\\program files\\myApp\\Northwind.mdb
```

The following connection string uses the settings that have been configured as a data source name (DSN) on the current machine.

```
DSN=My Application DataSource
```

The following is a connection to an Oracle database on the ORACLE8i7 servers. The name and password are passed in as well.

```
Driver={Microsoft ODBC for Oracle};
    Server=ORACLE8i7;
    UID=john;
    PWD=s3$W%1Xz
```

The following connection string uses the Excel driver to open the MyBook.xls file.

```
Driver={Microsoft Excel Driver (*.xls)};
   DBQ=C:\\Samples\\MyBook.xls
```

The following connection string uses the SQL Server driver to open the Northwind database on MyServer, using the passed-in user name and password.

```
DRIVER={SQL Server};
   SERVER=MyServer;
   UID=AppUserAccount;
   PWD=Zx%7$ha;
   DATABASE=Northwind;
```

This connection string uses the SQL Server driver to open the Northwind database on MyServer using SQL Server trusted security.

```
DRIVER={SQL Server};
   SERVER=MyServer;
   Trusted_Connection=yes
   DATABASE=Northwind;
```

Configuring an OLEDB Connection String

Another common but earlier technology used to access databases is Object Linking and Embedding for Databases (OLEDB). Table 2-3 describes the most common ODBC connection string settings.

TABLE 2-3 OLEDB Connection String Keywords

KEYWORD	DESCRIPTION
Data Source	The name of the database or physical location of the database file.
File Name	The physical location of a file that contains the real connection string.
Persist Security Info	If set to *true*, retrieving the connection string returns the complete connection string that was originally provided. If set to *false*, the connection string will contain the information that was originally provided, minus the security information.
Provider	The vendor-specific driver to use for connecting to the data store.

Sample OLEDB Connection Strings

This connection string uses the settings stored in the MyAppData.udl file. The .udl extension stands for *universal data link*.

```
FILE NAME=C:\Program Files\MyApp\MyAppData.udl
```

This connection string uses the Jet driver, which is the Access driver, and opens the demo database file. Retrieving the connection string from the connection will return the connection that was originally passed in, minus the security information.

```
Provider=Microsoft.Jet.OLEDB.4.0;
    Data Source=C:\Program Files\myApp\demo.mdb;
    Persist Security Info=False
```

Configuring an SQL Server Connection String

The SQL Server provider enables you to access SQL Server 7.0 and later. If you need to connect to SQL Server 6.5 and earlier, use the OLEDB provider. Table 2-4 describes the most common SQL Server connection string settings.

TABLE 2-4 SQL Server Connection String Keywords (not case sensitive)

KEYWORD	DESCRIPTION
Data Source, Addr, Address, Network Address, Server	The name or IP address of the database server (128 characters max). The default is an *empty string*.
Failover Partner	Provides support for database mirroring in SQL Server 2005 and later (128 characters max). The default is an *empty string*.
AttachDbFilename, extended properties, initial file name	The full or relative path and name of a file containing the database to which to be attached (260 characters max). The path supports the keyword string |*DataDirectory*|, which points to the application's data directory. (See "Attaching to a Local SQL Database File with SQL Express" later in this chapter.) The database must reside on a local drive. The log file name must be in the *<database-File-Name>_log.ldf* format, or it will not be found. If the log file is not found, a new log file is created. The default is an *empty string*.
Initial Catalog, Database	The name of the database to use (128 characters max). The default is an *empty string*.
Integrated Security, Trusted_Connection	Used to connect to SQL Server by using a secure connection when authentication is through the user's domain account. Can be set to *true*, *false*, or *sspi*. The default is *false*.
Persist Security Info, PersistSecurityInfo	If set to *true*, retrieving the connection string returns the complete connection string that was originally provided. If set to *false*, the connection string will contain the information that was originally provided, minus the security information. The default is *false*.

User ID, Uid, User	The user name to use to connect to the SQL server when not using a trusted connection (128 characters max).
Password, Pwd	The password to use to log on to SQL Server when not using a trusted connection (128 characters max). The default is an *empty string*.
Enlist	When set to *true*, the pooler automatically enlists the connection into the caller thread's ongoing transaction context. (See "Connection Pooling" later in this chapter.)
Pooling	When set to *true*, causes the request for a new connection to be drawn from the pool. If the pool does not exist, it is created. The default is *true*. (See "Connection Pooling" later in this chapter.)
Max Pool Size	Specifies the maximum allowed connections in the connection pool. The default is *100 connections*. (See "Connection Pooling" later in this chapter.)
Min Pool Size	Specifies the minimum number of connections to keep in the pool. The default is *0 connections*. (See "Connection Pooling" later in this chapter.)
Connection Reset	Indicates that the database connection will be reset when the connection is removed from the pool. The default is *true*. A setting of *false* results in fewer round-trips to the server when creating a connection, but the connection state is not updated. (See "Connection Pooling" later in this chapter.)
MultipleActiveResultSets	When set to *true*, allows for the retrieval of multiple forward-only, read-only result sets on the same connection. The default is *false*.
Replication	Used by SQL Server for replication. The default is *false*.
Connect Timeout, Connection Timeout, Timeout	The time in seconds to wait while an attempt is made to connect to the data store. The default is *15 seconds*.
Encrypt	If *Encrypt* is set to *true* and SQL Server has a certificate installed, all communication between the client and server will be SSL encrypted. The default is *false*.
Load Balance Timeout, Connection Lifetime	The maximum time in seconds that a pooled connection should live. The maximum time is checked only when the connection is returned to the pool. This setting is useful in load-balanced cluster configurations to force a balance between a server that is online and a server that has just started. The default is *0 (unlimited)*. (See "Connection Pooling" later in this chapter.)

Network Library, Net, Network	The network library DLL to use when connecting to SQL Server. Allowed libraries include dbmssocn (TCP/IP), dbnmpntw (Named Pipes), dbmsrpcn (Multiprotocol), dbmsadsn (Apple Talk), dbmsgnet (VIA), dbmsipcn (Shared Memory), and dbmsspxn (IPX/SPX).
	The default is dbmssocn (TCP/IP), but if a network is not specified and either "." or "(local)" is specified for the server, shared memory (i.e., Named Pipes) is the default.
Packet Size	The size in bytes for each packet sent to SQL Server. Valid values are between 512 and 32768. The default is *8000* bytes.
Application Name, App	The name of the application (80 character max). If not set, this defaults to *.NET SQL Client Data Provider*.
Current Language, Language	The SQL Server language record name (80 character max). The default is an *empty string.*
Workstation ID, Wsid	The name of the client computer connecting to SQL Server (128 characters max). The default is *null*.
Context Connection	Used with SQLCLR. When set to *true*, an in-process connection to SQL Server should be made. The default is *false.*
Transaction Binding	Controls connection association with an enlisted *System.Transactions.Transactions*. Valid values are *Implicit Unbind*, *Explicit Unbind*. The default is *Implicit Unbind*.
TrustServerCertificate	When set to *true*, the transport layer uses SSL to encrypt the channel and bypass exploring the certificate chain to validate trust. The default is *false*.
Type System Version	Specifies the client-side representation of SQL Server types to avoid potential problems that could cause an application to break if a different version of SQL Server is used. Possible values are *Latest*, *SQL Server 2000*, *SQL Server 2005*, and *SQL Server 2008*. The default is *Latest*.
User Instance	When set to *true*, starts an instance of SQL Express, using the current user's account. The default is *false*.

Sample SQL Server Connection Strings

The following connection string connects to the Northwind database on the current computer (localhost), using integrated security. This connection must be made within 30 seconds or an exception will be thrown. The security information will not be persisted.

```
Persist Security Info=False;
    Integrated Security=SSPI;
```

```
database=northwind;
server=localhost;
Connect Timeout=30
```

This next connection string uses the TCP sockets library (DBMSSOCN) and connects to the MyDbName database on the computer located at IP address 10.1.2.3, using port 1433. Authentication is based on using *MyUsername* as the user name and *x&1W$dF9* as the password.

```
Network Library=DBMSSOCN;
    Data Source=10.1.2.3,1433;
    Initial Catalog=MyDbName;
    User ID=myUsername;
    Password=x&1W$dF9
```

Attaching to a Local SQL Database File with SQL Express

SQL Express is a free database product that is easy to install and use and is based on SQL Server technology. When you're building small websites and single-user applications, SQL Express is a natural choice due to its XCOPY deployment capabilities, reliability, and high-performance engine. In addition, SQL Express databases can easily be attached to the full release of SQL Server. SQL Express is installed as part of the default Visual Studio .NET installation, which makes it an excellent database to use when you're developing applications destined to be used on SQL Express or SQL Server. To attach a local database file, you can use the following connection string.

```
Data Source=.\SQLEXPRESS;
    AttachDbFilename=C:\MyApplication\Northwind.MDF;
    Integrated Security=True;
    User Instance=True;
```

In this example, the data source is set to an instance of SQL Express called .\SQLEXPRESS. The database file name is set to the database file located at C:\MyApplication\Northwind. MDF. Note that the log file (Northwind_LOG.LDF) must also exist. Integrated security authenticates with SQL Express; setting *User Instance* to *true* starts an instance of SQL Express, using the current user's account.

Although you can use SQL Server to attach to a local file, SQL Server does not work with the *User Instance=true* setting. Also, SQL Server keeps the database attached when your application ends, so the next time you run SQL Server, an exception will be thrown because the data file is already attached.

AttachDBFile can also understand the keyword *|DataDirectory|* to use the application's data directory. Here is the revised connection string.

```
Data Source=.\SQLEXPRESS;
    AttachDbFilename=|DataDirectory|\Northwind.MDF;
    Integrated Security=True;
    User Instance=True
```

How *DataDirectory* Is Resolved

Internally, the System.Data.dll library contains a class called *System.Data.Common
.DbConnectionOptions*, which has a method called *ExpandDataDirectory*. This method in-
cludes code that resolves the |*DataDirectory*| keyword by executing code that looks some-
thing like the following.

Sample of Visual Basic Code

```
Dim path = AppDomain.CurrentDomain.GetData("DataDirectory")
If string.IsNullOrEmpty(path)) Then
     path = AppDomain.CurrentDomain.BaseDirectory
End If
Return path
```

Sample of C# Code

```
var path = (string)AppDomain.CurrentDomain.GetData("DataDirectory");
if (string.IsNullOrEmpty(path)))
{
     path = AppDomain.CurrentDomain.BaseDirectory;
}
return path;
```

What does this mean? The *ExpandDataDirectory* method tries to get the data directory
location from the current assembly. The data directory is set for every ClickOnce application
installed on a local computer. It's located in the user's Documents And Settings folder. If a
database file (.mdf) and its log file (.ldf) are included in a ClickOnce application and marked as
a "data" file, they are copied to this directory on application install. If the ClickOnce application is uninstalled, the application's data directory and the contents of the data directory are
destroyed.

EXAM TIP

For the exam, remember that you can include the database file in your project if you use
the *DataDirectory* keyword in your connection string.

The sample code uses the *BaseDirectory* of *CurrentDomain* if there is no data directory. *BaseDirectory* contains the compiled application. (When in development, this is the
bin\Debug under your project folder.) Instead of placing the database file directly in the
compiled application folder, it's better to place it in the project folder. In Solution Explorer,
click the file and, in the Properties window, set "Copy To Output Directory" to "Copy Always"
or "Copy If Newer."

Storing the Connection String in the Application Configuration File

You can store *ConnectionString* properties in the machine, application, or Web configuration file, so the connection strings can be changed without requiring a recompile of the application. You place the *<connectionStrings>* element under the *<configuration>* root element. This section supports the *<add>*, *<remove>*, and *<clear>* tags, as shown here:

XML Application Configuration File

```xml
<connectionStrings>
    <clear />
    <add name="nw"
        providerName="System.Data.SqlClient"
        connectionString=
        "Data Source=.\SQLEXPRESS;
            AttachDbFilename=|DataDirectory|Northwind.MDF;
            Integrated Security=True;
            User Instance=True"/>
</connectionStrings>
```

This example clears the list of connection settings that might have been defined in the machine configuration file and then adds a new connection string setting called *nw*. The connection strings can be accessed in code by using the static *ConnectionStrings* collection on the *ConfigurationManager* class (implemented in the System.Configuration.dll assembly), as shown in the following code sample.

Sample of Visual Basic Code

```vb
'Get the settings from the configuration file
Dim nw = ConfigurationManager.ConnectionStrings("nw")

'name = "nw"
Dim name = nw.Name

'provider = "System.Data.SqlClient"
Dim provider = nw.ProviderName

'cnString = "Data Source=.\SQLEXPRESS;AttachDbFilename=|DataDirectory|
'    \Northwind.MDF;Integrated Security=True;User Instance=True"
Dim cnString = nw.ConnectionString
MessageBox.Show("From App.Config: " & cnString)
```

Sample of C# Code

```csharp
//Get the settings from the configuration file
var nw = ConfigurationManager.ConnectionStrings["nw"];
var connection = new SqlConnection(nw.ConnectionString);

//name = "nw"
var name = nw.Name;

//provider = "System.Data.SqlClient"
var provider = nw.ProviderName;
```

```
//cnString = "Data Source=.\SQLEXPRESS;AttachDbFilename=|DataDirectory|
//   \Northwind.MDF;Integrated Security=True;User Instance=True"
var cnString = nw.ConnectionString;
MessageBox.Show("From App.Config: " + cnString);
```

Encrypted Communications to SQL Server

To enable encrypted communications between the client and SQL Server, a digital certificate must be installed at SQL Server, and then you can use the *Encrypt* setting in the connection string to turn on encryption.

The following is an example of a connection string that can turn on encrypted communications.

```
Data Source=.\SQLEXPRESS;
    AttachDbFilename=C:\MyApplication\Northwind.MDF;
    Integrated Security=True;
    User Instance=True;
    Encrypt=true
```

If you're using C#, don't forget that you must escape the strings with backslashes by using two backslashes (\\) for each single backslash, or by preceding the string with an at (@) symbol to turn off escape processing. The *Encrypt* setting is set to *true* so that all communication between the client and the server is encrypted.

Storing Encrypted Connection Strings in Web Applications

Web applications don't have an App.config file; they have a Web.config file. It's common practice to store connection strings in the Web.config file. This makes it easy to change the connection string without requiring a recompile of the application. However, connection strings can contain logon information such as user names and passwords. You certainly don't want this information to be easily readable by anyone. The solution is to encrypt the connection strings. You can do this by using the aspnet_regiis.exe utility to encrypt the *connectionStrings* section. You can use the */?* option to get help on the utility.

You encrypt and decrypt the contents of a Web.config file by using *System.Configuration.DPAPIProtectedConfigurationProvider*, which uses the Windows Data Protection API (DPAPI) to encrypt and decrypt data, or *System.Configuration.RSAProtectedConfigurationProvider*, which uses the RSA encryption algorithm to encrypt and decrypt data.

When you use the same encrypted configuration file on many computers in a Web farm, only *System.Configuration.RSAProtectedConfigurationProvider* enables you to export the encryption keys that encrypt the data and import them on another server. This is the default setting.

Implementing an Encrypted *ConnectionString* Property

You can encrypt the Web.config file by running the Visual Studio .NET command prompt and executing the following command, specifying the full path to your website folder:

```
aspnet_regiis -pef "connectionStrings" "C:\...\EncryptWebSite"
```

Note that the –pef switch requires you to pass the physical website path, which is the last parameter. Be sure to verify the path to your Web.config file.

If changes are made to the *connectionStrings* section—for example, if another connection is added using the GUI tools—the new connection will be encrypted; that is, you won't have to run the aspnet_regiis utility again.

You can decrypt the *connectionStrings* section by using the following command:

```
aspnet_regiis -pdf "connectionStrings" "C:\...\EncryptWebSite"
```

Connection Pooling

Creating a physical connection to the database is an expensive task. Connection pooling is reusing existing active connections with the same connection string instead of creating new connections when a request is made to the database. It involves the use of a connection manager that is responsible for maintaining a list, or pool, of available connections for a given connection string. Several pools exist if different connection strings ask for connection pooling.

When the connection manager receives a request for a new connection, it checks in the pool corresponding to the connection string for available connections. If a connection is available, it is returned. If no connections are available and the maximum pool size has not been reached, a new connection is created, added to the pool, and returned. If the maximum pool size has been reached, the connection request is added to a queue to wait until a connection becomes available and is returned. If the connection time-out defined in the connection string expires, an exception is raised.

Connection pooling is controlled by parameters placed into the connection string. The following parameters affect pooling:

- *Connection Timeout*
- *Min Pool Size*
- *Max Pool Size*
- *Pooling*
- *Connection Reset*
- *Load Balancing Timeout (Connection Lifetime)*
- *Enlist*

These parameters are defined in Table 2-4.

Abide by Pool Rules

To implement connection pooling, you must follow a few rules.

- The connection string must be the same for every user or service that participates in the pool. Each character must match in terms of lowercase and uppercase as well.

- The user ID must be the same for every user or service that participates in the pool. Even if you specify *integrated security=true*, the Windows user account of the process determines pool membership.

- The process ID must be the same. It has never been possible to share connections across processes, and this limitation extends to pooling.

> **NOTE   WHEN CAN YOU BENEFIT MOST FROM POOLING?**
>
> Pooling certainly has the most value when implemented on a Web server configured to use the same connection string with the same user account to access the database because many website users will benefit from the use of the pool.

Where's the Pool?

Connection pooling is a client-side technology. The database has no idea that one or more connection pools might be involved in your application. Client-side means that the connection pooling takes place on the machine initiating the *DbConnection* object's *Open* statement.

When Is the Pool Created?

The connection pool group is an object that manages the connection pools for a specific ADO.NET provider. When the first connection is instantiated, a connection pool group is created. However, a connection pool is not created until the first connection is opened. When a connection is closed or disposed, it goes back to the pool as available and will be returned when a new connection request is done.

How Long Will the Connection Stay in the Pool?

A connection is removed from the pool of available connections when used and then returned to the pool of available connections when the connection is closed. By default, when a connection is returned to the connection pool, it has an idle lifetime of 4 to 8 minutes (a time that is set somewhat randomly). This means the connection pool will not continue to hold on to idle connections indefinitely. If you want to make sure that at least one connection is available when your application is idle for long periods, you can set the connection string's *Min Pool Size* to one or more.

Load-Balancing Timeout (Connection Lifetime)

The connection string has a setting called *Load Balancing Timeout*, formerly known as *Connection Lifetime. Connection Lifetime* still exists for backward compatibility, but the new name describes this setting's intended use better. Use this setting only in an environment with clustered servers because it is meant to aid in load balancing database connections. This setting is examined only when the connection is closed. If the connection stays open longer than its *Load Balancing Timeout* setting, the connection is destroyed. Otherwise, it is added back into the pool.

Exceeding the Pool Size

The default maximum connection pool size is 100. You can modify this by changing the *Max Pool Size* connection string setting, although the default setting is fine for most scenarios. How do you know whether you need to change this value? You can use Performance Monitor to watch the .*NET DataProvider for SqlServer/NumberOfPooledConnections* counter. If the maximum pool size is reached, any new requests for a connection will be blocked until a connection frees up or the *Connection Timeout* connection string setting expires. The *Connection Timeout* setting has a default value of 15 seconds. If you exceed the *Connection Timeout* value, an *InvalidOperationException* will be thrown. This same exception is thrown if you try to connect to a database server and the server cannot be reached or if the server is found but the database service is down.

When to Turn Off Pooling

It's a good idea to keep pooling on at all times, but if you need to troubleshoot connection-related problems, you can turn it off. Pooling is on by default, but you can change the *Pooling* setting in the connection string to *false* to turn off pooling. Remember that performance will suffer because each *Open* statement creates a new connection to the database, and each *Dispose/Close* statement destroys the connection. Also, without any limits in terms of number of connections, the server might deny the requests for a connection if the licensing limit is exceeded or the administrator has set connection limits at the server.

Clearing the Pool

A database server might not always be available; it might have been removed from a cluster, or you might have needed to stop and start the service. When a database server becomes unavailable, the connections in the pool become corrupted.

You can use two methods in your code to recover from a corrupted connection pool: *ClearPool* and *ClearAllPools*. These are static methods on the *SqlConnection* and *OracleConnection* classes. If the database service is stopped and restarted, the previous code will cause a *SqlException* to be thrown, stating that a transport-level error has occurred. To recover from this exception silently, you can clean the pools and then re-execute the code.

In this practice, you continue the practice from Lesson 2 in Chapter 1 or use the beginning solution included on the companion CD for Lesson 1 in this chapter. You add code to read a connection string from the configuration file on application startup and test for connectivity. If a connection can be made, you display a message stating that the database server is available. In later practices, you will create a database and synchronize the data.

This practice is intended to focus on the classes that have been defined in this lesson, so the GUI will be minimal.

If you encounter a problem completing an exercise, the completed projects can be installed from the Code folder on the companion CD.

EXERCISE Open the Project

In this exercise, you open the project you created in Chapter 1, Lesson 2, and code to provide database connectivity status.

1. In Visual Studio .NET 2010, click File | Open | Project.

2. Locate the project you created in Chapter 1, Lesson 2, and click Open, or locate the beginning solution for Chapter 2, Lesson 1 on the companion CD.

3. Add a config file to the application.

   ■ **If you're using Visual Basic:** In Solution Explorer, click the project and then click Show All Files at the top of the Solution Explorer window. Your application already has an App.Config file. Right-click the App.config file and click Include In Project.

   ■ **If you're using C#:** In Solution Explorer, right-click the project and click Add | New Item | Application Configuration File | OK. Be sure to use App.Config as the file name.

4. Add the connection string to the config file. Inside the *<configuration>* element, add the following connection string:

   App.Config Connection

   ```
   <connectionStrings>
     <add name="db" connectionString=
       "Data Source=.\SQLEXPRESS;Integrated Security=True" />
   </connectionStrings>
   ```

   This connection string represents a minimum approach to connect to SQL Server Express on your local machine, using the default database setting. The default database is usually the master database, which exists on all versions of SQL Server. The master database should not be used for user-defined tables, so the connection string will be modified in the next lesson, when you create your database.

5. Add a reference to System.Configuration.DLL.

6. Add the following class-level variable to the top of your Windows form. This variable references your connection string after it's read from the configuration file.

Sample of Visual Basic Code

```
Private cnString As String
```

Sample of C# Code

```
private string cnString;
```

7. At the top of the *Form1_Load* event handler method, add code to retrieve the connection string from the configuration file and make a call to the *CheckConnectivity* method you will create in next step. The completed *Form1_Load* should look like the following.

Sample of Visual Basic Code

```
Private Sub Form1_Load(ByVal sender As System.Object, _
        ByVal e As System.EventArgs) Handles MyBase.Load
    cnString = ConfigurationManager _
                .ConnectionStrings("db") _
                .ConnectionString
    CheckConnectivity()
    PopulateDataSet()
    dgVehicles.DataSource = ds
    dgVehicles.DataMember = "Vehicles"
    dgRepairs.DataSource = ds
    dgRepairs.DataMember = "Vehicles.vehicles_repairs"
End Sub
```

Sample of C# Code

```
private void Form1_Load(object sender, EventArgs e)
{
    cnString = ConfigurationManager
                .ConnectionStrings["db"]
                .ConnectionString;
    CheckConnectivity();
    PopulateDataSet();
    dgVehicles.DataSource = ds;
    dgVehicles.DataMember = "Vehicles";
    dgRepairs.DataSource = ds;
    dgRepairs.DataMember = "Vehicles.vehicles_repairs";
}
```

> **NOTE ADD IMPORTS (C# *USING*) FOR NAMESPACES**
>
> For the next step to work properly, you must add *Imports* (C# *using*) statements for *System.Data.SqlClient* and *System.Configuration* at the top of your code.

8. Add the *CheckConnectivity* method, which will attempt to open *SqlConnection*, retrieve the version of SQL Server, and return true or false, based on whether the attempt was successful. Note how the *using* construct ensures that the connection object is always disposed. A message will be displayed to indicate success or failure.

```vb
Private Function CheckConnectivity() As Boolean
    Try
        Using cn = New SqlConnection(cnString)
            cn.Open()
            Dim version = cn.ServerVersion
            MessageBox.Show("Connectivity established! " & version)
        End Using
    Catch ex As Exception
        MessageBox.Show(ex.Message)
        Return False
    End Try
    Return True
End Function
```

Sample of C# Code

```csharp
private bool CheckConnectivity()
{
    try
    {
        using (var cn = new SqlConnection(cnString))
        {
            cn.Open();
            var version = cn.ServerVersion;
            MessageBox.Show("Connectivity established! " + version);
        }
    }
    catch (Exception ex)
    {
        MessageBox.Show(ex.Message);
        return false;
    }
    return true;
}
```

9. If you were to run this program as it is and end the program without adding any data, you would get an error indicating that the year of the vehicle cannot be null. This is because you are in edit mode in the grid, and you haven't added any data. To handle the error a bit more gracefully without masking it, add an error handler for the *dgVehicle* grid by selecting the *dgVehicles* grid in the Windows Forms designer and then, in the Properties window, click the Events (lightning bolt) button. In the *DataError* event, type **gridError** and press Enter to add an event handler method to your code.

In the new event handler method, add code to display the error gracefully. Your code should look like the following.

Sample of Visual Basic Code

```vb
Private Sub gridError(ByVal sender As System.Object, _
        ByVal e As System.Windows.Forms.DataGridViewDataErrorEventArgs) _
        Handles dgVehicles.DataError
    MessageBox.Show(e.Exception.Message)
End Sub
```

Sample of C# Code

```csharp
private void gridError(object sender, DataGridViewDataErrorEventArgs e)
{
    MessageBox.Show(e.Exception.Message);
}
```

10. To handle any error that might occur in the bottom grid gracefully, select the *dgRepairs* grid in the Windows Forms designer.

11. In the Properties window, select Events.

12. In the *DataError* property, click the drop-down list and select the *gridError* method you created in the previous step.

    Now, either grid will call the event handler method if either one has an error.

13. Build the application and correct any errors.

14. Test the application. Press F5 to run the application with the debugger.

    When the application starts, it will load the offline XML file if it exists. It will then check whether it can connect to SQL Server. If a connection can be made, you will see a message stating that connectivity exists. If you can't connect, you will see the error message.

Lesson Summary

This lesson provided a detailed overview of the ADO.NET connected classes.

- Connected classes, also known as provider classes, are responsible for movement of data between the data store and the disconnected classes. A valid instance of a class derived from *DbConnection* is required to use most of the primary provider classes.

- Connection strings can be stored in the App.config file or, for Web applications, the Web.config file.

- When working with Web applications, you can encrypt the connection strings stored in the Web.config file by using the aspnet_regiis.exe tool.

- Connections can be pooled to provide faster availability and better reuse.

Lesson Review

You can use the following questions to test your knowledge of the information in Lesson 1, "Connecting to the Data Store." The questions are also available on the companion CD if you prefer to review them in electronic form.

> **NOTE ANSWERS**
>
> Answers to these questions and explanations of why each answer choice is correct or incorrect are located in the "Answers" section at the end of the book.

1. You want to create a connection to an old SQL server. Upon investigation, you discover that its version is 6.5. Which .NET provider will you use to connect to this server?

    A. *Oracle*

    B. *SqlClient*

    C. *Oledb*

2. Before you can execute a command on a connection object, which method must you execute to prepare the connection?

    A. *Open*

    B. *BeginTransaction*

    C. *GetSchema*

    D. *Close*

3. You want to set up a secure connection between your application and SQL Server. SQL Server has a trusted certificate that is set up properly. What must you do?

    A. Execute *BeginTransaction* on the command object.

    B. Add *Encrypt=true* to the connection string.

    C. Encrypt the *CommandText* property on the command object.

    D. Close the connection before sending the command.

4. You want to secure the connection strings contained within your Web.config file to ensure that no one can open the file easily and see the connection information. Which tool must you use to encrypt the connection strings?

    A. ASPNET_REGSQL.EXE

    B. CASPOL.EXE

    C. INSTALLUTIL.EXE

    D. ASPNET_REGIIS.EXE.

Lesson 2: Reading and Writing Data

To execute commands to the database, you must have an open connection and a command object. The previous lesson covered connectivity, and this lesson describes how to create and use a command object.

> **After this lesson, you will be able to:**
> - Identify the ways to execute a command to a data store.
> - Execute a command to a data store.
> - Send updates back to the data store.
> - Use the *DbProviderFactory*-derived classes to create provider-agnostic code.
> - Handle exceptions with a try/catch block.
>
> **Estimated lesson time: 30 minutes**

DbCommand Object

You use the *DbCommand* object to send a Structured Query Language (SQL) command to the data store. *DbCommand* can be a Data Manipulation Language (DML) command to retrieve, insert, update, or delete data. The *DbCommand* object can also be a Data Definition Language (DDL) command, which enables you to create tables and modify schema information at the database. The *DbCommand* object requires a valid open connection to issue the command to the data store. A *DbConnection* object can be passed into the *DbCommand* object's constructor or attached to the *DbCommand* object's *Connection* property after *DbCommand* is created, but the best way to create a *DbCommand* object is to use the *CreateCommand* method on the *DbConnection* object so that provider-specific code is limited to the creation of the *DbConnection* object, and the *DbConnection* object automatically creates the appropriate provider-specific command object behind the scene.

DbCommand also requires a valid value for its *CommandText* and *CommandType* properties. The following code sample shows how to create and initialize a *DbCommand* object.

Sample of Visual Basic Code

```
Dim nw = ConfigurationManager.ConnectionStrings("nw")
Dim connection = New SqlConnection()
connection.ConnectionString = nw.ConnectionString
Dim cmd = connection.CreateCommand()
cmd.CommandType = CommandType.StoredProcedure
cmd.CommandText = "CustOrderHist"
'don't forget to close the connection!
```

Sample of C# Code

```
var nw = ConfigurationManager.ConnectionStrings["nw"];
var connection = new SqlConnection(nw.ConnectionString);
var cmd = connection.CreateCommand();
```

```
cmd.CommandType = CommandType.StoredProcedure;
cmd.CommandText = "CustOrderHist";
//don't forget to close the connection!
```

This code creates a *DbConnection* object that is an instance of *SqlConnection*. The *DbConnection* object is then used to create a *SqlCommand* object, which is assigned to *cmd*. The *DbConnection* object must be opened before any command can be submitted. If it executes a stored procedure, the *CommandText* property contains the name of the stored procedure, whereas *CommandType* indicates that this is a call to a stored procedure.

DbParameter Objects

Stored procedures typically require parameter values to be passed to them to execute. For example, a stored procedure called CustOrderHist might require a customer identification to retrieve information about the appropriate customer. You can create *System.Data.Common .DbParameter* objects by using the *Parameters.Add* method on the *Command* object, as shown here.

Sample of Visual Basic Code

```
Dim nw = ConfigurationManager.ConnectionStrings("nw")
Dim connection = New SqlConnection()
connection.ConnectionString = nw.ConnectionString
Dim cmd = connection.CreateCommand()
cmd.CommandType = CommandType.StoredProcedure
cmd.CommandText = "CustOrderHist"
Dim parm = cmd.CreateParameter()
parm.ParameterName = "@Id"
parm.Value = "ANATR"
cmd.Parameters.Add(parm)
Dim id = cmd.Parameters("@Id").Value
```

Sample of C# Code

```
var nw = ConfigurationManager.ConnectionStrings["nw"];
 var connection = new SqlConnection();
connection.ConnectionString = nw.ConnectionString;
var cmd = connection.CreateCommand();
cmd.CommandType = CommandType.StoredProcedure;
cmd.CommandText = "CustOrderHist";
DbParameter parm = cmd.CreateParameter();
parm.ParameterName = "@Id";
parm.Value = "ANATR";
cmd.Parameters.Add(parm);
```

This code creates a *DbConnection* object and a *DbCommand* object. It also configures the *DbCommand* object to execute a stored procedure called uspGetCustomerById, which requires a single parameter called *@Id* that is assigned the value *"ANATR."*

You can use the name assigned to the *DbParameter* object to access the parameter through code. For example, to retrieve the value currently in the @*Id* SQL parameter, use the following code:

Sample of Visual Basic Code

```
Dim id = cmd.Parameters("@Id").Value
```

Sample of C# Code

```
var id = (string)cmd.Parameters["@Id"].Value;
```

ExecuteNonQuery Method

You execute a *DbCommand* object differently depending on the data being retrieved or modified or the database object you are creating, altering, or dropping. You use the *ExecuteNonQuery* method when you don't expect a command to return any rows—an insert, update, or delete query, for example. This method returns an integer that represents the number of rows affected by the operation. The following example executes a SQL command to add 10% to the unit price of the product whose ProductID is 10, and it returns the number of rows that were updated.

Sample of Visual Basic Code

```
Private Sub menuExecuteNonQuery_Click(ByVal sender As System.Object, _
        ByVal e As System.EventArgs) _
        Handles ExecuteNonQueryToolStripMenuItem.Click
    Dim nw = ConfigurationManager.ConnectionStrings("nw")
    Dim count As Integer = 0
    Using connection = New SqlConnection()
        connection.ConnectionString = nw.ConnectionString
        Dim cmd = connection.CreateCommand()
        cmd.CommandType = CommandType.Text
        cmd.CommandText = _
            "UPDATE Products SET UnitPrice = UnitPrice * 1.1 WHERE ProductID = 10"
        connection.Open()
        count = cmd.ExecuteNonQuery()
    End Using
    MessageBox.Show(count.ToString())
End Sub
```

Sample of C# Code

```
private void menuExecuteNonQuery_Click(object sender, EventArgs e)
{
```

```
var nw = ConfigurationManager.ConnectionStrings["nw"];
int count = 0;
using (var connection = new SqlConnection())
{
    connection.ConnectionString = nw.ConnectionString;
    var cmd = connection.CreateCommand();
    cmd.CommandType = CommandType.Text;
    cmd.CommandText =
        "UPDATE Products SET UnitPrice = UnitPrice * 1.1 WHERE ProductID =
    connection.Open();
    count = cmd.ExecuteNonQuery();
}
MessageBox.Show(count.ToString());
}
```

ExecuteReader Method

The *ExecuteReader* method returns a *DbDataReader* instance. (*DbDataReader* is covered in more detail in the next section.) The *DbDataReader* object is a forward-only, read-only, server-side cursor. *DbDataReader* objects can be created only by executing one of the *ExecuteReader* methods on the *DbCommand* object. The following example uses the *ExecuteReader* method to create a *DbDataReader* object with the selection results and then continuously loops through the results until the end of data has been reached (when the *Read* method returns *false*).

Sample of Visual Basic Code

```
Dim nw = ConfigurationManager.ConnectionStrings("nw")
Dim connection = New SqlConnection()
connection.ConnectionString = nw.ConnectionString
Dim cmd = connection.CreateCommand()
cmd.CommandType = CommandType.Text
cmd.CommandText = "SELECT ProductID, UnitPrice FROM Products"
connection.Open()
Dim rdr = cmd.ExecuteReader()
While (rdr.Read())
    MessageBox.Show(rdr("ProductID") & ": " & rdr("UnitPrice"))
End While
connection.Close()
```

Sample of C# Code

```
var nw = ConfigurationManager.ConnectionStrings["nw"];
var connection = new SqlConnection();
connection.ConnectionString = nw.ConnectionString;
var cmd = connection.CreateCommand();
cmd.CommandType = CommandType.Text;
cmd.CommandText = "SELECT ProductID, UnitPrice FROM Products";
connection.Open();
DbDataReader rdr = cmd.ExecuteReader();
while (rdr.Read())
{
    MessageBox.Show(rdr["ProductID"] + ": " + rdr["UnitPrice"]);
}
connection.Close();
```

ExecuteScalar Method

Queries are often expected to return a single row with a single column. In these situations, the results can be treated as a single return value. For example, the following SQL returns a result that consists of a single row with a single column.

Sample SQL Statement

```
SELECT COUNT(*) FROM Products
```

If you use the *ExecuteScalar* method, the .NET Framework run time will not incur the overhead to produce objects that read the result stream, which means less resource usage and better performance. The following code shows how to use the *ExecuteScalar* method to easily retrieve the number of rows in the Sales table directly into a variable called *count*.

Sample of Visual Basic Code

```
Dim nw = ConfigurationManager.ConnectionStrings("nw")
Dim connection = New SqlConnection()
connection.ConnectionString = nw.ConnectionString
Dim cmd = connection.CreateCommand()
cmd.CommandType = CommandType.Text
cmd.CommandText = "SELECT COUNT(*) FROM Products"
connection.Open()
Dim count = cmd.ExecuteScalar()
connection.Close()
MessageBox.Show(count.ToString())
```

Sample of C# Code

```
var nw = ConfigurationManager.ConnectionStrings["nw"];
var connection = new SqlConnection();
connection.ConnectionString = nw.ConnectionString;
var cmd = connection.CreateCommand();
cmd.CommandType = CommandType.Text;
cmd.CommandText = "SELECT COUNT(*) FROM Products";
connection.Open();
int count = (int)cmd.ExecuteScalar();
connection.Close();
MessageBox.Show(count.ToString());
```

Notice how much simpler this is to implement than the previous example, which used *ExecuteReader*. If you can use this approach, you should.

DbDataReader Object

A *DbDataReader* object provides a high-performance method of retrieving data from the data store. It delivers a forward-only, read-only, server-side cursor. This makes the *DbDataReader* object an ideal choice for populating *ListBox* objects and *DropDownList* objects. When you run reports, you can use the *DbDataReader* object to retrieve the data from the data store, but it might not be a good choice when you are coding an operation that modifies data and needs to send the changes back to the database. For data modifications, the *DbDataAdapter* object, which is covered in the next section, might be a better choice.

The *DbDataReader* object contains a *Read* method that retrieves data into its buffer. Only one row of data is ever available at a time, which means that all the data from the database does not need to be completely read into the application before it is processed. For example, the sample code in the previous section created a *DbDataReader* and looped through the data, using a *while* loop that could have exited from the loop, pending some condition being met. This example, however, populates a new *DataTable* object directly with the list of Products from the Northwind database. The table is then bound to a *ComboBox* object called *cmbProducts*.

Sample of Visual Basic Code

```
Dim nw = ConfigurationManager.ConnectionStrings("nw")
Dim connection = New SqlConnection()
connection.ConnectionString = nw.ConnectionString
Dim cmd = connection.CreateCommand()
cmd.CommandType = CommandType.Text
cmd.CommandText = "SELECT ProductID, ProductName FROM Products"
connection.Open()
Dim rdr = cmd.ExecuteReader()
Dim products As New DataTable()
products.Load(rdr, LoadOption.Upsert)
connection.Close()
cmbProducts.DataSource = products
cmbProducts.DisplayMember = "ProductName"
cmbProducts.ValueMember = "ProductID"
```

Sample of C# Code

```
var nw = ConfigurationManager.ConnectionStrings["nw"];
var connection = new SqlConnection();
connection.ConnectionString = nw.ConnectionString;
var cmd = connection.CreateCommand();
cmd.CommandType = CommandType.Text;
cmd.CommandText = "SELECT ProductID, ProductName FROM Products";
connection.Open();
var rdr = cmd.ExecuteReader();
var products = new DataTable();
products.Load(rdr, LoadOption.Upsert);
connection.Close();
cmbProducts.DataSource = products;
cmbProducts.DisplayMember = "ProductName";
cmbProducts.ValueMember = "ProductID";
```

The *DataTable* object's *Load* method has a *LoadOption* parameter that gives you the option of deciding which *DataRowVersion* object should get the incoming data. For example, if you load a *DataTable* object, modify the data, and then save the changes back to the database, you might encounter concurrency errors if someone else has modified the data between the time you got the data and the time you attempted to save the data. One option is to load the *DataTable* object again, using the default *PreserveCurrentValues* enumeration value, which loads the original *DataRowVersion* object with the data from the database while leaving the current *DataRowVersion* object untouched. Next, you can simply execute the *Update* method again, and the database will be updated successfully.

For this to work properly, the *DataTable* object must have a defined primary key. Failure to define a primary key results in duplicate *DataRow* objects being added to the *DataTable* object. The *LoadOption* enumeration members are described in Table 2-5.

TABLE 2-5 *LoadOption* Enumeration Members

LOADOPTION MEMBER	DESCRIPTION
OverwriteChanges	Overwrites the original and current *DataRowVersion* objects and changes the row state to *Unchanged*. New rows will have a row state of *Unchanged* as well.
PreserveChanges (default)	Overwrites the original *DataRowVersion* object but does not modify the current *DataRowVersion* object. New rows will have a row state of *Unchanged* as well.
Upsert	Overwrites the current *DataRowVersion* object but does not modify the original *DataRowVersion* object. New rows will have a row state of *Added*. Rows that had a row state of *Unchanged* will have a row state of *Unchanged* if the current *DataRowVersion* object is the same as the original one, but if they are different, the row state will be *Modified*.

Using Multiple Active Result Sets (MARS) to Execute Multiple Commands on a Connection

Using the *DbDataReader* object is one of the fastest methods to retrieve data from the database, but one of the problems with *DbDataReader* is that it keeps an open server-side cursor while you are looping through the results of your query. If you try to execute another command while the first command is still executing, you will receive an *InvalidOperationException*, stating, "There is already an open DataReader associated with this Connection which must be closed first." You can avoid this exception by setting the *MultipleActiveResultSets* connection string option to *true* when connecting to Multiple Active Result Sets (MARS)–enabled hosts such as SQL Server 2005 and later. For example, the following connection string shows how this setting is added into a new connection string called *nwMars*.

XML Application Configuration File

```
<connectionStrings>
    <clear />
    <add name="nw"
        providerName="System.Data.SqlClient"
        connectionString=
        "Data Source=.\SQLEXPRESS;
            AttachDbFilename=|DataDirectory|Northwind.MDF;
            Integrated Security=True;
            User Instance=True"/>
    <add name="nwMars"
```

```
        providerName="System.Data.SqlClient"
        connectionString=
        "Data Source=.\SQLEXPRESS;
            AttachDbFilename=|DataDirectory|Northwind.MDF;
            Integrated Security=True;
            User Instance=True;
            MultipleActiveResultSets=True"/>
</connectionStrings>
```

MARS does not provide any performance gains, but it does simplify your coding efforts. Think of a scenario in which you execute a query to get a list of stores, and, while you loop through a list of stores that are returned, you want to execute a second query to get the total quantity of books sold.

> **NOTE** **BE CAREFUL ABOUT USING MARS**
>
> MARS is not performant; it is a feature that can simplify the code while minimizing the quantity of connections to the server.

MARS is not something that you can't live without; it simply makes your programming easier. As a matter of fact, setting *MultipleActiveResultSets=true* in the connection string has a negative performance impact, so you should not turn on MARS arbitrarily.

On a database server without MARS, you could first collect the list of stores into a collection and close the connection. After that, you can loop through the collection to get each store ID and execute a query to get the total quantity of books sold for that store. This means that you loop through the stores twice, once to populate the collection and again to get each store and execute a query to get the store's quantity of book sales. Another solution (and probably the best solution) is simply to create two connections: one for the store list and one for the quantity of books-sold query.

Another benefit MARS provides is that you might have purchased database client licenses based on the quantity of connections to the database. Without MARS, you would have to open a separate connection to the database for each command that needs to run at the same time, which means that you might need to purchase more client licenses.

The following code sample shows how MARS can perform the nested queries, using the Customers table to retrieve the count of Orders placed for each customer.

Sample of Visual Basic Code

```
Private Sub menuMars_Click( _
    ByVal sender As System.Object, _
    ByVal e As System.EventArgs) Handles MARSToolStripMenuItem.Click
    Dim nw = ConfigurationManager.ConnectionStrings("nwMars")
    Using connection = New SqlConnection()
        connection.ConnectionString = nw.ConnectionString
        Dim cmd = connection.CreateCommand()
        cmd.CommandType = CommandType.Text
        cmd.CommandText = "SELECT CustomerID, CompanyName FROM Customers"
        connection.Open()
        Dim rdr = cmd.ExecuteReader()
```

```
        While rdr.Read()
            Dim OrdersCmd = connection.CreateCommand()
            OrdersCmd.CommandType = CommandType.Text
            OrdersCmd.CommandText = _
                "SELECT COUNT(OrderID) FROM Orders WHERE (CustomerID = @CustId)"
            Dim parm = OrdersCmd.CreateParameter()
            parm.ParameterName = "@CustId"
            parm.Value = rdr("CustomerID")
            OrdersCmd.Parameters.Add(parm)
            Dim qtyOrders = OrdersCmd.ExecuteScalar()
            MessageBox.Show( _
                rdr("CompanyName").ToString() + ": " + qtyOrders.ToString())
        End While
    End Using
End Sub
```

Sample of C# Code

```
private void menuMars_Click(object sender, EventArgs e)
{
    var nw = ConfigurationManager.ConnectionStrings["nwMars"];
    using(var connection = new SqlConnection())
    {
        connection.ConnectionString = nw.ConnectionString;
        var cmd = connection.CreateCommand();
        cmd.CommandType = CommandType.Text;
        cmd.CommandText = "SELECT CustomerID, CompanyName FROM Customers";
        connection.Open();
        var rdr = cmd.ExecuteReader();
        while (rdr.Read())
        {
            var ordersCmd = connection.CreateCommand();
            ordersCmd.CommandType = CommandType.Text;
            ordersCmd.CommandText =
                "SELECT COUNT(OrderID) FROM Orders WHERE (CustomerID = @CustId)";
            var parm = ordersCmd.CreateParameter();
            parm.ParameterName = "@CustId";
            parm.Value = rdr["CustomerID"];
            ordersCmd.Parameters.Add(parm);
            var qtyOrders = ordersCmd.ExecuteScalar();
            MessageBox.Show(rdr["CompanyName"].ToString() + ": "
                            + qtyOrders.ToString());
        }
    }
}
```

Performing Bulk Copy Operations with a *SqlBulkCopy* Object

Often, you need to copy large amounts of data from one location to another. Most of the database servers provide a means to copy from one database to another, either by a Windows GUI interface such as the SQL Server Enterprise Manager or by a command-line tool such as the SQL Server Bulk Copy Program (BCP.exe). In addition to using the tools provided by the database vendor, you also can write your own bulk copy program, using the *SqlBulkCopy* class.

The *SqlBulkCopy* class provides a high-performance method for copying data to a table in a SQL Server database. The source of the copy is constrained by the overloads of the *WriteToServer* method, which can accept an array of *DataRow* objects, an object that implements the *IDataReader* interface, a *DataTable* object, or *DataTable* and *DataRowState*, as shown in Figure 2-2. This variety of parameters means you can retrieve data from most locations.

SqlBulkCopy Class

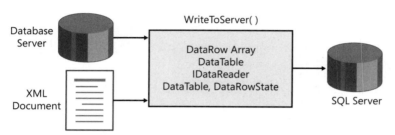

FIGURE 2-2 The *SqlBulkCopy* object can copy from a variety of sources to fill up a SQL Server table.

The following code shows how you can use a *SqlBulkCopy* object to copy data from the Customers table in the Northwind database to the CustomerList table in a SQL Server database called *BulkCopy*.

Sample of Visual Basic Code

```vb
Dim nw = ConfigurationManager.ConnectionStrings("nw")
Dim nwConnection = New SqlConnection()
nwConnection.ConnectionString = nw.ConnectionString
Dim bulkCopy = ConfigurationManager.ConnectionStrings("BulkCopy")
Dim bulkConnection = New SqlConnection()
bulkConnection.ConnectionString = bulkCopy.ConnectionString
Dim cmd = nwConnection.CreateCommand()
cmd.CommandType = CommandType.Text
cmd.CommandText = "SELECT CustomerID, CompanyName FROM Customers"
nwConnection.Open()
bulkConnection.Open()
Dim rdr = cmd.ExecuteReader()
Dim bc As New SqlBulkCopy(bulkConnection)
bc.DestinationTableName = "StoreList"
bc.WriteToServer(rdr)
nwConnection.Close()
bulkConnection.Close()
MessageBox.Show("Done with bulk copy")
```

Sample of C# Code

```csharp
var nw = ConfigurationManager.ConnectionStrings["nw"];
var nwConnection = new SqlConnection();
nwConnection.ConnectionString = nw.ConnectionString;
```

```
var bulkCopy = ConfigurationManager.ConnectionStrings["BulkCopy"];
var bulkConnection = new SqlConnection();
bulkConnection.ConnectionString = bulkCopy.ConnectionString;
var cmd = nwConnection.CreateCommand();
cmd.CommandType = CommandType.Text;
cmd.CommandText = "SELECT CustomerID, CompanyName FROM Customers";
nwConnection.Open();
bulkConnection.Open();
var rdr = cmd.ExecuteReader();
var bc = new SqlBulkCopy(bulkConnection);
bc.DestinationTableName = "CustomerList";
bc.WriteToServer(rdr);
nwConnection.Close();
bulkConnection.Close();
MessageBox.Show("Done with bulk copy");
```

Consider using the *IDataReader* overload whenever possible to get the best performance using the least resources. You can decide how much data should be copied based on the query you use. For example, the preceding code sample retrieved only the store names and could have had a WHERE clause to limit the data further.

DbDataAdapter Object

You use the *DbDataAdapter* object to retrieve and update data between a data table and a data store. *DbDataAdapter* is derived from the *DataAdapter* class and is the base class of the provider-specific *DbDataAdapter* classes, as shown in Figure 2-3.

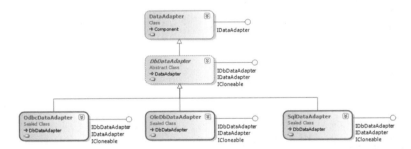

FIGURE 2-3 This figure shows the *DbDataAdapter* hierarchy with the *DataAdapter* base class and the provider-specific derived classes.

DbDataAdapter has a *SelectCommand* property you use when retrieving the data. *SelectCommand* must contain a valid *DbCommand* object, which must have a valid connection. Internally, *SelectCommand* has an *ExecuteReader* method, which is executed to get a *DbDataReader* object to populate a *DataTable* object.

DbDataAdapter also has *InsertCommand*, *UpdateCommand*, and *DeleteCommand* properties, which might contain *DbCommand* objects. You use these commands if you want to save *DataTable* changes back to the data store. You need not create these command objects if you need only to read data from the data store, but if you create one of these latter three commands, you must create all four of them (select, insert, update, and delete).

When *DbDataAdapter* is used to retrieve or update data, it examines the status of the connection. If the connection is open, the *DbDataAdapter* uses the open connection and leaves the connection open. If the connection is closed, *DbDataAdapter* opens the connection, uses it, and then closes it automatically. If you never open the connection, you don't have to close the connection. However, if you have many data adapters that will be used in one operation, you can get better performance by manually opening the connection before you call all the data adapters; just be sure to close the connection when you're done.

Using the *Fill* Method

The *Fill* method moves data from the data store to the *DataTable* object you pass into this method. The *Fill* method has several overloads, some of which accept only a data set as a parameter. When a data set is passed to the *Fill* method, a new *DataTable* object is created in the data set if a source *DataTable* object is not specified.

The following code sample shows how a data table can be loaded using the *Fill* method.

Sample of Visual Basic Code

```
Dim nw = ConfigurationManager.ConnectionStrings("nw")
Dim connection = New SqlConnection()
connection.ConnectionString = nw.ConnectionString
Dim cmd = CType(connection.CreateCommand(), SqlCommand)
cmd.CommandType = CommandType.Text
cmd.CommandText = "SELECT CustomerID, CompanyName FROM Customers"
Dim nwSet As New DataSet("nw")
Dim da As New SqlDataAdapter(cmd)
da.Fill(nwSet, "Customers")
MessageBox.Show("DataSet Filled")
```

Sample of C# Code

```
var nw = ConfigurationManager.ConnectionStrings["nw"];
var connection = new SqlConnection();
connection.ConnectionString = nw.ConnectionString;
var cmd = (SqlCommand)connection.CreateCommand();
cmd.CommandType = CommandType.Text;
cmd.CommandText = "SELECT CustomerID, CompanyName FROM Customers";
var da = new SqlDataAdapter(cmd);
var nwSet = new DataSet("nw");
da.Fill(nwSet, "Customers");
MessageBox.Show("DataSet Filled");
```

Many developers attempt to use a single *DbDataAdapter* class for all their queries or try to use a single *DbDataAdapter* class to execute a SQL statement that returns a result set from multiple tables that are joined together within the SQL query. If you need to store the data changes, consider using a separate *DbDataAdapter* class for each data table being loaded, as shown in Figure 2-4. If all you need is a read-only data table, you can simply use a *DbCommand* object and *DbDataReader* object to load the data table.

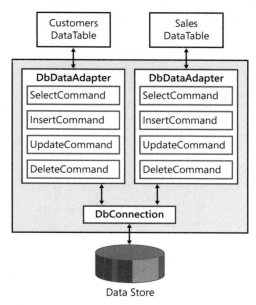

FIGURE 2-4 The *DbDataAdapter* class, which has four *DbCommand* objects, should be used to populate each data table if the data table will contain read-write data.

Saving Changes to the Database Using the *Update* Method

The *Update* method saves the data table modifications to the database by retrieving the changes from the data table and then using the respective *InsertCommand*, *UpdateCommand*, or *DeleteCommand* property to send the appropriate changes to the database on a row-by-row basis. The *Update* method retrieves the *DataRow* objects that have changed by looking at the *RowState* property of each row. If *RowState* is anything but *Unchanged*, the *Update* method sends the change to the database.

For the *Update* method to work, all four commands must be assigned to the *DbDataAdapter* object. Normally, this means creating individual *DbCommand* objects for each command. You can easily create the commands by using the DbDataAdapter Configuration Wizard, which starts when a *DbDataAdapter* object is dropped onto the Windows form. The wizard can generate stored procedures for all four commands.

Another way to populate the *DbDataAdapter* object's commands is to use the *DbCommandBuilder* object. This object creates the *InsertCommand*, *UpdateCommand*, and *DeleteCommand* properties as long as a valid *SelectCommand* property exists. *DbDataAdapter* is great for ad hoc changes and demos, but it's generally better to use stored procedures for all database access because, in SQL Server, it's easier to set permissions on stored procedures than it is to set permissions on tables. The following code demonstrates a simple update to the database, using *SqlDataAdapter*, which is the SQL Server–specific version of *DbDataAdapter*. After the changes are saved, the results are displayed on the *DataGridView* object, called *DataGridView2*.

Sample of Visual Basic Code

```vb
Dim nw = ConfigurationManager.ConnectionStrings("nw")
Dim connection = New SqlConnection()
connection.ConnectionString = nw.ConnectionString
Dim cmd = connection.CreateCommand()
cmd.CommandType = CommandType.Text
cmd.CommandText = "SELECT * FROM Customers"
Dim nwSet As New DataSet("nw")
Dim da As New SqlDataAdapter(cmd)
Dim bldr As New SqlCommandBuilder(da)
da.Fill(nwSet, "Customers")

'Modify existing row
Dim customersTable = nwSet.Tables("Customers")
Dim updRow = customersTable.Select("CustomerID='WOLZA'")(0)
updRow("CompanyName") = "New Wolza Company"

'Add new row
customersTable.Rows.Add( _
    "AAAAA", "Five A Company")

'Delete a row, note that you cannot delete a
'customer who has orders
Dim delRow = customersTable.Select("CustomerID='PARIS'")(0)
delRow.Delete()

'send changes to database
da.Update(nwSet, "Customers")
DataGridView2.DataSource = nwSet
DataGridView2.DataMember = "Customers"
MessageBox.Show("Update Complete")
```

Sample of C# Code

```csharp
var nw = ConfigurationManager.ConnectionStrings["nw"];
var connection = new SqlConnection();
connection.ConnectionString = nw.ConnectionString;
var cmd = connection.CreateCommand();
cmd.CommandType = CommandType.Text;
cmd.CommandText = "SELECT * FROM Customers";
var da = new SqlDataAdapter(cmd);
var nwSet = new DataSet("nw");
var bldr = new SqlCommandBuilder(da);
da.Fill(nwSet, "Customers");

//Modify existing row
var customersTable = nwSet.Tables["Customers"];
var updRow = customersTable.Select("CustomerID='WOLZA'")[0];
updRow["CompanyName"] = "New Wolza Company";

//Add new row
customersTable.Rows.Add(
    "AAAAA", "Five A Company");

//Delete a row, note that you cannot delete a
```

```
//customer who has orders
var delRow = customersTable.Select("CustomerID='PARIS'")[0];
delRow.Delete();

//send changes to database
da.Update(nwSet, "Customers");
dataGridView2.DataSource = nwSet;
dataGridView2.DataMember = "Customers";
MessageBox.Show("Update Complete");
```

> **NOTE DON'T EXECUTE TWICE!**
>
> If you execute this code twice, an exception will be thrown indicating that you are trying to insert duplicate rows. If you stop running the application and then run it again, you will be able to execute again because the Northwind database has the *Copy To Output Directory* property set to *Copy Always*, which means that you get a new clean copy of the database every time you build the project.

Saving Changes to the Database in Batches

If you have the SQL Profiler tool that is available when you install the full version of SQL Server on your computer, you can use this tool to view the update commands sent to SQL Server. You will notice that individual insert, update, and delete commands are sent to SQL Server on a row-by-row basis. One way to increase update performance is to send the changes to the database server in batches by assigning a value to the *DbDataAdapter* object's *UpdateBatchSize* property. This property defaults to *1*, which causes each change to be sent to the server on a row-by-row basis. Setting the value to *0* instructs the *DbDataAdapter* object to create the largest possible batch size for changes, or you can set the value to the number of changes you want to send to the server in each batch. Setting *UpdateBatchSize* to a number greater than the number of changes that need to be sent is equivalent to setting it to *0*.

> **NOTE FREE PERFORMANCE UPGRADE!**
>
> Setting *UpdateBatchSize* to *0* is a quick way to boost the update performance of the *DbDataAdapter* object.

One way to confirm that the changes are being sent to the database server in batches is to register a handler to the *RowUpdated* event of the *DbDataAdapter*-derived class instances. The event handler method receives the number of rows affected in the last batch. When *UpdateBatchSize* is set to *1*, the *RecordsAffected* property is always *1*. In the following code sample, the Customers table contains 91 rows. *nwDataSet* is filled, and then the CustomerName field is modified on all 91 rows. Before the *Update* method is executed, *UpdateBatchSize* is changed to *40*. When the *Update* method is executed, the changes are sent to the database as a batch of 40 changes, another batch of 40 changes, and, finally, a batch of 11 changes. This code contains a *RowUpdated* event handler to collect batch infor-mation, which is displayed after the *Update* method is executed. In this code, *SqlDataAdapter* is used because this event does not exist on the *DbDataAdapter* base class.

Sample of Visual Basic Code

```vbnet
Private WithEvents da As New SqlDataAdapter()
Private sb as New System.Text.StringBuilder()

private sub rowUpdated(byval sender as Object, _
      byval e as SqlRowUpdatedEventArgs) handles da.RowUpdated
   sb.Append("Rows: " & e.RecordsAffected.ToString() & vbCrLf)
End Sub

Private Sub menuUpdateBatch_Click(ByVal sender As System.Object, _
      ByVal e As System.EventArgs) _
      Handles UpdateBatchToolStripMenuItem.Click
   Dim nw = ConfigurationManager.ConnectionStrings("nw")
   Dim connection = New SqlConnection()
   connection.ConnectionString = nw.ConnectionString
   Dim cmd = connection.CreateCommand()
   cmd.CommandType = CommandType.Text
   cmd.CommandText = "SELECT * FROM Customers"
   Dim nwSet As New DataSet("nw")
   da.SelectCommand = cmd
   Dim bldr As New SqlCommandBuilder(da)
   da.Fill(nwSet, "Customers")

   'Modify data here
   For Each dr As DataRow In nwSet.Tables("Customers").Rows
       dr("CompanyName") = dr("CompanyName").ToString().ToUpper()
   Next
   sb.Clear()
   da.UpdateBatchSize = 40
   da.Update(nwSet, "Customers")
   MessageBox.Show(sb.ToString())
End Sub
```

Sample of C# Code

```csharp
private SqlDataAdapter da = new SqlDataAdapter();
private System.Text.StringBuilder sb = new System.Text.StringBuilder();

private void rowUpdated(object sender, SqlRowUpdatedEventArgs e )
{
    sb.Append("Rows: " + e.RecordsAffected.ToString() + "\r\n");
}

private void menuUpdateBatch_Click(object sender, EventArgs e)
{
    //event subscription is normally placed in constructor but is here
    //to encapsulate the sample
    da.RowUpdated += rowUpdated;
    var nw = ConfigurationManager.ConnectionStrings["nw"];
    var connection = new SqlConnection();
    connection.ConnectionString = nw.ConnectionString;
```

```
    var cmd = connection.CreateCommand();
    cmd.CommandType = CommandType.Text;
    cmd.CommandText = "SELECT * FROM Customers";
    da.SelectCommand = cmd;
    var nwSet = new DataSet("nw");
    var bldr = new SqlCommandBuilder(da);
    da.Fill(nwSet, "Customers");

    //Modify data here
    foreach (DataRow dr in nwSet.Tables["Customers"].Rows)
    {
        dr["CompanyName"] = dr["CompanyName"].ToString().ToUpper();
    }
    sb.Clear();
    da.UpdateBatchSize = 40;
    da.Update(nwSet, "Customers");

    //if event subscription is in the contructor, no need to
    //remove it here....
    da.RowUpdated -= rowUpdated;
    MessageBox.Show(sb.ToString());
}
```

DbProviderFactory Classes

There are many reasons for writing an application that does not require database provider–specific code. A company might want the flexibility to upgrade from one database product to another, such as for moving from Microsoft Access to SQL Server. Or a company might have a retail application that must allow connectivity to any data source. With earlier versions of ADO.NET, you can write a provider-independent application by using generic interfaces. The typical coding might look something like the following:

Sample of Visual Basic Code

```
Public Enum DbProvider
    SqlClient
    OleDb
    Odbc
End Enum

Public Function GetConnection() As IDbConnection
    'Get the provider from the config file
    Dim provider As DbProvider = [Enum].Parse( _
    GetType(DbProvider), _
        ConfigurationSettings.AppSettings("provider").ToString())

    Dim connection As IDbConnection = Nothing
    Select Case (provider)
        Case DbProvider.SqlClient
            connection = New System.Data.SqlClient.SqlConnection()
        Case DbProvider.OleDb
            connection = New System.Data.OleDb.OleDbConnection()
        Case DbProvider.Odbc
```

```vb
            connection = New System.Data.Odbc.OdbcConnection()
        Case DbProvider.Oracle
            connection = New System.Data.OracleClient.OracleConnection()
    End Select
    Return connection
End Function
```

Sample of C# Code

```csharp
public IDbConnection GetConnection()
{
    // Get the provider from the config file
    DbProvider provider = (DbProvider)Enum.Parse(
        typeof(DbProvider),
        (string)ConfigurationManager.AppSettings["provider"]);

    IDbConnection connection = null;
    switch (provider)
    {
        case DbProvider.SqlClient:
            connection = new System.Data.SqlClient.SqlConnection();
            break;
        case DbProvider.OleDb:
            connection = new System.Data.OleDb.OleDbConnection();
            break;
        case DbProvider.Odbc:
            connection = new System.Data.Odbc.OdbcConnection();
            break;
        case DbProvider.Oracle:
            connection = new System.Data.OracleClient.OracleConnection();
            break;
    }
    return connection;
}
public enum DbProvider
    { SqlClient, OleDb, Odbc, Oracle };
```

XML Application Configuration File

```xml
<configuration>
    <appSettings>
        <add key="provider" value="SqlClient" />
    </appSettings>
</configuration>
```

One problem with this approach is that you can't create interface instances directly, so provider-specific code exists to determine which type of connection to create. Another problem is that interfaces are immutable by definition, so new features can't be easily added without adding a new interface.

ADO.NET provides base classes from which the provider-specific classes inherit, as shown earlier in Table 2-1. The .NET Framework supports only single inheritance, so this approach has limitations if you want to create your own base class, but for classes that will expand, providing base class inheritance is better than providing interface implementation. Interfaces are still provided for backward compatibility.

The previous code listing addresses only the creation of the connection object. You would duplicate the code if you wanted to create many of the other provider objects, such as the data adapter and command objects. To keep from duplicating this conditional code for each of the provider objects, you can create a factory object that is responsible for creating the appropriate provider objects. This is when the *DbProviderFactory* is used. Each provider must supply a subclass of *DbProviderFactory* that can create instances of its provider classes. For example, you can use *SqlClientFactory* to create instances of any of the SQL Server classes. Figure 2-5 shows the *DbProviderFactory* and the *SqlClientFactory* classes, along with their properties and methods.

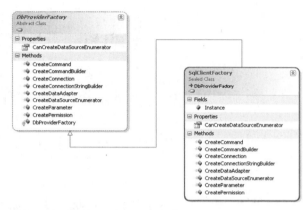

FIGURE 2-5 This figure shows the *DbProviderFactory* and *SqlClientFactory* classes.

The provider factory classes are implemented as singletons, in which each class provides an *Instance* property that enables you to access the methods and properties shown in Figure 2-5. For example, you can use the following code to create a new connection by using the *SqlClientFactory* class.

Sample of Visual Basic Code

```vb
'Get the singleton instance
Dim factory As DbProviderFactory = SqlClientFactory.Instance

Public Function GetProviderConnection() As DbConnection
    Dim connection = factory.CreateConnection()
    connection.ConnectionString = "Data Source=.\SQLEXPRESS;" _
        & "AttachDbFilename=|DataDirectory|PUBS.MDF;" _
        & "Integrated Security=True;User Instance=True"
    Return connection
End Function
```

Sample of C# Code

```csharp
//Get the singleton instance
DbProviderFactory factory = SqlClientFactory.Instance;

public DbConnection GetProviderConnection()
{
```

```
    var connection = factory.CreateConnection();
    connection.ConnectionString = @"Data Source=.\SQLEXPRESS;"
        + "AttachDbFilename=|DataDirectory|Northwind.MDF;"
        + "Integrated Security=True;User Instance=True";
    return connection;
}
```

You can use the factory variable to create any of the other SQL Server–specific objects. Note that *SqlDataReader* is created indirectly by creating a SQL command and then using the *ExecuteReader* method, as shown in the following code sample:

Sample of Visual Basic Code

```
Private Function GetData(ByVal commandText As String, _
        ByVal commandType As CommandType) As DataTable
    'get SqlDbCommand
    Dim command = factory.CreateCommand()
    command.Connection = GetProviderConnection()
    If (command.Connection Is Nothing) Then
        Return Nothing
    End If
    command.CommandText = commandText
    command.CommandType = commandType
    command.Connection.Open()
    Dim dataTable = New DataTable()

    'Get SqlDataReader and populate data table
    dataTable.Load(command.ExecuteReader())
    command.Connection.Close()
    Return dataTable
End Function
```

Sample of C# Code

```
private DataTable GetData(string commandText, CommandType commandType)
{
    //get SqlDbCommand
    var command = factory.CreateCommand();
    command.Connection = GetProviderConnection();
    if (command.Connection == null) return null;
    command.CommandText = commandText;
    command.CommandType = commandType;
    command.Connection.Open();
    var dataTable = new DataTable();

    //Get SqlDataReader and populate data table
    dataTable.Load(command.ExecuteReader());
    command.Connection.Close();
    return dataTable;
}
```

This code sample uses the factory variable to create a *DbCommand* class, which is then used to create the *DbDataReader* object.

Using *DbException* to Catch Provider Exceptions

All provider-specific exceptions inherit from a common base class called *DbException*. When working with a provider-neutral coding model, your *try/catch* block can simply catch *DbException* generically instead of trying to catch each provider-specific exception.

Working with SQL Server User-Defined Types (UDTs)

SQL Server 2005 and later provides hosting support for the .NET Framework common language runtime (SQLCLR), so you can use Visual Basic 2010 or C# to write code that will run in SQL Server. One of the features the SQLCLR provides is the ability to create user-defined types (UDTs) that enable objects and custom data structures to be stored in a SQL Server database. This can be in the form of a .NET Framework class or structure with methods and properties. UDTs can be specified as the column type in a table definition, they can be a variable's type in a T-SQL batch, or they can be the type for an argument of a T-SQL function or stored procedure.

Although you can write your own UDTs, Microsoft has been adding UDTs to SQL Server. For example, in SQL Server 2008, the new *Geography* and *Geometry* types are UDTs.

To get the most benefit from a UDT at the client, you will typically want to use a UDT on the client in a typed manner. This requires you to set a reference to the same assembly that contains the UDT registered in SQL Server. This means the assembly must be available to the client application, most commonly either by copying the assembly into the same folder as the client executable or by installing the assembly into the Global Assembly Cache (GAC). If you don't need typed access to the UDT, only the raw bytes of the UDT returned from SQL Server, you don't need to set a reference to the assembly. This could be used when you know the physical structure of the data, and you're going to parse the data and assign it to a different object.

The following example code demonstrates the creation of a table called Locations in SQL Server. Before creating the table, a command is executed to see whether the table already exists. If the table exists, it's dropped. After that, the Locations table is created.

Sample of Visual Basic Code

```
Dim nw = ConfigurationManager.ConnectionStrings("nw")
Dim nwConnection = New SqlConnection(nw.ConnectionString)
Dim cmd = nwConnection.CreateCommand()
cmd.CommandText = _
    "IF EXISTS (SELECT * FROM sys.Tables WHERE Name='Locations') " _
    & " DROP TABLE Locations"
nwConnection.Open()
cmd.ExecuteNonQuery()
cmd.CommandText = _
    "CREATE TABLE Locations(" _
    & " ZipCode char(5) PRIMARY KEY NOT NULL, Location Geography)"
cmd.ExecuteNonQuery()
nwConnection.Close()
MessageBox.Show("Location table created")
```

Sample of C# Code

```csharp
var nw = ConfigurationManager.ConnectionStrings["nw"];
var nwConnection = new SqlConnection(nw.ConnectionString);
var cmd = nwConnection.CreateCommand();
cmd.CommandText =
    "IF EXISTS (SELECT * FROM sys.Tables WHERE Name='Locations') "
    + " DROP TABLE Locations";
nwConnection.Open();
cmd.ExecuteNonQuery();
cmd.CommandText =
    "CREATE TABLE Locations("
    + " ZipCode char(5) PRIMARY KEY NOT NULL, Location Geography)";
cmd.ExecuteNonQuery();
nwConnection.Close();
MessageBox.Show("Location table created");
```

> **NOTE** **WORKING WITH A CLEAN COPY OF THE DATABASE**
>
> If your Copy To Output Directory settings on your database file are to Copy Always, every time you start the application you will get a new, clean database. You will need to re-create the table and then re-populate it. Then you can run other tests.

Now that the table is created, you might want to populate the table with some data. The problem is that the Location column is a UDT. To insert a *Geography* object, you must add a reference to the Microsoft.SqlServer.Types.dll assembly. If you have SQL Server 2008 installed on your computer, this assembly is in the GAC, but you can't add references directly to GAC assemblies. You must locate the assembly, which should be at the following location:

```
C:\Program Files (x86)\Microsoft SQL Server\100\SDK\Assemblies
```

This is the location if you have a 64-bit operating system, but you should be able to find it in the Program Files folder on a 32-bit operating system.

The following code adds three ZIP or postal codes with the corresponding *Geography* objects. Notice the magic number 4326 in the example. This is the Geocode for WGS84 round earth model that most people use.

Sample of Visual Basic Code

```vb
'add reference to Microsoft.SqlServer.Types.dll
'add imports to the top of this file:
'Imports Microsoft.SqlServer.Types

Dim nw = ConfigurationManager.ConnectionStrings("nw")
Dim nwConnection = New SqlConnection(nw.ConnectionString)
Dim cmd = nwConnection.CreateCommand()
cmd.CommandText = "INSERT Locations VALUES(@zip, @loc)"
Dim zip = New SqlParameter("@zip", "14710")  'Ashville NY
Dim loc = New SqlParameter("@loc", SqlDbType.Udt)
loc.UdtTypeName = "geography"
loc.Value = SqlGeography.STGeomFromText( _
    New SqlChars("POINT(42.1018 79.4144)"), 4326)
```

```
cmd.Parameters.Add(zip)
cmd.Parameters.Add(loc)
nwConnection.Open()
cmd.ExecuteNonQuery()

zip.Value = "44011"
loc.Value = SqlGeography.STGeomFromText( _
    New SqlChars("POINT(41.4484 82.0190)"), 4326)
cmd.ExecuteNonQuery()

zip.Value = "60609"
loc.Value = SqlGeography.STGeomFromText( _
    New SqlChars("POINT(41.8121 87.6542)"), 4326)
cmd.ExecuteNonQuery()

nwConnection.Close()
MessageBox.Show("Entries added")
```

Sample of C# Code

```
//add reference to Microsoft.SqlServer.Types.dll
//'add imports to the top of this file:
//using Microsoft.SqlServer.Types;
//using System.Data.SqlTypes;

var nw = ConfigurationManager.ConnectionStrings["nw"];
var nwConnection = new SqlConnection(nw.ConnectionString);
var cmd = nwConnection.CreateCommand();
cmd.CommandText = "INSERT Locations VALUES(@zip, @loc)";
var zip = new SqlParameter("@zip", "14710"); // Ashville NY
var loc = new SqlParameter("@loc", SqlDbType.Udt);
loc.UdtTypeName = "geography";
loc.Value = SqlGeography.STGeomFromText(
    new SqlChars("POINT(42.1018 79.4144)"), 4326);
cmd.Parameters.Add(zip);
cmd.Parameters.Add(loc);
nwConnection.Open();
cmd.ExecuteNonQuery();

zip.Value = "44011";
loc.Value = SqlGeography.STGeomFromText(
    new SqlChars("POINT(41.4484 82.0190)"), 4326);
cmd.ExecuteNonQuery();

zip.Value = "60609";
loc.Value = SqlGeography.STGeomFromText(
    new SqlChars("POINT(41.8121 87.6542)"), 4326);
cmd.ExecuteNonQuery();

nwConnection.Close();
MessageBox.Show("Entries added");
```

After the rows are inserted into the table, you can query for these rows and use them to perform tasks such as calculating the distance between two locations. Here is an example:

Sample of Visual Basic Code

```
Dim nw = ConfigurationManager.ConnectionStrings("nw")
Dim nwConnection = New SqlConnection()
nwConnection.ConnectionString = nw.ConnectionString
Dim cmd = nwConnection.CreateCommand()
cmd.CommandText = "SELECT Location FROM Locations WHERE ZipCode='14710'"
nwConnection.Open()
Dim ashvilleNY = cmd.ExecuteScalar()
cmd.CommandText = "SELECT Location FROM Locations WHERE ZipCode='44011'"
Dim avonOH = cmd.ExecuteScalar()
cmd.CommandText = "SELECT Location FROM Locations WHERE ZipCode='60609'"
Dim chicagoIL = cmd.ExecuteScalar()
nwConnection.Close()

MessageBox.Show(String.Format("Ashville to Chicago: {0}",
    ashvilleNY.STDistance(chicagoIL) / 1609.344)) '1609.344 meters/mile
MessageBox.Show(String.Format("Ashville to Avon: {0}",
    ashvilleNY.STDistance(avonOH) / 1609.344)) '1609.344 meters/mile
```

Sample of C# Code

```
var nw = ConfigurationManager.ConnectionStrings["nw"];
var nwConnection = new SqlConnection(nw.ConnectionString);
var cmd = nwConnection.CreateCommand();
cmd.CommandText = "SELECT Location FROM Locations WHERE ZipCode='14710'";
nwConnection.Open();
var ashvilleNY = (SqlGeography)cmd.ExecuteScalar();
cmd.CommandText = "SELECT Location FROM Locations WHERE ZipCode='44011'";
var avonOH = (SqlGeography)cmd.ExecuteScalar();
cmd.CommandText = "SELECT Location FROM Locations WHERE ZipCode='60609'";
var chicagoIL = (SqlGeography)cmd.ExecuteScalar();
nwConnection.Close();

MessageBox.Show(string.Format("Ashville to Chicago: {0}",
    ashvilleNY.STDistance(chicagoIL) / 1609.344)); //1609.344 meters/mile
MessageBox.Show(string.Format("Ashville to Avon: {0}",
    ashvilleNY.STDistance(avonOH) / 1609.344)); //1609.344 meters/mile
```

In this example, the *SqlGeography* object was retrieved from the database, and then the client application was able to execute methods on the UDT.

PRACTICE **Reading and Writing Data**

In this practice, you can continue the practice you began in the previous lesson or use the beginning Chapter 2, Lesson 2, solution included on the companion CD. If you're using the *CheckConnectivity* method from the previous lesson, if a connection can be made, you add code to create the tables if they don't exist. Next, you add code to synchronize with the database server on application startup and end. Synchronizing means that you send any client-side changes back to the database and get any server-side changes.

This practice is intended to focus on the classes that have been defined in this lesson, so the GUI will be minimal.

If you encounter a problem completing an exercise, the completed projects can be installed from the Code folder on the companion CD.

EXERCISE 1 Code to Provide Automatic Synchronization

In this exercise, you open the project from Lesson 1 and code to provide automatic synchronization to the database.

1. In Visual Studio .NET 2010, click File | Open | Project.

2. Locate the project you created in Chapter 2, Lesson 1, or locate the Chapter 2, Lesson 2 beginning solution on the companion CD and click Open.

3. Add a database file to your project.

   (Later, you can opt to attach this database to a remote database server, if needed, and then the connection string can be updated to point to the remote database server.)

4. In Solution Explorer, right-click the project node, click Add | New Item | Data | Service-based Database, and name the file **Maintenance.mdf.** Click Add.

   This will add the file, but it will also start a wizard to create a typed data set.

5. Click Cancel on the wizard page.

6. Select the newly created Maintenance.MDF file in Solution Explorer and then, in the Properties window, set the *Copy To Output Dir* property to *Copy If Newer*.

7. Modify the connection string in the config file to connect to your new database. In the *<configuration>* element, modify the connection string to look like the following.

   App.Config Connection

```
<connectionStrings>
  <add name="db" connectionString=
      "Data Source=.\SQLEXPRESS;AttachDbFilename=|DataDirectory|Maintenance.MDF;
      Integrated Security=True;User Instance=True" />
</connectionStrings>
```

8. Add the following class-level variables to the top of your Windows form that will reference the data adapters you will use to move data between your application and the database.

   Sample of Visual Basic Code

```
Private daVehicles As SqlDataAdapter
Private daRepairs As SqlDataAdapter
```

   Sample of C# Code

```
private SqlDataAdapter daVehicles;
private SqlDataAdapter daRepairs;
```

9. At the top of the *Form1_Load* event handler method, change the *CheckConnectivity* method call to call the *InitializeDataAdapters* method you will create in the next step. The completed *Form1_Load* should look like the following:

Sample of Visual Basic Code

```vb
Private Sub Form1_Load(ByVal sender As System.Object, _
        ByVal e As System.EventArgs) Handles MyBase.Load
    cnString = ConfigurationManager _
            .ConnectionStrings("db") _
            .ConnectionString
    InitializeDataAdapters()
    PopulateDataSet()
    dgVehicles.DataSource = ds
    dgVehicles.DataMember = "Vehicles"
    dgRepairs.DataSource = ds
    dgRepairs.DataMember = "Vehicles.vehicles_repairs"
End Sub
```

Sample of C# Code

```csharp
private void Form1_Load(object sender, EventArgs e)
{
    cnString = ConfigurationManager
        .ConnectionStrings["db"]
        .ConnectionString;
    InitializeDataAdapters();
    PopulateDataSet();
    dgVehicles.DataSource = ds;
    dgVehicles.DataMember = "Vehicles";
    dgRepairs.DataSource = ds;
    dgRepairs.DataMember = "Vehicles.vehicles_repairs";
}
```

The *InitializeDataAdapters* method will initialize a data adapter for the Vehicles table and a data adapter for the Repairs table. For the Vehicles table, the data adapter is initialized the easy way, using a *SqlCommandBuilder* object to create the *Insert*, *Update*, and *Delete* commands. For the Repairs table, the data adapter is initialized by creating each command object manually and explicitly setting the necessary properties. The following code shows the *InitializeDataAdapters* method.

Sample of Visual Basic Code

```vb
Public Sub InitializeDataAdapters()
    'do vehicles with the SQL Command Builder
    daVehicles = New SqlDataAdapter("SELECT * FROM Vehicles", cnString)
    Dim bldVehicles As New SqlCommandBuilder(daVehicles)

    'do repairs by creating all commands
    Dim cn As New SqlConnection(cnString)
    Dim cmdSelectRepairs = cn.CreateCommand()
    Dim cmdUpdateRepairs = cn.CreateCommand()
    Dim cmdDeleteRepairs = cn.CreateCommand()
    Dim cmdInsertRepairs = cn.CreateCommand()

    cmdSelectRepairs.CommandText = _
```

```
        "SELECT * FROM Repairs"

cmdInsertRepairs.CommandText = _
    "INSERT Repairs(VIN,Description, Cost) " _
    & " OUTPUT inserted.* " _
    & " VALUES( @VIN, @Description, @Cost); "

cmdInsertRepairs.Parameters.Add("@VIN", SqlDbType.VarChar, 20, "VIN")

cmdInsertRepairs.Parameters.Add("@Description", SqlDbType.VarChar, _
        60, "Description")

cmdInsertRepairs.Parameters.Add("@Cost", SqlDbType.Money, 0, "Cost")

cmdUpdateRepairs.CommandText = _
    "UPDATE Repairs SET " _
    & " VIN=@VIN, Description=@Description, Cost=@Cost " _
        & " WHERE ID=@OriginalID " _
        & " AND VIN=@OriginalVIN " _
        & " AND Description=@OriginalDescription " _
        & " AND Cost=@OriginalCost"

cmdUpdateRepairs.Parameters.Add("@OriginalID", SqlDbType.Int, 0, "ID") _
    .SourceVersion = DataRowVersion.Original

cmdUpdateRepairs.Parameters.Add("@VIN", SqlDbType.VarChar, 20, "VIN")

cmdUpdateRepairs.Parameters.Add("@OriginalVIN", SqlDbType.VarChar, _
        20, "VIN").SourceVersion = DataRowVersion.Original

cmdUpdateRepairs.Parameters.Add("@Description", SqlDbType.VarChar, _
        60, "Description")

cmdUpdateRepairs.Parameters.Add("@OriginalDescription", _
        SqlDbType.VarChar, 20, "Description") _
        .SourceVersion = DataRowVersion.Original

cmdUpdateRepairs.Parameters.Add("@Cost", SqlDbType.Money, 0, "Cost")

cmdUpdateRepairs.Parameters.Add("@OriginalCost", SqlDbType.Money, _
        0, "Cost").SourceVersion = DataRowVersion.Original

cmdDeleteRepairs.CommandText = _
    "DELETE Repairs " _
    & " WHERE ID=@OriginalID " _
    & " AND VIN=@OriginalVIN " _
    & " AND Description=@OriginalDescription " _
    & " AND Cost=@OriginalCost"

cmdDeleteRepairs.Parameters.Add("@OriginalID", SqlDbType.Int, 0, "ID") _
    .SourceVersion = DataRowVersion.Original

cmdDeleteRepairs.Parameters.Add("@OriginalVIN", SqlDbType.VarChar, _
        20, "VIN").SourceVersion = DataRowVersion.Original
```

```
        cmdDeleteRepairs.Parameters.Add("@OriginalDescription", _
            SqlDbType.VarChar, 20, "Description") _
            .SourceVersion = DataRowVersion.Original

        cmdDeleteRepairs.Parameters.Add("@OriginalCost", SqlDbType.Money, _
            0, "Cost").SourceVersion = DataRowVersion.Original

        daRepairs = New SqlDataAdapter(cmdSelectRepairs)
        daRepairs.InsertCommand = cmdInsertRepairs
        daRepairs.UpdateCommand = cmdUpdateRepairs
        daRepairs.DeleteCommand = cmdDeleteRepairs
End Sub
```

Sample of C# Code

```
public void InitializeDataAdapters()
{
    cnString = ConfigurationManager.ConnectionStrings["db"].ConnectionString;

    //do vehicles with the SQL Command Builder;
    daVehicles = new SqlDataAdapter("SELECT * FROM Vehicles", cnString);
    var bldVehicles = new SqlCommandBuilder(daVehicles);

    //do repairs by creating all commands
    var cn = new SqlConnection(cnString);
    var cmdSelectRepairs = cn.CreateCommand();
    var cmdUpdateRepairs = cn.CreateCommand();
    var cmdDeleteRepairs = cn.CreateCommand();
    var cmdInsertRepairs = cn.CreateCommand();

    cmdSelectRepairs.CommandText =
        "SELECT * FROM Repairs";

    cmdInsertRepairs.CommandText =
        "INSERT Repairs(VIN,Description, Cost) "
        + " OUTPUT inserted.* "
        + " VALUES( @VIN, @Description, @Cost); ";

    cmdInsertRepairs.Parameters.Add("@VIN", SqlDbType.VarChar, 20, "VIN");

    cmdInsertRepairs.Parameters.Add("@Description", SqlDbType.VarChar,
        60, "Description");

    cmdInsertRepairs.Parameters.Add("@Cost", SqlDbType.Money, 0, "Cost");

    cmdUpdateRepairs.CommandText =
        "UPDATE Repairs SET "
        + " VIN=@VIN, Description=@Description, Cost=@Cost "
            + " WHERE ID=@OriginalID "
            + " AND VIN=@OriginalVIN "
            + " AND Description=@OriginalDescription "
            + " AND Cost=@OriginalCost";

    cmdUpdateRepairs.Parameters.Add("@OriginalID", SqlDbType.Int, 0, "ID")
        .SourceVersion = DataRowVersion.Original;
```

```
cmdUpdateRepairs.Parameters.Add("@VIN", SqlDbType.VarChar, 20, "VIN");

cmdUpdateRepairs.Parameters.Add("@OriginalVIN", SqlDbType.VarChar,
        20, "VIN").SourceVersion = DataRowVersion.Original;

cmdUpdateRepairs.Parameters.Add("@Description", SqlDbType.VarChar,
        60, "Description");

cmdUpdateRepairs.Parameters.Add("@OriginalDescription",
        SqlDbType.VarChar, 20, "Description")
        .SourceVersion = DataRowVersion.Original;

cmdUpdateRepairs.Parameters.Add("@Cost", SqlDbType.Money, 0, "Cost");

cmdUpdateRepairs.Parameters.Add("@OriginalCost", SqlDbType.Money,
        0, "Cost").SourceVersion = DataRowVersion.Original;

cmdDeleteRepairs.CommandText =
    "DELETE Repairs "
    + " WHERE ID=@OriginalID "
    + " AND VIN=@OriginalVIN "
    + " AND Description=@OriginalDescription "
    + " AND Cost=@OriginalCost";

cmdDeleteRepairs.Parameters.Add("@OriginalID", SqlDbType.Int, 0, "ID")
    .SourceVersion = DataRowVersion.Original;

cmdDeleteRepairs.Parameters.Add("@OriginalVIN", SqlDbType.VarChar,
        20, "VIN").SourceVersion = DataRowVersion.Original;

cmdDeleteRepairs.Parameters.Add("@OriginalDescription",
        SqlDbType.VarChar, 20, "Description")
        .SourceVersion = DataRowVersion.Original;

cmdDeleteRepairs.Parameters.Add("@OriginalCost", SqlDbType.Money,
        0, "Cost").SourceVersion = DataRowVersion.Original;

daRepairs = new SqlDataAdapter(cmdSelectRepairs);
daRepairs.InsertCommand = cmdInsertRepairs;
daRepairs.UpdateCommand = cmdUpdateRepairs;
daRepairs.DeleteCommand = cmdDeleteRepairs;
}
```

In this method, it took only a couple lines of code to initialize the Vehicles data adapter. *SqlCommandBuilder* simplifies the initialization but doesn't have the same features that are available when writing all the code. This becomes apparent when initializing the Repairs data adapter. The Repairs table has an identity column that must be updated after inserts are done. The OUTPUT keyword in the SQL insert statement is the equivalent of executing a SELECT statement on the row that was inserted, which updates the identity column in the client application. The ID column had negative values and needed to be upgraded to the actual values that are generated in SQL Server when the insert takes place.

10. Add code into the *PopulateDataSet* method that will call to the *Synchronize* method you will add in the next step. Your completed *PopulateDataSet* method will look like the following.

Sample of Visual Basic Code

```
Private Sub PopulateDataSet()
    If File.Exists(xsdFile) Then
        ds = New DataSet()
        ds.ReadXmlSchema(xsdFile)
    Else
        CreateSchema()
    End If
    If File.Exists(xmlFile) Then
        ds.ReadXml(xmlFile, XmlReadMode.IgnoreSchema)
    End If
    Synchronize()
End Sub
```

Sample of C# Code

```
private void PopulateDataSet()
{
    if( File.Exists(xsdFile))
    {
        ds = new DataSet();
        ds.ReadXmlSchema(xsdFile);
    }
    else
    {
        CreateSchema();
    }
    if( File.Exists(xmlFile))
    {
        ds.ReadXml(xmlFile, XmlReadMode.IgnoreSchema);
    }
    Synchronize();
}
```

11. Add the *Synchronize* method, which will be called when the application starts and when it ends.

    This method will first check whether a connection can be made to the database server. If a connection can be made, the code verifies whether the tables exist; if they do not exist, the tables are created. The code then calls the *SyncData* method created in the next step to perform the synchronization. Your code should look like the following:

Sample of Visual Basic Code

```
Private Sub Synchronize()
    If CheckConnectivity() Then
        CreateTablesIfNotExisting()
        SyncData()
    End If
End Sub
```

Sample of C# Code

```csharp
private void Synchronize()
{
    if( CheckConnectivity())
    {
        CreateTablesIfNotExisting();
        SyncData();
    }
}
```

12. Modify the *CheckConnectivity* method, which will simply attempt to retrieve the version of SQL Server and return *true* or *false*, based on whether the attempt was successful. The messages have been removed so this method silently checks connectivity.

Sample of Visual Basic Code

```vb
Private Function CheckConnectivity() As Boolean
    Try
        Using cn = New SqlConnection(cnString)
            cn.Open()
            Dim version = cn.ServerVersion
        End Using
    Catch ex As Exception
        Return False
    End Try
    Return True
End Function
```

Sample of C# Code

```csharp
private bool CheckConnectivity()
{
    try
    {
        using(var cn = new SqlConnection(cnString))
        {
            cn.Open();
            var version = cn.ServerVersion;
        }
    }
    catch
    {
        return false;
    }
    return true;
}
```

13. Add the code for the *CreateTablesIfNotExisting* method. This method checks whether the Vehicles and Repairs tables exist on SQL Server and, if not, the tables are created.

Sample of Visual Basic Code

```vb
Private Sub CreateTablesIfNotExisting()
    Try
        Using cn = New SqlConnection(cnString)
            Using cmd = cn.CreateCommand()
                cn.Open()
```

```
                    cmd.CommandText = _
                        "IF NOT EXISTS ( " _
                        & " SELECT * FROM sys.Tables WHERE NAME='Vehicles') " _
                        & " CREATE TABLE Vehicles( " _
                        & " VIN varchar(20) PRIMARY KEY, " _
                        & " Make varchar(20), " _
                        & " Model varchar(20), Year int)"
                    cmd.ExecuteNonQuery()
                    cmd.CommandText = _
                        "IF NOT EXISTS ( " _
                        & " SELECT * FROM sys.Tables WHERE NAME='Repairs') " _
                        & " CREATE TABLE Repairs( " _
                        & " ID int IDENTITY PRIMARY KEY, " _
                        & " VIN varchar(20), " _
                        & " Description varchar(60), " _
                        & " Cost money)"
                    cmd.ExecuteNonQuery()
                End Using
            End Using
        Catch ex As Exception
            MessageBox.Show(ex.Message)
        End Try
    End Sub
```

Sample of C# Code

```
private void CreateTablesIfNotExisting()
{
    try
    {
        using( var cn = new SqlConnection(cnString))
        using( var cmd = cn.CreateCommand())
        {
            cn.Open();
            cmd.CommandText =
                "IF NOT EXISTS ( "
                + " SELECT * FROM sys.Tables WHERE NAME='Vehicles') "
                + " CREATE TABLE Vehicles( "
                + " VIN varchar(20) PRIMARY KEY, "
                + " Make varchar(20), "
                + " Model varchar(20), Year int)";
            cmd.ExecuteNonQuery();
            cmd.CommandText =
                "IF NOT EXISTS ( "
                + " SELECT * FROM sys.Tables WHERE NAME='Repairs') "
                + " CREATE TABLE Repairs( "
                + " ID int IDENTITY PRIMARY KEY, "
                + " VIN varchar(20), "
                + " Description varchar(60), "
                + " Cost money)";
            cmd.ExecuteNonQuery();
        }
    }
    catch(Exception ex)
    {
        MessageBox.Show(ex.Message);
```

```
        }
    }
```

14. Add the *SyncData* method that performs the actual data synchronization. This method needs to send client-side changes to the database and then receive all server-side changes.

Sample of Visual Basic Code

```vb
Private Sub SyncData()
    'send changes
    Try
        daVehicles.Update(ds, "Vehicles")
        daRepairs.Update(ds, "Repairs")
        ds.AcceptChanges()
    Catch ex As Exception
        MessageBox.Show(ex.Message)
    End Try

    'retrieve updates
    Dim tempVehicles As New DataTable()
    daVehicles.Fill(tempVehicles)
    ds.Tables("Vehicles").Merge(tempVehicles)

    'merge changes
    Dim tempRepairs As New DataTable()
    daRepairs.Fill(tempRepairs)
    ds.Tables("Repairs").Merge(tempRepairs)
End Sub
```

Sample of C# Code

```csharp
private void SyncData()
{
    //send changes
    try
    {
        daVehicles.Update(ds, "Vehicles");
        daRepairs.Update(ds, "Repairs");
        ds.AcceptChanges();
    }
    catch(Exception ex)
    {
        MessageBox.Show(ex.Message);
    }

    //retrieve updates
    var tempVehicles = new DataTable();
    daVehicles.Fill(tempVehicles);
    ds.Tables["Vehicles"].Merge(tempVehicles);

    //merge changes
    var tempRepairs = new DataTable();
    daRepairs.Fill(tempRepairs);
    ds.Tables["Repairs"].Merge(tempRepairs);
}
```

15. Add code to the *Form1_Closing* event to synchronize the data when the application is ending. Your completed *Form1_Closing* method should be as follows:

Sample of Visual Basic Code
```
Private Sub Form1_FormClosing(ByVal sender As System.Object, _
                    ByVal e As FormClosingEventArgs) _
                    Handles MyBase.FormClosing
    Synchronize()
    ds.WriteXml(xmlFile, XmlWriteMode.DiffGram)
End Sub
```

Sample of C# Code
```
private void Form1_FormClosing(object sender, FormClosingEventArgs e)
{
    Synchronize();
    ds.WriteXml(xmlFile, XmlWriteMode.DiffGram);
}
```

16. Build the application and correct any errors.

17. Test the application. Press F5 to run the application with the debugger.

When the application starts, it loads the offline XML file if it exists. It then checks whether it can connect to SQL Server. If a connection can be made, the application then creates the tables if they don't exist and attempts to synchronize the client-side data with the server-side data.

When you close the application, a call is made to synchronize the data, and then the data set is serialized to the offline XML file.

Lesson Summary

This lesson provided a detailed description of reading and writing data.

- SQL Express is an excellent database server for development because the .mdf database file can be placed into the project and the file can be configured to be copied to the output folder every time the application is built and run.

- You use the *DbCommand* object to send a SQL command to a data store. You can also create parameters and pass them to the *DbCommand* object.

- The *DbDataReader* object provides a high-performance method of retrieving data from a data store by delivering a forward-only, read-only, server-side cursor.

- The *SqlBulkCopy* object can copy data from a number of sources to a SQL Server table.

- You can use the *DbDataAdapter* object to retrieve and update data between a data table and a data store. *DbDataAdapter* can contain a single *SelectCommand* property for read-only data, or it can contain *SelectCommand*, *InsertCommand*, *UpdateCommand*, and *DeleteCommand* properties for fully updatable data.

- The *DbProviderFactory* object helps you create provider-independent code, which might be necessary when the data store needs to be changeable quickly.

Lesson Review

You can use the following questions to test your knowledge of the information in Lesson 2, "Reading and Writing Data." The questions are also available on the companion CD if you prefer to review them in electronic form.

> **NOTE ANSWERS**
>
> Answers to these questions and explanations of why each answer choice is correct or incorrect are located in the "Answers" section at the end of the book.

1. You are going to execute a *Select* command to SQL Server that returns several rows of customer data. You don't need a data table to hold the data because you will simply loop over the returned results to build a string of information that will be displayed to the user. You create and open a connection and then create the command and set its properties. Which method on the command will you execute to retrieve the results?

   A. *ExecuteScalar*

   B. *Close*

   C. *ExecuteReader*

   D. *ExecuteNonQuery*

2. You are calling a stored procedure in SQL Server 2008 that returns a UDT as an output parameter. This UDT, called *MyCompanyType*, was created by your company. The UDT has a method called *GetDetails* that you want to execute in your client application. What must you do to execute the method? (Each correct answer presents part of a complete solution. Choose three.)

   A. Set the *SqlDbType* of the parameter to *SqlDbType.Udt*.

   B. Set the *UdtTypeName* of the parameter to *MyCompanyType*.

   C. Call the *ExecuteXmlReader* method on the *SqlCommand* to serialize the UDT as XML.

   D. In the client application, set a reference to the assembly in which the UDT is.

3. You want to execute a SQL insert statement from your client application, so you set the *CommandText* property of the command object and open the connection. Which method will you execute on the command?

   A. *ExecuteScalar*

   B. *ExecuteXmlReader*

   C. *ExecuteReader*

   D. *ExecuteNonQuery*

Lesson 3: Working with Transactions

This lesson will help you understand what a transaction is and why you want to use transactions in your applications. It starts by defining the transaction and examining isolation levels, and then examines ADO.NET transactions. The lesson then moves beyond ADO.NET to a namespace called *System.Transactions*. This namespace actually is not part of ADO.NET; it was developed by the Enterprise Services team at Microsoft. This lesson discusses it because it offers a consistent, flexible programming model that's simply too significant to overlook.

After this lesson, you will be able to:

- Identify the attributes of a transaction.
- Indentify transaction isolation levels.
- Create a transaction by using the *SqlConnection* object.
- Create a distributed transaction by using the *System.Transactions* DLL and namespace.
- View the distributed transaction by using the Distributed Transaction Coordinator.

Estimated lesson time: 30 minutes

What Is a Transaction?

A transaction is an atomic unit of work that must be completed in its entirety. The transaction succeeds if it is committed and fails if it is aborted. Transactions have four essential attributes: atomicity, consistency, isolation, and durability (known as the ACID attributes).

- **Atomicity**   The work cannot be broken into smaller parts. Although a transaction might contain many SQL statements, they must be run as an all-or-nothing proposition, which means that if a transaction is half complete when an error occurs, the work reverts to its state prior to the start of the transaction.

- **Consistency**   A transaction must operate on a consistent view of the data and must leave the data in a consistent state. Any work in progress must not be visible to other transactions until the transaction has been committed.

- **Isolation**   A transaction should appear to be running by itself; the effects of other ongoing transactions must be invisible to this transaction, and the effects of this transaction must be invisible to other ongoing transactions.

- **Durability**   When a transaction is committed, it must be persisted so it will not be lost in the event of a power failure or other system failure. Only committed transactions are recovered during power-up and crash recovery; uncommitted work is rolled back.

Concurrency Models and Database Locking

The attributes of consistency and isolation are implemented by using the database's locking mechanism, which keeps one transaction from affecting another. If one transaction needs access to data with which another transaction is working, the data is locked until the first transaction is committed or rolled back. Transactions that must access locked data are forced to wait until the lock is released, which means that long-running transactions can affect performance and scalability. The use of locks to prevent access to the data is known as a "pessimistic" concurrency model.

In an "optimistic" concurrency model, locks are not used when the data is read. Instead, when updates are made, the data is checked to see whether the data has changed since it was read. If the data has changed, an exception is thrown and the application applies business logic to recover.

Transaction Isolation Levels

Complete isolation can be great, but it comes at a high cost. Complete isolation means that any data read or written during a transaction must be locked. Yes, even data that is read is locked because a query for customer orders should yield the same result at the beginning of the transaction and at the end of the transaction.

Depending on your application, you might not need complete isolation. By tweaking the transaction isolation level, you can reduce the amount of locking and increase scalability and performance. The transaction isolation level affects whether you experience the following:

- **Dirty read**   Being able to read data that has been changed by another transaction but not committed yet. This can be a big problem if the transaction that has changed data is rolled back.
- **Nonrepeatable read**   When a transaction reads the same row more than once with different results because another transaction has modified the row between reads.
- **Phantom read**   When a transaction reads a row that a different transaction will delete or when a second read finds a new row that has been inserted by another transaction.

Table 2-6 lists the transaction isolation levels along with their effects. It also shows the concurrency model the isolation level supports.

TABLE 2-6 Isolation Levels in SQL Server

LEVEL	DIRTY READ	NONREPEATABLE READ	PHANTOM READ	CONCURRENCY MODEL
Read Uncommitted	Yes	Yes	Yes	None
Read Committed with Locks	No	Yes	Yes	Pessimistic
Read Committed with Snapshots	No	Yes	Yes	Optimistic
Repeatable Read	No	No	Yes	Pessimistic
Snapshot	No	No	No	Optimistic
Serializable	No	No	No	Pessimistic

The following is a description of the concurrency levels that Table 2-6 shows.

- **Read Uncommitted** Queries inside one transaction are affected by uncommitted changes in another transaction. No locks are acquired, and no locks are honored when data is read.

- **Read Committed with Locks** The default setting in SQL Server. Committed updates are visible within another transaction. Long-running queries and aggregations are not required to be point-in-time consistent.

- **Read Committed with Snapshots** Only committed updates are visible within another transaction. No locks are acquired, and row versioning tracks row modifications. Long-running queries and aggregates are required to be point-in-time consistent. This level comes with the overhead of the version store (discussed further at the end of this list). The version store provides increased throughput with reduced locking contention.

- **Repeatable Read** Within a transaction, all reads are consistent; other transactions cannot affect your query results because they cannot complete until you finish your transaction and release your locks. This level is used primarily when you read data with the intention of modifying the data in the same transaction.

- **Snapshot** Used when accuracy is required on long-running queries and multi-statement transactions but there is no plan to update the data. No read locks are acquired to prevent modifications by other transactions because the changes will not be seen until the snapshot completes and the data modification transactions commit. Data can be modified within this transaction level at the risk of conflicts with transactions that have updated the same data after the snapshot transaction started.

- **Serializable** Places a range lock, which is a multi-row lock, on the complete row set accessed, preventing other users from updating or inserting rows into the data set until the transaction is complete. This data is accurate and consistent through the life of the transaction. This is the most restrictive of the isolation levels. Because of the large amount of locking in this level, you should use it only when necessary.

The version store retains row version records after the *update* or *delete* statement has committed until all active transactions have committed. The version store essentially retains row version records until all the following transaction types have committed or ended:

- Transactions that are running under Snapshot Isolation
- Transactions that are running under Read Committed with Snapshot Isolation
- All other transactions that started before the current transaction committed

Single Transactions and Distributed Transactions

A transaction is a unit of work that must be performed with a single durable resource (such as a database or a message queue). In the .NET Framework, a transaction typically represents all the work that can be done on a single open connection.

A distributed transaction spans multiple durable resources. In the .NET Framework, if you need a transaction to include work on multiple connections, you must perform a distributed transaction. A distributed transaction uses a two-phase commit protocol and a dedicated transaction manager. In Windows operating systems since Microsoft Windows NT, the dedicated transaction manager for managing distributed transactions is the Distributed Transaction Coordinator (DTC).

Creating a Transaction

The two types of transactions are *implicit* and *explicit*. Each SQL statement runs in its own implicit transaction. If you don't explicitly create a transaction, a transaction is implicitly created for you on a statement-by-statement basis. This ensures that a SQL statement that updates many rows is either completed as a unit or rolled back.

Creating a Transaction by Using T-SQL

An explicit transaction is one that you create in your program. You can create a transaction explicitly in T-SQL by using the following script:

SQL: Explicit Transaction

```
SET XACT_ABORT ON
BEGIN TRY
    BEGIN TRANSACTION
    --work code here
    COMMIT TRANSACTION
END TRY
BEGIN CATCH
    ROLLBACK TRANSACTION
    --cleanup code
END CATCH
```

The SQL *TRY/CATCH* block catches any errors and rolls back the transaction. This code sets XACT_ABORT to *On*, which ensures that all errors under severity level 21 are handled as transaction abort errors. Severity level 21 and higher is considered fatal and stops code execution, which also rolls back the transaction.

The scope of the transaction is limited to the statements in the *TRY* block, which can include calls to other stored procedures.

Creating a Transaction by Using the ADO.NET *DbTransaction* Object

Another way to create an explicit transaction is to put the transaction logic in your .NET Framework code. The *DbConnection* object has the *BeginTransaction* method, which creates a *DbTransaction* object. The following code sample shows how this is done.

Sample of Visual Basic Code

```vb
Private Sub BeginTransactionToolStripMenuItem_Click( _
        ByVal sender As System.Object, ByVal e As System.EventArgs) _
        Handles BeginTransactionToolStripMenuItem.Click
    Dim cnSetting As ConnectionStringSettings = _
        ConfigurationManager.ConnectionStrings("nw")
    Using cn As New SqlConnection()
        cn.ConnectionString = cnSetting.ConnectionString
        cn.Open()
        Using tran As SqlTransaction = cn.BeginTransaction()
            Try
                'work code here
                Using cmd As SqlCommand = cn.CreateCommand()
                    cmd.Transaction = tran
                    cmd.CommandText = "SELECT count(*) FROM employees"
                    Dim count As Integer = CInt(cmd.ExecuteScalar())
                    MessageBox.Show(count.ToString())
                End Using

                'if we made it this far, commit
                tran.Commit()
            Catch xcp As Exception
                tran.Rollback()
                'cleanup code
                MessageBox.Show(xcp.Message)
            End Try
        End Using
    End Using
End Sub
```

Sample of C# Code

```csharp
private void beginTransactionToolStripMenuItem_Click(object sender, EventArgs e)

{

    ConnectionStringSettings cnSetting =

        ConfigurationManager.ConnectionStrings["nw"];
    using (SqlConnection cn = new SqlConnection())
    {
        cn.ConnectionString = cnSetting.ConnectionString;
```

```
        cn.Open();
        using (SqlTransaction tran = cn.BeginTransaction())
        {
            try
            {
                //work code here
                using (SqlCommand cmd = cn.CreateCommand())
                {
                    cmd.Transaction = tran;
                    cmd.CommandText = "SELECT count(*) FROM employees";
                    int count = (int)cmd.ExecuteScalar();
                    MessageBox.Show(count.ToString());
                }

                //if we made it this far, commit
                tran.Commit();
            }
            catch (Exception xcp)
            {
                tran.Rollback();
                //cleanup code
                MessageBox.Show(xcp.Message);
            }
        }
    }
}
```

In this code, a *SqlConnection* object is created and opened, and then the connection object creates a transaction object by executing the *BeginTransaction* method. The *try* block does the work and commits the transaction. If an exception is thrown, the *catch* block rolls back the transaction. Although the data has been rolled back, if you need to reset any variables as a result of the rollback, you can do so at the Clean Up Code comment is. Also, the *SqlCommand* object must have its *Transaction* property assigned to the connection's transaction.

The scope of the transaction is limited to the code within the *try* block, but the transaction was created by a specific connection object, so the transaction cannot span to a different connection object.

Setting the Transaction Isolation Level

Each SQL Server connection (SQL session) can have its transaction isolation level set. The setting you assign remains until the connection is closed or until you assign a new setting. One way to assign the transaction isolation level is to add the SQL statement to your stored procedure. For example, to set the transaction isolation level to Repeatable Read, add the following SQL statement to your stored procedure.

SQL

```
SET TRANSACTION ISOLATION LEVEL REPEATABLE READ
```

Another way to set the transaction isolation level is to add a query hint to your SQL statement. For example, the following SQL statement overrides the current session's isolation setting and uses the Read Uncommitted isolation level to perform the query.

SQL

```
SELECT * FROM CUSTOMERS WITH (NOLOCK)
```

The transaction isolation level can also be set on the *DbTransaction* class, from which the *SqlTransaction* class inherits. Simply pass the desired transaction isolation level to the *BeginTransaction* method.

Introducing the *System.Transactions* Namespace

The *System.Transactions* namespace offers enhanced transactional support for managed code and makes it possible to handle transactions in a rather simple programming model. *System.Transactions* is designed to integrate well with SQL Server 2005 and later and offers automatic promotion of standard transactions to fully distributed transactions. Figure 2-6 shows the hierarchy of the *Transaction* class in the *System.Transactions* namespace. The *TransactionScope* class was added to the diagram to show that it is not related to the *Transaction* class but is used to create transactions.

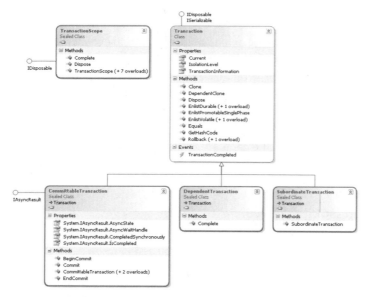

FIGURE 2-6 This figure shows the *System.Transactions.Transaction* class hierarchy.

Creating a Transaction by Using the *TransactionScope* Class

You can also create a transaction in your .NET Framework code by using classes in the *System.Transactions* namespace. The most commonly used class is the *TransactionScope* class; it creates a standard transaction called a "local lightweight transaction" that is automatically promoted to a full-fledged distributed transaction if required. This automatically promoted transaction is commonly referred to as an implicit transaction. The distinction is worth mentioning because it seems to give a somewhat different meaning to this term. Even in this context, you are not explicitly creating the transaction for the work and explicitly issuing a commit or rollback. Instead, you are creating a scope in which a transaction will exist and will automatically commit or roll back.

Sample of Visual Basic Code

```vb
Private Sub SystemTransactionToolStripMenuItem_Click(
        ByVal sender As System.Object, ByVal e As System.EventArgs) _
        Handles SystemTransactionToolStripMenuItem.Click
    Dim cnSetting As ConnectionStringSettings = _
        ConfigurationManager.ConnectionStrings("nw")
    Using ts As TransactionScope = New TransactionScope()
        Using cn As New SqlConnection()
            cn.ConnectionString = cnSetting.ConnectionString
            cn.Open()

            'work code here
            Using cmd As SqlCommand = cn.CreateCommand()
                cmd.CommandText = "SELECT count(*) FROM employees"
                Dim count As Integer = CInt(cmd.ExecuteScalar())
                MessageBox.Show(count.ToString())
            End Using

            'if we made it this far, commit
            ts.Complete()
        End Using
    End Using
End Sub
```

Sample of C# Code

```csharp
private void systemTransactionToolStripMenuItem_Click(
    object sender, EventArgs e)
{
    ConnectionStringSettings cnSetting =
        ConfigurationManager.ConnectionStrings["nw"];
    using (TransactionScope ts = new TransactionScope())
    {
        using (SqlConnection cn = new SqlConnection())
        {
            cn.ConnectionString = cnSetting.ConnectionString;
            cn.Open();

            //work code here
            using (SqlCommand cmd = cn.CreateCommand())
            {
```

```
        cmd.CommandText = "SELECT count(*) FROM employees";
        int count = (int)cmd.ExecuteScalar();
        MessageBox.Show(count.ToString());
    }

    //if we made it this far, commit
    ts.Complete();
    }
  }
}
```

This code starts by creating a *TransactionScope* object in a *using* block. If a connection is created, the *TransactionScope* object assigns a transaction to this connection so you don't need to add anything to your code to enlist this connection into the transaction. The *SqlCommand* object doesn't need to have the *Transaction* property assigned, but the *SqlCommand* object joins the transaction. If an exception is thrown within the *TransactionScope* object's *using* block, the transaction aborts, and all work is rolled back. The last line of the *TransactionScope* object's *using* block calls the *Complete* method to commit the transaction. This method sets an internal Boolean flag called *complete*. The *Complete* method can be called only once. This is a design decision that ensures that you won't continue adding code after a call to *Complete* and then try calling *Complete* again. A second call to *Complete* will throw an *InvalidOperationException*.

EXAM TIP

For the exam, you will be tested on the *TransactionScope*, so don't forget that you need to call the *Complete* method or your transaction will be rolled back.

The scope of the transaction is limited to the code within the *TransactionScope* object's *using* block, which includes any and all connections created within the block, even if the connections are created in methods called within the block. You can see that the *TransactionScope* object offers more functionality than ADO.NET transactions and is easy to code.

NOTE   NO DIFFERENCE IN PERFORMANCE

The code in this example performs as well as the previous examples showing ADO.NET transactions, so you should consider standardizing your code to use this programming model whenever you need transactional behavior, as long as you are using SQL Server 2005 or later. If you are using SQL Server 2000 or a different database product, you should continue to use the existing ADO.NET transaction because SQL Server 2000 and other database products don't know how to create a local lightweight transaction.

Setting the Transaction Options

You can set the isolation level and the transaction's timeout period on the *TransactionScope* object by creating a *TransactionOptions* object. The *TransactionOptions* structure has an *IsolationLevel* property you can use to deviate from the default isolation level of Serializable and employ another isolation level (such as Read Committed). The isolation level is merely a suggestion (hint) to the database. Most database engines try to use the suggested level if possible. The *TransactionOptions* type also has a *Timeout* property that can be used to deviate from the default of one minute.

The *TransactionScope* object's constructor also takes a *TransactionScopeOption* enumeration parameter. This parameter can be set to any of the following:

- **Required** If your application has already started a transaction, this *TransactionScope* object joins it. If there is no ongoing transaction, a new transaction is created. To help you understand the benefit of this setting, consider a *BankAccount* class that has *Deposit*, *Withdraw*, and *Transfer* methods. You want to create a transaction scope in all three methods, but when you get to the *Transfer* method, it calls the *Withdraw* and the *Deposit* methods that already have a transaction scope defined. The *Deposit* and *Withdraw* methods will be nested within the *Transfer* method. You can't remove *TransactionScope* from *Withdraw* and *Deposit* because you need the ability to call these methods directly, and you want them to execute within a transaction. With the *Required* setting, *Withdraw* and *Deposit* join the *Transfer* transaction. This is the default setting.

- **RequiresNew** This setting always starts a new transaction, even if there is an ongoing transaction. Expanding on the previous *BankAccount* scenario, you might want an audit record to be written, regardless of the outcome of the overall transaction. If you simply try to write an audit record and the transaction aborts, the audit record is rolled back as well. Use the *RequiresNew* setting to write the audit record regardless of the overall transaction state.

- **Suppress** This setting suppresses any transaction activity in this block. It provides a way to do nontransactional work while there is an ongoing transaction. The execution of the *Complete* method is not required in this block and has no effect.

The following code creates and configures a *TransactionOptions* object, which is passed to the constructor of the *TransactionScope* object.

Sample of Visual Basic Code

```
Private Sub TransactionOptionsToolStripMenuItem_Click( _
    ByVal sender As System.Object, ByVal e As System.EventArgs) _
    Handles TransactionOptionsToolStripMenuItem.Click
  Dim cnSetting As ConnectionStringSettings = _
    ConfigurationManager.ConnectionStrings("nw")
  Dim opt As New TransactionOptions()
  opt.IsolationLevel = IsolationLevel.Serializable
  Using ts As TransactionScope = _
      New TransactionScope(TransactionScopeOption.Required, opt)
    Using cn As New SqlConnection()
```

```
        cn.ConnectionString = cnSetting.ConnectionString
        cn.Open()

        'work code here
        Using cmd As SqlCommand = cn.CreateCommand()
            cmd.CommandText = "SELECT count(*) FROM employees"
            Dim count As Integer = CInt(cmd.ExecuteScalar())
            MessageBox.Show(count.ToString())
        End Using
    End Using

    'if we made it this far, commit
    ts.Complete()
  End Using
End Sub
```

Sample of C# Code

```
private void transactionScopeOptionsToolStripMenuItem_Click(
    object sender, EventArgs e)
{
    ConnectionStringSettings cnSetting =
        ConfigurationManager.ConnectionStrings["nw"];
    TransactionOptions opt = new TransactionOptions();
    opt.IsolationLevel = System.Transactions.IsolationLevel.Serializable;
    using (TransactionScope ts =
       new TransactionScope(TransactionScopeOption.Required, opt))
    {
        using (SqlConnection cn = new SqlConnection())
        {
            cn.ConnectionString = cnSetting.ConnectionString;
            cn.Open();

            //work code here
            using (SqlCommand cmd = cn.CreateCommand())
            {
                cmd.CommandText = "SELECT count(*) FROM employees";
                int count = (int)cmd.ExecuteScalar();
                MessageBox.Show(count.ToString());
            }
        }

        //if we made it this far, commit
        ts.Complete();
    }
}
```

Working with Distributed Transactions

Before the release of the classes in the *System.Transactions* namespace, developers had to create classes that inherited from the *ServicedComponent* class in the *System.EnterpriseServices*
namespace to perform distributed transactions, as shown in the following sample.

Sample of Visual Basic Code

```vb
Imports System.EnterpriseServices

<Transaction> _
Public Class MyClass
        Inherits ServicedComponent
    <AutoComplete()> _
    Public Sub MyMethod()
        ' calls to other serviced components
        ' and resource managers like SQL Server
    End Sub
End Class
```

Sample of C# Code

```csharp
using System.EnterpriseServices;

[Transaction]
public class MyClass : ServicedComponent
{
    [AutoComplete]
    public void MyMethod()
    {
        // calls to other serviced components
        // and resource managers like SQL Server
    }
}
```

> **NOTE THIS IS THE OLD WAY!**
>
> The sample code included with the companion CD does not include this example because it is an example of something you typically won't do anymore.

The *Transaction* and *AutoComplete* attributes ensure that any method called within the class is in a transactional context. The *AutoComplete* attribute makes it simple to commit a transaction in a declarative way, but you can also use the *ContextUtil* class for better control of the transaction from within your code.

The problem with this old approach is that you must inherit from the *ServicedComponent* class; that is, you lose the flexibility of inheriting from a class that might be more appropriate to your internal application's class model. Also, the DTC is always used, which is too resource intensive if you don't really need to execute a distributed transaction. Ideally, the DTC should be used only when necessary. This approach uses the COM+ hosting model, by which your component must be loaded into Component Services.

The *System.Transactions* namespace includes the Lightweight Transaction Manager (LTM) in addition to the DTC. Use the LTM to manage a single transaction to a durable resource manager such as SQL Server 2005 and later. Volatile resource managers, which are memory based, can also be enlisted in a single transaction. The transaction managers are intended to be invisible to the developer, who never needs to write code to access them.

Using the *TransactionScope* object and the same programming model you used for single transactions, you can easily create a distributed transaction. When you access your first durable resource manager, a lightweight committable transaction is created to support the single transaction. When you access a second durable resource manager, the transaction is promoted to a distributed transaction. When a distributed transaction is executed, the DTC manages the two-phase commit protocol to commit or roll back the transaction.

The LTM and the DTC represent their transaction by using the *System.Transactions .Transaction* class, which has a static (Visual Basic shared) property called *Current* that gives you access to the current transaction. The current transaction is known as the ambient transaction. This property is *null* (Visual Basic *Nothing*) if there is no ongoing transaction. You can access the *Current* property directly to change the transaction isolation level, roll back the transaction, or view the transaction status.

Promotion Details

When a transaction is first created, it always attempts to be a lightweight committable transaction, managed by the LTM. The LTM allows the underlying durable resource manager, such as SQL Server 2005 and later, to manage the transaction. A transaction managed by the underlying manager is known as a delegated transaction. The only thing the LTM does is monitor the transaction for a need to be promoted. If promotion is required, the LTM tells the durable resource manager to provide an object that is capable of performing a distributed transaction. To support the notification, the durable resource manager must implement the *IPromotableSinglePhaseNotification* interface. This interface, and its parent interface, the *ITransactionPromoter*, are shown here.

Sample of Visual Basic Code

```vb
Imports System
Namespace System.Transactions
    Public Interface IPromotableSinglePhaseNotification
            Inherits ITransactionPromoter
        Sub Initialize()
        Sub Rollback(ByVal singlePhaseEnlistment As _
            SinglePhaseEnlistment)
        Sub SinglePhaseCommit(ByVal singlePhaseEnlistment As _
            SinglePhaseEnlistment)
    End Interface
    Public Interface ITransactionPromoter
        Function Promote() As Byte()
    End Interface
End Namespace
```

Sample of C# Code

```csharp
using System;
namespace System.Transactions
{
    public interface IPromotableSinglePhaseNotification :
        ITransactionPromoter
    {
```

```
    void Initialize();
    void Rollback(SinglePhaseEnlistment
        singlePhaseEnlistment);
    void SinglePhaseCommit(SinglePhaseEnlistment
        singlePhaseEnlistment);
}
public interface ITransactionPromoter
{
    byte[] Promote();
}
}
```

> **NOTE** **REFERENCE CODE ONLY**
>
> This is only reference code; therefore, it will not be included with the companion CD.

For example, the System.Data.dll assembly contains an internal class called *SqlDelegatedTransaction* that implements these interfaces for use with SQL Server 2005 and later. SQL Server 2005 and later uses delegated transactions whenever possible. On the *SqlConnection.Open* method, a local promotable transaction is created using the internal *SqlDelegatedTransaction* class, not a distributed transaction, and it remains a local transaction with its accompanying performance implications until you require a distributed transaction.

A transaction can be promoted from a lightweight committable transaction to a distributed transaction in the following three scenarios:

- When a durable resource manager is used that doesn't implement the *IPromotableSinglePhaseNotification* interface, such as SQL Server 2000
- When two durable resource managers are enlisted in the same transaction
- When the transaction spans multiple application domains

Viewing Distributed Transactions

The DTC is available through Component Services (choose Start | Control Panel | Administrative Tools | Component Services | Computers | My Computer | Distributed Transaction Coordinator | LocalDTC | Transaction Statistics). Figure 2-7 shows the Component Services window with the Transaction Statistics node selected. The center of the screen shows no activity. If you run any of the previous code examples, the screen continues to show no activity because the examples use standard transactions; when a transaction is promoted to a distributed transaction, however, you see a change to the total transaction count as well as to the other counters.

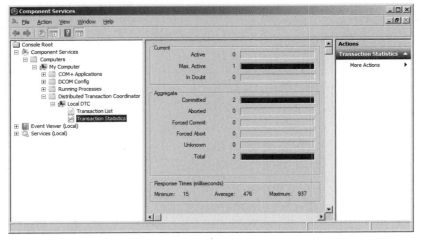

FIGURE 2-7 The DTC monitors distributed transactions.

Creating a Distributed Transaction

To create a distributed transaction, you can use the same *TransactionScope* programming model you used to create a standard transaction but add work to be performed on a different connection. The following code example uses two connections. Even though these connection objects use the same connection string, they are different connection objects, which will cause the single transaction to be promoted to a distributed transaction.

> **NOTE IS MICROSOFT DISTRIBUTED TRANSACTION COORDINATOR RUNNING?**
>
> Before running this code, verify that the DTC Windows service is started, or you will get an exception stating that the MSDTC is not available.

Sample of Visual Basic Code

```
Dim nwSetting As ConnectionStringSettings = _
    ConfigurationManager.ConnectionStrings("nw")
Dim bulkSetting As ConnectionStringSettings = _
    ConfigurationManager.ConnectionStrings("BulkCopy")
Using ts As TransactionScope = New TransactionScope()
    Using cn As New SqlConnection()
        cn.ConnectionString = nwSetting.ConnectionString
        cn.Open()

        'work code here
        Using cmd As SqlCommand = cn.CreateCommand()
            cmd.CommandText = _
                "Update Products SET UnitsInStock = UnitsInStock -1 " _
                & " Where ProductID=1"
            cmd.ExecuteNonQuery()
        End Using
    End Using
```

```vb
    Using cn As New SqlConnection()
        cn.ConnectionString = bulkSetting.ConnectionString
        cn.Open()

        'work code here
        Using cmd As SqlCommand = cn.CreateCommand()
            cmd.CommandText = _
                "Update Products SET UnitsInStock = UnitsInStock +1 " _
                & " Where ProductID=2"
            cmd.ExecuteNonQuery()
        End Using
    End Using

    'if we made it this far, commit
    'comment out ts.Complete() to simulate abort
    ts.Complete()
End Using

Dim dt As New DataTable()
Using cn As New SqlConnection()
    cn.ConnectionString = nwSetting.ConnectionString
    cn.Open()

    'work code here
    Using cmd As SqlCommand = cn.CreateCommand()
        cmd.CommandText = _
            "SELECT ProductID, UnitsInStock FROM Products " _
            & " WHERE ProductID = 1"
        dt.Load(cmd.ExecuteReader())
    End Using
End Using
Using cn As New SqlConnection()
    cn.ConnectionString = bulkSetting.ConnectionString
    cn.Open()

    'work code here
    Using cmd As SqlCommand = cn.CreateCommand()
        cmd.CommandText = _
            "SELECT ProductID, UnitsInStock FROM Products " _
            & " WHERE ProductID = 2"
        dt.Load(cmd.ExecuteReader())
    End Using
End Using
DataGridView2.DataSource = dt
```

Sample of C# Code

```csharp
var nwSetting = ConfigurationManager.ConnectionStrings["nw"];
var bulkSetting = ConfigurationManager.ConnectionStrings["BulkCopy"];
using (var ts = new TransactionScope())
{
    using (var cn = new SqlConnection())
    {
        cn.ConnectionString = nwSetting.ConnectionString;
        cn.Open();
```

```csharp
        //work code here
        using (var cmd = cn.CreateCommand())
        {
            cmd.CommandText =
                "Update Products SET UnitsInStock = UnitsInStock -1 "
                + " Where ProductID=1";
            cmd.ExecuteNonQuery();
        }
    }
    using (var cn = new SqlConnection())
    {
        cn.ConnectionString = bulkSetting.ConnectionString;
        cn.Open();

        //work code here
        using (var cmd = cn.CreateCommand())
        {
            cmd.CommandText =
                "Update Products SET UnitsInStock = UnitsInStock +1 "
                + " Where ProductID=2";
            cmd.ExecuteNonQuery();
        }
    }

    //if we made it this far, commit
    //comment out ts.Complete() to simulate abort
    ts.Complete();
}

var dt = new DataTable();
using (var cn = new SqlConnection())
{
    cn.ConnectionString = nwSetting.ConnectionString;
    cn.Open();

    //work code here
    using (var cmd = cn.CreateCommand())
    {
        cmd.CommandText =
            "SELECT ProductID, UnitsInStock FROM Products "
            + " WHERE ProductID = 1";
        dt.Load(cmd.ExecuteReader());
    }
}
using (var cn = new SqlConnection())
{
    cn.ConnectionString = bulkSetting.ConnectionString;
    cn.Open();

    //work code here
    using (var cmd = cn.CreateCommand())
    {
        cmd.CommandText =
            "SELECT ProductID, UnitsInStock FROM Products "
            + " WHERE ProductID = 2";
```

```
        dt.Load(cmd.ExecuteReader());
    }
}
dataGridView2.DataSource = dt;
```

Because this code uses multiple connections, the connections appear to the LTM as requiring multiple durable resource managers, and the transaction that was originally delegated to SQL Server 2005 and later is promoted to a distributed transaction.

PRACTICE Working with Transactions

In this practice, you can continue the practice from Lesson 2 or use the Begin Lesson 3 solution included on the companion CD. You modify the code to synchronize with the database server such that synchronization is performed using a transaction.

This practice is intended to focus on the classes that have been defined in this lesson, so the GUI will be minimal.

If you encounter a problem completing an exercise, the completed projects can be installed from the Code folder on the companion CD.

EXERCISE Provide Automatic Synchronization

In this exercise, you open the project from Lesson 2 and code to provide automatic synchronization to the database.

1. In Visual Studio .NET 2010, click File | Open | Project.

2. Locate the project you created in Lesson 2 and click Open.

3. In your project, add a reference to the System.Transactions.dll file by right-clicking the References node and click Add Reference. On the .NET tab, locate System.Transactions. Select it and click OK.

4. At the top of the Form1 code file, add *Imports System.Transactions* (C# *using System.Transactions*).

5. Locate the *SyncData* method that performs the actual data synchronization. Modify the code to perform the update within a transaction by using a *TransactionScope* object. Your modified *SyncData* method should look like the following:

Sample of Visual Basic Code
```
Private Sub SyncData()
    'send changes
    Using tran As New TransactionScope()
        Try
            daVehicles.Update(ds, "Vehicles")
            daRepairs.Update(ds, "Repairs")
            ds.AcceptChanges()
            tran.Complete()
        Catch ex As Exception
            MessageBox.Show(ex.Message)
        End Try
```

```vb
    End Using

    'retrieve updates
    Dim tempVehicles As New DataTable()
    daVehicles.Fill(tempVehicles)
    ds.Tables("Vehicles").Merge(tempVehicles)

    'merge changes
    Dim tempRepairs As New DataTable()
    daRepairs.Fill(tempRepairs)
    ds.Tables("Repairs").Merge(tempRepairs)
End Sub
```

Sample of C# Code

```csharp
private void SyncData()
{
    //send changes
    using(var tran = new TransactionScope())
    {
        try
        {
            daVehicles.Update(ds, "Vehicles");
            daRepairs.Update(ds, "Repairs");
            ds.AcceptChanges();
            tran.Complete();
        }
        catch(Exception ex)
        {
            MessageBox.Show(ex.Message);
        }
    }

    //retrieve updates
    var tempVehicles = new DataTable();
    daVehicles.Fill(tempVehicles);
    ds.Tables["Vehicles"].Merge(tempVehicles);

    //merge changes
    var tempRepairs = new DataTable();
    daRepairs.Fill(tempRepairs);
    ds.Tables["Repairs"].Merge(tempRepairs);
}
```

With these code changes, if the updates are not successful, the transaction will roll back, and the changes will exist only in the offline XML file until the next time synchronization is attempted.

6. Build the application and correct any errors.

7. Test the application. Choose Debug | Start Debugging to run the application with the debugger.

   When the application starts, it will load the offline XML file if it exists. It will then check whether it can connect to SQL Server. If a connection can be made, the application will create the tables if they don't exist and then attempt to synchronize the client-side data with the server-side data.

When you close the application, a call is made to synchronize the data within a transaction, and then the data set is serialized to the offline XML file.

Lesson Summary

This lesson provided a detailed overview of the ADO.NET connected classes.

- Transactions have four essential attributes: atomicity, consistency, isolation, and durability (know as ACID properties).
- The attributes of consistency and isolation are implemented by using the database's Lightweight Transaction Manager (LTM) locking mechanism, which keeps one transaction from affecting another.
- Instead of operating with complete isolation, you can modify the transaction isolation level. This reduces the amount of locking and increases scalability and performance.
- To create a transaction, you can use the *BeginTransaction* method on the *DbConnection* class.
- You can also use the *TransactionScope* class to create a promotable transaction.
- A promotable transaction starts as an explicit transaction, but this transaction can be promoted to a distributed transaction.

Lesson Review

You can use the following questions to test your knowledge of the information in Lesson 3, "Working with Transactions." The questions are also available on the companion CD if you prefer to review them in electronic form.

> **NOTE ANSWERS**
>
> Answers to these questions and explanations of why each answer choice is correct or incorrect are located in the "Answers" section at the end of the book.

1. In ADO.NET, which class can start an explicit transaction to update a SQL Server database?

   A. *SqlCommand*

   B. *SqlConnection*

   C. *SqlParameter*

   D. *SqlException*

2. In the *System.Transaction* namespace, which class can start an explicit promotable transaction to update a SQL Server database?

   A. *TransactionScope*

   B. *SqlConnection*

   C. *SqlTransaction*

3. You want to store the contents of a data set to an XML file so you can work on the data while disconnected from the database server. How should you store this data?

   A. As a SOAP file

   B. As a DataGram file

   C. As a WSDL file

   D. As an XML Schema file

Case Scenarios

In the following case scenarios, you will apply what you've learned about ADO.NET connected classes. You can find answers to these questions in the "Answers" section at the end of this book.

Case Scenario 1: Clustered Servers and Connection Pooling

Consider the scenario in which two database servers are clustered and appear to be heavily loaded, so a third database server is added. The original databases still seem overloaded and the new server has few or no connections. What happened? Connection pooling was doing its job by maintaining connections to the existing database servers. Answer the following questions.

1. After adding a new server to the cluster, how can you get the connection pooling to start using the third server now in the cluster?

2. Would you lose any performance by implementing a solution?

Case Scenario 2: The Daily Imports

Every evening, your company runs a process that imports all the sales from the SQL server at each branch office to the SQL server at headquarters. When the sales are received at headquarters, the sales are deleted from the branch office database. On several occasions, the network went down while the daily import was taking place. Sales are never lost, and the developers claim that the transfers are transactional, but some sales were at headquarters and some sales were at the branch office, so you have to figure out which sales made it to headquarters and which ones didn't. Answer the following questions regarding the application you might need to modify to support this daily import.

1. If the developers are stating that the transfers are transactional, why are some of the sales at headquarters and some of the sales at the branch office?

2. What could be done to ensure that either all sales make it to headquarters, or none are imported?

Suggested Practices

To help you successfully master the exam objectives presented in this chapter, complete the following tasks.

Create at least one application that accesses a database using the connected objects and performs transactional updates. This can be accomplished by completing the practices at the ends of Lesson 1, Lesson 2, and Lesson 3 or by completing the following practice exercises.

- **Practice 1** Create an application that requires you to collect data into at least two *DataTable* objects that are related. This could be customers who place orders, employees who have performance reviews, vehicles that have repairs, or contacts that have phone numbers. After collecting data, open a connection to the database and send the changes back to the database server.

- **Practice 2** Complete Practice 1 and then add code to ensure that all changes take place within a transaction.

Take a Practice Test

The practice tests on this book's companion CD offer many options. For example, you can test yourself on just the lesson review content, or you can test yourself on all the 70-516 certification exam content. You can set up the test so that it closely simulates the experience of taking a certification exam, or you can set it up in study mode so that you can look at the correct answers and explanations after you answer each question.

> **MORE INFO**   **PRACTICE TESTS**
>
> For details about all the practice test options available, see the "How to Use the Practice Tests" section in this book's introduction.

CHAPTER 3

Introducing LINQ

There always seems to be problems when it comes to moving data between the database and the client application. One of the problems stems from the differences in data types at both locations; another big problem is the handling of null values at each location. Microsoft calls this an impedance mismatch.

Yet another problem stems from passing commands to the database as strings. In your application, these strings compile as long as the quote is at each end of the string. If the string contains a reference to an unknown database object, or even a syntax error, the database server will throw an exception at run time instead of at compile time.

LINQ stands for Language Integrated Query. LINQ is the Microsoft solution to these problems, which LINQ solves by providing querying capabilities to the database, using statements that are built into LINQ-enabled languages such as Microsoft C# and Visual Basic 2010. In addition, these querying capabilities enable you to query almost any collection.

Exam objectives in this chapter:

- Create a LINQ query.

Lessons in this chapter:

Before You Begin

You must have some understanding of C# or Visual Basic 2010. This chapter requires only the hardware and software listed at the beginning of this book.

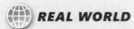 **REAL WORLD**

Glenn Johnson

There are many scenarios in which your application has collections of objects that you want to query, filter, and sort. In many cases, you might need to return the results of these queries as a collection of different objects that contain only the information needed—for instance, populating a grid on the user interface with a subset of the data. LINQ really simplifies these query problems, providing an elegant, language-specific solution.

Lesson 1: Understanding LINQ

This lesson starts by providing an example of a LINQ expression so you can see what a LINQ expression looks like, and some of the basic syntax is covered as well. This lesson also shows you the Microsoft .NET Framework features that were added to make LINQ work. The features can be used individually, which can be useful in many scenarios.

> **After this lesson, you will be able to:**
> - Use object initializers.
> - Implement implicitly typed local variables.
> - Create anonymous types.
> - Create lambda expressions.
> - Implement extension methods.
> - Understand the use of query extension methods.
>
> **Estimated lesson time: 60 minutes**

A LINQ Example

LINQ enables you to perform query, set, and transform operations within your programming language syntax. It works with any collection that implements the *IEnumerable* or the generic *IEnumerable<T>* interface, so you can run LINQ queries on relational data, XML data, and plain old collections.

So what can you do with LINQ? The following is a simple LINQ query that returns the list of colors that begin with the letter B, sorted.

Sample of Visual Basic Code

```
Dim colors() =
{
    "Red",
    "Brown",
    "Orange",
    "Yellow",
    "Black",
    "Green",
    "White",
    "Violet",
    "Blue"
}

Dim results as IEnumerable(Of String)=From c In colors _
          Where c.StartsWith("B") _
          Order By c _
          Select c
```

Sample of C# Code

```csharp
string[] colors =
{
    "Red",
    "Brown",
    "Orange",
    "Yellow",
    "Black",
    "Green",
    "White",
    "Violet",
    "Blue"
};

IEnumerable<string> results = from c in colors
            where c.StartsWith("B")
            orderby c
            select c;
```

The first statement in this example uses array initializer syntax to create an array of strings, populated with various colors, followed by the LINQ expression. Focusing on the right side of the equals sign, you see that the LINQ expression resembles a SQL statement, but the *from* clause is at the beginning, and the *select* clause is at the end.

You're wondering why Microsoft would do such a thing. SQL has been around for a long time, so why didn't Microsoft keep the same format SQL has? The reason for the change is that Microsoft could not provide IntelliSense if it kept the existing SQL command layout. By moving the *from* clause to the beginning, you start by naming the source of your data, and Visual Studio .NET can use that information to provide IntelliSense through the rest of the statement.

In the example code, you might be mentally equating the "from c in colors" with a *For Each* (C# *foreach*) loop; it is. Notice that *c* is the *loop* variable that references one item in the source collection for each of the iterations of the loop. What is *c*'s type and where is *c* declared? The variable called *c* is declared in the *from* clause, and its type is implicitly set to *string*, based on the source collection as an array of *string*. If your source collection is *ArrayList*, which is a collection of objects, *c*'s type would be implicitly set to *object*, even if *ArrayList* contained only strings. Like the *For Each* loop, you can set the type for *c* explicitly as well, and each element will be cast to that type when being assigned to *c* as follows:

Sample of Visual Basic Code

```vbnet
From c As String In colors _
```

Sample of C# Code

```csharp
from string c in colors
```

In this example, the source collection is typed, meaning it is an array of *string*, so there is no need to specify the type for *c* because the compiler can figure this out.

The *from* clause produces a generic *IEnumerable* object, which feeds into the next part of the LINQ statement, the *where* clause. Internally, imagine the *where* clause has code to iterate over the values passed into the *where* clause and output only the values that meet the specified criteria. The *where* clause also produces a generic *IEnumerable* object but contains logic to filter, and it is passed to the next part of the LINQ statement, the *order by* clause.

The *order by* clause accepts a generic *IEnumerable* object and sorts based on the criteria. Its output is also a generic *IOrderedEnumerable* object but contains the logic to sort and is passed to the last part of the LINQ statement, the *select* clause.

The *select* clause must always be the last part of any LINQ expression. This is when you can decide to return (select) the entire object with which you started (in this case, *c*) or something different. When selecting *c*, you are returning the whole string. In a traditional SQL statement, you might select * or select just the columns you need to get a subset of the data. You might select *c.SubString(0,2)* to return the first two characters of each of the colors to get a subset of the data or create a totally different object that is based on the string *c*.

Deferred Execution

A LINQ query is a generic *IEnumerable* object of what you select. The variable to which this result is assigned is known as the *range variable*. This is not a populated collection; it's merely a query object that can retrieve data. LINQ doesn't access the source data until you try to use the query object to work with the results. This is known as *deferred execution*.

EXAM TIP

For the exam, understand what deferred execution is because you can expect LINQ questions related to this topic.

The generic *IEnumerable* interface has only one method, *GetEnumerator*, that returns an object that implements the generic *IEnumerator* interface. The generic *IEnumerator* interface has a *Current* property, which references the current item in the collection, and two methods, *MoveNext* and *Reset*. *MoveNext* moves to the next element in the collection. *Reset* moves the iterator to its initial position—that is, before the first element in the collection.

The data source is not touched until you iterate on the query object, but if you iterate on the query object multiple times, you access the data source each time. For example, in the LINQ code example, a variable called *results* was created to retrieve all colors that start with B, sorted. In this example, code is added to loop over the *results* variable and display each color. Black in the original source data is changed to Slate. Then code is added to loop over the results again and display each color.

Sample of Visual Basic Code

```
For Each Color As String In results
    txtLog.AppendText(Color + Environment.NewLine)
Next
```

```
colors(4) = "Slate"

txtLog.AppendText("---------" + Environment.NewLine)
For Each Color As String In results
    txtLog.AppendText(Color + Environment.NewLine)
Next
```

Sample of C# Code
```
foreach (var color in results)
{
    txtLog.AppendText(color + Environment.NewLine);
}

colors[4] = "Slate";

txtLog.AppendText("---------" + Environment.NewLine);
foreach (var color in results)
{
    txtLog.AppendText(color + Environment.NewLine);
}
```

The second time the *results* variable was used, it displayed only Blue and Brown, not the original three matching colors (Black, Blue, and Brown), because the query was re-executed for the second loop on the updated collection in which Black was replaced by a color that does not match the query criteria. Whenever you use the *results* variable to loop over the results, the query re-executes on the same data source that might have been changed and, therefore, might return updated data.

You might be thinking of how that effects the performance of your application. Certainly, performance is something that must be considered when developing an application. However, you might be seeing the benefit of retrieving up-to-date data, which is the purpose of deferred execution. For users who don't want to re-run the query every time, use the resulting query object to produce a generic list immediately that you can use repeatedly afterward. The following code sample shows how to create a frozen list.

Sample of Visual Basic Code
```
Dim results As List(Of String) = (From c In colors _
            Where c.StartsWith("B") _
            Order By c _
            Select c).ToList()

For Each Color As String In results
    txtLog.AppendText(Color + Environment.NewLine)
Next

colors(4) = "Slate"

txtLog.AppendText("---------" + Environment.NewLine)
For Each Color As String In results
    txtLog.AppendText(Color + Environment.NewLine)
Next
```

Sample of C# Code

```
List<string> results = (from string c in colors
                             where c.StartsWith("B")
                             orderby c
                             select c).ToList();

foreach (var color in results)
{
    txtLog.AppendText(color + Environment.NewLine);
}

colors[4] = "Slate";

txtLog.AppendText("---------" + Environment.NewLine);
foreach (var color in results)
{
    txtLog.AppendText(color + Environment.NewLine);
}
```

In this code example, the result of the LINQ query is frozen by wrapping the expression in parentheses and adding the *ToList()* call to the end. The *results* variable now has a type of *List Of String*. The *ToList* method causes the query to execute and put the results into the variable called *results*; then the *results* collection can be used again without re-executing the LINQ expression.

LINQ Providers

In the previous examples, you can see that LINQ works with .NET Framework objects because the .NET Framework comes with a *LINQ to Objects* provider. Figure 3-1 shows the LINQ providers that are built into the .NET Framework. Each LINQ provider implements features focused on the data source.

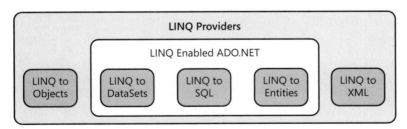

FIGURE 3-1 This figure shows the LINQ providers built into the .NET Framework.

The LINQ provider works as a middle tier between the data store and the language environment. In addition to the LINQ providers included in the .NET Framework, there are many third-party LINQ providers. To create a LINQ provider, you must implement the *IQueryable* interface. This has a *Provider* property whose type is *IQueryProvider*, which is called to initialize and execute LINQ expressions.

Features That Make Up LINQ

Now that you've seen a LINQ expression, it's time to see what was added to the .NET Framework to create LINQ. Each of these features can be used by itself, but all of them are required to create LINQ.

Object Initializers

You can use object initializers to initialize any or all of an object's properties in the same statement that instantiates the object, but you're not forced to write custom constructors.

You might have seen classes that have many constructors because the developer was trying to provide a simple way to instantiate and initialize the object. To understand this, consider the following code example of a *Car* class that has five automatic properties but doesn't have any custom constructors.

Sample of Visual Basic Code

```
Public Class Car
    Public Property VIN() As String
    Public Property Make() As String
    Public Property Model() As String
    Public Property Year() As Integer
    Public Property Color() As String
End Class
```

Sample of C# Code

```
public class Car
{
    public string VIN { get; set; }
    public string Make { get; set; }
    public string Model { get; set; }
    public int Year { get; set; }
    public string Color { get; set; }
}
```

To instantiate a *Car* object and populate the properties with data, you might do something like the following:

Sample of Visual Basic Code

```
Dim c As New Car()
c.VIN = "ABC123"
c.Make = "Ford"
c.Model = "F-250"
c.Year = 2000
```

Sample of C# Code

```
Car c = new Car();
c.VIN = "ABC123";
c.Make = "Ford";
c.Model = "F-250";
c.Year = 2000;
```

It took five statements to create and initialize the object, and *Color* wasn't initialized. If a constructor was provided, you could instantiate the object and implicitly initialize the properties with one statement, but what would you do if someone wanted to pass only three parameters? How about passing five parameters? Do you create constructors for every combination of parameters you might want to pass? The answer is to use object initializers.

By using object initializers, you can instantiate the object and initialize any combination of properties with one statement, as shown in the following example:

Sample of Visual Basic Code

```
Dim c As New Car() With {.VIN = "ABC123", .Make = "Ford", _
                         .Model = "F-250", .Year = 2000}
```

Sample of C# Code

```
Car c = new Car() { VIN = "ABC123", Make = "Ford",
                    Model = "F-250", Year = 2000 };
```

Conceptually, the *Car* object is being instantiated, and the default constructor generated by the compiler is executed. Each of the properties will be initialized with its default value. If you are using a parameterless constructor, as shown, the parentheses are optional, but if you are executing a constructor that requires parameters, the parentheses are mandatory.

Collection initializers are another form of object initializer, but for collections. Collection initializers have existed for arrays since the first release of the .NET Framework, but you can now initialize collections such as *ArrayList* and generic *List* using the same syntax. The following example populates a collection of cars, using both object initializers and collection initializers.

Sample of Visual Basic Code

```
Private Function GetCars() As List(Of Car)
    Return New List(Of Car) From
    {
        New Car() With {.VIN = "ABC123", .Make = "Ford",
                        .Model = "F-250", .Year = 2000},
        New Car() With {.VIN = "DEF123", .Make = "BMW",
                        .Model = "Z-3", .Year = 2005},
        New Car() With {.VIN = "ABC456", .Make = "Audi",
                        .Model = "TT", .Year = 2008},
        New Car() With {.VIN = "HIJ123", .Make = "VW",
                        .Model = "Bug", .Year = 1956},
        New Car() With {.VIN = "DEF456", .Make = "Ford",
                        .Model = "F-150", .Year = 1998}
    }
End Function
```

Sample of C# Code

```
private List<Car> GetCars()
{
    return new List<Car>
    {
        new Car {VIN = "ABC123",Make = "Ford",
```

```
                        Model = "F-250", Year = 2000},
            new Car {VIN = "DEF123",Make = "BMW",
                        Model = "Z-3",    Year = 2005},
            new Car {VIN = "ABC456",Make = "Audi",
                        Model = "TT",     Year = 2008},
            new Car {VIN = "HIJ123",Make = "VW",
                        Model = "Bug",    Year = 1956},
            new Car {VIN = "DEF456",Make = "Ford",
                        Model = "F-150", Year = 1998}
    };
}
```

The code example creates a generic *List* object and populates the list with five cars, all in one statement. No variables are needed to set the properties of each car because it's being initialized.

How are object initializers used in LINQ? They enable you to create some types of projections in LINQ. A *projection* is a shaping or transformation of the data in a LINQ query to produce what you need in the output with the *select* statement instead of including just the whole source object(s). For example, if you want to write a LINQ query that will search a color list for all the color names that are five characters long, sorted by the matching color, instead of returning an *IEnumerable* object of *string*, you might use object initializers to return an *IEnumerable* object of *Car* in which the car's color is set to the matching color, as shown here:

Sample of Visual Basic Code

```
Dim colors() =
    {
        "Red",
        "Brown",
        "Orange",
        "Yellow",
        "Black",
        "Green",
        "White",
        "Violet",
        "Blue"
    }

Dim fords As IEnumerable(Of Car) = From c In colors
                            Where c.Length = 5
                            Order By c
                            Select New Car() With
                                    {.Make = "Ford",
                                     .Color = c}

For Each car As Car In fords
    txtLog.AppendText(String.Format("Car: Make:{0} Color:{1}" _
                & Environment.NewLine, car.Make, car.Color))
Next
```

Sample of C# Code

```
string[] colors =
{
```

```
        "Red",
        "Brown",
        "Orange",
        "Yellow",
        "Black",
        "Green",
        "White",
        "Violet",
        "Blue"
};

IEnumerable<Car> fords = from c in colors
                        where c.Length == 5
                        orderby c
                        select new Car()
                            {
                                Make = "Ford",
                                Color = c
                            };

foreach (Car car in fords)
{
    txtLog.AppendText(String.Format("Car: Make:{0} Color:{1}"
                    + Environment.NewLine, car.Make, car.Color));
}
```

The whole idea behind this example is that you want to construct a collection of cars, but each car will have a color from the collection of colors that matches the five-letter-long criterion. The *select* clause creates the *Car* object and initializes its properties. The *select* clause cannot contain multiple statements. Without object initializers, you wouldn't be able to instantiate and initialize the *Car* object without first writing a constructor for the *Car* class that takes *Make* and *Color* parameters.

Implicit Typed Local Variable Declarations

Doesn't it seem like a chore to declare a variable as a specific type and then instantiate that type in one statement? You have to specify the type twice, as shown in the following example:

Sample of Visual Basic Code

```
Dim c as Car = New Car( )
```

Sample of C# Code

```
Car c = new Car( )
```

Visual Basic users might shout, "Hey, Visual Basic doesn't require me to specify the type twice!" But what about the example in which you make a call to a method that returns a generic *List Of Car*, but you still have to specify the type for the variable that receives the collection, as shown here?

Sample of Visual Basic Code

```
Dim cars As List(Of Car) = GetCars()
```

Sample of C# Code

```
List<Car> cars = GetCars();
```

In this example, would it be better if you could ask the compiler what the type is for this variable called *cars*? You can, as shown in this code example:

Sample of Visual Basic Code

```
Dim cars = GetCars()
```

Sample of C# Code

```
var cars = GetCars();
```

Instead of providing the type for your variable, you're asking the compiler what the type is, based on whatever is on the right side of the equals sign. That means there must be an equals sign in the declaration statement, and the right side must evaluate to a typed expression. You cannot have a null constant on the right side of the equals sign because the compiler would not know what the type should be.

If you're wondering whether this is the same as the older variant type that existed in earlier Visual Basic, the answer is no. As soon as the compiler figures out what the type should be, you can't change it. Therefore, you get IntelliSense as though you explicitly declared the variable's type.

Here are the rules for implicitly typed local variables:

- They can be implemented on local variables only.
- The declaration statement must have an equals sign with a non-null assignment.
- They cannot be implemented on method parameters.

Implicitly typed local variables can be passed to methods, but the method's parameter type must match the actual type that was inferred by the compiler.

Do you really need this feature? Based on this explanation, you can see that this feature is simply an optional way to save a bit of typing. You might also be wondering why implicitly typed local variables are required for LINQ: This feature is required to support anonymous types, which are used in LINQ.

Anonymous Types

Often, you want to group together some data in a somewhat temporary fashion. That is, you want to have a grouping of data, but you don't want to create a new type just for something that might be used in one method. To understand the problem that anonymous types solves, imagine that you are writing the graphical user interface (GUI) for your application, and a collection of cars is passed to you in which each car has many properties. If you bind the collection directly to a data grid, you'll see all the properties, but you needed to display only two of the properties, so that automatic binding is displaying more data than you want. This is when anonymous types can be used.

In the following code sample, you want to create an anonymous type that contains only *Make* and *Model* properties because these are the only properties you need.

Sample of Visual Basic Code

```vb
Dim x = New With {.Make = "VW", .Model = "Bug"}
txtLog.AppendText(x.Make & ", " & x.Model)
```

Sample of C# Code

```csharp
var x = new {Make = "VW", Model = "Bug"};
txtLog.AppendText(x.Make + ", " + x.Model);
```

If you type in this code, you see that in the second statement, when x is typed and you press the period key, the IntelliSense window is displayed and you see *Make* and *Model* as available selections. The variable called *x* is implicitly typed because you simply don't know what the name of the anonymous type is. The compiler, however, does know the name of the anonymous type. This is the benefit of getting IntelliSense for scenarios in which implicitly typed local variables are required.

Anonymous types are used in LINQ to provide projections. You might make a call to a method that returns a list of cars, but from that list, you want to run a LINQ query that retrieves the VIN as one property and make and year combined into a different property for displaying in a grid. Anonymous types help, as shown in this example:

Sample of Visual Basic Code

```vb
Dim carData = From c In GetCars()
    Where c.Year >= 2000
    Order By c.Year
    Select New With
            {
                c.VIN,
                .MakeAndModel = c.Make + " " + c.Model
            }

dgResults.DataSource = carData.ToList()
```

Sample of C# Code

```csharp
var carData = from c in GetCars()
            where c.Year >= 2000
            orderby c.Year
            select new
            {
                c.VIN,
                MakeAndModel = c.Make + " " + c.Model
            };

dgResults.DataSource = carData.ToList();
```

When this example is executed, the LINQ query will locate all the cars that have a *Year* property equal to or greater than 2000. This will result in finding three cars that are sorted by year. That result is then projected to an anonymous type that grabs the VIN and combines the make and model into a new property called *MakeAndModel*. Finally, the result is displayed in the grid, as shown in Figure 3-2.

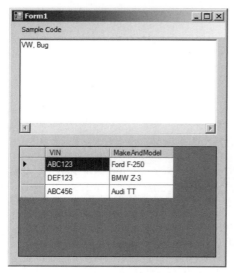

FIGURE 3-2 Anonymous types are displayed in the grid.

Lambda Expressions

Lambda expressions can be used anywhere delegates are required. They are very much like anonymous methods but have a much abbreviated syntax that makes them easy to use inline.

Consider the generic *List* class that has a *Find* method. This method accepts a generic *Predicate* delegate as a parameter. If you look up the generic *Predicate* delegate type, you find that this delegate is a reference to a method that accepts a single parameter of type *T* and returns a Boolean value. The *Find* method has code that loops though the list and, for each item, the code executes the method referenced through the *Predicate* parameter, passing the item to the method and receiving a response that indicates found or not found. Here is an example of using the *Find* method with a *Predicate* delegate:

Sample of Visual Basic Code

```
Dim yearToFind As Integer

Private Sub PredecateDelegateToolStripMenuItem_Click( _
        ByVal sender As System.Object, _
        ByVal e As System.EventArgs) _
    Handles PredecateDelegateToolStripMenuItem.Click

    yearToFind = 2000
    Dim cars = GetCars()
    Dim found = cars.Find(AddressOf ByYear)
    txtLog.AppendText(String.Format( _
        "Car VIN:{0} Make:{1} Year:{2}" & Environment.NewLine, _
```

```
        found.VIN, found.Make, found.Year))
End Sub

Private Function ByYear(ByVal c As Car) As Boolean
    Return c.Year = yearToFind
End Function
```

Sample of C# Code

```csharp
int yearToFind = 2000;

private void predecateDelegateToolStripMenuItem_Click(
    object sender, EventArgs e)
{
    var cars = GetCars();
    yearToFind = 2000;
    var found = cars.Find(ByYear);
    txtLog.AppendText(string.Format(
        "Car VIN:{0} Make:{1} Year{2}" + Environment.NewLine,
        found.VIN, found.Make, found.Year));
}

private bool ByYear(Car c)
{
    return c.Year == yearToFind;
}
```

In this example, the *yearToFind* variable is defined at the class level to make it accessible to both methods. That's typically not desirable because *yearToFind* is more like a parameter that needs to be passed to the *ByYear* method. The problem is that the *Predicate* delegate accepts only one parameter, and that parameter has to be the same type as the list's type. Another problem with this code is that a separate method was created just to do the search. It would be better if a method wasn't required.

The previous example can be rewritten to use a lambda expression, as shown in the following code sample:

Sample of Visual Basic Code

```
Private Sub LambdaExpressionsToolStripMenuItem_Click( _
        ByVal sender As System.Object, _
        ByVal e As System.EventArgs) _
        Handles LambdaExpressionsToolStripMenuItem.Click
    Dim cars = GetCars()
    Dim theYear = 2000
    Dim found = cars.Find(Function(c) c.Year = theYear)
    txtLog.AppendText(String.Format( _
            "Car VIN:{0} Make:{1} Year:{2}" & Environment.NewLine, _
            found.VIN, found.Make, found.Year))
End Sub
```

Sample of C# Code

```csharp
private void lambdaExpressionsToolStripMenuItem_Click(
    object sender, EventArgs e)
{
```

```
    var cars = GetCars();
    var theYear = 2000;
    var found = cars.Find(c => c.Year== theYear);
    txtLog.AppendText(string.Format(
        "Car VIN:{0} Make:{1} Year{2}" + Environment.NewLine,
        found.VIN, found.Make, found.Year));
}
```

You can think of the lambda expression as inline method. The left part declares the parameters, comma delimited. After the => sign, you have the expression. In this example, the lambda expression is supplied inline with the *Find* method. This eliminates the need for a separate method. Also, the variable called *theYear* is defined as a local variable in the enclosing method, so it's accessible to the lambda expression.

Formally, a lambda expression is an expression that has one input and contains only a single statement that is evaluated to provide a single return value; however, in the .NET Framework, multiple parameters can be passed to a lambda expression, and multiple statements can be placed into a lambda expression. The following example shows the multistatement lambda expression syntax.

Sample of Visual Basic Code

```
Dim found = cars.Find(Function(c As Car)
                          Dim x As Integer
                          x = theYear
                          Return c.Year = x
                      End Function)
```

Sample of C# Code

```
var found = cars.Find(c =>
{
    int x;
    x = theYear;
    return c.Year == x;
});
```

In C#, if the lambda expression takes multiple parameters, the parameters must be surrounded by parentheses, and if the lambda expression takes no parameters, you must provide an empty set of parentheses where the parameter would go.

How are lambda expressions used with LINQ? When you type your LINQ query, behind the scenes, parts of it will be converted into a tree of lambda expressions. Also, you must use lambda expressions with query extension methods, which are covered right after extension methods, which follows.

Extension Methods

Extension methods enable you to add methods to a type, even if you don't have the source code for the type.

To understand why you might want this, think of this simple scenario: You want to add an *IsNumeric* method to the *string* class, but you don't have the source code for the *string* class. What would you do?

One solution is to create a new class that inherits from *string*, maybe called *MyString*, and then add your *IsNumeric* method to this class. This solution has two problems. First, the *string* class is *sealed*, which means that you can't inherit from *string*. Even if you could inherit from *string* to create your custom class, you would need to make sure that everyone uses it and not the *string* class that's built in. You would also need to write code to convert strings you might receive when you make calls outside your application into your *MyString* class.

Another possible, and more viable, solution is to create a helper class, maybe called *StringHelper*, that contains all the methods you would like to add to the *string* class but can't. These methods would typically be static methods and take *string* as the first parameter. Here is an example of a *StringHelper* class that has the *IsNumeric* method:

Sample of Visual Basic Code

```
Public Module StringHelper
    Public Function IsNumeric(ByVal str As String) As Boolean
        Dim val As Double
        Return Double.TryParse(str, val)
    End Function
End Module
```

Sample of C# Code

```
public static class StringHelper
{
    public static bool IsNumeric(string str)
    {
        double val;
        return double.TryParse(str, out val);
    }
}
```

The following code uses the helper class to test a couple of strings to see whether they are numeric. The output will display *false* for the first call and *true* for the second call.

Sample of Visual Basic Code

```
Dim s As String = "abc123"
txtLog.AppendText(StringHelper.IsNumeric(s) & Environment.NewLine)
s = "123"
txtLog.AppendText(StringHelper.IsNumeric(s) & Environment.NewLine)
```

Sample of C# Code

```
string s = "abc123";
txtLog.AppendText(StringHelper.IsNumeric(s) + Environment.NewLine);
s = "123";
txtLog.AppendText(StringHelper.IsNumeric(s) + Environment.NewLine);
```

What's good about this solution is that the user doesn't need to instantiate a custom string class to use the *IsNumeric* method. What's bad about this solution is that the user needs to know that the helper class exists, and the syntax is clunky at best.

Prior to .NET Framework 3.5, the helper class solution was what most people implemented, so you will typically find lots of helper classes in an application, and, yes, you need to look for them and explore the helper classes so you know what's in them.

In .NET Framework 3.5, Microsoft introduced extension methods. By using extension methods, you can extend a type even when you don't have the source code for the type. In some respects, this is deceptive, but it works wonderfully, as you'll see.

In the previous scenario, another solution is to add the *IsNumeric* method to the *string* class by using an extension method, adding a public module (C# public *static* class) and creating public static methods in this class. In Visual Basic, you add the *<Extension()>* attribute before the method. In C#, you add the keyword *this* in front of the first parameter to indicate that you are extending the type of this parameter.

All your existing helper classes can be easily modified to become extension methods, but this doesn't break existing code. Here is the modified helper class, in which the *IsNumeric* method is now an extension method on *string*.

Sample of Visual Basic Code

```vb
Imports System.Runtime.CompilerServices

Public Module StringHelper
    <Extension()> _
    Public Function IsNumeric(ByVal str As String) As Boolean
        Dim val As Double
        Return Double.TryParse(str, val)
    End Function
End Module
```

Sample of C# Code

```csharp
public static class StringHelper
{
    public static bool IsNumeric(this string str)
    {
        double val;
        return double.TryParse(str, out val);
    }
}
```

You can see in this code example that the changes to your helper class are minimal. Now that the *IsNumeric* method is on the *string* class, you can call the extension method as follows.

Sample of Visual Basic Code

```vb
Dim s As String = "abc123"
txtLog.AppendText(s.IsNumeric() & Environment.NewLine)
s = "123"
txtLog.AppendText(s.IsNumeric() & Environment.NewLine)
```

Sample of C# Code

```
string s = "abc123";
txtLog.AppendText(s.IsNumeric() + Environment.NewLine);
s = "123";
txtLog.AppendText(s.IsNumeric() + Environment.NewLine);
```

You can see that this is much cleaner syntax, but the helper class syntax still works, so you can convert your helper class methods to extension methods but you're not forced to call the helper methods explicitly. Because the compiler is not able to find *IsNumeric* in the *string* class, it is looking for the extension methods that extend *string* with the right name and the right signature. Behind the scenes, it is simply changing your nice syntax into calls to your helper methods when you build your application, so the clunky syntax is still there (in the compiled code), but you can't see it. Performance is exactly the same as well. The difference is that the IntelliSense window now shows you the extension methods on any *string*, as shown in Figure 3-3. The icon for the extension method is a bit different from the icon for a regular method. In fact, there are already extension methods on many framework types. In Figure 3-3, the method called *Last* is also an extension method.

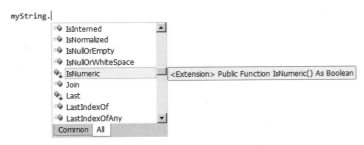

FIGURE 3-3 Extension methods for the *string* class are shown in the IntelliSense window.

In the previous code samples, did you notice that when a line needed to be appended in the *TextBox* class called *txtLog*, the string passed in is concatenated with *Environment. NewLine*? Wouldn't it be great if *TextBox* had a *WriteLine* method? Of course it would! In this example, a helper class called *TextBoxHelper* is added, as follows.

Sample of Visual Basic Code

```
Imports System.Runtime.CompilerServices

Public Module TextBoxHelper
    <Extension()> _
    Public Sub WriteLine(ByVal txt As TextBox, ByVal line As Object)
        txt.AppendText(line & Environment.NewLine)
    End Sub
End Module
```

Sample of C# Code

```
using System.Windows.Forms;

    public static class TextBoxHelper
```

```
    {
        public static void WriteLine(this TextBox txt, object line)
        {
            txt.AppendText(line + Environment.NewLine);
        }
    }
```

Using this new extension method on the *TextBox* class, you can change the code from the previous examples to use the *string* extension and the *TextBox* extension. This cleans up your code, as shown in the following example.

Sample of Visual Basic Code

```
Dim s As String = "abc123"
txtLog.WriteLine(s.IsNumeric())
s = "123"
txtLog.WriteLine(s.IsNumeric())
```

Sample of C# Code

```
string s = "abc123";
txtLog.WriteLine(s.IsNumeric());
s = "123";
txtLog.WriteLine(s.IsNumeric());
```

Here are some rules for working with extension methods:

- Extension methods must be defined in a Visual Basic module or C# static class.
- The Visual Basic module or C# static class must be *public*.
- If you define an extension method for a type, and the type already has the same method, the type's method is used and the extension method is ignored.
- In C#, the class and the extension methods must be *static*. Visual Basic modules and their methods are automatically static (Visual Basic *Shared*).
- The extension method works as long as it is in scope. This might require you to add an *imports* (C# *using*) statement for the namespace in which the extension method is to get access to the extension method.
- Although extension methods are implemented as *static* (Visual Basic *Shared*) methods, they are instance methods on the type you are extending. You cannot add static methods to a type with extension methods.

Query Extension Methods

Now that you've seen extension methods, you might be wondering why Microsoft needed extension methods to implement LINQ. To do so, Microsoft added extension methods to several types, but most important are the methods that were added to the generic *IEnumerable* interface. Extension methods can be added to any type, which is interesting when you think of adding concrete extension methods (methods that have code) to interfaces, which are abstract (can't have code).

Consider the following example code, in which an array of strings called *colors* is created and assigned to a variable whose type is *IEnumerable* of *string*.

Sample of Visual Basic Code

```
Dim colors() =
{
    "Red",
    "Brown",
    "Orange",
    "Yellow",
    "Black",
    "Green",
    "White",
    "Violet",
    "Blue"
}
Dim colorEnumerable As IEnumerable(Of String) = colors
```

Sample of C# Code

```
string[] colors =
{
    "Red",
    "Brown",
    "Orange",
    "Yellow",
    "Black",
    "Green",
    "White",
    "Violet",
    "Blue"
}
IEnumerable<string> colorEnumerable = colors;
```

Because the *colorEnumerable* variable's type is *IEnumerable* of *string*, when you type *colorEnumerable* and press the period key, the IntelliSense window is displayed and shows the list of methods available on the generic *IEnumerable* interface, as shown in Figure 3-4. These methods are known as *query extension methods*. In addition to the query extension methods that exist for *IEnumerable*, the generic *IEnumerable* interface also contains query extension methods.

FIGURE 3-4 This figure shows *Extension* methods on the *IEnumerable* interface.

Some of these extension methods are mapped directly to Visual Basic and C# keywords used in LINQ (also known as LINQ operators). For example, you'll find *Where* and *OrderBy* extension methods that map directly to the *where* and *orderby* (Visual Basic *Order By*) keywords.

Microsoft added these extension methods to the *IEnumerable* interface by implementing the extension methods in a class called *Enumerable*, which is in the *System.Linq* namespace. This class is in an assembly called *System.Core.dll* to which most project templates already have a reference.

> **NOTE** **TO USE LINQ AND QUERY EXTENSION METHODS**
>
> To use LINQ and query extension methods, your project must reference *System.Core.dll*, and, in your code, you must import (C# *using*) the *System.Linq* namespace.

The *Enumerable* class also has three static methods you might find useful: *Empty*, *Range*, and *Repeat*. Here is a short description of each of these methods.

- **Empty**   The generic *Empty* method produces a generic *IEnumerable* object with no elements.

- **Range**   The *Range* method produces a counting sequence of integer elements. This can be useful when you want to join a counter to another element sequence that should be numbered. This method takes two parameters: the starting number and the count of how many times to increment. If you pass 100,5 to this method, it will produce 100, 101, 102, 103, 104.

- **Repeat**   Use the generic *Repeat* method to produce an *IEnumerable<int>* object that has the same element repeated. This method accepts two parameters: *Element* and *Count*. The *element* parameter is the element to be repeated, and *count* specifies how many times to repeat the element.

The next section covers many of the query extension methods that are implemented on the *Enumerable* class to extend the generic *IEnumerable* interface.

ALL

The *All* method returns *true* when all the elements in the collection meet a specified criterion and returns *false* otherwise. Here is an example of checking whether all the cars returned from the *GetCars* method call have a year greater than 1960.

Sample of Visual Basic Code

```
txtLog.WriteLine(GetCars().All(Function(c) c.Year > 1960))
```

Sample of C# Code

```
txtLog.WriteLine(GetCars().All(c => c.Year > 1960));
```

ANY

The *Any* method returns *true* when at least one element in the collection meets the specified criterion and returns *false* otherwise. The following example checks whether there is a car that has a year of 1960 or earlier.

Sample of Visual Basic Code

```
txtLog.WriteLine(GetCars().Any(Function(c) c.Year <= 1960))
```

Sample of C# Code

```
txtLog.WriteLine(GetCars().Any(c => c.Year <= 1960));
```

ASENUMERABLE

To explain the *AsEnumerable* method, remember the rule mentioned earlier in this chapter for extension methods:

- If you define an extension method for a type, and the type already has the same method, the type's method will be used, and the extension method is ignored.

Use the *AsEnumerable* method when you want to convert a collection that implements the generic *IEnumerable* interface but is currently cast as a different type, such as *IQueryable*, to the generic *IEnumerable*. This can be desirable when the type you are currently casting has a concrete implementation of one of the extension methods you would prefer to get called.

For example, the *Table* class that represents a database table could have a *Where* method that takes the predicate argument and executes a SQL query to the remote database. If you don't want to execute a call to the database remotely, you can use the *AsEnumerable* method to cast to *IEnumerable* and execute the corresponding *Where* extension method.

In this example, a class called *MyStringList* inherits from *List Of String*. This class has a single *Where* method whose method signature matches the *Where* method on the generic *IEnumerable* interface. The code in the *Where* method of the *MyStringList* class is returning all elements but, based on the predicate that's passed in, is converting elements that match to uppercase.

Sample of Visual Basic Code

```
Public Class MyStringList
    Inherits List(Of String)
    Public Function Where(ByVal filter As Predicate(Of String)) As IEnumerable(Of
String)
        Return Me.Select(Of String)(Function(s) IIf(filter(s), s.ToUpper(), s))
    End Function
End Class
```

Sample of C# Code

```
public class MyStringList : List<string>
{
    public IEnumerable<string> Where(Predicate<string> filter)
    {
        return this.Select(s=>filter(s) ? s.ToUpper() : s);
```

```
    }
}
```

When the compiler looks for a *Where* method on a *MyStringList* object, it finds an implementation in the type itself and thus does not need to look for any extension method. The
following code shows an example:

Sample of Visual Basic Code

```
Dim strings As New MyStringList From {"orange", "apple", "grape", "pear"}
For Each item In strings.Where(Function(s) s.Length = 5)
    txtLog.WriteLine(item)
Next
```

Sample of C# Code

```
var strings = new MyStringList{"orange","apple","grape","pear"};
foreach (var item in strings.Where(s => s.Length == 5))
{
    txtLog.WriteLine(item);
}
```

This produces four items in the output, but the apple and grape will be uppercase. To call
the *Where* extension method, use *AsEnumerable* as follows:

Sample of Visual Basic Code

```
For Each item In strings.AsEnumerable().Where(Function(s) s.Length = 5)
    txtLog.WriteLine(item)
Next
```

Sample of C# Code

```
foreach (var item in strings.AsEnumerable().Where(s => s.Length == 5))
{
    txtLog.WriteLine(item);
}
```

This produces only two items, the apple and the grape, and they will not be uppercase.

ASPARALLEL

See "Parallel LINQ (PLINQ)" later in this chapter.

ASQUERYABLE

The *AsQueryable* extension method converts an *IEnumerable* object to an *IQueryable* object.
This might be needed because the *IQueryable* interface is typically implemented by query
providers to provide custom query capabilities such as passing a query back to a database for
execution.

The *IQueryable* interface inherits the *IEnumerable* interface so the results of a query can
be enumerated. Enumeration causes any code associated with an *IQueryable* object to be
executed. In the following example, the *AsQueryable* method is executed, and information is
now available for the provider.

Sample of Visual Basic Code

```vbnet
Private Sub asQueryableToolStripMenuItem_Click(ByVal sender As System.Object, _
        ByVal e As System.EventArgs) _
        Handles asQueryableToolStripMenuItem.Click
    Dim strings As New MyStringList From {"orange", "apple", "grape", "pear"}
    Dim querable = strings.AsQueryable()
    txtLog.WriteLine("Element Type:{0}", querable.ElementType)
    txtLog.WriteLine("Expression:{0}", querable.Expression)
    txtLog.WriteLine("Provider:{0}", querable.Provider)
End Sub
```

Sample of C# Code

```csharp
private void asQueryableToolStripMenuItem_Click(object sender, EventArgs e)
{
    IEnumerable<string> strings = new MyStringList
        { "orange", "apple", "grape", "pear" };
    var querable = strings.AsQueryable();
    txtLog.WriteLine("Element Type:{0}", querable.ElementType);
    txtLog.WriteLine("Expression:{0}", querable.Expression);
    txtLog.WriteLine("Provider:{0}", querable.Provider);
}
```

You can think of the *AsQueryable* method as the opposite of the *AsEnumerable* method.

AVERAGE

The *Average* extension method is an aggregate extension method that can calculate an average of a numeric property that exists on the elements in your collection. In the following example, the *Average* method calculates the average year of the cars.

Sample of Visual Basic Code

```vbnet
Dim averageYear = GetCars().Average(Function(c) c.Year)
txtLog.WriteLine(averageYear)
```

Sample of C# Code

```csharp
var averageYear = GetCars().Average(c => c.Year);
txtLog.WriteLine(averageYear);
```

CAST

Use the *Cast* extension method when you want to convert each of the elements in your source to a different type. The elements in the source must be coerced to the target type, or an *InvalidCastException* is thrown.

Note that the *Cast* method is not a filter. If you want to retrieve all the elements of a specific type, use the *OfType* extension method. The following example converts *IEnumerable* of *Car* to *IEnumerable* of *Object*.

Sample of Visual Basic Code

```vbnet
Private Sub castToolStripMenuItem_Click(ByVal sender As System.Object, _
        ByVal e As System.EventArgs) Handles castToolStripMenuItem.Click
    Dim cars As IEnumerable(Of Car) = GetCars()
```

```
    Dim objects As IEnumerable(Of Object) = cars.Cast(Of Object)()
End Sub
```

Sample of C# Code

```
private void castToolStripMenuItem_Click(object sender, EventArgs e)
{
    IEnumerable<Car> cars = GetCars();
    IEnumerable<Object> objects = cars.Cast<object>();
}
```

CONCAT

Use the *Concat* extension method to combine two sequences. This method is similar to the *Union* operator, but *Union* removes duplicates, whereas *Concat* does not remove duplicates.

The following example combines two collections to produce a result that contains all elements from both collections.

Sample of Visual Basic Code

```
Private Sub concatToolStripMenuItem_Click(ByVal sender As System.Object, _
        ByVal e As System.EventArgs) _
        Handles concatToolStripMenuItem.Click
    Dim lastYearScores As Integer() = New Integer() {88, 56, 23, 99, 65}
    Dim thisYearScores As Integer() = New Integer() {93, 78, 23, 99, 90}
    Dim item As Integer
    For Each item In lastYearScores.Concat(thisYearScores)
        Me.txtLog.WriteLine(item)
    Next
End Sub
```

Sample of C# Code

```
private void concatToolStripMenuItem_Click(object sender, EventArgs e)
{
    int[] lastYearScores = { 88, 56, 23, 99, 65 };
    int[] thisYearScores = { 93, 78, 23, 99, 90 };

    foreach (var item in lastYearScores.Concat(thisYearScores))
    {
        txtLog.WriteLine(item);
    }
}
```

The result:

```
88
56
23
99
65
93
78
23
99
90
```

CONTAINS

The *Contains* extension method determines whether an element exists in the source. If the element has the same values for all the properties as one item in the source, *Contains* returns *false* for a reference type but *true* for a value type. The comparison is done by reference for classes and by value for structures. The following example code gets a collection of cars, creates one variable that references one of the cars in the collection, and then creates another variable that references a new car.

Sample of Visual Basic Code

```
Private Sub containsToolStripMenuItem_Click(ByVal sender As System.Object, _
        ByVal e As System.EventArgs) _
        Handles containsToolStripMenuItem.Click
    Dim cars = Me.GetCars
    Dim c1 = cars.Item(2)
    Dim c2 As New Car
    txtLog.WriteLine(cars.Contains(c1))
    txtLog.WriteLine(cars.Contains(c2))
End Sub
```

Sample of C# Code

```
private void containsToolStripMenuItem_Click(object sender, EventArgs e)
{
    var cars = GetCars();
    Car c1 = cars[2];
    Car c2 = new Car();
    txtLog.WriteLine(cars.Contains(c1));
    txtLog.WriteLine(cars.Contains(c2));
}
```

The result:

```
True
False
```

COUNT

The *Count* extension method returns the count of the elements in the source. The following code example returns the count of cars in the source collection:

Sample of Visual Basic Code

```
Private Sub countToolStripMenuItem_Click(ByVal sender As System.Object, _
        ByVal e As System.EventArgs) _
        Handles countToolStripMenuItem.Click
    Dim cars = Me.GetCars
    txtLog.WriteLine(cars.Count())
End Sub
```

Sample of C# Code

```
private void countToolStripMenuItem_Click(object sender, EventArgs e)
{
    var cars = GetCars();
    txtLog.WriteLine(cars.Count());
}
```

The result:

5

DEFAULTIFEMPTY

Use the *DefaultIfEmpty* extension method when you suspect that the source collection might not have any elements, but you want at least one element corresponding to the default value of the type (*false* for Boolean, *0* for numeric, and *null* for a reference type). This method returns all elements in the source if there is at least one element in the source.

Sample of Visual Basic Code

```vbnet
Private Sub defaultIfEmptyToolStripMenuItem_Click(ByVal sender As System.Object, _
      ByVal e As System.EventArgs) _
      Handles defaultIfEmptyToolStripMenuItem.Click
   Dim cars As New List(Of Car)
   Dim oneNullCar = cars.DefaultIfEmpty()
   For Each car In oneNullCar
       txtLog.WriteLine(IIf((car Is Nothing), "Null Car", "Not Null Car"))
   Next
End Sub
```

Sample of C# Code

```csharp
private void defaultIfEmptyToolStripMenuItem_Click(object sender, EventArgs e)
{
    List<Car> cars = new List<Car>();
    IEnumerable<Car> oneNullCar = cars.DefaultIfEmpty();
    foreach (var car in oneNullCar)
    {
        txtLog.WriteLine(car == null ? "Null Car" : "Not Null Car");
    }
}
```

The result:

Null Car

DISTINCT

The *Distinct* extension method removes duplicate values in the source. The following code sample shows how a collection that has duplicate values is filtered by using the *Distinct* method. Matching to detect duplication follows the same rules as for *Contains*.

Sample of Visual Basic Code

```vbnet
Private Sub distinctToolStripMenuItem_Click(ByVal sender As System.Object, _
      ByVal e As System.EventArgs) _
      Handles distinctToolStripMenuItem.Click
   Dim scores = New Integer() {88, 56, 23, 99, 65, 93, 78, 23, 99, 90}
   For Each score In scores.Distinct()
       txtLog.WriteLine(score)
   Next
End Sub
```

Sample of C# Code

```csharp
private void distinctToolStripMenuItem_Click(object sender, EventArgs e)
{
    int[] scores = { 88, 56, 23, 99, 65, 93, 78, 23, 99, 90 };
    foreach (var score in scores.Distinct())
    {
        txtLog.WriteLine(score);
    }
}
```

The result:

```
88
56
23
99
65
93
78
90
```

ELEMENTAT

Use the *ElementAt* extension method when you know you want to retrieve the *n*th element in the source. If there is a valid element at that 0-based location, it's returned or an *ArgumentOutOfRangeException* is thrown.

Sample of Visual Basic Code

```vb
Private Sub elementAtToolStripMenuItem_Click(ByVal sender As System.Object, _
        ByVal e As System.EventArgs) _
        Handles elementAtToolStripMenuItem.Click
    Dim scores = New Integer() {88, 56, 23, 99, 65, 93, 78, 23, 99, 90}
    txtLog.WriteLine(scores.ElementAt(4))
End Sub
```

Sample of C# Code

```csharp
private void elementAtToolStripMenuItem_Click(object sender, EventArgs e)
{
    int[] scores = { 88, 56, 23, 99, 65, 93, 78, 23, 99, 90 };
    txtLog.WriteLine(scores.ElementAt(4));
}
```

The result:

```
65
```

ELEMENTATORDEFAULT

The *ElementAtOrDefault* extension method is the same as the *ElementAt* extension method except that an exception is not thrown if the element doesn't exist. Instead, the default value for the type of the collection is returned. The sample code attempts to access an element that doesn't exist.

Sample of Visual Basic Code

```vb
Private Sub elementAtOrDefaultToolStripMenuItem_Click( _
        ByVal sender As System.Object, _
        ByVal e As System.EventArgs) _
        Handles elementAtOrDefaultToolStripMenuItem.Click
    Dim scores = New Integer() {88, 56, 23, 99, 65, 93, 78, 23, 99, 90}
    txtLog.WriteLine(scores.ElementAtOrDefault(15))
End Sub
```

Sample of C# Code

```csharp
private void elementAtOrDefaultToolStripMenuItem_Click(
    object sender, EventArgs e)
{
    int[] scores = { 88, 56, 23, 99, 65, 93, 78, 23, 99, 90 };
    txtLog.WriteLine(scores.ElementAtOrDefault(15));
}
```

The result:

0

EXCEPT

When you have a sequence of elements and you want to find out which elements don't exist (as usual, by reference for classes and by value for structures) in a second sequence, use the *Except* extension method. The following code sample returns the differences between two collections of integers.

Sample of Visual Basic Code

```vb
Private Sub exceptToolStripMenuItem_Click(ByVal sender As System.Object, _
        ByVal e As System.EventArgs) _
        Handles exceptToolStripMenuItem.Click
    Dim lastYearScores As Integer() = New Integer() {88, 56, 23, 99, 65}
    Dim thisYearScores As Integer() = New Integer() {93, 78, 23, 99, 90}
    Dim item As Integer
    For Each item In lastYearScores.Except(thisYearScores)
        Me.txtLog.WriteLine(item)
    Next
End Sub
```

Sample of C# Code

```csharp
private void exceptToolStripMenuItem_Click(object sender, EventArgs e)
{
    int[] lastYearScores = { 88, 56, 23, 99, 65 };
    int[] thisYearScores = { 93, 78, 23, 99, 90 };

    foreach (var item in lastYearScores.Except(thisYearScores))
    {
        txtLog.WriteLine(item);
    }
}
```

The result:

88
56
65

FIRST

When you have a sequence of elements and you just need the first element, use the *First* extension method. This method doesn't care how many elements are in the sequence as long as there is at least one element. If no elements exist, an *InvalidOperationException* is thrown.

Sample of Visual Basic Code

```vb
Private Sub firstToolStripMenuItem_Click(ByVal sender As System.Object, _
      ByVal e As System.EventArgs) _
      Handles firstToolStripMenuItem.Click
   Dim scores = New Integer() {88, 56, 23, 99, 65, 93, 78, 23, 99, 90}
   txtLog.WriteLine(scores.First())
End Sub
```

Sample of C# Code

```csharp
private void firstToolStripMenuItem_Click(object sender, EventArgs e)
{
    int[] scores = { 88, 56, 23, 99, 65, 93, 78, 23, 99, 90 };
    txtLog.WriteLine(scores.First());
}
```

The result:

88

FIRSTORDEFAULT

The *FirstOrDefault* extension method is the same as the *First* extension method except that if no elements exist in the source sequence, the default value of the sequence type is returned. This example will attempt to get the first element when there are no elements.

Sample of Visual Basic Code

```vb
Private Sub firstOrDefaultToolStripMenuItem_Click(ByVal sender As System.Object, _
      ByVal e As System.EventArgs) _
      Handles firstOrDefaultToolStripMenuItem.Click
   Dim scores = New Integer() {}
   txtLog.WriteLine(scores.FirstOrDefault())
End Sub
```

Sample of C# Code

```csharp
private void firstOrDefaultToolStripMenuItem_Click(object sender, EventArgs e)
{
    int[] scores = { };
    txtLog.WriteLine(scores.FirstOrDefault());
}
```

The result:

0

GROUPBY

The *GroupBy* extension method returns a sequence of *IGrouping<TKey, TElement>* objects. This interface implements *IEnumerable<TElement>* and exposes a single *Key* property that represents the grouping key value. The following code sample groups cars by the *Make* property.

Sample of Visual Basic Code

```vb
Private Sub groupByToolStripMenuItem_Click(ByVal sender As System.Object, _
        ByVal e As System.EventArgs) _
        Handles groupByToolStripMenuItem.Click
    Dim cars = GetCars()
    Dim query = cars.GroupBy(Function(c) c.Make)
    For Each group As IGrouping(Of String, Car) In query
        txtLog.WriteLine("Key:{0}", group.Key)
        For Each c In group
            txtLog.WriteLine("Car VIN:{0} Make:{1}", c.VIN, c.Make)
        Next
    Next
End Sub
```

Sample of C# Code

```csharp
private void groupByToolStripMenuItem_Click(object sender, EventArgs e)
{
    var cars = GetCars();
    var query = cars.GroupBy(c => c.Make);
    foreach (IGrouping<string,Car> group in query)
    {
        txtLog.WriteLine("Key:{0}", group.Key);
        foreach (Car c in group)
        {
            txtLog.WriteLine("Car VIN:{0} Make:{1}", c.VIN, c.Make);
        }
    }
}
```

The result:

```
Key:Ford
Car VIN:ABC123 Make:Ford
Car VIN:DEF456 Make:Ford
Key:BMW
Car VIN:DEF123 Make:BMW
Key:Audi
Car VIN:ABC456 Make:Audi
Key:VW
Car VIN:HIJ123 Make:VW
```

Because there are two Fords, they are grouped together.

The *ToLookup* extension method provides the same result except that *GroupBy* returns a deferred query, whereas *ToLookup* executes the query immediately, and iterating on the result afterward will not change if the source changes. This is equivalent to the *ToList* extension method introduced earlier in this chapter, but for *IGrouping* instead of for *IEnumerable*.

GROUPJOIN

The *GroupJoin* extension method is similar to the SQL left outer join where it always produces one output for each input from the "outer" sequence. Any matching elements from the inner sequence are grouped into a collection that is associated with the outer element. In the following example code, a collection of *Makes* is provided and joined to the *cars* collection.

Sample of Visual Basic Code

```vb
Private Sub groupToolStripMenuItem_Click(ByVal sender As System.Object, _
        ByVal e As System.EventArgs) Handles groupToolStripMenuItem.Click
    Dim makes = New String() {"Audi", "BMW", "Ford", "Mazda", "VW"}
    Dim cars = GetCars()

    Dim query = makes.GroupJoin(cars, _
            Function(make) make, _
            Function(car) car.Make, _
            Function(make, innerCars) New With {.Make = make, .Cars = innerCars})

    For Each item In query
        txtLog.WriteLine("Make: {0}", item.Make)
        For Each car In item.Cars
            txtLog.WriteLine("Car VIN:{0}, Model:{1}", car.VIN, car.Model)
        Next
    Next
End Sub
```

Sample of C# Code

```csharp
private void groupToolStripMenuItem_Click(object sender, EventArgs e)
{
    var makes = new string[] { "Audi", "BMW", "Ford", "Mazda", "VW" };
    var cars = GetCars();

    var query = makes.GroupJoin(cars,
        make => make, car => car.Make,
        (make, innerCars) => new { Make = make, Cars = innerCars });

    foreach (var item in query)
    {
        txtLog.WriteLine("Make: {0}", item.Make);
        foreach (var car in item.Cars)
        {
            txtLog.WriteLine("Car VIN:{0}, Model:{1}", car.VIN, car.Model);
        }
    }
}
```

The result:

```
Make: Audi
Car VIN:ABC456, Model:TT
Make: BMW
Car VIN:DEF123, Model:Z-3
Make: Ford
Car VIN:ABC123, Model:F-250
Car VIN:DEF456, Model:F-150
```

```
Make: Mazda
Make: VW
Car VIN:HIJ123, Model:Bug
```

INTERSECT

When you have a sequence of elements in which you want to find out which exist in a second sequence, use the *Intersect* extension method. The following code example returns the common elements that exist in two collections of integers.

Sample of Visual Basic Code

```vb
Private Sub intersectToolStripMenuItem_Click(ByVal sender As System.Object, _
        ByVal e As System.EventArgs) Handles intersectToolStripMenuItem.Click
    Dim lastYearScores As Integer() = New Integer() {88, 56, 23, 99, 65}
    Dim thisYearScores As Integer() = New Integer() {93, 78, 23, 99, 90}
    Dim item As Integer
    For Each item In lastYearScores.Intersect(thisYearScores)
        Me.txtLog.WriteLine(item)
    Next
End Sub
```

Sample of C# Code

```csharp
private void intersectToolStripMenuItem_Click(object sender, EventArgs e)
{
    int[] lastYearScores = { 88, 56, 23, 99, 65 };
    int[] thisYearScores = { 93, 78, 23, 99, 90 };

    foreach (var item in lastYearScores.Intersect(thisYearScores))
    {
        txtLog.WriteLine(item);
    }
}
```

The result:

```
23
99
```

JOIN

The *Join* extension method is similar to the SQL inner join, by which it produces output only for each input from the outer sequence when there is a match to the inner sequence. For each matching element in the inner sequence, a resulting element is created. In the following sample code, a collection of *Makes* is provided and joined to the *cars* collection.

Sample of Visual Basic Code

```vb
Private Sub joinToolStripMenuItem_Click(ByVal sender As System.Object, _
        ByVal e As System.EventArgs) Handles joinToolStripMenuItem.Click
    Dim makes = New String() {"Audi", "BMW", "Ford", "Mazda", "VW"}
    Dim cars = GetCars()

    Dim query = makes.Join(cars, _
        Function(make) make, _
        Function(car) car.Make, _
```

```
            Function(make, innerCar) New With {.Make = make, .Car = innerCar})
    For Each item In query
        txtLog.WriteLine("Make: {0}, Car:{1} {2} {3}",
            item.Make, item.Car.VIN, item.Car.Make, item.Car.Model)
    Next
End Sub
```

Sample of C# Code

```csharp
private void joinToolStripMenuItem_Click(object sender, EventArgs e)
{
    var makes = new string[] { "Audi", "BMW", "Ford", "Mazda", "VW" };
    var cars = GetCars();

    var query = makes.Join(cars,
        make => make, car => car.Make,
        (make, innerCar) => new { Make = make, Car = innerCar });

    foreach (var item in query)
    {
        txtLog.WriteLine("Make: {0}, Car:{1} {2} {3}",
            item.Make, item.Car.VIN, item.Car.Make, item.Car.Model);
    }
}
```

The result:

```
Make: Audi, Car:ABC456 Audi TT
Make: BMW, Car:DEF123 BMW Z-3
Make: Ford, Car:ABC123 Ford F-250
Make: Ford, Car:DEF456 Ford F-150
Make: VW, Car:HIJ123 VW Bug
```

EXAM TIP

For the exam, expect to be tested on the various ways to join sequences.

LAST

When you want to retrieve the last element in a sequence, use the *Last* extension method. This method throws an *InvalidOperationException* if there are no elements in the sequence. The following sample code retrieves the last element.

Sample of Visual Basic Code

```vbnet
Private Sub lastToolStripMenuItem_Click(ByVal sender As System.Object, _
        ByVal e As System.EventArgs) Handles lastToolStripMenuItem.Click
    Dim scores = New Integer() {88, 56, 23, 99, 65, 93, 78, 23, 99, 90}
    txtLog.WriteLine(scores.Last())
End Sub
```

Sample of C# Code

```csharp
private void lastToolStripMenuItem_Click(object sender, EventArgs e)
{
    int[] scores = { 88, 56, 23, 99, 65, 93, 78, 23, 99, 90 };
```

```
    txtLog.WriteLine(scores.Last());
}
```

The result:

90

LASTORDEFAULT

The *LastOrDefault* extension method is the same as the *Last* extension method except that if no elements exist in the source sequence, the default value of the sequence type is returned. This example will attempt to get the last element when there are no elements.

Sample of Visual Basic Code

```
Private Sub lastOrDefaultToolStripMenuItem_Click(ByVal sender As System.Object, _
        ByVal e As System.EventArgs) Handles lastOrDefaultToolStripMenuItem.Click
    Dim scores = New Integer() {}
    txtLog.WriteLine(scores.LastOrDefault())
End Sub
```

Sample of C# Code

```
private void lastOrDefaultToolStripMenuItem_Click(object sender, EventArgs e)
{
    int[] scores = { };
    txtLog.WriteLine(scores.LastOrDefault());
}
```

The result:

0

LONGCOUNT

The *LongCount* extension method is the same as the *Count* extension method except that *Count* returns a 32-bit integer, and *LongCount* returns a 64-bit integer.

Sample of Visual Basic Code

```
Private Sub longCountToolStripMenuItem_Click(ByVal sender As System.Object, _
        ByVal e As System.EventArgs) Handles longCountToolStripMenuItem.Click
    Dim cars = Me.GetCars
    txtLog.WriteLine(cars.LongCount())
End Sub
```

Sample of C# Code

```
private void longCountToolStripMenuItem_Click(object sender, EventArgs e)
{
    var cars = GetCars();
    txtLog.WriteLine(cars.LongCount());
}
```

The result:

5

MAX

When you're working with a non-empty sequence of values and you want to determine which element is greatest, use the *Max* extension method. The *Max* extension has several overloads, but the following code sample shows two of the more common overloads that demonstrate the *Max* extension method's capabilities.

Sample of Visual Basic Code

```
Private Sub maxToolStripMenuItem_Click(ByVal sender As System.Object, _
        ByVal e As System.EventArgs) Handles maxToolStripMenuItem.Click
    Dim scores = New Integer() {88, 56, 23, 99, 65, 93, 78, 23, 99, 90}
    txtLog.WriteLine(scores.Max())

    Dim cars = GetCars()
    txtLog.WriteLine(cars.Max(Function(c) c.Year))
End Sub
```

Sample of C# Code

```
private void maxToolStripMenuItem_Click(object sender, EventArgs e)
{
    int[] scores = { 88, 56, 23, 99, 65, 93, 78, 23, 99, 90 };
    txtLog.WriteLine(scores.Max());

    var cars = GetCars();
    txtLog.WriteLine(cars.Max(c => c.Year));
}
```

The result:

99

In this example, the parameterless overload is called on a collection of integers and returns the maximum value of 99. The next overload example enables you to provide a selector that specifies a property that finds the maximum value.

MIN

When you're working with a non-empty sequence of values and you want to determine which element is the smallest, use the *Min* extension method, as shown in the following code sample.

Sample of Visual Basic Code

```
Private Sub maxToolStripMenuItem_Click(ByVal sender As System.Object, _
        ByVal e As System.EventArgs) Handles maxToolStripMenuItem.Click
    Dim scores = New Integer() {88, 56, 23, 99, 65, 93, 78, 23, 99, 90}
    txtLog.WriteLine(scores.Min())
End Sub
```

Sample of C# Code

```
private void maxToolStripMenuItem_Click(object sender, EventArgs e)
{
    int[] scores = { 88, 56, 23, 99, 65, 93, 78, 23, 99, 90 };
    txtLog.WriteLine(scores.Min());
}
```

The result:

23

OFTYPE

The *OfType* extension method is a filtering method that returns only objects that can be type cast to a specific type. The following sample code retrieves just the integers from the object collection.

Sample of Visual Basic Code

```vb
Private Sub ofTypeToolStripMenuItem_Click(ByVal sender As System.Object, _
        ByVal e As System.EventArgs) Handles ofTypeToolStripMenuItem.Click
    Dim items = New Object() {55, "Hello", 22, "Goodbye"}
    For Each intItem In items.OfType(Of Integer)()
        txtLog.WriteLine(intItem)
    Next
End Sub
```

Sample of C# Code

```csharp
private void ofTypeToolStripMenuItem_Click(object sender, EventArgs e)
{
    object[] items = new object[] { 55, "Hello", 22, "Goodbye" };
    foreach (var intItem in items.OfType<int>())
    {
        txtLog.WriteLine(intItem);
    }
}
```

The result:

55
22

ORDERBY, ORDERBYDESCENDING, THENBY, AND THENBYDESCENDING

When you want to sort the elements in a sequence, you can use the *OrderBy* or *OrderByDescending* extension methods, followed by the *ThenBy* and *ThenByDescending* extension methods. These extension methods are *nonstreaming*, which means that all elements in the sequence must be evaluated before any output can be produced. Most extension methods are *streaming*, which means that each element can be evaluated and potentially output without having to evaluate all elements.

All these extension methods return an *IOrderedEnumerable<T>* object, which inherits from *IEnumerable<T>* and enables the *ThenBy* and *ThenByDescending* operators. *ThenBy* and *ThenByDescending* are extension methods on *IOrderedEnumerable<T>* instead of on *IEnumerable<T>*, which the other extension methods extend. This can sometimes create unexpected errors when using the *var* keyword and type inference. The following code example creates a list of cars and then sorts them by make, model descending, and year.

Sample of Visual Basic Code

```vb
Private Sub orderByToolStripMenuItem_Click(ByVal sender As System.Object, _
```

```
        ByVal e As System.EventArgs) Handles orderByToolStripMenuItem.Click
    Dim cars = GetCars().OrderBy(Function(c) c.Make) _
                        .ThenByDescending(Function(c) c.Model) _
                        .ThenBy(Function(c) c.Year)
    For Each item In cars
        txtLog.WriteLine("Car VIN:{0} Make:{1} Model:{2} Year:{3}", _
        item.VIN, item.Make, item.Model, item.Year)
    Next
End Sub
```

Sample of C# Code

```csharp
private void orderByToolStripMenuItem_Click(object sender, EventArgs e)
{
    var cars = GetCars().OrderBy(c=>c.Make)
                        .ThenByDescending(c=>c.Model)
                        .ThenBy(c=>c.Year);
    foreach (var item in cars)
    {
        txtLog.WriteLine("Car VIN:{0} Make:{1} Model:{2} Year:{3}",
            item.VIN, item.Make, item.Model, item.Year);
    }
}
```

The result:

```
Car VIN:ABC456 Make:Audi Model:TT Year:2008
Car VIN:DEF123 Make:BMW Model:Z-3 Year:2005
Car VIN:ABC123 Make:Ford Model:F-250 Year:2000
Car VIN:DEF456 Make:Ford Model:F-150 Year:1998
Car VIN:HIJ123 Make:VW Model:Bug Year:1956
```

REVERSE

The *Reverse* extension method is an ordering mechanism that reverses the order of the sequence elements. This code sample creates a collection of integers but displays them in reverse order.

Sample of Visual Basic Code

```vb
Private Sub reverseToolStripMenuItem_Click(ByVal sender As System.Object, _
        ByVal e As System.EventArgs) Handles reverseToolStripMenuItem.Click
    Dim scores = {88, 56, 23, 99, 65, 93, 78, 23, 99, 90}

    For Each item In scores.Reverse()
        txtLog.WriteLine(item)
    Next
End Sub
```

Sample of C# Code

```csharp
private void reverseToolStripMenuItem_Click(object sender, EventArgs e)
{
    int[] scores = { 88, 56, 23, 99, 65, 93, 78, 23, 99, 90 };
    foreach (var item in scores.Reverse())
    {
        txtLog.WriteLine(item);
```

```
            }
      }
```

The result:

```
90
99
23
78
93
65
99
23
56
88
```

SELECT

The *Select* extension method returns one output element for each input element. Although *Select* returns one output for each input, the *Select* operator also enables you to perform a projection to a new type of element. This conversion or mapping mechanism plays an important role in most LINQ queries.

In the following example, a collection of *Tuple* types is queried to retrieve all the elements whose make (*Tuple.item2*) is *Ford*, but the *Select* extension method transforms these *Tuple* types into *Car* objects.

Sample of Visual Basic Code

```vb
Private Sub selectToolStripMenuItem_Click(ByVal sender As System.Object, _
        ByVal e As System.EventArgs) Handles selectToolStripMenuItem.Click
    Dim vehicles As New List(Of Tuple(Of String, String, Integer)) From { _
            Tuple.Create(Of String, String, Integer)("123", "VW", 1999), _
            Tuple.Create(Of String, String, Integer)("234", "Ford", 2009), _
            Tuple.Create(Of String, String, Integer)("567", "Audi", 2005), _
            Tuple.Create(Of String, String, Integer)("678", "Ford", 2003), _
            Tuple.Create(Of String, String, Integer)("789", "Mazda", 2003), _
            Tuple.Create(Of String, String, Integer)("999", "Ford", 1965) _
            }
    Dim fordCars = vehicles.Where(Function(v) v.Item2 = "Ford") _
        .Select(Function(v) New Car With { _
                                    .VIN = v.Item1, _
                                    .Make = v.Item2, _
                                    .Year = v.Item3 _
                            })
    For Each item In fordCars
        txtLog.WriteLine("Car VIN:{0} Make:{1} Year:{2}", _
                        item.VIN, item.Make, item.Year)
    Next
End Sub
```

Sample of C# Code

```csharp
private void selectToolStripMenuItem_Click(object sender, EventArgs e)
{
    var vehicles = new List<Tuple<string,string,int>>
```

```
    {
        Tuple.Create("123", "VW", 1999),
        Tuple.Create("234","Ford",2009),
        Tuple.Create("567","Audi", 2005),
        Tuple.Create("678","Ford", 2003),
        Tuple.Create("789","Mazda", 2003),
        Tuple.Create("999","Ford",1965)
    };

    var fordCars = vehicles
                    .Where(v=>v.Item2=="Ford")
                    .Select(v=>new Car
                    {
                        VIN=v.Item1,
                        Make=v.Item2,
                        Year=v.Item3
                    });
    foreach (var item in fordCars )
    {
        txtLog.WriteLine("Car VIN:{0} Make:{1} Year:{2}",
            item.VIN, item.Make, item.Year);
    }
}
```

The result:

```
Car VIN:234 Make:Ford Year:2009
Car VIN:678 Make:Ford Year:2003
Car VIN:999 Make:Ford Year:1965
```

SELECTMANY

When you use the *Select* extension method, each element from the input sequence can produce only one element in the output sequence. The *SelectMany* extension method projects a single output element into many output elements, so you can use the *SelectMany* method to perform a SQL inner join, but you can also use it when you are working with a collection of collections, and you are querying the outer collection but need to produce an output element for each element in the inner collection.

In the following code sample is a list of repairs in which each element in the *repairs* collection is a *Tuple* that contains the VIN of the vehicle as *item1* and a list of repairs as *item2*. *SelectMany* expands each *Tuple* into a sequence of repairs. *Select* projects each repair and the associated VIN into an anonymous type instance.

Sample of Visual Basic Code

```
Private Sub selectManyToolStripMenuItem_Click(ByVal sender As System.Object, _
        ByVal e As System.EventArgs) Handles selectManyToolStripMenuItem.Click
    Dim repairs = New List(Of Tuple(Of String, List(Of String))) From
            {
                Tuple.Create("ABC123",
                    New List(Of String) From {"Rotate Tires", "Change oil"}),
                Tuple.Create("DEF123",
                    New List(Of String) From {"Fix Flat", "Wash Vehicle"}),
                Tuple.Create("ABC456",
```

```
                        New List(Of String) From {"Alignment", "Vacuum", "Wax"}),
                Tuple.Create("HIJ123",
                        New List(Of String) From {"Spark plugs", "Air filter"}),
                Tuple.Create("DEF456",
                        New List(Of String) From {"Wiper blades", "PVC valve"})
            }
    Dim query = repairs.SelectMany(Function(t) _
        t.Item2.Select(Function(r) New With {.VIN = t.Item1, .Repair = r}))

    For Each item In query
        txtLog.WriteLine("VIN:{0} Repair:{1}", item.VIN, item.Repair)
    Next
End Sub
```

Sample of C# Code

```
private void selectManyToolStripMenuItem_Click(object sender, EventArgs e)
{
    var repairs = new List<Tuple<string, List<string>>>
                {
                    Tuple.Create("ABC123",
                        new List<string>{"Rotate Tires","Change oil"}),
                    Tuple.Create("DEF123",
                        new List<string>{"Fix Flat","Wash Vehicle"}),
                    Tuple.Create("ABC456",
                        new List<string>{"Alignment","Vacuum", "Wax"}),
                    Tuple.Create("HIJ123",
                        new List<string>{"Spark plugs","Air filter"}),
                    Tuple.Create("DEF456",
                        new List<string>{"Wiper blades","PVC valve"}),
                };
    var query = repairs.SelectMany(t =>
        t.Item2.Select(r => new { VIN = t.Item1, Repair = r }));

    foreach (var item in query)
    {
        txtLog.WriteLine("VIN:{0} Repair:{1}", item.VIN, item.Repair);
    }
}
```

The result:

```
VIN:ABC123 Repair:Rotate Tires
VIN:ABC123 Repair:Change oil
VIN:DEF123 Repair:Fix Flat
VIN:DEF123 Repair:Wash Vehicle
VIN:ABC456 Repair:Alignment
VIN:ABC456 Repair:Vacuum
VIN:ABC456 Repair:Wax
VIN:HIJ123 Repair:Spark plugs
VIN:HIJ123 Repair:Air filter
VIN:DEF456 Repair:Wiper blades
VIN:DEF456 Repair:PVC valve
```

SEQUENCEEQUAL

One scenario you might run into is when you have two sequences and want to see whether they contain the same elements in the same order. The *SequenceEqual* extension method can perform this task. It walks through two sequences and compares the elements inside for equality. You can also override the equality test by providing an *IEqualityComparer* object as a parameter. The following example code compares two sequences several times and displays the result.

Sample of Visual Basic Code

```vb
Private Sub sequenceEqualToolStripMenuItem_Click(ByVal sender As System.Object, _
        ByVal e As System.EventArgs) Handles sequenceEqualToolStripMenuItem.Click
    Dim lastYearScores = New List(Of Integer) From {93, 78, 23, 99, 91}
    Dim thisYearScores = New List(Of Integer) From {93, 78, 23, 99, 90}
    txtLog.WriteLine(lastYearScores.SequenceEqual(thisYearScores))
    lastYearScores(4) = 90
    txtLog.WriteLine(lastYearScores.SequenceEqual(thisYearScores))
    thisYearScores.Add(85)
    txtLog.WriteLine(lastYearScores.SequenceEqual(thisYearScores))
    lastYearScores.Add(85)
    txtLog.WriteLine(lastYearScores.SequenceEqual(thisYearScores))
    lastYearScores.Add(75)
    txtLog.WriteLine(lastYearScores.SequenceEqual(thisYearScores))
End Sub
```

Sample of C# Code

```csharp
private void sequenceEqualToolStripMenuItem_Click(object sender, EventArgs e)
{
    var lastYearScores = new List<int>{ 93, 78, 23, 99, 91 };
    var thisYearScores = new List<int>{ 93, 78, 23, 99, 90 };
    txtLog.WriteLine(lastYearScores.SequenceEqual(thisYearScores));
    lastYearScores[4] = 90;
    txtLog.WriteLine(lastYearScores.SequenceEqual(thisYearScores));
    thisYearScores.Add(85);
    txtLog.WriteLine(lastYearScores.SequenceEqual(thisYearScores));
    lastYearScores.Add(85);
    txtLog.WriteLine(lastYearScores.SequenceEqual(thisYearScores));
    lastYearScores.Add(75);
    txtLog.WriteLine(lastYearScores.SequenceEqual(thisYearScores));
}
```

The result:

```
False
True
False
True
False
```

SINGLE

The *Single* extension method should be used when you have a collection of one element and want to convert the generic *IEnumerable* interface to the single element. If the sequence contains more than one element or no elements, an exception is thrown. The following example code queries to retrieve the car with VIN HIJ123 and then uses the *Single* extension method to convert *IEnumerable* to the single *Car*.

Sample of Visual Basic Code

```
Private Sub singleToolStripMenuItem_Click(ByVal sender As System.Object, _
        ByVal e As System.EventArgs) Handles singleToolStripMenuItem.Click
    Dim cars = GetCars()
    Dim myCar As Car = cars.Where(Function(c) c.VIN = "HIJ123").Single()
    txtLog.WriteLine("Car VIN:{0}, Make:{1}, Model:{2}", _
        myCar.VIN, myCar.Make, myCar.Model)
End Sub
```

Sample of C# Code

```
private void singleToolStripMenuItem_Click(object sender, EventArgs e)
{
    var cars = GetCars();
    Car myCar = cars.Where(c => c.VIN == "HIJ123").Single();
    txtLog.WriteLine("Car VIN:{0}, Make:{1}, Model:{2}",
        myCar.VIN, myCar.Make, myCar.Model);
}
```

The result:

```
Car VIN:HIJ123, Make:VW, Model:Bug
```

SINGLEORDEFAULT

The *SingleOrDefault* extension method works like the *Single* extension method except that it doesn't throw an exception if no elements are in the sequence. It still throws an *InvalidOperationException* if more than one element exists in the sequence. The following sample code attempts to locate a car with an invalid VIN, so no elements exist in the sequence; therefore, the *myCar* variable will be *Nothing* (C# *null*).

Sample of Visual Basic Code

```
Private Sub singleOrDefaultToolStripMenuItem_Click(ByVal sender As System.Object, _
        ByVal e As System.EventArgs) Handles singleOrDefaultToolStripMenuItem.Click
    Dim cars = GetCars()
    Dim myCar = cars.Where(Function(c) c.VIN = "XXXXXX").SingleOrDefault()
    txtLog.WriteLine(myCar Is Nothing)
End Sub
```

Sample of C# Code

```
private void singleOrDefaultToolStripMenuItem_Click(object sender, EventArgs e)
{
    var cars = GetCars();
    Car myCar = cars.Where(c => c.VIN == "XXXXXX").SingleOrDefault();
    txtLog.WriteLine(myCar == null);
}
```

The result:

```
True
```

SKIP

The *Skip* extension method ignores, or jumps over, elements in the source sequence. This method, when combined with the *Take* extension method, typically produces paged result-sets to the GUI. The following sample code demonstrates the use of the *Skip* extension method when sorting scores and then skipping over the lowest score to display the rest of the scores.

Sample of Visual Basic Code

```
Private Sub skipToolStripMenuItem_Click(ByVal sender As System.Object, _
        ByVal e As System.EventArgs) Handles skipToolStripMenuItem.Click
    Dim scores = {88, 56, 23, 99, 65, 93, 78, 23, 99, 90}
    For Each score In scores.OrderBy(Function(i) i).Skip(1)
        txtLog.WriteLine(score)
    Next
End Sub
```

Sample of C# Code

```
private void skipToolStripMenuItem_Click(object sender, EventArgs e)
{
    int[] scores = { 88, 56, 23, 99, 65, 93, 78, 23, 99, 90 };
    foreach (var score in scores.OrderBy(i=>i).Skip(1))
    {
        txtLog.WriteLine(score);
    }
}
```

The result:

```
56
65
78
88
90
93
99
```

In this example, the score of 23 is missing because the *Skip* method jumped over that element.

SKIPWHILE

The *SkipWhile* extension method is similar to the *Skip* method except *SkipWhile* accepts a predicate that takes an element of the collection and returns a Boolean value to determine when to stop skipping over. The following example code skips over the scores as long as the score is less than 80.

Sample of Visual Basic Code

```
Private Sub skipWhileToolStripMenuItem_Click(ByVal sender As System.Object, _
        ByVal e As System.EventArgs) Handles skipWhileToolStripMenuItem.Click
    Dim scores = {88, 56, 23, 99, 65, 93, 78, 23, 99, 90}
    For Each score In scores.OrderBy(Function(i) i).SkipWhile(Function(s) s < 80)
        txtLog.WriteLine(score)
```

```
      Next
End Sub
```

Sample of C# Code

```csharp
private void skipWhileToolStripMenuItem_Click(object sender, EventArgs e)
{
    int[] scores = { 88, 56, 23, 99, 65, 93, 78, 23, 99, 90 };
    foreach (var score in scores.OrderBy(i => i).SkipWhile(s => s < 80))
    {
        txtLog.WriteLine(score);
    }
}
```

The result:

```
88
90
93
99
99
```

Note that if the scores were not sorted, the *Skip* method would not skip over any elements because the first element (88) is greater than 80.

SUM

The *Sum* extension method is an aggregate function that can loop over the source sequence and calculate a total sum based on the lambda expression passed into this method to select the property to be summed. If the sequence is *IEnumerable* of a numeric type, *Sum* can be executed without a lambda expression. The following example code displays the sum of all the scores.

Sample of Visual Basic Code

```vbnet
Private Sub sumToolStripMenuItem_Click(ByVal sender As System.Object, _
        ByVal e As System.EventArgs) Handles sumToolStripMenuItem.Click
    Dim scores = {88, 56, 23, 99, 65, 93, 78, 23, 99, 90}
    txtLog.WriteLine(scores.Sum())
End Sub
```

Sample of C# Code

```csharp
private void sumToolStripMenuItem_Click(object sender, EventArgs e)
{
    int[] scores = { 88, 56, 23, 99, 65, 93, 78, 23, 99, 90 };
    txtLog.WriteLine(scores.Sum());
}
```

The result:

```
714
```

TAKE

The *Take* extension method retrieves a portion of the sequence. You can specify how many elements you want with this method. It is commonly used with the *Skip* method to provide paging ability for data being displayed in the GUI. If you try to take more elements than are available, the *Take* method gracefully returns whatever it can without throwing an exception. The following code sample starts with a collection of integers called *scores*, sorts the collection, skips three elements, and then takes two elements.

Sample of Visual Basic Code

```
Private Sub takeToolStripMenuItem_Click(ByVal sender As System.Object, _
        ByVal e As System.EventArgs) Handles takeToolStripMenuItem.Click
    Dim scores = {88, 56, 23, 99, 65, 93, 78, 23, 99, 90}
    For Each item In scores.OrderBy(Function(i) i).Skip(3).Take(2)
        txtLog.WriteLine(item)
    Next
End Sub
```

Sample of C# Code

```
private void takeToolStripMenuItem_Click(object sender, EventArgs e)
{
    int[] scores = { 88, 56, 23, 99, 65, 93, 78, 23, 99, 90 };
    foreach (var item in scores.OrderBy(i => i).Skip(3).Take(2))
    {
        txtLog.WriteLine(item);
    }
}
```

The results:

65
78

TAKEWHILE

Just as the *SkipWhile* extension method enables you to skip while the provided predicate returns *true*, the *TakeWhile* extension method enables you to retrieve elements from your sequence as long as the provided predicate returns *true*.

Sample of Visual Basic Code

```
Private Sub takeWhileToolStripMenuItem_Click(ByVal sender As System.Object, _
        ByVal e As System.EventArgs) Handles takeWhileToolStripMenuItem.Click
    Dim scores = {88, 56, 23, 99, 65, 93, 78, 23, 99, 90}
    For Each item In scores.OrderBy(Function(i) i).TakeWhile(Function(s) s < 80)
        txtLog.WriteLine(item)
    Next
End Sub
```

Sample of C# Code

```
private void takeWhileToolStripMenuItem_Click(object sender, EventArgs e)
{
    int[] scores = { 88, 56, 23, 99, 65, 93, 78, 23, 99, 90 };
```

```
        foreach (var item in scores.OrderBy(i => i).TakeWhile(s => s < 80))
        {
            txtLog.WriteLine(item);
        }
    }
```

The result:

23
23
56
65
78

TOARRAY

The *ToArray* extension method executes the deferred query and converts the result to a con-crete array of the original sequence item's type. The following code creates a query to retrieve the even scores and converts the deferred query to an array of integers called *evenScores*. The third score is changed to two (even) and, when the even scores are displayed, the two is not in the array.

Sample of Visual Basic Code

```
Private Sub toArrayToolStripMenuItem_Click(ByVal sender As System.Object, _
        ByVal e As System.EventArgs) Handles toArrayToolStripMenuItem.Click
    Dim scores = {88, 56, 23, 99, 65, 93, 78, 23, 99, 90}
    Dim evenScores = scores.Where(Function(s) s Mod 2 = 0).ToArray()
    scores(2) = 2
    For Each item In evenScores
        txtLog.WriteLine(item)
    Next
End Sub
```

Sample of C# Code

```
private void toArrayToolStripMenuItem_Click(object sender, EventArgs e)
{
    int[] scores = { 88, 56, 23, 99, 65, 93, 78, 23, 99, 90 };
    var evenScores = scores.Where(s => s % 2 == 0).ToArray();
    scores[2] = 2;
    foreach (var item in evenScores)
    {
        txtLog.WriteLine(item);
    }
}
```

The result:

88
56
78
90

TODICTIONARY

The *ToDictionary* extension method executes the deferred query and converts the result to a dictionary with a key type inferred from the return type of the lambda passed as a parameter. The item associated with a dictionary entry is the value from the enumeration that computes the key.

The following code creates a query to retrieve the cars and converts them to a dictionary of cars with the *string* VIN used as the lookup key and assigns the dictionary to a *carsByVin* variable. The car with a VIN of HIJ123 is retrieved and displayed.

Sample of Visual Basic Code

```
Private Sub toDictionaryToolStripMenuItem_Click(ByVal sender As System.Object, _
        ByVal e As System.EventArgs) Handles toDictionaryToolStripMenuItem.Click
    Dim cars = GetCars()
    Dim carsByVin = cars.ToDictionary(Function(c) c.VIN)
    Dim myCar = carsByVin("HIJ123")
    txtLog.WriteLine("Car VIN:{0}, Make:{1}, Model:{2} Year:{3}", _
        myCar.VIN, myCar.Make, myCar.Model, myCar.Year)
End Sub
```

Sample of C# Code

```
private void toDictionaryToolStripMenuItem_Click(object sender, EventArgs e)
{
    var cars = GetCars();
    var carsByVin = cars.ToDictionary(c=>c.VIN);
    Car myCar = carsByVin["HIJ123"];
    txtLog.WriteLine("Car VIN:{0}, Make:{1}, Model:{2} Year:{3}",
        myCar.VIN, myCar.Make, myCar.Model, myCar.Year);
}
```

The result:

```
Car VIN:HIJ123, Make:VW, Model:Bug Year:1956
```

TOLIST

The *ToList* extension method executes the deferred query and stores each item in a *List<T>* where *T* is the same type as the original sequence. The following code creates a query to retrieve the even scores and converts the deferred query to a list of integers called *evenScores*. The third score is changed to two (even) and, when the even scores are displayed, the two is not in the list.

Sample of Visual Basic Code

```
Private Sub toListToolStripMenuItem_Click(ByVal sender As System.Object, _
        ByVal e As System.EventArgs) Handles toListToolStripMenuItem.Click
    Dim scores = {88, 56, 23, 99, 65, 93, 78, 23, 99, 90}
    Dim evenScores = scores.Where(Function(s) s Mod 2 = 0).ToList()
    scores(2) = 2
    For Each item In evenScores
        txtLog.WriteLine(item)
    Next
End Sub
```

Sample of C# Code

```csharp
private void toListToolStripMenuItem_Click(object sender, EventArgs e)
{
    int[] scores = { 88, 56, 23, 99, 65, 93, 78, 23, 99, 90 };
    var evenScores = scores.Where(s => s % 2 == 0).ToList();
    scores[2] = 2;
    foreach (var item in evenScores)
    {
        txtLog.WriteLine(item);
    }
}
```

The result:

```
88
56
78
90
```

TOLOOKUP

The *ToLookup* extension method returns *ILookup<TKey, TElement>*—that is, a sequence of *IGrouping<TKey, TElement>* objects. This interface specifies that the grouping object exposes a *Key* property that represents the grouping value. This method creates a new collection object, thus providing a frozen view. Changing the original source collection will not affect this collection. The following code sample groups cars by the *Make* property. After *ToLookup* is called, the original collection is cleared, but it has no impact on the collection produced by the *ToLookup* method.

Sample of Visual Basic Code

```vb
Private Sub toLookupToolStripMenuItem_Click(ByVal sender As System.Object, _
        ByVal e As System.EventArgs) Handles toLookupToolStripMenuItem.Click
    Dim cars = GetCars()
    Dim query = cars.ToLookup(Function(c) c.Make)
    cars.Clear()
    For Each group As IGrouping(Of String, Car) In query
        txtLog.WriteLine("Key:{0}", group.Key)
        For Each c In group
            txtLog.WriteLine("Car VIN:{0} Make:{1}", c.VIN, c.Make)
        Next
    Next
End Sub
```

Sample of C# Code

```csharp
private void toLookupToolStripMenuItem_Click(object sender, EventArgs e)
{
    var cars = GetCars();
    var query = cars.ToLookup(c => c.Make);
    cars.Clear();
    foreach (IGrouping<string, Car> group in query)
    {
        txtLog.WriteLine("Key:{0}", group.Key);
        foreach (Car c in group)
```

```
        {
            txtLog.WriteLine("Car VIN:{0} Make:{1}", c.VIN, c.Make);
        }
    }
}
```

The result:

```
Key:Ford
Car VIN:ABC123 Make:Ford
Car VIN:DEF456 Make:Ford
Key:BMW
Car VIN:DEF123 Make:BMW
Key:Audi
Car VIN:ABC456 Make:Audi
Key:VW
Car VIN:HIJ123 Make:VW
```

Because there are two Fords, they are grouped together. The *GroupBy* extension method provides the same result except that *GroupBy* is a deferred query, and *ToLookup* executes the query immediately to return a frozen sequence that won't change even if the original sequence is updated.

UNION

Sometimes, you want to combine two collections and work with the result. Be careful; this might not be the correct solution. You might want to use the *Concat* extension method, which fulfills the requirements of this scenario. The *Union* extension method combines the elements from two sequences but outputs the distinct elements. That is, it filters out duplicates. This is equivalent to executing *Concat* and then *Distinct*. The following code example combines two integer arrays by using the *Union* method and then sorts the result.

Sample of Visual Basic Code

```
Private Sub unionToolStripMenuItem_Click(ByVal sender As System.Object, _
        ByVal e As System.EventArgs) Handles unionToolStripMenuItem.Click
    Dim lastYearScores = {88, 56, 23, 99, 65, 56}
    Dim thisYearScores = {93, 78, 23, 99, 90, 99}
    Dim allScores = lastYearScores.Union(thisYearScores)
    For Each item In allScores.OrderBy(Function(s) s)
        txtLog.WriteLine(item)
    Next
End Sub
```

Sample of C# Code

```
private void unionToolStripMenuItem_Click(object sender, EventArgs e)
{
    int[] lastYearScores = { 88, 56, 23, 99, 65, 56 };
    int[] thisYearScores = { 93, 78, 23, 99, 90, 99 };
    var allScores = lastYearScores.Union(thisYearScores);
    foreach (var item in allScores.OrderBy(s=>s))
    {
        txtLog.WriteLine(item);
    }
}
```

The result:

```
23
56
65
78
88
90
93
99
```

WHERE

The *Where* extension method enables you to filter a source sequence. This method accepts a predicate lambda expression. When working with relational databases, this extension method typically translates to a SQL WHERE clause. The following sample code demonstrates the use of the *Where* method with a sequence of cars that are filtered on *Make* being equal to *Ford*.

Sample of Visual Basic Code

```vb
Private Sub whereToolStripMenuItem_Click(ByVal sender As System.Object, _
        ByVal e As System.EventArgs) Handles whereToolStripMenuItem.Click
    Dim cars = GetCars()
    For Each myCar In cars.Where(Function(c) c.Make = "Ford")
        txtLog.WriteLine("Car VIN:{0}, Make:{1}, Model:{2} Year:{3}", _
            myCar.VIN, myCar.Make, myCar.Model, myCar.Year)
    Next
End Sub
```

Sample of C# Code

```csharp
private void whereToolStripMenuItem_Click(object sender, EventArgs e)
{
    var cars = GetCars();
    foreach (var myCar in cars.Where(c => c.Make == "Ford"))
    {
        txtLog.WriteLine("Car VIN:{0}, Make:{1}, Model:{2} Year:{3}",
            myCar.VIN, myCar.Make, myCar.Model, myCar.Year);
    }
}
```

The result:

```
Car VIN:ABC123, Make:Ford, Model:F-250 Year:2000
Car VIN:DEF456, Make:Ford, Model:F-150 Year:1998
```

ZIP

The *Zip* extension method merges two sequences. This is neither *Union* nor *Concat* because the resulting element count is equal to the minimum count of the two sequences. Element 1 of sequence 1 is mated to element 1 of sequence 2, and you provide a lambda expression to define which kind of output to create based on this mating. Element 2 of sequence 1 is then mated to element 2 of sequence 2 and so on until one of the sequences runs out of elements.

The following sample code starts with a number sequence, using a starting value of *1* and an ending value of *1000*. The second sequence is a collection of *Car* objects. The *Zip* extension method produces an output collection of anonymous objects that contain the index number and the car.

Sample of Visual Basic Code

```vb
Private Sub zipToolStripMenuItem_Click(ByVal sender As System.Object, _
        ByVal e As System.EventArgs) Handles zipToolStripMenuItem.Click
    Dim numbers = Enumerable.Range(1, 1000)
    Dim cars = GetCars()
    Dim zip = numbers.Zip(cars, _
            Function(i, c) New With {.Number = i, .CarMake = c.Make})
    For Each item In zip
        txtLog.WriteLine("Number:{0} CarMake:{1}", item.Number, item.CarMake)
    Next
End Sub
```

Sample of C# Code

```csharp
private void zipToolStripMenuItem_Click(object sender, EventArgs e)
{
    var numbers = Enumerable.Range(1, 1000);
    var cars = GetCars();
    var zip = numbers.Zip(cars, (i, c) => new {
                Number = i, CarMake = c.Make });
    foreach (var item in zip)
    {
        txtLog.WriteLine("Number:{0} CarMake:{1}", item.Number, item.CarMake);
    }
}
```

The result:

```
Number:1 CarMake:Ford
Number:2 CarMake:BMW
Number:3 CarMake:Audi
Number:4 CarMake:VW
Number:5 CarMake:Ford
```

The ending range of *1000* on the first sequence was somewhat arbitrary but is noticeably higher than the quantity of *Car* objects in the second sequence. When the second sequence ran out of elements, the *Zip* method stopped producing output. If the ending range of the first sequence was set to 3, only three elements would be output because the first sequence would run out of elements.

PRACTICE **Working with LINQ-Enabling Features**

In this practice, you create a simple Vehicle Web application with a vehicles collection that is a generic list of *Vehicle*. This list will be populated with some vehicles to use object initializers, collection initializers, implicitly typed local variables, query extension methods, lambda expressions, and anonymous types.

This practice is intended to focus on the features that have been defined in this lesson, so the GUI will be minimal.

If you encounter a problem completing an exercise, the completed projects can be installed from the Code folder on the companion CD.

EXERCISE   Create a Web Application with a GUI

In this exercise, you create a Web Application project and add controls to the main Web form to create the graphical user interface.

1. In Visual Studio .NET 2010, choose File | New | Project.

2. Select your desired programming language and then select the ASP.NET Web Application template. For the project name, enter **VehicleProject**. Be sure to select a desired location for this project.

3. For the solution name, enter **VehicleSolution**. Be sure Create Directory For Solution is selected and then click OK.

   After Visual Studio .NET creates the project, the home page, Default.aspx, will be displayed.

> **NOTE**   **MISSING THE PROMPT FOR THE LOCATION**
>
> If you don't see a prompt for the location, it's because your Visual Studio .NET settings, set up to enable you to abort the project, automatically remove all files from your hard drive. To select a location, simply choose File | Save All after the project has been created. To change this setting, choose Tools | Options | Projects And Solutions | Save New Projects When Created. When this option is selected, you are prompted for a location when you create the project.

   There are two content tags, one called *HeaderContent* and one called *BodyContent*. The *BodyContent* tag currently has default markup to display a welcome message and help link.

4. If you haven't seen this Web Application template before, choose Debug | Start Debugging to build and run this Web application so that you can see the default template. After running the application, go back to the Default.aspx markup.

5. Delete the markup that's in the *BodyContent* tag.

6. Populate the *BodyContent* tag with the following markup, which will display filter and sort criteria and provide an execute button and a grid to display vehicles.

   ASPX Markup

   ```
   <asp:Content ID="BodyContent" runat="server" ContentPlaceHolderID="MainContent">
       <asp:Label ID="lblVin" runat="server" Width="100px" Text="VIN: "></asp:Label>
       <asp:TextBox ID="txtVin" runat="server"></asp:TextBox>
       <br />
       <asp:Label ID="lblMake" runat="server" Width="100px" Text="Make: "></
   ```

```
asp:Label>
    <asp:TextBox ID="txtMake" runat="server"></asp:TextBox>
    <br />
    <asp:Label ID="lblModel" runat="server" Width="100px" Text="Model: "></
asp:Label>
    <asp:TextBox ID="txtModel" runat="server"></asp:TextBox>
    <br />
    <asp:Label ID="lblYear" runat="server" Width="100px" Text="Year: "></
asp:Label>
    <asp:DropDownList ID="ddlYear" runat="server">
        <asp:ListItem Text="All Years" Value="0" />
        <asp:ListItem Text="> 1995" Value="1995" />
        <asp:ListItem Text="> 2000" Value="2000" />
        <asp:ListItem Text="> 2005" Value="2005" />
    </asp:DropDownList>
    <br />
    <asp:Label ID="lblCost" runat="server" Width="100px" Text="Cost: "></
asp:Label>
    <asp:DropDownList ID="ddlCost" runat="server">
        <asp:ListItem Text="Any Cost" Value="0" />
        <asp:ListItem Text="> 5000" Value="5000" />
        <asp:ListItem Text="> 20000" Value="20000" />
    </asp:DropDownList>
    <br />
    <asp:Label ID="lblSort" runat="server" Width="100px" Text="Sort Order: "></
asp:Label>
    <asp:DropDownList ID="ddlSort" runat="server">
        <asp:ListItem Text="" />
        <asp:ListItem Text="VIN" />
        <asp:ListItem Text="Make" />
        <asp:ListItem Text="Model" />
        <asp:ListItem Text="Year" />
        <asp:ListItem Text="Cost" />
    </asp:DropDownList>
    <br />
    <br />
    <asp:Button ID="btnExecute" runat="server" Text="Execute" />
    <br />
    <asp:GridView ID="gvVehicles" runat="server">
    </asp:GridView>
</asp:Content>
```

If you click the Design tab (bottom left), you should see the rendered screen as shown in Figure 3-5.

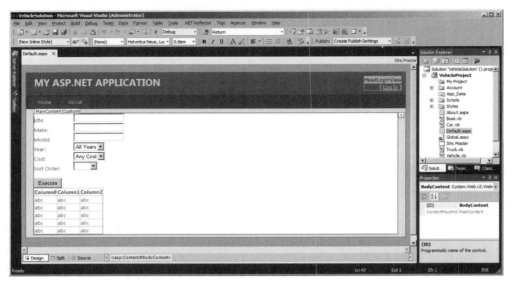

FIGURE 3-5 This is the rendered screen showing filter and sort settings.

7. Right-click the Design or Markup window and click View Code. This takes you to the code-behind page. There is already a *Page_Load* event handler method.

8. Before adding code to the *Page_Load* method, you must add some classes to the project. In Solution Explorer, right-click the VehicleProject icon, click Add, and then click Class. Name the class **Vehicle** and click Add. Add the following code to this class.

Sample of Visual Basic Code

```vb
Public Class Vehicle
    Public Property VIN As String
    Public Property Make As String
    Public Property Model As String
    Public Property Year As Integer
    Public Property Cost As Decimal
End Class
```

Sample of C# Code

```csharp
public class Vehicle
{
    public string VIN { get; set; }
    public string Make { get; set; }
    public string Model { get; set; }
    public int Year { get; set; }
    public decimal Cost { get; set; }
}
```

9. Add another class, named **Car**, that inherits from *Vehicle*, as shown in the following code sample:

Sample of Visual Basic Code

```
Public Class Car
    Inherits Vehicle
End Class
```

Sample of C# Code

```
public class Car : Vehicle
{
}
```

10. Add another class, named **Truck**, that inherits from *Vehicle,* as shown in the following code sample:

Sample of Visual Basic Code

```
Public Class Truck
    Inherits Vehicle
End Class
```

Sample of C# Code

```
public class Truck : Vehicle
{
}
```

11. Add another class, named **Boat**, that inherits from *Vehicle*, as shown in the following code sample:

Sample of Visual Basic Code

```
Public Class Boat
    Inherits Vehicle
End Class
```

Sample of C# Code

```
public class Boat : Vehicle
{
}
```

12. Above *Page_Load* (at the class level), add code to declare a variable called **vehicles** and instantiate it as a new **List Of Vehicles**. Your code should look like the following sample.

Sample of Visual Basic Code

```
Private Shared Vehicles As New List(Of Vehicle)
```

Sample of C# Code

```
private List<Vehicle> vehicles = new List<Vehicle>();
```

13. In the *Page_Load* method, add code to create a generic list of *Vehicle*. Populate the list with ten vehicles, which will give you something with which to experiment in this practice. The *Page_Load* method should look like the following example:

Sample of Visual Basic Code

```
Protected Sub Page_Load(ByVal sender As Object, _
        ByVal e As System.EventArgs) Handles Me.Load
    If (Vehicles.Count = 0) Then
        Vehicles.Add(New Truck With {.VIN = "AAA123", .Make = "Ford", _
                        .Model = "F-250", .Cost = 2000, .Year = 1998})
        Vehicles.Add(New Truck With {.VIN = "ZZZ123", .Make = "Ford", _
                        .Model = "F-150", .Cost = 10000, .Year = 2005})
        Vehicles.Add(New Car With {.VIN = "FFF123", .Make = "VW", _
                        .Model = "Bug", .Cost = 2500, .Year = 1997})
        Vehicles.Add(New Boat With {.VIN = "LLL123", .Make = "SeaRay", _
                        .Model = "Signature", .Cost = 12000, .Year = 1995})
        Vehicles.Add(New Car With {.VIN = "CCC123", .Make = "BMW", _
                        .Model = "Z-3", .Cost = 21000, .Year = 2005})
        Vehicles.Add(New Car With {.VIN = "EEE123", .Make = "Ford", _
                        .Model = "Focus", .Cost = 15000, .Year = 2008})
        Vehicles.Add(New Boat With {.VIN = "QQQ123", .Make = "ChrisCraft", _
                        .Model = "BowRider", .Cost = 102000, .Year = 1945})
        Vehicles.Add(New Truck With {.VIN = "PPP123", .Make = "Ford", _
                        .Model = "F-250", .Cost = 1000, .Year = 1980})
        Vehicles.Add(New Car With {.VIN = "TTT123", .Make = "Dodge", _
                        .Model = "Viper", .Cost = 95000, .Year = 2007})
        Vehicles.Add(New Car With {.VIN = "DDD123", .Make = "Mazda", _
                        .Model = "Miata", .Cost = 20000, .Year = 2005})
    End If
End Sub
```

Sample of C# Code

```
protected void Page_Load(object sender, EventArgs e)
{
    if (vehicles.Count == 0)
    {
        vehicles.Add(new Truck  {VIN = "AAA123", Make = "Ford",
                        Model = "F-250", Cost = 2000, Year = 1998});
        vehicles.Add(new Truck  {VIN = "ZZZ123", Make = "Ford",
                        Model = "F-150", Cost = 10000, Year = 2005});
        vehicles.Add(new Car  {VIN = "FFF123", Make = "VW",
                        Model = "Bug", Cost = 2500, Year = 1997});
        vehicles.Add(new Boat  {VIN = "LLL123", Make = "SeaRay",
                        Model = "Signature", Cost = 12000, Year = 1995});
        vehicles.Add(new Car  {VIN = "CCC123", Make = "BMW",
                        Model = "Z-3", Cost = 21000, Year = 2005});
        vehicles.Add(new Car  {VIN = "EEE123", Make = "Ford",
                        Model = "Focus", Cost = 15000, Year = 2008});
        vehicles.Add(new Boat  {VIN = "QQQ123", Make = "ChrisCraft",
                        Model = "BowRider", Cost = 102000, Year = 1945});
        vehicles.Add(new Truck  {VIN = "PPP123", Make = "Ford",
                        Model = "F-250", Cost = 1000, Year = 1980});
        vehicles.Add(new Car  {VIN = "TTT123", Make = "Dodge",
                        Model = "Viper", Cost = 95000, Year = 2007});
```

```
        vehicles.Add(new Car  {VIN = "DDD123", Make = "Mazda",
                     Model = "Miata", Cost = 20000, Year = 2005});
    }
}
```

14. Under the code you just added into the *Page_Load* method, insert code to filter the list of vehicles based on the data input. Use *method chaining* to create one statement that puts together all the filtering, as shown in the following code sample:

Sample of Visual Basic Code

```
Dim result = Vehicles _
        .Where(Function(v) v.VIN.StartsWith(txtVin.Text)) _
        .Where(Function(v) v.Make.StartsWith(txtMake.Text)) _
        .Where(Function(v) v.Model.StartsWith(txtModel.Text)) _
        .Where(Function(v) v.Cost > Decimal.Parse(ddlCost.SelectedValue)) _
        .Where(Function(v) v.Year > Integer.Parse(ddlYear.SelectedValue))
```

Sample of C# Code

```
var result = vehicles
    .Where(v => v.VIN.StartsWith(txtVin.Text))
    .Where(v => v.Make.StartsWith(txtMake.Text))
    .Where(v => v.Model.StartsWith(txtModel.Text))
    .Where(v => v.Cost > Decimal.Parse(ddlCost.SelectedValue))
    .Where(v => v.Year > int.Parse(ddlYear.SelectedValue));
```

15. Under the code you just added into the *Page_Load* method, add code to perform a sort of the results. This code calls a *SetOrder* method that will be created in the next step. You code should look like the following:

Sample of Visual Basic Code

```
result = SetOrder(ddlSort.SelectedValue, result)
```

Sample of C# Code

```
result = SetOrder(ddlSort.SelectedValue, result);
```

16. Add the *SetOrder* method, which has code to add an *OrderBy* query extension method based on the selection passed into this method. Your code should look like the following:

Sample of Visual Basic Code

```
Private Function SetOrder(ByVal order As String, _
        ByVal query As IEnumerable(Of Vehicle)) As IEnumerable(Of Vehicle)
    Select Case order
        Case "VIN"
            Return query.OrderBy(Function(v) v.VIN)
        Case "Make"
            Return query.OrderBy(Function(v) v.Make)
        Case "Model"
            Return query.OrderBy(Function(v) v.Model)
        Case "Year"
            Return query.OrderBy(Function(v) v.Year)
        Case "Cost"
            Return query.OrderBy(Function(v) v.Cost)
```

```
        Case Else
            Return query
    End Select
End Function
```

Sample of C# Code
```csharp
private IEnumerable<Vehicle> SetOrder(string order,
        IEnumerable<Vehicle> query)
{
    switch (order)
    {
        case "VIN":
            return query.OrderBy(v => v.VIN);
        case "Make":
            return query.OrderBy(v => v.Make);
        case "Model":
            return query.OrderBy(v => v.Model);
        case "Year":
            return query.OrderBy(v => v.Year);
        case "Cost":
            return query.OrderBy(v => v.Cost);
        default:
            return query;
    }
}
```

17. Finally, add code into the bottom of the *Page_Load* method to select an anonymous type that includes an index and all the properties in the *Vehicle* class and bind the result to *gvVehicles*. You code should look like the following example:

Sample of Visual Basic Code
```vbnet
gvVehicles.DataSource = result.Select(Function(v, i) New With
    {.Index = i, v.VIN, v.Make, v.Model, v.Year, v.Cost})
gvVehicles.DataBind()
```

Sample of C# Code
```csharp
gvVehicles.DataSource = result.Select((v, i)=> new
    {Index = i, v.VIN, v.Make, v.Model, v.Year, v.Cost});
gvVehicles.DataBind();
```

18. Choose Build | Build Solution to build the application. If you have errors, you can double-click the error to go to the error line and correct.

19. Choose Debug | Start Debugging to run the application. When the application starts, you should see a Web page with your GUI controls that enables you to specify filter and sort criteria. If you type the letter **F** into the Make text box and click Execute, the grid will be populated only with items that begin with F. If you set the sort order and click the Execute button again, you will see the sorted results.

Lesson Summary

This lesson provided detailed information about the features that comprise LINQ.

- Object initializers enable you to initialize public properties and fields without creating an explicit constructor.

- Implicitly typed local variables enable you to declare a variable without specifying its type, and the compiler will infer the type for you.

- In many cases, using implicitly typed local variables is an option, but, when working with anonymous types, it's a requirement.

- Anonymous types enable you to create a type inline. This enables you to group data without creating a class.

- Lambda expressions provide a much more abbreviated syntax than a method or anonymous method and can be used wherever a delegate is expected.

- Extension methods enable you to add methods to a type even when you don't have the source code for the type.

- Extension methods enable you to create concrete methods on interfaces; that is, all types that implement the interface will get these methods.

- Query extension methods are extension methods primarily implemented on the generic *IEnumerable* interface.

- The *Enumerable* class contains the query extension methods and static methods called *Empty*, *Range*, and *Repeat*.

Lesson Review

You can use the following questions to test your knowledge of the information in Lesson 1, "Understanding LINQ." The questions are also available on the companion CD if you prefer to review them in electronic form.

> **NOTE ANSWERS**
>
> Answers to these questions and explanations of why each answer choice is correct or incorrect are located in the "Answers" section at the end of the book.

1. To which of the following types can you add an extension method? (Each correct answer presents a complete solution. Choose five.)

    A. *Class*

    B. *Structure* (C# struct)

    C. *Module* (C# static class)

    D. *Enum*

    E. *Interface*

    F. *Delegate*

2. You want to page through an element sequence, displaying ten elements at a time, until you reach the end of the sequence. Which query extension method can you use to accomplish this? (Each correct answer presents part of a complete solution. Choose two.)

   A. *Skip*

   B. *Except*

   C. *SelectMany*

   D. *Take*

3. You have executed the *Where* query extension method on your collection, and it returned *IEnumerable* of *Car*, but you want to assign this to a variable whose type is *List Of Car*. How can you convert the *IEnumerable* of *Car* to *List Of Car*?

   A. Use *CType* (*C# cast*).

   B. It can't be done.

   C. Use the *ToList*() query extension method.

   D. Just make the assignment.

Lesson 2: Using LINQ Queries

The previous sections covered object initializers, implicitly typed local variables, anonymous types, lambda expressions, and extension methods. These features were created to support the implementation of LINQ. Now that you've seen all these, look at how LINQ is *language integrated*.

> **After this lesson, you will be able to:**
> - Identify the LINQ keywords.
> - Create a LINQ query that provides filtering.
> - Create a LINQ query that provides sorted results.
> - Create a LINQ query to perform an inner join on two element sequences.
> - Create a LINQ query to perform an outer join on two element sequences.
> - Implement grouping and aggregation in a LINQ query.
> - Create a LINQ query that defines addition loop variables using the *let* keyword.
> - Create a LINQ query that implements paging.
>
> **Estimated lesson time: 60 minutes**

Syntax-Based and Method-Based Queries

For basic queries, using LINQ in Visual Basic or C# is very easy and intuitive because both languages provide keywords that map directly to features that have been added through extension methods. The benefit is that you can write typed queries in a very SQL-like way, getting IntelliSense support all along the way.

In the following scenario, your schedule contains a list of days when you are busy, and you want to find out whether you are busy on a specific day. The following code demonstrates the implementation of a LINQ query to discover this.

Sample of Visual Basic Code

```
Private Function GetDates() As List(Of DateTime)
    Return New List(Of DateTime) From
                        {
                            New DateTime(11, 1, 1),
                            New DateTime(11, 2, 5),
                            New DateTime(11, 3, 3),
                            New DateTime(11, 1, 3),
                            New DateTime(11, 1, 2),
                            New DateTime(11, 5, 4),
                            New DateTime(11, 2, 2),
                            New DateTime(11, 7, 5),
                            New DateTime(11, 6, 30),
                            New DateTime(11, 10, 14),
                            New DateTime(11, 11, 22),
```

```
                    New DateTime(11, 12, 1),
                    New DateTime(11, 5, 22),
                    New DateTime(11, 6, 7),
                    New DateTime(11, 1, 4)
                 }
End Function
Private Sub BasicQueriesToolStripMenuItem_Click( _
        ByVal sender As System.Object, _
        ByVal e As System.EventArgs) _
        Handles BasicQueriesToolStripMenuItem.Click

    Dim schedule = GetDates()
    Dim areYouAvailable = new DateTime(11, 7, 10)

    Dim busy = From d In schedule
               Where d = areYouAvailable
               Select d

    For Each busyDate In busy
        txtLog.WriteLine("Sorry, but I am busy on {0:MM/dd/yy}", busyDate)
    Next
End Sub
```

Sample of C# Code

```
private List<DateTime> GetDates()
{
    return new List<DateTime>
                {
                  new DateTime(11, 1, 1),
                  new DateTime(11, 2, 5),
                  new DateTime(11, 3, 3),
                  new DateTime(11, 1, 3),
                  new DateTime(11, 1, 2),
                  new DateTime(11, 5, 4),
                  new DateTime(11, 2, 2),
                  new DateTime(11, 7, 5),
                  new DateTime(11, 6, 30),
                  new DateTime(11, 10, 14),
                  new DateTime(11, 11, 22),
                  new DateTime(11, 12, 1),
                  new DateTime(11, 5, 22),
                  new DateTime(11, 6, 7),
                  new DateTime(11, 1, 4)
                };
}
private void basicLINQToolStripMenuItem_Click(object sender, EventArgs e)
{
    var schedule = GetDates();
    var areYouAvailable = new DateTime(11,7, 5);

    var busy = from d in schedule
               where d == areYouAvailable
               select d;

    foreach(var busyDate in busy)
```

```
    {
        txtLog.WriteLine("Sorry, but I am busy on {0:MM/dd/yy}", busyDate);
    }
}
```

In the sample code, a LINQ query filtered the data, which returned an *IEnumerable<DateTime>* object as the result. Is there a simpler way to perform this query? You could argue that using the *Where* extension method would save some coding and would be simpler, as shown in this method-based code sample:

Sample of Visual Basic Code

```
Private Sub MethodbasedQueryToolStripMenuItem_Click( _
        ByVal sender As System.Object, _
        ByVal e As System.EventArgs) _
        Handles MethodbasedQueryToolStripMenuItem.Click

    Dim schedule = GetDates()
    Dim areYouAvailable = New DateTime(11,7,5)

    For Each busyDate In schedule.Where(Function(d) d = areYouAvailable)
        txtLog.WriteLine("Sorry, but I am busy on {0:MM/dd/yy}", busyDate)
    Next
End Sub
```

Sample of C# Code

```
private void methodbasedQueryToolStripMenuItem_Click(object sender, EventArgs e)
{
    var schedule = GetDates();
    var areYouAvailable = new DateTime(11,7,5);

    foreach (var busyDate in schedule.Where(d=>d==areYouAvailable))
    {
        txtLog.WriteLine("Sorry, but I am busy on {0:MM/dd/yy}", busyDate);
    }
}
```

This example eliminates the LINQ query and adds the *Where* extension method in the loop. This code block is smaller and more concise, but which is more readable? Decide for yourself. For a small query such as this, the extension method might be fine, but for larger queries, you probably will find it better to use the LINQ query. Performance is the same because both queries do the same thing.

Only a small subset of the query extension methods map to language keywords, so typically you will find yourself mixing LINQ queries with extension methods, as shown in the following rewrite of the previous examples:

Sample of Visual Basic Code

```
Private Sub MixingLINQAndMethodsToolStripMenuItem_Click( _
        ByVal sender As System.Object, _
        ByVal e As System.EventArgs) _
        Handles MixingLINQAndMethodsToolStripMenuItem.Click
    Dim schedule = GetDates()
```

```
        Dim areYouAvailable = New DateTime(11, 7, 5)

    Dim count = (From d In schedule
                Where d = areYouAvailable
                Select d).Count()

    If count > 0 Then
      txtLog.WriteLine("Sorry, but I am busy on {0:MM/dd/yy}", areYouAvailable)
    Else
      txtLog.WriteLine("Yay! I am available on {0:MM/dd/yy}", areYouAvailable)
    End If
End Sub
```

Sample of C# Code

```
private void mixingLINQAndMethodsToolStripMenuItem_Click(
    object sender, EventArgs e)
{
    var schedule = GetDates();
    var areYouAvailable = new DateTime(11, 7, 5);

    var count = (from d in schedule
                where d == areYouAvailable
                select d).Count();
    if (count > 0)
        txtLog.WriteLine("Sorry, but I am busy on {0:MM/dd/yy}",
            areYouAvailable);
    else
        txtLog.WriteLine("Yay! I am available on {0:MM/dd/yy}",
            areYouAvailable);
}
```

In the previous example, the *Count* extension method eliminates the *foreach* loop. In this example, an *if/then/else* statement is added to show availability. Also, parentheses are added to place the call to the *Count* method after the *select* clause.

LINQ Keywords

The LINQ-provided keywords can make your LINQ queries look clean and simple. Table 3-1 provides the list of available keywords, with a short description of each. Many of these keywords are covered in more detail in this section.

TABLE 3-1 Visual Basic and C# LINQ Keywords

KEYWORD	DESCRIPTION
from	Specifies a data source and a range variable
where	Filters source elements based on one or more Boolean expressions
select	Specifies the type and shape the elements in the returned sequence have when the query is executed

group	Groups query results according to a specified key value
into	Provides an identifier that can serve as a reference to the results of a *join*, *group*, or *select* clause
orderby (Visual Basic: *Order By*)	Sorts query results in ascending or descending order
join	Joins two data sources based on an equality comparison between two specified matching criteria
let	Introduces a range variable to store subexpression results in a query expression
in	Contextual keyword in a *from* or *join* clause to specify the data source
on	Contextual keyword in a *join* clause to specify the join criteria
equals	Contextual keyword in a *join* clause to join two sources
by	Contextual keyword in a *group* clause to specify the grouping criteria
ascending	Contextual keyword in an *orderby* clause
descending	Contextual keyword in an *orderby* clause

In addition to the keywords listed in Table 3-1, the Visual Basic team provided keywords that C# did not implement. These keywords are shown in Table 3-2 with a short description of each.

TABLE 3-2 Visual Basic Keywords That Are Not Implemented in C#

KEYWORD	DESCRIPTION
Distinct	Filters duplicate elements
Skip/Skip While	Jumps over elements before returning results
Take/Take While	Provides a means to limit how many elements will be retrieved
Aggregate	Includes aggregate functions in your queries
Into	Contextual keyword in the *Aggregate* clause that specifies what to do with the result of the aggregate
All	Contextual keyword in the *Aggregate* clause that determines whether all elements meet the specified criterion
Any	Contextual keyword in the *Aggregate* clause that determines whether any of the elements meet the specified criterion
Average	Contextual keyword in the *Aggregate* clause that calculates the average value

Count	Contextual keyword in the *Aggregate* clause that provides the count of elements that meet the specified criterion
Group	Contextual keyword in the *Aggregate* clause that provides access to the results of a *group by* or *group join* clause
LongCount	Contextual keyword in the *Aggregate* clause that provides the count (*as long*) of elements that meet the specified criterion
Max	Contextual keyword in the *Aggregate* clause that provides the maximum value
Min	Contextual keyword in the *Aggregate* clause that provides the minimum value
Sum	Contextual keyword in the *Aggregate* clause that provides the sum of the elements

All the query extension methods are available in both languages even if there isn't a language keyword mapping to the query extension method.

Projections

Projections enable you to transform the output of your LINQ query by using named or anonymous types. The following code example demonstrates projections in a LINQ query by using anonymous types.

Sample of Visual Basic Code

```vb
Private Sub LINQProjectionsToolStripMenuItem_Click(ByVal sender As System.Object, _
        ByVal e As System.EventArgs) Handles LINQProjectionsToolStripMenuItem.Click

    Dim cars = GetCars()
    Dim vinsAndMakes = From c In cars
        Select New With
                {
                    c.VIN,
                    .CarModel = c.Make
                }
    For Each item In vinsAndMakes
        txtLog.WriteLine("VIN:{0} Make:{1}", item.VIN, item.CarModel)
    Next
End Sub
```

Sample of C# Code

```csharp
private void lINQProjectionsToolStripMenuItem_Click(object sender, EventArgs e)
{
    var cars = GetCars();
    var vinsAndMakes = from c in cars
                       select new { c.VIN, CarModel = c.Model };
    foreach (var item in vinsAndMakes)
    {
        txtLog.WriteLine("VIN:{0} Make:{1}", item.VIN, item.CarModel);
```

```
        }
}
```

Using the *Let* Keyword to Help with Projections

You can use the *let* keyword to create a temporary variable within the LINQ query. Think of the *let* keyword as a variant of the *select* keyword used within the query. The following code sample shows how the *let* keyword can help with filtering and shaping the data.

Sample of Visual Basic Code

```vb
Private Sub LINQLetToolStripMenuItem_Click(ByVal sender As System.Object, _
        ByVal e As System.EventArgs) Handles LINQLetToolStripMenuItem.Click
    Dim cars = GetCars()
    Dim vinsAndMakes = From c In cars
                       Let makeModel = c.Make & " " & c.Model
                       Where makeModel.Contains("B")
                       Select New With
                                {
                                    c.VIN,
                                    .MakeModel = makeModel
                                }
    For Each item In vinsAndMakes
        txtLog.WriteLine("VIN:{0} Make and Model:{1}", item.VIN, item.MakeModel)
    Next
End Sub
```

Sample of C# Code

```csharp
private void lINQLetToolStripMenuItem_Click(object sender, EventArgs e)
{
    var cars = GetCars();
    var vinsAndMakes = from c in cars
                       let makeModel = c.Make + " " + c.Model
                       where makeModel.Contains('B')
                       select new { c.VIN, MakeModel=makeModel };
    foreach (var item in vinsAndMakes)
    {
      txtLog.WriteLine("VIN:{0} Make and Model:{1}", item.VIN, item.MakeModel);
    }
}
```

The result:

```
VIN:DEF123 Make and Model:BMW Z-3
VIN:HIJ123 Make and Model:VW Bug
```

Specifying a Filter

Both C# and Visual Basic have the *where* keyword that maps directly to the *Where* query extension method. You can specify a predicate (an expression that evaluates to a Boolean value) to determine the elements to be returned. The following code sample demonstrates the *where* clause with a *yearRange* variable being used as a parameter into the query.

Sample of Visual Basic Code

```vb
Private Sub LINQWhereToolStripMenuItem_Click(ByVal sender As System.Object, _
        ByVal e As System.EventArgs) Handles LINQWhereToolStripMenuItem.Click
    Dim yearRange = 2000
    Dim cars = GetCars()
    Dim oldCars = From c In cars
                  Where c.Year < yearRange
                  Select c

    For Each myCar In oldCars
        txtLog.WriteLine("Car VIN:{0}, Make:{1}, Model:{2} Year:{3}", _
            myCar.VIN, myCar.Make, myCar.Model, myCar.Year)
    Next
End Sub
```

Sample of C# Code

```csharp
private void lINQWhereToolStripMenuItem_Click(object sender, EventArgs e)
{
    int yearRange = 2000;
    var cars = GetCars();
    var oldCars = from c in cars
                  where c.Year < yearRange
                  select c;
    foreach (var myCar in oldCars)
    {
        txtLog.WriteLine("Car VIN:{0}, Make:{1}, Model:{2} Year:{3}",
            myCar.VIN, myCar.Make, myCar.Model, myCar.Year);
    }
}
```

The result:

```
Car VIN:HIJ123, Make:VW, Model:Bug Year:1956
Car VIN:DEF456, Make:Ford, Model:F-150 Year:1998
```

Specifying a Sort Order

It's very easy to sort using a LINQ query. The *orderby* keyword enables you to sort in ascending or descending order. In addition, you can sort on multiple properties to perform a compound sort. The following code sample shows the sorting of cars by *Make* ascending and then by *Model* descending.

Sample of Visual Basic Code

```vb
Private Sub LINQSortToolStripMenuItem_Click(ByVal sender As System.Object, _
        ByVal e As System.EventArgs) Handles LINQSortToolStripMenuItem.Click
    Dim cars = GetCars()
    Dim sorted = From c In cars
                 Order By c.Make Ascending, c.Model Descending
                 Select c

    For Each myCar In sorted
        txtLog.WriteLine("Car VIN:{0}, Make:{1}, Model:{2} Year:{3}", _
            myCar.VIN, myCar.Make, myCar.Model, myCar.Year)
```

```
    Next
End Sub
```

Sample of C# Code

```csharp
private void lINQSortToolStripMenuItem_Click(object sender, EventArgs e)
{
    var cars = GetCars();
    var sorted = from c in cars
                 orderby c.Make ascending, c.Model descending
                 select c;
    foreach (var myCar in sorted)
    {
        txtLog.WriteLine("Car VIN:{0}, Make:{1}, Model:{2} Year:{3}",
            myCar.VIN, myCar.Make, myCar.Model, myCar.Year);
    }
}
```

The result:

```
Car VIN:ABC456, Make:Audi, Model:TT Year:2008
Car VIN:DEF123, Make:BMW, Model:Z-3 Year:2005
Car VIN:ABC123, Make:Ford, Model:F-250 Year:2000
Car VIN:DEF456, Make:Ford, Model:F-150 Year:1998
Car VIN:HIJ123, Make:VW, Model:Bug Year:1956
```

Paging

The ability to look at data one page at a time is always a requirement when a large amount of data is being retrieved. LINQ simplifies this task with the *Skip* and *Take* extension methods. In addition, Visual Basic offers these query extension methods as keywords.

The following code example retrieves 25 rows of data and then provides paging capabilities to enable paging ten rows at a time.

EXAM TIP

For the exam, be sure that you fully understand how to perform paging.

Sample of Visual Basic Code

```vbnet
Private Sub LINQPagingToolStripMenuItem_Click(ByVal sender As System.Object, _
        ByVal e As System.EventArgs) Handles LINQPagingToolStripMenuItem.Click
    Dim pageSize = 10

    'create 5 copies of the cars - total 25 rows
    Dim cars = Enumerable.Range(1, 5) _
            .SelectMany(Function(i) GetCars() _
                .Select(Function(c) New With _
                    {.BatchNumber = i, c.VIN, c.Make, c.Model, c.Year}))

    'calculate page count
    Dim pageCount = (cars.Count() / pageSize)
    If (pageCount * pageSize < cars.Count()) Then pageCount += 1
```

```
        For i = 0 To pageCount
            txtLog.WriteLine("-----Printing Page {0}------", i)
            'Dim currentPage = cars.Skip(i * pageSize).Take(pageSize)
            Dim currentPage = From c In cars
                              Skip (i * pageSize)
                              Take pageSize
                              Select c
            For Each myCar In currentPage
                txtLog.WriteLine("#{0} Car VIN:{1}, Make:{2}, Model:{3} Year:{4}", _
                  myCar.BatchNumber, myCar.VIN, myCar.Make, myCar.Model, myCar.Year)
            Next
        Next
    Next
End Sub
```

Sample of C# Code

```
private void lINQPagingToolStripMenuItem_Click(object sender, EventArgs e)
{
    int pageSize = 10;

    //create 5 copies of the cars - total 25 rows
    var cars = Enumerable.Range(1,5)
        .SelectMany(i=>GetCars()
            .Select(c=>(new {BatchNumber=i, c.VIN, c.Make, c.Model, c.Year})));

    //calculate page count
    int pageCount = (cars.Count() / pageSize);
    if (pageCount * pageSize < cars.Count()) pageCount++;

    for(int i=0; i < pageCount; i++)
    {
        txtLog.WriteLine("-----Printing Page {0}------", i);
        var currentPage = cars.Skip(i * pageSize).Take(pageSize);

        foreach (var myCar in currentPage)
        {
            txtLog.WriteLine("#{0} Car VIN:{1}, Make:{2}, Model:{3} Year:{4}",
              myCar.BatchNumber, myCar.VIN, myCar.Make, myCar.Model, myCar.Year);
        }
    }
}
```

The result:

```
-----Printing Page 0------
#1 Car VIN:ABC123, Make:Ford, Model:F-250 Year:2000
#1 Car VIN:DEF123, Make:BMW, Model:Z-3 Year:2005
#1 Car VIN:ABC456, Make:Audi, Model:TT Year:2008
#1 Car VIN:HIJ123, Make:VW, Model:Bug Year:1956
#1 Car VIN:DEF456, Make:Ford, Model:F-150 Year:1998
#2 Car VIN:ABC123, Make:Ford, Model:F-250 Year:2000
#2 Car VIN:DEF123, Make:BMW, Model:Z-3 Year:2005
#2 Car VIN:ABC456, Make:Audi, Model:TT Year:2008
#2 Car VIN:HIJ123, Make:VW, Model:Bug Year:1956
#2 Car VIN:DEF456, Make:Ford, Model:F-150 Year:1998
-----Printing Page 1------
```

```
#3 Car VIN:ABC123, Make:Ford, Model:F-250 Year:2000
#3 Car VIN:DEF123, Make:BMW, Model:Z-3 Year:2005
#3 Car VIN:ABC456, Make:Audi, Model:TT Year:2008
#3 Car VIN:HIJ123, Make:VW, Model:Bug Year:1956
#3 Car VIN:DEF456, Make:Ford, Model:F-150 Year:1998
#4 Car VIN:ABC123, Make:Ford, Model:F-250 Year:2000
#4 Car VIN:DEF123, Make:BMW, Model:Z-3 Year:2005
#4 Car VIN:ABC456, Make:Audi, Model:TT Year:2008
#4 Car VIN:HIJ123, Make:VW, Model:Bug Year:1956
#4 Car VIN:DEF456, Make:Ford, Model:F-150 Year:1998
-----Printing Page 2------
#5 Car VIN:ABC123, Make:Ford, Model:F-250 Year:2000
#5 Car VIN:DEF123, Make:BMW, Model:Z-3 Year:2005
#5 Car VIN:ABC456, Make:Audi, Model:TT Year:2008
#5 Car VIN:HIJ123, Make:VW, Model:Bug Year:1956
#5 Car VIN:DEF456, Make:Ford, Model:F-150 Year:1998
```

This code sample starts by defining the page size as 10. Five copies of the cars are then created, which yields 25 cars. The five copies are created by using the *Enumerable* class to generate a range of values, 1 to 5. Each of these values is used with the *SelectMany* query extension method to create a copy of the cars. Calculating the page count is accomplished by dividing the count of the cars by the page size, but if there is a remainder, the page count is incremented. Finally, a *for* loop creates a query for each of the pages and then prints the current page.

In the Visual Basic example, the query for the page was written first to match the C# version, but that code is commented out and the query is rewritten using the Visual Basic *Skip* and *Take* keywords.

Joins

When working with databases, you commonly want to combine data from multiple tables to produce a merged result set. LINQ enables you to join two generic *IEnumerable* element sources, even if these sources are not from a database. There are three types of joins: inner joins, outer joins, and cross joins. Inner joins and outer joins typically match on a foreign key in a child source matching to a unique key in a parent source. This section examines these join types.

Inner Joins

Inner joins produce output only if there is a match between both join sources. In the following code sample, a collection of cars is joined to a collection of repairs, based on the VIN of the car. The resulting output combines some of the car information with some of the repair information.

Sample of Visual Basic Code

```
Public Class Repair
    Public Property VIN() As String
    Public Property Desc() As String
    Public Property Cost As Decimal
```

```
    End Class

    Private Function GetRepairs() As List(Of Repair)
        Return New List(Of Repair) From
        {
          New Repair With {.VIN = "ABC123", .Desc = "Change Oil", .Cost = 29.99},
          New Repair With {.VIN = "DEF123", .Desc = "Rotate Tires", .Cost = 19.99},
          New Repair With {.VIN = "HIJ123", .Desc = "Replace Brakes", .Cost = 200},
          New Repair With {.VIN = "DEF456", .Desc = "Alignment", .Cost = 30},
          New Repair With {.VIN = "ABC123", .Desc = "Fix Flat Tire", .Cost = 15},
          New Repair With {.VIN = "DEF123", .Desc = "Fix Windshield", .Cost = 420},
          New Repair With {.VIN = "ABC123", .Desc = "Replace Wipers", .Cost = 20},
          New Repair With {.VIN = "HIJ123", .Desc = "Replace Tires", .Cost = 1000},
          New Repair With {.VIN = "DEF456", .Desc = "Change Oil", .Cost = 30}
        }
    End Function

    Private Sub LINQInnerJoinToolStripMenuItem_Click( _
            ByVal sender As System.Object, _
            ByVal e As System.EventArgs) _
            Handles LINQInnerJoinToolStripMenuItem.Click
        Dim cars = GetCars()
        Dim repairs = GetRepairs()

        Dim carsWithRepairs = From c In cars
                              Join r In repairs
                              On c.VIN Equals r.VIN
                              Order By c.VIN, r.Cost
                              Select New With
                                  {
                                      c.VIN,
                                      c.Make,
                                      r.Desc,
                                      r.Cost
                                  }

        For Each item In carsWithRepairs
            txtLog.WriteLine("Car VIN:{0}, Make:{1}, Description:{2} Cost:{3:C}",
                item.VIN, item.Make, item.Desc, item.Cost)
        Next
    End Sub
```

Sample of C# Code

```
public class Repair
{
    public string VIN { get; set; }
    public string Desc { get; set; }
    public decimal Cost { get; set; }
}

private List<Repair> GetRepairs()
{
    return new List<Repair>
    {
        new Repair {VIN = "ABC123", Desc = "Change Oil", Cost = 29.99m},
```

```
                new Repair {VIN = "DEF123", Desc = "Rotate Tires",  Cost =19.99m},
                new Repair {VIN = "HIJ123", Desc = "Replace Brakes",  Cost = 200},
                new Repair {VIN = "DEF456", Desc = "Alignment", Cost = 30},
                new Repair {VIN = "ABC123", Desc = "Fix Flat Tire", Cost = 15},
                new Repair {VIN = "DEF123", Desc = "Fix Windshield",  Cost =420},
                new Repair {VIN = "ABC123", Desc = "Replace Wipers", Cost = 20},
                new Repair {VIN = "HIJ123", Desc = "Replace Tires",  Cost = 1000},
                new Repair {VIN = "DEF456", Desc = "Change Oil", Cost = 30}
        };
}

private void lINQInnerJoinToolStripMenuItem_Click(object sender, EventArgs e)
{
    var cars = GetCars();
    var repairs = GetRepairs();

    var carsWithRepairs = from c in cars
                          join r in repairs
                          on c.VIN equals r.VIN
                          orderby c.VIN, r.Cost
                          select new
                          {
                              c.VIN,
                              c.Make,
                              r.Desc,
                              r.Cost
                          };
    foreach (var item in carsWithRepairs)
    {
        txtLog.WriteLine("Car VIN:{0}, Make:{1}, Description:{2} Cost:{3:C}",
            item.VIN, item.Make, item.Desc, item.Cost);
    }
}
```

The result:

```
Car VIN:ABC123, Make:Ford, Description:Fix Flat Tire Cost:$15.00
Car VIN:ABC123, Make:Ford, Description:Replace Wipers Cost:$20.00
Car VIN:ABC123, Make:Ford, Description:Change Oil Cost:$29.99
Car VIN:DEF123, Make:BMW, Description:Rotate Tires Cost:$19.99
Car VIN:DEF123, Make:BMW, Description:Fix Windshield Cost:$420.00
Car VIN:DEF456, Make:Ford, Description:Alignment Cost:$30.00
Car VIN:DEF456, Make:Ford, Description:Change Oil Cost:$30.00
Car VIN:HIJ123, Make:VW, Description:Replace Brakes Cost:$200.00
Car VIN:HIJ123, Make:VW, Description:Replace Tires Cost:$1,000.00
```

This example shows the creation of the *Repair* class and the creation of a *GetRepairs* method that returns a generic list of *Repair* objects. Next is the creation of a *cars* variable populated with *Car* objects and a *repairs* variable populated with *Repair* objects. A *carsWithRepairs* variable is created, and the LINQ query is assigned to it. The LINQ query defines an outer element source in the *from* clause and then defines an inner element source using the *join* clause. The *join* clause must be immediately followed by the *on* clause that defines the linking between the two sources. Also, when joining the two sources, you must use the *equals* keyword, not the equals sign. If you need to perform a join on multiple keys, use the Visual Basic

And keyword or the *&&* C# operator. The LINQ query is sorting by the VIN of the car and the cost of the repair, and the returned elements are of an anonymous type that contains data from each element source.

When looking at the result of this query, the car with the VIN of ABC456 had no repairs, so there was no output for this car. If you want all cars to be in the output even if the car has no repairs, you must perform an outer join.

Another way to perform an inner join is to use the *Join* query extension method, which was covered earlier in this chapter.

Outer Joins

Outer joins produce output for every element in the outer source even if there is no match to the inner source. To perform an outer join by using a LINQ query, use the *into* clause with the *join* clause (Visual Basic *Group Join*). The *into* clause creates an identifier that can serve as a reference to the results of a *join*, *group*, or *select* clause. In this scenario, the *into* clause references the join and is assigned to the variable *temp*. The inner variable *rep* is out of scope, but a new *from* clause is provided to get the variable *r*, which references a repair, from *temp*. The *DefaultIfEmpty* method assigns *null* to *r* if no match can be made to a repair.

Sample of Visual Basic Code

```
Private Sub LINQOuterJoinToolStripMenuItem_Click( _
        ByVal sender As System.Object, _
        ByVal e As System.EventArgs) _
        Handles LINQOuterJoinToolStripMenuItem.Click
    Dim cars = GetCars()
    Dim repairs = GetRepairs()

    Dim carsWithRepairs = From c In cars
                          Group Join rep In repairs
                          On c.VIN Equals rep.VIN Into temp = Group
                             From r In temp.DefaultIfEmpty()
                          Order By c.VIN, If(r Is Nothing, 0, r.Cost)
                          Select New With
                              {
                                  c.VIN,
                                  c.Make,
                                  .Desc = If(r Is Nothing, _
                                             "***No Repairs***", r.Desc),
                                  .Cost = If(r Is Nothing, _
                                             0, r.Cost)
                              }
    For Each item In carsWithRepairs
    txtLog.WriteLine("Car VIN:{0}, Make:{1}, Description:{2} Cost:{3:C}",
            item.VIN, item.Make, item.Desc, item.Cost)
    Next
End Sub
```

Sample of C# Code

```
private void lINQOuterJoinToolStripMenuItem_Click(object sender, EventArgs e)
{
```

```
var cars = GetCars();
var repairs = GetRepairs();

var carsWithRepairs = from c in cars
                      join r in repairs
                      on c.VIN equals r.VIN into g
                         from r in g.DefaultIfEmpty()
                      orderby c.VIN, r==null?0:r.Cost
                      select new
                      {
                          c.VIN,
                          c.Make,
                          Desc = r==null?"***No Repairs***":r.Desc,
                          Cost = r==null?0:r.Cost
                      };
foreach (var item in carsWithRepairs)
{
    txtLog.WriteLine("Car VIN:{0}, Make:{1}, Description:{2} Cost:{3:C}",
        item.VIN, item.Make, item.Desc, item.Cost);
}
}
```

The result:

```
Car VIN:ABC123, Make:Ford, Description:Fix Flat Tire Cost:$15.00
Car VIN:ABC123, Make:Ford, Description:Replace Wipers Cost:$20.00
Car VIN:ABC123, Make:Ford, Description:Change Oil Cost:$29.99
Car VIN:ABC456, Make:Audi, Description:***No Repairs*** Cost:$0.00
Car VIN:DEF123, Make:BMW, Description:Rotate Tires Cost:$19.99
Car VIN:DEF123, Make:BMW, Description:Fix Windshield Cost:$420.00
Car VIN:DEF456, Make:Ford, Description:Alignment Cost:$30.00
Car VIN:DEF456, Make:Ford, Description:Change Oil Cost:$30.00
Car VIN:HIJ123, Make:VW, Description:Replace Brakes Cost:$200.00
Car VIN:HIJ123, Make:VW, Description:Replace Tires Cost:$1,000.00
```

The car with VIN = ABC456 is included in the result, even though it has no repairs. Another way to perform a left outer join is to use the *GroupJoin* query extension method, discussed earlier in this chapter.

Cross Joins

A cross join is a Cartesian product between two element sources. A Cartesian product will join each record in the outer element source with all elements in the inner source. No join keys are required with this type of join. Cross joins are accomplished by using the *from* clause multiple times without providing any link between element sources. This is often done by mistake.

In the following code sample, there is a *colors* element source and a *cars* element source. The *colors* source represents the available paint colors, and the *cars* source represents the cars that exist. The desired outcome is to combine the colors with the cars to show every combination of car and color available.

Sample of Visual Basic Code

```
Private Sub LINQCrossJoinToolStripMenuItem_Click( _
    ByVal sender As System.Object, _
```

```
         ByVal e As System.EventArgs) _
         Handles LINQCrossJoinToolStripMenuItem.Click
     Dim cars = GetCars()
     Dim colors() = {"Red", "Yellow", "Blue", "Green"}

     Dim carsWithRepairs = From car In cars
                           From color In colors
                           Order By car.VIN, color
                           Select New With
                               {
                                   car.VIN,
                                   car.Make,
                                   car.Model,
                                   .Color = color
                               }
     For Each item In carsWithRepairs
         txtLog.WriteLine("Car VIN:{0}, Make:{1}, Model:{2} Color:{3}",
             item.VIN, item.Make, item.Model, item.Color)
     Next
End Sub
```

Sample of C# Code

```
private void lINQCrossJoinToolStripMenuItem_Click(object sender, EventArgs e)
{
    var cars = GetCars();
    var colors = new string[]{"Red","Yellow","Blue","Green" };

    var carsWithRepairs = from car in cars
                          from color in colors
                          orderby car.VIN, color
                          select new
                          {
                              car.VIN,
                              car.Make,
                              car.Model,
                              Color=color
                          };
    foreach (var item in carsWithRepairs)
    {
        txtLog.WriteLine("Car VIN:{0}, Make:{1}, Model:{2} Color:{3}",
            item.VIN, item.Make, item.Model, item.Color);
    }
}
```

The result:

```
Car VIN:ABC123, Make:Ford, Model:F-250 Color:Blue
Car VIN:ABC123, Make:Ford, Model:F-250 Color:Green
Car VIN:ABC123, Make:Ford, Model:F-250 Color:Red
Car VIN:ABC123, Make:Ford, Model:F-250 Color:Yellow
Car VIN:ABC456, Make:Audi, Model:TT Color:Blue
Car VIN:ABC456, Make:Audi, Model:TT Color:Green
Car VIN:ABC456, Make:Audi, Model:TT Color:Red
Car VIN:ABC456, Make:Audi, Model:TT Color:Yellow
Car VIN:DEF123, Make:BMW, Model:Z-3 Color:Blue
Car VIN:DEF123, Make:BMW, Model:Z-3 Color:Green
```

```
Car VIN:DEF123, Make:BMW, Model:Z-3 Color:Red
Car VIN:DEF123, Make:BMW, Model:Z-3 Color:Yellow
Car VIN:DEF456, Make:Ford, Model:F-150 Color:Blue
Car VIN:DEF456, Make:Ford, Model:F-150 Color:Green
Car VIN:DEF456, Make:Ford, Model:F-150 Color:Red
Car VIN:DEF456, Make:Ford, Model:F-150 Color:Yellow
Car VIN:HIJ123, Make:VW, Model:Bug Color:Blue
Car VIN:HIJ123, Make:VW, Model:Bug Color:Green
Car VIN:HIJ123, Make:VW, Model:Bug Color:Red
Car VIN:HIJ123, Make:VW, Model:Bug Color:Yellow
```

The cross join produces an output for each combination of inputs, which means that the output count is the first input's count one multiplied by the second input's count.

Another way to implement a cross join is to use the *SelectMany* query extension method, covered earlier in this chapter.

Grouping and Aggregation

You will often want to calculate an aggregation such as the total cost of your repairs for each of your cars. LINQ enables you to calculate aggregates for each item by using the *group by* clause. The following code example demonstrates the use of the *group by* clause with the *Sum* aggregate function to output the VIN and the total cost of repairs.

Sample of Visual Basic Code

```vb
Private Sub LINQGroupByToolStripMenuItem_Click(ByVal sender As System.Object, _
        ByVal e As System.EventArgs) Handles LINQGroupByToolStripMenuItem.Click
    Dim repairs = From r In GetRepairs()
                Group By VIN = r.VIN
                Into grouped = Group, TotalCost = Sum(r.Cost)

    For Each item In repairs
        txtLog.WriteLine("Car VIN:{0}, TotalCost:{1:C}",
            item.VIN, item.TotalCost)
    Next
End Sub
```

Sample of C# Code

```csharp
private void lINQGroupByToolStripMenuItem_Click(object sender, EventArgs e)
{
    var repairs = from r in GetRepairs()
                group r by r.VIN into grouped
                select new
                {
                    VIN = grouped.Key,
                    TotalCost = grouped.Sum(c => c.Cost)
                };
    foreach (var item in repairs)
    {
        txtLog.WriteLine("Car VIN:{0}, Total Cost:{1:C}",
            item.VIN, item.TotalCost);
    }
}
```

The result:

```
Car VIN:ABC123, Total Cost:$64.99
Car VIN:DEF123, Total Cost:$439.99
Car VIN:HIJ123, Total Cost:$1,200.00
Car VIN:DEF456, Total Cost:$60.00
```

This query produced the total cost for the repairs for each car that had repairs, but one car had no repairs, so it's not listed. To list all the cars, you must left join the cars to the repairs and then calculate the sum of the repairs. Also, you might want to add the make of the car to the output and include cars that have no repairs. This requires you to perform a join and group on multiple properties. The following example shows how you can achieve the result.

Sample of Visual Basic Code

```
Private Sub LINQGroupBy2ToolStripMenuItem_Click( _
        ByVal sender As System.Object, _
        ByVal e As System.EventArgs) _
        Handles LINQGroupBy2ToolStripMenuItem.Click
    Dim cars = GetCars()
    Dim repairs = GetRepairs()

    Dim carsWithRepairs = From c In cars
                          Group c By Key = New With {c.VIN, c.Make}
                          Into grouped = Group
                          Group Join r In repairs On Key.VIN Equals r.VIN
                          Into joined = Group
                          Select New With
                              {
                                .VIN = Key.VIN,
                                .Make = Key.Make,
                                .TotalCost = joined.Sum(Function(x) x.Cost)
                              }
    For Each item In carsWithRepairs
        txtLog.WriteLine("Car VIN:{0}, Make:{1}, Total Cost:{2:C}", _
            item.VIN, item.Make, item.TotalCost)
    Next
End Sub
```

Sample of C# Code

```
private void lINQGroupBy2ToolStripMenuItem_Click(object sender, EventArgs e)
{
    var cars = GetCars();
    var repairs = GetRepairs();

    var carsWithRepairs = from c in cars
                          join rep in repairs
                          on c.VIN equals rep.VIN into temp
                          from r in temp.DefaultIfEmpty()
                          group r by new { c.VIN, c.Make } into grouped
                          select new
                          {
                              VIN = grouped.Key.VIN,
                              Make = grouped.Key.Make,
                              TotalCost =
```

```
                    grouped.Sum(c => c == null ? 0 : c.Cost)
                };
    foreach (var item in carsWithRepairs)
    {
        txtLog.WriteLine("Car VIN:{0}, Make:{1}, Total Cost:{2:C}",
            item.VIN, item.Make, item.TotalCost);
    }
}
```

The result:

```
Car VIN:ABC123, Make:Ford, Total Cost:$64.99
Car VIN:DEF123, Make:BMW, Total Cost:$439.99
Car VIN:ABC456, Make:Audi, Total Cost:$0.00
Car VIN:HIJ123, Make:VW, Total Cost:$1,200.00
Car VIN:DEF456, Make:Ford, Total Cost:$60.00
```

Parallel LINQ (PLINQ)

Parallel LINQ, also known as PLINQ, is a parallel implementation of LINQ to objects. PLINQ implements all the LINQ query extension methods and has additional operators for parallel operations. The degree of concurrency for PLINQ queries is based on the capabilities of the computer running the query.

In many, but not all, scenarios, PLINQ can provide a significant increase in speed by using all available CPUs or CPU cores. A PLINQ query can provide performance gains when you have CPU-intensive operations that can be paralleled, or divided, across each CPU or CPU core. The more computationally expensive the work is, the greater the opportunity for performance gain. For example, if the workload takes 100 milliseconds to execute, a sequential query over 400 elements will take 40 seconds to complete the work, whereas a parallel query on a computer with eight cores might take only 5 seconds. This yields a speedup of 35 seconds.

One problem with Windows applications is that when you try to update a control on your form from a thread other than the thread that created the control, an *InvalidOperationException* is thrown with the message, "Cross-thread operation not valid: Control 'txtLog' accessed from a thread other than the thread it was created on." To work with threading, update in a thread-safe way the following extension method for *TextBox* to the *TextBoxHelper* class.

Sample of Visual Basic Code

```
<Extension()> _
Public Sub WriteLine(ByVal txt As TextBox, _
                     ByVal format As String, _
                     ByVal ParamArray parms As Object())
    Dim line As String = String.Format((format & Environment.NewLine), parms)
    If txt.InvokeRequired Then
        txt.BeginInvoke(New Action(Of String)(AddressOf txt.AppendText), _
                        New Object() {line})
    Else
        txt.AppendText(line)
```

```
    End If
End Sub
```

Sample of C# Code
```csharp
public static void WriteLine(this TextBox txt,
            string format, params object[] parms)
{
    string line = string.Format(format + Environment.NewLine, parms);
    if (txt.InvokeRequired)
    {
        txt.BeginInvoke((Action<string>)txt.AppendText, line);
    }
    else
    {
        txt.AppendText(line);
    }
}
```

You use the *Invoke* or *BeginInvoke* method on the *TextBox* class to marshal the callback to the thread that was used to create the UI control. The *BeginInvoke* method posts an internal dedicated Windows message to the UI thread message queue and returns immediately, which helps avoid thread deadlock situations.

This extension method checks the *TextBox* object to see whether marshaling is required. If marshaling is required (i.e., when the calling thread is not the one used to create the *TextBox* object), the *BeginInvoke* method is executed. If marshaling is not required, the *AppendText* method is called directly on the *TextBox* object. The *BeginInvoke* method takes *Delegate* as a parameter, so *txt.AppendText* is cast to an action of *String*, a general-purpose delegate that exists in the framework, which represents a call to a method that takes a *string* parameter. Now that there is a thread-safe way to display information into the *TextBox* class, the *AsParallel* example can be performed without risking threading-related exceptions.

AsParallel Extension Method

The *AsParallel* extension method divides work onto each processor or processor core. The following code sample starts a stopwatch in the *System.Diagnostics* namespace to show you the elapsed time when completed, and then the *Enumerable* class produces a sequence of integers, from 1 to 10. The *AsParallel* method call is added to the source. This causes the iterations to be spread across the available processor and processor cores. Then a LINQ query retrieves all the even numbers, but in the LINQ query, the *where* clause is calling a *Compute* method, which has a one-second delay using the *Thread* class, which is in the *System.Threading* namespace. Finally, a *foreach* loop displays the results.

Sample of Visual Basic Code
```vbnet
Private Sub AsParallelToolStripMenuItem_Click(ByVal sender As System.Object, _
        ByVal e As System.EventArgs) _
        Handles AsParallelToolStripMenuItem.Click
    Dim sw As New Stopwatch
    sw.Start()
```

```
    Dim source = Enumerable.Range(1, 10).AsParallel()
    Dim evenNums = From num In source
                   Where Compute(num) Mod 2 = 0
                   Select num
    For Each ev In evenNums
        txtLog.WriteLine("{0} on Thread {1}", _
            New Object() {ev, Thread.CurrentThread.GetHashCode})
    Next
    sw.Stop()
    txtLog.WriteLine("Done {0}", New Object() {sw.Elapsed})
End Sub

Public Function Compute(ByVal num As Integer) As Integer
    txtLog.WriteLine("Computing {0} on Thread {1}", _
        New Object() {num, Thread.CurrentThread.GetHashCode})
    Thread.Sleep(1000)
    Return num
End Function
```

Sample of C# Code

```
private void asParallelToolStripMenuItem_Click(
    object sender, EventArgs e)
{
    Stopwatch sw = new Stopwatch();
    sw.Start();
    var source = Enumerable.Range(1, 10).AsParallel();
    var evenNums = from num in source
                   where Compute(num) % 2 == 0
                   select num;
    foreach (var ev in evenNums)
    {
        txtLog.WriteLine("{0} on Thread {1}", ev,
            Thread.CurrentThread.GetHashCode());
    }
    sw.Stop();
    txtLog.WriteLine("Done {0}", sw.Elapsed);
}

public int Compute(int num)
{
    txtLog.WriteLine("Computing {0} on Thread {1}", num,
        Thread.CurrentThread.GetHashCode());
    Thread.Sleep(1000);
    return num;
}
```

AsEnumerable results, showing even numbers, total time, and computing method:

```
6 on Thread 10
2 on Thread 10
4 on Thread 10
8 on Thread 10
10 on Thread 10
Done 00:00:05.0393262
Computing 1 on Thread 12
```

```
Computing 2 on Thread 11
Computing 3 on Thread 12
Computing 4 on Thread 11
Computing 5 on Thread 11
Computing 6 on Thread 12
Computing 7 on Thread 12
Computing 8 on Thread 11
Computing 9 on Thread 12
Computing 10 on Thread 11
```

The output from the *Compute* calls always shows after the *foreach* (Visual Basic *For Each*) loop output because *BeginInvoke* marshalls calls to the UI thread for execution when the UI thread is available. The *foreach* loop is running on the UI thread, so the thread is busy until the loop completes. The results are not ordered. Your result will vary as well, and, in some cases, the results might be ordered. In the example, you can see that the *foreach* loop displayed the even numbers, using the main thread of the application, which was thread 10 on this computer. The *Compute* method was executed on a different thread, but the thread is either 11 or 12 because this is a two-core processor. Although the *Compute* method has a one-second delay, it took five seconds to execute because only two threads were allocated, one for each core.

In an effort to get a clearer picture of PLINQ, the writing to a *TextBox* has been replaced in the following code. Instead of using *TextBox*, *Debug.WriteLine* is used, which removes the requirement to marshall calls back to the UI thread.

Sample of Visual Basic Code

```
Private Sub AsParallel2ToolStripMenuItem_Click( _
    ByVal sender As System.Object, ByVal e As System.EventArgs) _
    Handles AsParallel2ToolStripMenuItem.Click
    Dim sw As New Stopwatch
    sw.Start()
    Dim source = Enumerable.Range(1, 10).AsParallel()
    Dim evenNums = From num In source
                   Where Compute2(num) Mod 2 = 0
                   Select num
    For Each ev In evenNums
        Debug.WriteLine(String.Format("{0} on Thread {1}", _
            New Object() {ev, Thread.CurrentThread.GetHashCode}))
    Next
    sw.Stop()
    Debug.WriteLine(String.Format("Done {0}", New Object() {sw.Elapsed}))
End Sub
```

Sample of C# Code

```
private void asParallel2ToolStripMenuItem_Click(
    object sender, EventArgs e)
{
    Stopwatch sw = new Stopwatch();
    sw.Start();
    var source = Enumerable.Range(1, 10).AsParallel();
    var evenNums = from num in source
```

```
            where Compute2(num) % 2 == 0
            select num;
    foreach (var ev in evenNums)
    {
        Debug.WriteLine(string.Format("{0} on Thread {1}", ev,
            Thread.CurrentThread.GetHashCode()));
    }
    sw.Stop();
    Debug.WriteLine(string.Format("Done {0}", sw.Elapsed));
}

public int Compute2(int num)
{
    Debug.WriteLine(string.Format("Computing {0} on Thread {1}", num,
        Thread.CurrentThread.GetHashCode()));
    Thread.Sleep(1000);
    return num;
}
```

The result:

```
Computing 2 on Thread 10
Computing 1 on Thread 6
Computing 3 on Thread 10
Computing 4 on Thread 6
Computing 5 on Thread 10
Computing 6 on Thread 6
Computing 7 on Thread 10
Computing 8 on Thread 6
Computing 9 on Thread 10
Computing 10 on Thread 6
2 on Thread 9
4 on Thread 9
6 on Thread 9
8 on Thread 9
10 on Thread 9
Done 00:00:05.0632071
```

The result, which is in the Visual Studio .NET Output window, shows that there is no waiting for the UI thread. Once again, your result will vary based on your hardware configuration.

ForAll Extension Method

When the query is iterated by using a *foreach* (Visual Basic *For Each*) loop, each iteration is synchronized in the same thread, to be treated one after the other in the order of the sequence. If you just want to perform each iteration in parallel, without any specific order, use the *ForAll* method. It has the same effect as performing each iteration in a different thread. Analyze this technique to verify that you get the performance gain you expect. The following example shows the use of the *ForAll* method instead of the *For Each* (C# *foreach*) loop.

Sample of Visual Basic Code

```
Private Sub ForAllToolStripMenuItem_Click(ByVal sender As System.Object, _
        ByVal e As System.EventArgs) _
```

```
          Handles ForAllToolStripMenuItem.Click
    Dim sw As New Stopwatch
    sw.Start()
    Dim source = Enumerable.Range(1, 10).AsParallel()
    Dim evenNums = From num In source
                   Where Compute2(num) Mod 2 = 0
                   Select num
    evenNums.ForAll(Sub(ev) Debug.WriteLine(string.Format(
                        "{0} on Thread {1}", ev, _
                        Thread.CurrentThread.GetHashCode())))
    sw.Stop()
    Debug.WriteLine((string.Format("Done {0}", New Object() {sw.Elapsed}))
End Sub
```

Sample of C# Code

```
private void forAllToolStripMenuItem_Click(object sender, EventArgs e)
{
    Stopwatch sw = new Stopwatch();
    sw.Start();
    var source = Enumerable.Range(1, 10).AsParallel();
    var evenNums = from num in source
                   where Compute(num) % 2 == 0
                   select num;
    evenNums.ForAll(ev => Debug.WriteLine(string.Format(
                    "{0} on Thread {1}", ev,
                    Thread.CurrentThread.GetHashCode())));
    sw.Stop();
    Debug.WriteLine(string.Format("Done {0}", sw.Elapsed));
}
```

ForAll result, showing even numbers, total time, and computing method:

```
Computing 1 on Thread 9
Computing 2 on Thread 10
Computing 3 on Thread 9
2 on Thread 10
Computing 4 on Thread 10
Computing 5 on Thread 9
4 on Thread 10
Computing 6 on Thread 10
Computing 7 on Thread 9
6 on Thread 10
Computing 8 on Thread 10
Computing 9 on Thread 9
8 on Thread 10
Computing 10 on Thread 10
10 on Thread 10
Done 00:00:05.0556551
```

Like the previous example, the results are not guaranteed to be ordered, and there is no attempt to put the results in a particular order. This technique can give you better performance as long as this behavior is acceptable.

AsOrdered Extension Method

Sometimes, you must maintain the order in your query, but you still want parallel execution. Although this will come at a cost, it's doable by using the *AsOrdered* extension method. The following example shows how you can add this method call right after the *AsParallel* method to maintain order.

Sample of Visual Basic Code

```
Private Sub AsOrderedToolStripMenuItem_Click(ByVal sender As System.Object, _
        ByVal e As System.EventArgs) _
        Handles AsOrderedToolStripMenuItem.Click
    Dim sw As New Stopwatch
    sw.Start()
    Dim source = Enumerable.Range(1, 10).AsParallel().AsOrdered()
    Dim evenNums = From num In source
                   Where Compute2(num) Mod 2 = 0
                   Select num
    evenNums.ForAll(Sub(ev) Debug.WriteLine(string.Format(
                        "{0} on Thread {1}", ev, _
                        Thread.CurrentThread.GetHashCode())))
    sw.Stop()
    Debug.WriteLine(string.Format("Done {0}", New Object() {sw.Elapsed}))
End Sub
```

Sample of C# Code

```
private void asOrderedToolStripMenuItem_Click(object sender, EventArgs e)
{
    Stopwatch sw = new Stopwatch();
    sw.Start();
    var source = Enumerable.Range(1, 10).AsParallel().AsOrdered();
    var evenNums = from num in source
                   where Compute2(num) % 2 == 0
                   select num;

    evenNums.ForAll(ev => Debug.WriteLine(string.Format(
                        "{0} on Thread {1}", ev,
                        Thread.CurrentThread.GetHashCode())));
    sw.Stop();
    Debug.WriteLine(string.Format("Done {0}", sw.Elapsed));
}
```

AsOrdered result, showing even numbers, total time, and computing method:

```
Computing 2 on Thread 11
Computing 1 on Thread 10
2 on Thread 11
Computing 4 on Thread 11
Computing 3 on Thread 10
4 on Thread 11
Computing 6 on Thread 11
Computing 5 on Thread 10
6 on Thread 11
Computing 8 on Thread 11
Computing 7 on Thread 10
8 on Thread 11
```

```
Computing 9 on Thread 11
Computing 10 on Thread 10
10 on Thread 10
Done 00:00:05.2374586
```

The results are ordered, at least for the even numbers, which is what the *AsOrdered* extension method is guaranteeing.

PRACTICE Working with Disconnected Data Classes

In this practice, you convert the Web application from Lesson 1 to use LINQ queries instead of query extension methods. The result of this practice functions the same way, but you will see how using LINQ queries can improve readability.

If you encounter a problem completing an exercise, the completed projects can be installed from the Code folder on the companion CD.

EXERCISE 1 Converting from Query Extension Methods to LINQ Queries

In this exercise, you modify the Web application you created in Lesson 1 to use LINQ queries.

1. In Visual Studio .NET 2010, choose File | Open | Project. Open the project from Lesson 1 or locate and open the solution in the Begin folder for this lesson.

2. In Solution Explorer, right-click the Default.aspx file and select View Code to open the code-behind file containing the code from Lesson 1.

3. In the *Page_Load* method, locate the statement that contains all the *Where* method calls as follows:

Sample of Visual Basic Code

```
Dim result = Vehicles _
        .Where(Function(v) v.VIN.StartsWith(txtVin.Text)) _
        .Where(Function(v) v.Make.StartsWith(txtMake.Text)) _
        .Where(Function(v) v.Model.StartsWith(txtModel.Text)) _
        .Where(Function(v) v.Cost > Decimal.Parse(ddlCost.SelectedValue)) _
        .Where(Function(v) v.Year > Integer.Parse(ddlYear.SelectedValue))
```

Sample of C# Code

```
var result = vehicles
    .Where(v => v.VIN.StartsWith(txtVin.Text))
    .Where(v => v.Make.StartsWith(txtMake.Text))
    .Where(v => v.Model.StartsWith(txtModel.Text))
    .Where(v => v.Cost > Decimal.Parse(ddlCost.SelectedValue))
    .Where(v => v.Year > int.Parse(ddlYear.SelectedValue));
```

4. Convert the previous code to use a LINQ query. Your code should look like the following:

Sample of Visual Basic Code

```
Dim result = From v In Vehicles
             Where v.VIN.StartsWith(txtVin.Text) _
             And v.Make.StartsWith(txtMake.Text) _
```

```
                And v.Model.StartsWith(txtModel.Text) _
                And v.Cost > Decimal.Parse(ddlCost.SelectedValue) _
                And v.Year > Integer.Parse(ddlYear.SelectedValue) _
                Select v
```

Sample of C# Code

```
var result = from v in vehicles
                where v.VIN.StartsWith(txtVin.Text)
                &&    v.Make.StartsWith(txtMake.Text)
                &&    v.Model.StartsWith(txtModel.Text)
                &&    v.Cost > Decimal.Parse(ddlCost.SelectedValue)
                &&    v.Year > int.Parse(ddlYear.SelectedValue)
                select v;
```

Behind the scenes, these queries do the same thing as the previous code, which implemented many *Where* calls by using method chaining.

5. Locate the *SetOrder* method. Replace the code in this method to use LINQ expressions. Your code should look like the following:

Sample of Visual Basic Code

```
Private Function SetOrder(ByVal order As String, _
        ByVal query As IEnumerable(Of Vehicle)) As IEnumerable(Of Vehicle)
    Select Case order
        Case "VIN"
            Return From v In query Order By v.VIN Select v
        Case "Make"
            Return From v In query Order By v.Make Select v
        Case "Model"
            Return From v In query Order By v.Model Select v
        Case "Year"
            Return From v In query Order By v.Year Select v
        Case "Cost"
            Return From v In query Order By v.Cost Select v
        Case Else
            Return query
    End Select

End Function
```

Sample of C# Code

```
    private IEnumerable<Vehicle> SetOrder(string order,
        IEnumerable<Vehicle> query)
    {
        switch (order)
        {
            case "VIN":
                return from v in query orderby v.VIN select v;
            case "Make":
                return from v in query orderby v.Make select v;
            case "Model":
                return from v in query orderby v.Model select v;
            case "Year":
                return from v in query orderby v.Year select v;
            case "Cost":
```

```
                    return from v in query orderby v.Cost select v;
            default:
                return query;
        }
    }
```

6. Locate the data-binding code. This code uses the *Select* query extension method to instantiate an anonymous type, which is then bound to the grid as follows:

Sample of Visual Basic Code

```
gvVehicles.DataSource = result.Select(Function(v, i) New With
                {.Index = i, v.VIN, v.Make, v.Model, v.Year, v.Cost})
gvVehicles.DataBind()
```

Sample of C# Code

```
gvVehicles.DataSource = result.Select((v, i)=> new
    {Index = i, v.VIN, v.Make, v.Model, v.Year, v.Cost});
gvVehicles.DataBind();
```

Can you convert the previous code to a LINQ query? The LINQ *select* keyword doesn't support the index parameter value this code uses. You could spend time trying to find a way to convert this code, but it's better to leave this code as is.

7. Choose Build | Build Solution to build the application. If you have errors, you can double-click the error to go to the error line and correct.

8. Choose Debug | Start Debugging to run the application.

When the application starts, you should see a Web page with your GUI controls that enables you to specify filter and sort criteria. If you type the letter **F** into the Make text box and click Execute, the grid will be populated only with items that begin with F. If you set the sort order and click the Execute button again, you will see the sorted results.

Lesson Summary

This lesson provided a detailed overview of the ADO.NET disconnected classes.

- You can use LINQ queries to provide a typed method of querying any generic *IEnumerable* object.

- LINQ queries can be more readable than using query extension methods.

- Not all query extension methods map to LINQ keywords, so you might still be required to use query extension methods with your LINQ queries.

- Although the *Select* query extension method maps to the LINQ select keyword, the LINQ select keyword doesn't support the index parameter the *Select* query extension method has.

- LINQ queries enable you to filter, project, sort, join, group, and aggregate.

- PLINQ provides a parallel implementation of LINQ that can increase the performance of LINQ queries.

Lesson Review

You can use the following questions to test your knowledge of the information in Lesson 2, "Using LINQ Queries." The questions are also available on the companion CD if you prefer to review them in electronic form.

> **NOTE ANSWERS**
>
> Answers to these questions and explanations of why each answer choice is correct or incorrect are located in the "Answers" section at the end of the book.

1. Given the following LINQ query:

   ```
   from c in cars join r in repairs on c.VIN equals r.VIN …
   ```

   what kind of join does this perform?

   A. Cross join

   B. Left outer join

   C. Right outer join

   D. Inner join

2. In a LINQ query that starts with:

   ```
   from o in orderItems
   ```

   The *orderItems* collection is a collection of *OrderItem* with properties called *UnitPrice*, *Discount*, and *Quantity*. You want the query to filter out *OrderItem* objects whose *totalPrice* (UnitPrice * Quantity * Discount) result is less than 100. You want to sort by *totalPrice*, and you want to include the total price in your *select* clause. Which keyword can you use to create a *totalPrice* result within the LINQ query so you don't have to repeat the formula three times?

   A. *let*

   B. *on*

   C. *into*

   D. *by*

Case Scenarios

In the following case scenarios, you will apply what you've learned about LINQ as discussed in this chapter. You can find answers to these questions in the "Answers" section at the end of this book.

Case Scenario 1: Fibonacci Sequence

You were recently challenged to create an expression to produce the Fibonacci sequence for a predetermined quantity of iterations. An example of the Fibonacci sequence is:

0, 1, 1, 2, 3, 5, 8, 13, 21, 34, 55

The sequence starts with 0 and 1, known as the seed values. The next number is always the sum of the previous two numbers, so 0 + 1 = 1 to get the third element, 1 + 1 = 2 to get the fourth element, 2 + 1 = 3 for the fifth element, 3 + 2 = 5 for the sixth element, and so on.

Answer the following questions regarding the implementation of the Fibonacci sequence.

1. Can you write an expression using a LINQ query or query extension methods that will produce Fibonacci numbers for a predetermined quantity of iterations?

2. Instead of producing Fibonacci numbers for a predetermined quantity of iterations, how about producing Fibonacci numbers until you reach a desired maximum value?

Case Scenario 2: Sorting and Filtering Data

In your application, you are using a collection of *Customer*, a collection of *Order*, and a collection of *OrderItem*. Table 3-3 shows the properties of each of the classes. The total price for *OrderItem* is Quantity * Price * Discount. The *Order* amount is the sum of the total price of the order items. The *max Quantity* value is the maximum quantity of products purchased for a customer.

You must write a LINQ query that produces a generic *IEnumerable* result that contains *CustomerID*, *Name*, *OrderAmount*, and *MaxQuantity*. You produce this data only for orders whose amount is greater than $1,000. You want to sort by *OrderAmount* descending.

TABLE 3-3 Classes with Corresponding Properties

CUSTOMER	ORDER	ORDERITEM
CustomerID	OrderID	OrderItemID
Name	OrderDate	ProductID
Address	RequiredDate	Quantity
City	ShippedDate	Price
State		Discount

1. Can you produce a LINQ query that solves this problem?

2. Can you produce a solution to this problem by using query extension methods?

Suggested Practices

To help you successfully master the exam objectives presented in this chapter, complete the following tasks.

Create Query with Extension Methods

You should create at least one application that uses the LINQ and query extension methods. This can be accomplished by completing the practices at the end of Lesson 1 and Lesson 2 or by completing the following Practice 1.

- **Practice 1** Create an application that requires you to collect data into at least two generic collections in which the objects in these collections are related. This could be movies that have actors, artists who record music, or people who have vehicles. Add query extension methods to perform inner joins of these collections and retrieve results.

- **Practice 2** Complete Practice 1 and then add query extension methods to perform outer joins and *group by* with aggregations.

Create LINQ Queries

You should create at least one application that uses the LINQ and query extension methods. This can be accomplished by completing the practices at the end of Lesson 1 and Lesson 2 or by completing the following Practice 1.

- **Practice 1** Create an application that requires you to collect data into at least two generic collections in which the objects in these collections are related. This could be movies that have actors, artists who record music, or people who have vehicles. Add LINQ queries to perform inner joins of these collections and retrieve results.

- **Practice 2** Complete Practice 1 and then add query LINQ queries to perform outer joins and *group by* with aggregations.

Take a Practice Test

The practice tests on this book's companion CD offer many options. For example, you can test yourself on just the lesson review content, or you can test yourself on all the 70-516 certification exam content. You can set up the test so that it closely simulates the experience of taking a certification exam, or you can set it up in study mode so that you can look at the correct answers and explanations after you answer each question.

> **MORE INFO** **PRACTICE TESTS**
>
> For details about all the practice test options available, see the "How to Use the Practice Tests" section in this book's introduction.

CHAPTER 4

LINQ to SQL

In the past, one of the biggest problems developers have had with ADO.NET is that it forced everyone to create data-centric applications. This meant it was difficult to write an object-centric application that was focused on business objects because you had to think about the ADO.NET data-centric objects, such as *DataSet* and *DataTable*, and how you would use these objects to get proper persistence. These objects also caused problems when working with null values.

LINQ to SQL was released with Visual Studio 2008 as the first solution by Microsoft to the impedance mismatch between applications and data. LINQ to SQL enables you to access SQL Server by LINQ queries. In this chapter, you see how LINQ to SQL can put the fun back into programming data access.

Exam objectives in this chapter:

- Map entities and relationships by using LINQ to SQL.
- Create disconnected objects.
- Manage the *DataContext* and *ObjectContext*.
- Cache data.
- Create, update, or delete data by using *DataContext*.
- Create a LINQ query.

Lessons in this chapter:

Before You Begin

You must have some understanding of Microsoft C# or Visual Basic 2010. This chapter requires only the hardware and software listed at the beginning of this book.

 REAL WORLD

Glenn Johnson

Working with the classic ADO.NET classes such as *DataSet* and *DataTable* can be somewhat painful, especially when you have to deal with null values from the database. The first time I used LINQ to SQL was on a small project in which I needed to access a database that had several tables, and I needed to decide which technology to use for the data access. I decided to try LINQ to SQL. I was pleasantly surprised at how easy it was to set up and use.

Lesson 1: What Is LINQ to SQL?

LINQ to SQL provides a framework for managing relational data as objects, but you can still query the data. LINQ to SQL is an object-relational mapping (ORM) tool that enables you not only to query the data but also to insert, update, or delete the data. You can use an object-centric approach to manipulate the objects in your application while LINQ to SQL is in the background, tracking your changes.

In this lesson, you learn about modeling data.

> **After this lesson, you will be able to:**
> - Generate a LINQ to SQL model from an existing database.
> - Use the LINQ to SQL model to map stored procedures to methods.
> - Use a *DataContext* object to manage your database connection and context.
> - Understand how LINQ to SQL connects to your database.
> - Store information about objects and their state.
> - Understand object lifetime and how objects are cached.
> - Understand eager loading versus lazy loading.
>
> **Estimated lesson time: 45 minutes**

Modeling Your Data

Probably the best way to help you gain an understanding of LINQ to SQL is to start with some data modeling to help you see the big picture of the LINQ to SQL capabilities. This also helps by providing a visual model of your classes and how they relate to each other.

Generating a LINQ to SQL Model from an Existing Database

The easiest way to get started with LINQ to SQL is to generate a model from an existing database. This can be accomplished by right-clicking your project node in Solution Explorer, and choosing Add | New Item | LINQ to SQL Classes. Name the file **Northwind.dbml**, as shown in Figure 4-1.

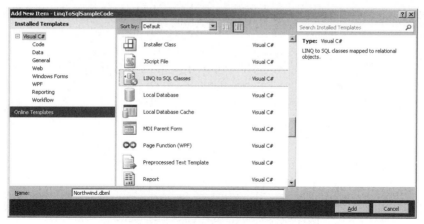

FIGURE 4-1 Select LINQ to SQL classes and name the file Northwind.dbml.

The file extension is .dbml (database markup language), which is an XML file that contains the model settings. After naming the file, click Add. The file will be rendered to your screen as a two-paned window in which the left side displays table entities and the right side displays stored procedures.

> **NOTE BE CAREFUL WHEN NAMING THE .DBML FILE**
>
> The name you assign to the file will also be used to create a *DataContext* object called *nameDataContext*. To ensure Pascal casing on your data context object, be sure to use Pascal casing on this file name. For example, if you name this file nOrThWiNd.dbml, the data context class that is created will be called nOrThWiNdDataContext. You can go to the *DataContext* properties to change the name if you make a mistake when naming the file, but being careful when naming the file will save you time.

From Server Explorer, you can drag tables to the left pane and drop them. This requires you to have a configured connection to Microsoft SQL Server. If you don't have a connection to the Northwind database, you can right-click the *Data Connections* node, click Add Connection, select Microsoft SQL Server, and click OK. In the Add Connection window, type your server name (for example, .\SQLExpress for your local SQL Server Express instance) and, in the Select Or Enter A Database Name drop-down list, select the Northwind database and click OK.

You can also drag stored procedures to the right pane and drop them. Figure 4-2 shows the model diagram after dragging and dropping the Customers, Orders, Order Details, and Employees tables and the CustOrderHist and CustOrdersDetail stored procedures.

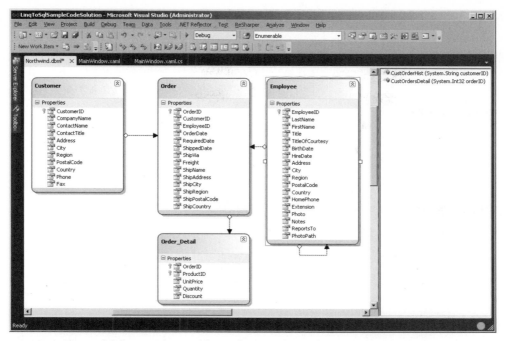

FIGURE 4-2 The model diagram shows tables as classes and stored procedures as methods.

Examining the Model

In Figure 4-2, the Customers table was added, but a class, *Customer* (singular), is shown. An instance of the *Customer* class represents a row in the Customers table. The LINQ to SQL designer automatically attempts to singularize plural table names. Most of the time, this works as expected, but it's not that smart. For example, a movies table will produce a *Movy* class instead of a *Movie* class. You can override the proposed name of any class by clicking the class in the design window and opening the Properties window to change the *Name* property to any valid class name.

In the Properties window, other properties can be configured. The *Insert*, *Update*, and *Delete* properties are defaulted to use the run time to generate the appropriate logic, but this can be changed to execute a stored procedure instead.

The primary key is also highlighted in the diagram by displaying a key beside all properties that make up the primary key. For example, notice that the *Order_Detail* class has two primary key properties to indicate that these properties are combined to produce a unique key.

The LINQ to SQL designer also imported the relationships into your diagram. For example, customers place orders, so you can see that an association line is drawn between the *Customer* class and the *Order* class. The association line shows a one-to-many relationship between the *Customer* class and the *Order* class. This also can be stated as "a customer has orders." You can use the Properties window to change the configuration of the associations.

Mapping Stored Procedures

With LINQ to SQL, you can easily access stored procedures as regular methods in your code, as shown in Figure 4-2, in which two stored procedures were added to the model by dragging and dropping them to the designer surface. The icon displayed in the designer is the standard method icon. If you click the CustOrderHist stored procedure, you'll see its properties, as shown in Figure 4-3.

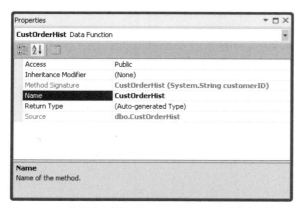

FIGURE 4-3 This figure displays the properties of the CustOrderHist stored procedure.

In Figure 4-3, the method signature is defined as CustOrderHist (System.String customerID), which means that a method called *CustOrderHist* will be created that accepts a string argument representing the customer ID.

> **NOTE** **WHAT DOES THE STORED PROCEDURE METHOD RETURN?**
>
> The designer will make an attempt to auto-define a new type that represents the output, but this works in simple scenarios only. If you have a stored procedure with conditional code that will return different result types based on a condition, the designer won't be smart enough to return the correct type. The design simply tries to execute the stored procedure with the SET FMTONLY ON option set, and it passes default values into the parameters to see what is returned. In the Properties window, you can specify the return type, but you can see that in some scenarios this will not be useful. Your solution will be either to rewrite the stored procedure or revert to traditional ADO.NET to get the returned result into a data table.

If you have a stored procedure that returns an entity type, for example, a stored procedure that returns a filtered list of customers, you can drag the stored procedure from Server Explorer and drop it on to the *Customer* entity. This will tell the designer that you want to return a list of *Customer* objects. If you've already added the stored procedure to the designer, you can set the Return Type in the Properties window, which informs the designer that you are returning an *IEnumerable* of the type you select.

Another example of using stored procedures with LINQ to SQL is when you want the *insert*, *update*, and *delete* statements to be executed as stored procedures instead of as dynamic SQL statements. This can be configured by clicking the appropriate entity class, for example, the *Customer* class, and setting *Insert*, *Update*, and *Delete* properties to the appropriate stored procedure, as shown in Figure 4-4.

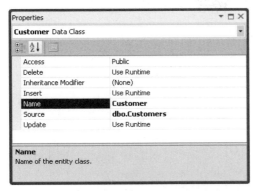

FIGURE 4-4 Each entity class has properties for *Insert*, *Update*, and *Delete*.

Figure 4-4 shows the default settings for *Insert*, *Update*, and *Delete*, but you can assign a stored procedure to these commands. In Figure 4-4, there is no property for *Select*. If you want to use a stored procedure for selecting customers, you can create the stored procedure and drag it to the design surface to create a method for selecting and then change the return type of the stored procedure to the *Customer* type.

Examining the Designer Output

When you save and close the LINQ to SQL designer, it creates types in your application that can access the entities and stored procedures in your model diagram. These types can be viewed by clicking the plus sign beside the Northwind.dbml file. If you don't have a plus sign beside the Northwind.dbml file, click the Show All Files button at the top of the Solution Explorer window. Under the Northwind.dbml file, you will see a Northwind.dbml.layout file, which is an XML file that contains layout information describing where the elements are on the design surface. The Northwind.dbml.vb (or Northwind.dbml.cs) file also contains the generated types. Open this file to see its contents.

The following classes are defined in this file: *Customer, CustOrderHistResult, CustOrderDetailsResult, Employee, NorthwindDataContext, Order*, and *Order_Detail*. The classes that have the "Result" suffix are auto-created to represent the results from the stored procedures.

Examining an *Entity* Class

The section focuses on one of the entity classes, the *Customer* class. All the other entity classes are implemented in a similar fashion. If you understand the *Customer* class, you should be able to understand the other entity classes.

When you locate the *Customer* class, you'll notice that this class is adorned with attributes, as shown in the following code sample:

Sample of Visual Basic Code

```
<Global.System.Data.Linq.Mapping.TableAttribute(Name:="dbo.Customers"), _
 Global.System.Runtime.Serialization.DataContractAttribute()> _
Partial Public Class Customer
      Implements System.ComponentModel.INotifyPropertyChanging,
                 System.ComponentModel.INotifyPropertyChanged
    ' more code here
End Class
```

Sample of C# Code

```
[global::System.Data.Linq.Mapping.TableAttribute(Name = "dbo.Customers")]
[global::System.Runtime.Serialization.DataContractAttribute()]
public partial class Customer : INotifyPropertyChanging, INotifyPropertyChanged
{
    //mode code here
}
```

The first attribute is *TableAttribute*, which LINQ to SQL uses to identify the table in SQL Server that this class represents. This means that *TableAttribute* links the *Customer* class to the dbo.Customers table in the database because the *Name* property specifies the exact name of the database table. If no *Name* property is supplied, LINQ to SQL assumes the database table has the same name as the class. Only instances of classes declared as tables are stored in the database. Instances of these types of classes are known as *entities*. The classes themselves are known as *entity classes*.

The second attribute is *DataContractAttribute*, which enables serialization of the *Customer* class when used with Windows Communication Foundation (WCF) services. This attribute exists because the *Serialization* property on *NorthwindDataContext* was set to *Unidirectional*. If you didn't set the *Serialization Mode* property, you won't see this attribute. (Read more about this in the "Examining the DataContext Class" section of this chapter).

The *Customer* class implements the *INotifyPropertyChanging* interface, which defines a *PropertyChanging* event. The *Customer* entity uses this interface to tell the LINQ to SQL change tracker when it has changed. If you don't implement *INotifyPropertyChanging*, the LINQ to SQL change tracker assumes that all objects queried will change, and it automatically keeps a copy of all queried objects.

The *Customer* class also implements the *INotifyPropertyChanged* interface, which has a *PropertyChanged* event. This interface is implemented for use with data binding. If your object will not be data-bound, it will not need this interface implementation.

Next, the *Customer* class has private fields and public properties for each column in the database table. The following code sample shows the *CustomerID*.

Sample of Visual Basic Code

```vb
Private _CustomerID As String

<Global.System.Data.Linq.Mapping.ColumnAttribute(Storage:="_CustomerID", _
        DbType:="NChar(5) NOT NULL", CanBeNull:=False, IsPrimaryKey:=True), _
    Global.System.Runtime.Serialization.DataMemberAttribute(Order:=1)> _
Public Property CustomerID() As String
    Get
        Return Me._CustomerID
    End Get
    Set(ByVal value As String)
        If (String.Equals(Me._CustomerID, value) = False) Then
            Me.OnCustomerIDChanging(value)
            Me.SendPropertyChanging()
            Me._CustomerID = value
            Me.SendPropertyChanged("CustomerID")
            Me.OnCustomerIDChanged()
        End If
    End Set
End Property
```

Sample of C# Code

```csharp
private string _CustomerID;

[global::System.Data.Linq.Mapping.ColumnAttribute(Storage="_CustomerID",
            DbType="NChar(5) NOT NULL", CanBeNull=false, IsPrimaryKey=true)]
[global::System.Runtime.Serialization.DataMemberAttribute(Order=1)]
public string CustomerID
{
    get
    {
        return this._CustomerID;
    }
    set
    {
        if ((this._CustomerID != value))
        {
            this.OnCustomerIDChanging(value);
            this.SendPropertyChanging();
            this._CustomerID = value;
            this.SendPropertyChanged("CustomerID");
            this.OnCustomerIDChanged();
        }
    }
}
```

In the code example, the *CustomerID* public property is adorned with *ColumnAttribute*. This attribute identifies each persistable property. Without this attribute, *CustomerID* will not be saved to the database. *ColumnAttribute* has several properties that can be set to change the persistence behavior slightly. In the code example, the *Storage* property identifies the private field that has the data. The *Name* property on *ColumnAttribute* can be set if, for example, the field name in the table does not match the property name.

The *CustomerID* property is also decorated by *DataMemberAttribute* to indicate to WCF services that this property's data can be serialized.

The property getter isn't doing anything other than returning the value of the private field. The setter has code that first attempts to call the partial *OnCustomerIDChanging* and *OnCustomerChanged* methods. If you decide to implement these methods, they will be called automatically to notify you before and after the change. The setter also has code to trigger the *PropertyChanging* and *PropertyChanged* events to notify anyone who has subscribed to these events.

An additional private field and public property for each child table is also referenced. In the *Customer* class, there is a private field and public property for the related orders because a customer has orders. The following code sample shows the private field and public property that represent the orders related to a customer.

Sample of Visual Basic Code

```vb
Private _Orders As EntitySet(Of [Order])

<Global.System.Data.Linq.Mapping.AssociationAttribute(Name:="Customer_Order", _
        Storage:="_Orders", ThisKey:="CustomerID", OtherKey:="CustomerID"), _
    Global.System.Runtime.Serialization.DataMemberAttribute(Order:=12, _
        EmitDefaultValue:=False)> _
Public Property Orders() As EntitySet(Of [Order])
    Get
        If (Me.serializing _
                AndAlso (Me._Orders.HasLoadedOrAssignedValues = False)) Then
            Return Nothing
        End If
        Return Me._Orders
    End Get
    Set(ByVal value As EntitySet(Of [Order]))
        Me._Orders.Assign(value)
    End Set
End Property
```

Sample of C# Code

```csharp
private EntitySet<Order> _Orders;

[global::System.Data.Linq.Mapping.AssociationAttribute(Name="Customer_Order", Storage="_
Orders", ThisKey="CustomerID", OtherKey="CustomerID")]
[global::System.Runtime.Serialization.DataMemberAttribute(Order=12,
EmitDefaultValue=false)]
public EntitySet<Order> Orders
{
    get
    {
        if ((this.serializing && (this._Orders.HasLoadedOrAssignedValues == false)))
        {
            return null;
        }
```

```
        return this._Orders;
    }
    set
    {
        this._Orders.Assign(value);
    }
}
```

At first glance, this code looks similar to the code example for *CustomerID*, but *ColumnAttribute* has been replaced by *AssociationAttribute*. This attribute identifies Customers_Order as the relationship that navigates from the Customers table to the Orders table. The attribute also identifies the key(s) used on the Customers and Orders tables.

The data type for Orders is a generic entity set of *Order*. The generic *EntitySet* is a specialized collection that provides deferred loading and relationship maintenance for the collection side of one-to-many and one-to-one relationships.

The getter has code to return nothing (C# *null*) if *Customer* is currently being serialized to keep from also serializing *Orders*. The getter also returns nothing (C# *null*) if no value has been assigned to this property or if this property has not been loaded.

The setter has simple code to pass the incoming value to the *Assign* method of the private field. *EntitySet* has a *ListChanged* event to which you can subscribe if you want to be notified when an assignment is made to this collection.

Examining the *DataContext* Class

The *NorthwindDataContext* class was created by the LINQ to SQL designer. This class inherits from the *DataContext* class that is part of the .NET Framework. The *DataContext* class is the main object for moving data to and from the database. You must instantiate the *NorthwindDataContext* class and then use its properties and methods to provide access to the database. To see the *DataContext* properties, click an empty area of the LINQ to SQL designer surface. Figure 4-5 shows the *DataContext* properties.

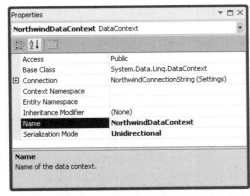

FIGURE 4-5 The *NorthwindDataContext* properties provide access to the connection string and other settings.

Of all the classes created by the LINQ to SQL designer, this is the only class that doesn't inherit from an object. The *Base Class* property provides the opportunity to create an intermediate class that inherits from *DataContext*, by which you add more functionality. You can then assign the intermediate class to the *Base Class* property.

EXAM TIP

You can expect to be tested on the *DataContext* class because it's explicitly called out in the exam objectives.

You also can set the namespace for the data context and entity classes so you can avoid naming collisions that could result if any of the created class names match the name of a class that already exists in your application.

If you are writing a WCF service, you might want to return instances of your entity classes from the service. This requires you to assign *DataContract* and *DataMember* attributes to the class and its properties by changing the *Serialization Mode* property from *None* to *Unidirectional*.

Looking at the *NorthwindDataContext* class that was produced by the LINQ to SQL designer, the following code example shows the class definition:

Sample of Visual Basic Code

```
<Global.System.Data.Linq.Mapping.DatabaseAttribute(Name:="Northwind")> _
Partial Public Class NorthwindDataContext
    Inherits System.Data.Linq.DataContext
    Private Shared mappingSource As System.Data.Linq.Mapping.MappingSource = _
        New AttributeMappingSource()
    'more members here
End Class
```

Sample of C# Code

```
[global::System.Data.Linq.Mapping.DatabaseAttribute(Name="Northwind")]
public partial class NorthwindDataContext : System.Data.Linq.DataContext
{
    private static System.Data.Linq.Mapping.MappingSource mappingSource = _
        new AttributeMappingSource();
    //more members here
}
```

This class is adorned with *DatabaseAttribute*, by which you specify the name of the database to which you will connect. This class inherits from *DataContext*.

This class also has a static field called *mappingSource*, which defaults to an instance of the *AttributeMappingSource* class. This field holds the mapping between the classes in the domain and the database as specified by attributes on the entity classes. You could opt to replace this object with an instance of *XmlMappingSource*, which would enable you to externalize the mappings to an XML file.

The *NorthwindDataContext* class contains a public property per type of entity class. The following code sample shows the *Customers* property:

Sample of Visual Basic Code

```vb
Public ReadOnly Property Customers() As System.Data.Linq.Table(Of Customer)
    Get
        Return Me.GetTable(Of Customer)()
    End Get
End Property
```

Sample of C# Code

```csharp
public System.Data.Linq.Table<Customer> Customers
{
    get
    {
        return this.GetTable<Customer>();
    }
}
```

Notice that the property type is the generic *Table* class of *Customer*. The *Table* class provides functionality for querying, inserting, updating, and deleting.

The *NorthwindDataContext* class also contains partial methods that you could implement for hooking into *insert*, *update*, and *delete* objects in any of the tables' properties on this class.

Managing Your Database Connection and Context Using *DataContext*

This section examines the connection string and how the *DataContext* object uses the connection string to connect to the database.

How LINQ to SQL Connects to Your Database

When you added items from Server Explorer, you automatically added the database connection string to your project as well. If you look in your config file, you will find the following connection string setting:

Config File

```xml
<connectionStrings>
    <add name="LinqToSqlSampleCode.Properties.Settings.NorthwindConnectionString"
        connectionString="Data Source=.;Initial Catalog=Northwind;Integrated
Security=True"
        providerName="System.Data.SqlClient" />
</connectionStrings>
```

LINQ to SQL uses the traditional ADO.NET *SqlConnection* class to open a connection to the SQL Server database. In this example, the data source property is set to a period, which means to connect to the local SQL Server instance. If you have only SqlExpress installed, your data source will be set to .\SQLEXPRESS, which means you want to connect to the SqlExpress instance of SQL Server on your local machine.

The *DataContext* object has a *Connection* property, and some of the constructors of the
NorthwindDataContext accept a connection string. The following code sample shows the
parameterless constructor for the *NorthwindDataContext* class:

Sample of Visual Basic Code

```
Public Sub New()
  MyBase.New(Global.LinqToSqlSampleCode.MySettings.Default.NorthwindConnectionString, _
      mappingSource)
  OnCreated()
End Sub
```

Sample of C# Code

```
public NorthwindDataContext() :
  base(global::LinqToSqlSampleCode.Properties.Settings.Default.
NorthwindConnectionString,
      mappingSource)
{
  OnCreated();
}
```

In this code example, the parameterless constructor makes a call to the base class
(*DataContext*) constructor but is passing *NorthwindConnectionString*, which is in the configuration file. This means that you can instantiate the *NorthwindDataContext* without passing
any parameter, and you automatically use the connection string that's in your config file. Also,
you can easily change the connection string in the config file without requiring a rebuild of
the application.

What's Sent to SQL Server, and When Is It Sent?

You might be wondering what kind of query is sent to SQL Server. Is the query efficient?
When is the query sent to SQL Server? This section explores a simple LINQ to SQL query to
answer these questions.

In the following code sample, a simple LINQ query is presented that retrieves a list of
employees whose last names start with "D" and binds the result to a Windows Presentation
Foundation (WPF) data grid.

Sample of Visual Basic Code

```
Private Sub mnuSimpleLinq_Click(ByVal sender As System.Object, _
                              ByVal e As System.Windows.RoutedEventArgs)
    Dim ctx = New NorthwindDataContext()
    Dim employees =  From emp In ctx.Employees
                  Where emp.LastName.StartsWith("D")
                  Select emp
```

```
      dg.ItemsSource = employees
End Sub
```

Sample of C# Code
```
private void mnuSimpleLinq_Click(object sender, RoutedEventArgs e)
{
    var ctx = new NorthwindDataContext();
    var employees = from emp in ctx.Employees
                    where emp.LastName.StartsWith("D")
                    select emp;
    dg.ItemsSource = employees;
}
```

This example shows the use of the parameterless constructor to create the *NorthwindDataContext* object. There is no reference to a connection in this code. *NorthwindDataContext* has an *Employees* property that can be used in your LINQ query. The LINQ query that follows creates the *IQueryable<Employee>* query object; however, remember that LINQ query execution is deferred until the result of the query is enumerated. The last statement assigns the employees query object to the *ItemsSource* property on the WPF data grid. The data grid will enumerate the employees query object, which will cause the query to execute and retrieve the two employees whose last names start with "D."

When the LINQ to SQL query is created by initializing the *employees* variable, connection pooling is initialized, but nothing has executed yet. When the *employees* variable is assigned to the *ItemsSource* property of the data grid, the LINQ to SQL query is executed, and two employees' names are returned, as shown in Figure 4-6.

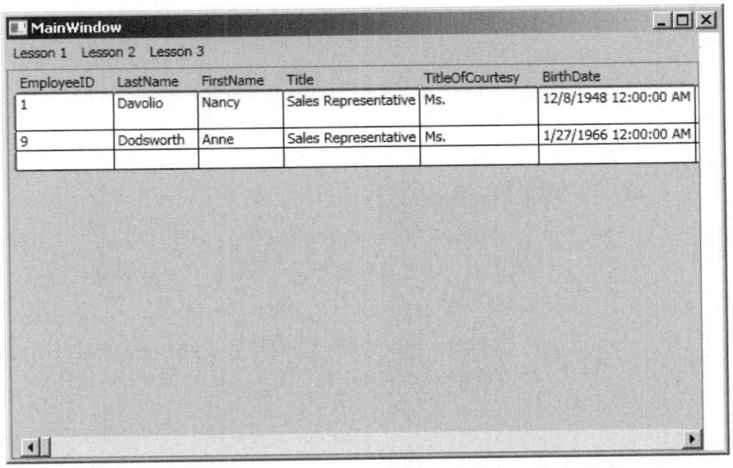

FIGURE 4-6 Two employees are returned from the LINQ to SQL query. In this example, *AutoGenerateColumns* is set to *true*.

How did this query work? Did LINQ to SQL send a query to SQL Server to retrieve all the employees and then filter the employees within your application? How can you find the answers to these questions?

One way to find the answers is to set a breakpoint in your program on the statement that assigns the employees query to the data grid. Run the application and, when you reach the break point, hover over the *employees* variable, and you'll see a tool tip with the SQL query that will be sent to SQL Server; however, it's difficult to see the whole query within the small tool tip.

> **NOTE LINQ TO SQL DEBUG VISUALIZER**
>
> You can find various LINQ to SQL debug visualizers on the Internet. After installing one of these visualizers, you will see a magnifying glass when hovering over the variable. Clicking the magnifying glass typically displays a pop-up window with the query in a much more readable format.

Another way to find the answers is to use the *Log* property on *NorthwindDataContext*. This property accepts a *TextWriter* object and will write out all queries so you can create a *StreamWriter* object that references a file so you can write everything to a file. You can also assign a *StringWriter* to the *Log* property, which will send the SQL queries to a memory stream, and then you can display the contents. The following code sample shows the creation of a *StringWriter* that is assigned to the *Log* property, and its contents are displayed after the query is executed.

Sample of Visual Basic Code

```
Private Sub mnuSimpleLinq_Click(ByVal sender As System.Object, _
                                ByVal e As System.Windows.RoutedEventArgs)
    Dim ctx = New NorthwindDataContext()
    Dim sw = New StringWriter()
    ctx.Log = sw
    Dim employees = From emp In ctx.Employees
                    Where emp.LastName.StartsWith("D")
                    Select emp
    dg.ItemsSource = employees
    MessageBox.Show(sw.GetStringBuilder().ToString())
End Sub
```

Sample of C# Code

```
private void mnuSimpleLinq_Click(object sender, RoutedEventArgs e)
{
    var ctx = new NorthwindDataContext();
    var sw =  new StringWriter();
    ctx.Log = sw;
    var employees = from emp in ctx.Employees
                    where emp.LastName.StartsWith("D")
                    select emp;
    dg.ItemsSource = employees;
    MessageBox.Show(sw.GetStringBuilder().ToString());
}
```

After running this code sample, a message box is displayed, as shown in Figure 4-7. This query is retrieving all columns from the Employees table, but the query includes a *where* clause to provide the filtering at the database. SQL Server then performs the filtering and returns two rows to your application, thus providing efficient SQL for your LINQ to SQL query.

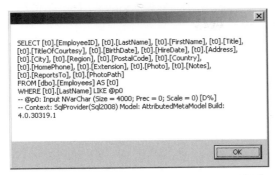

```
SELECT [t0].[EmployeeID], [t0].[LastName], [t0].[FirstName], [t0].[Title],
[t0].[TitleOfCourtesy], [t0].[BirthDate], [t0].[HireDate], [t0].[Address],
[t0].[City], [t0].[Region], [t0].[PostalCode], [t0].[Country],
[t0].[HomePhone], [t0].[Extension], [t0].[Photo], [t0].[Notes],
[t0].[ReportsTo], [t0].[PhotoPath]
FROM [dbo].[Employees] AS [t0]
WHERE [t0].[LastName] LIKE @p0
-- @p0: Input NVarChar (Size = 4000; Prec = 0; Scale = 0) [D%]
-- Context: SqlProvider(Sql2008) Model: AttributedMetaModel Build:
4.0.30319.1
```

FIGURE 4-7 Here is the SQL query that is sent to SQL Server.

Finally, another way to see the queries sent to SQL Server is to use the SQL Server Profiler tool that comes with the Developer edition of SQL Server. The SQL Server Profiler can capture all SQL statements sent to SQL Server. Although this tool isn't included with SQL Server Express, it does work with that edition.

To use the SQL Server Profiler, you must have administrator privileges on SQL Server, or the SQL Server administrator can grant permissions for you to run the profiler tool. This tool can store the captured statements to a file or a database table. Figure 4-8 shows the output when running the sample LINQ to SQL code.

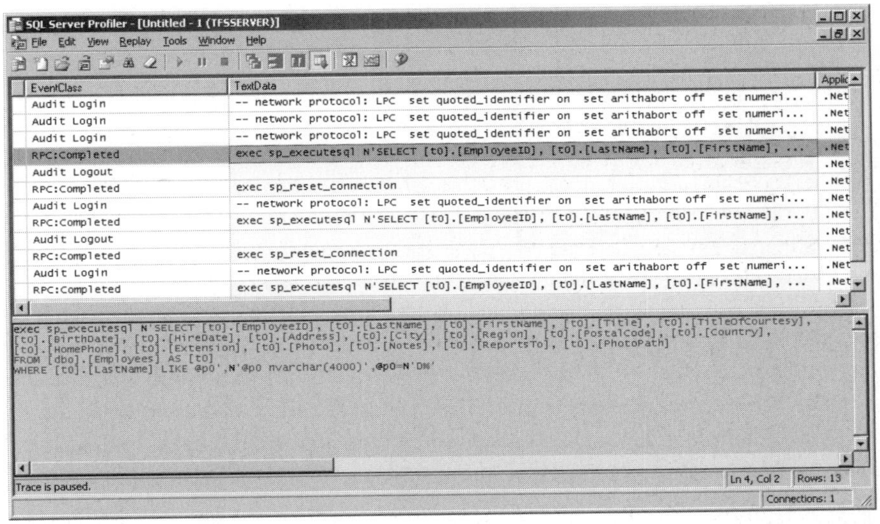

FIGURE 4-8 The SQL Server Profiler can capture all the traffic between the application and SQL Server.

The SQL Server Profiler can capture and display much more information than is shown in the *Log* property of *NorthwindDataContext*. In fact, in Figure 4-7, you can see that three select statements were sent to SQL Server. The first select statement is highlighted, and it matches the statement that was shown when using the *Log* property. The second SQL statement has a *where* clause to return only EmployeeID=2, and the third SQL statement has a *where* clause to return EmployeeID=5. These two queries were caused by the data grid in an effort to retrieve the most recent value for the employees.

Eager Loading vs. Lazy Loading

When specifying properties or associations for which to query on your entity, you can perform *eager loading* or *lazy loading*. Lazy loading is also known as delay loading. Eager loading is also known as pre-fetch loading. The default behavior is to perform eager loading of the properties, which means that a property is loaded when a query is executed that references the property.

Lazy loading is configured in the LINQ to SQL designer by selecting an entity and then, in the Properties window, setting the *Delay Loaded* property to *true*. Figure 4-9 shows the *Delay Loaded* property.

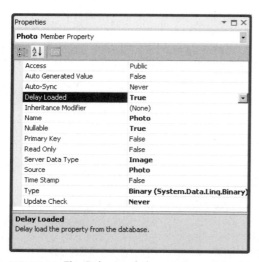

FIGURE 4-9 The *Delay Loaded* property can be set to *true* to perform lazy loading.

When using lazy loading, the property is not loaded until the property is accessed. When examining lazy loading, you need to think about performance and when you will you take the performance hit. In one extreme, if every property were lazy loaded, there would be a cost associated with establishing the connection each time and transferring the data. To the user, this might make the application feel choppy or erratic. If you're fairly certain that you will use the data, why not pull the properties in one call? You take a big hit, maybe when a page is displayed to the user, but the page feels crisp afterward. The choice you make depends on the how much data will be transferred and how certain you are that you will use the data. With lazy loading, you're making the decision to incur the performance cost to retrieve the data when you need it because you're fairly certain you won't need the data anyway. In

Figure 4-9, the Photo entry on the *Employee* entity is set to *Delay Loaded*. The following code example shows the effect of setting *Delay Loaded* to *true*:

Sample of Visual Basic Code

```vb
Private Sub mnuLazyLoading_Click(ByVal sender As System.Object, _
                                 ByVal e As System.Windows.RoutedEventArgs)
    Dim ctx = New NorthwindDataContext()
    Dim sw = New StringWriter()
    ctx.Log = sw
    Dim employee = (From emp In ctx.Employees
                    Where emp.LastName.StartsWith("D")
                    Select emp).First()
    MessageBox.Show(sw.GetStringBuilder().ToString())

    sw = New StringWriter()
    ctx.Log = sw
    Dim photo = New MemoryStream(Employee.Photo.ToArray())
    MessageBox.Show(sw.GetStringBuilder().ToString())
End Sub
```

Sample of C# Code

```csharp
private void mnuLazyLoading_Click(object sender, RoutedEventArgs e)
{
    var ctx = new NorthwindDataContext();
    var sw = new StringWriter();
    ctx.Log = sw;
    var employee = (from emp in ctx.Employees
                    where emp.LastName.StartsWith("Davolio")
                    select emp).First();
    MessageBox.Show(sw.GetStringBuilder().ToString());

    sw = new StringWriter();
    ctx.Log = sw;
    var photo = new MemoryStream(employee.Photo.ToArray());
    MessageBox.Show(sw.GetStringBuilder().ToString());
}
```

This code sample retrieves a single employee and displays the SQL statement that was generated. The code is then able to access the *Photo* property successfully, and the query that was run is displayed. Figure 4-10 shows the queries that were executed when this example code has been run.

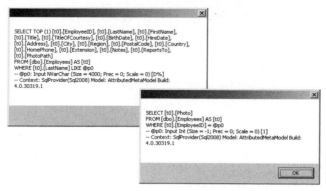

FIGURE 4-10 The SQL statements are shown that retrieve the employee name and then retrieve the employee's photo.

The first query that ran didn't include *Photo*, even though the LINQ expression requested the whole employee object. The *Photo* property was not included because the *Delay Loaded* property was set to *true*. When the *Photo* property was accessed, LINQ to SQL made a call to retrieve *Photo*. This is the second query displayed. When you use lazy loading, you're essentially betting that you're not going to need all columns' content, but if you do need the data, it will be automatically fetched for you.

PRACTICE Working with the LINQ to SQL Designer

In this practice, you create a new WPF application that accepts orders from customers, using the Northwind database. After creating the application, you use the LINQ to SQL designer to create an entity model for this application. In later exercises, you will add functionality to make the application operational.

This practice is intended to focus on the classes that have been defined in this lesson, so the graphical user interface (GUI) will be minimal.

If you encounter a problem completing an exercise, the completed projects can be installed from the Code folder on the companion CD.

EXERCISE Create the Project and LINQ to SQL Entity Model

In this exercise, you create a WPF Application project and the entity model, using the Northwind database.

1. In Visual Studio .NET 2010, choose File | New | Project.

2. Select a programming language and then select the WPF Application template. For the project name, enter **OrderEntryProject**. Be sure to select a location for this project.

3. For the solution name, enter **OrderEntrySolution**. Be sure that Create Directory For Solution is selected and then click OK.

    After Visual Studio .NET creates the project, the home page, MainWindow.xaml, is displayed.

4. In Solution Explorer, right-click the OrderEntryProject icon and choose Add | New Item. Select LINQ to SQL Classes and name the file **Northwind.dbml**. (Be sure to use the correct casing.)

5. Open Server Explorer by choosing View | Server Explorer.

6. Right-click the Data Connections icon and click Add Connection.

7. Depending on your Visual Studio configuration, you might be prompted with a window called Change Data Source. If so, select Microsoft SQL Server and click OK.

8. In the Add Connection window, at the Server Name prompt, type the name of the SQL Server instance. If you are using SQL Express on your local computer, type **./SqlExpress**.

9. At the Select Or Enter A Database Name prompt, select the Northwind database from the drop-down list and click OK. If you don't see the Northwind database in the drop-down list, install the Northwind database before going any further. If you don't have the Northwind database, a copy is included in the Chapter 4 sample code folder.

10. The Northwind database connection is now showing in the Server Explorer window. Beside the connection, click the plus sign to open the connection and then open the *Tables* node.

11. Drag the Customers, Orders, Order Details, and Products tables to the LINQ to SQL designer surface. Your window should look like the sample shown in Figure 4-11.

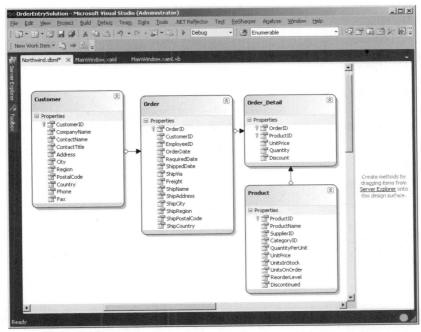

FIGURE 4-11 Here is the LINQ to SQL designer with the completed entity model.

12. Close and save the LINQ to SQL designer window.

Lesson Summary

This lesson provided detailed information about the LINQ to SQL designer.

- You can create an entity model easily by dragging and dropping database tables from Server Explorer.

- A table that is dropped on to the LINQ to SQL designer surface creates an entity class that represents each row in the table.

- You can drag and drop stored procedures to the LINQ to SQL designer surface, which creates methods that you can call from your application.

- Entity classes implement *INotifyPropertyChanging* and *INotifyPropertyChanged* to be tracked efficiently by the object tracking service.

- The *DataContext* object provides a property for each table and a method for each stored procedure.

- LINQ to SQL supports eager loading by default, but you can enable deferred loading, also known as lazy loading, to defer loading of the entity properties until you actually reference the property in your code.

Lesson Review

You can use the following questions to test your knowledge of the information in Lesson 1, "What Is LINQ to SQL?" The questions are also available on the companion CD if you prefer to review them in electronic form.

> **NOTE ANSWERS**
>
> Answers to these questions and explanations of why each answer choice is correct or incorrect are located in the "Answers" section at the end of the book.

1. When working with LINQ to SQL, what is the main object that moves data to and from the database?

   A. *DataSet*

   B. *SqlDataAdapter*

   C. *DataContext*

   D. *Entity*

2. You want to use LINQ to SQL to run queries on a table that contains a column that stores large photos. Most of the time, you won't need to view the photo, but occasionally you will need to see it. In the LINQ to SQL designer, which property can you set on the photo column to get the efficient loading of the data for most scenarios but still be able to retrieve the photo when needed?

A. *Skip*

B. *Delay Loaded*

C. *Take*

D. *Auto Generated Value*

Lesson 2: Executing Queries Using LINQ to SQL

In the previous lesson, you were introduced to the LINQ to SQL designer, the *DataContext* class, and an example entity class. In addition, a couple of LINQ to SQL queries were presented to demonstrate the operation of the *DataContext* class and lazy loading. You also saw how the LINQ to SQL provider queries only for the required data when *where* clauses are provided.

This lesson examines some of the more common types of LINQ to SQL queries you might perform.

After this lesson, you will be able to:

- Perform LINQ to SQL queries with filtering and sorting.
- Write LINQ to SQL statements that implement projections.
- Perform inner joins with LINQ to SQL.
- Perform outer joins with LINQ to SQL.
- Create and execute grouping and aggregation with LINQ to SQL.

Estimated lesson time: 45 minutes

Basic Query with Filter and Sort

Basic queries using the LINQ to SQL classes are very clean and readable. In addition, remember that LINQ to SQL classes retrieve only the data you request. The following code sample queries for a list of customers that contain the word "Restaurant" in the company name, sorted on postal code.

Sample of Visual Basic Code

```
private void mnuBasicQuery_Click(object sender, RoutedEventArgs e)
{
    var ctx = new NorthwindDataContext();
    var sw = new StringWriter();
    ctx.Log = sw;
    var customers = from c in ctx.Customers
                    where c.CompanyName.Contains("Restaurant")
                    orderby c.PostalCode
                    select c;
    dg.ItemsSource = customers;
    MessageBox.Show(sw.GetStringBuilder().ToString());
}
```

Sample of C# Code

```
private void mnuBasicQuery_Click(object sender, RoutedEventArgs e)
{
    var ctx = new NorthwindDataContext();
    var sw = new StringWriter();
    ctx.Log = sw;
```

```
    var customers = from c in ctx.Customers
                    where c.CompanyName.Contains("Restaurant")
                    orderby c.PostalCode
                    select c;
    dg.ItemsSource = customers;
    MessageBox.Show(sw.GetStringBuilder().ToString());
}
```

SQL Query

```
SELECT [t0].[CustomerID], [t0].[CompanyName], [t0].[ContactName], [t0].[ContactTitle],
[t0].[Address], [t0].[City], [t0].[Region], [t0].[PostalCode], [t0].[Country], [t0].
[Phone], [t0].[Fax]
FROM [dbo].[Customers] AS [t0]
WHERE [t0].[CompanyName] LIKE @p0
ORDER BY [t0].[PostalCode]
-- @p0: Input NVarChar (Size = 4000; Prec = 0; Scale = 0) [%Restaurant%]
```

The LINQ to SQL query sends a query to SQL Server that includes a *where* clause and an *order by* clause. Looking at the sample code, this looks like a very basic LINQ query, using the *Customers* property on the *NorthwindDataContext* object. The key here is that the LINQ to SQL provider is capable of constructing an efficient query to send to SQL Server.

Projections

One of the potential problems with the previous query is that all the column values from the Customers table are returned, but you might have needed to retrieve only CustomerID, CompanyName, and PostalCode. You can use a projection to limit the column values returned from SQL Server. The following code example demonstrates the use of projections to limit the returned column values from the Customers table.

Sample of Visual Basic Code

```
Private Sub mnuProjection_Click(ByVal sender As System.Object, _
                                ByVal e As System.Windows.RoutedEventArgs)
    Dim ctx = New NorthwindDataContext()
    Dim sw = New StringWriter()
    ctx.Log = sw
    Dim customers = From c In ctx.Customers
                    Where c.CompanyName.Contains("Restaurant")
                    Order By c.PostalCode
                    Select New With {c.CustomerID, c.CompanyName, c.PostalCode}
    dg.ItemsSource = customers
    MessageBox.Show(sw.GetStringBuilder().ToString())
End Sub
```

Sample of C# Code

```
private void mnuProjection_Click(object sender, RoutedEventArgs e)
{
    var ctx = new NorthwindDataContext();
    var sw = new StringWriter();
    ctx.Log = sw;
    var customers = from c in ctx.Customers
```

```
                    where c.CompanyName.Contains("Restaurant")
                    orderby c.PostalCode
                    select new
                            {
                                c.CustomerID,
                                c.CompanyName,
                                c.PostalCode
                            };
    dg.ItemsSource = customers;
    MessageBox.Show(sw.GetStringBuilder().ToString());
}
```

SQL Query

```
SELECT [t0].[CustomerID], [t0].[CompanyName], [t0].[PostalCode]
FROM [dbo].[Customers] AS [t0]
WHERE [t0].[CompanyName] LIKE @p0
ORDER BY [t0].[PostalCode]
-- @p0: Input NVarChar (Size = 4000; Prec = 0; Scale = 0) [%Restaurant%]
```

This code instantiates an anonymous type that filters out columns. Chapter 3, "Introducing LINQ," covers anonymous types and projections in more detail.

Inner Joins

An inner join produces output only when the two tables you are joining match on the unique key to foreign key. Inner joins can be implemented easily with LINQ to SQL by using the standard LINQ query syntax. The following LINQ query produces an inner join of the Customers table to the Orders table and retrieves CustomerID, CompanyName, OrderID, and OrderDate by using query extension methods.

Sample of Visual Basic Code

```
Private Sub mnuInnerJoin1_Click(ByVal sender As System.Object, _
                                ByVal e As System.Windows.RoutedEventArgs)
    Dim ctx = New NorthwindDataContext()
    Dim sw = New StringWriter()
    ctx.Log = sw
    Dim customers = ctx.Customers.Join(ctx.Orders, _
                                   Function(c) c.CustomerID, _
                                   Function(o) o.CustomerID, _
                                   Function(c, o) New With
                                                    {
                                                        c.CustomerID,
                                                        c.CompanyName,
                                                        o.OrderID,
                                                        o.OrderDate
                                                    }) _
                                .OrderBy(Function(r) r.CustomerID) _
                                .ThenBy(Function(r) r.OrderID)
    dg.ItemsSource = customers
    MessageBox.Show(sw.GetStringBuilder().ToString())
End Sub
```

Sample of C# Code

```csharp
private void mnuInnerJoin1_Click(object sender, RoutedEventArgs e)
{
    var ctx = new NorthwindDataContext();
    var sw = new StringWriter();
    ctx.Log = sw;
    var customers = ctx.Customers.Join(
        ctx.Orders,
        c => c.CustomerID,
        o => o.CustomerID,
        (c, o) => new
                    {
                        c.CustomerID,
                        c.CompanyName,
                        o.OrderID,
                        o.OrderDate
                    })
            .OrderBy(r=>r.CustomerID)
            .ThenBy((r=>r.OrderID));
    dg.ItemsSource = customers;
    MessageBox.Show(sw.GetStringBuilder().ToString());
}
```

SQL Query

```sql
SELECT [t0].[CustomerID], [t0].[CompanyName], [t1].[OrderID], [t1].[OrderDate]
FROM [dbo].[Customers] AS [t0]
INNER JOIN [dbo].[Orders] AS [t1] ON [t0].[CustomerID] = [t1].[CustomerID]
ORDER BY [t0].[CustomerID], [t1].[OrderID]
```

Using query extension methods to perform the join produced a nice, clean SQL query. Could this query be written as a LINQ query? It can, and the following code sample produces the same result.

Sample of Visual Basic Code

```vb
Private Sub mnuInnerJoin2_Click(ByVal sender As System.Object, _
                                ByVal e As System.Windows.RoutedEventArgs)
    Dim ctx = New NorthwindDataContext()
    Dim sw = New StringWriter()
    ctx.Log = sw
    Dim customers = From c In ctx.Customers
                    Join o In ctx.Orders
                    On c.CustomerID Equals o.CustomerID
                    Order By c.CustomerID, o.OrderID
                    Select New With
                        {
                            c.CustomerID,
                            c.CompanyName,
                            o.OrderID,
                            o.OrderDate
                        }
    dg.ItemsSource = customers
    MessageBox.Show(sw.GetStringBuilder().ToString())
End Sub
```

Sample of C# Code

```csharp
private void mnuInnerJoin_Click(object sender, RoutedEventArgs e)
{
    var ctx = new NorthwindDataContext();
    var sw = new StringWriter();
    ctx.Log = sw;
    var customers = from c in ctx.Customers
                    join o in ctx.Orders
                    on c.CustomerID equals o.CustomerID
                    orderby  c.CustomerID, o.OrderID
                    select new
                    {
                        c.CustomerID,
                        c.CompanyName,
                        o.OrderID,
                        o.OrderDate
                    };
    dg.ItemsSource = customers;
    MessageBox.Show(sw.GetStringBuilder().ToString());
}
```

SQL Query

```sql
SELECT [t0].[CustomerID], [t0].[CompanyName], [t1].[OrderID], [t1].[OrderDate]
FROM [dbo].[Customers] AS [t0]
INNER JOIN [dbo].[Orders] AS [t1] ON [t0].[CustomerID] = [t1].[CustomerID]
ORDER BY [t0].[CustomerID], [t1].[OrderID]
```

This is a clean-looking LINQ query, and it produced a nice, efficient SQL query. If you look through the results carefully, you might find that there are two customers who have not placed any orders. How would you know that? These two customers are missing from the output because they don't match up to any orders. The missing customer IDs are FISSA and PARIS. To see all customers, you need to write an outer join.

Outer Joins

An outer join produces output of the outer table, even if the outer table element doesn't match the inner table. To perform an outer join, you must provide code to indicate that you still want the outer table row, even if there is no match to the inner table. You can perform outer joins by using the *GroupJoin* extension method, as shown in the following sample code:

Sample of Visual Basic Code

```vbnet
Private Sub mnuOuterJoin1_Click(ByVal sender As System.Object, _
                                ByVal e As System.Windows.RoutedEventArgs)
    Dim ctx = New NorthwindDataContext()
    Dim sw = New StringWriter()
    ctx.Log = sw
    Dim customers = ctx.Customers.GroupJoin(ctx.Orders, _
            Function(c) c.CustomerID, _
            Function(o) o.CustomerID, _
            Function(c, o) New With
                      {
                          c.CustomerID,
```

```
                                c.CompanyName,
                                .Orders = o
                        }) _
        .SelectMany(Function(t) t.Orders.DefaultIfEmpty().Select( _
                Function(ord) New With
                        {
                            t.CompanyName,
                            t.CustomerID,
                            .OrderID = CType(ord.OrderID, Nullable(Of Integer)),
                            .OrderDate = CType(ord.OrderDate, Nullable(Of DateTime))
                        })) _
        .OrderBy(Function(r) r.CustomerID) _
        .ThenBy(Function(r) r.OrderID)
    dg.ItemsSource = customers
    MessageBox.Show(sw.GetStringBuilder().ToString())
End Sub
```

Sample of C# Code

```
private void mnuOuterJoin1_Click(object sender, RoutedEventArgs e)
{
    var ctx = new NorthwindDataContext();
    var sw = new StringWriter();
    ctx.Log = sw;
    var customers = ctx.Customers.GroupJoin(
        ctx.Orders,
        c => c.CustomerID,
        o => o.CustomerID,
        (c, o) => new
                    {
                        c.CustomerID,
                        c.CompanyName,
                        Orders = o
                    })
        .SelectMany(t=>t.Orders.DefaultIfEmpty().Select(ord=>
            new
            {
                t.CompanyName,
                t.CustomerID,
                OrderID=(int?)ord.OrderID,
                OrderDate=(DateTime?) ord.OrderDate}))
        .OrderBy(r => r.CustomerID).ThenBy((r => r.OrderID));

    dg.ItemsSource = customers;
    MessageBox.Show(sw.GetStringBuilder().ToString());
}
```

SQL Query

```
SELECT [t2].[CompanyName], [t2].[CustomerID],
[t2].[value] AS [OrderID2], [t2].[value2] AS [OrderDate]
FROM (
SELECT [t1].[OrderID] AS [value], [t1].[OrderDate] AS [value2],
[t0].[CompanyName], [t0].[CustomerID]
    FROM [dbo].[Customers] AS [t0]
    LEFT OUTER JOIN [dbo].[Orders] AS [t1] ON [t0].[CustomerID] = [t1].[CustomerID]
```

```
        ) AS [t2]
ORDER BY [t2].[CustomerID], [t2].[value]
```

This code sample turned out to be ugly, primarily because the goal was to bind this to the data grid and see the same results as the inner join but with an extra row for FISSA and PARIS. In the SQL query, although a left outer join was performed, it was nested in a subquery, and the only result the outer query provides is a reordering of the fields.

You can also perform an outer join by using a LINQ query with the *into* keyword with the join. The following is a rewrite of the previous query, done as a LINQ query.

Sample of Visual Basic Code

```
Private Sub mnuOuterJoin2_Click(ByVal sender As System.Object, _
                            ByVal e As System.Windows.RoutedEventArgs)
    Dim ctx = New NorthwindDataContext()
    Dim sw = New StringWriter()
    ctx.Log = sw
    Dim customers = From c In ctx.Customers
                    Group Join o In ctx.Orders
                    On c.CustomerID Equals o.CustomerID Into InJoin = Group
                    From outJoin In InJoin.DefaultIfEmpty()
                    Order By c.CustomerID, outJoin.OrderID
                    Select New With
                        {
                            c.CustomerID,
                            c.CompanyName,
                            .OrderID = CType(outJoin.OrderID, Nullable(Of Integer)),
                            .OrderDate = CType(outJoin.OrderDate, Nullable(Of DateTime))
                        }
    dg.ItemsSource = customers
    MessageBox.Show(sw.GetStringBuilder().ToString())
End Sub
```

Sample of C# Code

```
private void mnuOuterJoin2_Click(object sender, RoutedEventArgs e)
{
    var ctx = new NorthwindDataContext();
    var sw = new StringWriter();
    ctx.Log = sw;
    var customers = from c in ctx.Customers
                    join o in ctx.Orders
                    on c.CustomerID equals o.CustomerID into inJoin
                    from outJoin in inJoin.DefaultIfEmpty()
                    orderby c.CustomerID, outJoin.OrderID
                    select new
                    {
                        c.CustomerID,
                        c.CompanyName,
                        OrderID = (int?)outJoin.OrderID,
                        OrderDate = (DateTime?)outJoin.OrderDate
                    };w
    dg.ItemsSource = customers;
    MessageBox.Show(sw.GetStringBuilder().ToString());
}
```

```
SELECT [t0].[CustomerID], [t0].[CompanyName],
[t1].[OrderID] AS [OrderID2], [t1].[OrderDate] AS [OrderDate]
FROM [dbo].[Customers] AS [t0]
LEFT OUTER JOIN [dbo].[Orders] AS [t1] ON [t0].[CustomerID] = [t1].[CustomerID]
ORDER BY [t0].[CustomerID], [t1].[OrderID]
```

The LINQ query is much neater than the previous code example, which was implemented by extension methods. In addition, the SQL query is a nice, clean left outer join.

Grouping and Aggregation

LINQ to SQL also enables you to perform grouping operations to retrieve aggregate results. For example, you might want to retrieve the total amount of each order. To get the total of each order, get the sum of each order item in the Order_Details table. The following code sample shows how grouping and aggregation can solve this problem.

Sample of Visual Basic Code

```
Private Sub mnuAggregates_Click(ByVal sender As System.Object, _
                                ByVal e As System.Windows.RoutedEventArgs)
    Dim ctx = New NorthwindDataContext()
    Dim sw = New StringWriter()
    ctx.Log = sw
    Dim orders = From o In ctx.Order_Details
                 Group o By OrderID = o.OrderID Into grouped = Group
                 Select New With
                        {
                            .OrderID = OrderID,
                            .Total = grouped.Sum(Function(line) _
                                     line.Quantity * line.UnitPrice * _
                                     (1 - CType(line.Discount, Decimal)))
                        }
    dg.ItemsSource = orders
    MessageBox.Show(sw.GetStringBuilder().ToString())
End Sub
```

Sample of C# Code

```
private void mnuAggregates_Click(object sender, RoutedEventArgs e)
{
    var ctx = new NorthwindDataContext();
    var sw = new StringWriter();
    ctx.Log = sw;
    var orders = from o in ctx.Order_Details
                 group o by o.OrderID
                 into grouped
                 select new
                 {
                 OrderID = grouped.Key,
                 Total = grouped.Sum(
                    line=>line.Quantity * line.UnitPrice *
                        (1 - (decimal)line.Discount))
                 };
```

```
    dg.ItemsSource = orders;
    MessageBox.Show(sw.GetStringBuilder().ToString());
}
```

SQL Query

```
SELECT SUM([t1].[value]) AS [Total], [t1].[OrderID]
FROM (
    SELECT (CONVERT(Decimal(29,4),[t0].[Quantity])) * [t0].[UnitPrice] *
    (@p0 - (CONVERT(Decimal(33,4),[t0].[Discount]))) AS [value], [t0].[OrderID]
    FROM [dbo].[Order Details] AS [t0]
    ) AS [t1]
GROUP BY [t1].[OrderID]
-- @p0: Input Decimal (Size = -1; Prec = 33; Scale = 4) [1]
```

This code sample grouped the Order_Details rows by *OrderID* and then calculated the total of each order by calculating the sum of the line items of the order. To calculate the sum, each line had to be calculated by multiplying the quantity by the unit price and then multiplying by one minus the discount.

Paging

When writing an application that queries thousands or millions of rows of data, you will often run into problems when a query returns many more rows of data than you could possibly display. Having said that, what's the sense of waiting for all that data to be shipped from SQL Server to your application? For example, maybe you queried for the customers whose names begin with the letter A, but you didn't realize that this would return ten thousand rows of data.

Paging can be a useful way to minimize the amount of data returned from a query so you can see the first part of the data quickly and decide whether you want to continue viewing more data. To implement paging, you can use the *Skip* and *Take* extension methods with your LINQ query. In the following sample code, a scrollbar has been added to the WPF form, and its settings are configured to match the quantity of pages of customers. When scrolling, the *Scroll* event is triggered, and you see the previous or next page of customers. This code sample uses the *Skip* and *Take* methods:

Sample of Visual Basic Code

```
Private Const pageSize As Integer = 25
Private pageCount As Integer
Private customerCount As Integer
Private customers As IQueryable(Of Tuple(Of String, String))
Private sw As New StringWriter()

Private Sub mnuPaging_Click(ByVal sender As System.Object, _
        ByVal e As System.Windows.RoutedEventArgs)
    Dim ctx = New NorthwindDataContext()
    ctx.Log = sw
    customers = From c In ctx.Customers
                Order By c.CompanyName
```

```
                    Select New Tuple(Of String, String)(c.CustomerID, c.CompanyName)

    customerCount = customers.Count()
    pageCount = customerCount / pageSize
    If (pageCount * pageSize < customerCount) Then pageCount += 1

    scrData.Minimum = 0
    scrData.Maximum = pageCount
    scrData.Visibility = Visibility.Visible
    scrData.SmallChange = 1
    scrData_Scroll(Nothing, Nothing)
End Sub

Private Sub scrData_Scroll(ByVal sender As System.Object, _
        ByVal e As System.Windows.Controls.Primitives.ScrollEventArgs)
    Dim customersDisplay = From c In customers
                           Select New With {.ID = c.Item1, .Name = c.Item2}
    dg.ItemsSource = customersDisplay.Skip(CInt(scrData.Value) * pageSize).Take(pageSize)
End Sub
```

Sample of C# Code

```
private const int pageSize = 25;
private int pageCount;
private int customerCount;
private IQueryable<Tuple<string,string>> customers;
StringWriter sw = new StringWriter();

private void mnuPaging_Click(object sender, RoutedEventArgs e)
{
    var ctx = new NorthwindDataContext();
    ctx.Log = sw;
    customers = from c in ctx.Customers
                orderby c.CompanyName
                select
                    new Tuple<string,string>(c.CustomerID,c.CompanyName);

    customerCount = customers.Count();
    pageCount = customerCount / pageSize;
    if (pageCount * pageSize < customerCount) pageCount++;

    scrData.Minimum = 0;
    scrData.Maximum = pageCount;
    scrData.Visibility = Visibility.Visible;
    scrData.SmallChange = 1;
    scrData_Scroll(null, null);
}

private void scrData_Scroll(object sender,
               System.Windows.Controls.Primitives.ScrollEventArgs e)
{
    var customersDisplay = from c in customers
                           select new {ID = c.Item1, Name = c.Item2};
    dg.ItemsSource = customersDisplay.Skip((int)scrData.Value * pageSize).Take(pageSize);
}
```

SQL Query

```
SELECT COUNT(*) AS [value]
FROM [dbo].[Customers] AS [t0]
-- Context: SqlProvider(Sql2008) Model: AttributedMetaModel Build: 4.0.30319.1

SELECT [t1].[CustomerID] AS [item1], [t1].[CompanyName] AS [item2]
FROM (
    SELECT ROW_NUMBER() OVER (
            ORDER BY [t0].[CompanyName]) AS [ROW_NUMBER],
                          [t0].[CustomerID], [t0].[CompanyName]
    FROM [dbo].[Customers] AS [t0]
    ) AS [t1]
WHERE [t1].[ROW_NUMBER] BETWEEN @p0 + 1 AND @p0 + @p1
ORDER BY [t1].[ROW_NUMBER]
-- @p0: Input Int (Size = -1; Prec = 0; Scale = 0) [0]
-- @p1: Input Int (Size = -1; Prec = 0; Scale = 0) [25]
-- Context: SqlProvider(Sql2008) Model: AttributedMetaModel Build: 4.0.30319.1
```

Of the SQL queries that were run, the first query was to get the count of customers, which was executed when the *customers.Count()* call was made. The next SQL query was to retrieve the first page of customers. In this query, the two parameters are *@p0*, the current page, and *@p1*, the page size. These parameters are set to 0 and 25, respectively. The query itself uses the *ROW_NUMBER* function available in SQL Server 2005 and later, which is why using LINQ to SQL on SQL Server 2000 has limitations. As you page up and down, the second query executes but will substitute a different value for the current page (*@p0*).

In the Visual Basic 2010 and C# code, variables and constants are being defined outside the method for these variables to be accessible in all methods. The first method, *mnuPaging_Click*, executes when you select the Paging menu option. This method retrieves the count of customers and sets the LINQ to SQL query; it also configures the scroll bar and sets it to be visible. The next method, *scrData_Scroll*, is executed each time you click the scroll bar. This method retrieves the current page value from the scroll bar and uses the *Skip* and *Take* methods to retrieve a single page of data.

PRACTICE   Writing LINQ Queries to Display Data

In this practice, you continue the order entry application from Lesson 1, "What Is LINQ to SQL?" by adding a GUI and then LINQ queries to populate the GUI with data.

If you encounter a problem completing an exercise, the completed projects can be installed from the Code folder on the companion CD.

EXERCISE 1   Add the GUI

In this exercise, you modify the WPF application you created in Lesson 1 by creating the GUI. In the next exercise, you add the LINQ queries to populate the screen.

1. In Visual Studio .NET 2010, choose File | Open | Project. Open the project from Lesson 1 or locate and open the solution in the Begin folder for this lesson.

2. In Solution Explorer, double-click the MainWindow.xaml file to open the file in the WPF Form Designer window.

3. On the Window tab, add a *Loaded* event handler. When prompted for a new *EventHandler*, double-click the New EventHandler option. Your XAML should look like the following:

Sample of Visual Basic XAML

```
<Window x:Class="MainWindow"
        xmlns="http://schemas.microsoft.com/winfx/2006/xaml/presentation"
        xmlns:x="http://schemas.microsoft.com/winfx/2006/xaml"
        Loaded="Window_Loaded"
        Title="MainWindow" Height="350" Width="525">
    <Grid>
    </Grid>
</Window>
```

Sample of C# XAML

```
<Window x:Class="OrderEntryProject.MainWindow"
        xmlns="http://schemas.microsoft.com/winfx/2006/xaml/presentation"
        xmlns:x="http://schemas.microsoft.com/winfx/2006/xaml"
        Loaded="Window_Loaded"
        Title="MainWindow" Height="350" Width="525">
    <Grid>
    </Grid>
</Window>
```

4. The XAML code contains a *Grid* definition. Inside the grid, add three row definitions. The first two rows should have their *Height* property set to *Auto*, and the last row should have its *Height* property set to "*". Regardless of your programming language, your XAML for the grid should look like the following:

XAML

```
<Grid>
    <Grid.RowDefinitions>
        <RowDefinition Height="Auto" />
        <RowDefinition Height="Auto" />
        <RowDefinition Height="*" />
    </Grid.RowDefinitions>
</Grid>
```

5. In the XAML, before the end of the *Grid*, add a *Menu*. Inside the menu, add *Menu-Item* elements for Save called **mnuSave**, New Order called **mnuOrder**, and Exit called **mnuExit**. After adding these items, double-click each menu item to add the click event handler code. Your XAML should look like the following.

XAML

```
<Grid>
    <Grid.RowDefinitions>
        <RowDefinition Height="Auto" />
        <RowDefinition Height="Auto" />
        <RowDefinition Height="*" />
```

```
        </Grid.RowDefinitions>
        <Menu>
            <MenuItem Header="Save" Name="mnuSave" Click="mnuSave_Click" />
            <MenuItem Header="New Order" Name="mnuOrder" Click="mnuOrder_Click" />
            <MenuItem Header="Exit" Name="mnuExit" Click="mnuExit_Click" />
        </Menu>
    </Grid>
```

6. In XAML, under *Menu*, add a combo box called **cmbCustomers**. Configure the combo box to be in Grid.Row="1". Under that, add a list box called **lstOrders**. Configure *ListBox* to be in Grid.Row="2". Set the *Margin* property of both items to 5. Double-click the combo box to add a *SelectionChanged* event handler to your code. Your XAML should look like the following:

XAML

```
<Grid>
    <Grid.RowDefinitions>
        <RowDefinition Height="Auto" />
        <RowDefinition Height="Auto" />
        <RowDefinition Height="*" />
    </Grid.RowDefinitions>
    <Menu>
        <MenuItem Header="Save" Name="mnuSave" Click="mnuSave_Click" />
        <MenuItem Header="New Order" Name="mnuOrder" Click="mnuOrder_Click"/>
        <MenuItem Header="Exit" Name="mnuExit" Click="mnuExit_Click" />
    </Menu>
    <ComboBox Grid.Row="1"  Name="cmbCustomers" Margin="5"
            SelectionChanged="cmbCustomers_SelectionChanged"/>
    <ListBox Grid.Row="2" Name="lstOrders" Margin="5"/>
</Grid>
```

7. Extend markup in the list box element to configure a custom template to display OrderID, OrderDate, and RequiredDate from the Orders table. This will require the *ListBox* element to be converted to have separate start and end tags. Your XAML for the list box should look like the following, regardless of programming language:

XAML

```
<ListBox Grid.Row="2" Margin="5" Name="lstOrders">
    <ListBox.ItemTemplate>
        <DataTemplate>
            <Border CornerRadius="5" BorderThickness="2"
                    BorderBrush="Blue" Margin="3">
                <StackPanel Orientation="Horizontal">
                    <TextBlock Text="Order #"
                            TextAlignment="Right" Width="40"/>
                    <TextBlock Name="txtOrderID"
                            Text="{Binding Path=OrderID}" Margin="5,0,10,0"
                            Width="30"/>
                    <TextBlock Text="Order Date:"
                            TextAlignment="Right" Width="80"/>
                    <TextBlock Name="txtOrderDate"
                        Text="{Binding Path=OrderDate, StringFormat={}{0:MM/dd/yyyy}}"
                        Margin="5,0,10,0" Width="75"/>
```

```
                    <TextBlock Text="Required Date:"
                        TextAlignment="Right" Width="80"/>
                    <TextBlock Name="txtRequiredDate"
                        Text="{Binding Path=RequiredDate, StringFormat={}{0:MM/dd/
yyyy}}"
                        Margin="5,0,10,0" Width="75"/>
                </StackPanel>
            </Border>
        </DataTemplate>
    </ListBox.ItemTemplate>
</ListBox>
```

8. Choose Debug | Start Debugging to run this application.

   Although you haven't written any Visual Basic 2010 or C# code yet, you have entered enough XAML to produce a screen that can show a customer list in the combo box and the customer's orders in the data grid. Your main window should look like the sample in Figure 4-12. In the next exercise, you will add code to populate the window.

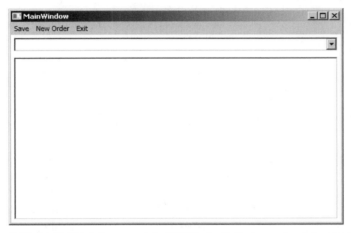

FIGURE 4-12 This is the completed GUI that will display customers and orders.

EXERCISE 2 Creating LINQ Queries to Display Data

In this exercise, you add code that includes LINQ queries to the WPF application you worked on in Exercise 1, "Add the GUI," of this lesson. This produces a running application for viewing the data, but in the next lesson, you'll add code to add an order to a customer and save it.

1. In Visual Studio .NET 2010, choose File | Open | Project. Open the project from the preceding exercise.

2. In Solution Explorer, double-click the MainWindow.xaml.vb or MainWindow.xaml.cs file to open the code-behind file for the main window.

3. Add a private field to the top of the *MainWindow* class, called *ctx*, and set its type to *NorthwindDataContext*; also, instantiate the class as shown in the following code sample:

Sample of Visual Basic Code

```vb
Private ctx As New NorthwindDataContext();
```

Sample of C# Code

```csharp
private NorthwindDataContext ctx = new NorthwindDataContext();
```

4. In the *Window_Loaded* event handler method, add code to save *ctx* to an application property called *ctx*, which makes the *ctx* object accessible from other windows. Also, add a LINQ query to populate *cmbCustomers* with a *Tuple* of *string*, a *string* that contains CustomerID and CompanyName from the Customers table. Set the *DisplayMemberPath* to display *Item2* of the *Tuple*. The *Window_Loaded* event handler should look like the following:

Sample of Visual Basic Code

```vb
Private Sub Window_Loaded(ByVal sender As System.Object, _
                          ByVal e As System.Windows.RoutedEventArgs)
    Application.Current.Properties("ctx") = ctx
    cmbCustomers.ItemsSource = From c In ctx.Customers
                               Select New Tuple(Of String, String)( _
                                   c.CustomerID, _
                                   c.CompanyName)
    cmbCustomers.DisplayMemberPath = "Item2"
End Sub
```

Sample of C# Code

```csharp
private void Window_Loaded(object sender, RoutedEventArgs e)
{
    App.Current.Properties["ctx"] = ctx;
    cmbCustomers.ItemsSource = from c in ctx.Customers
                               select new Tuple<string,string>
                                   (
                                       c.CustomerID,
                                       c.CompanyName
                                   );
    cmbCustomers.DisplayMemberPath = "Item2";
}
```

5. Add code to the *SelectionChanged* event handler method to retrieve the select customer information and use it to write a LINQ query for a list of OrderID, OrderDate, and RequestDate from the Orders table. Your code should look like the following.

Sample of Visual Basic Code

```vb
Private Sub cmbCustomers_SelectionChanged(ByVal sender As System.Object, _
            ByVal e As System.Windows.Controls.SelectionChangedEventArgs)
    Dim customer = CType(cmbCustomers.SelectedValue, Tuple(Of String, String))
    If (customer Is Nothing) Then Return
    lstOrders.ItemsSource =
        From o In ctx.Orders
        Where o.CustomerID = customer.Item1
        Select New With _
            { _
                o.OrderID, _
```

```
                    o.OrderDate, _
                    o.RequiredDate _
            }
    End Sub
```

Sample of C# Code
```csharp
private void cmbCustomers_SelectionChanged(object sender,
    SelectionChangedEventArgs e)
{
    var customer = (Tuple<string,string>)cmbCustomers.SelectedValue;
    if (customer == null) return;
    lstOrders.ItemsSource =
        from o in ctx.Orders
        where o.CustomerID == customer.Item1
        select new
            {
                o.OrderID,
                o.OrderDate,
                o.RequiredDate
            };
}
```

6. In the *Exit* event handler method, add code to end the application. Your code should look like the following:

    Sample of Visual Basic Code
    ```vbnet
    Private Sub mnuExit_Click(ByVal sender As System.Object, _
                            ByVal e As System.Windows.RoutedEventArgs)
        Application.Current.Shutdown()
    End Sub
    ```

    Sample of C# Code
    ```csharp
    private void mnuExit_Click(object sender, RoutedEventArgs e)
    {
        Application.Current.Shutdown();
    }
    ```

7. Choose Debug | Start Debugging to run the application. If you select a customer from the combo box, the list box will populate with the list of OrderID, OrderDate, and RequiredDate. Click Exit to shut down the application.

Lesson Summary

This lesson provided detailed information about how to run LINQ to SQL queries.

- You can use the table properties on the *DataContext* object to run LINQ queries.
- If you provide a *where* clause, LINQ to SQL will create a SQL query that includes the *where* clause to limit the rows returned to the application.
- If you provide a projection in your *select* clause to limit the properties that are selected, LINQ to SQL will create a SQL query that includes a matching column filter to limit the data returned to the application.

- LINQ to SQL supports both inner and outer joins.
- LINQ to SQL supports grouping and aggregation.
- You can use the *Skip* and *Take* extension methods to implement paging over data.

Lesson Review

You can use the following questions to test your knowledge of the information in Lesson 2, "Executing Queries Using LINQ to SQL." The questions are also available on the companion CD if you prefer to review them in electronic form.

> **NOTE ANSWERS**
>
> Answers to these questions and explanations of why each answer choice is correct or incorrect are located in the "Answers" section at the end of the book.

1. Which query extension methods can you use to implement paging over a LINQ to SQL query?

   A. *Contains* and *Intersect*

   B. *GroupBy* and *Last*

   C. *Skip* and *Take*

   D. *First* and *Last*

2. When using a LINQ query to join two tables, you must specify how the two tables are related by using which keyword?

   A. *let*

   B. *equals*

   C. *into*

   D. *by*

Lesson 3: Submitting Changes to the Database

Until now, the lessons have been focused on data retrieval, so you might be wondering about how to change data. LINQ itself is a query-based tool for data retrieval, but the LINQ to SQL classes do provide means for you perform insert, update, and delete operations on your data. This lesson focuses on that.

> **After this lesson, you will be able to:**
> - Understand how LINQ to SQL tracks changes and caches objects.
> - Know the life cycle a LINQ to SQL entity.
> - Modify LINQ to SQL entities.
> - Add new LINQ to SQL entities.
> - Delete LINQ to SQL entities.
> - Execute stored procedures using LINQ to SQL classes.
> - Submit all changes back to the database server.
> - Submit changes within a transaction.
>
> **Estimated lesson time: 60 minutes**

In the .NET Framework, classes are reference types, and an instance of a class is called an *object*. Each object has a unique identity, and many variables can refer to the same object. If two variables are referring to the same object, changes made through one variable are also visible through the other variable.

When working with relational database tables, a row has a primary key that is unique, so no two rows may share the same primary key. This is a constraint in the table. As long as you are working in the table, the primary key certainly feels like the unique identifier that objects have.

You start running into problems when retrieving data from the table for use in your application. When the data is retrieved as rows, there is no expectation that two rows representing the same data actually correspond to the same row objects that were retrieved. For example, if you query for a specific customer twice, you get two rows of data that contain the same information.

Using *DataContext* to Track Changes and Cache Objects

When working with objects, you typically expect that if you ask *DataContext* for the same information again, it will give you the same object instance. Certainly, this is the behavior you want, right? You want to make sure that if you have two variables that reference customer number 123, and you go through one of the variables to change the customer name, you will see the new name when going through the other variable to view the name. You don't want duplicate objects in memory just because you queried for the same customer twice.

The *DataContext* object manages object identity for you so that rows retrieved from the database table are automatically logged in the *DataContext* object's internal identity table by the row's primary key when the object is created. If the same row is retrieved again by this *DataContext* object, the original instance is handed back to you. Your application sees only the state of the row that was first retrieved. If, for example, you retrieve a row in your application and the row is modified in the database table by a different application, you won't get the updated data if you query for this row again because the row is delivered to you from the *DataContext* object's cache.

It might seem rather weird that querying for the same row returned the original state of the row, even though the row had been changed by another application. In essence, the new data was thrown away. The reason for this behavior is that LINQ to SQL needs this behavior to support optimistic concurrency. *DataContext* contains a method called *SubmitChanges*, which sends all your changes back to the database table. This is explained in more detail later in this lesson.

If the database contains a table without a primary key, LINQ to SQL allows queries to be submitted over the table, but it doesn't allow updates because the framework cannot identify which row to update, given the lack of a unique key.

EXAM TIP

The exam will contain questions related to modifying data using the *DataContext* class, so be sure you understand the role of *DataContext* when changes need to be sent to SQL Server.

If the object requested by the query is identified as one that has already been retrieved, no query is executed at all. The identity table acts as a cache, storing all previously retrieved objects.

The Life Cycle of an Entity

Consider the following scenario in which an object is retrieved by a LINQ to SQL query and modified, maybe several times, until your application is ready to send the changes back to the server. You might repeat this scenario until your application no longer needs the entity object information. If the entity object is no longer referenced by your application, the object will be reclaimed by the garbage collector, just like any other .NET Framework object. As long as you submitted the changes to the *DataContext* object by using its *SubmitChanges* method, the data is sent and remains in the database. Because of the database persistence, you can query the *DataContext* object for the same data, and you will receive an object that appears and behaves like the original object that was garbage-collected. From that perspective, the *DataContext* object provides the illusion that the lifetime of the object is beyond any single run-time instantiation.

This section focuses on a single instantiation of an entity object so that a cycle refers to the time span of that object instance within a particular run-time context. This cycle starts when the *DataContext* object becomes aware of a new instance and ends when the object or *DataContext* object is no longer needed.

When you retrieve objects from SQL Server by using the *DataContext* object, LINQ to SQL automatically stores information about the entity objects. The *DataContext* object provides an object-tracking service that tracks the state of your objects. LINQ to SQL objects always have a state, and Table 4-1 shows the states a LINQ to SQL object can have. In terms of performance and resource usage, object tracking using the *identity tracking service* is not costly, but making changes to the object by using the *change tracking service* can be costly.

TABLE 4-1 The States Available to LINQ to SQL Objects

STATE	DESCRIPTION
Untracked	An object not tracked by LINQ to SQL due to one of the following reasons:
	You instantiated the object yourself.
	The object was created through deserialization.
	The object came from a different *DataContext* object.
Unchanged	An object retrieved by using the current *DataContext* object and not known to have been modified since it was created.
PossiblyModified	An object that is attached to a *DataContext* object will be in this state unless you specify otherwise when you attach.
ToBeInserted	An object not retrieved by using the current *DataContext* object, which will send an *insert* statement to the database.
ToBeUpdated	An object known to have been modified since it was retrieved, which sends an *update* statement to the database.
ToBeDeleted	An object marked for deletion, which will send a *delete* statement to the database.
Deleted	An object that has been deleted in the database; this state is final and does not allow for additional transitions.

The following code retrieves a customer from the Northwind database. This customer will be used in the examples that follow.

Sample of Visual Basic Code

```
Dim customer As Customer
Dim ctx As New NorthwindDataContext()
Private Sub mnuCreateEntity_Click(ByVal sender As System.Object, _
                                  ByVal e As System.Windows.RoutedEventArgs)
    Dim sw = New StringWriter()
    ctx.Log = sw
    customer = (From c In ctx.Customers
```

```
             Where c.CustomerID = "ALFKI"
             Select c).First()
    MessageBox.Show(sw.GetStringBuilder().ToString())
End Sub
```

Sample of C# Code

```csharp
private Customer customer;
private NorthwindDataContext ctx = new NorthwindDataContext();
private void mnuCreateEntity_Click(object sender, RoutedEventArgs e)
{
    var sw = new StringWriter();
    ctx.Log = sw;
    customer = (from c in ctx.Customers
                where c.CustomerID == "ALFKI"
                select c).First();
    MessageBox.Show(sw.GetStringBuilder().ToString());
}
```

SQL Query

```sql
SELECT TOP (1) [t0].[CustomerID], [t0].[CompanyName],
[t0].[ContactName], [t0].[ContactTitle],
[t0].[Address], [t0].[City], [t0].[Region],
[t0].[PostalCode], [t0].[Country], [t0].[Phone], [t0].[Fax]
FROM [dbo].[Customers] AS [t0]
WHERE [t0].[CustomerID] = @p0
-- @p0: Input NVarChar (Size = 4000; Prec = 0; Scale = 0) [ALFKI]
```

In this example, there is a small difference in behavior between Visual Basic 2010 and C#. In Visual Basic 2010, every time you click the menu option to run this code, the query is sent to SQL Server. In C#, on the first click of the menu option, the SQL query is run, but subsequent clicks simply return the existing object that's in the cache. In either case, you won't see any changes that are made to the row in the database. Weird? Both languages use the same underlying .NET Framework classes, so you would think the behavior should be the same. If you reverse-engineer the compiled method, you'll find that the Visual Basic and C# code produce very different Intermediate Language (IL). Also, if you reverse-engineer the compiled Northwind.Designer.vb and the Northwind.Designer.cs code, you'll see that they produce very different IL code as well. The point is that the underlying framework is the same, but the designer-generated code, and the compiled C# and Visual Basic code, are different.

Modifying Existing Entities

When LINQ to SQL creates a new object, the object is in *Unchanged* state. If you modify the object, the *DataContext* object will change the state of the object to the *ToBeUpdated* state. This is what the *DataContext* object uses to determine which objects must be persisted when you submit your changes.

How does the *DataContext* object know when you change your object? Change notifications are accomplished through the *PropertyChanging* event that's in property setters. When

DataContext receives a change notification, it creates a copy of the object and changes its state to *ToBeUpdated*.

Recall that, as explained in Lesson 1, the entity class implements the *INotifyPropertyChanging* interface. You could create an entity class that does not implement *INotifyPropertyChanging*, and, in that scenario, *DataContext* maintains a copy of the values that objects had when they were first instantiated. When you call *SubmitChanges*, *DataContext* will compare the current and original values, field by field, to decide whether the object has been changed.

The following code sample modifies the customer object that was retrieved in the previous code example and then submits the change back to the database by using the *SubmitChanges* method on the *DataContext* object. Be sure to run the previous example to create the customer object first.

Sample of Visual Basic Code

```vb
Private Sub mnuModifyEntity_Click(ByVal sender As System.Object, _
                        ByVal e As System.Windows.RoutedEventArgs)
    customer.ContactName = "Marty " + DateTime.Now.ToLongTimeString()
    ctx.SubmitChanges()
End Sub
```

Sample of C# Code

```csharp
private void mnuModifyEntity_Click(object sender, RoutedEventArgs e)
{
    customer.ContactName = "Marty " + DateTime.Now.ToLongTimeString();
    ctx.SubmitChanges();
}
```

SQL Query

```sql
UPDATE [dbo].[Customers]
SET [ContactName] = @p10
WHERE ([CustomerID] = @p0) AND
        ([CompanyName] = @p1) AND
        ([ContactName] = @p2) AND
        ([ContactTitle] = @p3) AND
        ([Address] = @p4) AND
        ([City] = @p5) AND
        ([Region] IS NULL) AND
        ([PostalCode] = @p6) AND
        ([Country] = @p7) AND
        ([Phone] = @p8) AND
        ([Fax] = @p9)
-- @p0: Input NChar (Size = 5; Prec = 0; Scale = 0) [ALFKI]
-- @p1: Input NVarChar (Size = 4000; Prec = 0; Scale = 0) [Alfreds Futterkiste]
-- @p2: Input NVarChar (Size = 4000; Prec = 0; Scale = 0) [Maria Anders]
-- @p3: Input NVarChar (Size = 4000; Prec = 0; Scale = 0) [Sales Representative]
-- @p4: Input NVarChar (Size = 4000; Prec = 0; Scale = 0) [Obere Str. 57]
-- @p5: Input NVarChar (Size = 4000; Prec = 0; Scale = 0) [Berlin]
-- @p6: Input NVarChar (Size = 4000; Prec = 0; Scale = 0) [12209]
-- @p7: Input NVarChar (Size = 4000; Prec = 0; Scale = 0) [Germany]
-- @p8: Input NVarChar (Size = 4000; Prec = 0; Scale = 0) [030-0074321]
```

```
-- @p9: Input NVarChar (Size = 4000; Prec = 0; Scale = 0) [030-0076545]
-- @p10: Input NVarChar (Size = 4000; Prec = 0; Scale = 0) [Marty 11:44:30 AM]
-- Context: SqlProvider(Sql2008) Model: AttributedMetaModel Build: 4.0.30319.1
```

In this code sample, the *where* clause in the SQL query is not simply looking for a matching primary key; it's comparing all fields to find a match, and it's using the original values to perform the search. If someone modified that row in the database, your application will not find a match. This will generate a concurrency error.

If you make a change to a relationship, the object that has the foreign key, which is typically the child object, will have the authoritative information about the parent. Optionally, you can have a reference from the parent to the child. It's the generic *EntitySet* of *TEntity* and *EntityRef* of *TEntity* that maintain bidirectional references to ensure consistency of one-to-many and one-to-one relationships.

Adding New Entities to *DataContext*

A new object you instantiate yourself is unknown to *DataContext* and is in *Untracked* state because no *DataContext* class is aware of your object. You can use the *InsertOnSubmit* method, or you can assign your new object to an object that is already attached, and *DataContext* will discover the new object so that it can be saved to the database. You can also call the *InsertAllOnSubmit* method when you have many objects to insert.

The following sample code demonstrates the creation of an employee object that is then added to the *DataContext* object and submitted to the database.

Sample of Visual Basic Code

```vb
Private Sub mnuAddNewEntity_Click(ByVal sender As System.Object, _
                              ByVal e As System.Windows.RoutedEventArgs)
    Dim ctx = New NorthwindDataContext()
    Dim sw = New StringWriter()
    ctx.Log = sw
    Dim employee = New Employee With
                {
                    .FirstName = "John",
                    .LastName = "Smith"
                }
    ctx.Employees.InsertOnSubmit(employee)
    ctx.SubmitChanges()
    MessageBox.Show(sw.GetStringBuilder().ToString())
End Sub
```

Sample of C# Code

```csharp
private void mnuAddNewEntity_Click(object sender, RoutedEventArgs e)
{
    var ctx = new NorthwindDataContext();
    var sw = new StringWriter();
    ctx.Log = sw;
    var employee = new Employee
                {
                    FirstName = "John",
```

```
                    LastName = "Smith"
                };
    ctx.Employees.InsertOnSubmit(employee);
    ctx.SubmitChanges();
    MessageBox.Show(sw.GetStringBuilder().ToString());
}
```

SQL Query

```
INSERT INTO [dbo].[Employees]([LastName], [FirstName], [Title],
[TitleOfCourtesy], [BirthDate], [HireDate], [Address], [City], [Region],
 [PostalCode], [Country], [HomePhone], [Extension], [Photo],
[Notes], [ReportsTo], [PhotoPath])
VALUES (@p0, @p1, @p2, @p3, @p4, @p5, @p6, @p7, @p8,
 @p9, @p10, @p11, @p12, @p13, @p14, @p15, @p16)

SELECT CONVERT(Int,SCOPE_IDENTITY()) AS [value]
-- @p0: Input NVarChar (Size = 4000; Prec = 0; Scale = 0) [Smith]
-- @p1: Input NVarChar (Size = 4000; Prec = 0; Scale = 0) [John]
-- @p2: Input NVarChar (Size = 4000; Prec = 0; Scale = 0) [Null]
-- @p3: Input NVarChar (Size = 4000; Prec = 0; Scale = 0) [Null]
-- @p4: Input DateTime (Size = -1; Prec = 0; Scale = 0) [Null]
-- @p5: Input DateTime (Size = -1; Prec = 0; Scale = 0) [Null]
-- @p6: Input NVarChar (Size = 4000; Prec = 0; Scale = 0) [Null]
-- @p7: Input NVarChar (Size = 4000; Prec = 0; Scale = 0) [Null]
-- @p8: Input NVarChar (Size = 4000; Prec = 0; Scale = 0) [Null]
-- @p9: Input NVarChar (Size = 4000; Prec = 0; Scale = 0) [Null]
-- @p10: Input NVarChar (Size = 4000; Prec = 0; Scale = 0) [Null]
-- @p11: Input NVarChar (Size = 4000; Prec = 0; Scale = 0) [Null]
-- @p12: Input NVarChar (Size = 4000; Prec = 0; Scale = 0) [Null]
-- @p13: Input Image (Size = 8000; Prec = 0; Scale = 0) [Null]
-- @p14: Input NText (Size = -1; Prec = 0; Scale = 0) [Null]
-- @p15: Input Int (Size = -1; Prec = 0; Scale = 0) [Null]
-- @p16: Input NVarChar (Size = 4000; Prec = 0; Scale = 0) [Null]
-- Context: SqlProvider(Sql2008) Model: AttributedMetaModel Build: 4.0.30319.1
```

In this code sample, an employee object was created and populated with data. The employee object is then added to the Employees table on the *DataContext* object by using the *InsertOnSubmit* method. Finally, the *SubmitChanges* method on the *DataContext* object is called to send the new employee to the Employees database table. The SQL query performs the insert and then executes a *SELECT* statement to retrieve the *SCOPE_IDENTITY*, which is the value of the primary key that was created. The EmployeeID column is an identity column that automatically provides a new sequential number for each row added. After the code runs, you can look at the *EmployeeID* property to see the ID that was generated.

Deleting Entities

When you want to delete rows from a database table, you can call the *DeleteOnSubmit* or *DeleteAllOnSubmit* methods on the appropriate table property of the *DataContext* object. Deleting typically requires you to locate the item or items to be deleted and then pass them to the appropriate aforementioned method. The following is a code sample that shows how to delete an employee whose EmployeeID is 10.

Sample of Visual Basic Code

```vb
Private Sub mnuDeleteEntity_Click(ByVal sender As System.Object, _
                              ByVal e As System.Windows.RoutedEventArgs)
    Dim ctx = New NorthwindDataContext()
    Dim sw = New StringWriter()
    ctx.Log = sw
    Dim employee = (From emp In ctx.Employees
                    Where emp.EmployeeID = 10
                    Select emp).First()
    ctx.Employees.DeleteOnSubmit(employee)
    ctx.SubmitChanges()
    MessageBox.Show(sw.GetStringBuilder().ToString())
End Sub
```

Sample of C# Code

```csharp
private void mnuDeleteEntity_Click(object sender, RoutedEventArgs e)
{
    var ctx = new NorthwindDataContext();
    var sw = new StringWriter();
    ctx.Log = sw;
    var employee = (from emp in ctx.Employees
                    where emp.EmployeeID == 10
                    select emp).First();
    ctx.Employees.DeleteOnSubmit(employee);
    ctx.SubmitChanges();
    MessageBox.Show(sw.GetStringBuilder().ToString());
}
```

SQL Query

```sql
SELECT TOP (1) [t0].[EmployeeID], [t0].[LastName], [t0].[FirstName],
[t0].[Title], [t0].[TitleOfCourtesy], [t0].[BirthDate], [t0].[HireDate],
[t0].[Address], [t0].[City], [t0].[Region], [t0].[PostalCode], [t0].[Country],
[t0].[HomePhone], [t0].[Extension], [t0].[Notes],
[t0].[ReportsTo], [t0].[PhotoPath]
FROM [dbo].[Employees] AS [t0]
WHERE [t0].[EmployeeID] = @p0
-- @p0: Input Int (Size = -1; Prec = 0; Scale = 0) [10]
-- Context: SqlProvider(Sql2008) Model: AttributedMetaModel Build: 4.0.30319.1

DELETE FROM [dbo].[Employees] WHERE ([EmployeeID] = @p0) AND
([LastName] = @p1) AND
([FirstName] = @p2) AND ([Title] IS NULL) AND
([TitleOfCourtesy] IS NULL) AND ([BirthDate] IS NULL) AND
([HireDate] IS NULL) AND ([Address] IS NULL) AND
([City] IS NULL) AND ([Region] IS NULL) AND
([PostalCode] IS NULL) AND ([Country] IS NULL) AND
([HomePhone] IS NULL) AND ([Extension] IS NULL) AND
([ReportsTo] IS NULL) AND ([PhotoPath] IS NULL)
-- @p0: Input Int (Size = -1; Prec = 0; Scale = 0) [10]
-- @p1: Input NVarChar (Size = 4000; Prec = 0; Scale = 0) [Smith]
-- @p2: Input NVarChar (Size = 4000; Prec = 0; Scale = 0) [John]
-- Context: SqlProvider(Sql2008) Model: AttributedMetaModel Build: 4.0.30319.1
```

This code sample starts by querying for the employee whose EmployeeID is 10. If you had run the previous code sample that adds an employee named John Smith, you would have an employee with an EmployeeID of 10. Next, this code sample executes the *DeleteOnSubmit* method on the Employees *Table* property that's on the *DataContext* object. Finally, the call is made to the *SubmitChanges* method, which sends the *delete* command to the database.

In the SQL query, the row had to be retrieved to be deleted. If you want to delete an employee's name without retrieving it first, implement a stored procedure that takes the ID of the employee as a parameter.

LINQ to SQL does not support or recognize cascade-delete operations. If you want to delete a row in a table that has constraints against it, you have two options. The first option is to set the ON DELETE CASCADE rule in the foreign-key constraint in the database. This automatically deletes the child rows when a parent row is deleted. The other option is to write your own code to first delete the child objects that would otherwise prevent the parent object from being deleted.

Using Stored Procedures

In Lesson 1, you were introduced to the LINQ to SQL designer, and this lesson mentioned that you can add stored procedures to the LINQ to SQL designer. The stored procedures you add to the designer become methods on your *DataContext* object, which makes calling a stored procedure quite easy. The following sample code demonstrates the call to a stored procedure called *CustOrderHist*, which contains a *SELECT* statement that returns a list of all the products a customer has purchased.

Sample of Visual Basic Code

```
Private Sub mnuStoredProc_Click(ByVal sender As System.Object, _
                                ByVal e As System.Windows.RoutedEventArgs)
    Dim ctx = New NorthwindDataContext()
    Dim sw = New StringWriter()
    ctx.Log = sw
    dg.ItemsSource = ctx.CustOrderHist("ALFKI")
    MessageBox.Show(sw.GetStringBuilder().ToString())
End Sub
```

Sample of C# Code

```
private void mnuStoredProc_Click(object sender, RoutedEventArgs e)
{
    var ctx = new NorthwindDataContext();
    var sw = new StringWriter();
    ctx.Log = sw;
    dg.ItemsSource = ctx.CustOrderHist("ALFKI");
    MessageBox.Show(sw.GetStringBuilder().ToString());
}
```

SQL Query

```
EXEC @RETURN_VALUE = [dbo].[CustOrderHist] @CustomerID = @p0
```

```
-- @p0: Input NChar (Size = 5; Prec = 0; Scale = 0) [ALFKI]
-- @RETURN_VALUE: Output Int (Size = -1; Prec = 0; Scale = 0) [Null]
-- Context: SqlProvider(Sql2008) Model: AttributedMetaModel Build: 4.0.30319.1
```

This code is quite simple. You pass the customer ID of a customer (ALFKI in this case), and you get back a list of objects that can be easily bound to the data grid.

If you call stored procedures that have *OUTPUT* parameters, the method created defines parameters as *ByRef (C# ref)*, which gives you access to the returned value.

Using *DataContext* to Submit Changes

After you use LINQ to SQL to retrieve data, you might make many changes to the objects, but remember that these changes are made only to your in-memory objects. No changes are sent to the database until you call the *SubmitChanges* method on the *DataContext* object.

When you call the *SubmitChanges* method, the *DataContext* object tries to translate your changes into SQL commands. Although you can use your own custom logic to override these actions, the order of submission is orchestrated by a *change processor*.

The first thing the change processor will do is examine the set of known objects to determine whether new objects have been attached. If so, these new objects are added to the set of tracked objects.

Next, all objects that have pending changes are ordered into a sequence based on the dependencies between the objects. Objects whose changes depend on other objects will be located after their dependencies.

The *DataContext* object then starts a transaction to encapsulate the individual *insert*, *update*, and *delete* commands.

Finally, the changes to the objects are sent to the database server, one by one, as SQL commands. Any errors detected by the database cause the submission process to stop, and an exception is thrown. The transaction rolls back all changes to the database. *DataContext* still has all changes, so you can try to correct the problem and call *SubmitChanges* again if need be.

Following successful execution of *SubmitChanges*, all objects known to the *DataContext* object are in the *Unchanged* state. (The single exception is represented by those that have been successfully deleted from the database, which are in *Deleted* state and unusable in that *DataContext* instance.)

Submitting Changes in a Transaction

LINQ to SQL supports three transaction models when submitting your changes back to the database. This section covers these models in the order of checks performed.

- **Explicit Local Transaction**   If the *Transaction* property is set to a (*IDbTransaction*) transaction, the *SubmitChanges* call is executed in the context of the same transaction. In this scenario, you are responsible for committing or rolling back the transaction after execution of the transaction. Also, the connection that created the transaction must be the same connection used when instantiating *DataContext*. This throws an exception if a different connection is used.

- **Explicit Distributable Transaction** In this scenario, you can call any of the LINQ to SQL methods, including, but not limited to, the *SubmitChanges* method, in the scope of an active transaction. LINQ to SQL will detect that the call is in the scope of a transaction and will not create a new transaction. Also, the connection will not be closed. For example, you can perform queries and *SubmitChanges* executions in the context of this transaction.

- **Implicit Transaction** When you call *SubmitChanges*, LINQ to SQL automatically checks to see whether the call is already in the scope of a transaction or if the *Transaction* property (*IDbTransaction*) is set to a transaction that you started. If no transaction is found, LINQ to SQL starts a local transaction (*IDbTransaction*) and uses it to execute the generated SQL commands. When all SQL commands have been successfully completed, LINQ to SQL commits the local transaction and returns.

PRACTICE Writing LINQ Queries to Display Data

In this practice, you continue the order entry application from Lesson 2, "Executing Queries Using LINQ to SQL," by adding a graphical user interface (GUI) for order entry and then using LINQ to SQL to add the new order to the database.

If you encounter a problem completing an exercise, the completed projects can be installed from the Code folder on the companion CD.

EXERCISE 1 Add Order Entry to the Application

In this exercise, you modify the WPF application that you created in Lesson 2 by creating the GUI for order entry and then adding code to store the new order into the database by using LINQ to SQL.

1. In Visual Studio .NET 2010, choose File | Open | Project. Open the project from Lesson 2.

2. In Solution Explorer, right-click OrderEntryProject, choose Add | Window, and enter **OrderWindow.xaml** as the name of the new window.

3. In the XAML window, enter the following markup to create the window for entering the order information. Your XAML should look like the following:

Sample of Visual Basic XAML

```
<Window x:Class="OrderWindow"
        xmlns="http://schemas.microsoft.com/winfx/2006/xaml/presentation"
        xmlns:x="http://schemas.microsoft.com/winfx/2006/xaml"
        Title="OrderWindow" SizeToContent="WidthAndHeight">
    <Grid>
        <Grid.ColumnDefinitions>
            <ColumnDefinition Width="Auto" />
```

```
            <ColumnDefinition Width="Auto" />
        </Grid.ColumnDefinitions>
        <Grid.RowDefinitions>
            <RowDefinition Height="Auto" />
            <RowDefinition Height="Auto" />
            <RowDefinition Height="Auto" />
        </Grid.RowDefinitions>
        <DatePicker Grid.Column="1"  Margin="10" Name="dtOrder"  />
        <DatePicker Margin="10" Name="dtRequired" Grid.Column="1" Grid.Row="1" />
        <Button Content="Cancel" Grid.Row="2"  Margin="10"
            Name="btnCancel" Click="btnCancel_Click" />
        <Button Content="OK"  Margin="10" Name="btnOk"
            Grid.Column="1" Grid.Row="2" Click="btnOk_Click" />
        <TextBlock  Margin="10" Text="Order Date:"  />
        <TextBlock  Margin="10" Text="Required Date:" Grid.Row="1" />
    </Grid>
</Window>
```

Sample of C# XAML

```
<Window x:Class="OrderEntryProject.OrderWindow"
        xmlns="http://schemas.microsoft.com/winfx/2006/xaml/presentation"
        xmlns:x="http://schemas.microsoft.com/winfx/2006/xaml"
        Title="OrderWindow" SizeToContent="WidthAndHeight">
    <Grid>
        <Grid.ColumnDefinitions>
            <ColumnDefinition Width="Auto" />
            <ColumnDefinition Width="Auto" />
        </Grid.ColumnDefinitions>
        <Grid.RowDefinitions>
            <RowDefinition Height="Auto" />
            <RowDefinition Height="Auto" />
            <RowDefinition Height="Auto" />
        </Grid.RowDefinitions>
        <DatePicker Grid.Column="1"  Margin="10" Name="dtOrder"  />
        <DatePicker Margin="10" Name="dtRequired" Grid.Column="1" Grid.Row="1" />
        <Button Content="Cancel" Grid.Row="2"  Margin="10"
            Name="btnCancel" Click="btnCancel_Click" />
        <Button Content="OK"  Margin="10" Name="btnOk"
            Grid.Column="1" Grid.Row="2" Click="btnOk_Click" />
        <TextBlock  Margin="10" Text="Order Date:"  />
        <TextBlock  Margin="10" Text="Required Date:" Grid.Row="1" />
    </Grid>
</Window>
```

4. Right-click the OrderWindow.xaml file and click View Code to go to the code-behind window. Add a public *string* property called *CustomerID* to the top of the *OrderWindow* class. Your code should look like the following:

Sample of Visual Basic Code

```
Public Property CustomerID As String
```

Sample of C# Code

```
public string CustomerID { get; set; }
```

5. Double-click *btnCancel* to create the *btnCancel_Click* event handler method automatically and add a single line of code to call the *Close* method so this window will be closed.

6. Double-click *btnOk* to create the *btnOk_Click* event handler method automatically and add code to create a new *Order* object with the values from the main window. Use *DataContext* to go to the *Orders* collection and call *InsertOnSubmit* with the new order. Your completed window code should look like the following:

Sample of Visual Basic Code

```vb
Public Class OrderWindow

    Public Property CustomerID As String

    Private Sub btnOk_Click(ByVal sender As System.Object, _
                            ByVal e As System.Windows.RoutedEventArgs)
        Dim ctx = CType(Application.Current.Properties("ctx"), NorthwindDataContext)
        Dim Order = New Order With _
                    { _
                            .CustomerID = CustomerID, _
                            .OrderDate = dtOrder.SelectedDate, _
                            .RequiredDate = dtRequired.SelectedDate _
                    }
        ctx.Orders.InsertOnSubmit(Order)
        Close()
    End Sub

    Private Sub btnCancel_Click(ByVal sender As System.Object, _
                                ByVal e As System.Windows.RoutedEventArgs)
        Close()
    End Sub
End Class
```

Sample of C# Code

```csharp
using System.Windows;

namespace OrderEntryProject
{
    /// <summary>
    /// Interaction logic for OrderWindow.xaml
    /// </summary>
    public partial class OrderWindow : Window
    {
        public string CustomerID { get; set; }

        public OrderWindow()
        {
            InitializeComponent();
        }

        private void btnCancel_Click(object sender, RoutedEventArgs e)
        {
            Close();
```

```
            }

        private void btnOk_Click(object sender, RoutedEventArgs e)
        {
            var ctx = (NorthwindDataContext) App.Current.Properties["ctx"];
            Order order = new Order
                            {
                                CustomerID = this.CustomerID,
                                OrderDate = dtOrder.SelectedDate,
                                RequiredDate = dtRequired.SelectedDate
                            };
            ctx.Orders.InsertOnSubmit(order);
            this.Close();
        }
    }
}
```

7. Open the code-behind screen for *MainWindow* and add code to the *Save* event handler method to submit the *DataContext* changes to the database and display a message stating "Saved".

8. Call the customer combo box's *SelectionChanged* event handler method to force the *ListBox* to be updated. Your code should look like the following:

Sample of Visual Basic Code

```
Private Sub mnuSave_Click(ByVal sender As System.Object, _
                          ByVal e As System.Windows.RoutedEventArgs)
    ctx.SubmitChanges()
    MessageBox.Show("Saved")
    cmbCustomers_SelectionChanged(Nothing, Nothing)
End Sub
Private Sub mnuOrder_Click(ByVal sender As System.Object, _
                           ByVal e As System.Windows.RoutedEventArgs)
    Dim customer = CType(cmbCustomers.SelectedValue, Tuple(Of String, String))
    Dim window = New OrderWindow With {.CustomerID = customer.Item1}
    window.ShowDialog()
End Sub
```

Sample of C# Code

```
private void mnuSave_Click(object sender, RoutedEventArgs e)
{
    ctx.SubmitChanges();
    MessageBox.Show("Saved");
    cmbCustomers_SelectionChanged(null, null);
}
private void mnuOrder_Click(object sender, RoutedEventArgs e)
{
    var customer = (Tuple<string,string>)cmbCustomers.SelectedValue;
    OrderWindow window = new OrderWindow {CustomerID = customer.Item1};
    window.ShowDialog();
}
```

9. Choose Debug | Start Debugging to run your application.

10. Select a customer from the combo box. You should see a list of orders for that customer.

11. With a customer selected, click New Order on the menu. Enter an order date and required date and click OK.

12. Click Save. After you click OK to close the Saved window, you should see the updated list of orders, which includes your new order.

Lesson Summary

This lesson provided detailed information on how to send changes back to the database using LINQ to SQL.

- *DataContext* contains the identity tracking service that tracks objects created by *DataContext*.
- *DataContext* contains the change tracking service that keeps track of the state of your object to facilitate sending changes back to the database.
- The change tracking service will keep the original values of your objects, which enables *DataContext* to identify concurrency errors, such as when someone else modifies the same data with which you are working.
- You call the *SubmitChanges* method on the *DataContext* object to send all changes back to the database.
- To make *DataContext* aware of your object, call the *InsertOnSubmit* method on the appropriate table property of *DataContext* with your newly constructed object.
- To delete data from the database, call the *DeleteOnSubmit* method on the appropriate table property of *DataContext* with the entity object you want to delete.
- Changes that are sent back to the database are in an implicit transaction, but you can also create an explicit transaction for when you need other actions to be part of the same transaction.

Lesson Review

You can use the following questions to test your knowledge of the information in Lesson 2, "Executing Queries Using LINQ to SQL." The questions are also available on the companion CD if you prefer to review them in electronic form.

> **NOTE ANSWERS**
>
> Answers to these questions and explanations of why each answer choice is correct or incorrect are located in the "Answers" section at the end of the book.

1. You retrieved a row of data into an entity object by using a LINQ to SQL *DataContext* object. You haven't made any changes to the object, but you know that someone else has modified the data row in the database table, so you rerun your query, using the same LINQ to SQL *DataContext* object, to retrieve the updated data. What can be said about the result of the second query?

   A. It returns the updated data and you can use it immediately.

   B. The changes are thrown out and you use the cached data, so you don't see the changes.

   C. An exception is thrown due to the difference in data.

   D. An exception is thrown because you already have the object, so you can't re-query unless you create a new *DataContext* object.

2. You ran a LINQ to SQL query to retrieve the products that you are going to mark as discontinued. After running the query, you looped through the returned products and set their *Discontinued* property to *true*. What must you do to ensure that the changes go back to the database?

   A. Call the *Update* method on the *DataContext* object.

   B. Nothing; the changes are sent when you modify the object.

   C. Call the *Dispose* method on the *DataContext* object.

   D. Call the *SubmitChanges* method on the *DataContext* object.

Case Scenario

In the following case scenarios, you will apply what you've learned about using LINQ to SQL discussed in this chapter. You can find answers to these questions in the "Answers" section at the end of this book.

Case Scenario: Object-Oriented Data Access

Your boss has given you the task of designing a new software application. He is not a developer, but he read an article that described the benefits of object-oriented applications, so the only constraint that was conveyed to you was that the application must be an object-oriented application. The application will require you to store and modify data that will reside in a SQL Server database that you will also design. Answer the following questions regarding the implementation of the data access layer you will be creating.

1. If you chose to use traditional ADO.NET classes, such as *DataSet* and *SqlDataAdapter*, will that satisfy the requirement to be an object-oriented application? Does the use of LINQ to SQL satisfy the object-oriented requirement?

2. Describe some differences between these two technologies.

Suggested Practices

To help you successfully master the exam objectives presented in this chapter, complete the following tasks.

Create an Application That Uses LINQ to SQL Queries

You should create at least one application that uses the LINQ to SQL queries. This can be accomplished by completing the practices at the end of Lessons 1 and 2 or by completing the following Practice 1.

- **Practice 1**   Create an application that requires you to query a database for data from at least two tables that are related. This could be movies that have actors, artists who record music, or people who have vehicles. Add LINQ to SQL queries to provide searching and filtering of the data.

- **Practice 2**   Complete Practice 1 and then add LINQ to SQL queries that join the tables. Be sure to provide both inner and outer joins. Also, add queries that perform grouping and aggregates.

Create an Application That Modifies Data by Using LINQ to SQL

You should create at least one application that uses LINQ to SQL to modify data in the database. This can be accomplished by performing the practices at the end of Lessons 1, 2, and 3 or by completing the following Practice 1.

- **Practice 1**   Create an application that requires you to collect data into at least two database tables that are related. This could be movies that have actors, artists who record music, or people who have vehicles. Use LINQ to SQL to add, delete, and modify the data.

Take a Practice Test

The practice tests on this book's companion CD offer many options. For example, you can test yourself on just the lesson review content, or you can test yourself on all the 70-516 certification exam content. You can set up the test so that it closely simulates the experience of taking a certification exam, or you can set it up in study mode so that you can look at the correct answers and explanations after you answer each question.

> **MORE INFO**   **PRACTICE TESTS**
>
> For details about all the practice test options available, see the "How to Use the Practice Tests" section in this book's introduction.

CHAPTER 5

LINQ to XML

XML has been a rapidly growing technology because it provides a verbose means for transferring data that can be understood easily by computers as well as by people. You will often need to query the XML data.

Another common requirement is to transform XML into a different format. In some scenarios, you simply want to convert XML to a different form of XML. In other scenarios, you might want to convert XML into HTML. You might even want to convert XML into text.

This chapter's first lesson shows how you can use *XmlDocument* and *XmlReader* classes to query XML data. Lesson 2, "Querying with LINQ to XML," shows how you can use LINQ to XML to retrieve data from XML. Lesson 3, "Transforming XML Using LINQ to XML," uses LINQ to XML to transform XML data.

Exam objectives in this chapter:

- Query XML.

Lessons in this chapter:

Before You Begin

You must have some understanding of Microsoft C# or Visual Basic 2010, and you should be familiar with XPath query language, also known as XML Path Language. XPath is an XML technology that was created to provide a common syntax and semantics to address parts of an XML document. XPath has been a W3C (World Wide Web Consortium, *http://www.w3c.org*) recommendation since November 1999.

XPath uses a path notation for navigating through the hierarchical structure of an XML document that is similar to that used for navigating the folder hierarchy on your disk drive when you locate a file. Just as you can locate a file by specifying a relative or explicit path, you can locate parts of an XML document by supplying a relative or explicit path. Even the asterisk (*) is useful as the "all" wildcard when locating parts of an XML document. This chapter exposes you to simple XPath queries, but XPath is not the chapter's focus.

This chapter requires only the hardware and software listed at the beginning of this book.

 REAL WORLD

Glenn Johnson

I have worked on many projects that required the use of XML to transfer data to and from remote systems and web services. In the past, when an XML response was received, I would parse (shred) the XML using various XPath queries to retrieve the necessary data. With LINQ to XML, I can shred the XML by using LINQ queries to retrieve the necessary data.

Lesson 1: Working with the *XmlDocument* and *XmlReader* Classes

The *XmlDocument* and *XmlReader* classes have existed since Microsoft .NET Framework 1.0. This lesson explores each of these classes, showing benefits and drawbacks of using each in your code.

> **After this lesson, you will be able to:**
> - Create an *XmlDocument* object.
> - Iterate the nodes in an *XmlDocument* object.
> - Search for nodes in an *XmlDocument* object.
> - Implement the *XmlReader* class.
>
> **Estimated lesson time: 45 minutes**

The *XmlDocument* Class

The W3C has provided standards that define the structure and a standard programming interface called the Document Object Model (DOM) that can be used in a wide variety of environments and applications for XML documents. Classes that support the DOM typically are capable of random access navigation and modification of the XML document.

The XML classes are accessible by setting a reference to the System.Xml.dll file and adding the *Imports System.Xml* (C# *using System.Xml;*) directive to the code.

The *XmlDocument* class is an in-memory representation of XML using the DOM Level 1 and Level 2. This class can be used to navigate and edit the XML nodes.

There is another class, *XmlDataDocument*, which inherits from the *XmlDocument* class and represents relational data. The *XmlDataDocument* class, in the System.Data.dll assembly, can expose its data as a data set to provide relational and nonrelational views of the data. This lesson focuses on the *XmlDocument* class.

These classes provide many methods to implement the Level 2 specification and contain methods to facilitate common operations. The methods are summarized in Table 5-1. The *XmlDocument* class, which inherits from *XmlNode*, contains all the methods for creating XML elements and XML attributes.

TABLE 5-1 Summary of the *XmlDocument* Methods

METHOD	DESCRIPTION
CreateNode	Creates an XML node in the document. There are also specialized *Create* methods for each node type such as *CreateElement* or *CreateAttribute*.
CloneNode	Creates a duplicate of an XML node. This method takes a Boolean argument called *deep*. If *deep* is *false*, only the node is copied; if *deep* is *true*, all child nodes are recursively copied as well.
GetElementByID	Locates and returns a single node based on its *ID* attribute. This requires a document type definition (DTD) that identifies an attribute as being an *ID* type. An attribute with the name *ID* is not an *ID* type by default.
GetElementsByTagName	Locates and returns an *XmlNode* list containing all the descendant elements based on the element name.
ImportNode	Imports a node from a different *XmlDocument* class into the current document. The source node remains unmodified in the original *XmlDocument* class. This method takes a Boolean argument called *deep*. If *deep* is *false*, only the node is copied; if *deep* is *true*, all child nodes are recursively copied as well.
InsertBefore	Inserts an *XmlNode* list immediately before the referenced node. If the referenced node is *Nothing* (or *null* in C#), the new node is inserted at the end of the child list. If the node already exists in the tree, the original node is removed when the new node is inserted.
InsertAfter	Inserts an *XmlNode* list immediately after the referenced node. If the referenced node is *Nothing* (or *null* in C#), the new node is inserted at the beginning of the child list. If the node already exists in the tree, the original node is removed when the new node is inserted.
Load	Loads an XML document from a disk file, Uniform Resource Locator (URL), or stream.
LoadXml	Loads an XML document from a string.
Normalize	Ensures that there are no adjacent text nodes in the document. This is like saving the document and reloading it. This method can be desirable when text nodes are being programmatically added to an *XmlDocument* class, and the text nodes could be side by side. Normalizing combines the adjacent text nodes to produce a single text node.

PrependChild	Inserts a node at the beginning of the child node list. If the new node is already in the tree, it is removed before it is inserted. If the node is an *XmlDocument* fragment, the complete fragment is added.
ReadNode	Loads a node from an XML document by using an *XmlReader* object. The reader must be on a valid node before executing this method. The reader reads the opening tag, all child nodes, and the closing tag of the current element. This repositions the reader to the next node.
RemoveAll	Removes all children and attributes from the current node.
RemoveChild	Removes the referenced child.
ReplaceChild	Replaces the referenced child with a new node. If the new node is already in the tree, it is removed before it is inserted.
Save	Saves the XML document to a disk file, URL, or stream.
SelectNodes	Selects a list of nodes that match the XPath expression.
SelectSingleNode	Selects the first node that matches the XPath expression.
WriteTo	Writes a node to another XML document using an *XmlTextWriter* class.
WriteContentsTo	Writes a node and all its descendants to another XML document using an *XmlTextWriter* class.

Creating the *XmlDocument* Object

To create an *XmlDocument* object, start by instantiating an *XmlDocument* class. The *XmlDocument* object contains *CreateElement* and *CreateAttribute* methods that add nodes to the *XmlDocument* object. The *XmlElement* contains the *Attributes* property, which is an *XmlAttributeCollection* type. The *XmlAttributeCollection* type inherits from the *XmlNamedNodeMap* class, which is a collection of names with corresponding values.

The following code shows how an *XmlDocument* class can be created from the beginning and saved to a file. Note that *import System.Xml* (C# *using System.Xml;*) and *Import System.IO* (C# *using System.IO;*) was added to the top of the code file.

Sample of Visual Basic Code

```
Private Sub CreateAndSaveXmlDocumentToolStripMenuItem_Click( _
    ByVal sender As System.Object, ByVal e As System.EventArgs) _
    Handles CreateAndSaveXmlDocumentToolStripMenuItem.Click
  'Declare and create new XmlDocument
  Dim xmlDoc As New XmlDocument()

  Dim el As XmlElement
  Dim childCounter As Integer
  Dim grandChildCounter As Integer
```

```vbnet
        'Create the xml declaration first
        xmlDoc.AppendChild( _
         xmlDoc.CreateXmlDeclaration("1.0", "utf-8", Nothing))

        'Create the root node and append into doc
        el = xmlDoc.CreateElement("MyRoot")
        xmlDoc.AppendChild(el)

        'Child Loop
        For childCounter = 1 To 4
            Dim childelmt As XmlElement
            Dim childattr As XmlAttribute

            'Create child with ID attribute
            childelmt = xmlDoc.CreateElement("MyChild")
            childattr = xmlDoc.CreateAttribute("ID")
            childattr.Value = childCounter.ToString()
            childelmt.Attributes.Append(childattr)

            'Append element into the root element
            el.AppendChild(childelmt)
            For grandChildCounter = 1 To 3
               'Create grandchildren
               childelmt.AppendChild(xmlDoc.CreateElement("MyGrandChild"))
            Next
        Next

        'Save to file
        xmlDoc.Save(GetFilePath("XmlDocumentTest.xml"))
        txtLog.AppendText("XmlDocumentTest.xml Created" + vbCrLf)

    End Sub

    Private Function getFilePath(ByVal fileName As String) As String
        Return Path.Combine(Environment.GetFolderPath( _
              Environment.SpecialFolder.Desktop), fileName)
    End Function
```

Sample of C# Code

```csharp
private void createAndSaveXmlDocumentToolStripMenuItem_Click(
    object sender, EventArgs e)
{
    //Declare and create new XmlDocument
    var xmlDoc = new XmlDocument();

    XmlElement el;
    int childCounter;
    int grandChildCounter;

    //Create the xml declaration first
    xmlDoc.AppendChild(
        xmlDoc.CreateXmlDeclaration("1.0", "utf-8", null));

    //Create the root node and append into doc
    el = xmlDoc.CreateElement("MyRoot");
```

```
        xmlDoc.AppendChild(el);

        //Child Loop
        for (childCounter = 1; childCounter <= 4; childCounter++)
        {
            XmlElement childelmt;
            XmlAttribute childattr;

            //Create child with ID attribute
            childelmt = xmlDoc.CreateElement("MyChild");
            childattr = xmlDoc.CreateAttribute("ID");
            childattr.Value = childCounter.ToString();
            childelmt.Attributes.Append(childattr);

            //Append element into the root element
            el.AppendChild(childelmt);
            for (grandChildCounter = 1; grandChildCounter <= 3;
                grandChildCounter++)
            {
                //Create grandchildren
                childelmt.AppendChild(xmlDoc.CreateElement("MyGrandChild"));
            }
        }

        //Save to file
        xmlDoc.Save(getFilePath("XmlDocumentTest.xml"));
        txtLog.AppendText("XmlDocumentTest.xml Created\r\n");

}

private string getFilePath(string fileName)
{
    return Path.Combine(Environment.GetFolderPath(
        Environment.SpecialFolder.Desktop), fileName);
}
```

This code started by creating an instance of *XmlDocument*. Next, the XML declaration is created and placed inside the child collection. An exception is thrown if this is not the first child of *XmlDocument*. After that, the root element is created and the child nodes with corresponding attributes are created. Finally, a call is made to the *getFilePath* helper method to assemble a file path to save the file to your desktop. This helper method will be used in subsequent code samples. The following is the XML file that was produced by running the code sample:

XML File

```
<?xml version="1.0" encoding="utf-8"?>
<MyRoot>
    <MyChild ID="1">
        <MyGrandChild />
        <MyGrandChild />
        <MyGrandChild />
    </MyChild>
    <MyChild ID="2">
```

```
        <MyGrandChild />
        <MyGrandChild />
        <MyGrandChild />
    </MyChild>
    <MyChild ID="3">
        <MyGrandChild />
        <MyGrandChild />
        <MyGrandChild />
    </MyChild>
    <MyChild ID="4">
        <MyGrandChild />
        <MyGrandChild />
        <MyGrandChild />
    </MyChild>
</MyRoot>
```

Parsing an *XmlDocument* Object by Using the DOM

An *XmlDocument* object can be parsed by using a recursive routine to loop through all elements. The following code has an example of parsing *XmlDocument*. Note that *imports System.Text* (C# *using System.Text;*) was added.

Sample of Visual Basic Code

```
Private Sub ParsingAnXmlDocumentToolStripMenuItem_Click( _
      ByVal sender As System.Object, ByVal e As System.EventArgs) _
      Handles ParsingAnXmlDocumentToolStripMenuItem.Click
   Dim xmlDoc As New XmlDocument()
   xmlDoc.Load(getFilePath("XmlDocumentTest.xml"))
   RecurseNodes(xmlDoc.DocumentElement)
End Sub

Public Sub RecurseNodes(ByVal node As XmlNode)
   Dim sb As New StringBuilder()
   'start recursive loop with level 0
   RecurseNodes(node, 0, sb)
   txtLog.Text = sb.ToString()
End Sub

Public Sub RecurseNodes( _
      ByVal node As XmlNode, ByVal level As Integer, _
      ByVal sb As StringBuilder)
   sb.AppendFormat("{0,2} Type:{1,-9} Name:{2,-13} Attr:", _
      level, node.NodeType, node.Name)

   For Each attr As XmlAttribute In node.Attributes
      sb.AppendFormat("{0}={1} ", attr.Name, attr.Value)
   Next
   sb.AppendLine()

   For Each n As XmlNode In node.ChildNodes
      RecurseNodes(n, level + 1, sb)
   Next
 End Sub
```

Sample of C# Code

```csharp
private void parsingAndXmlDocumentToolStripMenuItem_Click(object sender, EventArgs e)
{
    XmlDocument xmlDoc = new XmlDocument();
    xmlDoc.Load(getFilePath("XmlDocumentTest.xml"));
    RecurseNodes(xmlDoc.DocumentElement);
}

public void RecurseNodes(XmlNode node)
{
    var sb = new StringBuilder();
    //start recursive loop with level 0
    RecurseNodes(node, 0, sb);
    txtLog.Text = sb.ToString();
}

public void RecurseNodes(XmlNode node, int level, StringBuilder sb)
{
    sb.AppendFormat("{0,2} Type:{1,-9} Name:{2,-13} Attr:",
        level, node.NodeType, node.Name);

    foreach (XmlAttribute attr in node.Attributes)
    {
        sb.AppendFormat("{0}={1} ", attr.Name, attr.Value);
    }
    sb.AppendLine();

    foreach (XmlNode n in node.ChildNodes)
    {
        RecurseNodes(n, level + 1, sb);
    }
}
```

This code starts by loading an XML file and then calling the *RecurseNodes* method, which is overloaded. The first call simply passes the *xmlDoc* root node. The recursive call passes the recursion level and a string builder object. Each time the *RecurseNodes* method executes, the node information is printed, and a recursive call is made for each child the node has. The following is the result.

Parsing Result

```
0 Type:Element    Name:MyRoot        Attr:
1 Type:Element    Name:MyChild       Attr:ID=1
2 Type:Element    Name:MyGrandChild  Attr:
2 Type:Element    Name:MyGrandChild  Attr:
2 Type:Element    Name:MyGrandChild  Attr:
1 Type:Element    Name:MyChild       Attr:ID=2
2 Type:Element    Name:MyGrandChild  Attr:
2 Type:Element    Name:MyGrandChild  Attr:
2 Type:Element    Name:MyGrandChild  Attr:
1 Type:Element    Name:MyChild       Attr:ID=3
2 Type:Element    Name:MyGrandChild  Attr:
2 Type:Element    Name:MyGrandChild  Attr:
2 Type:Element    Name:MyGrandChild  Attr:
1 Type:Element    Name:MyChild       Attr:ID=4
```

```
2 Type:Element    Name:MyGrandChild  Attr:
2 Type:Element    Name:MyGrandChild  Attr:
2 Type:Element    Name:MyGrandChild  Attr:
```

Searching the *XmlDocument* Object

The *SelectSingleNode* method can locate an element; it requires an XPath query to be passed into the method. The following code sample calls the *SelectSingleNode* method to locate the *MyChild* element, the ID of which is 3, by using an XPath query. The sample code is as follows:

Sample of Visual Basic Code

```vb
Private Sub SearchingAnXmlDocumentToolStripMenuItem_Click( _
     ByVal sender As System.Object, ByVal e As System.EventArgs) _
     Handles SearchingAnXmlDocumentToolStripMenuItem.Click

   Dim xmlDoc As New XmlDocument()
   xmlDoc.Load(getFilePath("XmlDocumentTest.xml"))

   Dim node = xmlDoc.SelectSingleNode("//MyChild[@ID='3']")
   RecurseNodes(node)
End Sub
```

Sample of C# Code

```csharp
private void searchingAnXmlDocumentToolStripMenuItem_Click(
   object sender, EventArgs e)
{
   var xmlDoc = new XmlDocument();
   xmlDoc.Load(getFilePath("XmlDocumentTest.xml"));

   var node = xmlDoc.SelectSingleNode("//MyChild[@ID='3']");
   RecurseNodes(node);
}
```

The *SelectSingleNode* method can perform an XPath lookup on any element or attribute. The following is a display of the result.

Search Result

```
0 Type:Element    Name:MyChild       Attr:ID=3
1 Type:Element    Name:MyGrandChild  Attr:
1 Type:Element    Name:MyGrandChild  Attr:
1 Type:Element    Name:MyGrandChild  Attr:
```

The *GetElementsByTagName* method returns an *XmlNode* list containing all matched elements. The following code returns a list of nodes with the tag name MyGrandChild.

Sample of Visual Basic Code

```vb
Private Sub GetElementsByTagNameToolStripMenuItem_Click( _
     ByVal sender As System.Object, ByVal e As System.EventArgs) _
     Handles GetElementsByTagNameToolStripMenuItem.Click

   Dim xmlDoc As New XmlDocument()
   xmlDoc.Load(getFilePath("XmlDocumentTest.xml"))
```

```
    Dim elmts = xmlDoc.GetElementsByTagName("MyGrandChild")

    Dim sb As New StringBuilder()
    For Each node As XmlNode In elmts
        RecurseNodes(node, 0, sb)
    Next
    txtLog.Text = sb.ToString()
End Sub
```

Sample of C# Code
```
private void getElementsByTagNameToolStripMenuItem_Click(
    object sender, EventArgs e)
{
    var xmlDoc = new XmlDocument();
    xmlDoc.Load(getFilePath("XmlDocumentTest.xml"));

    var elmts = xmlDoc.GetElementsByTagName("MyGrandChild");

    var sb = new StringBuilder();
    foreach (XmlNode node in elmts)
    {
        RecurseNodes(node, 0, sb);
    }
    txtLog.Text = sb.ToString();
}
```

This method works well, even for a single node lookup, when searching by tag name. The following is the execution result.

Search Result
```
0 Type:Element    Name:MyGrandChild    Attr:
0 Type:Element    Name:MyGrandChild    Attr:
0 Type:Element    Name:MyGrandChild    Attr:
0 Type:Element    Name:MyGrandChild    Attr:
0 Type:Element    Name:MyGrandChild    Attr:
0 Type:Element    Name:MyGrandChild    Attr:
0 Type:Element    Name:MyGrandChild    Attr:
0 Type:Element    Name:MyGrandChild    Attr:
0 Type:Element    Name:MyGrandChild    Attr:
0 Type:Element    Name:MyGrandChild    Attr:
0 Type:Element    Name:MyGrandChild    Attr:
0 Type:Element    Name:MyGrandChild    Attr:
```

The *SelectNodes* method, which requires an XPath query to be passed into the method, can also retrieve an *XmlNode* list. The previous code sample has been modified to call the *SelectNodes* method to achieve the same result, as shown in the following code:

Sample of Visual Basic Code
```
    Private Sub SelectNodesToolStripMenuItem_Click( _
        ByVal sender As System.Object, ByVal e As System.EventArgs) _
        Handles SelectNodesToolStripMenuItem.Click
    Dim xmlDoc As New XmlDocument()
    xmlDoc.Load(getFilePath("XmlDocumentTest.xml"))
```

```
    Dim elmts = xmlDoc.SelectNodes("//MyGrandChild")

    Dim sb As New StringBuilder()
    For Each node As XmlNode In elmts
        RecurseNodes(node, 0, sb)
    Next
    txtLog.Text = sb.ToString()
End Sub
```

Sample of C# Code

```
private void selectNodesToolStripMenuItem_Click(
    object sender, EventArgs e)
{
    var xmlDoc = new XmlDocument();
    xmlDoc.Load(getFilePath("XmlDocumentTest.xml"));

    var elmts = xmlDoc.SelectNodes("//MyGrandChild");

    var sb = new StringBuilder();
    foreach (XmlNode node in elmts)
    {
        RecurseNodes(node, 0, sb);
    }
    txtLog.Text = sb.ToString();
}
```

This method can perform an XPath lookup on any XML node, including elements, attributes, and text nodes. This provides much more querying flexibility, because the *SelectElementsByTagName* node is limited to a tag name.

The *XmlReader* Class

The *XmlReader* class is an abstract base class that provides methods to read and parse XML. One of the more common child classes of the *XmlReader* is *XmlTextReader*, which reads an XML file node by node.

The *XmlReader* class provides the fastest and least memory-consuming means to read and parse XML data by providing forward-only, noncaching access to an XML data stream. This class is ideal when it's possible that the desired information is near the top of the XML file and the file is large. If random access is required when accessing XML, use the *XmlDocument* class. The following code reads the XML file that was created in the previous example and displays information about each node:

Sample of Visual Basic Code

```
Private Sub ParsingWithXmlReaderToolStripMenuItem_Click( _
    ByVal sender As System.Object, ByVal e As System.EventArgs) _
    Handles ParsingWithXmlReaderToolStripMenuItem.Click

    Dim sb As New StringBuilder()
    Dim xmlReader As New _
        XmlTextReader(getFilePath("XmlDocumentTest.xml"))
```

```vb
        Do While xmlReader.Read()
            Select Case xmlReader.NodeType
                Case XmlNodeType.XmlDeclaration, _
                 XmlNodeType.Element, _
                 XmlNodeType.Comment
                    Dim s As String
                    sb.AppendFormat("{0}: {1} = {2}", _
                        xmlReader.NodeType, _
                        xmlReader.Name, _
                        xmlReader.Value)
                    sb.AppendLine()
                Case XmlNodeType.Text
                    Dim s As String
                    sb.AppendFormat(" - Value: {0}", _
                        xmlReader.Value)
                    sb.AppendLine()
            End Select

            If xmlReader.HasAttributes Then
                Do While xmlReader.MoveToNextAttribute()
                    sb.AppendFormat(" - Attribute: {0} = {1}", _
                        xmlReader.Name, xmlReader.Value)
                    sb.AppendLine()
                Loop
            End If
        Loop
        xmlReader.Close()
        txtLog.Text = sb.ToString()
End Sub
```

Sample of C# Code

```csharp
private void parsingWithXmlReaderToolStripMenuItem_Click(object sender, EventArgs e)
{
    var sb = new StringBuilder();
    var xmlReader = new XmlTextReader(getFilePath("XmlDocumentTest.xml"));

    while (xmlReader.Read())
    {
        switch (xmlReader.NodeType)
        {
            case XmlNodeType.XmlDeclaration:
            case XmlNodeType.Element:
            case XmlNodeType.Comment:
                sb.AppendFormat("{0}: {1} = {2}",
                                xmlReader.NodeType,
                                xmlReader.Name,
                                xmlReader.Value);
                sb.AppendLine();
                break;
            case XmlNodeType.Text:
                sb.AppendFormat(" - Value: {0}", xmlReader.Value);
                sb.AppendLine();
                break;
        }
```

```
      if (xmlReader.HasAttributes)
      {
         while (xmlReader.MoveToNextAttribute())
         {
            sb.AppendFormat(" - Attribute: {0} = {1}",
                                xmlReader.Name,
                                xmlReader.Value);
            sb.AppendLine();
         }
      }
   }
   xmlReader.Close();
   txtLog.Text = sb.ToString();
}
```

This code opens the file and then performs a simple loop, reading one element at a time until finished. For each node read, a check is made on *NodeType*, and the node information is printed. When a node is read, its corresponding attributes are read as well. A check is made to see whether the node has attributes, and they are displayed. The following is the result of the sample code execution.

Parse Result

```
XmlDeclaration: xml = version="1.0" encoding="utf-8"
 - Attribute: version = 1.0
 - Attribute: encoding = utf-8
Element: MyRoot =
Element: MyChild =
 - Attribute: ID = 1
Element: MyGrandChild =
Element: MyGrandChild =
Element: MyGrandChild =
Element: MyChild =
 - Attribute: ID = 2
Element: MyGrandChild =
Element: MyGrandChild =
Element: MyGrandChild =
Element: MyChild =
 - Attribute: ID = 3
Element: MyGrandChild =
Element: MyGrandChild =
Element: MyGrandChild =
Element: MyChild =
 - Attribute: ID = 4
Element: MyGrandChild =
Element: MyGrandChild =
Element: MyGrandChild =
```

When viewing the results, notice that many lines end with an equals sign because none of the nodes contained text. The *MyChild* elements have attributes that are displayed.

EXAM TIP

For the exam, understand that the *XmlReader* provides the fastest means to access XML data and is read-only, forward-only. *XmlDocument* provides the simplest means to access XML data and provides random access to any XML node.

PRACTICE   Work with the *XmlDocument* and *XmlReader* Classes

In this practice, you analyze an XML file, called Orders.xml, which contains order information. Your first objective is to write a program that can provide the total price of all orders. You also need to provide the total and the average freight cost, per order. Here is an example of what the file looks like.

Orders.xml File

```
<Orders>
  <Order OrderNumber="SO43659">
    <LineItem Line="1" PID="349" Qty="1" Price="2024.9940" Freight="50.6249" />
    <LineItem Line="2" PID="350" Qty="3" Price="2024.9940" Freight="151.8746" />
    <LineItem Line="3" PID="351" Qty="1" Price="2024.9940" Freight="50.6249" />
    <LineItem Line="4" PID="344" Qty="1" Price="2039.9940" Freight="50.9999" />
    <LineItem Line="5" PID="345" Qty="1" Price="2039.9940" Freight="50.9999" />
    <LineItem Line="6" PID="346" Qty="2" Price="2039.9940" Freight="101.9997" />
    <LineItem Line="7" PID="347" Qty="1" Price="2039.9940" Freight="50.9999" />
    <LineItem Line="8" PID="229" Qty="3" Price="28.8404" Freight="2.1630" />
    <LineItem Line="9" PID="235" Qty="1" Price="28.8404" Freight="0.7210" />
    <LineItem Line="10" PID="218" Qty="6" Price="5.7000" Freight="0.8550" />
    <LineItem Line="11" PID="223" Qty="2" Price="5.1865" Freight="0.2593" />
    <LineItem Line="12" PID="220" Qty="4" Price="20.1865" Freight="2.0187" />
  </Order>
  <Order OrderNumber="SO43660">
    <LineItem Line="1" PID="326" Qty="1" Price="419.4589" Freight="10.4865" />
    <LineItem Line="2" PID="319" Qty="1" Price="874.7940" Freight="21.8699" />
  </Order>
<!--Many more orders here -->
</Orders>
```

Your second objective is to determine whether it's faster to use *XmlDocument* or *XmlReader* to retrieve this data, because you need to process many of these files every day, and performance is critical.

This practice is intended to focus on the features that have been defined in this lesson, so a Console Application project will be implemented. The first exercise implements the solution based on *XmlDocument*, whereas the second exercise implements the solution based on *XmlReader*.

If you encounter a problem finishing an exercise, the completed projects can be installed from the Code folder on the companion CD.

EXERCISE 1 Creating the Project and Implementing the *XmlDocument* Solution

In this exercise, you create a Console Application project and add code to retrieve the necessary data by using the *XmlDocument* class.

1. In Visual Studio .NET 2010, choose File | New | Project.

2. Select your desired programming language and then the Console Application template. For the project name, enter **OrderProcessor**. Be sure to select a desired location for this project. For the solution name, enter **OrderProcessorSolution**. Be sure that Create Directory For Solution is selected and then click OK.

   After Visual Studio .NET finishes creating the project, Module1.vb (C# Program.cs) will be displayed.

3. In *Main*, declare a *string* variable for your file name and assign "Orders.xml" to it. Add the *parseWithXmlDocument* method and pass the file name as a parameter. Add this method to your code. Finally, add code to prompt the user to press Enter to end the application. Your code should look like the following:

Sample of Visual Basic Code

```vb
Module Module1
    Sub Main()
        Dim fileName = "Orders.xml"
        parseWithXmlDocument(fileName)

        Console.Write("Press <Enter> to end")
        Console.ReadLine()
    End Sub

    Private Sub parseWithXmlDocument(ByVal fileName As String)

    End Sub

End Module
```

Sample of C# Code

```csharp
namespace OrderProcessor
{
    class Program
    {
        static void Main(string[] args)
        {
            string fileName = "Orders.xml";
            parseWithXmlDocument(fileName);

            Console.Write("Press <Enter> to end");
            Console.ReadLine();
        }

        private static void parseWithXmlDocument(string fileName)
        {
```

```
            }
        }
    }
```

4. Add the Orders.xml file to your project. Right-click the *OrderProcessor* node in Solution Explorer and choose Add | Existing Item. In the bottom right corner of the Add Existing Item dialog box, click the drop-down list and select All Files (*.*). Navigate to the Begin folder for this exercise and select Orders.xml. If you don't see the Orders.xml file, check whether All Files (*.*) has been selected.

5. In Solution Explorer, click the Orders.xml file you just added. In the Properties window, set the *Copy to Output Directory* property to *Copy If Newer*.

   Because this file will reside in the same folder as your application, you will be able to use the file name without specifying a path.

6. In the *parseWithXmlDocument* method, instantiate a *Stopwatch* and assign the object to a variable. Start the stopwatch. Declare variables for the total order price, total freight cost, average freight cost, and order count. In C#, add *using System.Diagnostics;* to the top of the file. Your code should look like the following:

   Sample of Visual Basic Code
   ```
   Private Sub parseWithXmlDocument(ByVal fileName As String)
         Dim sw = New Stopwatch()
         sw.Start()
         Dim totalOrderPrice As Decimal = 0
         Dim totalFreightCost As Decimal = 0
         Dim orderQty As Integer = 0

   End Sub
   ```

   Sample of C# Code
   ```
   private static void parseWithXmlDocument(string fileName)
   {
       var sw = new Stopwatch();
       sw.Start();
       decimal totalOrderPrice = 0;
       decimal totalFreightCost = 0;
       decimal orderQty = 0;

   }
   ```

7. Add code to load the Orders.xml file into an *XmlDocument* object. You must also add *imports System.Xml.Linq* (C# *using System.Xml.Linq;*). Add code to get the order count by implementing an XPath query to get the *Order* elements and the count of elements returned. Your code should look like the following:

   Sample of Visual Basic Code
   ```
   Dim doc = New XmlDocument()
   doc.Load(fileName)
   orderQty = doc.SelectNodes("//Order").Count
   ```

```
var doc = new XmlDocument();
doc.Load(fileName);
orderQty = doc.SelectNodes("//Order").Count;
```

8. Add code to retrieve a node list containing all the line items by implementing an XPath query. Loop over all the line items and retrieve the freight and line price (quantity x price). Add the line price and the freight to the total order price. Add the freight to the total freight price. Your code should look like the following:

Sample of Visual Basic Code

```
For Each node As XmlNode In doc.SelectNodes("//LineItem")
    Dim freight = CDec(node.Attributes("Freight").Value)
    Dim linePrice = CDec(node.Attributes("Price").Value) _
                    * CDec(node.Attributes("Qty").Value)
    totalOrderPrice += linePrice + freight
    totalFreightCost += freight
Next
```

Sample of C# Code

```
foreach (XmlNode node in doc.SelectNodes("//LineItem"))
{
    var freight = decimal.Parse(node.Attributes["Freight"].Value);
    var linePrice = decimal.Parse(node.Attributes["Price"].Value)
        * decimal.Parse(node.Attributes["Qty"].Value);
    totalOrderPrice += linePrice + freight;
    totalFreightCost += freight;
}
```

9. Add code to display the total order price, the total freight cost, and the average freight cost per order. Stop the stopwatch and display the elapsed time. Your completed method should look like the following:

Sample of Visual Basic Code

```
Private Sub parseWithXmlDocument(ByVal fileName As String)
    Dim sw = New Stopwatch()
    sw.Start()
    Dim totalOrderPrice As Decimal = 0
    Dim totalFreightCost As Decimal = 0
    Dim averageFreightCost As Decimal = 0
    Dim orderQty As Integer = 0

    Dim doc = New XmlDocument()
    doc.Load(fileName)
    orderQty = doc.SelectNodes("//Order").Count

    For Each node As XmlNode In doc.SelectNodes("//LineItem")
        Dim freight = CDec(node.Attributes("Freight").Value)
        Dim linePrice = CDec(node.Attributes("Price").Value) _
                        * CDec(node.Attributes("Qty").Value)
        totalOrderPrice += linePrice + freight
        totalFreightCost += freight
```

```
    Next

    Console.WriteLine("Total Order Price: {0:C}", totalOrderPrice)
    Console.WriteLine("Total Freight Cost: {0:C}", totalFreightCost)
    Console.WriteLine("Average Freight Cost per Order: {0:C}", _
                    totalFreightCost / orderQty)

    sw.Stop()
    Console.WriteLine("Time to Parse XmlDocument: {0}", sw.Elapsed)
End Sub
```

Sample of C# Code

```
private static void parseWithXmlDocument(string fileName)
{
    var sw = new Stopwatch();
    sw.Start();
    decimal totalOrderPrice = 0;
    decimal totalFreightCost = 0;
    decimal averageFreightCost = 0;
    decimal orderQty = 0;

    var doc = new XmlDocument();
    doc.Load(fileName);
    orderQty = doc.SelectNodes("//Order").Count;

    foreach (XmlNode node in doc.SelectNodes("//LineItem"))
    {
        var freight = decimal.Parse(node.Attributes["Freight"].Value);
        var linePrice = decimal.Parse(node.Attributes["Price"].Value)
            * decimal.Parse(node.Attributes["Qty"].Value);
        totalOrderPrice += linePrice + freight;
        totalFreightCost += freight;
    }

    Console.WriteLine("Total Order Price: {0:C}", totalOrderPrice);
    Console.WriteLine("Total Freight Cost: {0:C}", totalFreightCost);
    Console.WriteLine("Average Freight Cost per Order: {0:C}",
        totalFreightCost/orderQty);

    sw.Stop();
    Console.WriteLine("Time to Parse XmlDocument: {0}", sw.Elapsed);
}
```

10. Run the application. Your total time will vary based on your machine configuration, but your output should look like the following:

Result

```
Total Order Price: $82,989,370.79
Total Freight Cost: $2,011,265.92
Average Freight Cost per Order: $529.84
Time to Parse XmlDocument: 00:00:01.3775482
Press <Enter> to end
```

EXERCISE 2 Implementing the *XmlReader* Solution

In this exercise, you extend the Console Application project from Exercise 1 by adding code to retrieve the necessary data using the *XmlReader* class.

1. In Visual Studio .NET 2010, choose File | Open | Project.

2. Select the project you created in Exercise 1.

3. In *Main*, after the call to *parseWithXmlDocument*, add the *parseWithXmlReader* method and pass the file name as a parameter. Add this method to your code. Your code should look like the following:

   Sample of Visual Basic Code

   ```
   Sub Main()
       Dim fileName = "Orders.xml"
       parseWithXmlDocument(fileName)
       parseWithXmlReader(fileName)
       Console.Write("Press <Enter> to end")
       Console.ReadLine()
   End Sub


   Private Sub parseWithXmlReader(ByVal fileName As String)

   End Sub
   ```

   Sample of C# Code

   ```
   static void Main(string[] args)
   {
       string fileName = "Orders.xml";
       parseWithXmlDocument(fileName);
       parseWithXmlReader(fileName);
       Console.Write("Press <Enter> to end");
       Console.ReadLine();
   }

   private static void parseWithXmlReader(string fileName)
   {

   }
   ```

4. In the *parseWithXmlReader* method, instantiate *Stopwatch* and assign the object to a variable. Start the stopwatch. Declare variables for the total order price, total freight cost, and order count. Your code should look like the following:

   Sample of Visual Basic Code

   ```
   Private Sub parseWithXmlReader(ByVal fileName As String)
       Dim sw = New Stopwatch()
       sw.Start()
       Dim totalOrderPrice As Decimal = 0
       Dim totalFreightCost As Decimal = 0
       Dim orderQty As Integer = 0

   End Sub
   ```

Sample of C# Code

```csharp
private static void parseWithXmlReader(string fileName)
{
    var sw = new Stopwatch();
    sw.Start();
    decimal totalOrderPrice = 0;
    decimal totalFreightCost = 0;
    decimal orderQty = 0;

}
```

5. Add a *using* statement to instantiate an *XmlTextReader* object and assign the object to a variable named *xmlReader*. In the *using* statement, add a *while* loop to iterate over all nodes. In the loop, add code to check the node type to see whether it is an element. Your code should look like the following:

Sample of Visual Basic Code

```vb
Using xmlReader As New XmlTextReader(fileName)
    Do While xmlReader.Read()
        If xmlReader.NodeType = XmlNodeType.Element Then

        End If
    Loop
End Using
```

Sample of C# Code

```csharp
using (var xmlReader = new XmlTextReader(fileName))
{
    while (xmlReader.Read())
    {
        if(xmlReader.NodeType==XmlNodeType.Element)
        {

        }
    }
}
```

6. Inside the *if* statement, add a *select* (C# *switch*) statement that increments the order quantity variable if the element's node name is *Order*. If the node name is *LineItem*, add code to retrieve the quantity, price, and freight. Add the freight to the total freight and add the total cost of the line to the total order cost variable. Your code should look like the following:

Sample of Visual Basic Code

```vb
Select Case xmlReader.Name
    Case "Order"
        orderQty += 1
    Case "LineItem"
        Dim qty = CDec(xmlReader.GetAttribute("Qty"))
        Dim price = CDec(xmlReader.GetAttribute("Price"))
        Dim freight = CDec(xmlReader.GetAttribute("Freight"))
        totalFreightCost += freight
```

```
        totalOrderPrice += (qty * price) + freight
End Select
```

Sample of C# Code

```csharp
switch(xmlReader.Name)
{
    case "Order":
        ++orderQty;
        break;
    case "LineItem":
        var qty = decimal.Parse(xmlReader.GetAttribute("Qty"));
        var price = decimal.Parse(xmlReader.GetAttribute("Price"));
        var freight = decimal.Parse(xmlReader.GetAttribute("Freight"));
        totalFreightCost += freight;
        totalOrderPrice += (qty * price) + freight;
        break;
}
```

7. Add code to display the total order price, the total freight cost, and the average freight cost per order. Stop the stopwatch and display the elapsed time. Your completed method should look like the following:

Sample of Visual Basic Code

```vb
Private Sub parseWithXmlReader(ByVal fileName As String)
    Dim sw = New Stopwatch()
    sw.Start()
    Dim totalOrderPrice As Decimal = 0
    Dim totalFreightCost As Decimal = 0
    Dim averageFreightCost As Decimal = 0
    Dim orderQty As Integer = 0

    Using xmlReader As New XmlTextReader(fileName)
        Do While xmlReader.Read()
            If xmlReader.NodeType = XmlNodeType.Element Then
                Select Case xmlReader.Name
                    Case "Order"
                        orderQty += 1
                    Case "LineItem"
                        Dim qty = CDec(xmlReader.GetAttribute("Qty"))
                        Dim price = CDec(xmlReader.GetAttribute("Price"))
                        Dim freight = CDec(xmlReader.GetAttribute("Freight"))
                        totalFreightCost += freight
                        totalOrderPrice += (qty * price) + freight
                End Select
            End If
        Loop
    End Using

    Console.WriteLine("Total Order Price: {0:C}", totalOrderPrice)
    Console.WriteLine("Total Freight Cost: {0:C}", totalFreightCost)
    Console.WriteLine("Average Freight Cost per Order: {0:C}", _
                    totalFreightCost / orderQty)
    sw.Stop()
```

```
        Console.WriteLine("Time to Parse XmlReader: {0}", sw.Elapsed)
    End Sub
```

Sample of C# Code

```csharp
private static void parseWithXmlReader(string fileName)
{
    var sw = new Stopwatch();
    sw.Start();
    decimal totalOrderPrice = 0;
    decimal totalFreightCost = 0;
    decimal averageFreightCost = 0;
    decimal orderQty = 0;

    using (var xmlReader = new XmlTextReader(fileName))
    {
        while (xmlReader.Read())
        {
            if (xmlReader.NodeType == XmlNodeType.Element)
            {
                switch (xmlReader.Name)
                {
                    case "Order":
                        ++orderQty;
                        break;
                    case "LineItem":
                        var qty = decimal.Parse(xmlReader.GetAttribute("Qty"));
                        var price = decimal.Parse(xmlReader.GetAttribute("Price"));
                        var freight = decimal.Parse(
                            xmlReader.GetAttribute("Freight"));
                        totalFreightCost += freight;
                        totalOrderPrice += (qty * price) + freight;
                        break;
                }
            }
        }
    }
    Console.WriteLine("Total Order Price: {0:C}", totalOrderPrice);
    Console.WriteLine("Total Freight Cost: {0:C}", totalFreightCost);
    Console.WriteLine("Average Freight Cost per Order: {0:C}",
        totalFreightCost / orderQty);

    sw.Stop();
    Console.WriteLine("Time to Parse XmlReader: {0}", sw.Elapsed);
}
```

8. Run the application. Your total time will vary based on your machine configuration, but you should find that *XmlReader* is substantially faster. Your output should look like the following, which includes the result from Exercise 1.

Result

```
Total Order Price: $82,989,370.79
Total Freight Cost: $2,011,265.92
Average Freight Cost per Order: $529.84
Time to Parse XmlDocument: 00:00:01.2218770
```

```
Total Order Price: $82,989,370.79
Total Freight Cost: $2,011,265.92
Average Freight Cost per Order: $529.84
Time to Parse XmlReader: 00:00:00.5919724
Press <Enter> to end
```

Lesson Summary

This lesson provided detailed information about the *XmlDocument* and the *XmlReader* classes.

- The *XmlDocument* class provides in-memory, random, read-write access to XML nodes.
- The *XmlReader* class provides fast-streaming, forward-only, read-only access to XML nodes.
- The *XmlDocument* class is easier to use, whereas the *XmlReader* class is faster.
- The *XmlDocument* class enables you to retrieve XML nodes by using the element name.
- The *XmlDocument* class enables you to retrieve XML nodes by using an XPath query.

Lesson Review

You can use the following questions to test your knowledge of the information in Lesson 1, "Working with the *XmlDocument* and *XmlReader* Classes." The questions are also available on the companion CD if you prefer to review them in electronic form.

> **NOTE ANSWERS**
>
> Answers to these questions and explanations of why each answer choice is correct or incorrect are located in the "Answers" section at the end of the book.

1. Given an XML file, you want to run several queries for data in the file based on filter criteria the user will be entering for a particular purpose. Which class would be more appropriate for these queries on the file?

   A. *XmlDocument*

   B. *XmlReader*

2. Every day, you receive hundreds of XML files. You are responsible for reading the file to retrieve sales data from the file and store it into a SQL database. Which class would be more appropriate for these queries on the file?

   A. *XmlDocument*

   B. *XmlReader*

3. You have a service that receives a very large XML-based history file once a month. These files can be up to 20GB in size, and you need to retrieve the header information that contains the history date range and the customer information on which this file is based. Which class would be more appropriate to retrieve the data in these files?

A. *XmlDocument*

B. *XmlReader*

Lesson 2: Querying with LINQ to XML

The use of LINQ to XML provides a powerful means to query XML data, using a language-based syntax that supports IntelliSense. LINQ to XML also enables you to transform XML in a very simple manner. This lesson covers the various aspects of querying XML by using LINQ to XML, and the next lesson explores transformations.

> **After this lesson, you will be able to:**
> - Understand the *XObject* class hierarchy.
> - Create *XDocument* objects.
> - Implement LINQ to XML queries.
> - Perform LINQ to XML queries with aggregates.
> - Execute LINQ to XML joins.
> - Use LINQ to XML with namespaces.
>
> **Estimated lesson time: 45 minutes**

Introducing the *XDocument* Family

In the quest to design a way to use LINQ over XML data, Microsoft needed to create a new set of classes that would simplify the task, so it created the *XDocument* classes: *XElement*, *XAttribute*, *XNamespace*, *XDirective*, and more. To use these classes, you must add a reference to the *System.Xml.Linq.dll* assembly, and then you can add an *imports* (C# *using*) *System.Xml.Linq* statement to your code. Figure 5-1 shows many of the classes that comprise the *XDocument* family.

As Figure 5-1 shows, many, but not all, classes inherit from the *XNode* class. In the class hierarchy, the *XAttribute* class is not an *XNode*. This lesson focuses on the *XDocument*, *XElement*, *XAttribute*, and *XNamespace* classes and their parent classes.

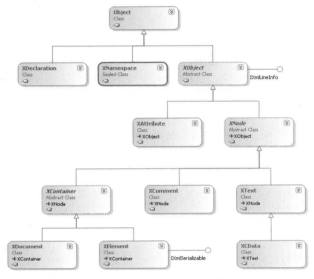

FIGURE 5-1 The *XDocument* class family simplifies LINQ access to XML data.

The *XObject* Class

Most of the *XDocument* classes derive from the *XObject* class. This is a *MustInherit* (C# *abstract*) class that contains the following members that will be inherited.

- **BaseUri**   A read-only property containing the base URI string for the current object.
- **Document**   A read-only property that references the *XDocument* object to which the current object belongs.
- **NodeType**   An abstract, read-only property that returns *XmlNodeType* of the current node. Child classes override this to return the proper node type.
- **Parent**   A read-only property that returns the *XElement* parent of the current node.
- **AddAnnotation**   A method for adding an annotation object to the object's annotations list. Think of an annotation as something like a notation—or, better yet, as an attachment. The annotation is not limited to being a string; it can be any object you want to attach to the current *XObject* instance. Annotations are not persisted and do not show when using the *ToString* method to retrieve the XML representation as a string.
- **Annotation**   Generic and non-generic methods that return the first annotation of the type passed to this method as a generic parameter or regular method parameter.
- **Annotations**   Generic and non-generic methods that return a collection of the type passed to this method as a generic parameter or regular method parameter.

- **RemoveAnnotations**   Generic and non-generic methods that remove the annotations of the type passed to this method as a generic parameter or regular method parameter.

- **Changed**   An event that occurs if the current *XObject* class or any of its descendents have changed.

- **Changing**   An event that occurs before the current *XObject* class or any of its descendents change.

In addition to these members, the *XObject* class explicitly implements the *IXmlLineInfo* interface, which contains *LineNumber* and *LinePosition* properties and the *HasLineInfo* method.

The *XAttribute* Class

The *XAttribute* object represents an XML attribute. The *XAttribute* class is derived from the *XObject* class, so it inherits all the members of the *XObject* class. In addition, the *XAttribute* class contains the following members.

- **EmptySequence**   A *shared* (C# *static*) read-only property that returns an empty generic *IEnumerable* of *XAttribute*.

- **IsNameSpaceDeclaration**   A read-only property that returns *true* if the current *XAttribute* object represents a namespace identifier.

- **Name**   A read-only property that returns the name of the XML attribute as a string.

- **NextAttribute**   A read-only property that returns a reference to the next XML attribute. Returns *null* if the current *XAttribute* object has no parent or if the current *XAttribute* object is the last XML attribute of the parent.

- **NodeType**   Overrides the inherited *NodeType* property from *XObject*. Returns *XmlNodeType.XAttribute*.

- **PreviousAttribute**   A read-only property that returns a reference to the previous XML attribute. Returns *null* if the current *XAttribute* object has no parent or if there is no previous XML attribute.

- **Value**   A string property that gets or sets the value of the XML attribute. When you attempt to set this property, the property is validated before the value is set. If you attempt to assign *Nothing* (C# *null*) to this property, an *ArgumentNullException* is thrown. Also, if this attribute is a namespace declaration, the namespace is validated. If validation succeeds, the *Changing* event inherited from *XObject* is raised, the value is set, and the *Changed* event is raised.

- **Operator**   A group of 25 explicit conversion operators that enable you to convert the *XAttribute* object to many types by using *CType* (C# *explicit cast*) based on the XML attribute's value. Internally, this uses the *XmlConvert* class to convert the value of the XML attribute to the desired type.

- **Remove**   A method that removes the current *XAttribute* object from the parent element. It throws an *InvalidOperationException* if the current *XAttribute* object has no parent.

- **SetValue**   A method that attempts to make the object parameter a string that is passed in and assigns the string to the current *XAttribute* object's value.

- **ToString**   A method that overrides the *ToString* method inherited from the *Object* class. This override emits the name and value of the XML attribute as you would expect to see it in an XML document.

The *XNode* Class

The *XNode* class is derived from the *XObject* class, so it contains all the *XObject* members. The *XNode* class contains the following members.

- **DocumentOrderComparer**   A *shared* (C# *static*), read-only property that returns a comparer of the type *XNodeDocumentOrderComparer*. This comparer can compare the relative positions of two nodes.

- **EqualityComparer**   A *shared* (C# *static*), read-only property that returns a comparer of the type *XNodeEqualityComparer*. This comparer can compare two nodes for equality.

- **NextNode**   A read-only property that returns a reference to the next node or *Nothing* (C# *null*) if there is no next node.

- **PreviousNode**   A read-only property that returns a reference to the previous node or *Nothing* (C# *null*) if there is no previous node.

- **AddAfterSelf**   A method that enables you to pass in content that should be added after the current node object.

- **AddBeforeSelf**   A method that enables you to pass in content that should be added before the current node object.

- **Ancestors**   A method that accepts a name parameter and returns a collection of the ancestor elements of the current node that have the specified name.

- **CompareDocumentOrder**   A *shared* (C# *static*) method that compares two nodes to determine their relative XML document order. This method accepts two *XNode* objects and returns an *Integer* (C# *int*) value by which *0* indicates that the two nodes are equal, *-1* indicates that the first node is before the second node, and *+1* indicates that the first node is after the second node.

- **CreateReader**   A method that returns an *XmlReader* that can read the contents of the current node and its descendents.

- **DeepEquals**   A *shared* (C# *static*) method that accepts two *XNode* parameters. This method compares the values of the two elements and the values of the descendents and returns *true* if the nodes are equal.

- **ElementsAfterSelf** A method that returns a collection of the sibling element nodes after this node, in document order. There is also an overload that accepts an *XName* object consisting of the name of the elements you want to return.

- **ElementsBeforeSelf** A method that returns a collection of the sibling element nodes before this node, in document order. There is also an overload that accepts an *XName* object consisting of the name of the elements you want to return.

- **IsAfter** A method that accepts an *XNode* parameter and returns *true* if the current node is after the *XNode* passed into this method.

- **IsBefore** A method that accepts an *XNode* parameter and returns *true* if the current node is before the *XNode* passed into this method.

- **NodeAfterSelf** A method that returns a reference to the node after the current node. Returns *Nothing* (C# *null*) if there is no node after the current node.

- **NodeBeforeSelf** A method that returns a reference to the node before the current node. Returns *Nothing* (C# *null*) if there is no node before the current node.

- **ReadFrom** A *shared* (C# *static*) method that accepts an *XmlReader* parameter and returns an *XNode* object that represents the first node encountered by *XmlReader*.

- **Remove** A method that removes the current node from its parent. This throws an *InvalidOperationException* if there is no parent.

- **ReplaceWith** A method that replaces the node with the specified content passed in as a parameter. The content can be simple content, a collection of content objects, a parameter list of content objects, or *null*.

- **ToString** A method that overrides the *ToString* method in *Object*. This returns the XML of the current node and its contents as a string.

- **WriteTo** A *MustImplement* (C# *abstract*) method that takes an *XmlWriter* parameter.

The *XContainer* Class

The *XContainer* class represents a node that can contain other nodes and is a *MustInherit* (C# *abstract*) class that derives from the *XNode* class. It inherits the members of *XNode* and *XObject*. The *XDocument* and *XElement* classes derive from this class. The following is a list of its members.

- **FirstNode** A read-only property that returns a reference to the first node in this container. If there are no nodes in the container, this property returns *Nothing* (C# *null*).

- **LastNode** A read-only property that returns a reference to the last node in this container. If there are no nodes in the container, this property returns *Nothing* (C# *null*).

- **Add** A method that accepts one or several content objects and adds them and their children to this container.

- **AddFirst** A method that accepts one or several content objects and adds them and their children to the current *XContainer* object as the first node.

- **CreateWriter** A method that returns an *XmlWriter* object that can be used to add elements or attributes to the current *XContainer* object.

- **DescendantNodes** A method that returns descendant elements plus leaf nodes contained in the current *XContainer* object.

- **Descendants** A method that returns references to the descendant nodes of the current *XContainer* object as a generic *IEnumerable* of *XElement*. There is also an overload that accepts a name as an *XName* parameter and returns references only to the descendant nodes that match the name parameter. This method does not return a reference to the current *XContainer* object.

- **Element** A method that accepts a name as an *XName* parameter and returns a reference to the first child element with a name that matches the name parameter or returns *null* if no match is found.

- **Elements** A method that returns references to all child elements of the current *XContainer* object as a generic *IEnumerable* of *XElement*. There is also an overload that accepts a name as an *XName* parameter and returns references only to the child nodes that match the name parameter.

- **Nodes** A method that returns a reference to all nodes in the current *XContainer* object as a generic *IEnumerable* of the *XNode* object.

- **RemoveNodes** A method that removes all nodes from the current *XContainer* object. Note that this method does not remove any attributes the *XContainer* object might have.

- **ReplaceNodes** A method that accepts one or several content objects as a parameter and replaces the existing content with the content parameter.

The *XElement* Class

The *XElement* class represents an XML element with a *Name* property of the type *XName*. The *XName* class is composed of a local name and a namespace. Optionally, *XElement* can contain XML attributes of type *XAttribute*, derives from *XContainer*, and inherits the members of *XContainer*, *XNode*, and *XObject*.

The *XElement* class explicitly implements the *IXmlSerializable* interface, which contains the *GetSchema*, *ReadXml*, and *WriteXml* methods so this object can be serialized. The following are members of the *XElement* class.

- **EmptySequence** A *shared* (C# *static*), read-only property that returns an empty generic *IEnumerable* of the *XElement* object.

- **FirstAttribute** A read-only property that returns a reference to the first XML attribute on this element or *null* if there are no attributes.

- **HasAttributes** A read-only property that returns *true* if the current element has at least one attribute.

- **HasElements**   A read-only property that returns *true* if the current element has at least one child element.

- **IsEmpty**   A read-only property that returns *true* if the current element has no child elements.

- **LastAttribute**   A read-only property that returns a reference to the last XML attribute on this element or *null* if there are no attributes.

- **Name**   A read–write property that contains the name of the current element as an *XName* object. The *XName* object contains a local name and a namespace.

- **NodeType**   A read-only property that returns *XmlNodeType.Element*.

- **Value**   A read–write string property that contains the text of the current element as an *XName* object. If the current element contains a mixture of text and child elements, the text of all children is concatenated and returned. If you pass an *XName* into the property setter, all existing content will be removed and replaced with the *XName* object.

- **AncestorsAndSelf**   A method that returns a generic *IEnumerable* of an *XElement* sequence containing references to the current element and all its ancestor elements. There is also an overload that accepts an *XName* parameter for the name of the elements you want to retrieve.

- **Attribute**   A method that accepts a name parameter as an *XName* and returns a reference to the attribute with a name that matches on the current element. This method returns *Nothing* (C# *null*) if no attribute is found.

- **Attributes**   A method that returns a generic *IEnumerable* of an *XAttribute* sequence containing references to all attributes of the current element. There is also an overload that accepts a name parameter as an *XName* and returns a reference to the attribute with a name that matches on the current element. This method returns an empty sequence if no attribute is found.

- **DescendantNodesAndSelf**   A method that returns a generic *IEnumerable* of an *XNode* sequence containing references to the current node and all its descendant nodes.

- **DescendantsAndSelf**   A method that returns a generic *IEnumerable* of an *XElement* sequence containing references to the current element and all its descendant elements. There is also an overload that accepts a string parameter for the name of the elements you want to retrieve.

- **GetDefaultNamespace**   A method that returns the default namespace of the current element as an *XNamespace* object. The *XNamespace* type has a *NamespaceName* property that contains the URI of the namespace. If there is no default namespace, this method returns the *XNamespace.None* value.

- **GetNamespaceOfPrefix**   A method that accepts a prefix parameter as a string and returns a reference to the associated namespace or *null* if the namespace is not found.

- **GetPrefixOfNamespace**   A method that returns the prefix of the current element as a string.

- **Load**   A *shared* (C# *static*) method that creates a new *XElement* object and initializes it with the contents passed into the method. There are eight overloads for this method that enable you to pass various objects as parameters, such as *Stream*, *TextReader*, *XmlReader*, or a *string* URI.

- **Operator**   There are 25 explicit conversion operators, which enable you to convert the *XElement* object to many types by using *CType* (C# *explicit cast*) based on the XML element's value. Internally, this uses the *XmlConvert* class to convert the value of the XML element to the desired type.

- **Parse**   A *shared* (C# *static*) method that creates a new *XElement* object and initializes it with the contents parameter as *string* passed into the method. There is also an overload for this method that enables you to pass load options to preserve white space.

- **RemoveAll**   A method that removes all attributes and all elements from the current element.

- **RemoveAttributes**   A method that removes all attributes from the current element.

- **ReplaceAll**   A method that replaces the child nodes and attributes of the current element with the content parameter passed into this method. The content can be simple content, a collection of content objects, a parameter list of content objects, or *null*.

- **ReplaceAttributes**   A method that replaces the attributes of the current element with the content parameter. The content can be simple content, a collection of content objects, a parameter list of content objects, or *null*.

- **Save**   A method that outputs the current element's XML tree to a file, *Stream*, *TextWriter*, or *XmlWriter* object.

- **SetElementValue**   A method that sets the value of a child element. The value is assigned to the first child element that matches the name parameter. If no child element with a matching name exists, a new child element is added. If the value is *null*, the first child element with the given name, if any, is deleted.

- **SetValue**   A method that assigns the *Object* parameter to the *Value* property of the current element by converting the given value to *string*.

- **WriteTo**   A method that writes the current element to the *XmlWriter* parameter.

The *XDocument* Class

The *XDocument* class represents an XML document that can contain a DTD, one root XML element, zero-to-many XML comments, and zero-to-many XML processing instructions. The *XDocument* class derives from *XContainer* and therefore inherits the members of *XContainer*, *XNode*, and *XObject*. The following are members of the *XDocument* class.

- **Declaration**   A read/write property of type *XDeclaration*. The *XDeclaration* class contains properties for *Encoding*, *Standalone*, and *Version*.

- **DocumentType**   A read-only property of *XDocumentType*, which is the Document Type Definition (DTD).

- **NodeType**   A read-only property that returns *XmlNodeType.Document*.

- **Root**   A read-only property that returns a reference to the first XML element in the XML document. The property returns *Nothing* (C# *null*) if there is no root element.

- **Load**   A *shared* (C# *static*) method that creates a new *XDocument* object and initializes it with the contents passed into the method. There are eight overloads for this method that enable you to load content from a *Stream*, *TextReader*, *XmlReader*, or *string* URI.

- **Parse**   A *shared* (C# *static*) method that creates a new *XDocument* object and initializes it with the XML passed as a *string* parameter. There is also an overload for this method that enables you to pass load options to preserve white space.

- **Save**   A method that outputs the current document's XML tree to a file or *XmlWriter*.

- **WriteTo**   A method that writes the current document to a *Stream*, *XmlWriter*, *TextWriter*, or file.

Using the *XDocument* Classes

The previous introduction to the *XDocument* classes described the members of the more common classes, whereas this section will implement the *XDocument* family of classes.

The *XDocument* class can be populated very easily by using the constructor, the *Load* method, or the *Parse* method. The following code sample uses the *Parse* method to load an XML string into an *XDocument* object. After that, the *Save* method saves the XML document to the XDocumentTest.xml file.

Sample of Visual Basic Code

```
Private Sub ParseXDocumentToolStripMenuItem_Click( _
      ByVal sender As System.Object, ByVal e As System.EventArgs) _
      Handles ParseXDocumentToolStripMenuItem.Click
    Dim xml = _
        "<CustomersOrders>" & _
        "  <Customer CustomerID='ALFKI' CompanyName='Alfreds Futterkiste'>" & _
        "    <Order OrderID='10643' Freight='29.4600'/>" & _
        "    <Order OrderID='10692' Freight='61.0200'/>" & _
        "    <Order OrderID='10702' Freight='23.9400'/>" & _
        "    <Order OrderID='10835' Freight='69.5300'/>" & _
        "    <Order OrderID='10952' Freight='40.4200'/>" & _
        "    <Order OrderID='11011' Freight='1.2100'/>" & _
        "  </Customer>" & _
        "  <Customer CustomerID='ANATR' CompanyName='Ana Trujillo'>" & _
        "    <Order OrderID='10308' Freight='1.6100'/>" & _
        "    <Order OrderID='10625' Freight='43.9000'/>" & _
        "    <Order OrderID='10759' Freight='11.9900'/>" & _
        "    <Order OrderID='10926' Freight='39.9200'/>" & _
        "  </Customer>" & _
        "  <Customer CustomerID='ANTON' CompanyName='Antonio Moreno'>" & _
        "    <Order OrderID='10365' Freight='22.0000'/>" & _
        "    <Order OrderID='10507' Freight='47.4500'/>" & _
```

```
            "        <Order OrderID='10535' Freight='15.6400'/>" & _
            "        <Order OrderID='10573' Freight='84.8400'/>" & _
            "        <Order OrderID='10677' Freight='4.0300'/>" & _
            "        <Order OrderID='10682' Freight='36.1300'/>" & _
            "        <Order OrderID='10856' Freight='58.4300'/>" & _
            "      </Customer>" & _
            "      <Customer CustomerID='AROUT' CompanyName='Around the Horn'>" & _
            "        <Order OrderID='10355' Freight='41.9500'/>" & _
            "        <Order OrderID='10383' Freight='34.2400'/>" & _
            "        <Order OrderID='10453' Freight='25.3600'/>" & _
            "        <Order OrderID='10558' Freight='72.9700'/>" & _
            "        <Order OrderID='10707' Freight='21.7400'/>" & _
            "        <Order OrderID='10741' Freight='10.9600'/>" & _
            "        <Order OrderID='10743' Freight='23.7200'/>" & _
            "        <Order OrderID='10768' Freight='146.3200'/>" & _
            "        <Order OrderID='10793' Freight='4.5200'/>" & _
            "        <Order OrderID='10864' Freight='3.0400'/>" & _
            "        <Order OrderID='10920' Freight='29.6100'/>" & _
            "        <Order OrderID='10953' Freight='23.7200'/>" & _
            "        <Order OrderID='11016' Freight='33.8000'/>" & _
            "      </Customer>" & _
            "</CustomersOrders>"
    Dim doc = XDocument.Parse(xml)
    doc.Save(getFilePath("XDocumentTest.xml"))
    MessageBox.Show("XDocument Saved")
End Sub
```

Sample of C# Code

```csharp
private void parseXDocumentToolStripMenuItem_Click(
    object sender, EventArgs e)
{
    string xml = @"
        <CustomersOrders>
            <Customer CustomerID='ALFKI' CompanyName='Alfreds Futterkiste'>
                <Order OrderID='10643' Freight='29.4600' />
                <Order OrderID='10692' Freight='61.0200' />
                <Order OrderID='10702' Freight='23.9400' />
                <Order OrderID='10835' Freight='69.5300' />
                <Order OrderID='10952' Freight='40.4200' />
                <Order OrderID='11011' Freight='1.2100' />
            </Customer>
            <Customer CustomerID='ANATR' CompanyName='Ana Trujillo'>
                <Order OrderID='10308' Freight='1.6100' />
                <Order OrderID='10625' Freight='43.9000' />
                <Order OrderID='10759' Freight='11.9900' />
                <Order OrderID='10926' Freight='39.9200' />
            </Customer>
            <Customer CustomerID='ANTON' CompanyName='Antonio Moreno'>
                <Order OrderID='10365' Freight='22.0000' />
                <Order OrderID='10507' Freight='47.4500' />
                <Order OrderID='10535' Freight='15.6400' />
                <Order OrderID='10573' Freight='84.8400' />
                <Order OrderID='10677' Freight='4.0300' />
                <Order OrderID='10682' Freight='36.1300' />
                <Order OrderID='10856' Freight='58.4300' />
```

```
      </Customer>
      <Customer CustomerID='AROUT' CompanyName='Around the Horn'>
          <Order OrderID='10355' Freight='41.9500' />
          <Order OrderID='10383' Freight='34.2400' />
          <Order OrderID='10453' Freight='25.3600' />
          <Order OrderID='10558' Freight='72.9700' />
          <Order OrderID='10707' Freight='21.7400' />
          <Order OrderID='10741' Freight='10.9600' />
          <Order OrderID='10743' Freight='23.7200' />
          <Order OrderID='10768' Freight='146.3200' />
          <Order OrderID='10793' Freight='4.5200' />
          <Order OrderID='10864' Freight='3.0400' />
          <Order OrderID='10920' Freight='29.6100' />
          <Order OrderID='10953' Freight='23.7200' />
          <Order OrderID='11016' Freight='33.8000' />
      </Customer>
    </CustomersOrders>
  ";
  var doc = XDocument.Parse(xml);
  doc.Save(getFilePath("XDocumentTest.xml"));
  MessageBox.Show("XDocument Saved");
}
```

Looking at the sample code, you might like the C# code better than the Visual Basic code because C# enables you to create a string that spans many rows. Visual Basic has an alternate way to load XML into an *XDocument*, as shown in the following code sample, which implements the *XDocument* constructor.

Sample of Visual Basic Code

```
Private Sub XDocumentConstructorToolStripMenuItem_Click( _
    ByVal sender As System.Object, ByVal e As System.EventArgs) _
    Handles XDocumentConstructorToolStripMenuItem.Click
  Dim doc As XDocument = _
    <?xml version="1.0" encoding="utf-8" standalone="yes"?>
    <CustomersOrders>
        <Customer CustomerID='ALFKI' CompanyName='Alfreds Futterkiste'>
            <Order OrderID='10643' Freight='29.4600'/>
            <Order OrderID='10692' Freight='61.0200'/>
            <Order OrderID='10702' Freight='23.9400'/>
            <Order OrderID='10835' Freight='69.5300'/>
            <Order OrderID='10952' Freight='40.4200'/>
            <Order OrderID='11011' Freight='1.2100'/>
        </Customer>
        <Customer CustomerID='ANATR' CompanyName='Ana Trujillo'>
            <Order OrderID='10308' Freight='1.6100'/>
            <Order OrderID='10625' Freight='43.9000'/>
            <Order OrderID='10759' Freight='11.9900'/>
            <Order OrderID='10926' Freight='39.9200'/>
        </Customer>
        <Customer CustomerID='ANTON' CompanyName='Antonio Moreno'>
            <Order OrderID='10365' Freight='22.0000'/>
            <Order OrderID='10507' Freight='47.4500'/>
            <Order OrderID='10535' Freight='15.6400'/>
            <Order OrderID='10573' Freight='84.8400'/>
```

```
                    <Order OrderID='10677' Freight='4.0300'/>
                    <Order OrderID='10682' Freight='36.1300'/>
                    <Order OrderID='10856' Freight='58.4300'/>
            </Customer>
            <Customer CustomerID='AROUT' CompanyName='Around the Horn'>
                    <Order OrderID='10355' Freight='41.9500'/>
                    <Order OrderID='10383' Freight='34.2400'/>
                    <Order OrderID='10453' Freight='25.3600'/>
                    <Order OrderID='10558' Freight='72.9700'/>
                    <Order OrderID='10707' Freight='21.7400'/>
                    <Order OrderID='10741' Freight='10.9600'/>
                    <Order OrderID='10743' Freight='23.7200'/>
                    <Order OrderID='10768' Freight='146.3200'/>
                    <Order OrderID='10793' Freight='4.5200'/>
                    <Order OrderID='10864' Freight='3.0400'/>
                    <Order OrderID='10920' Freight='29.6100'/>
                    <Order OrderID='10953' Freight='23.7200'/>
                    <Order OrderID='11016' Freight='33.8000'/>
            </Customer>
        </CustomersOrders>
    doc.Save(getFilePath("XDocumentTest.xml"))
    MessageBox.Show("XDocument Saved")
End Sub
```

Sample of C# Code

```csharp
private void xDocumentConstructorToolStripMenuItem_Click(
    object sender, EventArgs e)
{
    var doc = new XDocument(
        new XElement("CustomersOrders",
            new XElement("Customer",
                new XAttribute("CustomerID", "ALFKI"),
                new XAttribute("CompanyName", "Alfreds Futterkiste"),
                new XElement("Order",
                            new XAttribute("OrderID", "10643"),
                            new XAttribute("Freight", "29.4600")),
                new XElement("Order",
                            new XAttribute("OrderID", "10692"),
                            new XAttribute("Freight", "61.0200")),
                new XElement("Order",
                            new XAttribute("OrderID", "10702"),
                            new XAttribute("Freight", "23.9400")),
                new XElement("Order",
                            new XAttribute("OrderID", "10835"),
                            new XAttribute("Freight", "69.5300")),
                new XElement("Order",
                            new XAttribute("OrderID", "10952"),
                            new XAttribute("Freight", "40.4200")),
                new XElement("Order",
                            new XAttribute("OrderID", "11011"),
                            new XAttribute("Freight", "1.2100"))),
            new XElement("Customer",
                new XAttribute("CustomerID", "ANATR"),
                new XAttribute("CompanyName", "Ana Trujillo"),
                new XElement("Order",
```

```
                    new XAttribute("OrderID", "10308"),
                    new XAttribute("Freight", "1.6100")),
        new XElement("Order",
                    new XAttribute("OrderID", "10625"),
                    new XAttribute("Freight", "43.9000")),
        new XElement("Order",
                    new XAttribute("OrderID", "10759"),
                    new XAttribute("Freight", "11.9900")),
        new XElement("Order",
                    new XAttribute("OrderID", "10926"),
                    new XAttribute("Freight", "39.9200"))),
    new XElement("Customer",
        new XAttribute("CustomerID", "ANTON"),
        new XAttribute("CompanyName", "Antonio Moreno"),
        new XElement("Order",
                    new XAttribute("OrderID", "10365"),
                    new XAttribute("Freight", "22.0000")),
        new XElement("Order",
                    new XAttribute("OrderID", "10507"),
                    new XAttribute("Freight", "47.4500")),
        new XElement("Order",
                    new XAttribute("OrderID", "10535"),
                    new XAttribute("Freight", "15.6400")),
        new XElement("Order",
                    new XAttribute("OrderID", "10573"),
                    new XAttribute("Freight", "84.8400")),
        new XElement("Order",
                    new XAttribute("OrderID", "10677"),
                    new XAttribute("Freight", "4.0300")),
        new XElement("Order",
                    new XAttribute("OrderID", "10682"),
                    new XAttribute("Freight", "36.1300")),
        new XElement("Order",
                    new XAttribute("OrderID", "10856"),
                    new XAttribute("Freight", "58.5300"))),
    new XElement("Customer",
        new XAttribute("CustomerID", "AROUT"),
        new XAttribute("CompanyName", "Around the Horn"),
        new XElement("Order",
                    new XAttribute("OrderID", "10355"),
                    new XAttribute("Freight", "41.9500")),
        new XElement("Order",
                    new XAttribute("OrderID", "10383"),
                    new XAttribute("Freight", "34.2400")),
        new XElement("Order",
                    new XAttribute("OrderID", "10453"),
                    new XAttribute("Freight", "25.3600")),
        new XElement("Order",
                    new XAttribute("OrderID", "10558"),
                    new XAttribute("Freight", "72.9700")),
        new XElement("Order",
                    new XAttribute("OrderID", "10707"),
                    new XAttribute("Freight", "21.7400")),
        new XElement("Order",
                    new XAttribute("OrderID", "10741"),
```

```
                        new XAttribute("Freight", "10.9600")),
            new XElement("Order",
                        new XAttribute("OrderID", "10743"),
                        new XAttribute("Freight", "23.7200")),
            new XElement("Order",
                        new XAttribute("OrderID", "10768"),
                        new XAttribute("Freight", "146.3200")),
            new XElement("Order",
                        new XAttribute("OrderID", "10793"),
                        new XAttribute("Freight", "4.5200")),
            new XElement("Order",
                        new XAttribute("OrderID", "10864"),
                        new XAttribute("Freight", "3.0400")),
            new XElement("Order",
                        new XAttribute("OrderID", "10920"),
                        new XAttribute("Freight", "29.6100")),
            new XElement("Order",
                        new XAttribute("OrderID", "10953"),
                        new XAttribute("Freight", "23.7200")),
            new XElement("Order",
                        new XAttribute("OrderID", "11016"),
                        new XAttribute("Freight", "33.8000")))));
    doc.Save(getFilePath("XDocumentTest.xml"));
    MessageBox.Show("XDocument Saved");
}
```

In this code sample, the Visual Basic code is much simpler than the C# code. The Visual Basic compiler parses the XML literals and creates the same code that the C# compiler creates. This is very different from the previous example, in which the *Parse* method parsed an XML string. In this example, the code runs faster than the *Parse* example because there is no need to parse at run time.

Implementing LINQ to XML Queries

You can use many of the techniques covered in Chapter 3, "Introducing LINQ," to query an *XDocument* or *XElement* object. By using the XML from the previous examples, you might want to return the freight and customer ID for order ID 10677, which can be accomplished as shown in the following code sample:

Sample of Visual Basic Code
```
Private Sub LINQQueryToolStripMenuItem_Click( _
      ByVal sender As System.Object, ByVal e As System.EventArgs) _
      Handles LINQQueryToolStripMenuItem.Click
   Dim doc = XDocument.Load(getFilePath("XDocumentTest.xml"))
   Dim result = (From order In doc.Descendants("Order")
                 Where order.Attribute("OrderID").Value = "10677"
                 Select New With
                 {
                     .OrderID = CType(order.Attribute("OrderID"), Integer),
                     .CustomerID = CType(order.Parent.Attribute("CustomerID"), String),
                     .Freight = CType(order.Attribute("Freight"), Decimal)
                 }).FirstOrDefault()
   txtLog.Text = String.Format("OrderID:{0}  CustomerID:{1}  Freigth:{2:C}", _
```

```
        result.OrderID, result.CustomerID, result.Freight)
    End Sub
```

Sample of C# Code

```csharp
private void lINQQueryToolStripMenuItem_Click(
    object sender, EventArgs e)
{
    var doc = XDocument.Load(getFilePath("XDocumentTest.xml"));
    var result = (from order in doc.Descendants("Order")
                  where order.Attribute("OrderID").Value == "10677"
                  select new
                      {
                          OrderID=(int)order.Attribute("OrderID"),
                          CustomerID = (string)order.Parent.Attribute("CustomerID"),
                          Freight = (decimal)order.Attribute("Freight")
                      }).FirstOrDefault();
    txtLog.Text = string.Format("OrderID:{0}  CustomerID:{1}  Freigth:{2:C}",
        result.OrderID, result.CustomerID, result.Freight);
}
```

In this code sample, the *Load* method of the *XDocument* class is executed to retrieve the XML document from the previous examples, and then a LINQ query is applied to the *XDocument* object. The *select* clause creates an anonymous type containing *OrderID*, *CustomerID*, and *Freight*. The *FirstOrDefault* query extension method is implemented to return a single object of the anonymous type. The result is then displayed in the *txtLog* text box.

In the code sample, *CType* (C# *explicit cast*) converts the attribute to the appropriate type. The *XAttribute* class has 25 explicit conversion operators to convert the *XAttribute* object to a different .NET Framework type. This feature simplifies the syntax of the LINQ query.

Using LINQ to XML with Aggregates

If you want to query for the sum of the freight for each customer, you can use LINQ to XML as shown in the following code sample:

Sample of Visual Basic Code

```vb
Private Sub LINQQuerySumToolStripMenuItem_Click( _
    ByVal sender As System.Object, ByVal e As System.EventArgs) _
    Handles LINQQuerySumToolStripMenuItem.Click
    Dim doc = XDocument.Load(getFilePath("XDocumentTest.xml"))
    Dim result = From customer In doc.Descendants("Customer")
        Select New With
        {
            .CustomerID = CType(customer.Attribute("CustomerID"), String),
            .TotalFreight = customer.Descendants("Order") _
                .Sum(Function(o) CType(o.Attribute("Freight"), Decimal))
        }
    txtLog.Clear()
    For Each customer In result
        txtLog.AppendText( _
            String.Format("CustomerID:{0}  TotalFreight:{1,8:C}" + vbCrLf, _
                customer.CustomerID, customer.TotalFreight))
```

```
      Next
End Sub
```

Sample of C# Code

Sample of C# Code

```csharp
private void lINQQuerySumToolStripMenuItem_Click(
    object sender, EventArgs e)
{
    var doc = XDocument.Load(getFilePath("XDocumentTest.xml"));
    var result = from customer in doc.Descendants("Customer")
                 select new
                 {
                     CustomerID = (string)customer.Attribute("CustomerID"),
                     TotalFreight = customer.Descendants("Order")
                        .Sum(o=>(decimal)o.Attribute("Freight"))
                 };
    txtLog.Clear();
    foreach (var customer in result)
    {
        txtLog.AppendText( string.Format("CustomerID:{0}  TotalFreight:{1,8:C}\r\n",
            customer.CustomerID, customer.TotalFreight));
    }
}
```

The sample code starts by loading the XML file into an *XDocument* object. Next, a LINQ to XML query is created that retrieves *Customer* elements, but the *select* clause creates an anonymous type containing *CustomerID* and *TotalFreight*. *TotalFreight* is calculated by retrieving the *Order* elements of each customer and then executes the *Sum* query extension method by which the *Freight* attribute is converted to a decimal type to perform the aggregation.

Using LINQ to XML Joins

Joins can be accomplished between LINQ to XML and other LINQ providers such as LINQ to Objects. The following code sample starts with an array of orders to be retrieved. This array could have come from a multiple selection list box or some other customer input screen. The order array is then joined to the XML file that was used in the previous examples to retrieve the desired order information.

Sample of Visual Basic Code

```vb
Private Sub LINQQuerySumToolStripMenuItem_Click( _
        ByVal sender As System.Object, ByVal e As System.EventArgs) _
        Handles LINQQuerySumToolStripMenuItem.Click
    Dim orders() = {"10707", "10835", "10953"}
    Dim doc = XDocument.Load(getFilePath("XDocumentTest.xml"))
    Dim result = From order In doc.Descendants("Order")
                 Join selected In orders On
                 CType(order.Attribute("OrderID"), String) Equals selected
            Select New With
            {
                .OrderID = CType(order.Attribute("OrderID"), Integer),
                .CustomerID = CType(order.Parent.Attribute("CustomerID"), String),
                .Freight = CType(order.Attribute("Freight"), Decimal)
```

```
        }
    txtLog.Clear()
    For Each order In result
        txtLog.AppendText( _
            String.Format("OrderID:{0} CustomerID:{1}  TotalFreight:{2:C}" + vbCrLf, _
                order.OrderID, order.CustomerID, order.Freight))
    Next
End Sub
```

Sample of C# Code

```csharp
private void lINQQueryJoinToolStripMenuItem_Click(
    object sender, EventArgs e)
{
    string[] orders = {"10707","10835","10953"};

    var doc = XDocument.Load(getFilePath("XDocumentTest.xml"));
    var result = from order in doc.Descendants("Order")
                 join selected in orders
                     on (string) order.Attribute("OrderID") equals selected
                 select new
                 {
                     OrderID = (int) order.Attribute("OrderID"),
                     CustomerID = (string) order.Parent.Attribute("CustomerID"),
                     Freight = (decimal) order.Attribute("Freight")
                 };
    txtLog.Clear();
    foreach (var order in result)
    {
        txtLog.AppendText(
            string.Format("OrderID:{0}  CustomerID:{1}  Freight:{2:C}\r\n",
                    order.OrderID, order.CustomerID, order.Freight));
    }
}
```

Using LINQ to XML with Namespaces

LINQ to XML supports the use of namespaces, also known as the namespace URI, in addition to the local name of an XML node. Like .NET Framework namespaces, XML namespaces avoid naming collisions, especially when combining multiple XML documents that might have nodes that have the same name but different meanings. For example, a *Title* element would have a different meaning if it refers to a book and is compared to the *Title* element that refers to a person.

When working with XML namespaces, you can assign a prefix to the namespace. The prefixes can be the source of many problems because prefixes are scoped to their context, so a prefix of *abc* can be associated with namespace *x* in one part of the XML document and can be associated with namespace *y* in a different part of the document.

The following code sample uses an XML document that contains namespace definitions. Three queries are run against it.

Sample of Visual Basic Code

```vb
Private Sub LINQQueryNamespaceToolStripMenuItem_Click( _
        ByVal sender As System.Object, ByVal e As System.EventArgs) _
        Handles LINQQueryNamespaceToolStripMenuItem.Click
    Dim xml = "<Root xmlns:aw='http://www.adventure-works.com' " & _
             "    xmlns='http://www.xyz.com'> " & _
             "    <Child>1</Child> " & _
             "    <aw:Child>2</aw:Child> " & _
             "    <Child>3</Child> " & _
             "    <aw:Child>4</aw:Child> " & _
             "    <Child>5</Child> " & _
             "    <aw:Child>6</aw:Child> " & _
             "</Root>"
    Dim doc = XDocument.Parse(xml)
    txtLog.Clear()

    Dim result1 = From c In doc.Descendants("Child")
                  Select c
    txtLog.AppendText("Query for Child\r\n")
    For Each xElement In result1
        txtLog.AppendText(CType(xElement, String) + vbCrLf)
    Next

    Dim aw = XNamespace.Get("http://www.adventure-works.com")
    Dim result2 = From c In doc.Descendants(aw + "Child")
                  Select c
    txtLog.AppendText("Query for aw+Child" + vbCrLf)
    For Each xElement In result2
        txtLog.AppendText(CType(xElement, String) + vbCrLf)
    Next

    Dim defaultns = XNamespace.Get("http://www.xyz.com")
    Dim result3 = From c In doc.Descendants(defaultns + "Child")
                  Select c
    txtLog.AppendText("Query for defaultns+Child\r\n")
    For Each xElement In result3

        txtLog.AppendText(CType(xElement, String) + vbCrLf)
    Next

    txtLog.AppendText("Done" + vbCrLf)
End Sub
```

Sample of C# Code

```csharp
private void lINQQueryNamespaceToolStripMenuItem_Click(
    object sender, EventArgs e)
{
    var xml =
        @"<Root xmlns:aw='http://www.adventure-works.com'
                xmlns='http://www.xyz.com'>
                <Child>1</Child>
                <aw:Child>2</aw:Child>
                <Child>3</Child>
                <aw:Child>4</aw:Child>
```

```
                    <Child>5</Child>
                    <aw:Child>6</aw:Child>
            </Root>";

    var doc = XDocument.Parse(xml);
    txtLog.Clear();

    var result1 = from c in doc.Descendants("Child")
                  select c;
    txtLog.AppendText("Query for Child\r\n");
    foreach (var xElement in result1)
    {
        txtLog.AppendText((string)xElement + "\r\n");
    }

    var aw = XNamespace.Get("http://www.adventure-works.com");
    var result2 = from c in doc.Descendants(aw + "Child")
                  select c;
    txtLog.AppendText("Query for aw+Child\r\n");
    foreach (var xElement in result2)
    {
        txtLog.AppendText((string)xElement + "\r\n");
    }

    var defaultns = XNamespace.Get("http://www.xyz.com");
    var result3 = from c in doc.Descendants(defaultns + "Child")
                  select c;
    txtLog.AppendText("Query for defaultns+Child\r\n");
    foreach (var xElement in result3)
    {
        txtLog.AppendText((string)xElement + "\r\n");
    }

    txtLog.AppendText("Done\r\n");
}
```

In this code sample, the *XDocument* class is being populated by passing the XML string parameter to the *Parse* method, and the *txtLog* text box is cleared.

Next, the first query that produced *result1* is displayed. This query does not produce any elements because the query is looking for Child elements that are not in any namespace. In this example, all the Child elements are in a namespace; even the Child nodes that have no prefix are in the default namespace (*http://www.xyz.com*).

The second query is for the Child elements in the namespace defined by the *aw* prefix. For this example, an *aw* variable is created and assigned to the *http://www.adventure-works.com* names 2, 4, and 6.

The third query is for the Child elements in the default namespace. For this example, a *defaultns* variable is created and assigned to the *http://www.xyz.com* namespace. You can use the *defaultns* variable by adding the *defaultns* prefix to the local name (Child) by using the plus sign before the local name. This query produces the *result3* variable that enumerates as 1, 3, and 5.

Work with the *XDocument* Class

This practice is a continuation of the practice exercises in Lesson 1. In this practice, you analyze an XML file, called Orders.xml, which contains order information. Your first objective is to write a program that can provide the total price of all orders. You also need to provide the total and the average freight cost per order. In this exercise, you use the *XDocument* class and measure its performance by using the *Stopwatch* class.

EXERCISE   **Implementing the *XDocument* Solution**

In this exercise, you extend the Console Application project from Lesson 1 by adding code to retrieve the necessary data by using the *XmlReader* class.

1. In Visual Studio .NET 2010, choose File | Open | Project.

2. Select the project you created in Lesson 1 or open the project in the Begin folder for Lesson 2.

3. In *Main*, after the call to *parseWithXmlReader*, add a *parseWithXDocument* method and pass the file name as a parameter. Add this method to your code. Your code should look like the following:

Sample of Visual Basic Code

```vb
Sub Main()
    Dim fileName = "Orders.xml"
    parseWithXmlDocument(fileName)
    parseWithXmlReader(fileName)
    parseWithXDocument(fileName)
    Console.Write("Press <Enter> to end")
    Console.ReadLine()
End Sub

Private Sub parseWithXDocument (ByVal fileName As String)

End Sub
```

Sample of C# Code

```csharp
static void Main(string[] args)
{
    string fileName = "Orders.xml";
    parseWithXmlDocument(fileName);
    parseWithXmlReader(fileName);
    parseWithXDocument(fileName);
    Console.Write("Press <Enter> to end");
    Console.ReadLine();
}

private static void parseWithXDocument(string fileName)
{

}
```

4. In the *parseWithXDocument* method, instantiate a *Stopwatch*, assign the object to a variable, and start it. Declare variables for the total order price, the total freight cost, the average freight cost, and the order count. Add a line of code to load *XDocument* into memory. Add *imports System.Xml.Linq* (C# *using System.Xml.Linq;*) to the top of your file. Your code should look like the following:

Sample of Visual Basic Code

```vbnet
Private Sub parseWithXDocument(ByVal fileName As String)
    Dim sw = New Stopwatch()
    sw.Start()
    Dim totalOrderPrice As Decimal = 0
    Dim totalFreightCost As Decimal = 0
    Dim orderQty As Integer = 0
    Dim doc = XDocument.Load(fileName)

End Sub
```

Sample of C# Code

```csharp
private static void parseWithXDocument(string fileName)
{
    var sw = new Stopwatch();
    sw.Start();
    decimal totalOrderPrice = 0;
    decimal totalFreightCost = 0;
    decimal orderQty = 0;
    var doc = XDocument.Load(fileName);

}
```

5. Add a *for each* (C# *foreach*) loop to iterate over all *Order* elements. In the loop, increment the order quantity variable and add a nested *for each* (C# *foreach*) loop to iterate over all the *LineItem* elements of the current *Order*. In the nested loop, add code to retrieve the quantity, price, and freight from the line item. Add the freight to the total freight cost and add the line item cost to the total order price. Your code should look like the following:

Sample of Visual Basic Code

```vbnet
For Each order In doc.Descendants("Order")
    orderQty += 1
    For Each lineItem In order.Descendants("LineItem")
        Dim qty = CType(lineItem.Attribute("Qty"), Decimal)
        Dim price = CType(lineItem.Attribute("Price"), Decimal)
        Dim freight = CType(lineItem.Attribute("Freight"), Decimal)
        totalFreightCost += freight
        totalOrderPrice += (qty * price) + freight
    Next
Next
```

Sample of C# Code

```csharp
foreach (var order in doc.Descendants("Order"))
{
    ++orderQty;
```

```
        foreach (var lineItem in order.Descendants("LineItem"))
        {
            var qty = (decimal)lineItem.Attribute("Qty");
            var price = (decimal)lineItem.Attribute("Price");
            var freight = (decimal)lineItem.Attribute("Freight");
            totalFreightCost += freight;
            totalOrderPrice += (qty * price) + freight;
        }
    }
```

6. Add code to display the total order price, the total freight cost, and the average freight cost per order. Stop the stopwatch and display the elapsed time. Your completed method should look like the following:

Sample of Visual Basic Code

```
Private Sub parseWithXDocument(ByVal fileName As String)
    Dim sw = New Stopwatch()
    sw.Start()
    Dim totalOrderPrice As Decimal = 0
    Dim totalFreightCost As Decimal = 0
    Dim orderQty As Integer = 0
    Dim doc = XDocument.Load(fileName)

    For Each order In doc.Descendants("Order")
        orderQty += 1
        For Each lineItem In order.Descendants("LineItem")
            Dim qty = CType(lineItem.Attribute("Qty"), Decimal)
            Dim price = CType(lineItem.Attribute("Price"), Decimal)
            Dim freight = CType(lineItem.Attribute("Freight"), Decimal)
            totalFreightCost += freight
            totalOrderPrice += (qty * price) + freight
        Next
    Next

    Console.WriteLine("Total Order Price: {0:C}", totalOrderPrice)
    Console.WriteLine("Total Freight Cost: {0:C}", totalFreightCost)
    Console.WriteLine("Average Freight Cost per Order: {0:C}", _
                    totalFreightCost / orderQty)
    sw.Stop()
    Console.WriteLine("Time to Parse XDocument: {0}", sw.Elapsed)
End Sub
```

Sample of C# Code

```
private static void parseWithXDocument(string fileName)
{
    var sw = new Stopwatch();
    sw.Start();
    decimal totalOrderPrice = 0;
    decimal totalFreightCost = 0;
    decimal orderQty = 0;
    var doc = XDocument.Load(fileName);

    foreach (var order in doc.Descendants("Order"))
    {
```

```
        ++orderQty;
        foreach (var lineItem in order.Descendants("LineItem"))
        {
            var qty = (decimal)lineItem.Attribute("Qty");
            var price = (decimal)lineItem.Attribute("Price");
            var freight = (decimal)lineItem.Attribute("Freight");
            totalFreightCost += freight;
            totalOrderPrice += (qty * price) + freight;
        }
    }
    Console.WriteLine("Total Order Price: {0:C}", totalOrderPrice);
    Console.WriteLine("Total Freight Cost: {0:C}", totalFreightCost);
    Console.WriteLine("Average Freight Cost per Order: {0:C}",
        totalFreightCost / orderQty);

    sw.Stop();
    Console.WriteLine("Time to Parse XDocument: {0}", sw.Elapsed);
}
```

7. Run the application. Your total time will vary based on your machine configuration, but your output should look like the following:

Result

```
Total Order Price: $82,989,370.79
Total Freight Cost: $2,011,265.92
Average Freight Cost per Order: $529.84
Time to Parse XmlDocument: 00:00:00.7383706
Total Order Price: $82,989,370.79
Total Freight Cost: $2,011,265.92
Average Freight Cost per Order: $529.84
Time to Parse XmlReader: 00:00:00.3213059
Total Order Price: $82,989,370.79
Total Freight Cost: $2,011,265.92
Average Freight Cost per Order: $529.84
Time to Parse XDocument: 00:00:00.4891875
Press <Enter> to end
```

After coding and running this application, you see the results. The fastest test was *XmlReader*, after which are *XDocument* and *XmlDocument*. Because *XDocument* provides more capabilities using LINQ to XML, you probably want to use *XDocument* in most scenarios except when performance is most important.

Lesson Summary

This lesson provided detailed information about the *XDocument* class family.

- The *XDocument* class provides in-memory, random, read-write access to an XML document.
- The *XDocument* class provides access to the node by using LINQ to XML classes.
- When working with *XAttribute* objects, you can retrieve a typed value by using the *CType* (C# *explicit cast*) statement to convert the attribute value to the desired type.

- When working with *XElement* objects, you can retrieve a typed value by using the *CType* (C# *explicit cast*) statement to convert the element value to the desired type.

- The *XDocument* and *XElement* classes provide *Load* methods for loading from an *XmlReader* file.

- The *XDocument* and *XElement* classes provide a constructor that enables you to pass in *XNode* classes representing the content. The Visual Basic compiler enables you to specify the XML as a string, and it parses the string and generates statements to create the appropriate *XElement* and *XAttribute* objects.

- The *XDocument* and *XElement* classes provide a *Parse* method that enables you to pass in an XML string that will be parsed into the appropriate XML content.

Lesson Review

You can use the following questions to test your knowledge of the information in Lesson 2, "Querying with LINQ to XML." The questions are also available on the companion CD if you prefer to review them in electronic form.

> **NOTE ANSWERS**
>
> Answers to these questions and explanations of why each answer choice is correct or incorrect are located in the "Answers" section at the end of the book.

1. Given an XML file, you want to run several queries for data using LINQ to XML. Which class would be most appropriate for these queries on the file?

   A. *XmlDocument*

   B. *XmlReader*

   C. *XDocument*

2. In your code, you have a string variable that contains XML. Which method can you use to convert this into an *XDocument* class so you can run LINQ to XML queries?

   A. *Load*

   B. *Constructor*

   C. *WriteTo*

   D. *Parse*

Lesson 3: Transforming XML Using LINQ to XML

In addition to performing LINQ queries, another benefit of LINQ to XML is the ability to perform transformations. Prior to LINQ to XML, the best way to transform XML was to use XSLT, but you will certainly find that LINQ to XML is much easier to use than XSLT.

What can you transform XML to? You can transform it to a different form of XML, or to text, or to HTML, or to objects. Best of all is that you have complete control using Visual Basic or C#.

After this lesson, you will be able to:

- Transform XML to objects.
- Transform XML to text.
- Transform XML to XML.

Estimated lesson time: 45 minutes

Transforming XML to Objects

To transform XML to objects, you simply use all the techniques described in this chapter to load and query the XML and the techniques described in Chapter 3 to convert to objects.

The code sample that follows uses a *Customer* class and an *Order* class. These classes are defined as follows:

Sample of Visual Basic Code

```vb
Public Class Customer
    Public Property Id() As String
    Public Property Name() As String
    Public Property Orders() As List(Of Order)
End Class

Public Class Order
    Public Property Id() As Integer
    Public Property Freight() As Decimal
End Class
```

Sample of C# Code

```csharp
public class Customer
{
    public string Id { get; set; }
    public string Name { get; set; }
    public List<Order> Orders { get; set; }
}

public class Order
{
    public int Id { get; set; }
```

```
    public decimal Freight { get; set; }
}
```

In the following code sample, an XML document is loaded into an *XDocument* object from the XDocumentTest.xml file that was saved in the previous lesson examples. This XML document contains a list of customers with their orders, and then a LINQ query is provided to create a generic *IEnumerable* of *Customer*, but, within the *select* statement, a nested LINQ query is populating the *Orders* property of each customer. Finally, the results are displayed.

Sample of Visual Basic Code

```
Private Sub TransformToObjectsToolStripMenuItem_Click( _
      ByVal sender As System.Object, ByVal e As System.EventArgs) _
      Handles TransformToObjectsToolStripMenuItem.Click
    Dim doc = XDocument.Load(getFilePath("XDocumentTest.xml"))

    Dim CustomersOrders = _
       From c In doc.Descendants("Customer")
       Select New Customer With
       {
          .Id = CType(c.Attribute("CustomerID"), String),
          .Name = CType(c.Attribute("CompanyName"), String),
          .Orders = (From o In c.Elements("Order")
             Select New Order With
             {
                .Id = CType(o.Attribute("OrderID"), Integer),
                .Freight = CType(o.Attribute("Freight"), Decimal)
             }).ToList()
       }

    txtLog.Clear()
    For Each c In CustomersOrders
       txtLog.AppendText( _
          String.Format("ID:{0} Name:{1}", c.Id, c.Name) + vbCrLf)
       For Each o In c.Orders
          txtLog.AppendText( _
             String.Format("   OrderID:{0} Freight:{1,7:C}", _
                           o.Id, o.Freight) + vbCrLf)
       Next
    Next
End Sub
```

Sample of C# Code

```
private void transformToObjectsToolStripMenuItem_Click(
    object sender, EventArgs e)
{
    var doc = XDocument.Load(getFilePath("XDocumentTest.xml"));

    var CustomersOrders =
        from c in doc.Descendants("Customer")
        select new Customer
            {
                Id = (string)c.Attribute("CustomerID"),
                Name = (string)c.Attribute("CompanyName"),
```

```
                Orders = (from o in c.Elements("Order")
                          select new Order
                             {
                                 Id = (int)o.Attribute("OrderID"),
                                 Freight = (decimal)o.Attribute("Freight")
                             }).ToList()
            };

    txtLog.Clear();
    foreach (var c in CustomersOrders)
    {
        txtLog.AppendText(
            String.Format("ID:{0} Name:{1}\r\n", c.Id, c.Name));
        foreach (var o in c.Orders)
        {
            txtLog.AppendText(
                String.Format("    OrderID:{0} Freight:{1,7:C}\r\n",
                              o.Id, o.Freight));
        }
    }
}
```

Result

```
ID:ALFKI Name:Alfreds Futterkiste
    OrderID:10643 Freight: $29.46
    OrderID:10692 Freight: $61.02
    OrderID:10702 Freight: $23.94
    OrderID:10835 Freight: $69.53
    OrderID:10952 Freight: $40.42
    OrderID:11011 Freight:  $1.21
ID:ANATR Name:Ana Trujillo
    OrderID:10308 Freight:  $1.61
    OrderID:10625 Freight: $43.90
    OrderID:10759 Freight: $11.99
    OrderID:10926 Freight: $39.92
ID:ANTON Name:Antonio Moreno
    OrderID:10365 Freight: $22.00
    OrderID:10507 Freight: $47.45
    OrderID:10535 Freight: $15.64
    OrderID:10573 Freight: $84.84
    OrderID:10677 Freight:  $4.03
    OrderID:10682 Freight: $36.13
    OrderID:10856 Freight: $58.53
ID:AROUT Name:Around the Horn
    OrderID:10355 Freight: $41.95
    OrderID:10383 Freight: $34.24
    OrderID:10453 Freight: $25.36
    OrderID:10558 Freight: $72.97
    OrderID:10707 Freight: $21.74
    OrderID:10741 Freight: $10.96
    OrderID:10743 Freight: $23.72
    OrderID:10768 Freight:$146.32
    OrderID:10793 Freight:  $4.52
    OrderID:10864 Freight:  $3.04
    OrderID:10920 Freight: $29.61
```

```
OrderID:10953 Freight: $23.72
OrderID:11016 Freight: $33.80
```

The result shows that the transformation took place. In a real application, you would probably use the *Customer* and *Order* objects for a business purpose rather than simply to display them on the screen.

Transforming XML to Text

In the preceding code sample, if your only goal was to display the results, you could have simply converted the XML to a generic *IEnumerable* of *String* and then displayed the results. The following code sample demonstrates the use of LINQ to XML to convert XML to text.

Sample of Visual Basic Code

```vb
Private Sub TransformToTextToolStripMenuItem_Click( _
        ByVal sender As System.Object, ByVal e As System.EventArgs) _
        Handles TransformToTextToolStripMenuItem.Click
    Dim doc = XDocument.Load(getFilePath("XDocumentTest.xml"))

    Dim CustomersOrders = _
        From c In doc.Descendants("Customer")
        Select New With
        {
            .CustomerInfo = _
                String.Format("ID:{0} Name:{1}" + vbCrLf, _
                            CType(c.Attribute("CustomerID"), String),
                            CType(c.Attribute("CompanyName"), String)
                            ),
            .OrderInfo = From o In c.Elements("Order")
                    Select String.Format(
                        "   OrderID:{0} Freight:{1,7:C}" + vbCrLf, _
                            CType(o.Attribute("OrderID"), Integer),
                            CType(o.Attribute("Freight"), Decimal))
        }

    txtLog.Clear()
    For Each c In CustomersOrders
        txtLog.AppendText(c.CustomerInfo)
        For Each o In c.OrderInfo
            txtLog.AppendText(o)
        Next
    Next
End Sub
```

Sample of C# Code

```csharp
private void transformToTextToolStripMenuItem_Click(
    object sender, EventArgs e)
{
    var doc = XDocument.Load(getFilePath("XDocumentTest.xml"));
    var customersOrders =
        from c in doc.Descendants("Customer")
        select new
        {
```

```
        CustomerInfo = string.Format(
            "ID:{0} Name:{1}\r\n",
            c.Attribute("CustomerID"),
            c.Attribute("Name")),
        OrderInfo = from o in c.Elements("Order")
                    select string.Format(
                        "    OrderID:{0} Freight:{1,7:C}\r\n",
                        (int)o.Attribute("OrderID"),
                        (decimal)o.Attribute("Freight"))
    };
foreach (var c in customersOrders)
{
    txtLog.AppendText(c.CustomerInfo);
    foreach (var o in c.OrderInfo)
    {
        txtLog.AppendText(o);
    }
}
}
```

This code sample produces the same results as the preceding one. The difference is that
the string formatting is in the LINQ queries, and instead of creating a *Customer* and an *Order*
class, an anonymous type holds the result as strings, so the nested loop displaying the result
is much simpler.

Transforming XML to XML

You can use LINQ to XML to transform an XML document in one format into an XML document in a different format. Visual Basic really shines with its use of XML literals, to which you
were introduced in Lesson 1. Visual Basic implementation of XML literals can simplify XML to
XML transformations. C# users who want to use XML literals must learn Visual Basic, but don't
throw away your C# book. Instead, you can do all your XML literals in a separate Visual Basic
DLL project and then set a reference to the DLL in your C# code.

In the following sample, the XML document that contains customers and their orders is
transformed to an XML document that has the same information but is formatted differently.

Sample of Visual Basic Code

```
Private Sub TransformXMLToXMLToolStripMenuItem_Click( _
    ByVal sender As System.Object, ByVal e As System.EventArgs) _
    Handles TransformXMLToXMLToolStripMenuItem.Click
  Dim doc = XDocument.Load(getFilePath("XDocumentTest.xml"))
  Dim newXml = _
    <root>
      <%= From o In doc...<Order> _
        Select <Order CustID=<%= o.Parent.@CustomerID %>
                     CustName=<%= o.Parent.@CompanyName %>
                     OrdID=<%= o.@OrderID %>
                     OrdFreight=<%= o.@Freight %>/>
      %>
    </root>
```

```
        txtLog.Text = newXml.ToString()
End Sub
```

Sample of C# Code

```csharp
private void transformXMLToXMLToolStripMenuItem_Click(
    object sender, EventArgs e)
{
    var doc = XDocument.Load(getFilePath("XDocumentTest.xml"));
    var newXml = new XDocument(
        new XElement("root",
            from o in doc.Descendants("Order")
            select new XElement("Order",
                new XAttribute("CustID",o.Parent.Attribute("CustomerID").Value),
                new XAttribute("CustName", o.Parent.Attribute("CompanyName").Value),
                new XAttribute("OrdID", o.Attribute("OrderID").Value),
                new XAttribute("OrdFreight", o.Attribute("Freight").Value)
                )
            )
        );
    txtLog.Text = newXml.ToString();
}
```

Result

```xml
<root>
  <Order CustID="ALFKI" CustName="Alfreds Futterkiste" OrdID="10643"
OrdFreight="29.4600" />
  <Order CustID="ALFKI" CustName="Alfreds Futterkiste" OrdID="10692"
OrdFreight="61.0200" />
  <Order CustID="ALFKI" CustName="Alfreds Futterkiste" OrdID="10702"
OrdFreight="23.9400" />
  <Order CustID="ALFKI" CustName="Alfreds Futterkiste" OrdID="10835"
OrdFreight="69.5300" />
  <Order CustID="ALFKI" CustName="Alfreds Futterkiste" OrdID="10952"
OrdFreight="40.4200" />
  <Order CustID="ALFKI" CustName="Alfreds Futterkiste" OrdID="11011" OrdFreight="1.2100"
/>
  <Order CustID="ANATR" CustName="Ana Trujillo" OrdID="10308" OrdFreight="1.6100" />
  <Order CustID="ANATR" CustName="Ana Trujillo" OrdID="10625" OrdFreight="43.9000" />
  <Order CustID="ANATR" CustName="Ana Trujillo" OrdID="10759" OrdFreight="11.9900" />
  <Order CustID="ANATR" CustName="Ana Trujillo" OrdID="10926" OrdFreight="39.9200" />
  <Order CustID="ANTON" CustName="Antonio Moreno" OrdID="10365" OrdFreight="22.0000" />
  <Order CustID="ANTON" CustName="Antonio Moreno" OrdID="10507" OrdFreight="47.4500" />
  <Order CustID="ANTON" CustName="Antonio Moreno" OrdID="10535" OrdFreight="15.6400" />
  <Order CustID="ANTON" CustName="Antonio Moreno" OrdID="10573" OrdFreight="84.8400" />
  <Order CustID="ANTON" CustName="Antonio Moreno" OrdID="10677" OrdFreight="4.0300" />
  <Order CustID="ANTON" CustName="Antonio Moreno" OrdID="10682" OrdFreight="36.1300" />
  <Order CustID="ANTON" CustName="Antonio Moreno" OrdID="10856" OrdFreight="58.5300" />
  <Order CustID="AROUT" CustName="Around the Horn" OrdID="10355" OrdFreight="41.9500" />
  <Order CustID="AROUT" CustName="Around the Horn" OrdID="10383" OrdFreight="34.2400" />
  <Order CustID="AROUT" CustName="Around the Horn" OrdID="10453" OrdFreight="25.3600" />
  <Order CustID="AROUT" CustName="Around the Horn" OrdID="10558" OrdFreight="72.9700" />
  <Order CustID="AROUT" CustName="Around the Horn" OrdID="10707" OrdFreight="21.7400" />
  <Order CustID="AROUT" CustName="Around the Horn" OrdID="10741" OrdFreight="10.9600" />
```

```
<Order CustID="AROUT" CustName="Around the Horn" OrdID="10743" OrdFreight="23.7200" />
<Order CustID="AROUT" CustName="Around the Horn" OrdID="10768" OrdFreight="146.3200"
/>
<Order CustID="AROUT" CustName="Around the Horn" OrdID="10793" OrdFreight="4.5200" />
<Order CustID="AROUT" CustName="Around the Horn" OrdID="10864" OrdFreight="3.0400" />
<Order CustID="AROUT" CustName="Around the Horn" OrdID="10920" OrdFreight="29.6100" />
<Order CustID="AROUT" CustName="Around the Horn" OrdID="10953" OrdFreight="23.7200" />
<Order CustID="AROUT" CustName="Around the Horn" OrdID="11016" OrdFreight="33.8000" />
</root>
```

Both of these language samples produce the same result, but the C# version looks more obfuscated than the Visual Basic example. XML literals enable the Visual Basic programmer to simply embed the elements as literals in the code and use *<%= expression block %>* syntax in the code. This is very similar to expression blocks in ASP or ASP.NET applications. When referencing XML axes for navigation, Visual Basic enables you to use three dots instead of typing *Descendants*. You can also use dot notation to access a child element. This example code uses the dot notation to access an attribute by prefixing the attribute name with the @ symbol.

PRACTICE   Use LINQ to XML to Transform Data

In this practice, you transform an Orders.xml XML file, which contains order information, into a different format that management can use. Here is an example of what the file looks like:

Orders.xml File

```
<Orders>
  <Order OrderNumber="SO43659">
    <LineItem Line="1" PID="349" Qty="1" Price="2024.9940" Freight="50.6249" />
    <LineItem Line="2" PID="350" Qty="3" Price="2024.9940" Freight="151.8746" />
    <LineItem Line="3" PID="351" Qty="1" Price="2024.9940" Freight="50.6249" />
    <LineItem Line="4" PID="344" Qty="1" Price="2039.9940" Freight="50.9999" />
    <LineItem Line="5" PID="345" Qty="1" Price="2039.9940" Freight="50.9999" />
    <LineItem Line="6" PID="346" Qty="2" Price="2039.9940" Freight="101.9997" />
    <LineItem Line="7" PID="347" Qty="1" Price="2039.9940" Freight="50.9999" />
    <LineItem Line="8" PID="229" Qty="3" Price="28.8404" Freight="2.1630" />
    <LineItem Line="9" PID="235" Qty="1" Price="28.8404" Freight="0.7210" />
    <LineItem Line="10" PID="218" Qty="6" Price="5.7000" Freight="0.8550" />
    <LineItem Line="11" PID="223" Qty="2" Price="5.1865" Freight="0.2593" />
    <LineItem Line="12" PID="220" Qty="4" Price="20.1865" Freight="2.0187" />
  </Order>
  <Order OrderNumber="SO43660">
    <LineItem Line="1" PID="326" Qty="1" Price="419.4589" Freight="10.4865" />
    <LineItem Line="2" PID="319" Qty="1" Price="874.7940" Freight="21.8699" />
  </Order>
<!--Many more orders here -->
</Orders>
```

The resulting XML document is saved to a Results.xml file, and each *Order* element contains a *TotalFreight* attribute. The *LineItem* element is now called *Item*, the *Line* attribute is now called *Number*, the *PID* attribute is now called *ID*, and a *LineTotal* attribute has been added to each line item. The following is a sample of the Results.xml file.

Results.xml File

```
<ModifiedOrders>
  <Order OrderID="S043659" TotalFreight="514.1408">
    <Item Number="1" ID="349" Price="2024.9940" Qty="1" LineTotal="2024.994" />
    <Item Number="2" ID="350" Price="2024.9940" Qty="3" LineTotal="6074.982" />
    <Item Number="3" ID="351" Price="2024.9940" Qty="1" LineTotal="2024.994" />
    <Item Number="4" ID="344" Price="2039.9940" Qty="1" LineTotal="2039.994" />
    <Item Number="5" ID="345" Price="2039.9940" Qty="1" LineTotal="2039.994" />
    <Item Number="6" ID="346" Price="2039.9940" Qty="2" LineTotal="4079.988" />
    <Item Number="7" ID="347" Price="2039.9940" Qty="1" LineTotal="2039.994" />
    <Item Number="8" ID="229" Price="28.8404" Qty="3" LineTotal="86.5212" />
    <Item Number="9" ID="235" Price="28.8404" Qty="1" LineTotal="28.8404" />
    <Item Number="10" ID="218" Price="5.7000" Qty="6" LineTotal="34.2" />
    <Item Number="11" ID="223" Price="5.1865" Qty="2" LineTotal="10.373" />
    <Item Number="12" ID="220" Price="20.1865" Qty="4" LineTotal="80.746" />
  </Order>
  <Order OrderID="S043660" TotalFreight="32.3564">
    <Item Number="1" ID="326" Price="419.4589" Qty="1" LineTotal="419.4589" />
    <Item Number="2" ID="319" Price="874.7940" Qty="1" LineTotal="874.794" />
  </Order>
<!--Many more orders here -->
</ ModifiedOrders >
```

This project will be implemented as a simple Console application.

EXERCISE   Creating the Project and Implementing the Transformation

In this exercise, you create a Console Application project and then add code to the transformed *XDocument* class and save to the Result.xml file.

1. In Visual Studio .NET 2010, choose File | New | Project.

2. Select your desired programming language and then select the Console Application template. For the project name, enter **OrderTransformer**. Be sure to select a desired location for this project. For the solution name, enter **OrderTransformerSolution**. Be sure that Create Directory For Solution is selected and then click OK. After Visual Studio .NET finishes creating the project, Module1.vb (C# Program.cs) is displayed.

3. In *Main*, declare a *string* for your file name and assign Orders.xml to it. Add code to the bottom of *Main* to prompt the user to press Enter to end the application. Your code should look like the following:

Sample of Visual Basic Code

```
Module Module1
    Sub Main()
        Dim fileName = "Orders.xml"

        Console.Write("Press <Enter> to end")
        Console.ReadLine()
    End Sub
End Module
```

Sample of C# Code

```
namespace OrderTransformer
```

```
{
    class Program
    {
        static void Main(string[] args)
        {
            string fileName = "Orders.xml";

            Console.Write("Press <Enter> to end");
            Console.ReadLine();
        }
    }
}
```

4. Add the Orders.xml file to your project. Right-click the *OrderTransformer* node in Solution Explorer and choose Add | Existing Item. In the bottom right corner of the Add Existing Item dialog box, click the drop-down list and select All Files (*.*). Navigate to the Begin folder for this exercise and select Orders.xml. If you don't see the Orders. xml file, check whether All Files (*.*) has been selected.

5. In Solution Explorer, click the Orders.xml file you just added. In the Properties window, set the *Copy to Output Directory* property to *Copy If Newer*.

   Because this file will reside in the same folder as your application, you will be able to use the file name without specifying a path.

6. In the *Main* method, add code to load the Orders.xml file into an *XDocument* object and assign this object to a *doc* variable. For C#, add *using System.Xml.Linq;* to the top of your file. Your code should look like the following:

Sample of Visual Basic Code

```
Module Module1
    Sub Main()
        Dim fileName = "Orders.xml"
        Dim doc = XDocument.Load(fileName)

        Console.Write("Press <Enter> to end")
        Console.ReadLine()
    End Sub
End Module
```

Sample of C# Code

```
namespace OrderTransformer
{
    class Program
    {
        static void Main(string[] args)
        {
            string fileName = "Orders.xml";
            var doc = XDocument.Load(fileName);

            Console.Write("Press <Enter> to end");
            Console.ReadLine();
        }
```

```
      }
}
```

7. Declare a *result* variable and assign your LINQ to XML transformation to it. You need to iterate the *Order* elements to complete the transformation. If you're using Visual Basic, be sure to take advantage of XML literals. Your code should look like the following:

Sample of Visual Basic Code

```
Dim result = _
    <ModifiedOrders>
        <%= From o In doc...<Order> _
            Select <Order OrderID=<%= o.@OrderNumber %>
                    TotalFreight=<%= o.<LineItem>.Sum(
                        Function(li) CType(li.@Freight, Decimal)) %>>
                    <%= From li In o.<LineItem>
                        Select <Item Number=<%= li.@Line %>
                                    ID=<%= li.@PID %>
                                    Price=<%= li.@Price %>
                                    Qty=<%= li.@Qty %>
                                    LineTotal=<%= li.@Price * li.@Qty %>/>
                    %>
                </Order>
        %>
    </ModifiedOrders>
```

Sample of C# Code

```
var result = new XElement("ModifiedOrders",
        from o in doc.Descendants("Order")
        select new XElement("Order",
        new XAttribute("OrderID", (string)o.Attribute("OrderNumber")),
        new XAttribute("TotalFreight",
            o.Elements("LineItem").Sum(li=>(decimal) li.Attribute("Freight"))),
                from li in o.Elements("LineItem")
                select new  XElement("Item",
                    new XAttribute("Number",(int)li.Attribute("Line")),
                    new XAttribute("ID", (int)li.Attribute("PID")),
                    new XAttribute("Price",(decimal)li.Attribute("Price")),
                    new XAttribute("Qty", (int)li.Attribute("Qty")),
                    new XAttribute("LineTotal",
                        (decimal)li.Attribute("Price") *
                        (int)li.Attribute("Qty"))
                )
            )
    );
```

8. Add code to save the result to a Results.xml file on your desktop or to a location of your choice. Add *imports System.IO* (C# *using System.IO;*) to the top of your file. The completed *Main* method should look like the following.

Sample of Visual Basic Code

```
Sub Main()
    Dim fileName = "Orders.xml"
    Dim doc = XDocument.Load(fileName)
```

```vb
        Dim result = _
            <ModifiedOrders>
                <%= From o In doc...<Order> _
                    Select <Order OrderID=<%= o.@OrderNumber %>
                               TotalFreight=<%= o.<LineItem>.Sum(
                                    Function(li) CType(li.@Freight, Decimal)) %>>
                               <%= From li In o.<LineItem>
                                   Select <Item Number=<%= li.@Line %>
                                                ID=<%= li.@PID %>
                                                Price=<%= li.@Price %>
                                                Qty=<%= li.@Qty %>
                                                LineTotal=<%= li.@Price * li.@Qty %>/>
                               %>
                           </Order>
                %>
            </ModifiedOrders>
        result.Save(Path.Combine(Environment.GetFolderPath( _
                Environment.SpecialFolder.Desktop), "Results.xml"))
        Console.Write("Press <Enter> to end")
        Console.ReadLine()
End Sub
```

Sample of C# Code

```csharp
static void Main(string[] args)
{
    string fileName = "Orders.xml";
    var doc = XDocument.Load(fileName);
    var result = new XElement("ModifiedOrders",
            from o in doc.Descendants("Order")
            select new XElement("Order",
            new XAttribute("OrderID", (string)o.Attribute("OrderNumber")),
            new XAttribute("TotalFreight",
               o.Elements("LineItem").Sum(li=>(decimal) li.Attribute("Freight"))),
                 from li in o.Elements("LineItem")
                    select new  XElement("Item",
                        new XAttribute("Number",(int)li.Attribute("Line")),
                        new XAttribute("ID", (int)li.Attribute("PID")),
                        new XAttribute("Price",(decimal)li.Attribute("Price")),
                        new XAttribute("Qty", (int)li.Attribute("Qty")),
                        new XAttribute("LineTotal",
                           (decimal)li.Attribute("Price") *
                           (int)li.Attribute("Qty"))
                        )
                    )
            );
    result.Save(Path.Combine(Environment.GetFolderPath(
        Environment.SpecialFolder.Desktop), "Results.xml"));

    Console.Write("Press <Enter> to end");
    Console.ReadLine();
}
```

9. Run the application. You should see a message stating, "Press <Enter> to end." Press Enter to end the application. After running the application, locate the Results.xml file and open it. Your file should look like the following:

Results.xml

```xml
<?xml version="1.0" encoding="utf-8"?>
<ModifiedOrders>
  <Order OrderID="SO43659" TotalFreight="514.1408">
    <Item Number="1" ID="349" Price="2024.9940" Qty="1" LineTotal="2024.9940" />
    <Item Number="2" ID="350" Price="2024.9940" Qty="3" LineTotal="6074.9820" />
    <Item Number="3" ID="351" Price="2024.9940" Qty="1" LineTotal="2024.9940" />
    <Item Number="4" ID="344" Price="2039.9940" Qty="1" LineTotal="2039.9940" />
    <Item Number="5" ID="345" Price="2039.9940" Qty="1" LineTotal="2039.9940" />
    <Item Number="6" ID="346" Price="2039.9940" Qty="2" LineTotal="4079.9880" />
    <Item Number="7" ID="347" Price="2039.9940" Qty="1" LineTotal="2039.9940" />
    <Item Number="8" ID="229" Price="28.8404" Qty="3" LineTotal="86.5212" />
    <Item Number="9" ID="235" Price="28.8404" Qty="1" LineTotal="28.8404" />
    <Item Number="10" ID="218" Price="5.7000" Qty="6" LineTotal="34.2000" />
    <Item Number="11" ID="223" Price="5.1865" Qty="2" LineTotal="10.3730" />
    <Item Number="12" ID="220" Price="20.1865" Qty="4" LineTotal="80.7460" />
  </Order>
  <Order OrderID="SO43660" TotalFreight="32.3564">
    <Item Number="1" ID="326" Price="419.4589" Qty="1" LineTotal="419.4589" />
    <Item Number="2" ID="319" Price="874.7940" Qty="1" LineTotal="874.7940" />
  </Order>
  <!-- more orders here-->
</ModifiedOrders>
```

Lesson Summary

This lesson provided detailed information about transforming data by using LINQ to SQL.

- You can take advantage of LINQ projections to convert XML to objects.
- LINQ projections can also help convert XML to a generic *IEnumerable* of *string*.
- LINQ projections can also be used with the *XDocument* classes to convert XML to a different form of XML.
- If you use Visual Basic, you can take advantage of XML literals to simplify transformations.

Lesson Review

You can use the following questions to test your knowledge of the information in Lesson 3, "Transforming XML Using LINQ to XML." The questions are also available on the companion CD if you prefer to review them in electronic form.

> **NOTE ANSWERS**
>
> Answers to these questions and explanations of why each answer choice is correct or incorrect are located in the "Answers" section at the end of the book.

1. You have an XML file you want to transform to a different form of XML, and you want to use XML literals to simplify the transformation. Which language will you use?

   A. C#

   B. Visual Basic

   C. Either

Case Scenario

In the following case scenario, you will apply what you've learned in this chapter about querying data by using LINQ to XML. You can find answers to these questions in the "Answers" section at the end of this book.

Case Scenario: XML Web Service

You have been given the job of making a call to an XML web service and parsing the response. Your application is very object oriented, so you'll need to convert objects to an XML request, and, when you receive the XML response, you will need to parse the response back to business objects that you can use in the application. Answer the following questions regarding the implementation of the XML web service.

1. What approach will you take to create the XML web service request?
2. What approach will you take to parse the XML web service response?

Suggested Practices

To help you successfully master the exam objectives presented in this chapter, complete the following tasks. You should create at least one application that uses LINQ to XML for querying data. You can do this by completing the practices at the ends of Lessons 1 and 2 or by performing the following Practice 1.

- **Practice 1**   Create an application that queries XML data. This could be an application that reads RSS feeds or XML from a web service.

- **Practice 2**   Complete Practice 1 and then add code to produce a transformation of the XML to a different type.

Take a Practice Test

The practice tests on this book's companion CD offer many options. For example, you can test yourself on just the lesson review content, or you can test yourself on all the 70-516 certification exam content. You can set up the test so that it closely simulates the experience of taking a certification exam, or you can set it up in study mode so that you can look at the correct answers and explanations after you answer each question.

> **MORE INFO** **PRACTICE TESTS**
>
> For details about all the practice test options available, see the "How to Use the Practice Tests" section in this book's introduction.

CHAPTER 6

ADO.NET Entity Framework

In the previous chapters, you saw various aspects of Language Integrated Query (LINQ) for querying and transforming data. This chapter covers the most sophisticated and flexible implementation of LINQ, LINQ to Entities.

Exam objectives in this chapter:

- Map entities and relationships by using the Entity Data Model.
- Create and customize entity objects.
- Connect a POCO model to the Entity Framework.
- Create the database from the Entity Framework model.
- Create model-defined functions.
- Manage the *DataContext* and *ObjectContext*.
- Implement eager loading.
- Create, update, or delete data by using *ObjectContext*.
- Create an Entity SQL (ESQL) query.
- Manage transactions.

Lessons in this chapter:

Before You Begin

You must have some understanding of Microsoft Visual C# or Visual Basic 2010. This chapter requires only the hardware and software listed at the beginning of this book.

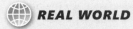

REAL WORLD

Glenn Johnson

When building object-oriented applications, the creation of business objects seems to go smoothly until it's time to persist the data to a database. I've been involved in applications that use data sets to persist the data. I've also used LINQ to SQL and various third-party object-relational mapping (ORM) products. There are always problems, but LINQ to Entities minimizes the ORM pain.

Lesson 1: What Is the ADO.NET Entity Framework?

When writing object-oriented applications, you want to think of the problem domain and write objects and code that are domain-centric. Writing data access code and creating data access objects that can talk to the database feel like distractions; they represent noise in your application. However, you need some means of persisting your domain objects to the database, which usually means creating a data model that represents your relational database. The Entity Framework can provide this.

> **After this lesson, you will be able to:**
> - Understand and explain the ADO.NET Entity Framework.
> - Explain the differences between LINQ to SQL and the ADO.NET Entity Framework.
> - Model data using the ADO.NET Entity Framework.
> - Implement the code first model.
> - Implement the database first model.
> - Retrieve data using the *ObjectContext* class.
> - Understand how the *ObjectContext* object connects to the database.
> - Comprehend the life cycle of an entity object.
> - Explain the difference between lazy loading, explicit loading, and eager loading.
> - Work with complex types.
> - Map stored procedures.
> - Implement Inheritance in the ADO.NET Entity Framework.
> - Use plain old CLR objects with the Entity Framework.
>
> **Estimated lesson time: 60 minutes**

Entity Framework Architecture Overview

The Entity Framework enables applications to access and change data that is represented as entities and relationships in the conceptual model. The Entity Framework translates object queries against entity types described in the conceptual model into database-specific queries by using information in the model and mapping files. When you execute a query, the results are materialized into objects managed by the Entity Framework. The diagram in Figure 6-1 shows the Entity Framework.

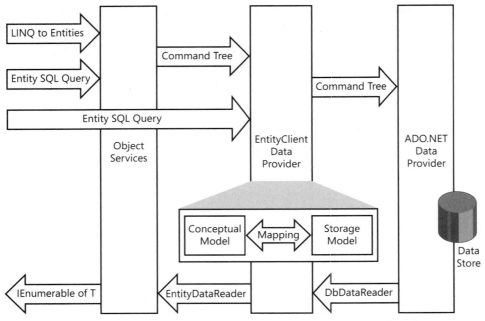

FIGURE 6-1 The Entity Framework diagram translates object queries into relational queries

The diagram shows that you can query a conceptual model and return objects by using LINQ to Entities or Entity SQL (ESQL).

LINQ to Entities provides LINQ support for querying entity types that are defined in a conceptual model.

ESQL is a storage-independent dialect of SQL that works directly with entities in the conceptual model. It can be used with object queries and queries that are executed by using the EntityClient provider.

The Object Services layer is a component of the Entity Framework that enables you to query, insert, update, and delete data, using common language runtime (CLR) objects that are instances of entity types. Object Services supports LINQ and ESQL queries against types that are defined in the conceptual model, is responsible for instantiating the returned data as objects, and propagates object changes back to the data source. Object Services provides change tracking and concurrency handling. The Object Services layer is implemented by classes in the *System.Data.Objects* and *System.Data.Objects.DataClasses* namespaces.

The Entity Framework includes the EntityClient data provider, which manages connections, translates entity queries into data source-specific queries, and returns a data reader the Entity Framework uses to materialize entity data into objects.

Traditional ADO.NET is still used to communicate to the underlying database. This is why it's still helpful to know this technology and the classes that were covered in Chapter 1, "ADO.NET Disconnected Classes," and Chapter 2, "ADO.NET Connected Classes."

Entity Framework vs. LINQ to SQL

In Chapter 4, "LINQ to SQL," you learned that LINQ to SQL provides a data model that simplifies persistence of your domain model to the relational database. So what's the difference between the Entity Framework and LINQ to SQL? This is a common question, and Table 6-1 provides a quick reference to the primary differences between the two technologies.

TABLE 6-1 A Comparison of LINQ to SQL and Entity Framework

CATEGORY	LINQ TO SQL	ENTITY FRAMEWORK
Complexity	Less complex	More complex
Model	Domain model	Conceptual data model
DB Server	SQL Server	Variety of database products
Development Time	Rapid application development	More time required but has mode features
Mapping Type	Class to single table	Class to multiple tables
Inheritance	Difficult to apply	Simple to apply
File Types	DBML files	EDMX, CDSL, MSL, SSDL files
Complex Type Support	No	Yes
Query Capability	LINQ to SQL through *DataContext*	LINQ to Entities, ESQL, Object Services, Entity Client
Performance	Slow for first query	Slow for first query but overall better than LINQ to SQL
Future Enhancements	No	Yes
Generate DB from Model	No	Yes

Following is a more detailed look at each of the categories:

- **Complexity** With more features comes more complexity, which is why LINQ to SQL, which has fewer features, is considered easier to use than the Entity Framework, which has more features.

- **Model** LINQ to SQL provides a one-to-one mapping of tables to classes. If you have Customers, Orders, and LineItems tables, you will have a *Customer*, *Order*, and *LineItem* class to match up with rows of each table. The Entity Framework enables you to have a *Customer* class whose data maps to several tables. This means the company name can be in one table, but the address can be in a different table, and the phone number can be in another table, and so on.

- **DB Server** LINQ to SQL supports only Microsoft SQL Server 2000 and later, but even SQL Server 2000 support has some limitations. The Entity Framework has support for IBM DB2, Sybase SqlAnywhere, Oracle, SQL Azure, and many others.

- **Development Time**   LINQ to SQL is simple to learn and implement for rapid application development, but LINQ to SQL has limitations that can cause problems in complex applications. The Entity Framework has more capabilities, which can take longer to learn and implement, but these features will minimize problems when creating complex applications.

- **Mapping Type**   With LINQ to SQL, each table maps to a single class. If your database has a join table, you must represent this as a class. Also, complex types cannot be easily represented without creating a separate table. For example, if a customer has an address and the Customers table has the address components in the table, you can't represent the address as a separate type. To represent the address as a separate type, you must extract the address to its own table. With the Entity Framework, a class can map to multiple tables. Regarding the address scenario, the address can be a type even if it's contained within the Customers table.

- **Inheritence**   LINQ to SQL supports Table per Class Hierarchy (TPH), whereas the Entity Framework supports TPH and Table per Type (TPT). The Entity Framework also provides limited support for Table per Concrete Class (TPC).

- **File Type**   LINQ to SQL uses a Database Markup Language (DBML extension) file that contains XML mappings of entities to tables. The Entity Framework uses four files. The first file is the Entity Data Model (EDMX extension), which the Entity Data Model designer uses. At compile time, the other three files are created from the EDMX file. The first of the three files is a Conceptual Schema Definition Language (CSDL extension) file that contains XML definition of the conceptual model. The second file is the Store Schema Definition Language (SSDL) file that contains XML definition of the storage model. The third file is the Mapping Specification Language (MSL extension) file that contains the mappings between the conceptual and storage models.

- **Complex Type Support**   A complex type is a nonscalar property of an entity type that does not have a key property. For example, a customer has a phone number, but you want the phone number to be defined as having a country code, an area code, a city code, a number, and an extension. LINQ to SQL doesn't support the creation of complex types, but the Entity Framework does.

- **Query Capability**   You can query the database by using LINQ to SQL through the *DataContext* object. With the Entity Framework, you can query the database by using LINQ to Entities through the *ObjectContext* object. The Entity Framework also provides ESQL, which is a SQL-like query language that is good for defining a query as part of the model definition. The Entity Framework also contains the *ObjectQuery* class, used with Object Services for dynamically constructing queries at run time. Last, the Entity Framework contains the EntityClient provider, which runs queries against the conceptual model.

- **Performance**   Both LINQ to SQL and the Entity Framework are slow when running the first query, but, after that, you should find that both provide acceptable performance, although the Entity Framework provides slightly better performance.

- **Future Enhancements**   Microsoft intended to obsolete LINQ to SQL after the Entity Framework release, but LINQ to SQL was popular due to its simplicity, so Microsoft responded to user feedback. You can expect that LINQ to SQL will not receive future enhancements, however.

- **Generate Database from Model**   LINQ to SQL has no capability of generating the database from the model. The Entity Framework supports two types of development, Database First and Code First. With Database First development, the database already exists, so there is no need to generate the database from the model. With Code First development, you create your model, and, from the model, you can generate your database.

Modeling Data

To use the Entity Framework, you must create an entity data model that defines your model classes and their mapping into the database schema. After the model is created, you can perform CRUD operations (create, retrieve, update, and delete) using LINQ to Entities and Object Services.

Mapping Scenarios

To create an entity data model, you must have a basic understanding of the mapping scenarios supported by the Entity Framework. The following is a description of each scenario supported by the Entity Framework:

- **Simple mapping**   Each entity in the conceptual model is mapped to a single table in the storage model. This is the Entity Data Model default mapping.

- **Entity splitting**   Properties from a single entity in the conceptual model are mapped to columns in two or more underlying tables that share a common primary key.

- **Horizontal partitioning in the conceptual model**   Multiple entity types in the conceptual model that have the same properties are mapped to a single table. A condition clause specifies which data in the table belongs to which entity type. This mapping is similar to TPH inheritance mapping.

- **TPH inheritance**   All types in an inheritance hierarchy are mapped to a single table. A condition clause defines the entity types.

- **TPT inheritance**   All types are mapped to individual tables. Properties that belong solely to a base type or a derived type are stored in a table that maps to that type.

- **TPC inheritance**   Nonabstract types are each mapped to an individual table. Each of these tables must have columns that map to all the properties of the derived type, including the properties inherited from the base type.

- **Multiple entity sets per type**   A single entity type is expressed in two or more entity sets in the conceptual model. Each entity set is mapped to a separate table in the storage model.

- **Complex types**   A complex type is a nonscalar property of an entity type that does not have a key property. A complex type can contain other nested complex types. Complex types are mapped to tables in the storage model.

- **Function import mapping**   A stored procedure in the storage model is mapped to a *FunctionImport* element in the conceptual model. This function is executed to return entity data, using the mapped stored procedure.

- **Modification function mapping**   Stored procedures are defined in the storage model to insert, update, and delete data. These functions are defined for an entity type to provide the update functionality for a specific entity type.

- **Defining query mapping**   A query is defined in the storage model that represents a table in the data source. The query is expressed in the native query language of the data source, such as Transact-SQL when mapping to a SQL Server database. This *DefiningQuery* element is mapped to an entity type in the conceptual model. The query is defined in the store-specific query language.

- **Query view mapping**   A read-only mapping is defined between entity types in the conceptual model and relational tables in the storage model. This mapping is defined based on an ESQL query against the storage model that returns entities in the conceptual model. When you use a query view, updates cannot be persisted to the data source by using the standard update process. Updates can be made by defining modification function mappings.

- **AssociationSet mapping**   Associations define relationships between entities. In a simple mapping with a one-to-one or one-to-many association, associations that define relationships in the conceptual model are mapped to associations in the storage model.

- **Many-to-many associations**   This is a special AssociationSet mapping by which both ends of the association are mapped to a link table in the storage model.

- **Self association**   A special AssociationSet mapping that supports an association between two entities of the same type, such as an *Employee* entity with an association to another *Employee* entity.

Code First Model vs. Database First Model

What is the Code First model? This is when you create your conceptual model before you create the database. Using the Code First model, you can generate the database from the conceptual model, but first you must create your conceptual model manually. The Database First model enables you to generate the conceptual model from the database schema, but first you must create the database schema manually.

Which model should you use? If the database or the conceptual model already exists, you will surely use the associated model. If nothing exists, simply take the path of least resistance and start working on the end with which you are most comfortable. It's that simple.

Implementing the Code First Model

To use the Code First model, add an ADO.NET Entity Data Model.edmx file to your project: Right-click the project node in Solution Explorer and choose Add | New Item. Select ADO.NET Entity Data Model. This template produces a file with an EDMX extension. Provide a name for your file. This example demonstrates the creation of a conceptual model for maintaining a list of vehicles with their associated repairs. After naming the file, click Add to start the Entity Data Model Wizard.

Figure 6-2 shows the first step in the Entity Data Model Wizard, which is to select whether you want to generate the model from the database (Database First) or start with an empty model (Code First). Select Empty Model and click Finish. You then see the empty Entity Data Model designer screen.

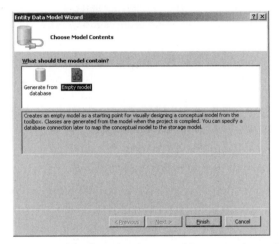

FIGURE 6-2 The first wizard step enables you to choose Database First or Code First.

Use the toolbox to drag an entity out and drop it on the Entity Data Model designer, as shown in Figure 6-3. When you drop the entity on the designer surface, the entity name will be *Entity1*, but you can click the name and type a new name. In Figure 6-3, the entity was renamed to *Vehicle*. The entity automatically gets an Id column.

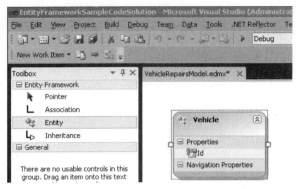

FIGURE 6-3 Dragging an entity from the toolbox to the designer surface.

Clicking the entity causes its properties to be displayed in the Properties window. The following is a list of entity properties.

- **Abstract**   Set to *true* if this entity will be a *MustInherit* (C# *abstract*) class. You set this to *true* when the entity will have derived entities, and you never want this entity to be instantiated directly. For example, you might have a *Pet* entity and *Cat* and *Dog* entities that inherit from *Pet*. You never want someone to instantiate *Pet* directly because you won't know what kind of pet this object represents, so you set *Abstract* to *true*, and no one will be able to instantiate *Pet*.

- **Access**   Sets the access modifier of generated class to either *Public* or *Internal*.

- **Base Type**   This property enables you to set the entity from which this entity will be derived.

- **Documentation**   You can enter XML comments for this property. The *summary* and *LongDescription* elements are supported.

- **Entity Set Name**   This property contains the name of the collection created on the custom *ObjectContext* class that is created. If you generate the database from this conceptual model, this is also the name of the table that will be generated. The name that is contained in this property is automatically pluralized, but be careful to verify that the pluralized name is valid. For example, entering *Quiz* for the name of the entity will cause Entity Set Name to be set to *Quizs*, but it should be *Quizzes*. You can change this property as needed.

- **Name**   This is the name of the current entity.

After you adjust the entity settings, you will want to add and adjust the user-defined properties. If you select the *Id* property and look at the Properties window, you will see the following property settings:

- **Concurrency Mode**   This setting defaults to *None*, which means that this column is not involved in concurrency checks. You can set the property to *Fixed*, which means that the original value of this property is sent as part of the WHERE clause in all update statements or delete statements to ensure that this property has not been modified since it was retrieved.

- **Default Value** This property setting enables you to enter a default initial value for the property.

- **Documentation** You can enter XML comments for this property. The *summary* and *LongDescription* elements are supported.

- **Entity Key** Set this to *true* if the current property is the primary key.

- **Getter** This sets the access modifier for the getter of the current property. Values are *Internal*, *Private*, *Protected*, and *Public*.

- **Name** This setting enables you to set the name of the current property.

- **Nullable** Setting this to *true* enables the current property to contain null values.

- **Setter** This sets the access modifier for the setter of the current property. Values are *Internal*, *Private*, *Protected*, and *Public*.

- **StoreGeneratedPattern** This setting enables you to indicate whether the property value will be auto-generated. *None* indicates that this property value will not be auto-generated. *Identity* indicates that this property value will be an auto-number column and tells the Entity Framework that it needs to get the generated value and feed it back into the entity after an insert. *Computed* indicates that this property value will be calculated after an insert or update. A column whose type is *timestamp* is an example of a column that should have its *StoreGeneratedPattern* property set to *Computed*, because *timestamp* columns get a new value after inserting or updating.

- **Type** Use this setting to set the data type of this property.

To add more properties, right-click the entity and choose Add | Scalar Property. Table 6-2 shows the entities and properties that have been added to the designer surface.

TABLE 6-2 Entities and Properties that Have Been Added to the Designer Surface

ENTITY NAME	PROPERTY NAME	CONCURRENCY MODE	TYPE	MAX LENGTH
Vehicle	Id	Fixed	Int32	
Vehicle	VIN	Fixed	String	17
Vehicle	Make	Fixed	String	20
Vehicle	Model	Fixed	String	20
Vehicle	Year	Fixed	Int32	
Repair	Id	Fixed	Int32	
Repair	VehicleId	Fixed	Int32	
Repair	Description	Fixed	String	100
Repair	Cost	Fixed	Decimal	

To show that two tables are related, add an association from the toolbox by choosing Association, the parent entity (*Vehicle*), and then the child entity (*Repair*). Although not mandatory, you'll find that this operation is best completed by pinning the toolbox open first because this will keep your tables from being covered by the floating toolbox. Pinning the toolbox is accomplished by clicking the thumbtack on the upper-right corner of the toolbox to make the thumbtack point downward (pinned).

After you add the association, check its settings. Simply double-click the association to display its *Referential Constraint* settings. Set the *Principal* property to *Vehicle*, and the *Dependent* property is automatically set to the *Repair* entity. You can also set the *Principal Key* and *Dependent Key* properties. Select *VehicleId* for the *Dependent Key* and click OK. Figure 6-4 shows the completed *Vehicle* (parent) and *Repair* (child) entities with the one-to-many association. Notice that each of the entities now contains *Navigation Properties*. *Navigation Properties* will exist on your classes, and they enable you to navigate easily from the entity with which you're working to either its parent or child entities.

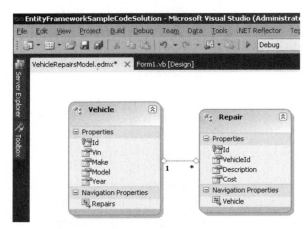

FIGURE 6-4 The completed *Vehicle* and *Repair* entities with the one-to-many association.

Now that this simple conceptual model is complete, create the database. The good news is that you can generate the database from the conceptual model: Right-click the Entity Framework designer surface and then choose Generate Database From Model. You are prompted for a database connection. Because this is a new database, you must click New Connection. Configure your connection to a valid database server and enter the name of the new database. You are prompted to create a new database. This database is named RepairDB. After you create the new database, you see the DDL (Data Definition Language) script and the file name. Click Finish to save the script to a file in your project.

 EXAM TIP

For the exam, remember that you can create the database from your model by right-click-ing the designer surface and choosing Generate Database From Model.

The script has been created and saved to a file, but it has not been executed. To execute the script, open the SQL script file, right-click in the opened script file window, and click Execute SQL. You are prompted for a database connection, and then the script executes.

You can view the new database from Server Explorer as shown in Figure 6-5, which shows the Vehicles and Repairs tables that were created and their corresponding columns. The table names came from the pluralized *Entity Set Name* property on each entity. Not shown is the creation of a relationship called FK_VehicleRepair with its foreign key constraint.

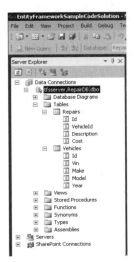

FIGURE 6-5 The created RepairDB contains the Vehicles and Repairs tables.

The database objects that were created are in the dbo schema, which might not be desirable. To change the database schema in which the database objects are created, click the Entity Framework designer surface, and you'll be able to set the general properties of the conceptual model. The properties are as follows:

- **Code Generation Strategy** This turns the default object-layer code generation on or off for the conceptual model. A value of *None* turns off the default code generation; a value of *Default* turns it on. Set the value to *None* when you add a custom text template to generate object-layer code. Custom text templates are covered later in this lesson, in the sections titled "The EntityObject Generator" and "The Self-Tracking Entity Generator."

- **Connection String** Displays the connection string information. To change the connection string, you must modify the .config file.

- **Database Generation Workflow** This is the path for the Window Workflow Foundation file the Generate Database uses from the Model wizard. You can copy and modify the existing file to change the behavior of the database generation.

- **Database Schema Name** The name of the schema to which all generated database objects are added. The default is dbo. If you change the schema name to a schema that does not exist, the schema is automatically created when you generate the database.

- **DDL Generation Template** This is the name of the T4 text template that transforms the SSDL to DDL when Generate Database from the Model wizard is run.
- **Entity Container Access** This is the access modifier of the entity container. Values can be *Public* or *Internal*. The entity container contains all instances of entities for the entity data model.
- **Entity Container Name** The name of the custom entity container created to hold all instances of entities. This class will derive from the *ObjectContext* class.
- **Lazy Loading Enabled** Set this property to *true* to perform just–in-time loading of data.
- **Metadata Artifact Processing** This property controls whether the model and mapping files (.csdl, .ssdl, and .msl files) are embedded in the compiled assembly (default) or simply copied to the output directory.
- **Namespace** This is the conceptual model's XML namespace.

> **NOTE** **CHANGING THE NAMESPACE**
>
> To change the namespace of your generated classes, in Solution Explorer, click the EDMX file. In Properties, set the Custom Tool Namespace. In Visual Basic, this entry is concatenated to the default namespace of the project. In C#, this is the absolute namespace of the generated classes.

- **Pluralize New Objects** This setting specifies whether new entity set names and navigation property names are pluralized. Default is *true*.
- **Transform Related Text Templates On Save** A text template is related to an .edmx file by inserting the name of the EDMX file into the text template. When set to *true* (default), all text templates related to the EDMX file are processed when the EDMX file is saved. When the property is set to *false*, none of the related text templates are processed.
- **Validate On Build** This setting specifies whether the model is validated when the project is built. Default is *true*.

Implementing the Database First Model

To use the Database First model, add an ADO.NET Entity Data Model.edmx file to your project: Right-click the project node in Solution Explorer and then choose Add | New Item. Select ADO.NET Entity Data Model. This template produces a file with an EDMX extension. Provide a name for your file. This example (Figure 6-6) demonstrates the creation of a conceptual model for the Northwind database. After naming the file NorthwindModel.edmx, click Add to start the Entity Data Model Wizard.

The previous section covered the Code First model but also covered many of the settings you might want to change even if you implement the Database First model.

Figure 6-2 showed the first step in the Entity Data Model Wizard, which is to select whether you want to generate the model from the database (Database First) or start with an empty model (Code First). Select Generate The Model from the database and click Next. The next step prompts you for a database connection. Configure the connection to reference the Northwind database and click Next. At the prompt, choose Select Your Database Objects, select All Tables, and click Finish.

Examining the Generated Model

Figure 6-6 shows the generated conceptual model of the Northwind database with the cardinality of each association. Notice some associations have a one-to-many relationship, whereas other associations have a zero-to-one-to-many relationship. This varies based on whether the foreign key allows null values.

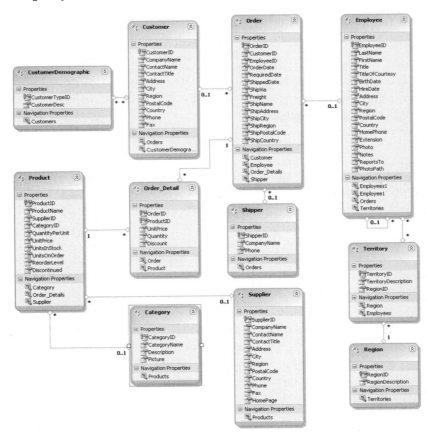

FIGURE 6-6 The Northwind conceptual model.

If you count the entities in Figure 6-6, you'll find that you have eleven, but you have thirteen tables in the database. The reason you're missing two entities is due to the many-to-many association. One of the tables not shown is the CustomerCustomerDemo table between Customer and CustomerDemographic. The other missing table is the EmployeeTerritories table between Employee and Territory. Because these tables exist simply to implement the many-to-many relationship, they are not shown on the conceptual model. You can see the missing table by clicking the many-to-many relationship and viewing the settings in the Mapping Details window. Figure 6-7 shows the selection of the relationship between Customer and CustomerDemographic. When this relationship is selected, the Mapping Details window shows that the CustomerCustomerDemo table implements this relationship.

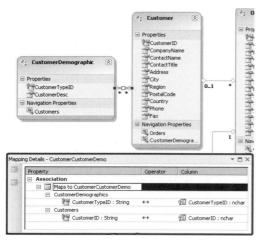

FIGURE 6-7 Select the relationship between Customer and CustomerDemographic to see the Customer-CustomerDemo table in the Mapping Details window.

Keys and Relationships

In Figure 6-7, you can see that the Mapping Details window shows the many-to-many relationship and the keys that join the tables in the relationship. This window is used whenever the join table is hidden when viewing the conceptual model. In addition, if you look at the Properties window, as shown in Figure 6-8, you will see the following properties:

- **Association Set Name**   The name of the table implemented to perform a many-to-many relationship or the name of the relationship that joins tables in a relationship other than many-to-many such as one-to-many. For example, in Figure 6-8, this property contains the CustomerCustomerDemo table name, but if you were to click the relationship between Customer and Order, you would find that this setting contains FK_Orders_Customers, which is the name of the database relationship that joins the Customers and Orders tables.

- **Documentation**   You can enter XML comments for this property. The *summary* and *LongDescription* elements are supported.

- **End1 Multiplicity**   Specifies the number of entities at this end of the association. Valid values are *0* (zero), *0..1* (zero-to-one), or * (many).

- **End1 Navigation Property**   Specifies the name of the *Navigation* property that returns values at this end. For example, if this property is set to *Customers*, there will be a property in the current entity called *Customers*, and you can use this property to retrieve a list of customers that relate to the current entity.

- **End1 OnDelete**   Specifies the action to perform on delete of an entity from *End1*. Look at *End1 Role Name* to identify the table to which table *End1* refers. Valid values are either *None*, which will not perform any delete action, or *Cascade*, which will delete the related items on *End2* when an entity on *End1* is deleted.

- **End1 Role Name**   Specifies the name of the table to which this end of the relationship is joined.

- **End2 Multiplicity**   Specifies the number of entities at this end of the association. Valid values are *0* (zero), *0..1* (zero-to-one), or * (many).

- **End2 Navigation Property**   Specifies the name of the *Navigation* property that returns values at this end. For example, if this property is set to *Orders*, there will be a property in the current entity called *Orders*, and you will be able to use this property to retrieve a list of orders that relate to the current entity.

- **End2 OnDelete**   Specifies the action to perform on delete of an entity from *End2*. Look at *End2 Role Name* to identify the table to which table *End2* refers. Valid values are either *None*, which will not perform any delete action, or *Cascade*, which will delete the related items on *End1* when an entity on *End2* is deleted.

- **End2 Role Name**   Specifies the name of the table to which this end of the relationship is joined.

- **Name**   The name of this relationship object.

- **Referential Constraint**   Shows the direction of the relationship.

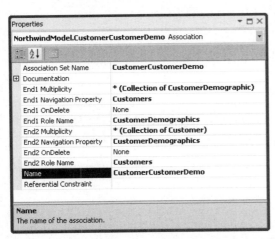

FIGURE 6-8 The relationship has settings in the Properties window that you can view and edit.

Managing your Database Connection and Context Using *ObjectContext*

So far, you've been introduced to data modeling using the Entity Framework, but you will inevitably want to retrieve some data. This is when *ObjectContext* is used. In this section, you will learn about *ObjectContext* and its features.

Retrieving Data with *ObjectContext*

You have created a conceptual model, and now you want to use it in your application. Start by instantiating *ObjectContext*. In the Northwind example, a *NorthwindEntities* class was created, which inherits from *ObjectContext*. You can instantiate the *NorthwindEntities* class and retrieve data very easily, as shown in the following sample code that retrieves the customers and assigns them to *DataGridView*.

Sample of Visual Basic Code

```
Private Sub UsingTheObjectContextToolStripMenuItem_Click( _
     ByVal sender As System.Object, ByVal e As System.EventArgs) _
     Handles UsingTheObjectContextToolStripMenuItem.Click
  Dim db As New NorthwindEntities()
  gv.DataSource = (From c In db.Customers
                   Select New With
                        {
                            .CompanyID = c.CustomerID,
                            .CompanyName = c.CompanyName
                        }).ToList()
End Sub
```

Sample of C# Code

```
private void usingTheObjectContextToolStripMenuItem_Click(
    object sender, EventArgs e)
{
    var db = new NorthwindEntities();
    gv.DataSource = (from c in db.Customers
                     select new
                          {
                              c.CustomerID,
                              c.CompanyName
                          }).ToList();
}
```

ObjectContext is the main object in the Entity Framework. The *NorthwindEntities* class derives from *ObjectContext* and adds properties for each of the entities collections, so, in the code sample, the *NorthwindEntities* object contains a *Customers* collection that can be queried.

How Entity Framework Connects to Your Database

The previous code sample used the *NorthwindEntities* class, which inherits from *ObjectContext*, to retrieve data by using a LINQ to Entities query and display the result in a data grid. You might be wondering where the connection is. The following is an abbreviated version of the source code that was generated by the Entity Framework designer to create the *NorthwindEntities* class.

Sample of Visual Basic Code

```vb
Public Partial Class NorthwindEntities
    Inherits ObjectContext

    Public Sub New()
        MyBase.New("name=NorthwindEntities", "NorthwindEntities")
        MyBase.ContextOptions.LazyLoadingEnabled = true
        OnContextCreated()
    End Sub

    Public Sub New(ByVal connectionString As String)
        MyBase.New(connectionString, "NorthwindEntities")
        MyBase.ContextOptions.LazyLoadingEnabled = true
        OnContextCreated()
    End Sub

    Public Sub New(ByVal connection As EntityConnection)
        MyBase.New(connection, "NorthwindEntities")
        MyBase.ContextOptions.LazyLoadingEnabled = true
        OnContextCreated()
    End Sub

    Public ReadOnly Property Categories() As ObjectSet(Of Category)
        Get
            If (_Categories Is Nothing) Then
                _Categories = MyBase.CreateObjectSet(Of Category)("Categories")
            End If
            Return _Categories
        End Get
    End Property

    Private _Categories As ObjectSet(Of Category)

    Public Function CustOrderHist(customerID As Global.System.String) As ObjectResult(Of
CustOrderHist_Result)
        Dim customerIDParameter As ObjectParameter
        If (customerID IsNot Nothing)
            customerIDParameter = New ObjectParameter("CustomerID", customerID)
        Else
            customerIDParameter = New ObjectParameter("CustomerID", GetType(Global.
System.String))
        End If

        Return MyBase.ExecuteFunction(Of CustOrderHist_Result)("CustOrderHist",
customerIDParameter)
```

```
      End Function

End Class
```

Sample of C# Code
```csharp
public partial class NorthwindEntities : ObjectContext
{
    public NorthwindEntities() : base("name=NorthwindEntities", "NorthwindEntities")
    {
        this.ContextOptions.LazyLoadingEnabled = true;
        OnContextCreated();
    }

    public NorthwindEntities(string connectionString)
        : base(connectionString, "NorthwindEntities")
    {
        this.ContextOptions.LazyLoadingEnabled = true;
        OnContextCreated();
    }

    public NorthwindEntities(EntityConnection connection)
        : base(connection, "NorthwindEntities")
    {
        this.ContextOptions.LazyLoadingEnabled = true;
        OnContextCreated();
    }

    public ObjectSet<Category> Categories
    {
        get
        {
            if ((_Categories == null))
            {
                _Categories = base.CreateObjectSet<Category>("Categories");
            }
            return _Categories;
        }
    }
    private ObjectSet<Category> _Categories;

    public ObjectResult<CustOrderHist_Result> CustOrderHist(global::System.String
customerID)
    {
        ObjectParameter customerIDParameter;
        if (customerID != null)
        {
            customerIDParameter = new ObjectParameter("CustomerID", customerID);
        }
        else
        {
            customerIDParameter = new ObjectParameter("CustomerID",
typeof(global::System.String));
        }
```

```
      return base.ExecuteFunction<CustOrderHist_Result>("CustOrderHist",
customerIDParameter);
    }
}
```

From this code sample, you can see that the *NorthwindEntities* class inherits from *ObjectContext*. There are three constructors for the class. The first constructor is the parameterless constructor, which is the one that was used in the previous code sample. This constructor calls the *ObjectContext* constructor and passes the name of the connection string stored in the App.Config file and the name of the default entity container. The entity container is a logical container for entity sets, association sets, and function imports. It's defined in the EDMX file. If you want to change the connection string, simply locate the connection information in the App.Config file and make the change.

The second constructor enables you to pass an explicit connection string as a parameter, which is passed to the *ObjectContext* constructor. This works well when you want to modify the connection string in your code and pass the modified connection string to *ObjectContext*.

The third constructor accepts an actual connection object and passes it to the *ObjectContext* constructor. This is especially useful when you are executing a local transaction and you want *ObjectContext* to join the ongoing transaction.

Provider and Connection String Information

Connection strings contain information passed from a data provider to a data source to initialize the connection. The connection string information varies, based on the provider. When working with the Entity Framework, connection strings contain information to connect to the underlying ADO.NET data provider that supports the Entity Framework.

The connection string also contains information about the model and mapping files that the *EntityClient* class uses to access the model, and mapping metadata when connecting to the data source. The following sample is the *NorthwindEntities* connection string.

Sample of Connection String
```
<add name="NorthwindEntities"
   connectionString="metadata=res://*/NorthwindModel.csdl|
      res://*/NorthwindModel.ssdl|
      res://*/NorthwindModel.msl;
      provider=System.Data.SqlClient;
      provider connection string=&quot;
      Data Source=.;Initial Catalog=Northwind;
      Integrated Security=True;
      MultipleActiveResultSets=True&quot;"
      providerName="System.Data.EntityClient" />
```

In this connection string, the metadata section references the .csdl, .ssdl, and .msl files, which are resources embedded in the compiled assembly. The format for the resource is as follows.

```
Metadata=res://<assemblyFullName>/<resourceName>.
```

AssemblyFullname is the full name of an assembly with the embedded resource. The name includes the simple name, version name, supported culture, and public key, as follows:

```
ResourceLib, Version=1.0.0.0, Culture=neutral, PublicKeyToken=null
```

Resources can be embedded in any assembly that is accessible by the application. You can also specify a wildcard (*) for *AssemblyFullName*, and the Entity Framework run time will search for resources in the following locations, in this order:

1. The calling assembly

2. The referenced assemblies

3. The assemblies in the bin directory of an application

If the files are not in one of these locations, an exception is thrown.

If your resources are in the current assembly, there is no harm in using the wildcard (*), but when you use the wildcard (*) to locate a resource in a different assembly, the Entity Framework has to look through all the assemblies for resources with the correct name. You can improve performance by specifying the assembly name instead of using the wildcard.

Storing Information about Objects and Their State

When a query is executed, the returned objects must be monitored for changes in state for the Entity Framework to have knowledge of the object's need to be persisted. The change-tracking information for the returned objects is stored in *ObjectStateEntry* objects, which *ObjectContext* creates for each retrieved or attached object. The *ObjectStateEntry* class is in the *System.Data.Objects* namespace. Table 6-3 shows the information the *ObjectStateEntry* object stores.

TABLE 6-3 The *ObjectStateEntry* Properties

PROPERTY NAME	DESCRIPTION
CurrentValues	Gets the current property values of the object or relationship associated with this *ObjectStateEntry*
Entity	Gets a reference to the tracked object that's associated with this *ObjectStateEntry*
EntityKey	Gets the entity key that's associated with this *ObjectStateEntry*
EntitySet	Gets the *EntitySetBase* class of the entity or relationship that's associated with this *ObjectStateEntry*
IsRelationship	Gets a Boolean value that indicates whether the entity associated with this entity is a relationship
ObjectStateManager	Gets the *ObjectStateManager* class for this *ObjectStateEntry*
Original Values	Gets the read-only version of the original property values of the object or relationship associated with this *ObjectStateEntry*. Objects in an *Added* state don't have original values

RelationshipManager	Gets a reference to the *RelationshipManager* class instance for the object represented by the entry
State	Gets the state of the entity associated with this *ObjectStateEntry*

ObjectContext has a *SaveChanges* method that you can call when you're ready to save all changed objects. To find whether the value of a property has changed between the calls to *SaveChanges*, query the collection of changed property names returned by the *GetModifiedProperties* method on the *ObjectStateEntry* object. The *GetModifiedProperties* method returns a generic *IEnumerable* of *string* containing the names of the properties that have changed.

The state of an entity object can be any of the values described in Table 6-4. To gain access to the state information for a given entity object, use *ObjectContext*, which has an *ObjectStateManager* property. *ObjectStateManager* has a *GetObjectStateEntry* method that accepts an entity parameter and returns the *ObjectStateEntry* object containing a *State* property of type *EntityState* that can take the values defined in Table 6-4.

TABLE 6-4 The *EntityState* Enumeration

MEMBER	DESCRIPTION
Added	The object has been instantiated and has been added to *ObjectContext*, and the *SaveChanges* method has not been called. After the changes are saved, the object state changes to *Unchanged*. Objects in the *Added* state do not have original values in *ObjectStateEntry*.
Deleted	The object has been deleted from *ObjectContext*. After the changes are saved, the object state changes to *Detached*.
Modified	At least one scalar property on the object has been modified, and the *SaveChanges* method has not been called. After the changes are saved, the object state changes to *Unchanged*.
Detached	The object exists but is not being tracked by *ObjectContext*. An entity is in this state immediately after it has been instantiated and before it is added to *ObjectContext*. If an entity has been removed from *ObjectContext* by calling the *Detach* method, it is also in this state. Also, an object might be in this state if it is loaded by using *NoTracking MergeOption*. No *ObjectStateEntry* instance is associated with objects in the *Detached* state.
Unchanged	The object has not been modified since it was attached to the context or since the last time the *SaveChanges* method was called.

EXAM TIP

Expect to be tested on the various entity states of an entity object.

ObjectContext Life Cycle

One of the things you must consider is the lifetime of your *ObjectContext*. When *ObjectContext* is referencing many objects to provide change tracking, its memory footprint could become quite large. Otherwise, change tracking and object caching provide value. Here are some guidelines to consider when you're developing an application that requires *ObjectContext*:

- **Memory Usage**   The memory footprint must be considered. *ObjectContext* grows in size as it is used because it holds a reference to all the entities it's tracking. Although *ObjectContext* grows, it might be better to have a single shared *ObjectContext* than to have many *ObjectContext* objects in your application.

- **Dispose**   *ObjectContext* does implement the *IDisposable* interface, so you might consider instantiating the object within a *using* block. Thus, you would use the *ObjectContext* object to perform a single action. This might not give you the functionality you want because you'll lose object tracking. If you can possibly retrieve your data, modify it, and send the changes back to the database within a single method call, you can use the *using* block within the method. If you can't use the *using* block, you can still benefit from explicitly calling the *Dispose* method whenever you know you're done with the object.

- **Cost Of Construction**   Don't be too concerned with the cost to reconstruct *ObjectContext* because this cost is small.

- **Thread Safety**   If you are trying to share an *ObjectContext* object across threads, don't. *ObjectContext* is not thread safe. You could explicitly synchronize access to a shared *ObjectContext* object, but you must analyze your scenario and decide whether it's better to have an *ObjectContext* object per thread or incur the cost to synchronize a shared *ObjectContext* object.

- **Stateless**   If you are creating a stateless environment, such as a web service, you should not reuse *ObjectContext* across method calls. Therefore, this scenario lends itself to implementing the *using* block, but the contents of the *using* block might be code to requery the data that was retrieved in a previous call, so modify the data and then save it.

Lazy Loading vs. Explicit Loading vs. Eager Loading

Lazy loading refers to delaying the loading of data until the data is needed. Lazy loading is also known as just-in-time loading, lazy initialization, on-demand loading, and deferred loading. In many applications, you will want lazy loading when the data is not retrieved until it's required. In Entity Framework 4, lazy loading is enabled by default, so if you execute the following code sample that retrieves the first *Order* object for the customer whose CustomerID is ALFKI and then retrieves the list of order details for that *Order* object, the three order detail objects are displayed.

Sample of Visual Basic Code

```
Private Sub LazyLoadingToolStripMenuItem_Click( _
  ByVal sender As System.Object, ByVal e As System.EventArgs) _
  Handles LazyLoadingToolStripMenuItem.Click
  MessageBox.Show("Don't forget to set the Lazy Loading Enabled " & _
              "property on the EDMX file to true!")
  Dim db As New NorthwindEntities()
  Dim order = db.Orders.Where(Function(o) o.CustomerID = "ALFKI").First()
  gv.DataSource = order.Order_Details.ToList()
End Sub
```

Sample of C# Code

```
private void lazyLoadingToolStripMenuItem_Click(
    object sender, EventArgs e)
{
    MessageBox.Show("Don't forget to set the Lazy Loading Enabled " +
                    "property on the EDMX file to true!");
    var db = new NorthwindEntities();
    var order = db.Orders.Where(o => o.CustomerID == "ALFKI").First();
    gv.DataSource = order.Order_Details.ToList();
}
```

In this example, the order detail objects were not retrieved until the *ToList* method was executed. This lazy loading worked properly—as you expected—because lazy loading is enabled.

From a best practices perspective, turn off lazy loading to ensure that you are not loading data inadvertently. To turn off lazy loading, open your EDMX file, click the designer surface, and, in the Properties window, set the *Lazy Loading Enabled* property to *false*.

EXAM TIP

For the exam, be sure you understand lazy loading. You can expect to get questions related to activating and deactivating lazy loading.

After turning off lazy loading, if you run the query again, no order details are displayed because no data was retrieved. Note that no exception was thrown, which means that you must pay attention to result sets to verify that the results of your queries match what is expected.

At this point, you must decide whether you want to load the order detail objects *explicitly* just before calling the *ToList* method or *eagerly* load the order detail objects when you run the initial query for the order.

To use eager loading, use the *Include* method to include the order detail objects when running the query for the order, as shown in the following code sample.

```vb
Private Sub EagerLoadingToolStripMenuItem_Click( _
    ByVal sender As System.Object, ByVal e As System.EventArgs) _
    Handles EagerLoadingToolStripMenuItem.Click
  MessageBox.Show("Don't forget to set the Lazy Loading Enabled " & _
            "property on the EDMX file to false!")
  Dim db As New NorthwindEntities()
  Dim order = db.Orders.Include("Order_Details") _
            .Where(Function(o) o.CustomerID = "ALFKI").First()
  gv.DataSource = order.Order_Details.ToList()
End Sub
```

Sample of C# Code

```csharp
private void eagerLoadingToolStripMenuItem_Click(
    object sender, EventArgs e)
{
  MessageBox.Show("Don't forget to set the Lazy Loading Enabled " +
 "property on the EDMX file to false!");
  var db = new NorthwindEntities();
  var order = db.Orders.Include("Order_Details").Where(
            o => o.CustomerID == "ALFKI").First();
  gv.DataSource = order.Order_Details.ToList();
}
```

To use explicit loading, use the *Load* method to load the order detail objects before executing the *ToList* method. Note that the *Load* method is a *Sub* (C# returns *void*), so the *Load* method can't be *chained* like many of the other query extension methods.

Sample of Visual Basic Code

```vb
Private Sub ExplicitLoadingToolStripMenuItem_Click( _
    ByVal sender As System.Object, ByVal e As System.EventArgs) _
    Handles ExplicitLoadingToolStripMenuItem.Click
    MessageBox.Show("Don't forget to set the Lazy Loading Enabled " & _
        "property on the EDMX file to false!")
    Dim db As New NorthwindEntities()
    Dim orders = db.Orders.Where(Function(o) o.CustomerID = "ALFKI").First()
    orders.Order_Details.Load()
    gv.DataSource = orders.Order_Details.ToList()
  End Sub
```

Sample of C# Code

```csharp
private void explicitLoadingToolStripMenuItem_Click(
    object sender, EventArgs e)
{
  MessageBox.Show("Don't forget to set the Lazy Loading Enabled " +
        "property on the EDMX file to false!");
  var db = new NorthwindEntities();
  var order = db.Orders.Where(o => o.CustomerID == "ALFKI").First();
  order.Order_Details.Load();
  gv.DataSource = order.Order_Details.ToList();
}
```

More Modeling and Design

In the next part of this chapter, you are introduced to more concepts that you need to understand in order to be able to implement a LINQ to Entities solution.

Working with Complex Types

Complex types are nonscalar properties of entities that enable scalar properties to be organized within entities. Complex types consist of scalar properties or other complex type properties. Complex types do not have keys, so they cannot be managed by the Entity Framework except through the parent object.

Classes generated by the Entity Framework tools inherit from *EntityObject*. Complex types that are generated inherit from *ComplexObject*. These classes inherit from a common base class, *StructuralObject*. Scalar properties of complex type objects can be accessed like other scalar properties.

You can create and modify complex types by using the Model Browser window, typically viewable when the EDMX file is open. In the Model Browser window, right-click the Complex Types folder and choose Create Complex Type. A new complex type is added to the folder with a default name, but the default name is selected, so you can simply type in the new name. In this example, a complex type called *Address* is created.

After the complex type has been added, you can add scalar or complex properties. For *Address*, five scalar properties will be added: *AddressLine1*, *AddressLine2*, *City*, *State*, and *PostalCode*. Figure 6-9 shows the completed complex type called *Address*.

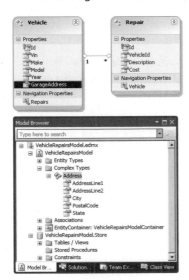

FIGURE 6-9 You can use the Model Browser window to create complex types.

After you create a complex type, you can use it on an entity or another complex type. In this example, a *GarageAddress* property is added to the *Vehicle* entity.

You can also create a complex type from existing properties on an existing entity. Using the Entity Framework designer, select one or more properties on an entity, right-click, and select Refactor Into New Complex Type. This adds a new complex type with the selected properties to the Model Browser. The complex type is given a default name, which you can rename. In addition, the complex property of the newly created type replaces the selected properties, and all property mappings are preserved.

Complex types do not support inheritance and cannot contain navigation properties. It's permissible for a complex type's scalar properties to be null, but a complex type property cannot be null. If *SaveChanges* is called on *ObjectContext* to persist a null complex type property, an *InvalidOperationException* is thrown.

When any property is changed anywhere in the object graph of a complex type, the property of the parent type is marked as changed, and all properties in the object graph of the complex type are updated when *SaveChanges* is called.

When the object layer is generated by the Entity Data Model tools, complex objects are instantiated when the complex type property is accessed and not when the parent object is instantiated.

Mapping Stored Procedures

There are two primary scenarios for mapping a stored procedure into a conceptual model. In one scenario, you simply want to expose a stored procedure and return either entities or complex types. In another scenario, you want to map insert, update, and delete operations for an entity type to stored procedures.

Adding a stored procedure to a conceptual model is also known as adding a function import, which enables you to call the corresponding stored procedure easily from your application code by executing a method on *ObjectContext*. A function import can return collections of simple types, entity types, or complex types, or return no value.

To add existing stored procedures to the conceptual model, right-click the Entity Framework designer surface and choose Update Model From Database. On the Add tab, select the stored procedures you want to add to the conceptual model and click Finish. In this example, all the Northwind stored procedures have been added.

In the Model Browser window, double-click the stored procedure you expose as a method, which opens the Add Function Import dialog box, as shown in Figure 6-10, when double-clicking the CustOrderHist stored procedure.

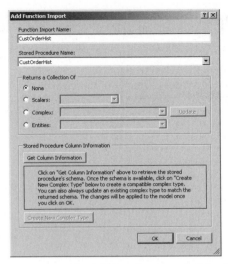

FIGURE 6-10 The Add Function Import dialog box maps a stored procedure to a function import.

In the Add Function Import dialog box, specify the return type of the stored procedure. You can specify a complex type or an entity. If the stored procedure executes a custom SQL statement, you can click Get Column Information to retrieve the schema information. After the schema information has been retrieved, you can click Create New Complex Type to create a complex type to match the returned schema. After you add the function import, you can use it as shown in the following code sample.

Sample of Visual Basic Code

```vb
Private Sub ExecuteStoredProcedureToolStripMenuItem_Click( _
      ByVal sender As System.Object, ByVal e As System.EventArgs) _
      Handles ExecuteStoredProcedureToolStripMenuItem.Click
   Dim db As New NorthwindEntities()
   gv.DataSource = db.CustOrderHist("ALFKI").ToList()
End Sub
```

Sample of C# Code

```csharp
   private void executeStoredProcedureToolStripMenuItem_Click(
   object sender, EventArgs e)
{
   var db = new NorthwindEntities();
   gv.DataSource = db.CustOrderHist("ALFKI");
}
```

The other scenario in which you might use stored procedures is for insert, update, and delete of entities. The *ObjectContext* class exposes a *SaveChanges* method that triggers updates to the underlying database. By default, these updates use SQL statements that are automatically generated, but the updates can use stored procedures that you specify. The good news is that the application code you use to create, update, and delete entities is the same whether or not you use stored procedures to update the database.

To map stored procedures to entities, in the Entity Framework designer, right-click the entity and choose Stored Procedure Mapping. In the Mapping Details window, as shown in Figure 6-11, assign a stored procedure for insert, update, and delete.

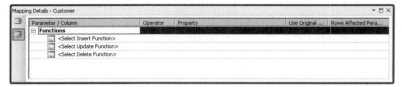

FIGURE 6-11 The Mapping Details window stores procedure mapping

Partial Classes and Methods

The Entity Framework generates classes that contain the properties defined in the conceptual model and do not contain any methods. These generated classes are partial, which means that you can extend these classes by adding your own methods and properties in a separate source file. When you add your code to a separate source file, you don't have to worry about losing your customization if the files are regenerated.

Consider the Northwind database, which has an Order Details table; this table has columns for Quantity, UnitPrice, and Discount. You want to display this information in a data grid, but you also want to include the total price for each row. You might start with a LINQ to Entities query that looks like the following.

Sample of Visual Basic Code

```
Private Sub orderDetailsWoCustomMethodToolStripMenuItem_Click( _
      ByVal sender As System.Object, ByVal e As System.EventArgs) _
      Handles orderDetailsWoCustomMethodToolStripMenuItem.Click
   Dim db As New NorthwindEntities()
   gv.DataSource = (From od In db.Order_Details.AsEnumerable()
           Where od.Order.CustomerID = "ALFKI"
           Select New With
               {
                   od.OrderID,
                   od.ProductID,
                   od.Quantity,
                   od.Discount,
                   .DetailTotal = (1 - CType(od.Discount, Decimal)) *
                       (od.Quantity * od.UnitPrice)
               }).ToList()
End Sub
```

Sample of C# Code

```
private void orderDetailsWoCustomMethodToolStripMenuItem_Click(
   object sender, EventArgs e)
{
   var db = new NorthwindEntities();

   gv.DataSource = (from od in db.Order_Details.AsEnumerable()
```

```
                 where od.Order.CustomerID == "ALFKI"
                 select new
                        {
                            od.OrderID,
                            od.ProductID,
                            od.Quantity,
                            od.Discount,
                            DetailTotal = (1 - (decimal)od.Discount) *
                                        (od.Quantity * od.UnitPrice)
                        }).ToList();
}
```

In this example, the total for each order detail is calculated in the LINQ to Entities query and assigned to a *DetailTotal* property on the anonymous type in the query. However, you might want access to *DetailTotal* in many places within the application.

A solution to this problem is to add a new property, *DetailTotal*, to the *Order_Detail* class. To add the new method without the risk of losing the method when the classes are regenerated, add a new file to your project that contains a partial class that has the same name as the class that is generated and that must be in the same namespace. In the following example, a new file has been added called NorthwindExtensions.vb (C# NorthwindExtensions.cs) that contains the *Order_Detail* partial class and the *DetailTotal* method.

Sample of Visual Basic Code

```
Partial Public Class Order_Detail
    Public ReadOnly Property DetailTotal() As Decimal
        Get
            Return (1 - CType(Discount, Decimal)) *
                            (Quantity * UnitPrice)
        End Get
    End Property
End Class
```

Sample of C# Code

```
namespace EntityFrameworkSampleCode
{
    public partial class Order_Detail
    {
        public double DetailTotal
        {
            get
            {
                return (1 - Discount) *
                        (double)(Quantity * UnitPrice);
            }
        }
    }
}
```

Now that you've add this file with the *Order_Detail* partial class to your project, you can change your LINQ query to use the new property. The following code sample shows the revised query, using the new *DetailTotal* property.

```vb
Private Sub orderDetailsWithCustomMethodToolStripMenuItem_Click( _
      ByVal sender As System.Object, ByVal e As System.EventArgs) _
      Handles orderDetailsWithCustomMethodToolStripMenuItem.Click
   Dim db As New NorthwindEntities()
   gv.DataSource = (From od In db.Order_Details.AsEnumerable()
   Where od.Order.CustomerID = "ALFKI"
                    Select New With
                          {
                              od.OrderID,
                              od.ProductID,
                              od.Quantity,
                              od.Discount,
                              od.DetailTotal
                          }).ToList()
End Sub
```

Sample of C# Code

```csharp
private void orderDetailsWithCustomMethodToolStripMenuItem_Click(
   object sender, EventArgs e)
{
   var db = new NorthwindEntities();
   gv.DataSource = (from od in db.Order_Details.AsEnumerable()
                    where od.Order.CustomerID == "ALFKI"
                    select new
                    {
                        od.OrderID,
                        od.ProductID,
                        od.Quantity,
                        od.Discount,
                        od.DetailTotal
                    }).ToList();
}
```

Another area of extensibility is with the partial methods created on each entity type. There is a pair of partial methods called *OnXxxChanging* and *OnXxxChanged* for each property, in which *Xxx* is the name of the property. The *OnXxxChanging* method executes before the property has changed, and the *OnXxxChanged* method executes after the property has changed. To implement any of the partial methods, create a partial class as shown in the previous example and add the appropriate partial method with implementation code. In the following code sample, the *OnQuantityChanging* and *OnQuantityChanged* methods have been implemented in the partial class from the previous example.

Sample of Visual Basic Code

```vb
Private Sub OnQuantityChanging(ByVal value As Global.System.Int16)
   Debug.WriteLine(String.Format( _
         "Changing quantity from {0} to {1}", Quantity, value))
End Sub

Private Sub OnQuantityChanged()
   Debug.WriteLine(String.Format( _
      "Changed quantity to {0}", Quantity))
```

```
End Sub
```

Sample of C# Code

```csharp
partial void OnQuantityChanging(global::System.Int16 value)
{
    Debug.WriteLine(string.Format(
        "Changing quantity from {0} to {1}", Quantity, value));
}

partial void OnQuantityChanged()
{
    Debug.WriteLine(string.Format(
        "Changed quantity to {0}", Quantity));
}
```

Implementing Inheritance in the Entity Framework

One of the problems with connecting an object-oriented application to a relational database is that the relational database has no concept of inheritance. There are three basic ways to solve this problem when implementing an object-relational mapping (ORM) solution: Table per Class Hierarchy (TPH), Table per Type (TPT), and Table per Concrete Class (TPC). This section covers all three solutions.

TPH

Of the different solutions, probably the simplest and easiest to implement is TPH, which is also known as Single Table Inheritance. To implement this solution, all concrete types in the inheritance hierarchy are stored on one table. The Entity Framework needs to know which type each row is, so you must define a discriminator column that identifies the concrete type to which a specific row is mapped.

Although this solution is simplistic from a database administrator's perspective, this model is not normalized because you typically have columns that have many null values. This is because some types need columns that others don't need, so you must mark columns that are unique per data type as being nullable even if they are not nullable when you are working with a type that requires the column.

This approach is not as efficient regarding disk space consumed, but the trade-off is simplicity and fewer joins to other tables, which can yield better performance.

To demonstrate this solution, consider the scenario in which your application tracks vehicles, and there are many types of vehicles. To keep the example manageable, there is a *Vehicle* base class, a *Car* object that inherits from *Vehicle*, and a *Boat* object that inherits from *Vehicle*. *Vehicle* is abstract and contains *Id*, *Vin*, *Make*, *Model*, and *Year* properties. *Car* inherits from *Vehicle* and has a *TireSize* property. *Boat* inherits from *Vehicle* and has a *PropellerSize* property. All this data is stored in a single table called Vehicles, as shown in Figure 6-12.

Vehicles

	Column Name	Data Type	Allow Nulls
🔑	Id	int	☐
	Type	varchar(10)	☐
	Vin	char(17)	☐
	Make	varchar(50)	☐
	Model	varchar(50)	☐
	Year	int	☐
	TireSize	varchar(50)	☑
	PropSize	varchar(50)	☑
			☐

FIGURE 6-12 The Vehicles table contains data for the *Vehicle*, *Car*, and *Boat* entities.

The *Id* property is the primary key for all types that this table contains. The Type column is the column discriminator, which specifies the object a row represents. Vin, Make, Model, and Year are common to all vehicles, so they are contained in a *Vehicle* base class with the Id. The TireSize column is mandatory for all instances of *Car* and is defined on the *Car* class, but because *Boat* instances don't have tires, this column allows nulls. PropSize is mandatory for all *Boat* instances and is defined on the *Boat* class, but *Car* objects don't have propellers, so the PropSize column must allow nulls.

After the table is created, a TablePerHierarchyModel.edmx ADO.NET Entity Data Model is added, and, in the wizard, Generate From Database is selected, the connection and database are selected, and the Vehicles table is selected.

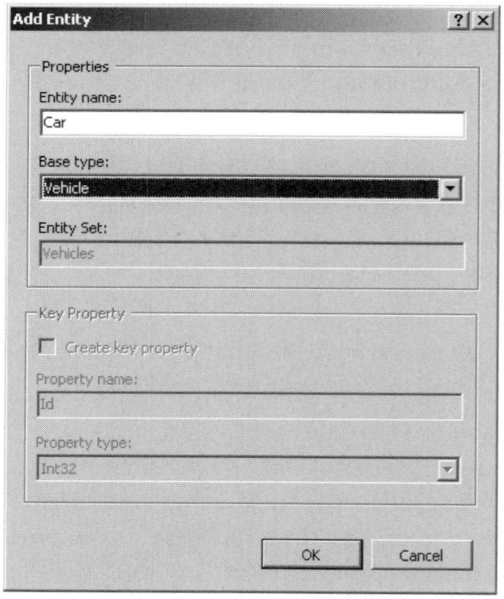

FIGURE 6-13 The Add Entity screen for *Car*.

The Entity Framework designer is displayed with the *Vehicle* entity. Right-click the designer surface and choose Add | Entity. Set Entity Name to *Car* and Base Type to *Vehicle*, as shown in Figure 6-13. Right-click the designer surface again and choose Add | Entity. Set Entity Name to *Boat* and Base Type to *Vehicle*.

At this point, you should be able to see the inheritance hierarchy, but the *TireSize* and *PropSize* properties are still in the *Vehicle* class. Right-click TireSize and select Cut; right-click the properties node on the *Car* entity and choose Paste. Next, right-click PropSize and choose Cut; right-click the properties node on the *Boat* entity and choose Paste. Your inheritance hierarchy should look like Figure 6-14.

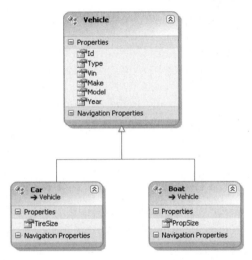

FIGURE 6-14 The inheritance hierarchy is shown with the *TireSize* and *PropSize* properties on the correct entities.

Now that the properties are on the correct entities, it's time to set up the mapping of the *TireSize* and *PropSize* properties. Select the *TireSize* property and note that the Mapping Details window is blank. Under the *Tables* node, click Add A Table Or View. From the drop-down list, select the Vehicles table. The TireSize column is automatically mapped to the *TireSize* property. You must also specify when a row should map to a *Car* entity. Click Add A Condition and, in the drop-down list, select Type. Next, click <Empty String> and type **Car**. Your mapping should look like Figure 6-15.

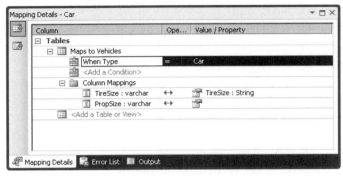

FIGURE 6-15 The Mapping Details window shows the mapping of *Car* to the Vehicles table.

Select the *PropSize* property and note that the Mapping Details window is blank. Under the *Tables* node, click Add A Table Or View. From the drop-down list, select the Vehicles table. The PropSize column is automatically mapped to the *PropSize* property. You must also specify when a row should map to a *Boat* entity. Click Add A Condition and, in the drop-down list, select the type. Next, click <Empty String> and type **Boat**.

Ensure that your generated classes are in an isolated namespace. In Solution Explorer, click the EDMX file. In the Properties window, set the Custom Tool Namespace for Visual Basic to *TablePerHierarchy* or, for C#, to *EntityFrameworkSampleCode.TablePerHierarchy*.

If you try to build your application, you will see the following build error: "Error 159: EntityType 'TablePerHierarchyModel.Vehicle' has no key defined." Define the key for EntityType. Click the *Id* property and, in the Properties window, set the *Entity Key* property to *true*.

If you try to build again, you will see a new error: Error 3023: "Problem in mapping fragments starting at lines 56, 66, 73: Column Vehicles. Type has no default value and is not nullable. A column value is required to store entity data. An Entity with Key (PK) will not round-trip when PK is in 'Vehicles' EntitySet AND Entity is type [TablePerHierarchyModel.Vehicle]." To correct this error, select the *Vehicle* entity and, in the Properties window, set the *Abstract* property to *true*.

If you try to build again, you will see a new error: "Error 3032: Problem in mapping fragments starting at line 56: Condition member 'Vehicles.Type' with a condition other than 'IsNull=False' is mapped. Either remove the condition on Vehicles.Type or remove it from the mapping." To correct this problem, remove the *Type* property from the *Vehicle* entity because the discriminator property should not be mapped. You should then be able to build the project.

To test this, either enter the following data into the table as shown in Table 6-5 or use the sample code that contains this data.

TABLE 6-5 Sample Data in the Vehicles Table

ID	TYPE	VIN	MAKE	MODEL	YEAR	TIRESIZE	PROPSIZE
1	*Car*	ABC123	BMW	Z-4	2009	225/45R17	NULL
2	*Boat*	DEF234	SeaRay	SunDeck	2005	NULL	14.75 x 21 SS
3	*Car*	GHI345	VW	Bug	2007	205/55R16	NULL
4	*Boat*	JKL456	Harris	FloatBoat	2000	NULL	14-1/2" x 18" LH

The following code sample will display the *Car* objects in a data grid.

Sample of Visual Basic Code

```
Private Sub tPHDisplayCarsToolStripMenuItem_Click( _
     ByVal sender As System.Object, ByVal e As System.EventArgs) _
     Handles tPHDisplayCarsToolStripMenuItem.Click
  Dim db = New TablePerHierarchy.TablePerHierarchyEntities()
  gv.DataSource = (From b In db.Vehicles.OfType(Of TablePerHierarchy.Car)()
                   Select b).ToList()
End Sub
```

Sample of C# Code

```
private void tPHDisplayCarsToolStripMenuItem_Click(object sender, EventArgs e)
{
   var db = new TablePerHierarchy.TablePerHierarchyEntities();
   gv.DataSource = (from c in db.Vehicles.OfType< TablePerHierarchy.Car>()
                   select c).ToList();
}
```

With a small tweak to change the type to *Boat*, you can retrieve the *Boat* objects as shown in the following code sample.

Sample of Visual Basic Code

```
Private Sub tPHDisplayBoatsToolStripMenuItem_Click( _
     ByVal sender As System.Object, ByVal e As System.EventArgs) _
     Handles tPHDisplayBoatsToolStripMenuItem.Click
  Dim db = New TablePerHierarchy.TablePerHierarchyEntities()
  gv.DataSource = (From b In db.Vehicles.OfType(Of TablePerHierarchy.Boat)()
                   Select b).ToList()
End Sub
```

Sample of C# Code

```
private void tPHDisplayBoatsToolStripMenuItem_Click(object sender, EventArgs e)
{
   var db = new TablePerHierarchy.TablePerHierarchyEntities();
   gv.DataSource = (from b in db.Vehicles.OfType<TablePerHierarchy.Boat>()
                   select b).ToList();
}
```

TPT

Of the different inheritance solutions, probably the most efficient is TPT. To implement this solution, each type in the inheritance hierarchy is stored in its own table. With a one-to-one mapping of type to table, this solution might also feel the most logical. Also, because of the one-to-one mapping, this solution is typically the most normalized.

One of the potential drawbacks to this solution is the increase in the number of joins you need to get the data. Joins are expensive, but if you're careful about creating indexes on foreign keys where necessary, performance issues can be minimized.

To demonstrate this solution, consider the same scenario described previously in the TPH section, in which your application tracks vehicles and there are many types of vehicles. To keep the example manageable, there is a *Vehicle* base class, a *Car* object that inherits from *Vehicle*, and a *Boat* object that inherits from *Vehicle*. *Vehicle* is abstract and contains *Id*, *Vin*, *Make*, *Model*, and *Year* properties. *Car* inherits from *Vehicle* and has a *TireSize* property. *Boat* inherits from *Vehicle* and has a *PropellerSize* property. All this data is stored in three tables named Vehicles, Cars, and Boats, as shown in Figure 6-16.

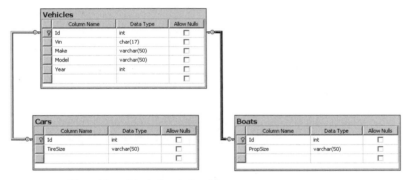

FIGURE 6-16 The tables with their relationships.

Id is the primary key for all types these tables contain. On the Vehicles table, the *Id* property is configured to be an auto-number (identity) column. On the Car and Boat tables, the *Id* property is not an auto-number column because *Car Id* and *Boat Id* get their values from the Vehicle Id column. *Vin*, *Make*, *Model*, and *Year* are common to all vehicles, so they are contained in a *Vehicle* base class with the *Id* property. *TireSize* is mandatory for all instances of *Car* and is defined on the *Car* class and on the Cars table. *Null* values cannot exist in *TireSize*. *PropSize* is mandatory for all *Boat* instances and is defined on the *Boat* class on the Boats table. *PropSize* does not allow null values.

After the tables are created, an ADO.NET Entity Data Model, TablePerTypeModel.edmx, is added in the wizard, and the Vehicles, Cars, and Boats tables are selected. The result is shown in Figure 6-17.

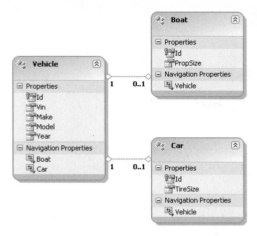

FIGURE 6-17 Updating the model from the database produces entities with associations.

The conceptual model generated from the database shows associations where you want inheritance instead. If you select the *Boat* entity, in the Properties window you will be able to set the *Base Type* property to *Vehicles*. Do the same for *Car* and then click the two associations and delete them. Also delete the *Id* property from *Boat* and *Car* because *Id* is inherited. Click the TablePerTypeModel.edmx file and, in the Properties window, set Custom Tool Namespace to *TablePerType*. Last, click the vehicle and set the *Abstract* property to *true*. Figure 6-18 shows the completed conceptual model.

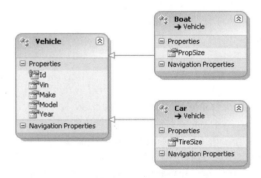

FIGURE 6-18 The completed TPT conceptual model.

The following code sample displays the *Car* objects in a data grid.

Sample of Visual Basic Code

```
Private Sub TPTDisplayCarsToolStripMenuItem_Click( _
    ByVal sender As System.Object, ByVal e As System.EventArgs) _
    Handles TPTDisplayCarsToolStripMenuItem.Click
  Dim db = New TablePerType.TablePerTypeEntities()
  gv.DataSource = (From b In db.Vehicles.OfType(Of TablePerType.Car)()
                Select b).ToList()
```

```
      End Sub
```

Sample of C# Code

```csharp
private void tPTDisplayCarsToolStripMenuItem_Click(
   object sender, EventArgs e)
{
   var db = new TablePerType.TablePerTypeEntities();
   gv.DataSource = (from c in db.Vehicles.OfType<TablePerType.Car>()
                    select c).ToList();
}
```

With a small tweak to change the type to *Boat*, you can retrieve the *Boat* objects as shown in the following code sample.

Sample of Visual Basic Code

```vb
Private Sub TPTDisplayBoatsToolStripMenuItem_Click( _
     ByVal sender As System.Object, ByVal e As System.EventArgs) _
     Handles TPTDisplayBoatsToolStripMenuItem.Click
   Dim db = New TablePerType.TablePerTypeEntities()
   gv.DataSource = (From b In db.Vehicles.OfType(Of TablePerType.Boat)()
                    Select b).ToList()
End Sub
```

Sample of C# Code

```csharp
private void tPTDisplayBoatsToolStripMenuItem_Click(
   object sender, EventArgs e)
{
   var db = new TablePerType.TablePerTypeEntities();
   gv.DataSource = (from b in db.Vehicles.OfType<TablePerType.Boat>()
                    select b).ToList();
}
```

TPC

TPC is another method of implementing inheritance with the Entity Framework. In this solution, you provide a table for each concrete class but no table for the abstract class. To clarify terminology, the abstract class is the base class from which the concrete child classes inherit. Typically, you would instantiate the concrete class in your application. If there is no table for the abstract class, where is the data that is in the abstract class stored? It is included with each of the concrete classes, so you will have the same base-class columns definition in each of the concrete classes.

One of the potential drawbacks to this solution is the duplication of columns in each concrete class. If you add a new property to the abstract class, you must add a column to every concrete class table. Also, if you need to access only values that are in the abstract class, you must create a query that performs a union of all concrete tables. For example, if the *Vin*, *Make*, *Model*, and *Year* are in the abstract class, and you want a list of all vehicles whose year is 2000, you must union all the concrete tables together to get the desired result. This inheritance solution is not used often, relative to TPH and TPT.

To demonstrate this solution, consider the same scenario described in the TPH and TPT sections, in which your application tracks vehicles and there are many types of vehicles. To keep the example manageable, there will be a *Vehicle* base class, a *Car* object that inherits from *Vehicle*, and a *Boat* object that inherits from *Vehicle*. *Vehicle* is abstract and contains *Id*, *Vin*, *Make*, *Model*, and *Year* properties. *Car* inherits from *Vehicle* and has a *TireSize* property. *Boat* inherits from *Vehicle* and has a *PropellerSize* property. All this data is stored in two tables, Cars and Boats, as shown in Figure 6-19.

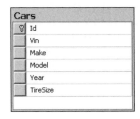
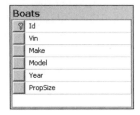

FIGURE 6-19 Implementing TPC shows tables with duplicate column names for base class storage.

The *Id* property on both tables is the primary key and is configured to be an auto-number (identity) column. The *Vin*, *Make*, *Model*, and *Year* properties are common to all vehicles, so they are contained in a *Vehicle* base class with *Id* even if the base class data is stored with the concrete class. The *TireSize* property is mandatory for all instances of *Car* and is defined on the *Car* class as well as on the *Cars* entity. Null values cannot exist in *TireSize*. *PropSize* is mandatory for all *Boat* instances and is defined on the *Boat* class and on the Boats table. *PropSize* does not allow null values.

TPC class solution is not supported in the Entity Framework designer but can be implemented by editing the EDMX file with an XML editor. Also, you'll find it quite difficult to find documentation on this, so here is a step-by-step walkthrough:

- **Create the database tables** In this example, a new folder called TablePerConcrete was added to the project. A service-based database was added to the TablePerConcrete. mdf folder; the Cars and Boats tables were added as shown in Figure 6-19, and these tables were populated with the data as defined in Table 6-4.

- **Add an ADO.NET Entity Data Model** Right-click the TablePerConcrete folder, choose Add | New Item | ADO.NET Entity Data Model, name it TablePerConcreteModel.edmx, and click Add. This starts the Entity Data Model Wizard, which displays the Generate From Database or Empty Model prompt. Select Generate From Database and click Next. On the Choose Your Data Connection page, select TablePerConcrete.mdf as the connection and click Next. If you are informed that the connection uses a local data file that's not in the project, click Yes to add the data file to the project. On the Choose Your Database Objects page, open the *Tables* node, select Boats and Cars, and click Finish. In Solution Explorer, select the TablePerConcreteModel.edmx file and, in the Properties window, set the *Custom Tool Namespace* property to *TablePerConcrete*. At this point, the Entity Framework designer shows the *Boat* and *Car* entities with properties that match the columns in the tables. The problem is that you want to use inheritance for the columns that exist in both entities.

■ **Add the Vehicle Abstract Entity** From the toolbox, drag an entity to the designer surface and name it *Vehicle*. While *Vehicle* is selected, in the Properties window, set the *Abstract* property to *true*. From either the *Boat* or the *Car* entity, select *Make*, *Model*, *Vin*, and *Year*, copy these properties, and then right-click the *Vehicle* entity and click Paste. Click the *Boat* entity and, in the Properties window, choose the Base Type and select *Vehicle*. Click the *Car* entity and, in the Properties window, choose the Base Type and select *Vehicle*. Now that *Boat* and *Car* inherit from *Vehicle*, you can delete the *Id*, *Vin*, *Make*, *Model*, and *Year* properties from the Boat and the Car columns. Your conceptual model should look like Figure 6-20.

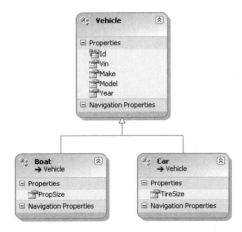

FIGURE 6-20 The completed TPC conceptual model is shown with the base *Vehicle* entity.

■ **Edit the EDMX file with an XML Editor** If you click the *Boat* or *Car* entity and look at the Mapping Details window, you'll notice that all of the table columns are shown, but only the *PropSize* and *TireSize* properties are mapped. If you try to map the *Id*, *Vin*, *Make*, *Model*, or *Year* properties, you'll find that the designer won't let you map to a property in the base class. At this point, you've done as much as you can with the Entity Framework designer, so save and close the EDMX file. Next, right-click the EDMX file, choose Open With, and select XML (Text) Editor. Figure 6-21 shows the collapsed structure of the EDMX file.

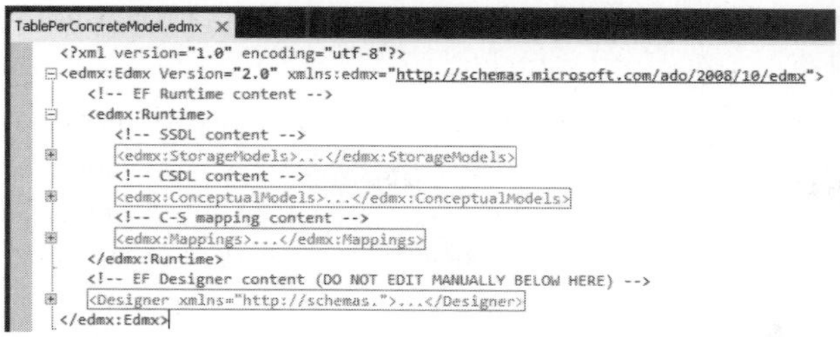

FIGURE 6-21 The collapsed view of the EDMX file shows the sections that comprise this file.

The Store Schema Definition Language (SSDL) content is good because this is the SSDL section that defines the database tables. The CSDL content needs only a small change because this is the CSDL section that represents the conceptual model you just modi-fied in the designer. The following change must be made because the current concep-tual model is defining a *Vehicles* collection on the *ObjectContext* class, but you need *Cars* and *Boats* collections instead.

Sample of Existing XML

```xml
<EntityContainer Name="TablePerConcreteEntities"
      annotation:LazyLoadingEnabled="true">
  <EntitySet Name="Vehicles" EntityType="TablePerConcreteModel.Vehicle" />
</EntityContainer>
```

Sample of New XML

```xml
<EntityContainer Name="TablePerConcreteEntities"
      annotation:LazyLoadingEnabled="true">
  <EntitySet Name="Cars" EntityType="TablePerConcreteModel.Car" />
  <EntitySet Name="Boats" EntityType="TablePerConcreteModel.Boat" />
</EntityContainer>
```

The CDSL-to-SSDL (C–S) mapping content needs to be changed. There are two issues with this section. First, it doesn't contain the mappings for all the columns of the Cars and Boats tables to the abstract class columns. Second, it shows the Cars and Boats columns nested inside Vehicles, so you would see only a *Vehicles* property on the *ObjectContext* class, but you want *Cars* and *Boats* to be exposed explicitly on the *ObjectContext* class. Modify this section to look like the following.

Sample of Updated C–S Mapping

```xml
<!-- C-S mapping content -->
<edmx:Mappings>
  <Mapping Space="C-S"
          xmlns="http://schemas.microsoft.com/ado/2008/09/mapping/cs">
    <EntityContainerMapping
        StorageEntityContainer="TablePerConcreteModelStoreContainer"
        CdmEntityContainer="TablePerConcreteEntities">

        <EntitySetMapping Name="Cars">
         <EntityTypeMapping
            TypeName="IsTypeOf(TablePerConcreteModel.Car)">
```

```
        <MappingFragment StoreEntitySet="Cars">
           <ScalarProperty Name="Id" ColumnName="Id" />
           <ScalarProperty Name="Vin" ColumnName="Vin" />
           <ScalarProperty Name="Make" ColumnName="Make" />
           <ScalarProperty Name="Model" ColumnName="Model" />
           <ScalarProperty Name="Year" ColumnName="Year" />
           <ScalarProperty Name="TireSize" ColumnName="TireSize" />
        </MappingFragment>
      </EntityTypeMapping>
    </EntitySetMapping>

    <EntitySetMapping Name="Boats">
       <EntityTypeMapping
          TypeName="IsTypeOf(TablePerConcreteModel.Boat)">
          <MappingFragment StoreEntitySet="Boats">
             <ScalarProperty Name="Id" ColumnName="Id" />
             <ScalarProperty Name="Vin" ColumnName="Vin" />
             <ScalarProperty Name="Make" ColumnName="Make" />
             <ScalarProperty Name="Model" ColumnName="Model" />
             <ScalarProperty Name="Year" ColumnName="Year" />
             <ScalarProperty Name="PropSize" ColumnName="PropSize" />
          </MappingFragment>
       </EntityTypeMapping>
    </EntitySetMapping>

  </EntityContainerMapping>
 </Mapping>
</edmx:Mappings>
```

- **Add Implementation Code to View Cars**   The following code sample retrieves a list of cars and binds the return value to a data grid.

Sample of Visual Basic Code

```vb
Private Sub TOCDisplayCarsToolStripMenuItem_Click( _
     ByVal sender As System.Object, ByVal e As System.EventArgs) _
     Handles TOCDisplayCarsToolStripMenuItem.Click
  Dim db = New TablePerConcrete.TablePerConcreteEntities()
  gv.DataSource = (From b In db.Cars
                    Select b).ToList()
End Sub
```

Sample of C# Code

```csharp
private void tPCDisplayCarsToolStripMenuItem_Click(
   object sender, EventArgs e)
{
   var db = new TablePerConcrete.TablePerConcreteEntities();
   gv.DataSource = (from c in db.Cars
                    select c).ToList();
}
```

- **Add Implementation Code to View Boats**   The following code sample retrieves a list of boats and binds the return value to a data grid.

Sample of Visual Basic Code

```vb
Private Sub TOCDisplayBoatsToolStripMenuItem_Click( _
        ByVal sender As System.Object, ByVal e As System.EventArgs) _
        Handles TOCDisplayBoatsToolStripMenuItem.Click
    Dim db = New TablePerConcrete.TablePerConcreteEntities()
    gv.DataSource = (From b In db.Boats
                        Select b).ToList()
End Sub
```

Sample of C# Code

```csharp
private void tPCDisplayBoatsToolStripMenuItem_Click(
    object sender, EventArgs e)
{
    var db = new TablePerConcrete.TablePerConcreteEntities();
    gv.DataSource = (from b in db.Boats
                        select b).ToList();
}
```

Updating the Database Schema

If you make changes to the conceptual model, you will want to update the database schema to match the model. To update the database, right-click the Entity Framework designer surface and choose Generate Database From Model. The Generate Database Wizard produces a SQL script file that you can edit and execute.

Be aware that the Generate Database Wizard does not create a "differencing" script that simply sends only the modifications to the database. In the created script, you'll see that the script drops the tables and re-creates them.

If you download the Entity Designer Database Generation Power Pack, you'll find that this tool gives you more control of the database generation scripts.

The EntityObject Generator

When reading the database to generate entities, you might want more control over the entities that are generated. For example, maybe you want to implement a custom interface on all your entity classes, or you want every entity class to contain a custom constructor. You can create and edit templates by using Text Template Transformation Toolkit (T4) Code Generation. T4 Code Generation is built into Microsoft Visual Studio .NET so that you can use T4 Code Generation immediately. When you create a T4 template, it has a TT extension, which stands for Text Template.

Microsoft is including various T4 templates in Visual Studio .NET as a way of rapidly developing templates that help get the job done quickly. The EntityObject Generator is a T4 template you can use to generate entity classes that enable you to customize the entities that are created by actually modifying the template that generates the Visual Basic or C# code.

To use the ADO.NET EntityObject Generator, create or open an EDMX file and right-click the Entity Framework designer surface. Click Add Code Generation Item, as shown in Figure 6-22. The next screen shows the ADO.NET EntityObject Generator. When you select it, notice that a file with a TT extension is created, which indicates that this uses T4 Code Generation. The next screen is a security warning stating that running the T4 template can cause harm to your computer. Clicking OK causes the T4 template to execute and create entities that can be customized.

FIGURE 6-22 The Add Code Generation Item menu option enables you to add a T4 template to achieve more control over the generated entities.

Here are some notes about using the EntityObject Generator template:

- The name of the template file determines the name of the code file it generates. For example, if the text template is named TextTemplate.tt, the generated file will be named TextTemplate.vb or TextTemplate.cs.

- The *Custom Tool* property of the targeted .edmx file must be empty.

- The SourceCsdlPath initialization below must be set to either the path of the targeted .edmx or .csdl file or to the path of the targeted .edmx or .csdl file relative to the template path.

After you add the ADO.NET EntityObject Generator, look at the Visual Basic or C# file that normally exists under the EDMX file: The file is essentially empty except for a note stating that default code generation is disabled. The *Code Generation Strategy* property on the EDMX file can be changed from *None* back to *Default* if you want to discontinue using the EntityObject Generation template.

Where are the generated entities? They are in the Visual Basic or C# file located under the T4 text template file. What value did this provide? You can have the template that creates the entities so you can modify the template that creates the entities, which means that you get a great amount of power and flexibility that you didn't have before. Prior to the implementation of the T4 template, you had to rely entirely on the template that was built into Visual Studio .NET. Now, you can modify the EntityObject Generator text template, and code generation will be produced based on the modified text template contents.

The Self-Tracking Entity Generator

Until now, when working with the Entity Framework, you created entities that are tracked by *ObjectContext*. If you change any of your entities, *ObjectContext* knows about the change, and it can persist the change when you call the *SaveChanges* method on *ObjectContext*. What happens if *ObjectContext* is disposed? What happens if you serialize your entities and send them across tiers, such as when you have an N-tier application? In these scenarios, the entity objects and *ObjectContext* become disconnected.

The ADO.NET Self-Tracking Entity Generator text template generates the object-layer code that consists of a custom typed *ObjectContext* and entity classes that contain self-tracking state logic so that the entities themselves keep track of their state instead of *ObjectContext* doing so. Probably the best usage of self-tracking entities is when working with N-tier applications.

You add the ADO.NET Self-Tracking Entity (STE) Generator text template to an EDMX file the same way as you add the EntityObject Generator: with an open EDMX file, you right-click the designer surface, choose Add Code Generation Item, and then select the ADO.NET Self-Tracking Entity Generator. When you add the ADO.NET Self-Tracking Entity Generator, you get two text template (.tt) files. The first file is the <model name>.tt, which generates the self-tracking entity types. The second file is the <model name>.Context.tt, which generates the typed *ObjectContext* class.

After you add the STE Generator, the Visual Basic or C# file under the EDMX file will be empty. The STE classes are created as separate class files under the <model name>.tt file. If you open one of the STE class files, you'll find much more code than the amount of code that was in the original entity class files, because the STE classes contain the code to track the state of the object.

The following extension methods can be called on self-tracking entities:

- ***StartTracking* Method**   This method instructs the change tracker on the entity to start recording any changes applied to scalar properties, collections, and references to other entities. Tracking starts automatically when an STE is deserialized into the client through the Windows Communication Foundation (WCF). Tracking is also turned on for newly created entities when a relationship is created between the new entity and an entity that is already tracking changes. Tracking is also turned on when any of the *MarkAs* methods are executed.

- ***StopTracking* Method**   The *StopTracking* method stops recording changes.

- ***MarkAs* Methods**   All the *MarkAs* methods turn tracking on. These extension methods facilitate changing the state of an entity explicitly to *Added*, *Modified*, *Deleted*, or *Unchanged*. The *MarkAs[State]* methods return the same entity to which they are applied, with the modified state.

- ***MarkAsAdded* Method**   This method changes the state of the entity to *Added*. When new self-tracking entities are created, they are in the *Added* state with change tracking not enabled.

- **MarkAsDeleted Method**   This method changes the state of the entity to *Deleted* and clears the navigation properties on the entity that is being marked for deletion, essentially severing the relationship(s). If the navigation property is a reference object, the property is set to *null*. If the navigation property represents a collection, its *Clear* method is called. When *MarkAsDeleted* is called on an object that is part of a collection, the object is removed from the collection. To mark each object in a collection as deleted, mark the objects in a copy of the collection. You can create a copy of a collection by calling the *ToArray()* or *ToList()* method on the collection.

- **MarkAsModified Method**   This method changes the state of the entity to *Modified*. Modifying the value of a property on an entity that has change tracking enabled also sets the state to *Modified*.

- **MarkAsUnchanged Method**   This method changes the state of the entity to *Unchanged*. *AcceptChanges* also clears the change-tracking information for an entity and moves its state to *Unchanged*.

- **AcceptChanges Method**   This method clears the change-tracking information for an entity and changes its state to *Unchanged*. If you want to reset the state of a relationship, call *AcceptChanges* on both entities that participate in the relationship.

Commonly, you will be using self-tracking entities to transfer objects across tiers, using WCF. In this scenario, there are some items for which you should specifically watch. Consider the following items:

- Be sure that your client project has a reference to the assembly containing the entity types. If you don't have a reference to the assembly with the entity types, and you add the WCF service reference to the client project, the client project will use the WCF proxy types that were created by adding the service reference and not the actual self-tracking entity types. This is a problem because the WCF proxy types that are created contain only the data and don't contain any methods that the STEs have, so you will not get the automated notification features that manage the tracking of the entities on the client. If you intentionally do not want to include the entity types, you must set change-tracking information manually on the client for the changes to be sent back to the service.

- Calls to the service operation should be stateless and should create a new *ObjectContext* instance. *ObjectContext* implements *IDisposable*, so consider creating *ObjectContext* in a *using* block.

- You might have to send a modified object graph from the client to the service but then intend to continue working with the same graph on the client. In this scenario, you have to iterate through the object graph manually and call the *AcceptChanges* method on each object to reset the change tracker. If objects in your object graph contain properties that are populated with database-generated values such as identity values, the Entity Framework replaces values of these properties with the database-generated values after the *SaveChanges* method is called. You might want to implement your service operation to return saved objects or a list of generated property values for the objects back to the client. The client could then replace the object instances or object property values with the objects or property values returned from the service operation.

- Merging object graphs from multiple service requests can introduce objects with duplicate key values in the resulting graph. The Entity Framework does not remove objects with duplicate keys. When you call the *ApplyChanges* method, an exception is thrown.

- When you change the relationship between objects by setting the foreign key property, the reference navigation property is set to *null* and not synchronized to the appropriate principal entity on the client. After the object graph is attached to the *ObjectContext* class and you call the *ApplyChanges* method, the foreign key properties and navigation properties will be synchronized.

- Not having a reference navigation property synchronized with the appropriate principal object is a problem if you have specified cascade delete on the foreign key relationship. If you delete the principal object, the delete is not propagated to the dependent objects. If you have cascade deletes specified, use the navigation properties to change relationships instead of setting the foreign key property.

- Self-tracking entities cannot perform lazy loading.

- Binary serialization and serialization to ASP.NET state management objects are not supported by self-tracking entities, but you can modify the text template to add binary serialization support as needed.

POCO Entities

POCO stands for Plain Old CLR Objects, which essentially means you can use the classes you create, and the Entity Framework enables you to use your classes without making any modifications to the classes themselves as long as the names of the entity types, complex types, and properties in the custom data classes match the names of the entity types, complex types, and properties in the conceptual model. This enables you to use domain objects with your data model.

When the Entity Framework was first released (.NET 3.5 SP1), many restrictions were imposed on entity classes. Entity classes had to be subclasses of *EntityObject* or had to implement a set of interfaces, referred to as IPOCO. These interfaces include *IEntityWithKey*, *IEntityWithChangeTracker*, and *IEntityWithRelationships*. The many restrictions became a problem when trying to create domain classes that were truly independent of persistence concerns.

Entity Framework 4.0 supports POCO types that don't need to inherit from a base class or implement any interfaces to get persistence. There is also no need for metadata or mapping attributes on type members, so you can create simple entity classes that are coded as shown. The following code sample defines POCO classes for working with Northwind Customers and Orders tables.

Sample of Visual Basic Code

```vb
Public Class Customer
    Public Property CustomerID As String
    Public Property CompanyName As String
    Public Property ContactName As String
    Public Property ContactTitle As String
    Public Property Address As String
    Public Property City As String
    Public Property Region As String
    Public Property PostalCode As String
    Public Property Country As String
    Public Property Phone As String
    Public Property Fax As String
    Public Property Orders() As List(Of Order)
End Class

Public Class Order
    Public Property OrderID As Integer
    Public Property CustomerID As String
    Public Property EmployeeID As Nullable(Of Integer)
    Public Property OrderDate As Nullable(Of DateTime)
    Public Property RequiredDate As Nullable(Of DateTime)
    Public Property ShippedDate As Nullable(Of DateTime)
    Public Property ShipVia As Nullable(Of Integer)
    Public Property Freight As Nullable(Of Decimal)
    Public Property ShipName As String
    Public Property ShipAddress As String
    Public Property ShipCity As String
    Public Property ShipRegion As String
    Public Property ShipPostalCode As String
    Public Property ShipCountry As String
    Public Property Customer As Customer
End Class
```

Sample of C# Code

```csharp
    public class Customer
    {
        public string CustomerID { get; set; }
        public string CompanyName { get; set; }
        public string ContactName { get; set; }
        public string ContactTitle { get; set; }
        public string Address { get; set; }
        public string City { get; set; }
        public string Region { get; set; }
        public string PostalCode { get; set; }
        public string Country { get; set; }
        public string Phone { get; set; }
        public string Fax { get; set; }
        public List<Order> Orders { get; set; }
    }

    public class Order
    {
        public int OrderID  { get; set; }
```

```
            public string CustomerID { get; set; }
            public int? EmployeeID { get; set; }
            public DateTime? OrderDate { get; set; }
            public DateTime? RequiredDate { get; set; }
            public DateTime? ShippedDate { get; set; }
            public int? ShipVia { get; set; }
            public decimal? Freight { get; set; }
            public string ShipName { get; set; }
            public string ShipAddress { get; set; }
            public string ShipCity { get; set; }
            public string ShipRegion { get; set; }
            public string ShipPostalCode { get; set; }
            public string ShipCountry { get; set; }
            public Customer Customer { get; set; }
        }
```

You can then use the Entity Framework to query and instantiate these types from the database, and you'll automatically get change tracking, updating, and all other services the .NET Framework offers. The compelling aspect of this scenario is that you might already have your POCO classes in your existing code, so adding an EDMX file and generating the conceptual model from the database can be quick and easy. Simply make sure that the names on your POCO classes match the names of your conceptual entities.

To get started with POCO classes, be aware of the following factors:

- An EDMX file that contains the conceptual model is still required.

- You must turn off the building of .NET classes on the EDMX file by clearing the *Custom Tool* property on the EDMX file. (In Solution Explorer, click the EDMX file to see this setting in the Properties window.)

- You cannot use non-POCO EDMX (an EDMX file with the *Custom Tool* property still set) files and POCO EDMX files in the same project because a non-POCO EDMX file generates an assembly-level attribute, *EdmSchemaAttribute*, that can't exist in an assembly that has a POCO EDMX file. The solution is to create a separate class library project for the POCO or non-POCO EDMX files. In the sample code for this chapter, many examples have already been presented with non-POCO EDMX files, so the POCO example code will be placed in a separate class library project, which is referenced by the sample code project.

- When using POCO, the Entity Framework will search the assembly that contains the POCO EDMX file to locate classes that have the same name as the conceptual model entities. This is done without considering the namespace the POCO classes are in. Therefore, if you have a *Customer* class that's in the *Data* namespace (*Data.Customer*) and another *Customer* class that's in the *ViewModel* namespace (*ViewModel.Customer*), the Entity Framework throws an exception, stating that there is an ambiguous match on the *Customer* class. Once again, the solution is to place your POCO classes and your POCO EDMX file in a separate assembly with a dedicated namespace and reference that assembly from your project.

Getting Started with POCO Entities

After you decide which project will be the home of your POCO EDMX file and POCO classes, you can right-click the project node, choose Add | New Item, and add the ADO.NET Entity Data Model file; in these examples, it's called NorthwindPoco.edmx. This starts the Entity Data Model Wizard, which prompts you to select either Generate From Database or Empty Model. In this example, Generate From Database is selected. The next page prompts for a database connection and a connection settings name. Select a connection to the Northwind database and name the NorthwindPocoEntities connection setting. On the next page, Choose Database Objects, select the Customers and Orders tables and set Model Name to NorthwindPocoModel. Click Finish. The conceptual model is displayed, as shown in Figure 6-23.

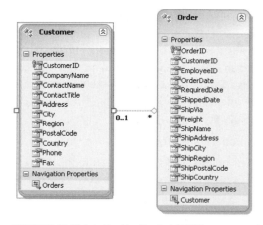

FIGURE 6-23 This is the Northwind POCO conceptual model.

Now that you've added the EDMX file, it's time to configure it. In Solution Explorer, click the EDMX file and then, in the Properties window, clear the *Custom Tool* property to turn off the automatic generation of .NET classes for your conceptual model.

Add the *Customer* and *Order* classes to this project. These classes contain the code from the previous code sample. Be sure they are in the same project as your EDMX file.

Create a custom *ObjectContext* class. The following code sample defines a simple *NorthwindPocoContext* class.

Sample of Visual Basic Code

```
Imports System.Data.Objects

Public Class NorthwindPocoContext
    Inherits ObjectContext

    Public Sub New()
        MyBase.New("name= NorthwindPocoEntities", "NorthwindPocoEntities")
        Me._customers = MyBase.CreateObjectSet(Of Customer)()
```

```
        Me._orders = MyBase.CreateObjectSet(Of Order)()
    End Sub

    Public ReadOnly Property Customers As ObjectSet(Of Customer)
        Get
            Return Me._customers
        End Get
    End Property
    Private _customers As ObjectSet(Of Customer)

    Public ReadOnly Property Orders As ObjectSet(Of Order)
        Get
            Return Me._orders
        End Get
    End Property
    Private _orders As ObjectSet(Of Order)
End Class
```

Sample of C# Code

```
public class NorthwindPocoContext : ObjectContext
{
    public NorthwindPocoContext()
        : base("name=NorthwindPocoEntities", "NorthwindPocoEntities")
    {
        _customers = CreateObjectSet<Customer>();
        _orders = CreateObjectSet<Order>();
    }

    public ObjectSet<Customer> Customers
    {
        get
        {
            return _customers;
        }
    }
    private ObjectSet<Customer> _customers;

    public ObjectSet<Order> Orders
    {
        get
        {
            return _orders;
        }
    }
    private ObjectSet<Order> _orders;
}
```

If you added the POCO EDMX file to a class library project, the connection information was stored in an App.Config file within that project. Copy your connection from the App.Config file in your library project to the App.Config file in your executable project.

This completes the setup of a simple POCO scenario. Use the following code to retrieve a list of customers and their orders.

Sample of Visual Basic Code

```vb
Private Sub pOCODisplayCustomersOrdersToolStripMenuItem_Click( _
        ByVal sender As System.Object, ByVal e As System.EventArgs) _
        Handles pOCODisplayCustomersOrdersToolStripMenuItem.Click
    Dim db = New PocoLibrary.NorthwindPocoContext()
    gv.DataSource = (From c In db.Customers
                        Join o In db.Orders
                            On c.CustomerID Equals o.CustomerID
                        Select New With
                                {
                                    c.CustomerID,
                                    c.CompanyName,
                                    o.OrderID,
                                    o.OrderDate
                                }).ToList()
End Sub
```

Sample of C# Code

```csharp
private void pOCODisplayCustomersOrdersToolStripMenuItem_Click(
    object sender, EventArgs e)
{
    var db = new PocoLibrary.NorthwindPocoContext();
    gv.DataSource = (from c in db.Customers
                        join o in db.Orders
                            on c.CustomerID equals o.CustomerID
                        select new
                                {
                                    c.CustomerID,
                                    c.CompanyName,
                                    o.OrderID,
                                    o.OrderDate
                                }).ToList();
}
```

Other POCO Considerations

It was relatively easy to set up and configure POCO support by using the Entity Framework. Now that you have a working POCO sample, you might consider the following:

- Instead of manually creating the POCO classes, you could set up a T4 text template to generate POCO classes for you.

- Your POCO class getters and setters can have any access modifier (*public*, *private*, and so on), but none of the mapped properties can be *overrideable* (C# *virtual*), and you can't specify that you require partial trust support.

- Any collection type that implements the generic *ICollection* interface can be used as a collection when creating your POCO types. If you don't initialize a collection when instantiating a POCO class that has a collection, a generic *List* will be created.

- In many object-oriented applications, it's common to have only one-way navigability between objects. For example, from the *Customer* object, you can navigate to the

Order objects the customer has, but you can't navigate to the *Customer* object from an *Order* object. This one-way navigability is supported as long as your conceptual model shows the same behavior.

- POCO does support lazy (just-in-time) data loading, but only through the creation of proxy types that implement lazy-loading behavior on top of your POCO classes.

Model-Defined Functions

You create a model-defined function within the conceptual model of your EDMX file to provide extra functionality within your LINQ to Entity queries.

An example of a model-defined function would be an instance when you want to retrieve the total price of a line from the Order Details table in the Northwind database. This table contains a row for each line in an order but provides only the quantity, unit price, and discount of each item, not the total price for the line. The same scenario was considered earlier in this chapter in the "Partial Classes and Methods" section. Although a solution was proposed, it used a client-side extension method and required the *AsEnumerable* extension method to call the method. In this example, a model-defined method is created, and the function executes server-side.

To add a model-defined function, open the EDMX file with the XML editor by right-clicking the EDMX file, which, in this case, is the NorthwindModel.edmx file, choose Open With | XML (Text) Editor, and click OK. The EDMX file is displayed as XML.

Scroll down until you locate the conceptual model, which is the *edmx:ConceptualModels* tag. Just inside that tag is a *Schema* tag. You add model-defined functions inside the *Schema* tag. Add the following XML inside the *Schema* tag.

Sample of XML

```xml
<Function Name="DetailTotal" ReturnType="Decimal">
    <Parameter Name="od" Type="NorthwindModel.Order_Detail" />
    <DefiningExpression>
        (od.UnitPrice * od.Quantity) * CAST(1 - od.Discount AS DECIMAL)
    </DefiningExpression>
</Function>
```

This function is called *DetailTotal*, and it returns a decimal value. The function accepts one parameter, *od*, that is of *NorthwindMode.Order_Detail* type. The *DefiningExpression* tag contains the function's expression. In this expression, the *SQL CAST* function, a model-defined function, will be run server-side. Close and save the EDMX file.

The model-defined function has been created in the conceptual model, but you still need a way to connect your code to it. To do so, add a function into your Visual Basic or C# code, which will have to be annotated with the *EdmFunctionAttribute* attribute. This function can be another instance method of the class itself, but best practice is to create a separate class and define this method as *shared* (C# *static*). In the following sample code, a *ModelDefinedFunctions* class has been created, and a *DetailTotal* method has been added.

Sample of Visual Basic Code

```vb
Public Class ModelDefinedFunctions
    <EdmFunction("NorthwindModel", "DetailTotal")>
    Public Shared Function DetailTotal(ByVal orderDetail As Order_Detail) As Decimal
        Throw New NotSupportedException( _
            "DetailTotal can only be used in a LINQ to Entities query")
    End Function
End Class
```

Sample of C# Code

```csharp
public class ModelDefinedFunctions
{
    [EdmFunction("NorthwindModel", "DetailTotal")]
    public static decimal DetailTotal(Order_Detail orderDetail)
    {
        throw new NotSupportedException(
            "DetailTotal can only be used in a LINQ to Entities query");
    }
}
```

The completed model-defined function can be used in a LINQ to Entities query, and the function will be executed server-side. The following code sample demonstrates the query for order details and uses the *DetailTotal* function.

Sample of Visual Basic Code

```vb
Private Sub ModelDefinedFunctionsToolStripMenuItem_Click( _
        ByVal sender As System.Object, ByVal e As System.EventArgs) _
        Handles ModelDefinedFunctionsToolStripMenuItem.Click
    Dim db As New NorthwindEntities()
    gv.DataSource = (From od In db.Order_Details
    Where od.Order.CustomerID = "ALFKI"
            Select New With
                {
                    od.OrderID,
                    od.ProductID,
                    od.Quantity,
                    od.Discount,
                    od.UnitPrice,
                    .DetailTotal = ModelDefinedFunctions.DetailTotal(od)
                }).ToList()
End Sub
```

Sample of C# Code

```csharp
private void modelDefinedFunctionsToolStripMenuItem_Click(
    object sender, EventArgs e)
{
    var db = new NorthwindEntities();
    gv.DataSource = (from od in db.Order_Details
                    where od.Order.CustomerID == "ALFKI"
                    select new
                    {
                        od.OrderID,
                        od.ProductID,
```

```
        od.Quantity,
        od.Discount,
        od.UnitPrice,
        DetailTotal = ModelDefinedFunctions.DetailTotal(od)
    }).ToList();
}
```

In some scenarios, model-defined functions can increase performance. For example, in the previous code sample, the quantity, unit price, and discount were displayed. If you need to display only the value returned by the *DetailTotal* function, the quantity, unit price, and discount don't need to be sent to your client application. When this scenario was covered earlier in the chapter, in the "Partial Classes and Methods" section, the quantity, unit price, and discount were needed because the extension method was being executed in your client application. In that example, you needed those columns, even if they were not displayed.

PRACTICE   **Design a Database to Track Music**

In this practice, you design a database for tracking your music by album and song name. You use the Code First model to design the conceptual model and then generate the database from the conceptual model.

This practice generates the data-access layer by using the Entity Framework designer, but the result of this practice will be used as the starting point for the next practice.

If you encounter a problem completing an exercise, the completed projects can be installed from the Code folder on the companion CD.

EXERCISE   Creating the Project and the Data-Access Layer

In this exercise, you create a Windows Presentation Foundation (WPF) application project and use the ADO.NET Entity Data Model to configure the conceptual model and generate the database.

1. In Visual Studio .NET 2010, choose File | New | Project.

2. Select your desired programming language and then select the WPF Application template. For the project name, enter **MusicTracker**. Be sure to select a desired location for this project. For the solution name, enter **MusicTrackerSolution**. Be sure that Create Directory For Solution is selected and then click OK. After Visual Studio .NET finishes creating the project, the home page, MainWindow.xaml, is displayed.

> **NOTE**   **CHECK YOUR VISUAL STUDIO .NET SETTINGS**
>
> If you don't see a prompt for the location, it's because your Visual Studio .NET settings are set up to enable you to abort the project and automatically remove all files from your hard drive. To select a location, simply choose File | Save All after the project has been created. To change this setting, choose Tools | Options | Projects and Solutions | Save New Projects When Created. When this option is selected, you are prompted for a location when you create the project.

3   You won't add anything to the MainWindow.xaml file in this practice, so you can close the file.

4. Add a service-based database to the project by right-clicking the *Project* node in Solution Explorer and choose Add | New Item | Data | Service-Based Database. Name the database **MusicDatabase.mdf** and click Add. This starts the Data Source Configuration Wizard.

5. On the Data Source Configuration page, select Entity Data Model and click Next. This starts the Entity Data Model Wizard.

6. The next prompt is to choose either Generate From Database or Empty Model.

    Be careful here; although you will be working with an empty model, selecting Generate From Database will attach the database connection string to the EDMX file.

7. Select Generate From Database and click Next.

8. The next page prompts for a connection, and the MusicDatabase.mdf file is already selected. Click Next.

9. On the Choose Your Database Objects page, click Finish because the database is currently empty.

    The MusicDatabase.mdf and Model1.edmx files are now in your project, and the Entity Data Model designer is open.

10. In Solution Explorer, change to the name of the new Model1.edmx file to **MusicModel.edmx**.

11. Drag an entity from the toolbox and drop it onto the designer surface. Change the name to **Album**.

12. Drag another entity from the toolbox and drop it onto the designer surface. Change the name to **Song**.

13. On these entities, right-click each entity, choose Add | Scalar Property, and name the new property **Name**.

14. In the toolbox, select Association, click the *Album* entity, and then click the *Song* entity. You should see the new association. In the Properties window, change *End1 Multiplicity* to 0..1 and *End2 Multiplicity* to an asterisk.

    An album can have many songs, and a song can be on one album, many albums, or no album. Your conceptual model should look Figure 6-24.

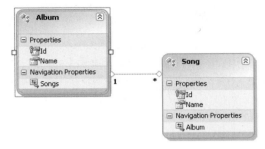

FIGURE 6-24 The MusicTracker conceptual model.

15. You're ready to generate the database from your conceptual model. Right-click an empty location on the Entity Data Model designer surface and click Generate Database From Model.

16. On the next page, the Generate Database Wizard shows the SQL script that creates the database. Click Finish. The SQL script is open for editing and execution.

17. Because you are working with an automatically mounted database, you don't need the *USE* statement in the script, so locate and delete the following statement:

```
USE [MusicDatabase];
```

18. Before you execute the script, devise a connection string that references the database in your project.

In the App.Config file, you'll see a reference to |DataDirectory| before MusicDatabase. mdf, which indicates that at run time, ADO.NET looks for the database in the folder that contains your executable file. If this were a web application, ADO.NET would look in the Data directory for the database. This location is good at run time, but when the database is generated, you must reference the MusicDatabase physical location in the project.

19. To get a proper connection string for database generation, double-click the MusicDatabase.mdf file in Solution Explorer. This opens the database in Server Explorer.

20. In Server Explorer, select MusicDatabase.mdf and, in the Properties window, copy the contents of the connection string to the clipboard. You can copy the connection string even though the property is read-only. You're now ready to execute the SQL script.

21. Right-click an empty part of the SQL Script file and then click Execute SQL. When the Connect To Database screen is displayed, click Options, click the Additional Connection Parameters tab, paste the connection string into this window, and click Connect. This executes your SQL script, and you should see a message stating that the execution succeeded. Figure 6-25 shows the created MusicDatabase with two tables.

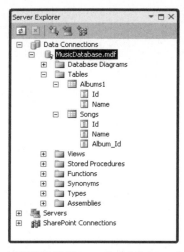

FIGURE 6-25 The created database shows the new tables and includes the join tables.

22. Build your solution; it should be successful.

You now have a database with an Entity Data Model that can query and modify data.

Lesson Summary

This lesson provided detailed information about the Entity Framework, covering basic architecture, data modeling, and connectivity with *ObjectContext*.

- The Object Services layer converts LINQ to Entities and some ESQL queries to a pure Entity SQL command tree.
- EntityClient provider handles the mapping from the conceptual model to the storage model to create an ADO.NET command tree.
- ADO.NET is the underlying technology to communicate to the database.
- You can implement a Code First model by which to create the conceptual model and then generate the database from the conceptual mode.
- You can implement a Database First model by which to generate the conceptual model from the existing database.
- *ObjectContext* is the central object to use for executing queries and updates to the database.
- Lazy loading of data is also called just-in-time loading, when the data doesn't load until you reference it.
- Eager loading is using the *Include* extension method to load child table data when the parent table is being loaded.
- Explicit loading of data is using the *Load* extension method explicitly to load child table data before you use it.

- The Entity Framework supports mapping to complex types and stored procedures.

- The generated entity classes are partial classes and include partial methods.

- The Entity Framework supports Table per Class Hierarchy (TPH) and Table per Type (TPT) inheritance.

- The Entity Framework supports Table per Concrete Class (TPC) inheritance, but the Entity Framework designer does not support it.

- You can modify the conceptual model and send the changes back to the database.

- You can use the Text Template Transformation Toolkit (T4) to generate your entity classes, and Visual Studio .NET provides the T4 EntityObject Generator template by which you can control the entity object generation. Visual Studio .NET also provides the T4 SelfTracking Entity Generator template by which you can create and control the self-tracking entity classes.

- The Entity Framework provides support for the creation of Plain Old CLR Objects (POCO) that can be tracked.

- The Entity Framework enables you to create model-defined functions by which you can create server-side functions that can be called from within a LINQ query.

Lesson Review

You can use the following questions to test your knowledge of the information in Lesson 1, "What Is the ADO.NET Entity Framework?" The questions are also available on the companion CD if you prefer to review them in electronic form.

> **NOTE ANSWERS**
>
> Answers to these questions and explanations of why each answer choice is correct or incorrect are located in the "Answers" section at the end of the book.

1. You are creating a new application that will use a database that already exists. Which model will you use to create your Entity Data Model?

   A. The Code First model

   B. The Database First model

2. You have a created *Customer* entity but it comprises properties that are spread across two tables in the database. What should you do?

   A. Use LINQ to SQL classes.

   B. Use LINQ to XML.

   C. Use the Entity Framework.

3. You have created entity classes from your conceptual model, but you can't add a custom method to one of the classes. Which would be the best approach to adding this method?

A. Create a T4 text template and the method.

B. Add an EntityObject Generator to your project and add the new modification to the text template.

C. Add a new partial class to your project and add the method to this class.

D. Open the created entity class and add the method.

4. In your application, you have existing classes that represent the conceptual model. How can the Entity Framework be configured to use these classes?

   A. You can use these classes by making the classes inherit from *ObjectContext*.

   B. You can use these classes, but you must make the EDMX-generated entity classes inherit from each of your existing classes.

   C. You can implement a POCO EDMX file.

5. You have created a conceptual model manually by using the Entity Framework designer. Can you use the Entity Framework designer to generate a new database from the completed conceptual model?

   A. Yes

   B. No

6. In your application, you want to define a function to be called in your LINQ to Entities query and executed server-side, but you don't have permission to create objects in the database server. How can you solve this problem?

   A. Create a model-defined function.

   B. Extend the entity class and add a method to it.

   C. Create a stored procedure.

7. In the Entity Framework, which is the primary object you use to query and modify data?

   A. *ObjectContext*

   B. *DataContext*

   C. *ObjectStateEntry*

   D. *EntityObject*

8. Adding a call to the *Include* extension method in a query for data is an example of what kind of loading strategy?

   A. Lazy loading

   B. Eager loading

   C. Explicit loading

Lesson 2: Querying and Updating with the Entity Framework

In Lesson 1, you learned how the Entity Framework enables you to create a conceptual model of your data and provides the mapping between the entity classes and the storage. Now you will use the Entity Framework to query for data.

> **After this lesson, you will be able to:**
> - Execute LINQ to Entity queries.
> - Execute Entity SQL queries.
> - Execute queries using the database's query language.
> - Create a LINQ query to perform an inner join on two element sequences.
>
> **Estimated lesson time: 30 minutes**

Using LINQ to Entities to Query Your Database

In Chapter 3, "Introducing LINQ," you learned about LINQ and query extension methods. Everything you learned in Chapter 3 is applicable when working with LINQ to Entities.

Query Execution

When you execute a LINQ query, LINQ to Entities converts LINQ queries to command-tree queries. The command-tree query is executed against *ObjectContext*, and the returned objects can be used by both the Entity Framework and LINQ.

The procedure the Entity Framework follows when executing a LINQ query is as follows.

1. *ObjectContext* creates an *ObjectQuery* instance. The *ObjectQuery* class is a generic class that represents a query that returns zero to many typed objects. The *ObjectQuery* instance belongs to the *ObjectContext* class and gets connection information from *ObjectContext*. The *ObjectQuery* class implements the *IQueryable* interface, which defines many methods that can be used to create an object that queried and enumerated to get the query result. This *IQueryable* interface is a generic interface that inherits from the generic *IEnumerable* interface.

2. Using the *ObjectQuery* instance, *ObjectContext* composes a LINQ to Entities query in Visual Basic or C#. The following code sample demonstrates the use of the *ObjectQuery* object and the *IQueryable* interface.

Sample of Visual Basic Code

```
Private Sub ObjectQueryToolStripMenuItem_Click( _
    ByVal sender As System.Object, ByVal e As System.EventArgs) _
    Handles ObjectQueryToolStripMenuItem.Click
  Dim db As New NorthwindEntities()
```

```
    Dim customers As ObjectQuery(Of Customer) = db.Customers
    Dim result As IQueryable(Of Customer) =
        From c In customers
        Where c.CustomerID.StartsWith("S")
        Select c
    gv.DataSource = result.ToList()
End Sub
```

Sample of C# Code
```
private void objectQueryToolStripMenuItem_Click(
    object sender, EventArgs e)
{
    var db = new NorthwindEntities();
    ObjectQuery<Customer> customers = db.Customers;
    IQueryable<Customer> result = from c in customers
                                  where c.CustomerID.StartsWith("S")
                                  select c;
    gv.DataSource = result.ToList();
}
```

3. The LINQ query operators and expressions are converted to command-tree represen-
   tations that can be executed against the Entity Framework. LINQ to Entities queries
   contain query operators and expressions; example query operators are *select* and
   where. Example expressions are *x >= 0* and *c.CustomerName.StartsWith("S")*. In LINQ,
   operators are defined as methods on a class, whereas expressions can contain anything
   allowed by the types defined in the *System.Linq.Expressions* namespace and anything
   that can be represented by a lambda function. The Entity Framework allows a subset of
   LINQ, basically allowing only operations that are run on the database and supported
   by *ObjectQuery*. Be aware that LINQ defines a number of query operators that are not
   supported by LINQ to Entities. One example of an unsupported LINQ query operator is
   the *Where* query extension method, which has an overload that passes in two parameters: the generic item and the corresponding index in the sequence. However, only
   the single parameter *Where* query extension method typically used is supported. If you
   attempt to use an unsupported operator, an exception will be thrown.

4. The command-tree representation of the query is executed against the data source.
   Like LINQ, LINQ to Entities queries provide deferred execution.

5. Return the query results to the client as objects. This is known as *materialization*.
   Materialization never returns data rows to the client; instead, CLR objects are always
   instantiated (materialized) and returned.

Difference in Query Execution

Just like LINQ, the Entity Framework supports both LINQ to Entities (also known as query expression syntax) queries and extension method (also known as method-based query syntax)
queries. Because LINQ to Entities is a subset of LINQ, it's appropriate to explore things that
are unsupported in LINQ to Entities. The following are areas of unsupported items:

- **Projections** The transforming of returned data to a desired result is known as a projection. Projections are supported by the *Select* and *SelectMany* query extension methods. Most overloads of *Select* and *SelectMany* are supported in LINQ to Entities, with the exception of those that accept a positional index argument.

- **Filters** The *Where* query extension method provides the ability to filter. Most overloads of *Where* are supported in LINQ to Entities except those that accept a positional index argument. The following sample code attempts to return every other customer by using the index number of the current customer but throws a *NotSupportedException* because the *Where* overload that has the positional index argument is not supported.

Sample of Visual Basic Code
```
Private Sub UnsupportedToolStripMenuItem1_Click( _
    ByVal sender As System.Object, ByVal e As System.EventArgs) _
    Handles UnsupportedToolStripMenuItem1.Click
  Dim db As New NorthwindEntities()
  Dim result = db.Customers.Where(Function(c, i) i Mod 2 = 0)
  gv.DataSource = result.ToList()
End Sub
```

Sample of C# Code
```
private void unsupportedToolStripMenuItem_Click(
    object sender, EventArgs e)
{
    var db = new NorthwindEntities();
    var result = db.Customers.Where((c, i) => i % 2 == 0);
    gv.DataSource = result.ToList();
}
```

- **Sorting** The query extension methods that support sorting are *OrderBy*, *OrderByDescending*, *ThenBy*, *ThenByDescending*, and *Reverse*. Most overloads of these extension methods are supported except overloads that accept an *IComparer* because this can't be translated to the data source.

- **Joining** The query extension methods that support joining are *Join* and *GroupJoin*. Most overloads of *Join* and *GroupJoin* are supported except overloads that accept an *IEqualityComparer* because the *IEqualityComparer* can't be translated to the data source.

- **Paging** A paging operation returns a single, specific element from a sequence. The supported methods are *First*, *FirstOrDefault*, *Skip*, and *Take*. The unsupported methods are *ElementAt*, *ElementAtOrDefault*, *Last*, *LastOrDefault*, *Single*, *SingleOrDefault*, *SkipWhile*, and *TakeWhile*.

- **Grouping** The grouping method is *GroupBy*. Most overloads of the grouping methods are supported, with the exception of those that use an *IEqualityComparer* because the comparer cannot be translated to the data source.

If you attempt to use any of the unsupported methods, a *NotSupportedException* will be thrown. In many cases, you might be able to execute the desired operation client-side by adding *AsEnumerable* to the beginning of the query, but using *AsEnumerable* could cause performance problems if executing a method client-side means copying much more data to the client or making many more server calls. The following code sample uses the *AsEnumerable* method to work around the exception that was thrown in the previous example.

Sample of Visual Basic Code

```
Private Sub SupportedToolStripMenuItem1_Click( _
      ByVal sender As System.Object, ByVal e As System.EventArgs) _
      Handles SupportedToolStripMenuItem1.Click
   Dim db As New NorthwindEntities()
   Dim result = db.Customers.AsEnumerable() _
                .Where(Function(c, i) i Mod 2 = 0)
   gv.DataSource = result.ToList()
End Sub
```

Sample of C# Code

```
private void supportedToolStripMenuItem_Click(
   object sender, EventArgs e)
{
   var db = new NorthwindEntities();
   var result = db.Customers.AsEnumerable()
                .Where((c, i) => i % 2 == 0);
   gv.DataSource = result.ToList();
}
```

Although this code sample fixes the problem, you'll find that the SQL statement, as follows, simply queries for all customers. That means SQL Server sent twice as many rows to the client.

SQL Query

```
SELECT
[Extent1].[CustomerID] AS [CustomerID],
[Extent1].[CompanyName] AS [CompanyName],
[Extent1].[ContactName] AS [ContactName],
[Extent1].[ContactTitle] AS [ContactTitle],
[Extent1].[Address] AS [Address],
[Extent1].[City] AS [City],
[Extent1].[Region] AS [Region],
[Extent1].[PostalCode] AS [PostalCode],
[Extent1].[Country] AS [Country],
[Extent1].[Phone] AS [Phone],
[Extent1].[Fax] AS [Fax]
FROM [dbo].[Customers] AS [Extent1]
```

This problem could be solved by implementing a stored procedure, as shown in the following SQL code sample.

SQL Stored Procedure

```
CREATE PROC EveryOtherCustomer
AS
WITH RowData as
(
        SELECT ROW_NUMBER() OVER( ORDER BY CustomerID) as Row, *
```

```
      FROM Customers
)
SELECT CustomerID ,CompanyName ,ContactName
      ,ContactTitle ,Address ,City
      ,Region ,PostalCode ,Country
      ,Phone ,Fax
  FROM RowData
  WHERE Row % 2 = 0
```

This stored procedure uses the *WITH* statement to create a common table expression that feeds into the next statement. The next statement returns the Customer rows but filters out every other row. After adding the stored procedure to the EDMX file, you can call the stored procedure, as shown in the following code sample.

Sample of Visual Basic Code

```
Private Sub StoredProcedureToolStripMenuItem_Click( _
      ByVal sender As System.Object, ByVal e As System.EventArgs) _
      Handles StoredProcedureToolStripMenuItem.Click
   Dim db As New NorthwindEntities()
   gv.DataSource = db.EveryOtherCustomer().ToList()
End Sub
```

Sample of C# Code

```
private void storedProcedureToolStripMenuItem_Click(
   object sender, EventArgs e)
{
   var db = new NorthwindEntities();
   gv.DataSource = db.EveryOtherCustomer().ToList();
}
```

SQL Statement

```
exec [dbo].[EveryOtherCustomer]
```

This was an example of how you might run into incompatibilities and what to do to solve this problem. In addition to some of the more common differences described in this section, there are many other incompatibilities and differences between LINQ and LINQ to Entities due to the difference in behavior between the CLR and the data source. For more information, be sure to investigate the MSDN documentation.

Introducing Entity SQL

The Entity Framework enables developers to write object-based queries that target the Entity Data Model without the need to know the logical schema of the database, which could have varying degrees of normalization, as well as different schema styles and different naming conventions for tables and columns, based on who creates the schema. The Entity Data Model insulates developers from the low-level details of the logical model and frees them to focus on the problem at hand.

SQL is the time-tested query language for data access, but the Entity Data Model introduces an enhanced data model that builds on entities, rich types, and relationships. Entity

SQL (ESQL) provides a query language that enables programmers to write queries in terms of Entity Data Model abstractions. ESQL was designed to address this need by supporting types in a clean and expressive way. If you already know SQL, working with ESQL will feel natural. One of the best uses of ESQL is to create complex dynamic queries.

ESQL is not SQL, but you can use ESQL to pass standard SQL queries to the database. It provides access to data as *EntitySet* collections of a given entity type. Using the Northwind database and EDMX file that was created in Lesson 1, NorthwindEntities.Customers is a valid query that returns the collection of all *Customers*, whereas {1,2,3} is an inline collection of integers. Tables in the database are just collections of a given entity type. Collections can be created, nested, and projected just like any other Entity Data Model type.

When you're working with ESQL, you are working with the EntityClient data provider, as shown in Figure 6-26. Because you are at an abstract level, you can expect ESQL to be provider-independent, so queries written in ESQL can be reused across different database products.

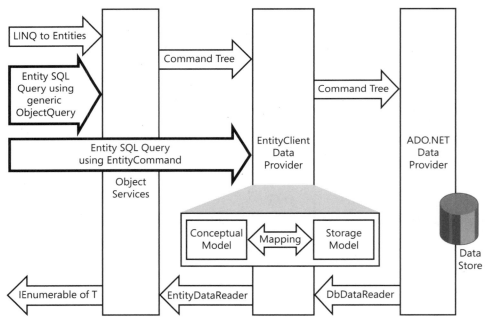

FIGURE 6-26 ESQL can target Object Services and the EntityClient data provider.

When using ESQL, there are two ways of executing queries: You can use *EntityCommand* or the generic *ObjectQuery* class. Both of these are covered in this lesson, but you must first know how to open an entity connection.

Opening an ESQL Connection

To use ESQL, you need an *EntityConnection* object. *EntityConnection* is in the *System.Data. EntityClient* namespace. The connection needs a connection string as well. If the connection is created dynamically or from the beginning, you can use *EntityConnectionStringBuilder* to create the connection string. The connection string must include the metadata that references the .csdl, .ssdl, and .msl files, a subject that was covered in the Lesson 1 section, "Provider and Connection String Information," of this chapter.

If you already have a connection string stored in your application's config file, you can set the connection string easily by using "name=NorthwindEntities" as the connection string, where NorthwindEntities is the name of the connection in the config file. The following code sample creates a connection that can be used with ESQL.

Sample of Visual Basic Code

```
Private Sub EntitySQLConnectionToolStripMenuItem_Click( _
    ByVal sender As System.Object, ByVal e As System.EventArgs) _
    Handles EntitySQLConnectionToolStripMenuItem.Click
  Using conn As New EntityConnection("name=NorthwindEntities")
    conn.Open()
    MessageBox.Show("Connected!")
  End Using
End Sub
```

Sample of C# Code

```
private void entitySQLConnectionToolStripMenuItem_Click(
    object sender, EventArgs e)
{
    using (EntityConnection conn =
        new EntityConnection("name=NorthwindEntities"))
    {
        conn.Open();
        MessageBox.Show("Connected!");
    }
}
```

The *EntityCommand* Object

The *EntityCommand* class inherits from the *DbCommand* class that you learned about in Chapter 2, "ADO.NET Connected Classes," so coding with an *EntityCommand* object looks like traditional ADO.NET programming. Queries written using the *EntityCommand* object are targeted toward the EntityClient data provider, as shown in Figure 6-26. When you use *EntityCommand*, there is no entity materialization. This means that querying for all customers will not return *Customer* objects; you simply get a *DbDataReader* object, which gives you a stream of row data. The following code sample demonstrates the use of the *EntityCommand* class.

Sample of Visual Basic Code

```
Private Sub EntityCommandToolStripMenuItem_Click( _
    ByVal sender As System.Object, ByVal e As System.EventArgs) _
```

```vbnet
        Handles EntityCommandToolStripMenuItem.Click
    Using conn As New EntityConnection("name = NorthwindEntities")
        conn.Open()
        Dim myQuery = "SELECT c.CustomerID FROM NorthwindEntities.Customers AS c"
        Using cmd As New EntityCommand(myQuery, conn)
            Dim customerIds = New List(Of String)()
            Dim reader = cmd.ExecuteReader(CommandBehavior.SequentialAccess)
            While reader.Read()
                customerIds.Add(reader.GetString(0))
            End While
            gv.DataSource = (From id In customerIds
                             Select New With {.ID = id}).ToList()
        End Using
    End Using
End Sub
```

Sample of C# Code

```csharp
private void entityCommandToolStripMenuItem_Click(object sender, EventArgs e)
{
    using (EntityConnection conn = new EntityConnection("name = NorthwindEntities"))
    {
        conn.Open();
        string myQuery = "SELECT c.CustomerID FROM NorthwindEntities.Customers AS c";
        using (EntityCommand cmd =
            new EntityCommand(myQuery, conn ))
        {
            var customerIds = new List<string>();
            var reader = cmd.ExecuteReader(CommandBehavior.SequentialAccess);
            while (reader.Read())
            {
                customerIds.Add((string)reader[0]);
            }
            gv.DataSource = (from id in customerIds
                             select new {ID=id}).ToList();
        }
    }
}
```

This example contains an ESQL query that retrieves a list of customer IDs by using the *NorthwindEntities* container that was defined in the Entity Data Model. You can use dot notation to access the Customers *EntitySet* collection. When you create an alias, you must use the *AS* keyword. In the example, the reader populates a generic list of string objects called *customerIds*. To display *customerIds* in the data grid, a LINQ query creates a generic list of anonymous types that have an *ID* property. In ESQL, you can't use the asterisk (*) to indicate all columns. When *ExecuteReader* is called to retrieve a stream of rows, you must include *CommandBehavior.SequentialAccess*.

The *ObjectQuery* Class

The generic *ObjectQuery* class targets the object services layer, as shown in Figure 6-26, which enables you to write queries that use your conceptual model entities. Unlike the *EntityCommand* class, you can use the *ObjectQuery* class to retrieve materialized entities, so you can query for a list of customers and get a collection of *Customer* objects. Using the query from the previous code sample, you can run the same query as with *ObjectQuery*, as follows.

Sample of Visual Basic Code

```
Private Sub ObjectQueryToolStripMenuItem1_Click( _
      ByVal sender As System.Object, ByVal e As System.EventArgs) _
      Handles ObjectQueryToolStripMenuItem1.Click
  Using ctx = New ObjectContext("name=NorthwindEntities")
      ctx.Connection.Open()
      Dim myQuery = "SELECT c.CustomerID FROM NorthwindEntities.Customers AS c"
      Dim customerIds = New ObjectQuery(Of DbDataRecord)(myQuery, ctx).ToList()
      gv.DataSource = (From id In customerIds
                       Select New With {.ID = id.GetString(0)}).ToList()
  End Using
End Sub
```

Sample of C# Code

```
private void objectQueryToolStripMenuItem1_Click(object sender, EventArgs e)
{
    using (ObjectContext ctx = new ObjectContext("name=NorthwindEntities"))
    {
        ctx.Connection.Open();
        string myQuery = "SELECT c.CustomerID FROM NorthwindEntities.Customers AS c";
        var customerIds = new ObjectQuery<DbDataRecord>(myQuery, ctx).ToList();
        gv.DataSource = (from id in customerIds
                         select new { ID = id.GetString(0) }).ToList();
    }
}
```

This code sample shows that *ObjectQuery* is a bit more simplistic than *EntityCommand*. The query string is exactly the same as the previous code sample, but this sample is easier to execute.

The *ROW* Function

The Entity Data Model defines three kinds of types: primitive types such as *Int32* and *String*; nominal types that are defined in the schema, such as *Entity* and *Relationship*; and transient types that are anonymous types, such as *collection*, *row*, and *ref*.

In your query, you can create a *row* instance by using the *ROW* function. This enables you to construct rows without accessing a table. The following code sample demonstrates the creation of a *row* instance.

Sample of Visual Basic Code

```
Private Sub RowToolStripMenuItem_Click( _
      ByVal sender As System.Object, ByVal e As System.EventArgs) _
      Handles RowToolStripMenuItem.Click
  Using ctx = New ObjectContext("name=NorthwindEntities")
      ctx.Connection.Open()
      Dim myQuery = "ROW(1 AS MyIndex, 'ALFKI' AS MyId)"
      Dim myStuff = New ObjectQuery(Of DbDataRecord)(myQuery, ctx).ToList()
```

```
                gv.DataSource = (From i In myStuff
                            Select New With
                                    {
                                        .Index = i.GetInt32(0),
                                        .Id = i.GetString(1)
                                    }).ToList()
        End Using
    End Sub
```

Sample of C# Code

```
private void rowToolStripMenuItem_Click(object sender, EventArgs e)
{
    using (ObjectContext ctx = new ObjectContext("name=NorthwindEntities"))
    {
      ctx.Connection.Open();
      string myQuery = "ROW(1 AS MyIndex, 'ALFKI' AS MyId)";
      var myStuff = new ObjectQuery<DbDataRecord>(myQuery, ctx).ToList();
      gv.DataSource = (from item in myStuff
                        select new
                                {
                                    Index = item.GetInt32(0),
                                    Id = item.GetString(1)
                                }).ToList();
    }

}
```

The *MULTISET* Collection

Collections can be created by using the *MULTISET* keyword. For example, *MULTISET(1,2,3,4,5)*
creates a collection of five integers. You can also create collections simply by using curly
braces {}. For example, *{1,2,3,4,5}* is the same as *MULTISET(1,2,3,4,5)*. You can use a collection
in your query, as shown in the following code sample.

Sample of Visual Basic Code

```
Private Sub MultiSetToolStripMenuItem_Click( _
        ByVal sender As System.Object, ByVal e As System.EventArgs) _
        Handles MultiSetToolStripMenuItem.Click
    Using ctx = New ObjectContext("name=NorthwindEntities")
        ctx.Connection.Open()
        Dim myQuery = "SELECT i FROM {1,2,3,4,5} AS i"
        Dim myStuff = New ObjectQuery(Of DbDataRecord)(myQuery, ctx).ToList()
        gv.DataSource = (From i In myStuff
                            Select New With
                                    {
                                        .Index = i.GetInt32(0)
                                    }).ToList()
        End Using
    End Sub
```

Sample of C# Code

```
private void multiSetToolStripMenuItem_Click(object sender, EventArgs e)
{
```

```
using (ObjectContext ctx = new ObjectContext("name=NorthwindEntities"))
{
    ctx.Connection.Open();
    string myQuery = "SELECT i FROM {1,2,3,4,5} AS i";
    var myStuff = new ObjectQuery<DbDataRecord>(myQuery, ctx).ToList();
    gv.DataSource = (from item in myStuff
                     select new
                     {
                         Index = item.GetInt32(0),
                     }).ToList();
}
}
```

Working with the *REF*, *CREATEREF*, and *DEREF* Functions

The *REF* function returns an entity reference to a persisted entity. An entity reference is a form of lightweight entity in which you don't need to consume resources to create and maintain the full entity state until it is really necessary. An entity reference consists of the entity key and an entity set name. Different entity sets can be based on the same entity type, so a particular entity key can appear in multiple entity sets, but an entity reference is always unique. If the input expression represents a persisted entity, a reference to this entity is returned. If the input expression is not a persisted entity, a null reference is returned.

When you are ready to use the referenced entity, you can dereference it by using the *DEREF* function explicitly, or you can dereference it implicitly by just invoking a property of the entity. The following code sample uses *REF* to obtain a reference to a customer and then implicitly dereferences it back to a customer by using the dot (.) to access *CompanyName*.

Sample of Visual Basic Code

```
Private Sub RefDerefToolStripMenuItem_Click( _
    ByVal sender As System.Object, ByVal e As System.EventArgs) _
    Handles RefDerefToolStripMenuItem.Click
    Using ctx = New ObjectContext("name=NorthwindEntities")
        ctx.Connection.Open()
        Dim myQuery = _
            "SELECT REF(c).CompanyName FROM NorthwindEntities.Customers as c"
        Dim myStuff = New ObjectQuery(Of DbDataRecord)(myQuery, ctx).ToList()
        gv.DataSource = (From i In myStuff
                         Select New With
                             {
                                 .Name = i.GetString(0)
                             }).ToList()
    End Using
End Sub
```

Sample of C# Code

```
private void refCreateRefDerefToolStripMenuItem_Click(
    object sender, EventArgs e)
{
    using (ObjectContext ctx = new ObjectContext("name=NorthwindEntities"))
    {
        ctx.Connection.Open();
```

```
string myQuery =
    "SELECT REF(c).CompanyName FROM NorthwindEntities.Customers as c";
var myStuff =  new ObjectQuery<DbDataRecord>(myQuery, ctx).ToList();
gv.DataSource = (from item in myStuff
                 select new
                 {
                     Name = item.GetString(0),
                 }).ToList();
    }
}
```

The *CREATEREF* function also returns a reference to a persisted entity, but this function requires an additional parameter, which is the key of the entity you want to locate. The key parameter is passed as a *ROW* function. The following sample code demonstrates the use of *CREATEREF* to create a reference to a single customer by passing in the primary key value as the second parameter. The code then uses the *DEREF* function to return the actual *Customer* object.

Sample of Visual Basic Code

```
Private Sub CreateRefDerefToolStripMenuItem_Click( _
    ByVal sender As System.Object, ByVal e As System.EventArgs) _
    Handles CreateRefDerefToolStripMenuItem.Click
  Using ctx = New ObjectContext("name=NorthwindEntities")
    ctx.Connection.Open()
    Dim myQuery = _
        "DEREF(CREATEREF(NorthwindEntities.Customers, ROW('ALFKI')))"
    gv.DataSource = New ObjectQuery(Of Customer)(myQuery, ctx).ToList()
  End Using
End Sub
```

Sample of C# Code

```
private void createRefDerefToolStripMenuItem_Click(object sender, EventArgs e)
{
    using (ObjectContext ctx = new ObjectContext("name=NorthwindEntities"))
    {
        ctx.Connection.Open();
        string myQuery = "DEREF(CREATEREF(NorthwindEntities.Customers, ROW('ALFKI')))";
        gv.DataSource = new ObjectQuery<Customer>(myQuery, ctx).ToList();
    }
}
```

Working with Entity Sets

Entities are at the core of the Entity Data Model, and an entity set is like a table except that it's within the Entity Data Model. An entity container is like a database. If you want to retrieve all entities in an entity set, you can write a simple ESQL such as the following.

Sample of Visual Basic Code

```
Private Sub EntitySetToolStripMenuItem_Click( _
    ByVal sender As System.Object, ByVal e As System.EventArgs) _
    Handles EntitySetToolStripMenuItem.Click
  Using ctx = New ObjectContext("name=NorthwindEntities")
```

```
        ctx.Connection.Open()
        Dim myQuery = "NorthwindEntities.Customers"
        gv.DataSource = New ObjectQuery(Of Customer)(myQuery, ctx).ToList()
    End Using
End Sub
```

Sample of C# Code

```
private void entitySetToolStripMenuItem_Click(object sender, EventArgs e)
{
    using (ObjectContext ctx = new ObjectContext("name=NorthwindEntities"))
    {
        ctx.Connection.Open();
        string myQuery = "NorthwindEntities.Customers";
        gv.DataSource = new ObjectQuery<Customer>(myQuery, ctx).ToList();
    }
}
```

This example simply specified the name of the container (*NorthwindEntities*) and the entity set (*Customers*). When executed as *ObjectQuery*, the results were materialized, meaning that *Customer* objects were created.

Using Query Builder Methods

The generic *ObjectQuery* object has many extension methods that can perform projection. When you use these methods, you can use the *it* keyword to reference the current entity. The following code sample demonstrates the use of query builder methods to filter the *Customers* entity set and then sort and create a projection that returns only the company name and contact name.

Sample of Visual Basic Code

```
Private Sub QueryBuilderMethodsToolStripMenuItem_Click( _
        ByVal sender As System.Object, ByVal e As System.EventArgs) _
        Handles QueryBuilderMethodsToolStripMenuItem.Click
    Using ctx = New ObjectContext("name=NorthwindEntities")
        ctx.Connection.Open()
        Dim myQuery = "NorthwindEntities.Customers"
        Dim results = New ObjectQuery(Of DbDataRecord)(myQuery, ctx) _
            .Where("StartsWith(it.CompanyName,'A')") _
            .Select("it.CompanyName, it.ContactName") _
            .OrderBy("it.ContactName") _
            .ToList()
        gv.DataSource = (From i In results
            Select New With
                    {
                        .Company = i(0),
                        .Contact = i(1)
                    }).ToList()
    End Using
End Sub
```

Sample of C# Code

```
private void queryBuilderMethodsToolStripMenuItem_Click(object sender, EventArgs e)
{
```

```
using (ObjectContext ctx = new ObjectContext("name=NorthwindEntities"))
{
    ctx.Connection.Open();
    string myQuery = "NorthwindEntities.Customers";
    var results = new ObjectQuery<DbDataRecord>(myQuery, ctx)
        .Where("StartsWith(it.CompanyName,'A')")
        .Select("it.CompanyName, it.ContactName")
        .OrderBy("it.ContactName")
        .ToList();

    gv.DataSource = (from i in results
                     select new
                            {
                                Company=(string)i[0],
                                Contact=(string)i[1]
                            }).ToList();
}
}
```

Using *ObjectContext* to Submit Changes to the Database

This chapter has examined the Entity Data Model and various ways of retrieving data by using the Entity Framework. The following section examines modifying data. The balance of this chapter focuses on submitting changes to the database.

Modifying Existing Entities

In Lesson 1, you learned about the *ObjectContext* object and how it tracks changes. You also learned how to model and retrieve entities. So how do you change one of the entities you've retrieved? You simply modify the entity and call the *SaveChanges* method on the *ObjectContext* object you used to retrieve the entity. The following code sample retrieves a single customer whose CustomerID is ALFKI and modifies the *ContactTitle* property. Next, the *SaveChanges* method is called on *ObjectContext* to persist the change back to the database.

Sample of Visual Basic Code

```
Private Sub ModifyExistingDataToolStripMenuItem_Click( _
    ByVal sender As System.Object, ByVal e As System.EventArgs) _
    Handles ModifyExistingDataToolStripMenuItem.Click
    Dim db = New NorthwindEntities()
    Dim customer = (From c In db.Customers
                    Where c.CustomerID = "ALFKI"
                    Select c).First()
    customer.ContactTitle = "President " + DateTime.Now
    db.SaveChanges()
    MessageBox.Show("Customer Saved")
End Sub
```

Sample of C# Code

```
private void updateExistingDataToolStripMenuItem_Click(
    object sender, EventArgs e)
{
```

```
var db = new NorthwindEntities();
var customer = (from c in db.Customers
                where c.CustomerID=="ALFKI"
                select c).First();
customer.ContactTitle = "President " + DateTime.Now;
db.SaveChanges();
MessageBox.Show("Customer Saved");
}
```

When the *SaveChanges* method is called, the *ObjectContext* object locates all entities whose *EntityState* property is *Added*, *Deleted*, or *Modified* and executes the appropriate *Insert*, *Delete*, or *Update* command to the database. The valid values for *EntityState* are shown in Table 6-4.

The Entity Data Model Generator creates classes in which each property contains *OnPropertyChanging* and *OnPropertyChanged* events. You can extend the entity class to add code that subscribes to these events as needed. Any change to a scalar property causes the entity's *EntityState* property to be *Modified*.

Entities in the *Detached* state are not persisted. You must attach the entity to an *ObjectContext* object to enable change tracking.

Adding New Entities to an *ObjectContext* Class

Before you save a new entity to the database, you must create it. You can use the *new* keyword to instantiate the class and populate all non-nullable properties before saving. If you're working with the Entity Framework–generated classes, they have a static *CreateObjectName* method that can instantiate the class. This method accepts parameters for each non-nullable property. The *CreateObjectName* method does not attach the newly created object to an *ObjectContext* object.

When creating POCO objects, you should use the *CreateObject* method of *ObjectContext* because this creates a proxy object wrapper that inherits from the entity you are creating. The proxy object handles the object tracking.

When you create a new entity such as *Employee*, its initial *EntityState* will be *Detached*. You can populate the *Employee* object with data, but its *EntityState* will still be *Detached* until you attach the entity to an *ObjectContext* object. You can use any of the following methods to attach an entity to an *ObjectContext* object:

- **AddToXxx** Use the *AddToXxx* method on *ObjectContext*, where Xxx is the entity collection name, and the method accepts a single typed entity parameter.
- **AddObject** The *AddObject* method of *ObjectContext* accepts two parameters. The first parameter is a string containing the name of the entity set. The second parameter's type is *object* and references the entity you want to add.
- **AddObject** The *AddObject* method of *ObjectSet*, which is the entity set's type, accepts a single typed parameter containing the entity to be added to an *ObjectSet*.
- **Add** The *Add* method on the *EntityCollection*, which is the type used for a property that represents the "many" end of a relationship, accepts one typed entity parameter.

Before you can save a new entity, you must set all properties that do not support null values. The Entity Framework generates a temporary key value for every new object when it's created. After *SaveChanges* is called, the temporary key value is replaced by the identity value assigned at the database.

If the database is not configured to generate a key value, you should assign a unique value. If multiple objects have the same user-specified key value, an *InvalidOperationException* is thrown when *SaveChanges* is called.

In the following code sample, a new *Employee* entity is created using the *CreateObjectName* method to populate the non-nullable properties. The new entity is passed to the *AddObject* method of the *Employees ObjectSet* to attach the new entity to the *ObjectContext* object. Finally, the *SaveChanges* method is called to persist the new entity to the database.

Sample of Visual Basic Code

```
Private Sub AddNewEntitiesToolStripMenuItem_Click( _
      ByVal sender As System.Object, ByVal e As System.EventArgs) _
      Handles AddNewEntitiesToolStripMenuItem.Click
   Dim db = New NorthwindEntities()
   Dim emp = Employee.CreateEmployee(-1, "John", "Smith")
   MessageBox.Show(emp.EntityState.ToString())
   db.Employees.AddObject(emp)
   MessageBox.Show(emp.EntityState.ToString())
   db.SaveChanges()
   MessageBox.Show("Employee Saved")
   MessageBox.Show(emp.EntityState.ToString())
End Sub
```

Sample of C# Code

```
private void addingNewEntitesToolStripMenuItem_Click(
   object sender, EventArgs e)
{
   var db = new NorthwindEntities();
   var emp = Employee.CreateEmployee(-1, "John", "Smith");
   MessageBox.Show(emp.EntityState.ToString());
   db.Employees.AddObject(emp);
   MessageBox.Show(emp.EntityState.ToString());
   db.SaveChanges();
   MessageBox.Show("Employee Saved");
   MessageBox.Show(emp.EntityState.ToString());
}
```

When this code executes, an *Employee* object is created, and its *EntityState* is displayed as *Detached*. The *Employee* object is added to the *Employees* entity set, which attaches it to the *ObjectContext*, and the *EntityState* is displayed as *Added*. Finally, the *SaveChanges* method is called, and the *Employee* object is saved. You are notified that the *Employee* object has been saved, and the *EntityState* is displayed as *Unchanged*. The *Unchanged* state indicates that no changes have been made to the *Employee* object since it was saved.

Notice that a temporary value is supplied for the *Employee* object, but after the save *EmployeeID* would contain the value assigned to the *Employee* object at the database, which is a positive number.

Attaching Entities to an *ObjectContext*

When a new entity is created, you use one of the *Add* methods described in the previous section to attach the new entity to the *ObjectContext*. This procedure works well if the key has never been assigned, but if the key already has a value, an exception will be thrown. This can happen when an entity is retrieved from the database with the *NoTacking* option or if the entity was detached using the *Detach* method. You might also attach an entity to an *ObjectContext* when the entity comes from a different *ObjectContext* object.

You can use any of the following methods to attach an entity that has a key to an *ObjectContext* object:

- **Attach**   Use the *Attach* method of *ObjectContext* where the method accepts a single typed entity parameter.

- **AttachTo**   The *AttachTo* method of *ObjectContext* accepts two parameters. The first parameter is a string containing the name of the entity set. The second parameter's type is *object* and references the entity you want to add.

- **Attach**   The *Attach* method of *ObjectSet*, which is the entity set's type, accepts a single typed parameter containing the entity to be added to the *ObjectSet*.

The following code is an example of retrieving an entity, detaching it, and then attaching it to a new *ObjectContext* object so that the entity is modified and saved.

Sample of Visual Basic Code

```
Private Sub AttachToolStripMenuItem_Click( _
        ByVal sender As System.Object, ByVal e As System.EventArgs) _
        Handles AttachToolStripMenuItem.Click
    Dim db = New NorthwindEntities()
    Dim customer = (From c In db.Customers
                        Where c.CustomerID = "ALFKI"
                        Select c).First()
    MessageBox.Show(customer.EntityState.ToString())
    db.Detach(customer)
    MessageBox.Show(customer.EntityState.ToString())
    db = New NorthwindEntities()
    db.Customers.Attach(customer)
    MessageBox.Show(customer.EntityState.ToString())
    customer.ContactTitle = "Pres " + DateTime.Now
    MessageBox.Show(customer.EntityState.ToString())
    db.SaveChanges()
    MessageBox.Show("Customer Saved")
    MessageBox.Show(customer.EntityState.ToString())
End Sub
```

Sample of C# Code

```
private void attachToolStripMenuItem_Click(
    object sender, EventArgs e)
```

```
{
    var db = new NorthwindEntities();
    var customer = (from c in db.Customers
                        where c.CustomerID == "ALFKI"
                        select c).First();
    MessageBox.Show(customer.EntityState.ToString());
    db.Detach(customer);
    MessageBox.Show(customer.EntityState.ToString());
    db = new NorthwindEntities();
    db.Customers.Attach(customer);
    MessageBox.Show(customer.EntityState.ToString());
    customer.ContactTitle = "Pres " + DateTime.Now;
    MessageBox.Show(customer.EntityState.ToString());
    db.SaveChanges();
    MessageBox.Show("Customer Saved");
    MessageBox.Show(customer.EntityState.ToString());
}
```

When the sample code is executed, an *ObjectContext* object is created (of type *NorthwindEntities*), a customer is retrieved, and a pop-up shows *EntityState* as *Unchanged*. The customer is then detached from the *ObjectContext*, and a pop-up shows *EntityState* as *Detached*. Next, a new *ObjectContext* object is created, and the customer is attached by using the *Attach* method on the *ObjectSet Customers* property of this new *ObjectContext*. A pop-up shows *EntityState* is now *Unchanged*. Attaching a detached entity always changes *EntityState* to *Unchanged* even if the entity was changed while detached. The customer is modified, and a pop-up shows its *EntityState* property as *Modified*. Finally, the *SaveChanges* method is called on the *ObjectContext*, and a pop-up shows the customer was saved. Another pop-up shows that *EntityState* is back to *Unchanged*, which implies that the state of the customer is in sync with the database.

When working with POCO, you must call the *DetectChanges* method on the *ObjectContext* to attach the POCO entity to the *ObjectContext*. Be sure to call *DetectChanges* prior to calling *SaveChanges*.

EXAM TIP

For the exam, expect to be tested on saving POCO entities. Remember that you must call the *DetectChanges* method on the *ObjectContext*.

Deleting Entities

When it's time to delete an entity, call the *DeleteObject* method of the *ObjectSet* property or the *DeleteObject* method of the *ObjectContext* to mark the specified entity for deletion. The row is not deleted from the database until *SaveChanges* is called. The following code sample shows the deletion of an *Order_Detail* object.

Sample of Visual Basic Code

```
Private Sub DeleteToolStripMenuItem_Click( _
    ByVal sender As System.Object, ByVal e As System.EventArgs) _
```

```
      Handles DeleteToolStripMenuItem.Click
   Dim db = New NorthwindEntities()
   Dim itemToDelete = db.Order_Details.First()
   MessageBox.Show(itemToDelete.EntityState.ToString())
   db.Order_Details.DeleteObject(itemToDelete)
   MessageBox.Show(itemToDelete.EntityState.ToString())
   db.SaveChanges()
   MessageBox.Show("Order Detail Deleted")
   MessageBox.Show(itemToDelete.EntityState.ToString())
End Sub
```

Sample of C# Code

```
private void deleteToolStripMenuItem_Click(
   object sender, EventArgs e)
{
   var db = new NorthwindEntities();
   var itemToDelete = db.Order_Details.First();
   MessageBox.Show(itemToDelete.EntityState.ToString());
   db.Order_Details.DeleteObject(itemToDelete);
   MessageBox.Show(itemToDelete.EntityState.ToString());
   db.SaveChanges();
   MessageBox.Show("Order Detail Deleted");
   MessageBox.Show(itemToDelete.EntityState.ToString());
}
```

After *SaveChanges* is called, if you still hold a reference to the deleted entity, its *EntityState* will be *Detached*. You should not reuse the entity, because if you attach the entity, its *EntityState* will be *Unchanged*, and if you then modify the entity and call *SaveChanges*, an attempt to modify a nonexistent row will throw an *OptimisticConcurrencyException*.

Cascading Deletes

When an entity has associations to other entities, and you are trying to delete the entity, consider the following factors.

If the entity you deleted has dependent entities (foreign key association), and the foreign key on the dependent entities is nullable, the Entity Framework sets the foreign key of the dependent entities to *null* when the principal entity is deleted.

If a primary key of the principal entity is part of the primary key of the dependent entity, deleting the principal entity also deletes all the loaded dependent entities, which is essentially an implicit cascading delete for which you don't need to define a cascading delete rule on the relationship.

You can also set up a delete rule in your EDMX file. In the Entity Data Model designer, click the desired relationship and, in the Properties window, locate the *1* or *0..1* multiplicity end of the relationship. Set the *Delete* property to *Cascade* as shown in Figure 6-27, in which a cascading delete is being configured on the relationship between *Customers* and *Orders*.

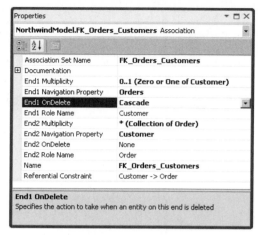

FIGURE 6-27 A Cascading delete is configured on the *1* or *0..1* multiplicity end.

It's important to note that a cascading delete in the Entity Framework works only if the dependent entity objects are loaded. This can be accomplished using the *Include* or *Load* methods. If you don't load the dependent entities, an *UpdateException* will be thrown. Also, don't forget to load dependents of dependents and so on. For example, if you set up *Customers* to cascade the deletion of *Orders*, deleting a customer will fail if you haven't loaded the dependent *Orders* and the dependent *Order_Details* as well.

To demonstrate a cascading delete, one has been configured for the relationship between *Customers* and *Orders*, as shown in Figure 6-27, and the following code sample will delete the first customer, which will delete the customer's orders, which will delete the orders' *Order_Details* values.

Sample of Visual Basic Code

```
Private Sub CascadeDeleteToolStripMenuItem_Click( _
      ByVal sender As System.Object, ByVal e As System.EventArgs) _
      Handles CascadeDeleteToolStripMenuItem.Click
   Dim db = New NorthwindEntities()
   Dim itemToDelete = db.Customers _
         .Include("Orders") _
         .Include("Orders.Order_Details") _
         .First()
   db.Customers.DeleteObject(itemToDelete)
   db.SaveChanges()
   MessageBox.Show("Customer Deleted!")
End Sub
```

Sample of C# Code

```
private void cascadingDeleteToolStripMenuItem_Click(
   object sender, EventArgs e)
{
   var db = new NorthwindEntities();
   var itemToDelete = db.Customers
```

```
            .Include("Orders")
            .Include("Orders.Order_Details")
            .First();
    db.Customers.DeleteObject(itemToDelete);
    db.SaveChanges();
    MessageBox.Show("Customer Deleted!");
}
```

Notice that the *Include* method loads the *Order* objects for each *Customer* by passing "Orders" to the *Include* method. The *Include* method is used again to load *Order_Details* for each *Customer* by passing "Orders.Order_Details" to the *Include* method.

Using Stored Procedures

You've learned that the Entity Framework generates a class that inherits from *ObjectContext* to represent the entity container in the conceptual model. In most of the previous examples, this is the *NorthwindEntities* class. You've also learned that *ObjectContext* exposes a *SaveChanges* method that sends updates to the underlying database. So far, these updates have been using SQL statements that are automatically generated by the system, but you can develop and use custom stored procedures instead. Your application code will stay the same; you're simply remapping the update operations to use stored procedures instead of dynamic SQL.

When you decide to use stored procedures, you must map all three of the insert, update, and delete operations of an entity to stored procedures. If you don't map all three operations, the unmapped operations will fail when executed at run time, and an *UpdateException* will be thrown.

To map the insert, update, and delete operations to stored procedures, open your EDMX file. Right-click the desired entity and click Stored Procedure Mapping. This opens the Mapping Details window in Function mapping view. After you select the stored procedure to map to one of the operations (insert, update, or delete), you'll see the parameter list by which you can map entity properties to each property. For each mapping, you can choose whether to use the current value or the original value.

Submitting Changes in a Transaction

When working with the Entity Framework, you might wonder what happens when you execute the *SaveChanges* method and an exception is thrown after half of the changes have already been sent to the database.

By default, the Entity Framework automatically sends all changes back to the database in the context of a transaction, so if an exception is thrown, all changes are rolled back. In some scenarios, you need more control over the transaction. The most common scenario is when you have multiple *ObjectContext* objects, and they all need to participate in a transaction. Why multiple *ObjectContext* objects? One *ObjectContext* object accesses mainframe data while the other *ObjectContext* object is accessing SQL Server data. Alternately, maybe your code was written to create the *ObjectContext* object in a just-in-time fashion, so the method creates an *ObjectContext* object for its operation, and then the method creates a new *ObjectContext* object for its operation. This scenario is addressed in the following sample code.

In your application, you might have an *addToInventory* method that accepts a *productId* parameter and a *quantity* parameter. This method creates an *ObjectContext* object, retrieves the product, and adds to its *UnitsInStock* property based on the quantity passed to the method. You might have a matching *removeFromInventory* method that does the same thing except that it subtracts from *UnitsInStock*. Also, a helper *displayUnitsInStock* method enables you to easily display the current value of the *UnitsInStock* property. The following sample code shows these methods.

Sample of Visual Basic Code

```vb
Private Sub displayUnitsInStock(ByVal productId As Integer)
    Dim db = New NorthwindEntities()
    Dim Product = db.Products _
    .Where(Function(p) p.ProductID = productId) _
    .First()
    MessageBox.Show(String.Format( _
        "Product ID: {0}  UnitsInStock: {1}", _
        productId, Product.UnitsInStock))
End Sub

Private Sub addToInventory( _
        ByVal productId As Integer, ByVal quantity As Short)
    Dim db = New NorthwindEntities()
    Dim Product = db.Products _
    .Where(Function(p) p.ProductID = productId) _
    .First()
    Product.UnitsInStock += quantity
    db.SaveChanges()
End Sub

Private Sub removeFromInventory( _
        ByVal productId As Integer, ByVal quantity As Short)
    Dim db = New NorthwindEntities()
    Dim Product = db.Products _
    .Where(Function(p) p.ProductID = productId) _
    .First()
    Product.UnitsInStock -= quantity
    db.SaveChanges()
End Sub
```

Sample of C# Code

```csharp
private void displayUnitsInStock(int productId )
{
    var db = new NorthwindEntities();
    var product = db.Products
        .Where(p => p.ProductID == productId)
        .First();
    MessageBox.Show(String.Format(
        "Product ID: {0}  UnitsInStock: {1}",
```

```
            productId, Product.UnitsInStock));
}

private void addToInventory(int productId, short quantity)
{
    var db = new NorthwindEntities();
    var product = db.Products
        .Where(p => p.ProductID == productId)
        .First();
    product.UnitsInStock += quantity;
    db.SaveChanges();
}

private void removeFromInventory(int productId, short quantity)
{
    var db = new NorthwindEntities();
    var product = db.Products
        .Where(p => p.ProductID == productId)
        .First();
    product.UnitsInStock -= quantity;
    db.SaveChanges();
}
```

Each of these methods modifies *UnitsInStock* in the context of its own transaction, but you want to add a new method, *transferInventory*, that accepts *fromProductId* and *toProductId* parameters and a quantity. This enables a customer to exchange one product for another. You want this operation to be treated as a transaction so you can use the *TransactionScope* class to wrap the complete transfer in a transaction. The *TransactionScope* class was covered in more detail in Chapter 2.

In the following code sample, a *transferInventory* method makes the call to the *addToInventory* and *removeFromInventory* methods to perform the transaction. These calls are wrapped in a *TransactionScope* object, which is in a *try/catch* block. For the purpose of the demonstration, *transferInventory* will also accept a Boolean value to indicate whether a failure should be simulated.

Sample of Visual Basic Code

```
Private Sub FailToolStripMenuItem_Click( _
      ByVal sender As System.Object, ByVal e As System.EventArgs) _
      Handles FailToolStripMenuItem.Click
    transferInventory(1, 2, 1, True)
End Sub

Private Sub SuccessToolStripMenuItem_Click( _
      ByVal sender As System.Object, ByVal e As System.EventArgs) _
      Handles SuccessToolStripMenuItem.Click
    transferInventory(1, 2, 1, False)
End Sub

Private Sub transferInventory( _
      ByVal fromProductId As Integer, _
      ByVal toProductId As Integer, _
```

```
      ByVal quantity As Integer, _
      ByVal causeError As Boolean)

   displayUnitsInStock(fromProductId)
   displayUnitsInStock(toProductId)

   Try
      Using tran As New TransactionScope()
         removeFromInventory(fromProductId, quantity)
         addToInventory(toProductId, quantity)
         If causeError Then
            Throw New EntitySqlException("Simulated Exception")
         End If
         tran.Complete()
         MessageBox.Show("Success")
      End Using
   Catch ex As Exception
      MessageBox.Show(ex.Message)
   End Try

   displayUnitsInStock(fromProductId)
   displayUnitsInStock(toProductId)
End Sub
```

Sample of C# Code

```csharp
private void failToolStripMenuItem_Click(object sender, EventArgs e)
{
   transferInventory(1,2,1,true);
}

private void successToolStripMenuItem_Click(object sender, EventArgs e)
{
   transferInventory(1, 2, 1, false);
}

private void transferInventory(
   int fromProductId,
   int toProductId,
   short quantity,
   bool causeError)
{

   displayUnitsInStock(fromProductId);
   displayUnitsInStock(toProductId);

   try
   {
      using (var tran = new TransactionScope())
      {
         removeFromInventory(fromProductId, quantity);
         addToInventory(toProductId, quantity);
         if(causeError)
         {
            throw new EntitySqlException("Simulated Exception");
```

```
        }
        tran.Complete();
        MessageBox.Show("Success");
    }
}
catch (Exception ex)
{
    MessageBox.Show(ex.Message);
}

    displayUnitsInStock(fromProductId);
    displayUnitsInStock(toProductId);
}
```

PRACTICE   Retrieve and Save Data

In this practice, you continue the design of an application and database for tracking your music. You want to track your music by album, song name, artist, and genre. You use the Code First model to design the conceptual model and then generate the database from the conceptual model.

The previous practice generated the data-access layer by using the Entity Framework designer, and the result of that practice is the starting point for this practice.

In this practice, you create the graphical user interface (GUI) and provide code to retrieve data from and save data to the database.

If you encounter a problem completing an exercise, the completed projects can be installed from the Code folder on the companion CD.

EXERCISE   Creating the GUI

In this exercise, you modify the WPF application you created in Lesson 1 by creating the GUI.

1. In Visual Studio .NET 2010, select File | Open | Project. Open the project from Lesson 1 or locate and open the solution in the Begin folder for this lesson.

2. In Solution Explorer, double-click the MainWindow.xaml file to open it in the WPF Form Designer window.

3. In the *Window* tag, add a *Loaded* event handler. When prompted for a new event handler, double-click New EventHandler. Your XAML should look like the following.

    Sample of Visual Basic XAML

    ```
    <Window x:Class="MainWindow"
            xmlns="http://schemas.microsoft.com/winfx/2006/xaml/presentation"
            xmlns:x="http://schemas.microsoft.com/winfx/2006/xaml"
            Loaded="Window_Loaded"
            Title="MainWindow" Height="350" Width="525">
        <Grid>
        </Grid>
    </Window>
    ```

Sample of C# XAML

```xaml
<Window x:Class="MusicTracker.MainWindow"
        xmlns="http://schemas.microsoft.com/winfx/2006/xaml/presentation"
        xmlns:x="http://schemas.microsoft.com/winfx/2006/xaml"
        Loaded="Window_Loaded"
        Title="MainWindow" Height="350" Width="525">
    <Grid>
    </Grid>
</Window>
```

4. The XAML contains a *Grid* definition. Inside the grid, add three row definitions. The first row should have its *Height* property set to *Auto*, and the last two rows should have their *Height* property set to *"*"*. Regardless of your programming language, your XAML for the grid should look like the following.

Sample of XAML

```xaml
<Grid>
    <Grid.RowDefinitions>
        <RowDefinition Height="Auto" />
        <RowDefinition Height="*" />
        <RowDefinition Height="*" />
    </Grid.RowDefinitions>
</Grid>
```

5. In the XAML, before the end of the *Grid* tag name, add *Menu*. Inside the menu, add *MenuItem* elements for *Save*, called *mnuSave*, and for *Exit*, called *mnuExit*. After adding these items, double-click each *MenuItem* element to add the click event handler code. Your XAML should look like the following.

Sample of XAML

```xaml
<Grid>
    <Grid.RowDefinitions>
        <RowDefinition Height="Auto" />
        <RowDefinition Height="*" />
        <RowDefinition Height="*" />
    </Grid.RowDefinitions>
    <Menu>
        <MenuItem Header="Save" Name="mnuSave" Click="mnuSave_Click" />
        <MenuItem Header="Exit" Name="mnuExit" Click="mnuExit_Click" />
    </Menu>
</Grid>
```

6. Add *Albums* to *Grid*. To display the Data Sources panel, select Data | Show Data Sources. The *MusicDatabaseEntities ObjectContext* object is displayed, and it contains the *Albums* and *Songs* entity sets.

7. Drag *Albums* to the WPF designer surface and drop it in the second row. This adds resources and code to your project to wire the entity set to this data grid.

8. Resize *DataGrid* so it fits within the first row and then modify the *DataGrid* XAML code to clean up the sizing, hide the Id column, and set the Name column to take all

available space on the row. Your XAML for the data grid should look like the following, regardless of programming language.

Sample of XAML

```xml
<DataGrid AutoGenerateColumns="False" EnableRowVirtualization="True"
        ItemsSource="{Binding}"  Name="AlbumsDataGrid" Margin="5"
        RowDetailsVisibilityMode="VisibleWhenSelected"  Grid.Row="1">
   <DataGrid.Columns>
      <DataGridTextColumn x:Name="IdColumn" Binding="{Binding Path=Id}"
          Header="Id" Visibility="Hidden" />
      <DataGridTextColumn x:Name="NameColumn" Binding="{Binding Path=Name}"
          Header="Album Name" Width="*" />
   </DataGrid.Columns>
</DataGrid>
```

9. Add *Songs* for the current *Album* to the grid. (Don't use the *Songs* entity set directly under *MusicDatabaseEntities*.)

10. Click the plus sign beside Albums; Songs appears. This represents the songs an album contains. Drag that *Songs* entity set to the third row of the grid.

11. Resize *DataGrid* to fit within the bottom row. Modify the XAML to clean up the resizing, make the Id column invisible, and set the Name column to take all available space on the row. Your XAML for this data grid should look like the following, based on programming language.

Sample of Visual Basic XAML

```xml
<DataGrid AutoGenerateColumns="False" EnableRowVirtualization="True"
        Grid.Row="2"  Margin="5"
        ItemsSource="{Binding Source={StaticResource AlbumsSongsViewSource}}"
        Name="SongsDataGrid" RowDetailsVisibilityMode="VisibleWhenSelected" >
   <DataGrid.Columns>
      <DataGridTextColumn x:Name="IdColumn1" Binding="{Binding Path=Id}"
                     Header="Id" Visibility="Hidden" />
      <DataGridTextColumn x:Name="NameColumn1" Binding="{Binding Path=Name}"
                     Header="Song Name" Width="*" />
   </DataGrid.Columns>
</DataGrid>
```

Sample of C# XAML

```xml
<DataGrid AutoGenerateColumns="False" EnableRowVirtualization="True"
        Grid.Row="2"  Margin="5"
        ItemsSource="{Binding Source={StaticResource albumsSongsViewSource}}"
        Name="SongsDataGrid" RowDetailsVisibilityMode="VisibleWhenSelected" >
   <DataGrid.Columns>
      <DataGridTextColumn x:Name="IdColumn1" Binding="{Binding Path=Id}"
                     Header="Id" Visibility="Hidden" />
      <DataGridTextColumn x:Name="NameColumn1" Binding="{Binding Path=Name}"
                     Header="Song Name" Width="*" />
   </DataGrid.Columns>
</DataGrid>
```

A *Windows.Resources* element contains the resource information to which your *DataGrid* controls are binding. The XAML is a bit different between programming languages, so here is the completed XAML, based on programming language.

Sample of Visual Basic XAML

```
<Window x:Class="MainWindow"
    xmlns="http://schemas.microsoft.com/winfx/2006/xaml/presentation"
    xmlns:x="http://schemas.microsoft.com/winfx/2006/xaml"
    Loaded="Window_Loaded"
    Title="MainWindow" Height="350" Width="525" mc:Ignorable="d"
    xmlns:d="http://schemas.microsoft.com/expression/blend/2008"
    xmlns:mc="http://schemas.openxmlformats.org/markup-compatibility/2006"
    xmlns:my="clr-namespace:MusicTracker">
    <Window.Resources>
        <CollectionViewSource x:Key="AlbumsViewSource" d:DesignSource=
            "{d:DesignInstance my:Album, CreateList=True}" />
        <CollectionViewSource x:Key="AlbumsSongsViewSource" Source=
            "{Binding Path=Songs, Source={StaticResource AlbumsViewSource}}" />
    </Window.Resources>
    <Grid DataContext="{StaticResource AlbumsViewSource}">
        <Grid.RowDefinitions>
            <RowDefinition Height="Auto" />
            <RowDefinition Height="*" />
            <RowDefinition Height="*" />
        </Grid.RowDefinitions>
        <Menu>
            <MenuItem Header="Save" Name="mnuSave" Click="mnuSave_Click" />
            <MenuItem Header="Exit" Name="mnuExit" Click="mnuExit_Click" />
        </Menu>
        <DataGrid AutoGenerateColumns="False" EnableRowVirtualization="True"
                ItemsSource="{Binding}"  Name="AlbumsDataGrid" Margin="5"
                RowDetailsVisibilityMode="VisibleWhenSelected"  Grid.Row="1">
            <DataGrid.Columns>
                <DataGridTextColumn x:Name="IdColumn"
                                    Binding="{Binding Path=Id}"
                                    Header="Id" Visibility="Hidden" />
                <DataGridTextColumn x:Name="NameColumn"
                                    Binding="{Binding Path=Name}"
                                    Header="Album Name" Width="*" />
            </DataGrid.Columns>
        </DataGrid>
        <DataGrid AutoGenerateColumns="False" EnableRowVirtualization="True"
                Grid.Row="2"  Margin="5" ItemsSource=
                "{Binding Source={StaticResource AlbumsSongsViewSource}}"
                Name="SongsDataGrid"
                RowDetailsVisibilityMode="VisibleWhenSelected" >
            <DataGrid.Columns>
                <DataGridTextColumn x:Name="IdColumn1"
                                    Binding="{Binding Path=Id}"
                                    Header="Id" Visibility="Hidden" />
                <DataGridTextColumn x:Name="NameColumn1"
                                    Binding="{Binding Path=Name}"
                                    Header="Song Name" Width="*" />
            </DataGrid.Columns>
```

```
        </DataGrid>
    </Grid>
</Window>


Sample of C# XAML

<Window x:Class="MusicTracker.MainWindow"
        xmlns="http://schemas.microsoft.com/winfx/2006/xaml/presentation"
        xmlns:x="http://schemas.microsoft.com/winfx/2006/xaml"
        Loaded="Window_Loaded"
        Title="MainWindow" Height="350" Width="525" mc:Ignorable="d"
        xmlns:d="http://schemas.microsoft.com/expression/blend/2008"
        xmlns:mc="http://schemas.openxmlformats.org/markup-compatibility/2006"
        xmlns:my="clr-namespace:MusicTracker">
    <Window.Resources>
        <CollectionViewSource x:Key="albumsViewSource" d:DesignSource=
            "{d:DesignInstance my:Album, CreateList=True}" />
        <CollectionViewSource x:Key="albumsSongsViewSource" Source=
            "{Binding Path=Songs, Source={StaticResource albumsViewSource}}" />
    </Window.Resources>
    <Grid DataContext="{StaticResource albumsViewSource}">
        <Grid.RowDefinitions>
            <RowDefinition Height="Auto" />
            <RowDefinition Height="*" />
            <RowDefinition Height="*" />
        </Grid.RowDefinitions>
        <Menu>
            <MenuItem Header="Save" Name="mnuSave" Click="mnuSave_Click" />
            <MenuItem Header="Exit" Name="mnuExit" Click="mnuExit_Click" />
        </Menu>
        <DataGrid AutoGenerateColumns="False" EnableRowVirtualization="True"
                ItemsSource="{Binding}"  Name="AlbumsDataGrid" Margin="5"
                RowDetailsVisibilityMode="VisibleWhenSelected"  Grid.Row="1">
            <DataGrid.Columns>
                <DataGridTextColumn x:Name="IdColumn" Binding="{Binding Path=Id}"
                                Header="Id" Visibility="Hidden" />
                <DataGridTextColumn x:Name="NameColumn"
                                Binding="{Binding Path=Name}"
                                Header="Album Name" Width="*" />
            </DataGrid.Columns>
        </DataGrid>
        <DataGrid AutoGenerateColumns="False" EnableRowVirtualization="True"
                Grid.Row="2"  Margin="5"
                ItemsSource=
                    "{Binding Source={StaticResource albumsSongsViewSource}}"
                Name="SongsDataGrid"
                RowDetailsVisibilityMode="VisibleWhenSelected" >
            <DataGrid.Columns>
                <DataGridTextColumn x:Name="IdColumn1"
                                Binding="{Binding Path=Id}"
                                Header="Id" Visibility="Hidden" />
                <DataGridTextColumn x:Name="NameColumn1"
                                Binding="{Binding Path=Name}"
                                Header="Song Name" Width="*" />
            </DataGrid.Columns>
        </DataGrid>
```

```
        </Grid>
    </Window>
```

12. Double-click the Save menu item. This takes you to the code-behind file. Code is already in this file from dropping Albums and Songs on the XAML designer surface. *Window_Loaded* contains code to instantiate *MusicDatabaseEntities*, but you need access to that object from within the *mnuSave_Click* method, so cut that line and paste it just inside the class. Your code should look like the following.

Sample of Visual Basic Code

```
Class MainWindow
    Dim MusicDatabaseEntities As MusicTracker.MusicDatabaseEntities = _
        New MusicTracker.MusicDatabaseEntities()

    Private Sub Window_Loaded(ByVal sender As System.Object, _
                            ByVal e As System.Windows.RoutedEventArgs)

        'Load data into Albums. You can modify this code as needed.
        Dim AlbumsViewSource As System.Windows.Data.CollectionViewSource = _
            CType(Me.FindResource("AlbumsViewSource"), _
                System.Windows.Data.CollectionViewSource)
        Dim AlbumsQuery As System.Data.Objects.ObjectQuery( _
                    Of MusicTracker.Album) _
                    = Me.GetAlbumsQuery(MusicDatabaseEntities)
        AlbumsViewSource.Source = AlbumsQuery.Execute( _
            System.Data.Objects.MergeOption.AppendOnly)
    End Sub

    Private Sub mnuSave_Click( _
        ByVal sender As System.Object, _
        ByVal e As System.Windows.RoutedEventArgs)

    End Sub

    Private Sub mnuExit_Click( _
        ByVal sender As System.Object, _
        ByVal e As System.Windows.RoutedEventArgs)

    End Sub

    Private Function GetAlbumsQuery( _
        ByVal MusicDatabaseEntities As MusicTracker.MusicDatabaseEntities) _
        As System.Data.Objects.ObjectQuery(Of MusicTracker.Album)

        Dim AlbumsQuery As System.Data.Objects.ObjectQuery( _
            Of MusicTracker.Album) = MusicDatabaseEntities.Albums
        'Update the query to include Songs data in Albums.
        'You can modify this code as needed.
        AlbumsQuery = AlbumsQuery.Include("Songs")
        'Returns an ObjectQuery.
        Return AlbumsQuery
    End Function
End Class
```

Sample of C# Code

```csharp
using System;
using System.Collections.Generic;
using System.Collections.ObjectModel;
using System.Linq;
using System.Text;
using System.Windows;
using System.Windows.Controls;
using System.Windows.Data;
using System.Windows.Documents;
using System.Windows.Input;
using System.Windows.Media;
using System.Windows.Media.Imaging;
using System.Windows.Navigation;
using System.Windows.Shapes;

namespace MusicTracker
{
    /// <summary>
    /// Interaction logic for MainWindow.xaml
    /// </summary>
    public partial class MainWindow : Window
    {
        MusicTracker.MusicDatabaseEntities musicDatabaseEntities =
            new MusicTracker.MusicDatabaseEntities();

        public MainWindow()
        {
            InitializeComponent();
        }

        private void Window_Loaded(object sender, RoutedEventArgs e)
        {

            // Load data into Albums. You can modify this code as needed.
            System.Windows.Data.CollectionViewSource albumsViewSource =
                ((System.Windows.Data.CollectionViewSource)
                (this.FindResource("albumsViewSource")));
            System.Data.Objects.ObjectQuery<MusicTracker.Album> albumsQuery =
                this.GetAlbumsQuery(musicDatabaseEntities);
            albumsViewSource.Source =
                albumsQuery.Execute(System.Data.Objects.MergeOption.AppendOnly);
        }

        private void mnuSave_Click(object sender, RoutedEventArgs e)
        {

        }

        private void mnuExit_Click(object sender, RoutedEventArgs e)
        {

        }

        private System.Data.Objects.ObjectQuery<Album> GetAlbumsQuery(
```

```
        MusicDatabaseEntities musicDatabaseEntities)
    {
        // Auto generated code

        System.Data.Objects.ObjectQuery<MusicTracker.Album> albumsQuery =
            musicDatabaseEntities.Albums;
        // Update the query to include Songs data in Albums.
        //You can modify this code as needed.
        albumsQuery = albumsQuery.Include("Songs");
        // Returns an ObjectQuery.
        return albumsQuery;
    }
  }
}
```

13. Add the following code to the *mnuSave_Click* method to save all changes to the database and display a saved message or an error message.

Sample of Visual Basic Code

```vb
Private Sub mnuSave_Click( _
  ByVal sender As System.Object, _
  ByVal e As System.Windows.RoutedEventArgs)

  Try
      MusicDatabaseEntities.SaveChanges()
      MessageBox.Show("Saved")
  Catch ex As Exception
      MessageBox.Show(ex.Message)
  End Try
End Sub
```

Sample of C# Code

```csharp
private void mnuSave_Click(object sender, RoutedEventArgs e)
{
    try
    {
        musicDatabaseEntities.SaveChanges();
        MessageBox.Show("Saved");
    }
    catch (Exception ex)
    {
        MessageBox.Show(ex.Message);
    }
}
```

14. Add code to the *mnuExit_Click* method to exit the application. The exit method first saves all changes and then exits. If an error is thrown during the save operation, display the error but continue exiting the application. Your code should look like the following.

Sample of Visual Basic Code

```vb
Private Sub mnuExit_Click( _
    ByVal sender As System.Object, _
    ByVal e As System.Windows.RoutedEventArgs)
```

```vbnet
    Try
        MusicDatabaseEntities.SaveChanges()
    Catch ex As Exception
        MessageBox.Show(ex.Message)
    End Try
    Application.Current.Shutdown()
End Sub
```

Sample of C# Code

```csharp
private void mnuExit_Click(object sender, RoutedEventArgs e)
{
    try
    {
        musicDatabaseEntities.SaveChanges();
    }
    catch (Exception ex)
    {
        MessageBox.Show(ex.Message);
    }
    Application.Current.Shutdown();
}
```

15. Press F5 to run this application. Your main window should look the one in Figure 6-28. You should be able to enter albums by simply typing the album name and pressing Enter. As you add albums, you might want to add songs; simply type each song name and press Enter.

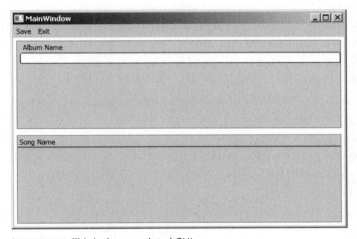

FIGURE 6-28 This is the completed GUI.

Lesson Summary

This lesson provided detailed information about querying the Entity Frameworks and covered LINQ to Entities and ESQL querying.

- LINQ to Entities queries are converted to command trees that are executed against *ObjectContext* objects.
- You use *ObjectQuery* to compose a LINQ to Entities query.
- LINQ to Entities provides deferred execution of queries.
- *Materialization* is the creation of objects that represent the result.
- Not all implementations of LINQ operators are supported in LINQ to Entities, due to the varying types of data stores that LINQ to Entities supports.
- Use the *AsEnumerable* query extension method to cast to the generic *IEnumerable* interface, which bypasses LINQ to Entities, but code executes client-side.
- Instead of using *AsEnumerable*, you can implement a stored procedure that executes server-side and might perform better to solve a problem .
- ESQL provides an SQL-like syntax for building queries that are database independent.
- One of the biggest benefits of using ESQL is the ability to create dynamic queries that target any supported database.
- ESQL queries can target Object Services and the EntityClient data provider.
- *ObjectContext* can send changes back to the database.
- The *SaveChanges* method on the *ObjectContext* object locates all changed objects and sends the appropriate *Insert*, *Update*, or *Delete* command to the database.
- An entity has an *EntityState* property that can be set to *Detached*, *Unchanged*, *Modified*, *Added*, or *Deleted*.
- If an existing entity (entity that has a primary key) is detached, you can use the *Attach* method to attach the entity to an *ObjectContext* object.
- Deleting an entity simply marks the entity for deletion. The entity is not deleted until you call the *SaveChanges* method on the *ObjectContext* object.
- You can configure a relationship to perform cascading deletes by setting the *1* or *1..0* end of a relationship to *Cascade*.
- You can map stored procedures to insert, delete, and change operations.
- *ObjectContext* automatically sends the updates within a transaction context.
- You can wrap operations that use multiple *ObjectContext* objects within a *TransactionScope* class.

Lesson Review

You can use the following questions to test your knowledge of the information in Lesson 2, "Querying and Updating with the Entity Framework." The questions are also available on the companion CD if you prefer to review them in electronic form.

> **NOTE ANSWERS**
>
> Answers to these questions and explanations of why each answer choice is correct or incorrect are located in the "Answers" section at the end of the book.

1. When working with the Entity Framework, which method do you execute to send changes back to the database?

    A. *SubmitChanges*

    B. *SaveChanges*

2. You are writing an Entity SQL query that requires you to construct a row from various data. Which function will you use to construct the row?

    A. *CREATEREF*

    B. *MULTISET*

    C. *ROW*

3. You have just set up the Entity Framework cascading delete, and you are now trying to use it, but you keep getting an *UpdateException*. What is the most logical cause of this exception?

    A. You must make sure that all dependent objects are loaded.

    B. Your database does not support cascading deletes.

    C. You have not defined a cascading delete at the database server.

4. You are working with an *ObjectContext* object that targets the mainframe and another *ObjectContext* object that targets SQL Server. When it's time to save the changes, you want all changes to be sent to the mainframe and to SQL Server as one transaction. How can you accomplish this?

    A. Just save both *ObjectContext* objects because they automatically join the same transaction.

    B. Save to the mainframe and use an *if* statement to verify that the changes were successful. If successful, save to SQL Server.

    C. Wrap the saving of both *ObjectContext* objects within a *TransactionScope* object that is implemented in a *using* statement in which the last line executes the *Complete* method on the *TransactionScope* class.

    D. Use a Boolean flag to indicate the success of each save, which will tell you whether the save was successful.

Case Scenarios

In the following case scenarios, you apply what you've learned about the Entity Framework. You can find answers to these questions in the "Answers" section at the end of this book.

Case Scenario 1: Choosing an Object-Relational Mapper

You have been assigned the task of choosing an object-relational mapper, and your choices are LINQ to SQL or LINQ to Entities. The application will be using SQL Server 2008 R2, and the database will have a small number of tables (fewer than 10) but will also occasionally need to send transactions to an existing Oracle server. Your team will be designing the database while the application is being created. Your application takes advantage of inheritance and poly-morphism wherever possible.

1. Does anything in this scenario force you to choose a particular ORM?
2. Which ORM would you choose?
3. What are the reasons for your choice?

Case Scenario 2: Using the Entity Framework

You are creating a new application, but you have to connect to an existing database. However, your team has no control over that schema. Your team wants to work in an object-centric environment in which the focus is on the domain model, not on the data model. Answer the following questions regarding this application and the use of the Entity Framework.

1. Can you describe a feature of the Entity Framework that will help you when the data-base already exists?
2. Can you describe a feature of the Entity Framework that will help you when you have no control of the database schema?
3. Can you describe a feature of the Entity Framework that will help you when you see that different kinds of employees (managers, salespeople) have additional data in other tables?

Suggested Practices

To help you successfully master the exam objectives presented in this chapter, complete the following tasks.

Create an Application That Uses LINQ to Entities Queries

Create at least one application that uses LINQ to Entities. This can be accomplished by performing the practices at the ends of Lesson 1 and Lesson 2, or you can complete the following Practice 1.

- **Practice 1**   Create an application that requires you to query a database for data from at least two tables by using LINQ to Entities when the tables are related. This could be movies that have actors, artists who record music, or people who have vehicles. Add LINQ to Entities queries to search and filter the data.

- **Practice 2**   Complete Practice 1 and then add LINQ to Entities queries that join the tables. Be sure to provide both inner and outer joins. Also, add queries that perform grouping and aggregates. Try at least one Entity SQL query.

Create an Application That Modifies Data by Using LINQ to Entities

Create at least one application that uses LINQ to Entities to modify data in the database. This can be accomplished by performing the practices at the ends of Lesson 1 and Lesson 2 or by completing the following practice.

- **Practice**   Create an application that requires you to collect data into at least two database tables when the data tables are related. This could be movies that have actors, artists who record music, or people who have vehicles. Use LINQ to Entities to add, delete, and modify the data.

Take a Practice Test

The practice tests on this book's companion CD offer many options. For example, you can test yourself on just the lesson review content, or you can test yourself on all the 70-516 certification exam content. You can set up the test so that it closely simulates the experience of taking a certification exam, or you can set it up in study mode so that you can look at the correct answers and explanations after you answer each question.

> **MORE INFO**   **PRACTICE TESTS**
>
> For details about all the practice test options available, see the "How to Use the Practice Tests" section in this book's introduction.

CHAPTER 7

WCF Data Services

Originally code named "Astoria" and formally known as ADO.NET Data Services, WCF Data Services is part of the .NET Framework that provides the ability to create Windows Communication Foundation (WCF) services that use the Atom Publishing protocol (AtomPub) and Open Data protocol (OData) to expose and consume data over the web. WCF Data Services exposes data by using the semantics of representational state transfer (REST). OData provides the ability to perform create, retrieve, update, and delete (CRUD) operations and can be used on a variety of sources such as relational databases, file systems, content management systems, and traditional websites.

Exam objectives in this chapter:

- Query data by using ADO.NET Data Services.
- Configure ADO.NET Data Services.
- Implement eager loading.

Lessons in this chapter:

Before You Begin

You must have some understanding of Microsoft Visual C# or Visual Basic 2010. This chapter requires only the hardware and software listed at the beginning of this book. You should also have access to the Northwind database, which is one of the Microsoft "sandbox" databases. The Northwind database can be downloaded from the Microsoft website and is included on the companion disk.

 REAL WORLD

Glenn Johnson

OData provides a means of accessing data on the web that's very simple to work with. Simple is the key here because OData does not provide all the features available when using Web Services Security. Many companies are exposing an OData interface for customers to access their data. With OData, you can query eBay's catalog to find auction items. You can also query Netflix to retrieve the complete catalog of movie titles. Using a URI such as *http://odata.netflix.com/Catalog /Titles* displays a list of movies in the browser but, if you right-click the web page and click View Source, you see that the browser has rendered an XML response from the OData interface. You can create applications that consume data from many disparate OData services.

Lesson 1: What Is WCF Data Services?

WCF Data Services is the Microsoft implementation of OData, which is an open-format specification for accessing data. Microsoft Visual Studio .NET facilitates creating a WCF data service
by using an ADO.NET Entity Framework data model. WCF Data Services includes an object-
based client library for .NET Framework client applications. Also included is an object-based
client library specifically for Microsoft Silverlight-based applications.

> **After this lesson, you will be able to:**
> - Create a WCF data service.
> - Execute a simple query to a WCF data service.
> - Work with filters and query expressions.
> - Perform eager data loading.
>
> **Estimated lesson time: 30 minutes**

Introducing OData

OData is an open protocol for sharing data that builds on Atom Publishing protocol
(AtomPub), which is used with feeds such as blogs. It provides a way to access and essentially
break down data silos to increase the shared value of data so that consumers can interoperate
with data producers in a very powerful way.

OData provides a consistent interface, which means that the way you construct or address
items in an OData feed, and how you interact with a service using HTTP verbs, is the same
across any OData service, regardless of the data it exposes. This consistent interface enables
code reuse against your data services so that reusable client libraries and UI widgets can be
created.

Interactions with an OData feed are performed by using URIs to address resources and
standard HTTP verbs (GET, POST, PUT, DELETE) to act on those resources. Compared with
SQL, the GET verb selects, the POST verb inserts, the PUT verb updates, and the DELETE verb
deletes.

EXAM TIP

For the exam, you can expect to be tested on the HTTP verbs required to perform selects,
inserts, updates, and deletes to the database.

Creating a WCF Data Service

WCF Data Services is designed to provide access to your data, but it's important to under-stand that you don't need to get the data from a database server. The data might be in an XML file or somewhere else; WCF Data Services simply enables data sharing across the Internet in a simplistic way. To gain an understanding of WCF Data Services, this section de-scribes how to create a WCF data service.

Consider a scenario in which you have a list of *Car* objects you want to expose on the Internet. It doesn't matter that the *Car* objects will be instantiated and populated within the sample code; the *Car* objects could have come from a SQL Server database as well.

This demonstration starts by creating an empty solution called WcfDataServicesSolution, and then a standard ASP.NET web application, called WcfDataServicesLibrary, is added to the solution.

A class called *Car* is then added to the WcfDataServiceLibrary. This class contains the fol-lowing code.

Sample of Visual Basic Code

```vb
<DataServiceKey("VIN")> _
Public Class Car
    Public Property VIN As String
    Public Property Make As String
    Public Property Model As String
    Public Property Year As Integer
End Class
```

Sample of C# Code

```csharp
[DataServiceKey("VIN")]
public class Car
{
    public string VIN { get; set; }
    public string Make { get; set; }
    public string Model { get; set; }
    public int Year { get; set; }
}
```

The *Car* class contains properties for the *VIN*, *make*, *model*, and *year*. In addition, the *Car* class has a *DataServiceKey* class attribute, which OData uses to access a specific item. The *DataServiceKey* attribute expects a string containing the name of a property that contains unique values. You must add a reference to the System.Data.Services.Client.dll assembly and use the *System.Data.Services.Common* namespace.

In the WcfDataServicesLibrary project, add the WCF data service by right-clicking the WcfDataServicesLibrary project and then choosing Add | New Item. Select the WCF Data Service template and name it **CarService.svc**, as shown in Figure 7-1.

FIGURE 7-1 Add a WCF data service to an ASP.NET Web application.

The CarService.svc file represents the exposed endpoint URI you will call from the Internet. This file contains a single line that references a class, which is in the code-behind file, CarService.svc.cs or CarService.svc.vb. The code-behind file is opened and contains the following class code.

Sample of Visual Basic Code

```vb
Public Class CarService
    ' TODO: replace [[class name]] with your data class name
    Inherits DataService (Of [[class name]])

    ' This method is called only once to initialize service-wide policies.
    Public Shared Sub InitializeService(ByVal config As DataServiceConfiguration)
        ' TODO: set rules to indicate which entity sets and service operations
        '        are visible, updatable, etc.
        ' Examples:
        ' config.SetEntitySetAccessRule("MyEntityset", EntitySetRights.AllRead)
        ' config.SetServiceOperationAccessRule("MyServiceOperation", _
            ServiceOperationRights.All)
        config.DataServiceBehavior.MaxProtocolVersion = DataServiceProtocolVersion.V2
    End Sub

End Class
```

Sample of C# Code

```csharp
public class CarService :
    DataService< /* TODO: put your data source class name here */ >
{
    // This method is called only once to initialize service-wide policies.
    public static void InitializeService(DataServiceConfiguration config)
    {
        // TODO: set rules to indicate which entity sets and service
        //       operations are visible, updatable, etc.
        // Examples:
        // config.SetEntitySetAccessRule("MyEntityset", EntitySetRights.AllRead);
```

```
//  config.SetServiceOperationAccessRule("MyServiceOperation",
        ServiceOperationRights.All);
    config.DataServiceBehavior.MaxProtocolVersion =
        DataServiceProtocolVersion.V2;
    }
}
```

The code-behind class inherits from the generic *DataService* class. A comment appears where the parameter type is expected, *CarService* in this case.

Configuring WCF Data Services (ADO.NET Data Services)

The *CarService* class contains an *InitializeService* method by which you set up the service configuration, using the passed-in *config* parameter whose data type is *DataServiceConfiguration*. This class has a *SetEntitySetAccessRule* method that accepts two parameters. The first parameter represents the name of the entity set on which you want to set permission. This parameter also accepts the asterisk (*) wildcard to set permissions on all entity sets. The second parameter is an *EntitySetRights* enumeration value that represents the permissions you want to assign to the entity set. Table 7-1 contains a list of the *EntitySetRights* values. For this demonstration, the parameter name is set to asterisk and the permission is set to *AllRead*.

TABLE 7-1 The *EntitySetRights* Enumeration Values

VALUE	DESCRIPTION
All	Provides authorization to create, read, update, and delete data.
AllRead	Provides authorization to read data.
AllWrite	Provides authorization to write data.
None	Denies all rights to access data.
ReadMultiple	Provides authorization to perform multiple item queries to read from the entity set.
ReadSingle	Provides authorization to perform single item queries to read from the entity set.
WriteAppend	Provides authorization to write new items to the entity set.
WriteDelete	Provides authorization to delete items from the entity set.
WriteMerge	Provides authorization to perform merge-based updates, in which the payload must be an entity and needs only to contain the properties being modified. If a property is not included, the value currently present in the server will be preserved.
WriteReplace	Provides authorization to perform replace-based updates, in which the payload must be an entity and should contain all the properties of the entity. If a property is not included, the value is reset on the server to the default value for the property.

In the previous code sample, the generated code contains commented sample code that references the *config* object. The *config* object sets permissions on the operations by providing a *ServiceOperationRights* enumeration value to the *SetServiceOperationAccessRule* method. The possible values for the *ServiceOperationRights* enumeration are described in Table 7-2.

TABLE 7-2 The *ServiceOperationRights* Enumeration Values

VALUE	DESCRIPTION
All	All rights are granted
AllRead	Grants permission to read all items returned from the operation
None	Does not grant permissions to the operation
OverrideEntitySetRights	Overrides permissions that have been explicitly set on the entity with the operation permissions
ReadMultiple	Grants permission to read multiple items that are returned from the operation
ReadSingle	Grants permission to read only a single item that is returned from the operation

The *SetServiceOperationAccessRule* method isn't used in this example but will be used in the next section of this chapter, "Accessing Database Data."

Next, the *CarService* class must contain properties to expose data, so a *Cars* property is added to *CarService*. This property gets data from a hard-coded list of cars but could certainly get its data from a back-end SQL Server or other source. The property's data type must be of generic *IQueryable*. The following code sample shows the completed *CarService* class with the *Cars* property.

Sample of Visual Basic Code

```vb
Public Class CarService
    Inherits DataService(Of CarService)

    Public ReadOnly Property Cars As IQueryable(Of Car)
        Get
            Return (New List(Of Car) From
        {
            New Car() With {.VIN = "ABC123", .Make = "Ford",
                            .Model = "F-250", .Year = 2000},
            New Car() With {.VIN = "DEF123", .Make = "BMW",
                            .Model = "Z-3", .Year = 2005},
            New Car() With {.VIN = "ABC456", .Make = "Audi",
                            .Model = "TT", .Year = 2008},
            New Car() With {.VIN = "HIJ123", .Make = "VW",
                            .Model = "Bug", .Year = 1956},
            New Car() With {.VIN = "DEF456", .Make = "Ford",
                            .Model = "F-150", .Year = 1998}
```

```
        }).AsQueryable()
      End Get
    End Property

    Public Shared Sub InitializeService( _
          ByVal config As DataServiceConfiguration)
      config.SetEntitySetAccessRule("*", EntitySetRights.AllRead)
      config.DataServiceBehavior.MaxProtocolVersion = _
        DataServiceProtocolVersion.V2
    End Sub

End Class
```

Sample of C# Code

```
public class CarService : DataService<CarService>
{

    public IQueryable<Car> Cars
    {
      get
      {
        return (new List<Car>
        {
          new Car {VIN = "ABC123",Make = "Ford",
            Model = "F-250", Year = 2000},
          new Car {VIN = "DEF123",Make = "BMW",
            Model = "Z-3",   Year = 2005},
          new Car {VIN = "ABC456",Make = "Audi",
            Model = "TT",    Year = 2008},
          new Car {VIN = "HIJ123",Make = "VW",
            Model = "Bug",   Year = 1956},
          new Car {VIN = "DEF456",Make = "Ford",
            Model = "F-150", Year = 1998}
        }).AsQueryable();

      }
    }

    public static void InitializeService(DataServiceConfiguration config)
    {
      config.SetEntitySetAccessRule("*", EntitySetRights.AllRead);
      config.DataServiceBehavior.MaxProtocolVersion = DataServiceProtocolVersion.V2;
    }
}
```

Before running this, right-click the CarServer.svc file and choose Set As Start Page. Next, open Microsoft Internet Explorer and turn off Feed Viewing by choosing Tools | Internet Options | Content. Under the Feeds and Web Slices section of the screen, click Settings and clear the Turn option on the Feed reading view. Run the application, and the browser opens and displays the OData service, as shown in Figure 7-2.

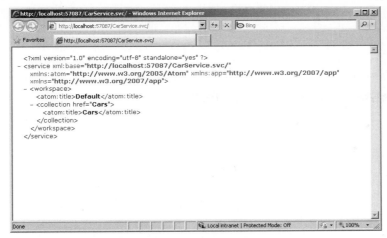

FIGURE 7-2 The OData service information is displayed.

The browser shows an XML representation of the service. In the defined namespaces, the atom namespace is defined. This is the namespace that is used for RSS feeds. The *Cars* collection is defined as a relative URI location, so adding *Cars* to the end of the URI will display an XML feed containing the list of cars, as shown in Figure 7-3. The list of cars is shown in a feed. With each *Car* description, you see a relative URI that indicates how to retrieve this *Car* description. For example, the second *Car* entry has href="Cars('DEF123')", so instead of adding *Cars* to the end of the URI, you can add the parentheses and the VIN to retrieve a single *Car*.

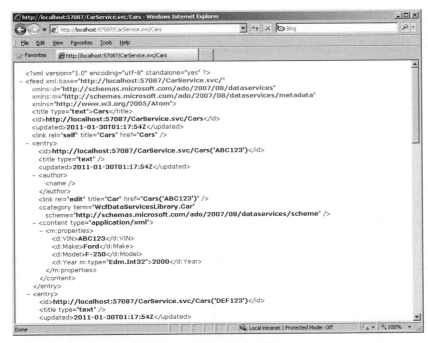

FIGURE 7-3 To query for all the cars, add *Cars* to the URI.

You might also want to retrieve the schema information that describes the entities exposed by the service. For example, with ASMX web services, you could add ?WSDL to the end of the URI to get the schema information. With WCF Data Services, you add /$metadata to the end of the URI, as shown in Figure 7-4. In Figure 7-4, the root element is using the *EDMX* namespace. You saw this in the previous chapter, "ADO.NET Entity Framework," when working with EDMX files that describe the Entity Data Model. The metadata describes the *Car* entity with its properties. Also described is the *EntityContainer*, called *CarService*, which has an *EntitySet* called *Cars*.

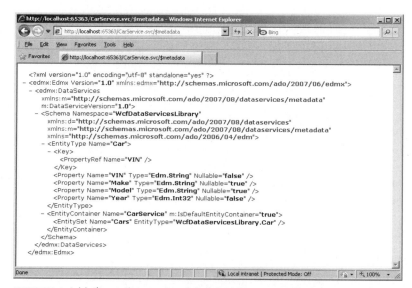

FIGURE 7-4 Add /$metadata to the end of the URI to retrieve schema information.

Accessing Database Data

You've seen an example of creating a WCF data service to provide access to data that is not in a database. In this section, you see an example of exposing database data by using WCF Data Services.

First, an ADO.NET Entity Data Model is added to the project by right-clicking the project node in Solution Explorer and then choosing Add | New Item. Select ADO.NET Entity Data Model, set the file name to **NorthwindModel.edmx**, and click Add. This starts the Entity Data Model Wizard. Select Generate from Database, and the connection is configured to reference the Northwind database. All tables and *CustOrderHist* stored procedures are selected; keep the default namespace of *NorthwindModel* and click Finish. This displays the Entity Framework designer.

The stored procedure must be exposed as a function import before it can be called. In the Model Browser window, right-click the *CustOrderHist* stored procedure and click Add Function Import. In the Add Function Import window, click Get Column Information and then click Create New Complex Type, which creates a new entity, *CustOrderHist_Result*. Click OK and then save and close the designer.

Next, add a WCF data service by right-clicking the project node in Solution Explorer and then choosing Add | New Item. Select WCF Data Service, set the file name to NorthwindService.svc, and then click Add. You now see the code-behind class for *NorthwindService*. The *NorthwindService* class must be configured to inherit from the generic *DataService* of *NorthwindEntities*.

You can't directly access the *CustOrderHist* function import from the WCF data service, but you can add a method to the *NorthwindService* class that will provide access. Methods that are added to the service class are called *service operations*. Service operations can accept parameters, but the parameters must be input (Visual Basic *ByVal*) parameters, and the parameters must be primitive types. Service operations must return either a primitive type, *IEnumerable*, *IQueryable*, or void (Visual Basic *Sub* instead of *Function*).

Service operations must also have either a *WebGet* or *WebInvoke* attribute. The *WebGet* attribute works with the HTTP GET verb, and the *WebInvoke* attribute works with the HTTP POST verb. This example uses the *WebGet* attribute, which enables you to execute the service operation from the URI.

In this example, all permissions will be granted, which include permissions for service operations. The following code sample shows the completed *NorthwindService* class.

Sample of Visual Basic Code

```
Public Class NorthwindService
    Inherits DataService(Of NorthwindEntities)
    Public Shared Sub InitializeService( _
          ByVal config As DataServiceConfiguration)
       config.SetEntitySetAccessRule("*", EntitySetRights.All)
       config.SetServiceOperationAccessRule("*", _
          ServiceOperationRights.All)
       config.DataServiceBehavior.MaxProtocolVersion = _
          DataServiceProtocolVersion.V2
    End Sub

    <WebGet()> _
    Public Function CustOrderHist(ByVal customerID As String) _
          As IQueryable(Of CustOrderHist_Result)
       Using db As New NorthwindEntities()
          Return db.CustOrderHist(customerID).ToList().AsQueryable()
       End Using
    End Function
End Class
```

Sample of C# Code

```
public class NorthwindService : DataService<NorthwindEntities>
{
    // This method is called only once to initialize service-wide policies.
    public static void InitializeService(DataServiceConfiguration config)
    {
       config.SetEntitySetAccessRule("*",
```

```
        EntitySetRights.All);
    config.SetServiceOperationAccessRule("*",
        ServiceOperationRights.All);
    config.DataServiceBehavior.MaxProtocolVersion =
        DataServiceProtocolVersion.V2;
}

[WebGet]
public IQueryable<CustOrderHist_Result> CustOrderHist(string customerID)
{
    using(NorthwindEntities db = new NorthwindEntities())
    {
        return  db.CustOrderHist(customerID).ToList().AsQueryable();
    }
}
}
```

In the previous code sample, the *config* object sets permissions on the operations by providing a *ServiceOperationRights* enumeration value to the *SetServiceOperationAccessRule* method. The possible values for the *ServiceOperationRights* enumeration were described previously, in Table 7-2.

Before running the application, right-click the NorthwindService.svc file and choose Set As Start Page. Next, run the application. The browser window opens and displays the available entity collections. If you add the entity collection name to the end of the URI, you see the items in the collection as shown in the following sample URIs.

Sample URIs to Access Entities

```
http://localhost:65363/NorthwindService.svc/Customers
http://localhost:65363/NorthwindService.svc/Employees
http://localhost:65363/NorthwindService.svc/Orders
```

These URIs return the *Customer*, *Employees*, and *Orders* classes, respectively. To execute the *CustOrderHist* service operation, provide the name of the operation and then specify the parameter and its value in the query string. If you have multiple parameters, use the ampersand (&) to separate each parameter. The following example executes the *CustOrderHist* service operation.

Sample URI to Execute Service Operation

```
http://localhost:65363/NorthwindService.svc/CustOrderHist?customerID='ALFKI'
```

This URI executes the *CustOrderHist* service operation with the *customerID* parameter being set to *ALFKI*. The service operation then makes a call to the *CustOrderHist* stored procedure, passing the parameter. The result is converted to a list, and then the *AsQueryable* method is executed to return a result that can be used with sorting, paging, and filtering.

Querying Data through WCF Data Services

Now that you have learned how to create a WCF data service, you will want to perform queries against the data. Some queries will require filtering, whereas other queries require joining operations. This section examines many of the aspects of querying your WCF data service for data.

Accessing the WCF Data Service

By now, you might see that you can perform queries and service operations by constructing an appropriate URI. You also learned that specifying /Cars('DEF123') at the end of the URI passes DEF123 as the key to locate and returns the single *Car* that has a VIN of DEF123. For service operations, you learned that you can specify the name of the service operation followed by a question mark and the name of the parameter, with their respective values.

A URI used by an OData service has up to three significant parts: the service root URI, the resource path, and query options. Figure 7-5 shows the basic layout of the URI. You've seen the use of the service root URI, the resource path, and the query string. Figure 7-5 shows the implementation of a filter to retrieve customers whose Country equals USA.

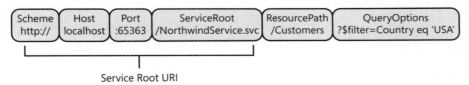

FIGURE 7-5 The URI layout has a service root URI, a resource path, and query options.

Executing a Simple Query

Executing simple queries for entities can be accomplished by constructing the proper URI to access the entity set in which you are interested. The following are examples of queries to the *NorthwindService* class to return entity sets.

Retrieve All Customers

```
http://localhost:65363/NorthwindService.svc/Customers
```

Retrieve All Products

```
http://localhost:65363/NorthwindService.svc/Products
```

Retrieve the Customer Whose CustomerID (primary key) is WOLZA

```
http://localhost:65363/NorthwindService.svc/Customers('WOLZA')
```

Retrieve the Products Whose ProductID (primary key) is 10

```
http://localhost:65363/NorthwindService.svc/Products(10)
```

Addressing Properties to Retrieve

You might also be interested in retrieving a single property from a query. You can specify single properties as well as other keywords at the end of the URI, such as in the following examples.

Retrieve the CompanyName from the Customer Whose CustomerID (primary key) is QUICK

```
http://localhost:57087/NorthwindService.svc/Customers('QUICK')/CompanyName
```

Retrieve the Orders (navigation property) for the Customer Whose CustomerID (primary key) is QUICK

```
http://localhost:57087/NorthwindService.svc/Customers('QUICK')/Orders
```

Retrieve the Supplier's CompanyName from the Supplier (navigation property) of Product 1 (primary key)

```
http://localhost:57087/NorthwindService.svc/Products(1)/Supplier/CompanyName
```

In the previous examples, you saw that you can access navigation properties to retrieve data. You are able to navigate from parent to child in the example where the orders are retrieved for the customer whose ID is QUICK. You are able also to navigate from child to parent in the example where Supplier is retrieved for the product whose ID is 1.

You can also use the *$count* keyword to retrieve the count of entities in the query, as shown in the following example.

Retrieve the Count of Orders for the Customer Whose CustomerID (primary key) is QUICK

```
http://localhost:57087/NorthwindService.svc/Customers('QUICK')/Orders/$count
```

You can also use the *$value* keyword to retrieve the *raw value* of a property explicitly, although *$value* is implied if you don't specify it.

Retrieve the CompanyName Value from the Customer Whose CustomerID (primary key) is QUICK

```
http://localhost:57087/NorthwindService.svc/Customers('QUICK')/CompanyName/$value
```

In addition to the previous examples that retrieve a single property value such as the *CompanyName* property of a customer, you can also specify multiple properties to return by using the *$select* keyword in the query string, as shown in the following examples.

Retrieve the ProductID, ProductName, and UnitPrice for the Product Whose ProductID is 1(primary key)

```
http://localhost:57087/NorthwindService.svc/Products(1)
    ?$select=ProductID,ProductName,UnitPrice
```

Retrieve the CustomerID and CompanyName for all Customers

```
http://localhost:57087/NorthwindService.svc/Customers?$select=CustomerID,CompanyName
```

Setting Result Order

You can use the *$orderby* keyword in the query options to specify an expression for determining which values are used to order the collection of entities identified by the Resource Path section of the URI. The *$orderby* keyword is supported only when the resource path identifies a collection of entities. The following are examples of using the *$orderby* keyword.

Retrieve Customers Ordered By ContactName

```
http://localhost:57087/NorthwindService.svc/Customers?$orderby=ContactName
```

Retrieve Employees Ordered By LastName, FirstName

```
http://localhost:57087/NorthwindService.svc/Employees?$orderby=LastName,FirstName
```

Retrieve Products Ordered By UnitPrice Descending

```
http://localhost:57087/NorthwindService.svc/Products?$orderby=UnitPrice desc
```

Retrieving the Top *x* Entities

Often, you have a query that returns many entities, but you are interested in only the first three entities. The *$top* keyword can limit the quantity of entities returned from a query. This subset is formed by selecting only the first *n* items of the entities that would have been returned, where *n* is a positive integer specified.

If the data service URI contains the *$top* keyword but doesn't contain the *$orderby* keyword, the entities in the set first need to be fully ordered by the data service. The *$orderby* keyword isn't mandated, but, to ensure repeatable results, a data service must always use the same semantics to obtain a full ordering across requests. The following are examples of using the *$top* keyword.

Retrieve First 3 Customers

```
http://localhost:57087/NorthwindService.svc/Customers?$top=3
```

Retrieve Top 3 of Highest Priced Products

```
http://localhost:57087/NorthwindService.svc/Products?$orderby=UnitPrice desc&$top=3
```

The *$orderby* and *$top* keywords are combined in the second example by using the ampersand (&) character.

Skipping Over Entities

You can use the *$skip* keyword to jump over, or skip past, a subset of entities that would have been returned as identified by the Resource Path section of the URI. Probably the most beneficial use of the *$skip* keyword is in the implementation of paging scenarios, in which you skip *n* and take *x* entities to display a page of data.

Although not mandated, a query that contains the *$skip* keyword should have the *$orderby* keyword to ensure the same semantics across paging requests. The following is an example of retrieving data by using the *$skip* keyword.

Retrieve 3 Customers after Skipping 18 Customers

```
http://localhost:57087/NorthwindService.svc/Customers?
    $orderby=CustomerID&$skip=18&$top=3
```

Working with Filters

How do you query for Customers in the USA? This requires you to provide a filter expression in the URI. You can use the *$filter* keyword in the query option to identify a subset of the items you want to retrieve from the entity set identified in the Resource Path section of the URI. The subset is determined by selecting only the entities that satisfy the predicate expression specified by the query option.

The expression you provide in the *$filter* keyword supports references to properties and literals. The literal can be a string enclosed in single quotes, a number, or a Boolean value (*true* or *false*). The operators supported in the *$filter* expression are shown in Table 7-3.

TABLE 7-3 The *$filter* Operators

OPERATOR	DESCRIPTION
eq	Equality comparison
ne	Not equals comparison
gt	Greater than comparison
ge	Greater than or equal to
lt	Less than comparison
le	Less than or equal to
and	And logical operator
or	Or logical operator
Not	Not logical operator
Add	Mathematical addition
Sub	Mathematical subtraction
mul	Mathematical multiplication
div	Mathematical division
mod	Mathematical modulus
( )	Precedence grouping

The following sample URIs demonstrate queries you can perform to retrieve data by using the *$filter* operators.

Retrieve Products Whose Unit Price Is Greater than 10

```
http://localhost:65363/NorthwindService.svc/Products?$filter=UnitPrice gt 10
```

Retrieve Orders Where the CustomerID Equals ALFKI

```
http://localhost:65363/NorthwindService.svc/Orders?$filter=CustomerID eq 'ALFKI'
```

Retrieve Products Whose UnitsInStock Is Less than or Equal to 2

```
http://localhost:65363/NorthwindService.svc/Products?$filter=UnitsInStock le 2
```

Retrieve Discontinued Product Whose UnitPrice Is Greater than or Equal to 50

```
http://localhost:65363/NorthwindService.svc/Products?$filter=Discontinued eq true
    and UnitPrice ge 50
```

EXAM TIP

For the exam, make sure you understand how to write filters because you will be tested on these.

In addition to using the filter operators, you can also take advantage of the string functions specified in Table 7-4.

TABLE 7-4 The OData String Functions

FUNCTION	DESCRIPTION
bool substringof(string p0, string p1)	Returns *true* if p0 is contained within p1, else *false*
bool endswith(string p0, string p1)	Returns *true* if p0 ends with p1, else *false*
bool startswith(string p0, string p1)	Returns *true* if p0 starts with p1, else *false*
int length(string p0)	Returns the length of p0
int indexof(string p0, string p1)	Returns the location of p1 in p0
string replace(string p0, string pFind, string pReplace)	Replaces *pFind* in p0 with *pReplace* and returns the result
string substring(string p0, int pos)	Returns the string part of p0 starting at pos to the end of the string
string substring(string p0, int pos, int length)	Returns the string part of p0 starting at pos to the length
string tolower(string p0)	Converts the string p0 to lowercase and returns the result
string toupper(string p0)	Converts the string p0 to uppercase and returns the result
string trim(string p0)	Trims leading and trailing spaces from p0 and returns the result
string concat(string p0, string p1)	Concatenates p0 and p1 and returns the result

The following sample URIs demonstrate queries that you can perform to retrieve data by using string functions.

Retrieve Products Whose ProductName Starts with C

```
http://localhost:65363/NorthwindService.svc/Products?$filter=startswith(ProductName,'C')
```

Retrieve Customers Whose CompanyName Contains restaurant

```
http://localhost:65363/NorthwindService.svc/Customers?$filter=
    substringof('restaurant',CompanyName)
```

Date and time functions are also available for use with *$filter* operations. Table 7-5 describes the date and time functions.

TABLE 7-5 The OData Date and Time Functions

FUNCTION	DESCRIPTION
int day(DateTime p0)	Returns the day of the month from p0
int hour(DateTime p0)	Returns the hour of the day from p0
int minute(DateTime p0)	Returns the minute of the hour from p0
int month(DateTime p0)	Returns the month of the year from p0
int second(DateTime p0)	Returns the second of the minute from p0
int year(DateTime p0)	Returns the year of the date from p0

The following sample URIs demonstrate queries you can perform to retrieve data by using date and time functions.

Retrieve Orders Placed in 1998

```
http://localhost:65363/NorthwindService.svc/Orders?$filter=year(OrderDate) eq 1998
```

Retrieve Orders Placed in February of 1998

```
http://localhost:65363/NorthwindService.svc/Orders?$filter=year(OrderDate) eq 1998
    and month(OrderDate) eq 2
```

Math functions are also available for use with *$filter* operations. Table 7-6 describes the math functions.

TABLE 7-6 The OData Math Functions

FUNCTION	DESCRIPTION
double round(double p0) *decimal round(decimal p0)*	Rounds p0 to the nearest whole number and returns the result. A .5 value will always round away from zero. For positive numbers, this will be the next highest whole number. For negative numbers, this will be the next lowest whole number.
double floor(double p0) *decimal floor(decimal p0)*	Returns the whole number that is just under p0.
double ceiling(double p0) *decimal ceiling(decimal p0)*	Returns the whole number that is just over p0.

The following sample URIs demonstrate queries you can perform to retrieve data by using math functions.

Retrieve Products Whose UnitPrice Floor Is 19

```
http://localhost:65363/NorthwindService.svc/Products?$filter=floor(UnitPrice) eq 19
```

Retrieve Products Whose UnitPrice Rounds to 29

```
http://localhost:65363/NorthwindService.svc/Products?$filter=round(UnitPrice) eq 29
```

Retrieve Products Whose UnitPrice Ends with .5

```
http://localhost:65363/NorthwindService.svc/Products?$filter=
    UnitPrice sub floor(UnitPrice) eq 0.5
```

Type functions are also available for use with *$filter* operations. Table 7-7 describes the type functions.

TABLE 7-7 The OData Type Functions

FUNCTION	DESCRIPTION
bool IsOf(type p0)	Returns *true* if entity being queried is of the type p0, else returns *false*
bool IsOf(expression p0, type p1)	Returns *true* if expression p0 is of type p1, else returns *false*

The *IsOf* functions are useful when you are returning instances of derived classes and you want to return only the elements that are of one of the types. For example, your query might ask for all the Accounts, which will return *CheckingAccount* and *SavingsAccount* entities. You can use *$function=IsOf('MyModel.SavingsAccount')* to return *SavingsAccounts*.

Eager Loading of Entities

You might want to retrieve a *Customer* entity and then retrieve the *Order* entities for that *Customer*. Rather than execute two queries, you can execute a single query by using the *$expand* keyword. A URI with an *$expand* keyword indicates that entities associated with the entity or collection of entities identified by the resource path section of the URI must be eagerly loaded.

The syntax of an *$expand* keyword is a comma-separated list of *Navigation* properties. Additionally, each *Navigation* property can be followed by a forward slash and another *Navigation* property to enable identifying a multilevel relationship.

Retrieve the Customer Whose CustomerID Is QUICK and the Orders for QUICK

```
http://localhost:57087/NorthwindService.svc/Customers('QUICK')?$expand=Orders
```

Retrieve the Customer Whose CustomerID Is ALFKI and the Orders and Order_Details for ALFKI

```
http://localhost:57087/NorthwindService.svc/Customers('ALFKI')
    ?$expand=Orders/Order_Details
```

Create a WCF Data Service

In this practice, you create a WCF data service to expose and share data to applications that have Internet access. This WCF data service will be used in Lesson 2, "Consuming WCF Data Services."

If you encounter a problem completing an exercise, the completed projects can be installed from the Code folder on the companion CD.

EXERCISE **Creating a Web Application with WCF Data Services**

In this exercise, you create a web application project, the WCF data service, and an Entity Data Model that represents the Northwind Customers and Orders tables.

1. In Visual Studio .NET 2010, choose File | New | Project.

2. Select your desired programming language and then select the ASP.NET Web Application template. For the project name, enter **OrderEntryServices**. Be sure to select a desired location for this project.

3. For the solution name, enter **OrderEntrySolution**. Be sure Create Directory For Solution is selected and then click OK.

   After Visual Studio .NET creates the project, the home page, Default.aspx, is displayed.

4. Delete the Default.aspx file, which should also cause the corresponding code-behind file to be deleted.

5. Add the Northwind Entity Data Model by right-clicking the project node in Solution Explorer. Choose Add | New Item | Data and select ADO.NET Entity Data Model. Set the file name to **NorthwindModel.edmx** and click Add. This starts the Entity Data Model Wizard.

6. Select Generate from the database and click Next. Configure your connection to reference the Northwind database and click Next.

7. On the Choose Your Database Objects screen, select the Customers, Orders, Order_ Details, and Products tables and click Finish.

8. Add the Northwind Data Service by right-clicking the project node in Solution Explorer. Choose Add | New Item | Web, select WCF Data Service, and set the file name to **NorthwindDataService.svc**. Click Add.

9. In the code-behind file for NorthwindDataService, set the *DataService* generic parameter to *NorthwindDataService*. Also, add code to call the config object's *SetEntitySetAccessRule* method, passing all (*) and the *EntitySetRights.All* enumeration. Your code should look like the following.

Sample of Visual Basic Code

```
Public Class NorthwindDataService
    Inherits DataService(Of NorthwindEntities)

    Public Shared Sub InitializeService(ByVal config As DataServiceConfiguration)
        config.SetEntitySetAccessRule("*", EntitySetRights.All)
```

```
        config.DataServiceBehavior.MaxProtocolVersion =
DataServiceProtocolVersion.V2
    End Sub

End Class
```

Sample of C# Code
```csharp
public class NorthwindDataService : DataService<NorthwindEntities >
{
    public static void InitializeService(DataServiceConfiguration config)
    {
        config.SetEntitySetAccessRule("*", EntitySetRights.All);
        config.DataServiceBehavior.MaxProtocolVersion =
            DataServiceProtocolVersion.V2;
    }
}
```

10. In Solution Explorer, right-click the NorthwindDataService.svc file and click Set As Start Page.

11. Before running the application, configure your browser so that it does not render feeds. Open Internet Explorer and choose Tools | Internet Options | Content. In the Feeds and Web Slices section, click Settings. Clear Turn On Feed Reading View and click OK.

12. Run the application. You should see the browser window open and the output of the NorthwindDataService.svc displayed.

13. Try running some queries by changing the URI. Add customers to the end of the URI to see the Customers list. Try the same for Order, Order_Details, and Products.

Lesson Summary

This lesson provided detailed information about creating, configuring, and querying WCF Data Services.

- WCF Data Services was formerly known as ADO.NET Data Services.
- WCF Data Services uses Atom Publishing protocol and Open Data protocol (OData).
- WCF Data Services uses the semantics of representational state transfer (REST).
- URIs that you simply enter in the browser address bar perform an HTTP GET, which enables you to query for data.
- You can use *EntitySetRights* enumeration to set access permissions to data.
- You can use the *ServiceOperationRights* enumeration to set the access permissions to service operations.
- The *$metadata* keyword retrieves the entire schema, which defines all data being exposed.
- You can expose any data with a WCF data service.
- You can expose an Entity Data Model with a WCF data service.

- You cannot directly call a stored procedure or function import from WCF Data Services. You must create a service operation to gain access to a stored procedure through a function import.
- When calling a service operation, the parameters are passed in the query string and separated with the ampersand (&).
- The *$count* keyword can retrieve a count of entities that meet a query criterion.
- The *$orderby* keyword can specify a sort order.
- The *$top* keyword can retrieve the first *n* entities from a query result.
- The *$skip* keyword can be used when paging to skip over *n* entities before returning a query result.
- The *$filter* keyword limits the entities to be returned from a query.
- The *$expand* keyword eager loads entities when executing a query.

Lesson Review

You can use the following questions to test your knowledge of the information in Lesson 1, "What Is WCF Data Services?" The questions are also available on the companion CD if you prefer to review them in electronic form.

> **NOTE ANSWERS**
>
> Answers to these questions and explanations of why each answer choice is correct or incorrect are located in the "Answers" section at the end of the book.

1. Which of the following keywords is used to implement eager loading of data when executing a query?

    A. *$skip*

    B. *$value*

    C. *$expand*

    D. *$filter*

2. You want to configure your WCF data service to allow only a single row lookup from the *Customers* entities and not allow queries that return all entities from *Customers*. How can you configure the WCF data service?

    A. config.SetEntitySetAccessRule("Customers", *EntitySetRights.ReadSingle*)

    B. config.SetEntitySetAccessRule("Customers", *EntitySetRights.ReadMultiple*)

    C. config.SetEntitySetAccessRule("Customers", *EntitySetRights.AllRead*)

3. The URI to your WCF data service is *http://www.northwind.com/DataServices.svc*. What can you add to the end of the URI to retrieve only a list of *Order* entities for the *Customer* entity whose CustomerID is 'BONAP'?

   A. /Customers('BONAP')?$expand=Orders

   B. /Customers?$filter=CustomerID eq 'BONAP'&$expand=Orders

   C. /Customers/Orders?$filter=CustomerID eq 'BONAP'

   D. /Customers('BONAP')/Orders

Lesson 2: Consuming WCF Data Services

Now that you've learned how to create, configure, and query a WCF data service, you must bind it to an application. In this lesson, a simple application is added to the example project from Lesson 1, and you will find that it's relatively easy to use WCF Data Services.

Adding a client application enables you to consume and display the data as needed. In this demonstration, a WPF client is added to the existing solution to access the WCF data service, but keep in mind that the client application could be any kind of application, including web or console applications.

> **After this lesson, you will be able to:**
> - Create a WPF application that binds to a WCF data service.
> - Add a WCF data service reference to an application.
> - Bind a WCF data service to a WPF *DataGrid*.
> - Specify a payload format.
> - Create a query interceptor.
>
> **Estimated lesson time: 30 minutes**

Adding a Client Application

In Lesson 1, a sample solution was created called WcfDataServicesSolution. It contains a WcfDataServicesLibrary web application. Add a WPF WpfClient application to the solution by right-clicking the solution node in Solution Explorer, choose Add | New Project | Windows, and select the WPF Application template. Name the project **WpfClient** and click OK.

When the client application is loaded, you see the MainWindows.xaml file. Add a row to the *Grid* control for a *Menu* control and a second row to the *Grid* control for a *DataGrid* control. Add the *Menu* and *DataGrid* controls. Name the *DataGrid* control **dg** and set the *AutoGenerateColumns* property to *true*. In *Menu*, add a *MenuItem* element for Lesson 2 and a *MenuItem* element to retrieve the *Customers* collection and display it in the *DataGrid* control. Finally, click the *MenuItem* element for retrieving the *Customers* collection and, in the Properties window, click Events. Locate the *Click* event, type **getCustomers**, and press Enter. This creates the *getCustomers* method in the code. Your XAML for the *Grid* control should look like the following.

Sample of XAML

```
<Grid>
  <Grid.RowDefinitions>
    <RowDefinition Height="Auto"/>
    <RowDefinition Height="*"/>
  </Grid.RowDefinitions>
  <Menu>
```

```
        <MenuItem Header="Lesson 2">
            <MenuItem Header="Get Customers" Click="getCustomers" />
            <MenuItem Header="Save"/>
        </MenuItem>
    </Menu>
    <DataGrid AutoGenerateColumns="True" Grid.Row="1" Name="dg"  />
</Grid>
```

Referencing the WCF Data Service

Now that a basic GUI has been created that can be expanded upon, tell the client application where the data is by adding a service reference to the WpfClient application.

To add the service reference, in the WpfClient application, right-click the project node and choose Add Service Reference. When the Service window is displayed, click Discover, which causes Visual Studio .NET to look through the solution for web and WCF services. CarService and NorthwindService will be displayed. Select NorthwindService by making sure that the radio button is selected. Also, note the address or copy it to the clipboard because you'll need it soon. At the bottom of the screen, set the namespace to *NorthwindServiceReference*, as shown in Figure 7-6.

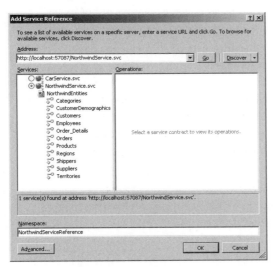

FIGURE 7-6 The Service Reference screen alerts your application to the WCF data service.

Click OK to add the reference. This creates proxy classes in your application that appear and behave like the classes that exist in the WCF data service. You will be able to use the proxy classes to communicate to the WCF data service. If you want to see the proxy classes, they are in Reference.datasvcmap/Reference.cs file under the *NorthwindServiceReference* node and can be found by clicking the plus sign (+) beside *NorthwindServiceReference*. If the *NorthwindServiceReference* node does not have a plus sign beside it, you can click Show All Files at the top of the Solution Explorer window.

If you look at the proxy classes, you'll notice that the *NorthwindEntities* class inherits from *DataServiceContext* instead of from *ObjectContext*. The *DataServiceContext* class is the proxy class that behaves like *ObjectContext* except that it's at the client. *DataServiceContext* has many of the same methods *ObjectContext* has, but, typically, you'll find changes to the parameters due to *DataServiceContext* being a client-side object. For example, the constructor requires the URI of the WCF data service.

Binding to the WCF Data Service with *DataServiceCollection*

When binding your data to a WPF or Silverlight *DataGrid* control, you normally assign the data to the *ItemsSource* property. This works if your data is read-only, but you might want to modify the data in *DataGrid* and save the changes. In that scenario, if you bind an entity set directly to the *ItemsSource* property, when you execute the *SaveChanges* method on the *DataServiceContext* object, nothing will be saved because *DataServiceContext* won't know that changes actually took place—*DataGrid* doesn't notify *DataServiceContext* of changes.

WCF Data Services provides the generic *DataServiceCollection* class to support two-way binding of data to controls in client applications. This class inherits from the generic *ObservableCollection* class, which implements the *INotifyCollectionChanged* interface. This is the primary data-binding mechanism for WPF and Silverlight-based applications.

To bind the *Customers* collection to the *DataGrid* control when you click the Get Customers menu item, add code to instantiate the *NorthwindEntities* class and assign the object to the *db* field. Next, in the *getCustomers* method, add code to create a *DataServiceCollection* object and pass *db.Customers* into the constructor. Assign this object to the *source* local variable. Next, add code to assign *source* to *DataGrid* (*dg*). Your code should look like the following example.

Sample of Visual Basic Code

```
Imports System.Data.Services.Client
Imports WpfClient.NorthwindServiceReference

Class MainWindow
    Dim db As New NorthwindEntities( _
        New Uri("http://localhost:65363/NorthwindService.svc"))

    Private Sub getCustomers(ByVal sender As System.Object, _
        ByVal e As System.Windows.RoutedEventArgs)
        Dim source = New DataServiceCollection(Of Customer)(db.Customers)
        dg.ItemsSource = source
    End Sub
End Class
```

Sample of C# Code

```
using System;
using System.Data.Services.Client;
using System.Windows;
using WpfClient.NorthwindServiceReference;
```

```
namespace WpfClient
{
    /// <summary>
    /// Interaction logic for MainWindow.xaml
    /// </summary>
    public partial class MainWindow : Window
    {

        private NorthwindEntities db = new NorthwindEntities(
            new Uri("http://localhost:57087/NorthwindService.svc"));

        public MainWindow()
        {
            InitializeComponent();
        }

        private void getCustomers(object sender, RoutedEventArgs e)
        {
            var source = new DataServiceCollection<Customer>(db.Customers);
            dg.ItemsSource = source;
        }
    }
}
```

Before running your application, right-click the WcfClient application and click Set As Startup Project. If you run the application and click the Get Customers menu item, you should see the customer data in the data grid, as shown in Figure 7-7.

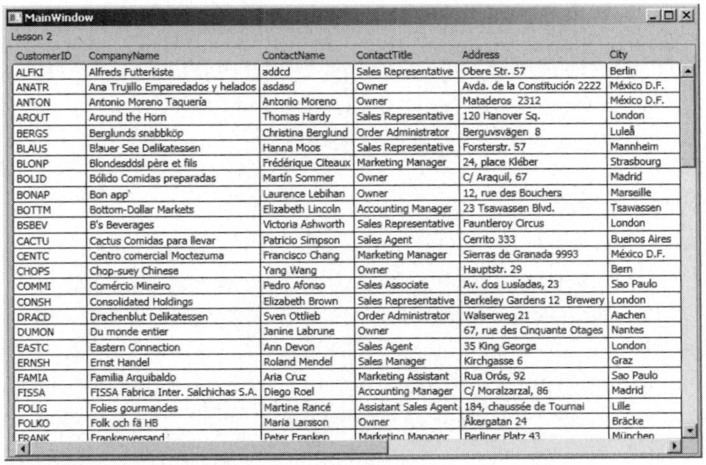

FIGURE 7-7 *DataServiceCollection* binds WCF Data Services to data grids.

To be able to save changes back to the database, you can execute the *SaveChanges* method on the *DataServiceContext* object. The *SaveChanges* method contains an overload that enables you to pass a *SaveChangesOption* enumeration value that provides the following options:

- **None** This is the default. Changes are sent to the server by using multiple requests, and the operation aborts on the first failure.
- **Batch** All changes are sent to the server in a single batch.
- **ContinueOnError** Changes are sent to the server by using multiple requests, and the operation continues even if errors occur.
- **ReplaceOnUpdate** Updates are made by replacing all values on the entity with the values from the client.

Click within the XAML definition of the Save *MenuItem* and, in the Properties window, click Events. In the *Click* event, type **saveToDatabase** and press Enter. This adds the *saveToDatabase* method to the code-behind file. In this method, call the *SaveChanges* method and display a Saved message. Your code should look like the following sample code.

Sample of Visual Basic Code

```
Private Sub saveToDatabase(ByVal sender As System.Object, _
   ByVal e As System.Windows.RoutedEventArgs)
   db.SaveChanges()
   MessageBox.Show("Saved")
End Sub
```

Sample of C# Code

```
private void saveToDatabase(object sender, RoutedEventArgs e)
{
   db.SaveChanges();
   MessageBox.Show("Saved");
}
```

Run the application and get the customer list. Modify some of the contact names and click Save. You should see the Saved message. If you stop the application and restart, viewing the customers displays the modified customer that has been persisted.

Specifying a Payload Format

When passing messages between the client and the WCF data service, the supported formats are AtomPub and JSON. AtomPub is a specially formatted XML format used with feeds, and JSON is JavaScript Object Notation, which competes with XML when objects can be represented with JSON. Instead of *begin* and *end* tags, JSON uses curly braces { }. The *DataServiceContext* object supports only AtomPub format, but if you use the *WebClient* class to send requests, you can specify a header of Accept=application/json. Table 7-8 shows the supported formats.

TABLE 7-8 The Supported Payload Formats

REQUESTED MIME TYPE	RESPONSE MIME TYPE	SERIALIZATION FORMAT
/	*application/atom+xml*	AtomPub
text/*	*Not supported*	N/A

application/*	Not supported	N/A
text/xml	text/xml	AtomPub
application/xml	application/xml	AtomPub
application/atom+xml	application/atom+xml	AtomPub
application/json	application/json	JSON

Another menu item has been added to the sample client application to retrieve a customer by using the AtomPub format and JSON format. The following code samples show how to use the *System.Net.WebClient* class to call a WCF data service.

Sample of Visual Basic Code

```vb
Private Sub getCustomerWebClient(ByVal sender As System.Object, _
    ByVal e As System.Windows.RoutedEventArgs)
  Dim uri = db.BaseUri.ToString() + "/Customers('ALFKI')"
  Using client = New WebClient()
    Dim result = client.DownloadString(uri)
    MessageBox.Show(result)
  End Using
  Using client = New WebClient()
    client.Headers("Accept") = "application/json"
    Dim result = client.DownloadString(uri)
    MessageBox.Show(result)
  End Using
End Sub
```

Sample of C# Code

```csharp
private void getCustomerWebClient(object sender, RoutedEventArgs e)
{
    var uri = db.BaseUri.ToString() + "/Customers('ALFKI')";
    using (WebClient client = new WebClient())
    {
        var result = client.DownloadString(uri);
        MessageBox.Show(result);
    }
    using (WebClient client = new WebClient())
    {
        client.Headers["Accept"] = "application/json";
        var result = client.DownloadString(uri);
        MessageBox.Show(result);
    }
}
```

EXAM TIP

For the exam, make sure you understand how to make JSON calls to WCF Data Services.

Using Interceptors

You can hook into WCF Data Services by using interceptors to gain access to the request messages so that you can add custom logic to an operation. To intercept a message, you add *QueryInterceptorAttribute* or *ChangeInterceptorAttribute* over the desired methods in the data service. The *interceptor* attribute requires a *string* parameter that specifies the entity set to which the interceptor applies.

Add the following sample code to the NorthwindService.svc code-behind file. This code shows how you can use *QueryInterceptorAttribute* to intercept calls to retrieve *Customers* collections and provide a lambda expression that filters the customers to return only the customers that are in the United States.

Sample of Visual Basic Code

```vb
<QueryInterceptor("Customers")> _
Public Function OnQueryCustomers() _
      As Expression(Of Func(Of Customer, Boolean))
    Return Function(c) c.Country = "USA"
End Function
```

Sample of C# Code

```csharp
[QueryInterceptor("Customers")]
public Expression<Func<Customer, bool>> OnQueryCustomers()
{
    return c => c.Country=="USA";
}
```

ChangeInterceptorAttribute can intercept changes and perform validation or constraint checking before the modification takes place. In your method, you can decide to abort the modification by throwing a *DataServiceException* in your code.

Sample of Visual Basic Code

```vb
<ChangeInterceptor("Products")> _
Public Sub OnChangeProducts(ByVal product As Product, _
                        ByVal operations As UpdateOperations)
    If operations = UpdateOperations.Add OrElse _
          operations = UpdateOperations.Change Then
        ' Reject changes to discontinued products.
        If product.Discontinued Then
          Throw New DataServiceException(400, _
            String.Format( _
                "Modifications not allowed on discontinued product ID:{0} Name:{1}", _
                product.ProductID, product.ProductName))
        End If
    ElseIf operations = UpdateOperations.Delete Then
        ' Block the delete and instead set the Discontinued flag.
        Throw New DataServiceException(400, _
            String.Format( _
                "Deletion not allowed on discontinued product " + _
                "ID:{0} Name:{1} set Discontinued to true", _
                product.ProductID, product.ProductName))
    End If
End Sub
```

Sample of C# Code

```csharp
[ChangeInterceptor("Products")]
public void OnChangeProducts(Product product, UpdateOperations operations)
{
    if (operations == UpdateOperations.Add ||
        operations == UpdateOperations.Change)
    {
        // Reject changes to discontinued products.
        if (product.Discontinued)
        {
            throw new DataServiceException(400,
                string.Format(
                    "Modifications not allowed on discontinued product " +
                    "ID:{0} Name:{1}",
                    product.ProductID, product.ProductName));
        }
    }
    else if (operations == UpdateOperations.Delete)
    {
        // Block the delete and instead set the Discontinued flag.
        throw new DataServiceException(400,
            string.Format(
                "Deletion not allowed on discontinued product " +
                "ID:{0} Name:{1} set Discontinued to true",
                product.ProductID, product.ProductName));
    }
}
```

PRACTICE   Add a WPF Client

In this practice, you add a new WPF project to the solution you created in Lesson 1. The project will be almost the same as the project you created in Chapter 4, "LINQ to SQL," except that you use this project to connect to remote data by using WCF Data Services instead of connecting to local data by using LINQ to SQL classes.

If you encounter a problem completing an exercise, the completed projects can be installed from the Code folder on the companion CD.

EXERCISE 1   Adding the WPF Project

In this exercise, you modify the solution you created in Lesson 1 by adding a WPF application to enter orders.

1. In Visual Studio .NET 2010, choose File | Open | Project. Open the project from Lesson 1 or locate and open the solution in the Begin folder for this lesson.

2. In Solution Explorer, right-click the solution node and choose Add | New Project, select the desired programming language, and then select Windows. In the project templates window, select WPF Application.

3. Name the project **OrderEntryProject** and click OK. The New WPF Application window is displayed. Click OK. When the new project finishes loading, the MainPage.xaml file is displayed.

4. On the *Window* tag, add a *Loaded* event handler. When prompted for a new event handler, double-click New EventHandler. Your XAML should look like the following.

Sample of Visual Basic XAML

```
<Window x:Class="OrderEntryProject.MainWindow"
        xmlns="http://schemas.microsoft.com/winfx/2006/xaml/presentation"
        xmlns:x="http://schemas.microsoft.com/winfx/2006/xaml"
        Loaded="Window_Loaded"
        Title="MainWindow" Height="350" Width="525">
    <Grid>
    </Grid>
</Window>
```

Sample of C# XAML

```
<Window x:Class="OrderEntryProject.MainWindow"
        xmlns="http://schemas.microsoft.com/winfx/2006/xaml/presentation"
        xmlns:x="http://schemas.microsoft.com/winfx/2006/xaml"
        Loaded="Window_Loaded"
        Title="MainWindow" Height="350" Width="525">
    <Grid>
    </Grid>
</Window>
```

5. The XAML code contains a *Grid* definition. Inside the grid, add three row definitions. The first two rows should have their *Height* property set to *Auto*, and the last row should have its *Height* property set to "*". Regardless of your programming language, your XAML for the grid should look like the following:

Sample of XAML

```
<Grid>
    <Grid.RowDefinitions>
        <RowDefinition Height="Auto" />
        <RowDefinition Height="Auto" />
        <RowDefinition Height="*" />
    </Grid.RowDefinitions>
</Grid>
```

6. In XAML, before the end of *Grid*, add a menu. Inside *Menu*, add a *MenuItem* tag for Save called *mnuSave*, a *MenuItem* tag for New Order called *mnuOrder*, and a *MenuItem* tag for Exit called *mnuExit*. After adding these items, double-click each menu item to add the click event handler code. Your XAML should look like the following, regardless of programming language.

Sample of XAML

```
<Grid>
    <Grid.RowDefinitions>
        <RowDefinition Height="Auto" />
        <RowDefinition Height="Auto" />
```

```
            <RowDefinition Height="*" />
        </Grid.RowDefinitions>
        <Menu>
            <MenuItem Header="Save" Name="mnuSave" Click="mnuSave_Click" />
            <MenuItem Header="New Order" Name="mnuOrder" Click="mnuOrder_Click" />
            <MenuItem Header="Exit" Name="mnuExit" Click="mnuExit_Click" />
        </Menu>
    </Grid>
```

7. In XAML, under Menu, add a *cmbCustomers* combo box control. Configure the combo box to be in Grid.Row="1". Under that, add a *lstOrders* list box control. Configure *ListBox* to be in Grid.Row="2". Set the *Margin* property of both items to **5**. Double-click the combo box to add a *SelectionChanged* event handler to your code. Your XAML should look like the following:

Sample of XAML

```
<Grid>
    <Grid.RowDefinitions>
        <RowDefinition Height="Auto" />
        <RowDefinition Height="Auto" />
        <RowDefinition Height="*" />
    </Grid.RowDefinitions>
    <Menu>
        <MenuItem Header="Save" Name="mnuSave" Click="mnuSave_Click" />
        <MenuItem Header="New Order" Name="mnuOrder" Click="mnuOrder_Click" />
        <MenuItem Header="Exit" Name="mnuExit" Click="mnuExit_Click" />
    </Menu>
    <ComboBox Grid.Row="1"  Name="cmbCustomers" Margin="5"
            SelectionChanged="cmbCustomers_SelectionChanged" />
    <ListBox Grid.Row="2" Margin="5" Name="lstOrders" />
</Grid>
```

8. Extend markup in the list box element to configure a custom template to display OrderID, OrderDate, and RequiredDate from the Orders table. This requires the *ListBox* element to be converted to have separate start and end tags. Your XAML for the list box should look like the following, regardless of programming language:

Sample of XAML

```
<ListBox Grid.Row="2" Margin="5" Name="lstOrders">
    <ListBox.ItemTemplate>
        <DataTemplate>
            <Border CornerRadius="5" BorderThickness="2"
                    BorderBrush="Blue" Margin="3">
                <StackPanel Orientation="Horizontal">
                    <TextBlock Text="Order #"
                            TextAlignment="Right" Width="40"/>
                    <TextBlock Name="txtOrderID"
                            Text="{Binding Path=OrderID}" Margin="5,0,10,0"
                            Width="30"/>
                    <TextBlock Text="Order Date:"
                            TextAlignment="Right" Width="80"/>
                    <TextBlock Name="txtOrderDate"
                        Text="{Binding Path=OrderDate,
```

```
              StringFormat={}{0:MM/dd/yyyy}}"
              Margin="5,0,10,0" Width="75"/>
      <TextBlock Text="Required Date:"
          TextAlignment="Right" Width="80"/>
      <TextBlock Name="txtRequiredDate"
          Text="{Binding Path=RequiredDate,
              StringFormat={}{0:MM/dd/yyyy}}"
          Margin="5,0,10,0" Width="75"/>
    </StackPanel>
  </Border>
  </DataTemplate>
</ListBox.ItemTemplate>
</ListBox>
```

9. Add the service reference to NorthwindDataService.svc in *OrderEntryServices*. In Solution Explorer, right-click the *OrderEntryProject* node and click Add Service Reference.

10. Click Discover, which will locate WCF services in your solution. Select NorthwindDataService.svc, swipe the URI in the address window, and copy it to the clipboard (for use in later steps). In the Namespace text box, enter **NorthwindServiceReference** and click OK.

11. At the top of the code-behind file, add code to import the *OrderEntryProject. NorthwindServiceReference* namespace as shown.

    Sample of Visual Basic Code

    ```
    Imports OrderEntryProject.NorthwindServiceReference
    ```

    Sample of C# Code

    ```
    using OrderEntryProject.NorthwindServiceReference;
    ```

12. In the code-behind file, add a *ctx* private field to the top of the *MainWindow* class, set its type to **NorthwindEntities,** and instantiate the class as follows:

    Sample of Visual Basic Code

    ```
    Private ctx As New NorthwindEntities(New Uri());
    ```

    Sample of C# Code

    ```
    private NorthwindEntities ctx = new NorthwindEntities(new Uri());
    ```

13. In the constructor of the *NorthwindEntities* object, pass the URI to the WCF data service. If you don't have the URI in the clipboard, you can right-click the project, choose Add Service Reference, and then click Discover. You will see NorthwindDataService. Swipe the URI in the address window and copy it to the clipboard. Paste the URI into the Uri constructor.

14. In the *Window_Loaded* event handler method, add code to save *ctx* to an application property called "ctx", which makes the *ctx* object accessible from other windows. Add *imports System.Data.Services.Client* (C# *using System.Data.Service.Client;*). Next, create an instance of *DataServiceCollection* and assign it to a local *source* variable. Assign the

source variable to *cmbCustomers*. Set *DisplayMemberPath* to display *CompanyName*. The *Window_Loaded* event handler should look like the following:

Sample of Visual Basic Code

```vb
Private Sub Window_Loaded(ByVal sender As System.Object, _
                          ByVal e As System.Windows.RoutedEventArgs)
    Application.Current.Properties("ctx") = ctx
    Dim source = New DataServiceCollection(Of Customer)(ctx.Customers)
    cmbCustomers.ItemsSource = source
    cmbCustomers.DisplayMemberPath = "CompanyName"
End Sub
```

Sample of C# Code

```csharp
private void Window_Loaded(object sender, RoutedEventArgs e)
{
    Application.Current.Properties["ctx"] = ctx;
    var source = new DataServiceCollection<Customer>(ctx.Customers);
    cmbCustomers.ItemsSource = source;
    cmbCustomers.DisplayMemberPath = "CompanyName";
}
```

15. Add code to the *SelectionChanged* event handler method to retrieve the selected customer information and use it to write a LINQ query for a list of OrderID, OrderDate, and RequestDate from the Orders table. Your code should look like the following.

Sample of Visual Basic Code

```vb
Private Sub cmbCustomers_SelectionChanged(ByVal sender As System.Object, _
            ByVal e As System.Windows.Controls.SelectionChangedEventArgs)
    Dim customer = CType(cmbCustomers.SelectedValue, Customer)
    If (customer Is Nothing) Then Return
    lstOrders.ItemsSource =
        From o In ctx.Orders
        Where o.CustomerID = customer.CustomerID
        Select New With _
            { _
                o.OrderID, _
                o.OrderDate, _
                o.RequiredDate _
            }
End Sub
```

Sample of C# Code

```csharp
private void cmbCustomers_SelectionChanged(object sender,
    SelectionChangedEventArgs e)
{
    var customer = (Customer)cmbCustomers.SelectedValue;
    if (customer == null) return;
    lstOrders.ItemsSource =
        from o in ctx.Orders
        where o.CustomerID == customer.CustomerID
        select new
            {
                o.OrderID,
```

```
            o.OrderDate,
            o.RequiredDate
        };
}
```

16. In the *Exit* event handler method, add code to end the application. Your code should look like the following:

Sample of Visual Basic Code

```
Private Sub mnuExit_Click(ByVal sender As System.Object, _
                            ByVal e As System.Windows.RoutedEventArgs)
    Application.Current.Shutdown()
End Sub
```

Sample of C# Code

```
private void mnuExit_Click(object sender, RoutedEventArgs e)
{
    Application.Current.Shutdown();
}
```

17. Choose Debug | Start Debugging to run the application. If you select a customer from the combo box, the list box populates with the list of OrderID, OrderDate, and RequiredDate. Click Exit to shut down the application.

EXERCISE 2   Adding Order Entry to the Application

In this exercise, you modify the WPF application you created in Lesson 1 by creating the GUI for order entry and then adding code to store the new order in the database.

1. In Visual Studio .NET 2010, choose File | Open | Project. Open the project from Lesson 1.

2. In Solution Explorer, right-click OrderEntryProject, choose Add | Window, and enter **OrderWindow.xaml** as the name of the new window.

3. In the XAML window, enter the following markup to create the window for entering the order information. Your XAML should look like the following:

Sample of Visual Basic XAML

```
<Window x:Class="OrderEntryProject.OrderWindow"
        xmlns="http://schemas.microsoft.com/winfx/2006/xaml/presentation"
        xmlns:x="http://schemas.microsoft.com/winfx/2006/xaml"
        Title="OrderWindow" SizeToContent="WidthAndHeight">
    <Grid>
        <Grid.ColumnDefinitions>
            <ColumnDefinition Width="Auto" />
            <ColumnDefinition Width="Auto" />
        </Grid.ColumnDefinitions>
        <Grid.RowDefinitions>
            <RowDefinition Height="Auto" />
            <RowDefinition Height="Auto" />
            <RowDefinition Height="Auto" />
        </Grid.RowDefinitions>
        <DatePicker Grid.Column="1"  Margin="10" Name="dtOrder"  />
```

```
              <DatePicker Margin="10" Name="dtRequired" Grid.Column="1" Grid.Row="1" />
              <Button Content="Cancel" Grid.Row="2"  Margin="10"
                  Name="btnCancel" Click="btnCancel_Click" />
              <Button Content="OK"  Margin="10" Name="btnOk"
                  Grid.Column="1" Grid.Row="2" Click="btnOk_Click" />
              <TextBlock  Margin="10" Text="Order Date:"  />
              <TextBlock  Margin="10" Text="Required Date:" Grid.Row="1" />
          </Grid>
      </Window>
```

Sample of C# XAML

```
<Window x:Class="OrderEntryProject.OrderWindow"
        xmlns="http://schemas.microsoft.com/winfx/2006/xaml/presentation"
        xmlns:x="http://schemas.microsoft.com/winfx/2006/xaml"
        Title="OrderWindow" SizeToContent="WidthAndHeight">
    <Grid>
        <Grid.ColumnDefinitions>
          <ColumnDefinition Width="Auto" />
          <ColumnDefinition Width="Auto" />
        </Grid.ColumnDefinitions>
        <Grid.RowDefinitions>
          <RowDefinition Height="Auto" />
          <RowDefinition Height="Auto" />
          <RowDefinition Height="Auto" />
        </Grid.RowDefinitions>
        <DatePicker Grid.Column="1"  Margin="10" Name="dtOrder"  />
        <DatePicker Margin="10" Name="dtRequired" Grid.Column="1" Grid.Row="1" />
        <Button Content="Cancel" Grid.Row="2"  Margin="10"
            Name="btnCancel" Click="btnCancel_Click" />
        <Button Content="OK"  Margin="10" Name="btnOk"
            Grid.Column="1" Grid.Row="2" Click="btnOk_Click" />
        <TextBlock  Margin="10" Text="Order Date:"  />
        <TextBlock  Margin="10" Text="Required Date:" Grid.Row="1" />
    </Grid>
</Window>
```

4. Right-click the OrderWindow.xaml file and click View Code to go to the code-behind window. Add a *CustomerID* public *string* property to the top of the *OrderWindow* class. Your code should look like the following.

Sample of Visual Basic Code

```
Public Property CustomerID As String
```

Sample of C# Code

```
public string CustomerID { get; set; }
```

5. Double-click *btnCancel* to create the *btnCancel_Click* event handler method automatically and add a single line of code to call the *Close* method so this window will be closed.

6. Double-click *btnOk* to create the *btnOk_Click* event handler method automatically and add code to create a new *Order* object with the values from the main window. Use

DataContext to go to the *Orders* collection and call *InsertOnSubmit* with the new order. Your completed window code should look like the following.

Sample of Visual Basic Code

```vb
Imports OrderEntryProject.NorthwindServiceReference

Public Class OrderWindow

    Public Property CustomerID As String

    Private Sub btnOk_Click(ByVal sender As System.Object, _
                            ByVal e As System.Windows.RoutedEventArgs)
        Dim ctx = CType(Application.Current.Properties("ctx"), NorthwindEntities)
        Dim Order = New Order With _
                    { _
                        .CustomerID = CustomerID, _
                        .OrderDate = dtOrder.SelectedDate, _
                        .RequiredDate = dtRequired.SelectedDate _
                    }
        ctx.AddToOrders(Order)
        Close()
    End Sub

    Private Sub btnCancel_Click(ByVal sender As System.Object, _
                                ByVal e As System.Windows.RoutedEventArgs)
        Close()
    End Sub
End Class
```

Sample of C# Code

```csharp
using System.Windows;
using OrderEntryProject.NorthwindServiceReference;

namespace OrderEntryProject
{

    public partial class OrderWindow : Window
    {
        public string CustomerID { get; set; }

        public OrderWindow()
        {
            InitializeComponent();
        }

        private void btnCancel_Click(object sender, RoutedEventArgs e)
        {
            Close();
        }

        private void btnOk_Click(object sender, RoutedEventArgs e)
        {
            var ctx = (NorthwindEntities) App.Current.Properties["ctx"];
            Order order = new Order
```

```
                    {
                        CustomerID = this.CustomerID,
                        OrderDate = dtOrder.SelectedDate,
                        RequiredDate = dtRequired.SelectedDate
                    };
            ctx.AddToOrders(order);
            this.Close();
        }
    }
}
```

7. Open the code-behind screen for *MainWindow* and add code to the *Save* event handler method to submit the *NorthwindEntities* changes to the database and display a message stating "Saved."

8. Call the customer combo box's *SelectionChanged* event handler method to force *ListBox* to be updated. Your code should look like the following.

Sample of Visual Basic Code

```
Private Sub mnuSave_Click(ByVal sender As System.Object, _
                        ByVal e As System.Windows.RoutedEventArgs)
    ctx.SaveChanges()
    MessageBox.Show("Saved")
    cmbCustomers_SelectionChanged(Nothing, Nothing)
End Sub

Private Sub mnuOrder_Click(ByVal sender As System.Object, _
                        ByVal e As System.Windows.RoutedEventArgs)
    Dim customer = CType(cmbCustomers.SelectedValue, Customer)
    Dim window = New OrderWindow With {.CustomerID = customer.CustomerID}
    window.ShowDialog()
End Sub
```

Sample of C# Code

```
private void mnuSave_Click(object sender, RoutedEventArgs e)
{
    ctx.SaveChanges();
    MessageBox.Show("Saved");
    cmbCustomers_SelectionChanged(null, null);
}

private void mnuOrder_Click(object sender, RoutedEventArgs e)
{
    var customer = (Customer)cmbCustomers.SelectedValue;
    OrderWindow window = new OrderWindow {CustomerID = customer.CustomerID};
    window.ShowDialog();
}
```

9. Choose Debug | Start Debugging to run your application.

10. Select a customer from the combo box. You should see a list of orders for that customer.

11. With a customer selected, click New Order on the menu. Enter an order date and required date and click OK.

12. Click Save. After you click OK to close the Saved window, you should see the updated list of orders, which includes your new order.

Lesson Summary

This lesson provided a detailed overview of WCF Data Services.

- WCF Data Services supports data connectivity to any application that has network access to the data, which includes Silverlight, WPF, and Windows Forms.
- You can access a WCF data service by adding a service reference to your project.
- Use *DataServiceCollection* to perform a two-way binding to *DataGrid* controls.
- With WCF Data Services, you can specify the payload format to be JSON or AtomPub.
- Interceptors can intercept a query request before the results are returned and intercept a service operation before it's executed.

Lesson Review

You can use the following questions to test your knowledge of the information in Lesson 2, "Consuming WCF Data Services." The questions are also available on the companion CD if you prefer to review them in electronic form.

NOTE ANSWERS

Answers to these questions and explanations of why each answer choice is correct or incorrect are located in the "Answers" section at the end of the book.

1. You are writing a WCF data service that will be included in a large project that has many other WCF data services. Your WCF data service will provide access to a SQL server using the Entity Framework. The EDMX file already exists in the project and is used by other services. One of the tables exposed by your service is the Contacts table, which contains the list of employees and the list of external contacts, which are denoted by the IsEmployee column that can be set to *1* or *0*. You want to configure your WCF data service to return the external contacts whenever someone queries the *Contacts* entity set through WCF Data Services. What is the best way to solve this problem?

   A. Modify the *Contacts* entity set in the EDMX file.

   B. Add a stored procedure to SQL Server and modify the EDMX file to create a function import that you can call.

   C. Add a method to your WCF data service class and adorn the method with a *QueryInterceptorAttribute* of *Contacts*. In the method, provide the filter.

   D. Add a lazy loader to the WCF data service that will filter out the employees.

2. Which payload formats can be specified if you are making an AJAX call to a WCF data service? (Each correct answer provides a complete solution. Choose two.)

   A. SOAP

   B. JSON

   C. WSDL

   D. AtomPub

Case Scenario

In the following case scenario, you will apply what you've learned about WCF Data Services discussed in this chapter. You can find answers to these questions in the "Answers" section at the end of this book.

Case Scenario: Exposing Data

You want to expose your data to the web in a way that clients can easily consume and query the data in their applications. You have no idea what the client application type is, but you want to ensure that your data is consumable by a broad range of clients. Answer the following questions regarding the implementation of a solution:

1. Can WCF Data Services solve this problem?

2. Which WCF Data Services features and drawbacks would you consider when trying to decide whether it's a viable solution?

Suggested Practices

To help you successfully master the exam objectives presented in this chapter, complete the following tasks.

You should create at least one WCF data service that exposes at least two related entity sets and then create an application that consumes the WCF data service. This can be accomplished by completing the practices at the ends of Lesson 1 and Lesson 2 or by completing the following Practice 1.

- **Practice 1** Create an application that requires you to display data from at least two related database tables that are located on a remote database server where you will access these tables by creating a WCF data service. This could be movies that have actors, artists who record music, or people who have vehicles.

- **Practice 2** Complete Practice 1 and then provide additional code to enable modification to the data.

Take a Practice Test

The practice tests on this book's companion CD offer many options. For example, you can test yourself on just the lesson review content, or you can test yourself on all the 70-516 certification exam content. You can set up the test so that it closely simulates the experience of taking a certification exam, or you can set it up in study mode so that you can look at the correct answers and explanations after you answer each question.

> **MORE INFO** **PRACTICE TESTS**
>
> For details about all the practice test options available, see the "How to Use the Practice Tests" section in this book's introduction.

CHAPTER 8

Developing Reliable Applications

The previous chapters have presented various ways to access data, starting with the traditional data classes such as *DataSet* and *DbDataAdapter* and then examining LINQ, LINQ to SQL, LINQ to XML, LINQ to Entities, and WCF Data Services. Many more topics related to data access need to be covered. This chapter covers these surrounding topics to help round out your data access needs.

Exam objectives in this chapter:

- Monitor and collect performance data.
- Handle exceptions.
- Protect data.
- Synchronize data.

Lessons in this chapter:

Before You Begin

You must have some understanding of Microsoft Visual C# or Visual Basic 2010. This chapter requires only the hardware and software listed at the beginning of this book. You should also have access to the Northwind database, which is one of the Microsoft "sandbox" databases. The Northwind database can be downloaded from the Microsoft website and is included on the companion disk.

 REAL WORLD

Glenn Johnson

It's relatively easy to create an application that provides access to data, but you typically run into problems when the application needs to support hundreds or thousands of users. What do you do if users are complaining that queries are either running too slowly or are failing? You need a way to monitor your application for problems that can affect performance and overall reliability. Reliability is closely associated with availability and performance. Many of the topics in this chapter will help you increase the reliability of your application.

Lesson 1: Monitoring and Collecting Performance Data

Trace logging provides a detailed record of system and application events when activities such as a disk I/O operation or a committed transaction occurs. In this lesson, you learn some of the ways you can implement tracing.

> **After this lesson, you will be able to:**
> - Set up a trace log.
> - Generate a trace log.
> - Access performance counters.
>
> **Estimated lesson time: 20 minutes**

Implementing Instrumentation

Instrumentation enables you to determine the running state of a system after it's been deployed. You instrument your application at development time by creating an instrumentation policy at the beginning of the development process to determine what should be instrumented, as well as why, where, and how.

Instrumentation is performed using a wide variety of available technologies that provide support and diagnostic information from within an application itself. These technologies include event logging, debug tracing, and performance counters. This lesson covers the use of these technologies.

Logging Queries

ADO.NET provides various ways to access and log the queries that are executed. This section explores an implementation of logging by using the LINQ to SQL classes and the Entity Framework.

Accessing SQL Generated by LINQ to SQL

When working with LINQ to SQL classes, you can easily assign an object that inherits from *TextWriter* to the *Log* property of the *DataContext* object so that you can create a *StreamWriter* object that fills up a log file, assigns it to the *Log* property, and starts running queries.

EXAM TIP

For the exam, remember that the *Log* property is used on the *DataContext* object to capture all SQL statements when they are executed.

Logging every executed query is certainly costly in terms of performance and disk space, so you might want to control logging from your .config file. To accomplish this, you can add a BooleanSwitch to your .config file and set the value to turn logging on or off.

To set up logging in a way that is controllable, a new class is created that takes advantage of the *DataContext Log* property and the *Trace* framework in the *System.Diagnostics* namespace. The new class is called *LinqToSqlTraceWriter*, and it inherits from *TextWriter*, so it can be assigned to the *Log* property of the *DataContext* object. This class overrides the *Write* method that accepts a *character* parameter, which is the data to be written. This method is called from all other overloads of the *Write* and *WriteLine* methods, so this override provides a way for you to intercept all data and pass the data to the *Trace.Write* method, but only if the BooleanSwitch is enabled in the .config file. Also, the *Close* and *Flush* methods are overridden to call *Trace.Close* and *Trace.Flush*, respectively. The following code contains the *LinqToSqlTraceWriter* class.

Sample of Visual Basic Code

```vb
Imports System.IO
Imports System.Text

Public Class LinqToSqlTraceWriter
    Inherits TextWriter

    Private logSwitch As BooleanSwitch

    Public Sub New(ByVal switchName As String)
        logSwitch = New BooleanSwitch(switchName, switchName)
    End Sub

    Public Overrides ReadOnly Property Encoding As Encoding
        Get
            Throw New NotImplementedException()
        End Get
    End Property

    Public Overrides Sub Write(ByVal value As Char)
        If (logSwitch.Enabled) Then
            Trace.Write(value)
        End If
    End Sub


    Public Overrides Sub Flush()
        Trace.Flush()
    End Sub

    Public Overrides Sub Close()
        Trace.Close()
    End Sub

End Class
```

Sample of C# Code

```csharp
using System;
using System.Diagnostics;
using System.Text;
using System.IO;

namespace ReliableApplication.LinqToSql
{
    public class LinqToSqlTraceWriter : TextWriter
    {
        private BooleanSwitch logSwitch;
        public LinqToSqlTraceWriter(string switchName)
        {
            logSwitch = new BooleanSwitch(switchName, switchName);
        }

        public override Encoding Encoding
        {
            get { throw new NotImplementedException(); }
        }

        public override void Write(char value)
        {
            if (logSwitch.Enabled)
            {
                Trace.Write(value);
            }
        }

        public override void Flush()
        {
            Trace.Flush();
        }

        public override void Close()
        {
            Trace.Close();
        }
    }
}
```

Now that this class is created, you can add LINQ to SQL classes to your project and execute a LINQ to SQL query to log the results. The following code sample shows a simple query for *IEnumerable* of *Customer*.

Sample of Visual Basic Code

```vb
Private Sub mnuLinqToSqlTrace_Click(ByVal sender As System.Object, _
    ByVal e As System.Windows.RoutedEventArgs) _
    Handles mnuLinqToSqlTrace.Click

    Dim db = New LinqToSql.NorthwindDataContext()
    db.Log = New LinqToSqlTraceWriter("LinqToSqlSwitch")
```

```
    Dim cust = From c In db.Customers
               Where c.CompanyName.StartsWith("A") _
               And c.Country = "UK"
               Order By c.CompanyName
               Select c
    Dim items = cust.ToList()'force execution
    MessageBox.Show("Done")
End Sub
```

Sample of C# Code

```
private void mnuLinqToSqlTrace_Click(
    object sender, RoutedEventArgs e)
{
    var db = new LinqToSql.NorthwindDataContext();
    db.Log = new LinqToSqlTraceWriter("LinqToSqlSwitch");

    var cust = from c in db.Customers
               where c.CompanyName.StartsWith("A")
                     && c.Country == "UK"
               orderby c.CompanyName
               select c;

    var items = cust.ToList();//force execution
    MessageBox.Show("Done");
}
```

When you run this code, you won't see anything special because you must turn on tracing in your .config file. The following must be added to your .config file to turn on tracing.

Sample of Config File

```
<configuration>
    <system.diagnostics>
        <switches>
            <add name="LinqToSqlSwitch" value="1"/>
        </switches>
    </system.diagnostics>
</configuration>
```

If any of these sections already exist, you must merge this into the existing sections so the section isn't listed twice. For example, many of the default Visual Basic templates already contain *system.diagnostics* namespaces and switches, so you must add the *add* element into the existing *switches* element.

This .config sample shows the declaration of a switch named *LinqToSqlSwitch* and sets its value to *1*, which enables the switch in the code.

When you run the code to execute a LINQ to SQL query, you see the SQL statement in your Visual Studio .NET Output window because a default listener is configured that sets the trace output to the Output window. Figure 8-1 shows the Output window. The TRACE compiler constant, which is defined by default, must also be defined.

FIGURE 8-1 The LINQ to SQL query is written to the Output window by default.

You might also want to change the location of the log or add other log locations, such as file logging or logging to the Windows EventLog. This can be done from within the .config file, so you can decide where to place the log file without rebuilding the application. The following is an example of adding a trace listener, one for writing to a text file and another for writing to the Windows Event Log.

Sample of Config File

```
<configuration>
    <system.diagnostics>
        <trace autoflush="true">
            <listeners>
                <add name="LinqToSql"
                     initializeData="C:\Logs\CsLinqToSql.log"
                     type="System.Diagnostics.TextWriterTraceListener"/>
                <add name="LinqToSqlEventLog"
                     initializeData="VbLinqToSqlTraceLog"
                     type="System.Diagnostics.EventLogTraceListener"/>
            </listeners>
        </trace>
    </system.diagnostics>
</configuration>
```

Accessing SQL Generated by the Entity Framework

When working with the Entity Framework, you might want to see the SQL that is generated when you execute a LINQ query. Do this by using the *ToTraceString* method on the generic *ObjectQuery* class.

Most LINQ to Entities queries return a generic *IQueryable* object, which can be converted to a generic *ObjectQuery* class. To implement this, you can create an extension method for *IQueryable* that performs the conversion and executes the *ToTraceString* method. Here is an example of such a method that also adds the date and time to the returned string.

Sample of Visual Basic Code

```
Imports System.Runtime.CompilerServices
Imports System.Data.Objects
```

```
Module ExtensionMethods
    <Extension()>
    Public Function ToTraceString(Of T)(ByVal query As IQueryable(Of T)) As String
        Dim objQuery = CType(query, ObjectQuery(Of T))
        If (Not objQuery Is Nothing) Then
            Return String.Format("{0}{2}{1}{2}{2}", _
                DateTime.Now, objQuery.ToTraceString(), _
                Environment.NewLine)
        End If
        Return String.Emp
    End Function
End Module
```

Sample of C# Code

```csharp
using System;
using System.Data.Objects;
using System.Linq;

namespace ReliableApplication
{
    public static class ExtensionMethods
    {
        public static string ToTraceString<T>(this IQueryable<T> query)
        {
            var objQuery = query as ObjectQuery<T>;
            if (objQuery != null)
                return string.Format("{0}{2}{1}{2}{2}",
                    DateTime.Now, objQuery.ToTraceString(),
                    Environment.NewLine);
            return string.Empty;
        }
    }
}
```

EXAM TIP

For the exam, remember that the *ToTraceString* method retrieves the SQL for LINQ to Entities, and calling this method does not execute the query.

This code sample returns a string containing the date and time on the first line, followed by the SQL being sent to the server, followed by two new lines. To test this code, add code to perform a LINQ query, call this new extension method, and append the results to a log file as shown in the following example.

Sample of Visual Basic Code

```vb
Private Sub mnuEntityFrameworkTrace_Click(ByVal sender As System.Object, _
        ByVal e As System.Windows.RoutedEventArgs) _
        Handles mnuEntityFrameworkTrace.Click
    Dim traceFile = Environment.GetFolderPath( _
        Environment.SpecialFolder.Desktop) _
        + "\EntityFrameworkTrace.log"
```

```vb
    Dim db = New NorthwindEntities()
    Dim cust = From c In db.Customers
               Where c.CompanyName.StartsWith("A") _
               And c.Country = "UK"
               Order By c.CompanyName
               Select c
    File.AppendAllText(traceFile, cust.ToTraceString())
    MessageBox.Show("Done")

End Sub
```

Sample of C# Code

```csharp
private void mnuEntityFrameworkTrace_Click(
    object sender, RoutedEventArgs e)
{
    var traceFile = Environment.GetFolderPath(
        Environment.SpecialFolder.Desktop)
        + @"\EntityFrameworkTrace.log";

    var db = new NorthwindEntities();
    var cust = from c in db.Customers
                where c.CompanyName.StartsWith("A")
                    && c.Country == "UK"
                orderby c.CompanyName
                select c;
    File.AppendAllText(traceFile, cust.ToTraceString());
    MessageBox.Show("Done");
}
```

After running the code sample several times, stop the application and open the EntityFrameworkTrace.log file that's located on your desktop. The result should look like the following.

EntityFrameworkTrace.log File

```
2/5/2011 7:17:36 PM
SELECT
[Extent1].[CustomerID] AS [CustomerID],
[Extent1].[CompanyName] AS [CompanyName],
[Extent1].[ContactName] AS [ContactName],
[Extent1].[ContactTitle] AS [ContactTitle],
[Extent1].[Address] AS [Address],
[Extent1].[City] AS [City],
[Extent1].[Region] AS [Region],
[Extent1].[PostalCode] AS [PostalCode],
[Extent1].[Country] AS [Country],
[Extent1].[Phone] AS [Phone],
[Extent1].[Fax] AS [Fax]
FROM [dbo].[Customers] AS [Extent1]
WHERE ([Extent1].[CompanyName] LIKE N'A%') AND (N'UK' = [Extent1].[Country])
ORDER BY [Extent1].[CompanyName] ASC
```

Accessing and Implementing Performance Counters

Performance counters provide data about how your application uses resources. At run time, you use the Performance utility that's part of Microsoft Windows to provide a graphical view of the counters.

Microsoft has also implemented many performance counters in the .NET Framework that you can view with the Windows Performance Monitor utility. To start this tool, choose Start | Control Panel | Administrative Tools and double-click Performance Monitor.

After Performance Monitor starts, you can open the *Monitoring Tools* node to see Performance Monitor, as shown in Figure 8-2. By default, clicking Performance Monitor reveals a graph that's constantly updated with the current value of the percent processor time, a performance counter that's implemented in Windows.

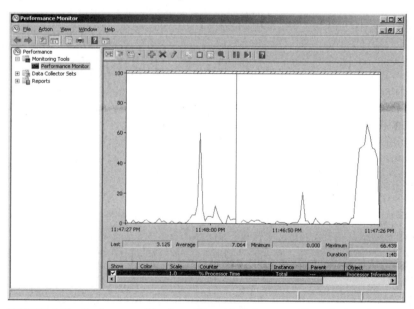

FIGURE 8-2 The Performance Monitor utility with % Processor Time displayed.

At the top of the Performance Monitor screen is a large green plus sign you can click to add more counters to the graph. Clicking the plus sign opens the Add Counters window. In the Add Counters part of the screen is a drop-down list from which you can select the computer you want to monitor. Under that, you'll find a list of Performance Monitor categories. One of the first categories is the .NET CLR Data category, as shown in Figure 8-3.

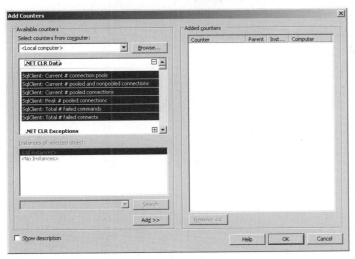

FIGURE 8-3 The .NET CLR Data category contains counters you might want to monitor.

There is a category for .NET Data Provider for Microsoft SQL Server as well. You can add any of the counters to the graph to display the counter's value constantly.

You can create your own Performance Monitor counters for your application by using classes in the *System.Diagnostics* namespace. Before adding a custom performance counter, you typically want to add a *PerformanceCounterCategory* for your counter, but verify that the category doesn't exist before you create it, or your code will throw an *InvalidOperationException*. After you verify that the category needs to be created, create the category and the counter. You can do this in a single statement, as shown in the following code sample.

Sample of Visual Basic Code

```vbnet
Private Sub mnuPerformanceMonitorCategory_Click( _
     ByVal sender As System.Object, _
     ByVal e As System.Windows.RoutedEventArgs) _
     Handles mnuPerformanceMonitorCategory.Click

   Dim catName = "MyAppCategory"
   If Not PerformanceCounterCategory.Exists(catName) Then
      PerformanceCounterCategory.Create(catName, _
         "Here is the category help.", _
         PerformanceCounterCategoryType.SingleInstance, _
         "MyCounter", _
         "Here is the counter help.")
      MessageBox.Show("Category and counter created")
```

```
    Else
        MessageBox.Show("Category and counter already exist")
    End If
End Sub
```

Sample of C# Code
```csharp
private void mnuPerformanceMonitorCategory_Click(
    object sender, RoutedEventArgs e)
{
    var catName = "MyAppCategory";
    if (!PerformanceCounterCategory.Exists(catName))
    {
        PerformanceCounterCategory.Create(catName,
            "Here is the category help.",
            PerformanceCounterCategoryType.SingleInstance,
            "MyCounter",
            "Here is the counter help.");
        MessageBox.Show("Category and counter created");
    }
    else
    {
        MessageBox.Show("Category and counter already exist");
    }
}
```

This sample code checks to see whether the category exists. If the category doesn't exist, the counter doesn't exist either which is why you can execute a single statement to create the category and the counter. The *Create* method accepts a *PerformanceCounterCategoryType* that can be set as *SingleInstance*, which means there is only a single *PerformanceCounter* instance to represent all applications that are running and using the counter. You can also set this to *MultipleInstances* so that you can see each application (instance) that is running and using the counter.

Now that you've created the category and counter, you can implement it in your code by instantiating *PerformanceMonitorCounter*, as shown in the following code sample.

Sample of Visual Basic Code
```vb
Private Sub mnuPerformanceCounter_Click( _
        ByVal sender As System.Object, _
        ByVal e As System.Windows.RoutedEventArgs) _
        Handles mnuPerformanceCounter.Click
    Dim pc = New PerformanceCounter("MyAppCategory", "MyCounter", False)
    Dim db = New LinqToSql.NorthwindDataContext()
    db.Log = New LinqToSqlTraceWriter("LinqToSqlSwitch")

    Dim cust = From c In db.Customers
                Where c.CompanyName.StartsWith("A") _
                And c.Country = "UK"
                Order By c.CompanyName
                Select c
    Dim items = cust.ToList() 'force execution
```

```
        pc.IncrementBy(items.Count)
        MessageBox.Show("Done")
End Sub
```

Sample of C# Code

```csharp
private void mnuPerformanceCounter_Click(
    object sender, RoutedEventArgs e)
{
    var db = new LinqToSql.NorthwindDataContext();
    db.Log = new LinqToSqlTraceWriter("LinqToSqlSwitch");
    var pc = new PerformanceCounter("MyAppCategory", "MyCounter", false);
    var cust = from c in db.Customers
               where c.CompanyName.StartsWith("A")
                    && c.Country == "UK"
               orderby c.CompanyName
               select c;
    var items = cust.ToList();//force execution
    pc.IncrementBy(items.Count);
    MessageBox.Show("Done");
}
```

If you run the application and click Performance Monitor Category, the MyCategory category and the MyCounter counter will be created. Next, start the Performance Monitor utility and navigate through the monitoring tools to reveal the *Performance Monitor* node. Click the plus sign and open MyCategory. Add MyCounter to the Performance Monitor view. In your application, click Performance Monitor to run the query in the previous sample code, which will increment the counter by the quantity of items returned. Each time you execute this code, you should see the Performance Monitor counter value increase, as shown in Figure 8-4.

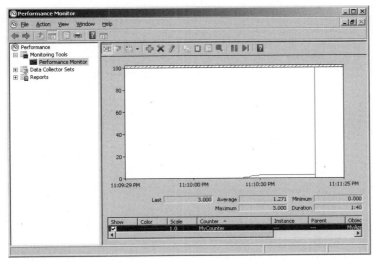

FIGURE 8-4 The MyCounter counter displays the total quantity of items returned.

In this practice, you instrument the application you created in Chapter 4 by adding tracing. When completed, you will be able to enable or disable the trace logging by using a trace switch.

If you encounter a problem completing an exercise, the completed projects can be installed from the Code folder on the companion CD.

EXERCISE   Opening the Existing Windows Presentation Foundation Project

In this exercise, you modify the solution you created in Chapter 4 by adding a tracing.

1. In Microsoft Visual Studio .NET 2010, choose File | Open | Project. The completed project from Chapter 4 has been copied to the Begin folder of Chapter 8, "Developing Reliable Applications," Lesson 1. Open the project.

2. Right-click the project node and choose Add | Class. Name the class **LinqToSqlTraceWriter** and click Add.

3. In the new class, add code to inherit from *TextWriter* and, in the class, add a *logSwitch* field whose type is *BooleanSwitch*.

4. Add a constructor that contains code to instantiate *logSwitch*.

5. Override the read-only *Encoding* property by adding a getter that throws a *NotImplementedException*.

6. Override the *Write* method that accepts a character parameter and add code that calls the *Write* method of the *Trace* object if *logSwitch* is enabled.

7. Override the *Flush* method and add code to call the *Trace.Flush* method.

8. Override the *Close* method and add code to call the *Trace.Close* method. Your code should look like the following.

Sample of Visual Basic Code

```vb
Imports System.IO
Imports System.Text

Public Class LinqToSqlTraceWriter
    Inherits TextWriter

    Private logSwitch As BooleanSwitch

    Public Sub New(ByVal switchName As String)
        logSwitch = New BooleanSwitch(switchName, switchName)
    End Sub

    Public Overrides ReadOnly Property Encoding As Encoding
        Get
            Throw New NotImplementedException()
        End Get
    End Property
```

```vb
    Public Overrides Sub Write(ByVal value As Char)
        If (logSwitch.Enabled) Then
            Trace.Write(value)
        End If
    End Sub

    Public Overrides Sub Flush()
        Trace.Flush()
    End Sub

    Public Overrides Sub Close()
        Trace.Close()
    End Sub

End Class
```

Sample of C# Code

```csharp
using System;
using System.Diagnostics;
using System.Text;
using System.IO;

namespace ReliableApplication.LinqToSql
{
    public class LinqToSqlTraceWriter : TextWriter
    {
        private BooleanSwitch logSwitch;
        public LinqToSqlTraceWriter(string switchName)
        {
            logSwitch = new BooleanSwitch(switchName, switchName);
        }

        public override Encoding Encoding
        {
            get { throw new NotImplementedException(); }
        }

        public override void Write(char value)
        {
            if (logSwitch.Enabled)
            {

                Trace.Write(value);
            }
        }

        public override void Flush()
        {
            Trace.Flush();
        }

        public override void Close()
        {
```

```
            Trace.Close();
        }
    }
}
```

9. Open the code-behind file for the MainWindow.xaml page.

10. Add a statement to the top of the *Window_Loaded* method that sets the *Log* property of the *ctx* object to a new *LinqToSqlTraceWriter* object, as shown in the following code sample.

Sample of Visual Basic Code

```
Private Sub Window_Loaded(ByVal sender As System.Object, _
                         ByVal e As System.Windows.RoutedEventArgs)
    ctx.Log = New LinqToSqlTraceWriter("DataLogging")
    Application.Current.Properties("ctx") = ctx
    cmbCustomers.ItemsSource = From c In ctx.Customers
                           Select New Tuple(Of String, String)( _
                               c.CustomerID, _
                               c.CompanyName)
    cmbCustomers.DisplayMemberPath = "Item2"
End Sub
```

Sample of C# Code

```
private void Window_Loaded(object sender, RoutedEventArgs e)
{
    ctx.Log = new LinqToSqlTraceWriter("DataLogging");
    App.Current.Properties["ctx"] = ctx;
    cmbCustomers.ItemsSource = from c in ctx.Customers
                           select new Tuple<string,string>
                               (
                                   c.CustomerID,
                                   c.CompanyName
                               );
    cmbCustomers.DisplayMemberPath = "Item2";
}
```

11. Open the App.config file, add a *DataLogging* trace switch, and set its value to *1*, as shown in the following sample.

Sample of Config File

```
<configuration>
    <system.diagnostics>
        <switches>
            <add name="DataLogging" value="1"/>
        </switches>
    </system.diagnostics>
</configuration>
```

12. Add a trace listener to the App.config file and set the log file location to a path to which you have permissions to write, for example, c:\logs\LinqToSql.log. Be sure to create the folder if it doesn't exist. The result should look like the following example.

Sample of Config File

```
<configuration>
   <system.diagnostics>
      <trace autoflush="true">
         <listeners>
            <add name="LinqToSql"
                 initializeData="C:\Logs\LinqToSql.log"
                 type="System.Diagnostics.TextWriterTraceListener"/>
         </listeners>
      </trace>
   </system.diagnostics>
</configuration>
```

13. Run the application. Add an Order and then save and end the application.

14. Locate and open the log file. You should see the SQL statements that were sent to the server.

Lesson Summary

This lesson provided a detailed overview of monitoring and collecting performance data.

- When using LINQ to SQL classes, you can use the *Log* property of the *DataContext* object to collect all the SQL statements sent to the database server when the application is running.

- When working with the Entity Framework, you must use the *ToTraceString* method on the *ObjectQuery* object.

- To access the *ToTraceString* method, you must typically convert your query to *ObjectQuery*, using the Visual Basic *CType* statement or the C# casting syntax.

- You can use the *Trace* framework that is part of the .NET Framework to write data to the trace listeners, based on a trace switch setting.

- The Performance Monitor utility can be used while the application is running to watch the performance monitor counters.

Lesson Review

You can use the following questions to test your knowledge of the information in Lesson 1, "Monitoring and Collecting Performance Data." The questions are also available on the companion CD if you prefer to review them in electronic form.

> **NOTE ANSWERS**
>
> Answers to these questions and explanations of why each answer choice is correct or incorrect are located in the "Answers" section at the end of the book.

1. When working with the Entity Framework, what can you use to retrieve the SQL of a query?

    A. Add a *TextWriter* object to the *Log* property of *ObjectContext*.

    B. Set the *Connection* property of *ObjectContext* to a *TextWriter* object.

    C. Use the *ToTraceString* method on the *ObjectQuery* object.

2. You create a *PerformanceCounter* object to view the SQL statements sent to the database server. True or false?

    A. True

    B. False

Lesson 2: Handling Exceptions

Before you learn about handling exceptions, consider being proactive: Prevent the exception from being thrown when possible. If you can't prevent an exception, handle the exception gracefully. In this lesson, you learn about areas in which you prevent exceptions and implement error handling to improve the behavior of your application when errors occur.

There are two primary reasons for handling exceptions in your applications. One is to recover gracefully from an exception that you are aware might occur. In this scenario, you have identified that a *SqlException* is thrown when attempting to connect to the database server while it's being restarted. You might want to offer the ability to retry or simply try three times before ending the application.

The other reason is to minimize the amount of information that might be conveyed to a malicious user. For example, if such a user is causing an exception to occur, you certainly don't want to display a detailed error message that includes source code. It's important to display a user-friendly message that has little information about the error and log as much information as possible.

> **After this lesson, you will be able to:**
> - Prevent certain connection and query exceptions.
> - Handle connection and query exceptions.
> - Handle exceptions when submitting changes.
>
> **Estimated lesson time: 20 minutes**

Preventing Connection and Command Exceptions

When opening a connection to the database server, an exception might be thrown because the server is not available. The connection timeout defaults to 15 seconds, and you should consider your scenario to decide whether to increase or decrease this time. For fast networks, you might lower this time so you can fail quickly. Why wait more than five seconds to fail when you know that most of your connections take only one second? However, if you're on a slow connection, you might set the connection timeout to a higher value.

You set the connection timeout in your connection string, as shown in the following connection string sample that sets the connection timeout to 30 seconds.

Sample of Connection String

```
"server=.;database=northwind;integrated security=true;connection timeout=30"
```

You might also have a scenario in which certain queries are throwing an exception because they take too long to execute. You can set the *CommandTimeout* property to give more time for commands to execute before the timeout exception is thrown. In all these examples, the default value is 30, in seconds.

To set the command timeout with traditional ADO.NET classes, *DbCommand* has a *CommandTimeout* property you can set.

Sample of Visual Basic Code

```
Private Sub mnuAdoNetCommandTimeout_Click( _
      ByVal sender As System.Object, _
      ByVal e As System.Windows.RoutedEventArgs) _
      Handles mnuAdoNetCommandTimeout.Click
   Dim cnSetting = ConfigurationManager.ConnectionStrings("nw")
   Using cn = New SqlConnection(), cmd = cn.CreateCommand()
      cn.ConnectionString = cnSetting.ConnectionString
      cmd.CommandTimeout = 60
      cmd.CommandText = "Select @@version"
      cn.Open()
      MessageBox.Show(cmd.ExecuteScalar().ToString())
   End Using
End Sub
```

Sample of C# Code

```
private void mnuAdoNetCommandTimeout_Click(
   object sender, RoutedEventArgs e)
{
   var cnSetting = ConfigurationManager.ConnectionStrings["nw"];
   using(var cn = new SqlConnection())
   using(var cmd = cn.CreateCommand())
   {

      cn.ConnectionString = cnSetting.ConnectionString;
      cmd.CommandTimeout = 60;
      cmd.CommandText = "Select @@version";
      cn.Open();
      MessageBox.Show(cmd.ExecuteScalar().ToString());
   }
}
```

When working with LINQ to SQL classes, you can set the *CommandTimeout* property of the *DataContext* object.

Sample of Visual Basic Code

```
Private Sub mnuLinqToSqlCommandTimeout_Click( _
    ByVal sender As System.Object, _
    ByVal e As System.Windows.RoutedEventArgs) _
    Handles mnuLinqToSqlCommandTimeout.Click

   Using db = New LinqToSql.NorthwindDataContext()
      db.CommandTimeout = 60
      Dim count = db.Employees.Count()
      MessageBox.Show(String.Format("Employee Count:{0}", count))
   End Using
End Sub
```

```csharp
private void mnuLinqToSqlCommandTimeout_Click(object sender, RoutedEventArgs e)
{
    using(var db = new LinqToSql.NorthwindDataContext())
    {
        db.CommandTimeout = 60;
        var count = db.Employees.Count();
        MessageBox.Show(String.Format("Employee Count:{0}", count));
    }
}
```

When working with the Entity Framework, the *ObjectContext* object contains a *CommandTimeout* that you can set.

Sample of Visual Basic Code

```vbnet
Private Sub mnuEntityFrameworkCommandTimeout_Click( _
    ByVal sender As System.Object, _
    ByVal e As System.Windows.RoutedEventArgs) _
    Handles mnuEntityFrameworkCommandTimeout.Click

    Using db = New NorthwindEntities()
        db.CommandTimeout = 60
        Dim count = db.Employees.Count()
        MessageBox.Show(String.Format("Employee Count:{0}", count))
    End Using
End Sub
```

Sample of C# Code

```csharp
private void mnuEntityFrameworkCommandTimeout_Click(
    object sender, RoutedEventArgs e)
{
    using (var db = new NorthwindEntities())
    {
        db.CommandTimeout = 60;
        var count = db.Employees.Count();
        MessageBox.Show(String.Format("Employee Count:{0}", count));
    }
}
```

Handling Connection and Query Exceptions

There are many scenarios in which you can't prevent an exception proactively. For example, you might be readying data from the database server and the server loses power. This throws an exception, and you'll need a way to catch it. This is when you can benefit from the *try/catch* block in your code.

The *try* block should contain all the "happy path" code, meaning that all the code that should execute if no errors take place should be in the *try* block. The *catch* blocks contain the alternate code paths that execute if an exception is thrown.

If an exception is thrown, you should have *catch* blocks for each type of exception for which you have specific handling. Also, you should consider a *catch* block that catches *Exception*, which is the default if there is no match to any of the other *catch* blocks you have. Why would you want to catch an exception? If you don't know what the exception is, how can you recover from it? In many scenarios, it's more appropriate to catch only exceptions from which you know how to recover. You could, however, catch an exception for the purpose of logging the exception just before ending the application.

The following code sample demonstrates the use of a *try/catch* block when working with traditional ADO.NET classes.

Sample of Visual Basic Code

```vb
Private Sub mnuAdoNetTryCatch_Click( _
     ByVal sender As System.Object, _
     ByVal e As System.Windows.RoutedEventArgs) _
     Handles mnuAdoNetTryCatch.Click
   Try
      Dim cnSetting = ConfigurationManager.ConnectionStrings("nw")
      Using cn = New SqlConnection(), cmd = cn.CreateCommand()
         cn.ConnectionString = cnSetting.ConnectionString
         cmd.CommandTimeout = 60
         cmd.CommandText = "Select @@version"
         cn.Open()
         MessageBox.Show(cmd.ExecuteScalar().ToString())
      End Using
   Catch ex As SqlException
      MessageBox.Show("SQL Exception: " + ex.Message)
   Catch ex As Exception
      MessageBox.Show("Exception: " + ex.Message)
   End Try
End Sub
```

Sample of C# Code

```csharp
private void mnuAdoNetTryCatch_Click(
    object sender, RoutedEventArgs e)
{
    try
    {
        var cnSetting = ConfigurationManager.ConnectionStrings["nw"];
        using (var cn = new SqlConnection())
        using (var cmd = cn.CreateCommand())
        {

            cn.ConnectionString = cnSetting.ConnectionString;
            cmd.CommandTimeout = 60;
            cmd.CommandText = "Select @@version";
            cn.Open();
            MessageBox.Show(cmd.ExecuteScalar().ToString());
        }
    }
```

```
    catch (SqlException ex)
    {
        MessageBox.Show("SQL Exception: " + ex.Message);
    }
    catch (Exception ex)
    {
        MessageBox.Show("Exception: " + ex.Message);
    }
}
```

In this example, the *using* block is inside the *try* block, so if an error occurs, *SqlCommand* and *SqlConnection* will be disposed before the *catch* block is called. Also, you could certainly use a *finally* block to dispose *SqlCommand* and *SqlConnection*, but you would be required to declare the *cn* and *cmd* variables outside the *try/catch/finally* block to access these variables in a *finally* block.

The following code sample demonstrates the use of a *try/catch* block when working with LINQ to SQL classes.

Sample of Visual Basic Code
```
Private Sub mnuLinqToSqlTryCatch_Click( _
    ByVal sender As System.Object, _
    ByVal e As System.Windows.RoutedEventArgs) _
    Handles mnuLinqToSqlTryCatch.Click
    Try
        Using db = New LinqToSql.NorthwindDataContext()
            db.CommandTimeout = 60
            Dim count = db.Employees.Count()
            MessageBox.Show(String.Format("Employee Count:{0}", count))
        End Using
    Catch ex As SqlException
        MessageBox.Show("SQL Exception: " + ex.Message)
    Catch ex As Exception
        MessageBox.Show("Exception: " + ex.Message)
    End Try
End Sub
```

Sample of C# Code
```
private void mnuLinqToSqlTryCatch_Click(
    object sender, RoutedEventArgs e)
{
    try
    {
        using (var db = new LinqToSql.NorthwindDataContext())
        {
            db.CommandTimeout = 60;
            var count = db.Employees.Count();
            MessageBox.Show(String.Format("Employee Count:{0}", count));
        }
    }
```

```
    catch (SqlException ex)
    {
        MessageBox.Show("SQL Exception: " + ex.Message);
    }
    catch (Exception ex)
    {
        MessageBox.Show("Exception: " + ex.Message);
    }
}
```

Like the previous code sample, the *using* block in this sample is inside the *try* block, so if an error occurs, *SqlCommand* and *SqlConnection* will be disposed before the *catch* block is called.

The following code sample demonstrates the use of a *try/catch* block when working with the Entity Framework.

Sample of Visual Basic Code

```
Private Sub mnuEntityFrameworkTryCatch_Click( _
        ByVal sender As System.Object, _
        ByVal e As System.Windows.RoutedEventArgs) _
        Handles mnuEntityFrameworkTryCatch.Click

    Try
        Using db = New NorthwindEntities()
            db.CommandTimeout = 60
            Dim count = db.Employees.Count()
            MessageBox.Show(String.Format("Employee Count:{0}", count))
        End Using
    Catch ex As SqlException
        MessageBox.Show("SQL Exception: " + ex.Message)
    Catch ex As Exception
        MessageBox.Show("Exception: " + ex.Message)
    End Try
End Sub
```

Sample of C# Code

```
private void mnuEntityFrameworkTryCatch_Click(
    object sender, RoutedEventArgs e)
{
    try
    {
        using (var db = new NorthwindEntities())
        {
            db.CommandTimeout = 60;
            var count = db.Employees.Count();
            MessageBox.Show(String.Format("Employee Count:{0}", count));
        }
    }
    catch (SqlException ex)
    {
        MessageBox.Show("SQL Exception: " + ex.Message);
    }
```

```
catch (Exception ex)
{
    MessageBox.Show("Exception: " + ex.Message);
}
}
```

Once again, the *using* block is inside the *try* block, so if an error occurs, *SqlCommand* and *SqlConnection* will be disposed before the *catch* block is called.

Handling Exceptions When Submitting Changes

Handling exceptions when submitting changes to the database requires a bit more work. First, ensure that your changes are saved as part of a transaction. Next, consider what you will do if you can't submit changes successfully. Finally, if the changes have been submitted successfully, reset the state of your data to *Unchanged*. By resetting the state, you are essentially declaring that you are now in sync with the database.

The following code sample demonstrates handling exceptions with the traditional ADO.NET classes when submitting changes. First, a *DataTable* object is loaded, then changes are made, and, finally, the changes are submitted within a transaction.

Sample of Visual Basic Code

```
Private Sub mnuAdoNetSubmitChanges_Click( _
        ByVal sender As System.Object, _
        ByVal e As System.Windows.RoutedEventArgs) _
        Handles mnuAdoNetSubmitChanges.Click

    Dim cnSetting = ConfigurationManager.ConnectionStrings("nw")
    Dim sql = "SELECT * FROM PRODUCTS"
    Dim da = New SqlDataAdapter(sql, cnSetting.ConnectionString)
    Dim bldr = New SqlCommandBuilder(da)
    Dim dt = New DataTable("Products")

    'retrieve data
    Try
        da.Fill(dt)
    Catch ex As SqlException
        MessageBox.Show("SQL Exception: " + ex.Message)
        Return
    Catch ex As Exception
        MessageBox.Show("Exception: " + ex.Message)
        Return
    End Try

    'modify
    For Each row In dt.Rows
        Dim price = CType(row("UnitPrice"), Decimal)
        row("UnitPrice") = price * 1.1
    Next
```

```vb
        'submit changes
        Try
            Using tran As New TransactionScope()
                da.ContinueUpdateOnError = False
                da.Update(dt)
                dt.AcceptChanges()
                tran.Complete()
            End Using
        Catch ex As SqlException
            MessageBox.Show("SQL Exception: " + ex.Message)
            Return
        Catch ex As Exception
            MessageBox.Show("Exception: " + ex.Message)
            Return
        End Try
        MessageBox.Show("Update Complete")
End Sub
```

Sample of C# Code

```csharp
private void mnuAdoNetSubmitChanges_Click(
    object sender, RoutedEventArgs e)
{
    var cnSetting = ConfigurationManager.ConnectionStrings["nw"];
    var sql = "SELECT * FROM PRODUCTS";
    var da = new SqlDataAdapter(sql, cnSetting.ConnectionString);
    var bldr = new SqlCommandBuilder(da);
    var dt = new DataTable("Products");

    //retrieve data
    try
    {
        da.Fill(dt);
    }
    catch (SqlException ex)
    {
        MessageBox.Show("SQL Exception: " + ex.Message);
        return;
    }
    catch (Exception ex)
    {
        MessageBox.Show("Exception: " + ex.Message);
        return;
    }

    //modify
    foreach (DataRow row in dt.Rows)
    {
        var price = (decimal)row["UnitPrice"];
        row["UnitPrice"] = price * 1.1m;
    }

    //submit the changes
    try
```

```
    {
        using (var tran = new TransactionScope())
        {
            da.ContinueUpdateOnError = false;
            da.Update(dt);
            dt.AcceptChanges();
            tran.Complete();
        }
    }
    catch (SqlException ex)
    {
        MessageBox.Show("SQL Exception: " + ex.Message);
        return;
    }
    catch (Exception ex)
    {
        MessageBox.Show("Exception: " + ex.Message);
        return;
    }
    MessageBox.Show("Update Complete");
}
```

When working with the LINQ to SQL classes, the submission of changes to the database is automatically handled within a transaction when you call the *SubmitChanges* method on the *DataContext* object. Also, the *AcceptChanges* method is automatically called if no exception is thrown when updating, which will reset the state of all objects to *Unchanged*. Although the *SubmitChanges* method is executed within a transaction, you might need to create your own transaction if you must perform other operations within the same transaction. The following code sample demonstrates handling exceptions with LINQ to SQL classes when submitting changes.

Sample of Visual Basic Code

```
Private Sub mnuLinqToSqlSubmitChanges_Click( _
      ByVal sender As System.Object, _
      ByVal e As System.Windows.RoutedEventArgs) _
      Handles mnuLinqToSqlSubmitChanges.Click

   Using db = New LinqToSql.NorthwindDataContext()
      'retrieve and update
      Try
         For Each P In db.Products
            P.UnitPrice *= 1.1
         Next
      Catch ex As SqlException
         MessageBox.Show("SQL Exception: " + ex.Message)
         Return
      Catch ex As Exception
         MessageBox.Show("Exception: " + ex.Message)
         Return
      End Try

      'submit the changes
```

```
        Try
            db.SubmitChanges()
        Catch ex As SqlException
            MessageBox.Show("SQL Exception: " + ex.Message)
            Return
        Catch ex As Exception
            MessageBox.Show("Exception: " + ex.Message)
            Return
        End Try
    End Using
End Sub
```

Sample of C# Code

```csharp
private void mnuLinqToSqlSubmitChanges_Click(
    object sender, RoutedEventArgs e)
{

    using (var db = new LinqToSql.NorthwindDataContext())
    {
        //retrieve and update
        try
        {
            foreach (var p in db.Products)
            {
                p.UnitPrice *= 1.1m;
            }
        }
        catch (SqlException ex)
        {
            MessageBox.Show("SQL Exception: " + ex.Message);
            return;
        }
        catch (Exception ex)
        {
            MessageBox.Show("Exception: " + ex.Message);
            return;
        }

        //submit the changes
        try
        {
            db.SubmitChanges();
        }
        catch (SqlException ex)
        {
            MessageBox.Show("SQL Exception: " + ex.Message);
            return;
        }
        catch (Exception ex)
        {
            MessageBox.Show("Exception: " + ex.Message);
            return;
        }
    }
}
```

When working with the Entity Framework, the submission of changes to the database is automatically handled within a transaction when you call the *SaveChanges* method on the *ObjectContext* object. Also, the *AcceptAllChanges* method is automatically called if no exception is thrown when updating, which will reset the state of all objects to *Unchanged*. Although the *SaveChanges* method is executed within a transaction, you might need to create your own transaction if you need to perform other operations within the same transaction. The following code sample demonstrates handling exceptions with the Entity Framework when submitting changes.

Sample of Visual Basic Code

```vb
Private Sub mnuEntityFrameworkSubmitChanges_Click( _
      ByVal sender As System.Object, _
      ByVal e As System.Windows.RoutedEventArgs) _
      Handles mnuEntityFrameworkSubmitChanges.Click

   Using db = New NorthwindEntities()
      'retrieve and update
      Try
         For Each P In db.Products
            P.UnitPrice *= 1.1
         Next
      Catch ex As SqlException
         MessageBox.Show("SQL Exception: " + ex.Message)
         Return
      Catch ex As Exception
         MessageBox.Show("Exception: " + ex.Message)
         Return
      End Try

      'submit the changes
      Try
         db.SaveChanges()
      Catch ex As SqlException
         MessageBox.Show("SQL Exception: " + ex.Message)
         Return
      Catch ex As Exception
         MessageBox.Show("Exception: " + ex.Message)
         Return
      End Try
   End Using
End Sub
```

Sample of C# Code

```csharp
private void mnuEntityFrameworkSubmitChanges_Click(
   object sender, RoutedEventArgs e)
{
   using (var db = new NorthwindEntities())
   {
      //retrieve and update
      try
      {
         foreach (var p in db.Products)
         {
```

```
            p.UnitPrice *= 1.1m;
        }
    }
    catch (SqlException ex)
    {
        MessageBox.Show("SQL Exception: " + ex.Message);
        return;
    }
    catch (Exception ex)
    {
        MessageBox.Show("Exception: " + ex.Message);
        return;
    }

    //submit the changes
    try
    {
        db.SaveChanges();
    }
    catch (SqlException ex)
    {
        MessageBox.Show("SQL Exception: " + ex.Message);
        return;
    }
    catch (Exception ex)
    {
        MessageBox.Show("Exception: " + ex.Message);
        return;
    }
    }
}
```

PRACTICE   Handle Exceptions

In this practice, you add global exception handling and specific exception handling code to the application you modified in Lesson 1. When completed, your code will contain exception handling to exit the application gracefully when unhandled exceptions occur and will log the exception to the Windows Application Event Log.

If you encounter a problem completing an exercise, the completed projects can be installed from the Code folder on the companion CD.

EXERCISE   Adding Exception Handling to the Existing WPF Project

1. In Visual Studio .NET 2010, choose File | Open | Project. Open the project in the Begin folder of Chapter 8, Lesson 2.

2. Open the code-behind file for the MainWindow.xaml file.

3. Add a private method called *unhandledException* that accepts a *sender* object and a *DispatcherUnhandledExceptionEventArgs* called e. In this method, add code to retrieve the exception from e and format the message.

4. Add code to write the formatted message to the Windows Application Event Log.

5. Add code to display a user-friendly message and end the application. Your code should look like the following.

Sample of Visual Basic Code

```vb
Private Sub unhandledException( _
    ByVal sender As Object, _
    ByVal e As DispatcherUnhandledExceptionEventArgs)
  Dim ex = e.Exception
  Dim message = String.Format( _
        "Exception Type:{0}{1}Message:{2}{1}Stack Trace:{3}{1}", _
        ex.GetType().Name, Environment.NewLine, _
        ex.Message, _
        ex.StackTrace)
  EventLog.WriteEntry( _
    Assembly.GetExecutingAssembly().GetName().Name, _
    message, _
    EventLogEntryType.Error)
  MessageBox.Show( _
"This application has encountered an error and will shutdown." _
      + " Please contact your administrator.")
  Application.Current.Shutdown()
End Sub
```

Sample of C# Code

```csharp
private void unhandledException(
    object sender,DispatcherUnhandledExceptionEventArgs e)
{
    var ex = e.Exception;
    string message = string.Format(
        "Exception Type:{0}{1}Message:{2}{1}Stack Trace:{3}{1}",
        ex.GetType().Name, Environment.NewLine,
        ex.Message,
        ex.StackTrace);
    EventLog.WriteEntry(
        Assembly.GetExecutingAssembly().GetName().Name,
        message,
        EventLogEntryType.Error);
    MessageBox.Show(
"This application has encountered an error and will shutdown."
        + " Please contact your administrator.");
    Application.Current.Shutdown();
}
```

6. If you don't have a parameterless constructor for the *MainWindow* class, add one. In the paramaterless constructor, add code to attach to this *unhandledException* method by subscribing to the *DispatcherUnhandledException* event, which will be fired if an exception is thrown but is not caught by your code. Your code should look like the following.

Sample of Visual Basic Code

```vb
Public Sub New()
    InitializeComponent()
```

```
      AddHandler Application.Current.DispatcherUnhandledException, _
          AddressOf unhandledException
End Sub
```

Sample of C# Code

```
public MainWindow()
{
    InitializeComponent();
    Application.Current.DispatcherUnhandledException +=
        new DispatcherUnhandledExceptionEventHandler(
            unhandledException);
}
```

7. Modify the code in the Save menu item event handler. Add a *try/catch* block to catch a *SqlException* and prompt to retry. Wrap the *try/catch* block in a *while* loop to keep retrying until it is successful or until Cancel is selected when the error message is displayed. Your code should look like the following.

Sample of Visual Basic Code

```
Private Sub mnuSave_Click(ByVal sender As System.Object, _
                          ByVal e As System.Windows.RoutedEventArgs)
    Dim done As Boolean = False
    While (Not done)
       Try
          ctx.SubmitChanges()
          MessageBox.Show("Saved")
          cmbCustomers_SelectionChanged(Nothing, Nothing)
          done = True
       Catch ex As SqlException
          Dim result = MessageBox.Show("Error Saving Changes. Retry?", _
                         "Save Error", MessageBoxButton.OKCancel)
          If result = MessageBoxResult.Cancel Then
              Return
          End If
       End Try
    End While
End Sub
```

Sample of C# Code

```
private void mnuSave_Click(object sender, RoutedEventArgs e)
{
    var done = false;
    while (!done)
    {
       try
       {
          ctx.SubmitChanges();
          MessageBox.Show("Saved");
          cmbCustomers_SelectionChanged(null, null);
          done = true;
       }
       catch (SqlException ex)
       {
```

```
                var result = MessageBox.Show("Error Saving Changes. Retry?",
                                             "Save Error",
                                             MessageBoxButton.OKCancel);
                if (result == MessageBoxResult.Cancel)
                {
                    return;
                }
            }
        }
    }
```

8. Shut down SQL Server and run the application. After 15 seconds, you see the global error handler message that states an error occurred. Click OK, and the application ends.

9. Start SQL Server and run the application. The main window is displayed. Click the DropDownList to reveal the Customer list, thus proving that SQL Server is available. Add several orders.

10. While the application is still running, stop SQL Server.

11. Attempt to save the new orders. The Save Error screen should appear after 15 seconds. Click OK a couple of times to see that the code attempts to retry until you click Cancel.

12. Start SQL Server. Attempt to save the new orders. The save should be successful.

Lesson Summary

This lesson provided detailed information about handling exceptions with the traditional ADO.NET classes, the LINQ to SQL classes, and the Entity Framework.

- Always be proactive and test for a potential exception instead of letting the exception take place.

- Set *Connection Timeout* in the connection string to help avoid exceptions when connecting to the database server.

- Set the *CommandTimeout* property on *DbCommand*, *DataContext*, or *ObjectContext* to avoid exceptions from long-running queries.

- Use *try/catch* blocks to catch exceptions and handle any exceptions gracefully.

Lesson Review

You can use the following questions to test your knowledge of the information in Lesson 2, "Handling Exceptions." The questions are also available on the companion CD if you prefer to review them in electronic form.

> **NOTE ANSWERS**
>
> Answers to these questions and explanations of why each answer choice is correct or incorrect are located in the "Answers" section at the end of the book.

1. What must you use to capture an exception that might occur when you are sending changes to the database server?

A. A *using* block.

B. A *try/catch* block.

C. A *while* statement.

D. You can't capture exceptions.

Lesson 3: Protecting Your Data

In this lesson, you learn about basic cryptography and how it protects data. This lesson starts with the most basic cryptography, symmetric cryptography. From there, the lesson builds on symmetric cryptography, adding asymmetric cryptography, hashing, salted hashes, and digital signatures. This provides the basis for learning about encrypted protocols such as Secure Sockets Layer (SSL).

System.Security.Cryptography is the primary namespace for cryptography, so you typically need to add an *imports* (C# *using*) statement to the top of your code to set a lookup to this namespace.

Cryptography works with bits and bytes, so you usually must convert data to binary before encrypting. After decrypting, you must convert the decrypted bytes back to the original type.

After this lesson, you will understand:

- Symmetric cryptography.
- Asymmetric cryptography.
- Hashing.
- Salted hashes.
- Digital signatures.
- Digital certificates.
- Secure Sockets Layer (SSL) protocol.

Estimated lesson time: 30 minutes

Encoding vs. Encryption

Before getting into encryption, understand that encoding is not encryption. An encoding mechanism such as base 64 encoding does not require a key for encoding or decoding. Base 64 encoding is used when you need to represent binary data in a text-based environment. For example, Simple Mail Transfer Protocol (SMTP) is a text-based protocol for sending email. If it's a text-based protocol, how can you send a binary attachment? You must base 64 encode the attachment.

Base 64 encoding converts every three bytes of binary into four characters. Figure 8-5 shows how three 8-bit bytes are converted to four 6-bit characters. Six bits has sixty-four combinations of zeros and ones (hence the name base 64). The sixty-four combinations are represented by the twenty-six uppercase characters, the twenty-six lowercase characters, the ten numeric digits, and the plus and division signs. Because three bytes are converted to four characters, the encoded data is always larger than the binary data.

Binary data can't always be split evenly into three-byte blocks. You often have one or two bytes remaining at the end of the message. If two bytes remain, four characters are created, but the last character is an equals sign. If one byte remains, four characters are created, but the last two characters are equals signs.

Use the *Convert* class to convert to and from base 64 encoding. The following example demonstrates the use of the *Convert* class to base 64 encode a binary array and to base 64 decode the binary array.

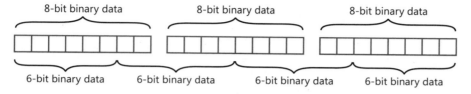

6 bits = 64 combinations of 0s and 1s
How is this represented?

Characters	Combinations
A-Z	26
a-z	26
0-9	10
+/	2
Total	64

FIGURE 8-5 Base 64 encoding converts binary data into characters.

Sample of Visual Basic Code

```
Private Sub mnuBase64_Click(ByVal sender As System.Object, _
    ByVal e As System.Windows.RoutedEventArgs) _
    Handles mnuBase64.Click
  Dim binary = New Byte() {1, 2, 3, 4, 5}
  Dim encoded = Convert.ToBase64String(binary)
  Dim backToBinary = Convert.FromBase64String(encoded)
  MessageBox.Show(String.Format("Encoded:{0}{2}Binary Equal?{1}", _
                  encoded, binary.SequenceEqual(backToBinary), _
                  Environment.NewLine))
End Sub
```

Sample of C# Code

```
private void mnuBase64_Click(object sender, RoutedEventArgs e)
{
    var binary = new Byte[] {1, 2, 3, 4, 5};
    var encoded = Convert.ToBase64String(binary);
    var backToBinary = Convert.FromBase64String(encoded);
    MessageBox.Show(String.Format("Encoded:{0}{2}Binary Equal?{1}",
                    encoded, binary.SequenceEqual(backToBinary),
                    Environment.NewLine));
}
```

If you run the sample code, the encoded value of 1,2,3,4,5 is AQIDBAU=. In binary, 1,2,3,4,5 is represented as follows.

00000001 | 00000010 | 00000011 | 00000100 | 00000101

This value is broken up into 6-bit blocks to get the following.

000000 | 010000 | 001000 | 000011 | 000001 | 000000 | 0101

To get the first base 64 encoded character, you use the first 6 bits to look up a value. The first 6 bits is 000000, which translates to the letter A. The second character gets its value from the next 6-bit block, 010000 (16), which translates to Q. The next character gets its value from the third 6-bit block, 001000 (8), which translates to the letter I. The fourth letter comes from 000011(3), which translates to the letter D. The next letter comes from 000001(1), which translates to the letter B. The next letter comes from 000000, which translates to the letter A. The next letter comes from the last block of bits, but there are not enough bits to make this character, so additional zero bits are added to the end. Therefore, 0101(5) becomes 010100(20), which translates to the letter U. In addition, the equals sign is added to the end to signal that the quantity of input bytes is not evenly divisible by 3. The shortage of 1 byte is represented by one equals sign. If you were short by two bytes, two equals signs would be added to the end.

Symmetric Cryptography

Symmetric cryptography provides the fastest and most basic type of encryption. In this type of encryption, you use the same secret key to encrypt and decrypt data. Symmetric cryptography dates back to ancient Egypt, and the Caesar Cipher was a well-known way of performing symmetric cryptography that dates back to Julius Caesar. You've heard of the secret decoder ring; you use the same secret decoder ring to encrypt messages and decrypt messages.

Symmetric cryptography is fast. There are many symmetric algorithms, and such an algorithm is complex but efficient, which is why it's still at the core of many encrypted communication protocols.

Symmetric cryptography uses relatively small keys, usually fewer than 256 bits. What's the significance of small keys? Generally speaking, the larger the key, the stronger the encryption, but this also requires more resources to perform the encryption and decryption. To help you understand, consider the extreme: if a key is only one bit, you could break the cryptography by trying to decrypt with 0 for the key and then trying to decrypt with 1 for the key. Because of the trade-off between strength and resources, you don't usually create keys that are, for instance, one megabyte in size. This might provide super-strong encryption, but it would take a significant length of time to encrypt or decrypt a message.

The big disadvantage of symmetric cryptography is key management and distribution. If you use the same key to encrypt and decrypt data, how do you transfer the key to someone so he or she can decrypt the data you encrypted? If a malicious user intercepts the key, he or she can decrypt your messages.

Another disadvantage of symmetric cryptography is that you don't know whether the author of a message is the person from whom the message was sent or if it was intercepted by a malicious user. If an unexpected user intercepts the key, he or she can also encrypt messages in an effort to provide disinformation.

You can mitigate the disadvantages of symmetric cryptography by adding layers of security on top of symmetric cryptography.

The Federal Information Processing Standard (FIPS) 140-1 provides a means to validate vendors' cryptographic products. It provides standard implementations of several widely used cryptographic algorithms, and it judges whether a vendor's products implement the algorithms according to the standard. If you plan to sell your software to the U.S. federal government, you must use FIPS 140-1–approved algorithms. Many of the algorithms in the .NET Framework are FIPS 140-1 approved, but some, such as Data Encryption Standard (DES), are in the .NET Framework for backward compatibility and are not FIPS approved.

To protect your data and keep it secret, the protection algorithm must be public. What sounds like a paradox can be best understood by analyzing the selection process for the new Advanced Encryption Standard (AES). When the American National Institute of Standards and Technology (NIST) started looking for a successor to the widespread DES, it invited anyone to submit a more complex encryption algorithm that would be called Advanced Encryption Standard. After 15 potential algorithms were submitted, NIST made the algorithms public and invited everyone to break them. It was amazing how quickly many of these algorithms were broken, meaning that someone was able to decrypt a message without knowing the secret key. Although the submitters were sure that their algorithm couldn't be broken for at least 30 years, as required by NIST, the first candidate was broken almost immediately. Three other candidates were eliminated soon after that, and just five algorithms made it to the final selection round.

This example demonstrates that there is no better measure of security than extensive public testing. A group of technicians might not think of a way to break an algorithm, but that doesn't guarantee that at least one unconventional user somewhere in the world can't. Only time and real-life testing by as many people as possible can show whether an algorithm really serves its purpose. That's what makes encryption standards so valuable: although widely deployed and, thereby, often a target of malicious users, they have been shown to withstand these attacks. DES, for example, started its career in 1977. It took twenty years and an enormous increase in computing power before it was shown in 1997 that DES had become vulnerable.

AES is the current encryption standard (FIPS-197), intended to be used by U.S. government organizations to protect sensitive (and even secret and top secret) information. It is also becoming the unofficial global standard for commercial software and hardware that uses encryption or other security features.

On October 2, 2000, NIST selected Rijndael as the Advanced Encryption Standard (FIPS-197) and thus destined it for massive worldwide usage. The .NET Framework contains the Rijndael algorithm, which you should use for all new projects that require symmetric cryptography.

You can use the *RijndaelManaged* class to perform symmetric encryption and decryption. This class requires you to provide a key and *initialization vector* (*IV*). The IV helps ensure that encrypting the same message multiple times produces different *ciphertext*s. The encrypted message is commonly known as the *ciphertext*. To decrypt data, you must use the same key and IV you used to encrypt the data.

The key must consist of data bytes that make up the total key length. For example, a 128-bit key comprises 16 bytes. If the key is generated by the application, using bytes for the key is not a problem; however, if a human being is generating a key, it's common to want the key to consist of a word or phrase. This can be accomplished by using the *Rfc2898DeriveBytes* class, which can derive a key from a password you provide.

The following code sample demonstrates the use of the *RijndaelManaged* class to encrypt data.

Sample of Visual Basic Code

```vb
Dim myData = "hello"
Dim myPassword = "OpenSesame"
Dim cipherText As Byte()
Dim salt() As Byte = {&H0, &H1, &H2, &H3, &H4, &H5, &H6, &H5, &H4, &H3, &H2, &H1, &H0}

Private Sub mnuSymmetricEncryption_Click(ByVal sender As System.Object, _
    ByVal e As System.Windows.RoutedEventArgs) _
    Handles mnuSymmetricEncryption.Click

    Dim key As New Rfc2898DeriveBytes(myPassword, salt)

    ' Encrypt the data.
    Dim algorithm = New RijndaelManaged()
    algorithm.Key = key.GetBytes(16)
    algorithm.IV = key.GetBytes(16)
    Dim sourceBytes() As Byte = New System.Text.UnicodeEncoding().GetBytes(myData)
    Using sourceStream = New MemoryStream(sourceBytes)
        Using destinationStream As New MemoryStream()
            Using crypto As New CryptoStream(sourceStream, _
                                            algorithm.CreateEncryptor(), _
                                            CryptoStreamMode.Read)
                moveBytes(crypto, destinationStream)
                cipherText = destinationStream.ToArray()
            End Using
        End Using
    End Using
    MessageBox.Show(String.Format( _
                "Data:{0}{1}Encrypted and Encoded:{2}", _
                myData, Environment.NewLine, _
                Convert.ToBase64String(cipherText)))
End Sub
```

```
Private Sub moveBytes(ByVal source As Stream, ByVal dest As Stream)
    Dim bytes(2048) As Byte
    Dim count = source.Read(bytes, 0, bytes.Length - 1)
    While (0 <> count)
        dest.Write(bytes, 0, count)
        count = source.Read(bytes, 0, bytes.Length - 1)
    End While
End Sub
```

Sample of C# Code

```
private string myData = "hello";
private string myPassword = "OpenSesame";
private byte[] cipherText;
private byte[] salt =
    { 0x0, 0x1, 0x2, 0x3, 0x4, 0x5, 0x6, 0x5, 0x4, 0x3, 0x2, 0x1, 0x0 };

private void mnuSymmetricEncryption_Click(
    object sender, RoutedEventArgs e)
{
    var key = new Rfc2898DeriveBytes(myPassword, salt);

    // Encrypt the data.
    var algorithm = new RijndaelManaged();
    algorithm.Key = key.GetBytes(16);
    algorithm.IV = key.GetBytes(16);
    var sourceBytes = new System.Text.UnicodeEncoding().GetBytes(myData);
    using (var sourceStream = new MemoryStream(sourceBytes))
    using (var destinationStream = new MemoryStream())
    using (var crypto = new CryptoStream(sourceStream,
                                  algorithm.CreateEncryptor(),
                                  CryptoStreamMode.Read))
    {
        moveBytes(crypto, destinationStream);
        cipherText = destinationStream.ToArray();
    }
    MessageBox.Show(String.Format(
        "Data:{0}{1}Encrypted and Encoded:{2}",
        myData, Environment.NewLine,
        Convert.ToBase64String(cipherText)));
}

private void moveBytes(Stream source, Stream dest)
{
    byte[] bytes = new byte[2048];
    var count = source.Read(bytes, 0, bytes.Length);
    while (0 != count)
    {
        dest.Write(bytes, 0, count);
        count = source.Read(bytes, 0, bytes.Length);
    }
}
```

In this code sample, the data to be encrypted is stored in *myData*, and the result ends up in *ciphertext*. In between, *myPassword* and *salt* create a key, thanks to the *Rfc2898DeriveBytes* class. You must use the same *salt* value to decrypt. Next, the *RijndaelManaged* class is instantiated, and the *Key* and *IV* properties are populated from the *key* object. It might look like *Key* and *IV* are populated with the same value, but each time you call *key.GetBytes*, you get different bytes back, so to decrypt your message, you must perform the same sequence: First call *Key*, then call *GetBytes* to populate *Key*, and, finally, call *key.GetBytes* to populate *IV.*

The next task is to convert the data to binary so it can be encrypted, which is done using the *UnicodeEncoding* class.

Three streams are created for moving the data. The first stream is a *MemoryStream* object and represents the source that is populated with the bytes of the data. The next stream is a *CryptoStream* object, and this is where the work is accomplished. The *CryptoStream* object's constructor accepts a *Stream* object, which represents the stream to which the *CryptoStream* object will be bound (*sourceStream* in this example). The second parameter is an object that implements the *ICryptoTransform* interface, which is created by using the *algorithm* object's *CreateEncryptor* method. The third parameter is an enumeration value that indicates the type of binding to the stream that is passed in, which is *Read* or *Write*. Because the *sourceStream* object is passed in, *Read* is passed as the third parameter. In this case, you are pulling encrypted bytes from the *CryptoStream*, and the *CryptoStream* will in turn pull (*Read*) bytes from *sourceStream* until the end of the stream is reached. You could write this code to bind *CryptoStream* to *destinationStream*. To do this, you would pass the destination stream as the first parameter, and *Write* would be the third parameter. In that scenario, you would be pushing bytes into *CryptoStream*, which would encrypt the bytes and push (*Write*) them into the *destinationStream* object.

A *moveBytes* helper method copies the bytes from a source stream to a destination stream. The *crypto* stream object is passed to *moveBytes* as the source, and the *destinationStream* object is passed to *moveBytes* as the destination.

After calling *moveBytes*, the *destinationStream* object contains the encrypted data. This data is retrieved from the *destinationStream* object by calling its *ToArray* method, and the resulting bytes are stored in the *cipherText* variable.

Finally, a message is displayed containing *myData* and the encrypted and encoded *cipherText*.

Decrypting *cipherText* is almost the same as encrypting *myData*, as shown in the following code sample.

Sample of Visual Basic Code

```
Private Sub mnuSymmetricDecryption_Click(ByVal sender As System.Object, _
        ByVal e As System.Windows.RoutedEventArgs) _
        Handles mnuSymmetricDecryption.Click

    If (cipherText Is Nothing) Then
        MessageBox.Show("Encrypt Data First!")
        Return
    End If
```

```vb
        Dim key As New Rfc2898DeriveBytes(myPassword, salt)

        ' Try to decrypt, thus showing it can be round-tripped.
        Dim algorithm = New RijndaelManaged()
        algorithm.Key = key.GetBytes(16)
        algorithm.IV = key.GetBytes(16)
        Using sourceStream = New MemoryStream(cipherText)
            Using destinationStream As New MemoryStream()
                Using crypto As New CryptoStream(sourceStream, _
                                            algorithm.CreateDecryptor(), _
                                            CryptoStreamMode.Read)
                    moveBytes(crypto, destinationStream)
                    Dim decryptedBytes() As Byte = destinationStream.ToArray()
                    Dim decryptedMessage = New UnicodeEncoding().GetString( _
                        decryptedBytes)
                    MessageBox.Show(decryptedMessage)
                End Using
            End Using
        End Using
End Sub
```

Sample of C# Code

```csharp
private void mnuSymmetricDecryption_Click(
    object sender, RoutedEventArgs e)
{
    if (cipherText == null)
    {
        MessageBox.Show("Encrypt Data First!");
        return;
    }

    var key = new Rfc2898DeriveBytes(myPassword, salt);

    // Try to decrypt, thus showing it can be round-tripped.
    var algorithm = new RijndaelManaged();
    algorithm.Key = key.GetBytes(16);
    algorithm.IV = key.GetBytes(16);
    using (var sourceStream = new MemoryStream(cipherText))
    using (var destinationStream = new MemoryStream())
    using (var crypto = new CryptoStream(sourceStream,
                                    algorithm.CreateDecryptor(),
                                    CryptoStreamMode.Read))
    {
        moveBytes(crypto, destinationStream);
        var decryptedBytes = destinationStream.ToArray();
        var decryptedMessage = new UnicodeEncoding().GetString(
            decryptedBytes);
        MessageBox.Show(decryptedMessage);
    }
}
```

This code sample starts by checking to see whether you encrypted the data first. If *cipherText* is *Nothing* (C# *null*), a message is displayed to indicate that you need to encrypt first, and then you exit the method.

Next, the *key* object and the *algorithm* object are created just like in the encryption sample.

After that, the streams are created: a *MemoryStream* object for the source *cipherText*, a *MemoryStream* object for the *destinationStream* object, and the *CryptoStream* object that works with the algorithm to encrypt and decrypt data. The second parameter of the *CryptoStream* object is created by calling the *algorithm.CreateDecryptor* method.

Finally, a call is made to the *moveBytes* helper method, and the *destinationStream* object contains the decrypted bytes that are read, converted to a string, and displayed.

Asymmetric Cryptography

Asymmetric cryptography provides a very secure mechanism for encrypting and decrypting data, due to its use of a pair of keys called the private and public keys. The private key is held by one entity and securely locked down. It should never be passed to another entity. The public key is the opposite; you can give the public key to anyone who requests it.

Asymmetric cryptography encrypts a message using just one of the keys (public or private), but you must use the opposite key to decrypt the message. For example, you ask the bank for its public key, and you encrypt a message using that public key. Who can decrypt the message? Only the holder of the private key, which is the bank, can decrypt the message. This offers strong protection because the private key never crosses the network, which is very different from symmetric cryptography, in which the recipient needs your key to decrypt.

As a side note, if the bank encrypts a message using its private key, who can decrypt it? Anyone can decrypt this message because the bank's public key is required to decrypt, and the bank will give the public key to anyone. This doesn't sound too useful; however, if you try to decrypt with an invalid key, or if the message is corrupted, an exception is thrown. If you can decrypt a message successfully using the bank's public key, it proves that the message came from the bank. You encrypt a message with your private key to prove your identity; this forms the basis for digital signatures, which are covered later in this lesson.

The RSA algorithm is the most common asymmetric algorithm used today. RSA was created by Rivest, Shamir, and Adleman who, at the time, were all at MIT. The latter authors published their work in 1978, and the algorithm appropriately came to be known as RSA. RSA uses exponentiation modulo, a product of two large primes, to encrypt and decrypt, performing both public key encryption and public key digital signature. Its security is based on the presumed difficulty of factoring large integers.

RSA is all about mathematics; it's a simple equation with big numbers (as opposed to a complex equation with small numbers, which more closely resembles symmetric cryptography). What you are encrypting is only a value in the equation. By default, RSA uses 1024-bit key pairs, so your value must have 128 bytes (1024 bits, 8 bits/byte).

Next comes the padding. Raw encryption, without padding, is not secure because your (128 bytes) number could be very small. Raw encryption isn't possible using the Microsoft .NET Framework; the *EncryptValue* and *DecryptValue* methods of the

RSACryptoServiceProvider throw an *UnsupportedException*. This is a restriction of *CryptoAPI* used in *RSACryptoServiceProvider*.

The most common padding mechanism for asymmetric keys is PKCS#1 version 1.5. Because the PKCS#1 padding length is 11 bytes, the maximum message size is 128 bytes minus the 11 bytes of padding, which gives you a maximum of 117 bytes for encryption.

A newer padding mechanism is Optimal Asymmetric Encryption Padding (OAEP). It's considered to be a more advanced padding algorithm. It's not used much in standards right now, but the padding algorithm has been proven secure. *CryptoAPI* supports OAEP only for Windows XP and later operating systems.

You can see that key exchange is not a problem with asymmetric cryptography like it is with symmetric cryptography. This might lead you to believe that you should always use asymmetric cryptography. However, asymmetric algorithms such as RSA are extremely slow compared to symmetric algorithms, such as AES, which are fast. Encrypting data by using a symmetric algorithm makes sense from a performance perspective. You can solve the key exchange problem of symmetric cryptography by adding an asymmetric layer that can encrypt the symmetric key by using asymmetric cryptography and can send the encrypted symmetric key to the recipient. The recipient can decrypt the symmetric key by using asymmetric cryptography and then symmetric cryptography can be used for encrypted data transfer.

Figure 8-6 shows an example of asymmetric cryptography. In this example, the bank has an asymmetric key pair. Alice's browser generates a random number that is the symmetric key used for performant-encrypted communications using symmetric cryptography. Alice's browser requests the public key from the bank, and the bank responds with the public key. Alice's browser uses the bank's public key to encrypt the symmetric key by using the RSA asymmetric algorithm. Next, Alice's browser sends the encrypted symmetric key to the bank.

Because the bank's private key is required to decrypt the symmetric key and the private key is locked down, only the bank can decrypt the symmetric key. The bank uses its private key and the RSA algorithm to decrypt the symmetric key. Finally, Alice and the bank are able to communicate using symmetric cryptography.

When using the asymmetric cryptography, you don't choose your keys. Instead, the public and private key pair is generated automatically for you the first time you reference the keys. How are the keys created? The public and private keys are mathematically related—you use the opposite key to decrypt, so the keys must be mathematically related. To generate the keys, *CryptoAPI* starts by generating two very large random prime numbers, called p and q. These aren't the keys, but they generate the keys. For all practical purposes, the public key is the product of p and q. Other factors go into the creation of the public key, but this is the important one. The private key formula is more complicated, but it's well known.

If the public key is the product of p and q, and the private key is also derived from p and q, then, given a public key—if you can factor it back to p and q—you could theoretically calculate the private key. Although this is true, these numbers are so large that you can't factor the public key back to p and q in your lifetime. If computers get fast enough for this to be a problem, the size of these numbers can be increased.

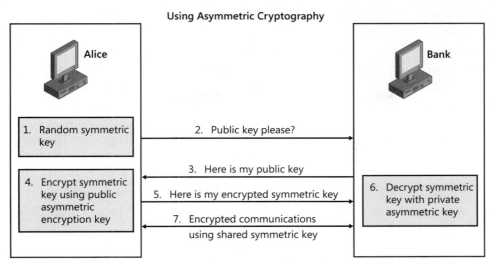

FIGURE 8-6 Asymmetric cryptography performs symmetric key exchange.

In the following code sample, the RSA encryption algorithm encrypts a small message. Remember that you should not encrypt large messages with asymmetric encryption due to its lack of performance; it is about 1000 times slower than the symmetric algorithm of comparable strength.

Sample of Visual Basic Code

```
Dim rsaCipherText As Byte()
Private Sub mnuAsymmetricEncryption_Click( _
    ByVal sender As System.Object, _
    ByVal e As System.Windows.RoutedEventArgs) _
    Handles mnuAsymmetricEncryption.Click

    Dim rsa = 1

    ' Encrypt the data.
    Dim cspParms = New CspParameters(rsa)
    cspParms.Flags = CspProviderFlags.UseMachineKeyStore
    cspParms.KeyContainerName = "My Keys"

    Dim algorithm = New RSACryptoServiceProvider(cspParms)

    Dim sourceBytes() As Byte = New System.Text.UnicodeEncoding().GetBytes(myData)
    rsaCipherText = algorithm.Encrypt(sourceBytes, True)
    MessageBox.Show(String.Format( _
                "Data: {0}{1}Encrypted and Encoded: {2}", _
                myData, Environment.NewLine, _
                Convert.ToBase64String(rsaCipherText)))
End Sub
```

Sample of C# Code

```csharp
private byte[] rsaCipherText;

private void mnuAsymmetricEncryption_Click(
    object sender, RoutedEventArgs e)
{
    var rsa = 1;

    // Encrypt the data.
    var cspParms = new CspParameters(rsa);
    cspParms.Flags = CspProviderFlags.UseMachineKeyStore;
    cspParms.KeyContainerName = "My Keys";

    var algorithm = new RSACryptoServiceProvider(cspParms);

    var sourceBytes = new UnicodeEncoding().GetBytes(myData);
    rsaCipherText = algorithm.Encrypt(sourceBytes, true);
    MessageBox.Show(String.Format(
        "Data: {0}{1}Encrypted and Encoded: {2}",
        myData, Environment.NewLine,
        Convert.ToBase64String(rsaCipherText)));
}
```

You can see that this sample code is very different from the symmetric cryptography's sample code. No streams are used in this code because, as a general rule, you shouldn't be encrypting large messages.

This code starts by setting the RSA variable to a value of *1*, which is the RSA Full provider. This magic number indicates which provider you want to use. The registered provider types can be found in the registry at the following location.

Registry Location of Provider Types

```
HKEY_LOCAL_MACHINE\SOFTWARE\Microsoft\Cryptography\Defaults\Provider Types
```

Next, an instance of the *CspParameters* class is created, its settings are set to use the computer's key store, and a name for the key container is assigned. The computer's key store refers to a location on your hard drive in which all the keys are stored that are scoped to the computer, as opposed to the user's key store, which has user-scoped keys. This location differs based on your operating system. On a Windows 7 and Windows 2008 Server, the key store is located at C:\Users\All Users\Microsoft\Crypto\RSA\MachineKeys. When a key pair is created, you see a new file in this folder that contains the private and public keys.

The *RSACryptoServiceProvider* is then instantiated with the parameters. The keys are generated the first time you reference the "My Keys" key container. Subsequent references to the key container use the existing keys.

Finally, the data is converted to bytes and encrypted.

Decryption is very similar to encryption. The following code sample decrypts *rsaCipherText*.

Sample of Visual Basic Code

```vb
Private Sub mnuAsymmetricDecryption_Click( _
        ByVal sender As System.Object, _
```

```
         ByVal e As System.Windows.RoutedEventArgs) _
         Handles mnuAsymmetricDecryption.Click

    If (rsaCipherText Is Nothing) Then
        MessageBox.Show("Encrypt first!")
        Return
    End If

    Dim rsa = 1

    ' Encrypt the data.
    Dim cspParms = New CspParameters(rsa)
    cspParms.Flags = CspProviderFlags.UseMachineKeyStore
    cspParms.KeyContainerName = "My Keys"

    Dim algorithm = New RSACryptoServiceProvider(cspParms)

    Dim unencrypted = algorithm.Decrypt(rsaCipherText, True)
    MessageBox.Show(New UnicodeEncoding().GetString(unencrypted))
End Sub
```

Sample of C# Code

```csharp
private void mnuAsymmetricDecryption_Click(
    object sender, RoutedEventArgs e)
{
    if(rsaCipherText==null)
    {
        MessageBox.Show("Encrypt First!");
        return;
    }

    var rsa = 1;

    // decrypt the data.
    var cspParms = new CspParameters(rsa);
    cspParms.Flags = CspProviderFlags.UseMachineKeyStore;
    cspParms.KeyContainerName = "My Keys";

    var algorithm = new RSACryptoServiceProvider(cspParms);

    var unencrypted = algorithm.Decrypt(rsaCipherText, true);
    MessageBox.Show(new UnicodeEncoding().GetString(unencrypted));
}
```

Hashing and Salting

A cryptographic hash function takes a block of data of arbitrary size and returns a fixed-size set of binary bits, known as the hash value, which represents the block of data; if you change the original block of data in any way, the calculated hash value changes. If a single bit is changed in the original data, at least fifty percent of the calculated hash value's bits change. If the data has not changed and you calculate the hash value over and over, the hash value will be the same. If you copy the data and calculate its hash value, it'll be the same.

Although it's possible to calculate a hash value of data, it's not possible to convert from hash value back to the original data, which is why hashing functions are also known as one-way functions. The hash calculation is complex and one-way, but it is very efficient.

One of the main purposes of using hashing functions is to determine whether data has changed, either by accident or through a malicious act. Hashing does not encrypt your data. In fact, hashing is most commonly used for data that is public, when the reader of the public data wants to verify that the data hasn't changed.

Another use for hashing functions is when you want to store passwords but you don't want anyone to be able to see the passwords. If you encrypt the passwords before storing them, you have to worry about the location of the key. If someone can gain access to the key, he or she is able to decrypt all passwords. If you store a hash of the passwords, when a person attempts to logs in, a hash of the password typed into the logon screen is calculated. If this hash matches the hash that has been stored, the user is authenticated.

Salted Hashes

When you are storing hashes of passwords in a database table, anyone looking at the table is able to see the logon names and the hash values of the passwords. This seems secure because you can't reverse-engineer the hash to get the password. Table 8-1 shows an example of the data in the database table.

TABLE 8-1 Sample of a Database Table Containing Hash Values

LOGINID	HASH
JoePresident	AEB0FC9FCEA137CF9BBC594BBC97991C10CD9138
MaryDeveloper	DEFAFC9FCEA137C12345694BBC97991C10123456
TomNewHire	AEB0FC9FCEA137CF9BBC594BBC97991C10CD9138

Do you see anything wrong? As it turns out, JoePresident has the same password as Tom-NewHire. Although it's acceptable for multiple people to have the same password, if someone finds out that TomNewHire has the same password as JoePresident, he or she could ask TomNewHire what his password is—for a fee. TomNewHire could then change his password, but JoePresident's password has been compromised.

How can you mitigate this problem? You can add a *salt* value to your password, a value you add to the password before calculating the hash value, because any change to the password will cause the hash value to change dramatically. This is usually a random value of sufficient size to ensure that you don't have duplicate values. To generate a random number for the *salt*, you can use the *RNGCryptoServiceProvider* class that provides cryptographically secure random numbers. In some scenarios, globally unique identifiers are used. The *salt* must be stored with the hash to recalculate the hash when someone is logging on. Table 8-2 shows the modified database table containing a third column for the *salt*. In this example,

JoePresident and TomNewHire still have the same password, but you can't tell that they are the same.

TABLE 8-2 Sample of a Database Table Containing Salted Hash Values

LOGINID	HASH	SALT
JoePresident	876ABD9FCEA137CF9BBC594B-BC97991C10CD9138	5d8a2052-1f3e-4fe1-9ca4-7c891a980592
MaryDeveloper	ADCAD79FCEA137C12345694B-BC97991C10987650	38011b98-3ce5-4f62-a959-415ce93ed7bb
TomNewHire	BC89129FCEA137CF9BBC594BBC-97991C10BDCA09	fd05e0fe-d17c-4d6c-8a55-06445bb5613c

Various hashing algorithms exist. The most commonly used algorithm is the SHA-1 algorithm, which produces a 20-byte (160 bit) hash value. In 2005, a security flaw was discovered by a team of scientists from Shandong University in China, causing many companies to move to SHA-256, which produces a 32-byte (256 bit) hash value.

In the .NET Framework, the *SHA256Managed* class computes hash values. This class has *ComputeHash* method overloads that accept byte arrays or a stream. The following sample code demonstrates use of the *SHA256Managed* class.

Sample of Visual Basic Code

```vb
Private Sub mnuHash_Click(ByVal sender As System.Object, _
    ByVal e As System.Windows.RoutedEventArgs) _
    Handles mnuHash.Click

    Dim data = "The quick brown fox jumped over the lazy dog."
    Dim bytes() = New UnicodeEncoding().GetBytes(data)

    Dim sha = New SHA256Managed()
    Dim hash = sha.ComputeHash(bytes)

    MessageBox.Show(ToHexString(hash))
End Sub

Public Function ToHexString(ByVal bytes As Byte()) As String
    Dim hex = New StringBuilder()
    For Each b In bytes
        hex.AppendFormat("{0:x2}", b)
    Next
    Return hex.ToString()
End Function
```

Sample of C# Code

```csharp
private void mnuHash_Click(object sender, RoutedEventArgs e)
{
    var data = "The quick brown fox jumped over the lazy dog.";
    var bytes = new UnicodeEncoding().GetBytes(data);
```

```
    var sha = new SHA256Managed();
    var hash = sha.ComputeHash(bytes);

    MessageBox.Show(ToHexString(hash));
}

public string ToHexString(byte[] bytes)
{
    var hex = new StringBuilder();
    foreach (byte b in bytes)
    {
        hex.AppendFormat("{0:x2}", b);
    }
    return hex.ToString();
}
```

In this sample code, the hash value was created and then displayed by using the
ToHexString helper method.

Digital Signatures

A digital signature proves that a message hasn't been modified and proves the identity of
its author. This is an essential combination of two topics that have been covered in this lesson: asymmetric encryption using the private key, and hashing. A digital signature is created
by calculating a hash of data, followed by encrypting the hash, with a private asymmetric
encryption key.

The following code sample shows the use of *RSACryptoServiceProvider* and the *SHA256*
hashing algorithm.

Sample of Visual Basic Code

```
Dim signature() As Byte

Private Sub mnuDigitlSignature_Click( _
      ByVal sender As System.Object, _
      ByVal e As System.Windows.RoutedEventArgs) _
      Handles mnuDigitlSignature.Click

   Dim data = "The quick brown fox jumped over the lazy dog."

   Dim rsa = 24
   ' create signature.
   Dim cspParms = New CspParameters(rsa)
   cspParms.Flags = CspProviderFlags.UseMachineKeyStore
   cspParms.KeyContainerName = "My Keys"

   Dim algorithm = New RSACryptoServiceProvider(cspParms)

   Dim sourceBytes() As Byte = _
                 New System.Text.UnicodeEncoding().GetBytes(data)
   signature = algorithm.SignData(sourceBytes, "SHA256")

   MessageBox.Show(ToHexString(signature))
End Sub
```

Sample of C# Code

```csharp
private byte[] signature;

private void mnuDigitlSignature_Click(
    object sender, RoutedEventArgs e)
{
    var data = "The quick brown fox jumped over the lazy dog.";

    var rsa = 24;
    // create signature
    var cspParms = new CspParameters(rsa);
    cspParms.Flags = CspProviderFlags.UseMachineKeyStore;
    cspParms.KeyContainerName = "My Keys";

    var algorithm = new RSACryptoServiceProvider(cspParms);

    var sourceBytes =
        new System.Text.UnicodeEncoding().GetBytes(data);
    signature = algorithm.SignData(sourceBytes, "SHA256");

    MessageBox.Show(ToHexString(signature));
}
```

The RSA number has been changed from *1* to *24*. This change enables you to use the SHA256 hashing algorithm.

To verify a digital signature, you use the *VerifyData* method instead of the *SignData* method, as shown in the following code sample.

Sample of Visual Basic Code

```vbnet
Private Sub mnuVerifySignature_Click( _
        ByVal sender As System.Object, _
        ByVal e As System.Windows.RoutedEventArgs) _
        Handles mnuVerifySignature.Click

    If signature Is Nothing Then
        MessageBox.Show("Create signature first")
        Return
    End If

    Dim data = "The quick brown fox jumped over the lazy dog."

    Dim rsa = 24
    ' verify signature.
    Dim cspParms = New CspParameters(rsa)
    cspParms.Flags = CspProviderFlags.UseMachineKeyStore
    cspParms.KeyContainerName = "My Keys"

    Dim algorithm = New RSACryptoServiceProvider(cspParms)

    Dim sourceBytes() As Byte = _
                New System.Text.UnicodeEncoding().GetBytes(data)
    Dim valid = algorithm.VerifyData(sourceBytes, _
                "SHA256", signature)
```

```
      MessageBox.Show(valid.ToString())
End Sub
```

Sample of C# Code
```
private void mnuVerifySignature_Click(
   object sender, RoutedEventArgs e)
{
   var data = "The quick brown fox jumped over the lazy dog.";

   var rsa = 24;
   // verify signature
   var cspParms = new CspParameters(rsa);
   cspParms.Flags = CspProviderFlags.UseMachineKeyStore;
   cspParms.KeyContainerName = "My Keys";

   var algorithm = new RSACryptoServiceProvider(cspParms);

   var sourceBytes =
      new System.Text.UnicodeEncoding().GetBytes(data);
   var valid = algorithm.VerifyData(sourceBytes, "SHA256", signature);

   MessageBox.Show(valid.ToString());
}
```

Encrypting Connections and Configuration Files

When creating applications that access data, you frequently work with data that is considered to be sensitive. You must ensure that you've taken the appropriate actions to protect this data. Some of it can exist in a database, whereas other data might be in files on your file system. This section explores the various aspects of ensuring data privacy.

Encrypted Communications to SQL Server

To enable encrypted communications between the client and SQL Server, a digital certificate must be installed at SQL Server. You can then use the *Encrypt* setting in the connection string to turn on encryption. In addition, you can set the *TrustServerCertificate* setting to *true* so that the complete certificate hierarchy is not examined to validate the digital certificate. The following connection string turns on SSL communications and does not go through the certificate hierarchy to validate the certificate chain.

```
Data Source=.\SQLEXPRESS;
   AttachDbFilename=C:\MyApplication\Northwind.MDF;
   Integrated Security=True;
   User Instance=True;
   Encrypt=true;
   TrustServerCertificate=yes
```

If you're using C#, don't forget that the strings that have backslashes must be escaped by using two backslashes (\\) for each single backslash, or you can precede the string with an at

(@) symbol to turn off escape processing. The *Encrypt* setting is set to *true*, so all communication between the client and the server will be encrypted.

Storing Encrypted Connection Strings in Web Applications

Web applications don't have an App.config file; they have a Web.config file. It's common practice to store connection strings in the Web.config file to change the connection string without requiring a recompile of the application. However, connection strings can contain logon information such as user names and passwords. You certainly don't want this information to be easily readable by anyone. The solution is to encrypt the connection strings by using the aspnet_regiis.exe utility to encrypt the *connectionStrings* section. This utility is part of the .NET Framework and can be accessed by using the Visual Studio .NET command prompt. You can use the /? option to get help on the utility.

You encrypt and decrypt the contents of a Web.config file by using *System.Configuration .DPAPIProtectedConfigurationProvider* from the *System.Configuration.dll* assembly, which uses the Windows Data Protection API (DPAPI) to encrypt and decrypt data, or by using *System .Configuration.RSAProtectedConfigurationProvider*, which uses the RSA encryption algorithm to encrypt and decrypt data.

When you use the same encrypted configuration file on many computers in a web farm, only *System.Configuration.RSAProtectedConfigurationProvider* enables you to export the encryption keys that encrypt the data and import them on another server. This is the default setting.

Storing Encrypted Connection Strings for Non-Web Applications

For non-web applications, you can use the same technique as with web applications by renaming your .config file to Web.config and then using the *–pef* switch with the aspnet _regiis.exe utility. Rename the Web.config file back to the original name.

You can also encrypt or decrypt connection strings on any application by using the *ConfigurationManager* class in your code. The following sample code encrypts the connection strings in the current application.

Sample of Visual Basic Code

```
Private Sub mnuEncryptConnectionStrings_Click( _
     ByVal sender As System.Object, _
     ByVal e As System.Windows.RoutedEventArgs) _
     Handles mnuEncryptConnectionStrings.Click

  Dim config = ConfigurationManager.OpenExeConfiguration( _
     ConfigurationUserLevel.None)
  Dim section = CType(config.GetSection("connectionStrings"), _
     ConnectionStringsSection)
  section.SectionInformation.ProtectSection( _
     "RsaProtectedConfigurationProvider")
  ' Save the encrypted section.
  section.SectionInformation.ForceSave = True
  config.Save(ConfigurationSaveMode.Full)
```

```
        MessageBox.Show("Connection strings encrypted on file "
                        + section.CurrentConfiguration.FilePath)
End Sub
```

Sample of C# Code

```
private void mnuEncryptConnectionStrings_Click(
    object sender, RoutedEventArgs e)
{
    var config = ConfigurationManager.OpenExeConfiguration(
        ConfigurationUserLevel.None);
    var section = (ConnectionStringsSection)config.GetSection(
        "connectionStrings");
    section.SectionInformation.ProtectSection(
        "RsaProtectedConfigurationProvider");
    // Save the encrypted section.
    section.SectionInformation.ForceSave = true;
    config.Save(ConfigurationSaveMode.Full);

    MessageBox.Show("Connection strings encrypted on file "
                    + section.CurrentConfiguration.FilePath);

}
```

Implementing an Encrypted *ConnectionString* Property

You can encrypt the Web.config file by running the Visual Studio .NET command prompt and executing the following command, specifying the full path to your website folder:

```
aspnet_regiis -pef "connectionStrings" "C:\...\EncryptWebSite"
```

The *–pef* switch requires you to pass the physical website path, which is the last parameter. Be sure to verify the path to your Web.config file.

If changes are made to the *connectionStrings* section—for example, if another connection is added by using the GUI tools—the new connection will be encrypted; that is, you won't have to run the aspnet_regiis utility again.

You can decrypt the *connectionStrings* section by using the following command:

```
aspnet_regiis -pdf "connectionStrings" "C:\...\EncryptWebSite"
```

Principle of Least Privilege

When creating large applications, you frequently need to set up services that require the service to access resources. This typically means that you create a logon account for the service and assign the necessary permissions to the account.

The principle of least privilege mandates that every service must be able to access only the data and resources that are necessary for its legitimate purpose. This means giving logon accounts only those permissions that are absolutely essential, regardless of whether the logon accounts are used by services or by actual people.

Be especially careful about assigning administrator permissions to logon accounts. If a malicious user finds a way to exploit this account, the result could be disastrous.

You should frequently review the Administrators, Domain Administrators, and Enterprise Administrators groups to see who is a member and to adjust as necessary. This is especially important, and you might be surprised to find others adding accounts to these groups. Every account in one of these groups is a high risk. Less permission equals less risk.

PRACTICE   Encrypt Connection Strings

In this practice, you encrypt the connection strings in the .config file for the application you modified in Lesson 2. When completed, your .config file will contain an encrypted section with the connection string information, and your application will decrypt this section transparently as needed.

If you encounter a problem completing an exercise, the completed projects can be installed from the Code folder on the companion CD.

EXERCISE   Encrypting the Config File of the Existing WPF Project

1. From the Windows Start menu, open the Visual Studio .NET command prompt.

2. Use the *cd* command to change the Begin folder of Chapter 8, Lesson 3. Use the *cd* command to navigate into the project folder.

3. In the Project folder, rename the App.config file to **Web.config**.

4. Execute the following command to encrypt the connection strings in this file, where D is the drive letter, and . . . is the full path to the to the project folder.

   ```
   aspnet_regiis /pef "connectionStrings" "d:\..."
   ```

5. If you open the Web.config file with a text editor, you see that the *connectionStrings* section is now encrypted as follows.

   Sample of Config File

   ```
   <connectionStrings configProtectionProvider="RsaProtectedConfigurationProvider">
       <EncryptedData Type="http://www.w3.org/2001/04/xmlenc#Element"
           xmlns="http://www.w3.org/2001/04/xmlenc#">
       <EncryptionMethod Algorithm=
           "http://www.w3.org/2001/04/xmlenc#tripledes-cbc" />
       <KeyInfo xmlns="http://www.w3.org/2000/09/xmldsig#">
           <EncryptedKey xmlns="http://www.w3.org/2001/04/xmlenc#">
               <EncryptionMethod Algorithm=
                   "http://www.w3.org/2001/04/xmlenc#rsa-1_5" />
               <KeyInfo xmlns="http://www.w3.org/2000/09/xmldsig#">
               <KeyName>Rsa Key</KeyName>
               </KeyInfo>
               <CipherData>
   <CipherValue>ZuLRNk8cB7lkIUhjxgWosaDQIDPaq9jtG/emMwILg8gnCCrHFPzYzW
   Qb5218h5+P4yHIfp3yforrAZ/77d8m9ydbUoMS/PYG/wo1mfaTCzXOa/334hYuBt8ca
   wtzuDBAuq/XiQ1jh9/kQtpasGOlsOs5g2gYKwE1qFlcFdJHhEc=</CipherValue>
               </CipherData>
   ```

```
            </EncryptedKey>
        </KeyInfo>
        <CipherData>
            <CipherValue>AQIn1f+FAWbp634DFxp8oyEjDBmjQMJs7mgVyMCN/vQ=
            </CipherValue>
        </CipherData>
    </EncryptedData>
</connectionStrings>
```

6. Rename the Web.config file to **App.config**.

7. Open Visual Studio .NET and load this solution. Run the application. Click the drop-down list to see that it's populated with customer data from the database, indicating that the .NET Framework was able to decrypt the .config file transparently.

Lesson Summary

This lesson provided detailed information about protecting your data.

- Encoding is not encryption because there is no secret key.

- Symmetric cryptography uses the same key to encrypt and decrypt a message; its biggest benefit is performance, but its biggest drawback is the key exchange requirement.

- The *RijndaelManaged* class provides a symmetric algorithm, which is the Advanced Encryption Standard (AES).

- The *Rfc2898DeriveBytes* class retrieves a key as bytes when a password is supplied.

- The *CryptoStream* class performs symmetric encryption and decryption.

- Asymmetric cryptography uses a pair of keys known as public and private keys; its biggest benefit is that the private key does not need to be transferred across the Internet, so key disclosure risk is minimized. Its biggest drawback is its lack of performance.

- A hashing function determines whether data has been modified.

- A *salt* ensures that no two hashes of passwords are the same.

- A digital signature proves the identity of its author and proves that a message hasn't been modified.

- Use the aspnet_regiis.exe utility to encrypt .config files.

- Always assign the least privileges for any logon account that is created.

Lesson Review

You can use the following questions to test your knowledge of the information in Lesson 3, "Protecting Your Data." The questions are also available on the companion CD if you prefer to review them in electronic form.

1. Which of the following are valid encryption algorithms that can be selected when encrypting the connection strings in your .config files? (Each correct answer presents a complete solution. Choose two.)

   A. *DpapiProtectedConfigurationProvider*

   B. *RNGCryptoServiceProvider*

   C. *SHA256Managed*

   D. *RsaProtectedConfigurationProvider*

   E. *RijndaelManaged*

2. Which of the following is a valid symmetric encryption algorithm?

   A. *RNGCryptoServiceProvider*

   B. *RNGCryptoServiceProvider*

   C. *SHA256Managed*

   D. *RijndaelManaged*

Lesson 4: Synchronizing Data

The need to access data from all types of devices is a growing concern for many organizations every day. Companies need to ensure that users have information access regardless of where they are or what device they are using. In this lesson, you learn about the Microsoft Sync Framework.

After this lesson, you will be able to:

- Understand how change tracking works when using the Microsoft Sync Framework.
- Comprehend how conflict resolution operates.
- Perform inner joins with LINQ to SQL.
- Implement the Microsoft Sync Framework.

Estimated lesson time: 30 minutes

The Microsoft Sync Framework

When connectivity to mobile devices such as laptops is required, consider the implementation of an occasionally connected application (OCA), which enables a remote worker to continue to access information because the information is stored in a local database on the user's device. The OCA typically includes data synchronization capabilities to populate the local database, to periodically synchronize the information stored in the client database (such as SQL Server Compact), and to synchronize changes with a server database (such as SQL Server). Thus, a synchronization-based solution does not require a constant network connection to the database server because the data is stored locally.

Synchronization between data stores has never been an easy task; it consumes a lot of time and resources. This is where the Microsoft Sync Framework enters the picture. The Microsoft Sync Framework simplifies the integration of application data synchronization from any data store.

With the Microsoft Sync Framework, Microsoft released Microsoft Synchronization Services for ADO.NET, Synchronization Services for File Systems, and Synchronization Services for FeedSync. These services enable developers to perform synchronizations for specific environments, whereas the Microsoft Sync Framework is used for building synchronization logic within your application.

Change Tracking

A method of change tracking is required to make data synchronization efficient. Change tracking is the ability to maintain a list of the inserts, updates, and deletes that have been made to the local database. With change tracking at the client, you don't need to send all data back to the server; you send only the changes. With change tracking at the server, the server needs to send changes only to the client.

SQL Server 2008 contains a method for tracking changes called SQL Server 2008 Change Tracking. With this method, the database administrator can identify specific tables to be monitored for changes. SQL Server 2008 will then keep track of the inserts, updates, or deletes. When the client application requests changed data, SQL Server 2008 will provide all the changes that have occurred since the last successful download by the requester.

In an OCA environment, the Microsoft Sync Framework takes advantage of SQL Server 2008 Change Tracking by not requiring schema changes to enable change tracking. Triggers aren't even required, which translates to significantly better performance than trigger-based change tracking solutions. The overhead of enabling SQL Server 2008 change tracking on a table is conceptually the same as the overhead of maintaining a second index.

Conflict Detection

With OCA, conflicts are an issue that arises when two or more databases change the same piece of data and then the synchronization engine tries to apply those changes in a single database. What should happen if the traveling salesperson updates a customer record while the home office personnel update the same customer record? The traveling salesperson has the original customer record, and then the home office successfully updates the central database. In the meantime, the traveling salesperson changes the customer record and attempts to synchronize the update to the main database, which causes a conflict because the current state of the row is different from what the synchronization engine expected.

To resolve conflicts, business rules must be implemented because conflict resolution will be based on the problem domain. One way to resolve the conflict is to implement a business rule stating that the last change sent to the database server is the one that wins. Another resolution is a rule stating that the winner can be based on location (headquarters or remote office) or title (president versus salesperson).

The Microsoft Sync Framework provides conflict detection and resolution capabilities out of the box. Furthermore, SQL Server 2008 decreases the complexity associated with recognizing conflicts. Using the built-in conflict detection, the home office personnel successfully upload the change to the central server because this is the first change. When the traveling salesperson uploads the change, a conflict is detected because the change version in the central server does not exist in the current salesperson database. Logic in the remote application determines how to handle the conflict.

Data Prioritization

With slow network connections, you'll be looking for ways to optimize the exchange of data. You can prioritize data by defining the set of data that has a high priority or is critical. This causes critical changes to be synchronized immediately and leaves less important data to be synchronized later. The Microsoft Sync Framework enables your remote application to synchronize on a table-by-table basis and on an upload-only or download-only basis.

The Microsoft Sync Framework supports synchronization by using a background thread. If you are using a local database such as SQL Server Compact, synchronization can be executed in the background.

Implementing the Microsoft Sync Framework

You can add synchronization support to your application by using Sync Services for ADO.NET, which uses SQL Server Compact 3.5 to create a lightweight data store on your local file system. SQL Server Compact uses a file as its repository.

Before you implement Synchronization Services for ADO.NET, you must decide how to track changes in your data. In Synchronization Services for ADO.NET, you can use the SQL Server 2008 integrated change tracking, or you can use custom tracking by managing change tracking yourself in the application database. Integrated change tracking does not work with SQL Server Express.

To add synchronization services to your application, in Solution Explorer, right-click the project node and choose Add | New Item. Select your language and click Data. In the data templates window, select Local Database Cache, change the name to **NorthwindLocalDataCache.sync**, and click Add. The Configure Data Synchronization window opens, as shown in Figure 8-7, with the Advanced drop-down list selected.

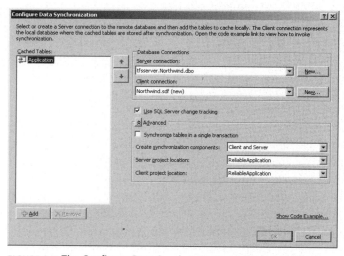

FIGURE 8-7 The Configure Data Synchronization window's settings.

If you select a connection to a SQL Server 2008 database (not SQL Express), the Use SQL Server change tracking check box will be accessible, as shown in Figure 8-7. Use this option to enable integrated change tracking.

The Advanced section enables you to force changes to occur within a single transaction. You might select that option when you want to ensure that either all or none of the changes are persisted, but, often, you want to save as much data as possible and be notified of problems. For those scenarios, leave the check box cleared.

In the Cached Tables list box, click Add to configure the tables to be cached locally. This opens the Configure Tables For Offline Use window, as shown in Figure 8-8. In this window, select the tables of which you want to keep local copies. In this example, the Customers table has been selected. The Data To Download drop-down list enables you to select between incremental synchronization of changes or synchronization by copying the complete table. The Compare Updates, Deletes, and Inserts drop-down lists are disabled if you opt to use SQL Server change tracking, but if you didn't choose SQL Server change tracking, these drop-down lists would be accessible for you to select a column that can confirm that a change took place.

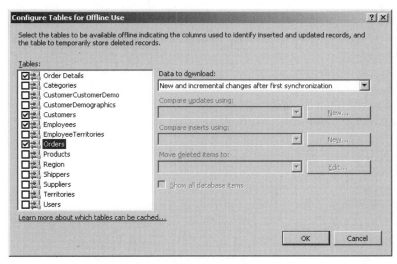

FIGURE 8-8 Select the tables that will be available offline.

After selecting the desired tables to be cached, click OK to go back to the Configure Data Synchronization screen shown in Figure 8-7. This screen has a Show Code Example link. Click the link to display sample code. Click Copy Code To The Clipboard and close the window. Click OK, and the Generate SQL Scripts window is displayed, as shown in Figure 8-9. SQL Server needs its settings updated to perform change tracking, and you might want to keep the scripts in your project for future use on your QA or production database. Click OK to execute the scripts.

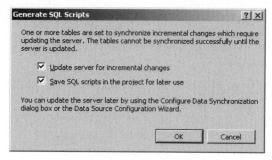

FIGURE 8-9 The Generate SQL Scripts window enables you to update the server and store the scripts.

When the scripts execute on SQL Server 2008, tables that are enabled for integrated change tracking log every data change in a change tracking log table. When you synchronize, the Sync Services look at the log to identify changes since the last synchronization. You don't need to change the database schema to enable synchronization.

If you're not using SQL Server 2008, as is the case for applications using SQL Server Express or SQL Server 2005, integrated change tracking is not available. Consider using custom change tracking, which identifies insertions and updates of records in a table with the help of columns and identifies deletions with the help of a tombstone table. To help Sync Services identify rows that have been updated or inserted since the last update, add new columns to each table you want to track. These columns are Update Originator, Update Time, Create Originator, and Create Time. You must also create a tombstone table to keep a log of all rows that are removed. Within the table, you need at least two pieces of information: the time of deletion and the row's original primary key. The tombstone table is where Sync Services finds entries that must be removed from the destination store because they have been removed from the source. All this information helps Sync Services identify the changes since last synchronization.

The next screen is the DataSource Configuration Wizard. This window enables you to choose between implementing a typed data set or using the Entity Framework. Select *DataSet* and, on the next screen, select the *Tables* node, which selects the Customers table and the offline overhead tables.

After the wizard has completed, you can add traditional ADO.NET code to load a data set with the customers and bind the *Customers DataTable* to a *DataGrid*, as shown in the following code sample.

Sample of Visual Basic Code

```vb
Private northwindDataSet = New NorthwindDataSet()
Private northwindDataSetCustomersTableAdapter = _
        New CustomersTableAdapter()

Private Sub mnuGetOfflineData_Click( _
        ByVal sender As System.Object, _
        ByVal e As System.Windows.RoutedEventArgs) _
        Handles mnuGetOfflineData.Click
```

```
northwindDataSetCustomersTableAdapter.Fill( _
    northwindDataSet.Customers)
dg.ItemsSource = northwindDataSet.Customers
End Sub
```

Sample of C# Code

```
private NorthwindDataSet northwindDataSet = new NorthwindDataSet();
private CustomersTableAdapter northwindDataSetCustomersTableAdapter
    = new CustomersTableAdapter();

private void mnuGetOfflineData_Click(
    object sender, RoutedEventArgs e)
{
    northwindDataSetCustomersTableAdapter.Fill(
        northwindDataSet.Customers);
    dg.ItemsSource = northwindDataSet.Customers;
}
```

When running this code, you will see that the *DataGrid* control, called *dg*, is populated with customers. The customers came from the local cache, but this local cache is not being updated. You can verify that the local cache is not being updated by changing the *ContactName* of the first customer and then restarting the program. You'll see that the change was not persisted. The following code saves the changes to the local cache.

Sample of Visual Basic Code

```
Private Sub mnuSaveOfflineData_Click( _
    ByVal sender As System.Object, _
    ByVal e As System.Windows.RoutedEventArgs) _
    Handles mnuSaveOfflineData.Click
    northwindDataSetCustomersTableAdapter.Update( _
        northwindDataSet.Customers)
    MessageBox.Show("Saved")
End Sub
```

Sample of C# Code

```
private void mnuSaveOfflineData_Click(
    object sender, RoutedEventArgs e)
{
    northwindDataSetCustomersTableAdapter.Update(
        northwindDataSet.Customers);
    MessageBox.Show("Saved");
}
```

This code sample saves the customers to the local cache. If you run the application, make changes, and then click the menu option to save, you see a message stating that the customers were saved. If you stop running the application and restart the application, you see the changed data, thus proving that the changes were persisted.

The only problem with the previous code sample is that the changes were saved only to the local cache; the changes weren't sent to SQL Server. If you open SQL Management Studio and look at the Customers table, you see that *Customer* still has the original values for all columns. To synchronize the local cache with SQL Server, add the following sample code.

Sample of Visual Basic Code

```vb
Private Sub mnuSyncOfflineData_Click( _
      ByVal sender As System.Object, _
      ByVal e As System.Windows.RoutedEventArgs) _
      Handles mnuSyncOfflineData.Click

   Dim syncAgent = New NorthwindLocalDataCacheSyncAgent()
   syncAgent.Customers.SyncDirection = SyncDirection.Bidirectional
   Dim syncStats = syncAgent.Synchronize()
   northwindDataSet.Customers.Merge( _
      northwindDataSetCustomersTableAdapter.GetData())
   MessageBox.Show("In Sync")
End Sub
```

Sample of C# Code

```csharp
private void mnuSyncOfflineData_Click(object sender, RoutedEventArgs e)
{
   var syncAgent = new NorthwindLocalDataCacheSyncAgent();
   syncAgent.Customers.SyncDirection = SyncDirection.Bidirectional;
   var syncStats = syncAgent.Synchronize();
   northwindDataSet.Customers.Merge(
      northwindDataSetCustomersTableAdapter.GetData());
   MessageBox.Show("In Sync");
}
```

If you run this code sample, the local cache will be synchronized with the SQL Server database. This code starts by creating a *NorthwindLocalDataCacheSyncAgent* object. This class was created by the wizard and inherits from the *SqlCeClientSyncProvider* class. You provide each table with an enumeration value that specifies *SyncDirection*. The values are shown in Table 8-3.

TABLE 8-3 The *SyncDirection* Enumeration Values

VALUE	DESCRIPTION
Bidirectional	The first synchronization downloads the schema and data from the server. Subsequent synchronizations upload changes from the client, followed by downloading changes from the server.
UploadOnly	The first synchronization downloads the schema and data from the server. Subsequent synchronizations upload changes from the client.
DownloadOnly	The first synchronization downloads the schema and data from the server. Subsequent synchronizations download changes from the server.
Snapshot	The client downloads the complete set of data every time synchronization takes place.

After setting *SynchDirection*, the *Synchronize* method is called to perform the synchronization.

Latest Version of Microsoft Sync Services

Although Visual Studio .NET 2010 shipped with Microsoft Sync Services 2.1, development continues and, at this time of writing, Microsoft Sync Framework 4.0 October 2010 CTP has been released.

Microsoft Sync Framework 4.0 October 2010 CTP is built on top of Sync Framework 2.1. It defines OData + Sync as a synchronization protocol that makes it easy to build offline applications on any client platform capable of caching data. This release enables synchronization of data stored in SQL Server/SQL Azure over an open-standard network format by a remote synchronization service handling all sync-specific computations. Moving all synchronization logic off the client enables clients that do not have the Sync Framework runtime installed to cache data and participate in a synchronization topology. Earlier versions of Sync Framework required clients to have Windows systems with Sync Framework runtime installed on them. This CTP enables other Microsoft platforms such as Silverlight, Windows Phone 7, and Windows Mobile, and third-party platforms such as HTML5, iPhone, Android, and other devices with no Sync Framework runtime installed on them as clients.

PRACTICE   Synchronize Data

In this practice, you create an application for a vendor who supplies the products to Northwind Traders. The vendor is a distributer of various products, so the vendor's representatives are always on the road, updating, adding, and discontinuing products. Products are never deleted because they might be part of existing orders. This application will be written as an OCA. When completed, your application will synchronize with the vendor's SQL Server when the application starts and when it ends.

If you encounter a problem completing an exercise, the completed projects can be installed from the Code folder on the companion CD.

EXERCISE   Synchronizing Data

In this exercise, you create a Windows application project and then add the local cache and typed *DataSet* with a *Products DataTable*. This *DataTable* will be available offline and will be synchronized at startup and shutdown.

1.   In Visual Studio .NET 2010, choose File | New | Project.

2.   Select your desired programming language and then select the WPF Application template.

3. For the project name, enter **VendorProducts**. Be sure to select a desired location for this project.

4. For the solution name, enter **VendorProductsSolution**. Be sure that Create Directory For Solution is selected and then click OK.

   After Visual Studio .NET finishes creating the project, MainWindow.xaml is displayed, using the WPF Forms designer.

5. Add the local cache file by right-clicking the project node in Solution Explorer and choosing Add | New Item. Under your language, click Data and select the Local Database Cache template. Name this **NorthwindLocalDataCache.sync** and click Add. This opens the Configure Data Synchronization screen.

6. For the server connection, configure a connection to your Northwind database. If you don't have the Northwind database, it's provided in the companion content as a script and as an MDF file to which you can attach.

7. Add the Products table to the cached table list by clicking Add and selecting the Products table. Click OK and then click OK again to close the window.

8. The Generate SQL Scripts window opens. Click OK. This generates SQL Server scripts and executes them. The local cache table is created and populated.

9. The Data Source Configuration Wizard starts. Select DataSet and click Next. In the next window, select the *Tables* node to select all tables and then click Finish. This creates a typed *DataSet* with a *Products DataTable*.

10. In the XAML for the MainWindow.xaml file, change Window Height to 600 and change Window Width to 1000.

11. Double-click the title bar of the MainWindow file to create a *Window_Loaded* event handler method in the code-behind file.

12. In the WPF designer, click the title bar of the MainWindow file and, in the Properties window, click Events to display the events for the MainWindow file. Locate the *Closing* event and double-click it to add an event handler for the *Closing* event.

13. The XAML contains a Grid definition. Inside the grid, add two row definitions. The first row should have its *Height* property set to *Auto*, and the last row should have its *Height* property set to "*". Regardless of your programming language, your XAML for the Grid should look like the following.

    Sample of XAML

    ```
    <Grid>
        <Grid.RowDefinitions>
            <RowDefinition Height="Auto" />
            <RowDefinition Height="*" />
        </Grid.RowDefinitions>
    </Grid>
    ```

14. In the XAML, before the end of the Grid, add a menu. Inside the menu, add *MenuItem* elements for **Save**, called **mnuSave**, and for **Exit**, called **mnuExit**. After adding these

items, double-click each menu item to add the click event handler code. Your XAML should look like the following.

Sample of XAML

```xaml
<Grid>
    <Grid.RowDefinitions>
        <RowDefinition Height="Auto" />
        <RowDefinition Height="*" />
    </Grid.RowDefinitions>
    <Menu>
        <MenuItem Header="Save" Name="mnuSave" Click="mnuSave_Click" />
        <MenuItem Header="Exit" Name="mnuExit" Click="mnuExit_Click" />
    </Menu>
</Grid>
```

15. Click the Data menu and then click Show Data Sources. This opens the Data Source window. With the MainWindow screen displayed in the WPF designer, drag the Products table out and drop it into the middle of the MainWindow screen. Next, modify the *DataGrid* XAML code to clean up the sizing and hide the Id column and make the Name column take all available space on the row. Also, set the *CanUserDeleteRows* property of *DataGrid* to *false*. Your XAML for the MainWindow screen should look like the following.

Sample of Visual Basic XAML

```xaml
<Window x:Class="MainWindow"
    xmlns="http://schemas.microsoft.com/winfx/2006/xaml/presentation"
    xmlns:x="http://schemas.microsoft.com/winfx/2006/xaml"
    Title="MainWindow" Height="600" Width="1000"
    Loaded="Window_Loaded"  Closing="Window_Closing"
    xmlns:my="clr-namespace:VendorProducts">
    <Window.Resources>
        <my:NorthwindDataSet x:Key="NorthwindDataSet" />
        <CollectionViewSource x:Key="ProductsViewSource"
Source="{Binding Path=Products, Source={StaticResource NorthwindDataSet}}" />
    </Window.Resources>
    <Grid DataContext="{StaticResource ProductsViewSource}">
        <Grid.RowDefinitions>
            <RowDefinition Height="Auto" />
            <RowDefinition Height="*" />
        </Grid.RowDefinitions>
        <Menu>
            <MenuItem Header="Save" Name="mnuSave" Click="mnuSave_Click" />
            <MenuItem Header="Exit" Name="mnuExit" Click="mnuExit_Click" />
        </Menu>
        <DataGrid AutoGenerateColumns="False" EnableRowVirtualization="True"
                ItemsSource="{Binding}" Margin="5" Name="productsDataGrid"
                RowDetailsVisibilityMode="VisibleWhenSelected" Grid.Row="1"
                CanUserDeleteRows="False">
            <DataGrid.Columns>
                <DataGridTextColumn x:Name="productIDColumn"
                                Binding="{Binding Path=ProductID}"
                                Header="Product ID"
                                IsReadOnly="True"
```

```
                                    Width="SizeToHeader" />
            <DataGridTextColumn x:Name="productNameColumn"
                                Binding="{Binding Path=ProductName}"
                                Header="Product Name"
                                Width="*" />
            <DataGridTextColumn x:Name="supplierIDColumn"
                                Binding="{Binding Path=SupplierID}"
                                Header="Supplier ID"
                                Width="SizeToHeader" />
            <DataGridTextColumn x:Name="categoryIDColumn"
                                Binding="{Binding Path=CategoryID}"
                                Header="Category ID"
                                Width="SizeToHeader" />
            <DataGridTextColumn x:Name="quantityPerUnitColumn"
                                Binding="{Binding Path=QuantityPerUnit}"
                                Header="Quantity Per Unit"
                                Width="SizeToHeader" />
            <DataGridTextColumn x:Name="unitPriceColumn"
                                Binding="{Binding Path=UnitPrice}"
                                Header="Unit Price"
                                Width="SizeToHeader" />
            <DataGridTextColumn x:Name="unitsInStockColumn"
                                Binding="{Binding Path=UnitsInStock}"
                                Header="Units In Stock"
                                Width="SizeToHeader" />
            <DataGridTextColumn x:Name="unitsOnOrderColumn"
                                Binding="{Binding Path=UnitsOnOrder}"
                                Header="Units On Order"
                                Width="SizeToHeader" />
            <DataGridTextColumn x:Name="reorderLevelColumn"
                                Binding="{Binding Path=ReorderLevel}"
                                Header="Reorder Level"
                                Width="SizeToHeader" />
            <DataGridCheckBoxColumn x:Name="discontinuedColumn"
                                    Binding="{Binding Path=Discontinued}"
                                    Header="Discontinued"
                                    Width="SizeToHeader" />
        </DataGrid.Columns>
      </DataGrid>
    </Grid>
</Window>
```

Sample of C# XAML

```
<Window x:Class="VendorProducts.MainWindow"
        xmlns="http://schemas.microsoft.com/winfx/2006/xaml/presentation"
        xmlns:x="http://schemas.microsoft.com/winfx/2006/xaml"
        Title="MainWindow" Height="600" Width="1000"
        Loaded="Window_Loaded" Closing="Window_Closing"
        xmlns:my="clr-namespace:VendorProducts" >
    <Window.Resources>
        <my:NorthwindDataSet x:Key="northwindDataSet" />
        <CollectionViewSource x:Key="productsViewSource"
Source="{Binding Path=Products, Source={StaticResource northwindDataSet}}" />
    </Window.Resources>
    <Grid DataContext="{StaticResource productsViewSource}">
```

```xml
<Grid.RowDefinitions>
    <RowDefinition Height="Auto" />
    <RowDefinition Height="*" />
</Grid.RowDefinitions>
<Menu>
    <MenuItem Header="Save" Name="mnuSave" Click="mnuSave_Click" />
    <MenuItem Header="Exit" Name="mnuExit" Click="mnuExit_Click" />
</Menu>
<DataGrid AutoGenerateColumns="False" EnableRowVirtualization="True"
          ItemsSource="{Binding}" Margin="5" Name="productsDataGrid"
          RowDetailsVisibilityMode="VisibleWhenSelected" Grid.Row="1"
          CanUserDeleteRows="False">
    <DataGrid.Columns>
        <DataGridTextColumn x:Name="productIDColumn"
                            Binding="{Binding Path=ProductID}"
                            Header="Product ID"
                            IsReadOnly="True"
                            Width="SizeToHeader" />
        <DataGridTextColumn x:Name="productNameColumn"
                            Binding="{Binding Path=ProductName}"
                            Header="Product Name"
                            Width="*" />
        <DataGridTextColumn x:Name="supplierIDColumn"
                            Binding="{Binding Path=SupplierID}"
                            Header="Supplier ID"
                            Width="SizeToHeader" />
        <DataGridTextColumn x:Name="categoryIDColumn"
                            Binding="{Binding Path=CategoryID}"
                            Header="Category ID"
                            Width="SizeToHeader" />
        <DataGridTextColumn x:Name="quantityPerUnitColumn"
                            Binding="{Binding Path=QuantityPerUnit}"
                            Header="Quantity Per Unit"
                            Width="SizeToHeader" />
        <DataGridTextColumn x:Name="unitPriceColumn"
                            Binding="{Binding Path=UnitPrice}"
                            Header="Unit Price"
                            Width="SizeToHeader" />
        <DataGridTextColumn x:Name="unitsInStockColumn"
                            Binding="{Binding Path=UnitsInStock}"
                            Header="Units In Stock"
                            Width="SizeToHeader" />
        <DataGridTextColumn x:Name="unitsOnOrderColumn"
                            Binding="{Binding Path=UnitsOnOrder}"
                            Header="Units On Order"
                            Width="SizeToHeader" />
        <DataGridTextColumn x:Name="reorderLevelColumn"
                            Binding="{Binding Path=ReorderLevel}"
                            Header="Reorder Level"
                            Width="SizeToHeader" />
        <DataGridCheckBoxColumn x:Name="discontinuedColumn"
                                Binding="{Binding Path=Discontinued}"
                                Header="Discontinued"
                                Width="SizeToHeader" />
```

```
          </DataGrid.Columns>
        </DataGrid>
    </Grid>
</Window>
```

16. Before adding code, run the application. You should see *Products* in *DataGrid*. There is no code for the Save or Exit menu items, so if you make changes to *Products*, the changes won't be persisted.

17. In the code-behind file, the *Window_Loaded* method has code that was inserted when you dropped the Products table onto MainWindow. Rework the code and move the *northwindDataSet* and *ProductsTableAdapter* declarations to the class to have access to these objects anywhere in MainWindow. Your code should look like the following sample.

Sample of Visual Basic Code

```
Dim NorthwindDataSet As VendorProducts.NorthwindDataSet
Dim NorthwindDataSetProductsTableAdapter = _
   New VendorProducts.NorthwindDataSetTableAdapters.ProductsTableAdapter()

Private Sub Window_Loaded(ByVal sender As System.Object, _
      ByVal e As System.Windows.RoutedEventArgs)
   NorthwindDataSet = _
      CType(Me.FindResource("NorthwindDataSet"), _
      VendorProducts.NorthwindDataSet)
   NorthwindDataSetProductsTableAdapter.Fill(NorthwindDataSet.Products)

   Dim ProductsViewSource As System.Windows.Data.CollectionViewSource = _
      CType(Me.FindResource("ProductsViewSource"), _
         System.Windows.Data.CollectionViewSource)
   ProductsViewSource.View.MoveCurrentToFirst()
End Sub
```

Sample of C# Code

```
private VendorProducts.NorthwindDataSet northwindDataSet;
private VendorProducts.NorthwindDataSetTableAdapters.ProductsTableAdapter
   northwindDataSetProductsTableAdapter =
   new VendorProducts.NorthwindDataSetTableAdapters.ProductsTableAdapter();

private void Window_Loaded(object sender, RoutedEventArgs e)
{
   northwindDataSet = ((VendorProducts.NorthwindDataSet)
      (this.FindResource("northwindDataSet")));
   northwindDataSetProductsTableAdapter.Fill(northwindDataSet.Products);

   var productsViewSource =
      ((System.Windows.Data.CollectionViewSource)
      (this.FindResource("productsViewSource")));
   productsViewSource.View.MoveCurrentToFirst();
}
```

18. Add code to the Save menu to save the changes that are currently in the data set to the local cache, thus saving the data to the local hard drive.

Sample of Visual Basic Code

```vb
Private Sub mnuSave_Click(ByVal sender As System.Object, _
      ByVal e As System.Windows.RoutedEventArgs)
   NorthwindDataSetProductsTableAdapter.Update( _
      NorthwindDataSet.Products)
   MessageBox.Show("Saved")
End Sub
```

Sample of C# Code

```csharp
private void mnuSave_Click(object sender, RoutedEventArgs e)
{
   northwindDataSetProductsTableAdapter.Update(
      northwindDataSet.Products);
   MessageBox.Show("Saved");
}
```

19. Create a *SyncData* public method to synchronize your local cache with the SQL Server database. Be sure to wrap this code in a *try/catch* block because this code will fail if SQL Server is unavailable. Set the synchronization to be bidirectional. Write a message to the Windows Application Event Log, indicating success or failure. Your code should look like the following.

Sample of Visual Basic Code

```vb
Private Sub SyncData()
   Try
      Dim syncAgent = New NorthwindLocalDataCacheSyncAgent()
      syncAgent.Products.SyncDirection = SyncDirection.Bidirectional
      Dim syncStats = syncAgent.Synchronize()
      NorthwindDataSet.Products.Merge( _
         NorthwindDataSetProductsTableAdapter.GetData())
      EventLog.WriteEntry("VendorProducts", "Synchronized Successfully", _
         EventLogEntryType.Information)
   Catch xcp As Exception
      EventLog.WriteEntry("VendorProducts", "SyncError: " + _
            xcp.Message, EventLogEntryType.Error)
   End Try
End Sub
```

Sample of C# Code

```csharp
public void SyncData()
{
   try
   {
      var syncAgent = new NorthwindLocalDataCacheSyncAgent();
      syncAgent.Products.SyncDirection = SyncDirection.Bidirectional;
      var syncStats = syncAgent.Synchronize();
      northwindDataSet.Products.Merge(
         northwindDataSetProductsTableAdapter.GetData());
      EventLog.WriteEntry("VendorProducts", "Synchronized Successfully",
         EventLogEntryType.Information);
```

```
            }
            catch (Exception xcp)
            {
                EventLog.WriteEntry("VendorProducts", "SyncError: " +
                    xcp.Message, EventLogEntryType.Error);
            }
        }
```

20. In the *mnuExit_Click* event handler, add a call to the *Shutdown* method on the current applicaton.

21. In the *Window_Closing* event handler, add a call to the *SyncData* method.

22. In the *Window_Loaded* event handler, add a call to the *SyncData* method. This call should be inserted right after the code to fill *DataSet* to the top of the *Window_Loaded* method. When completed, your code-behind file should look like the following.

Sample of Visual Basic Code

```
Imports Microsoft.Synchronization.Data
Imports Microsoft.Synchronization

Class MainWindow

    Dim NorthwindDataSet As VendorProducts.NorthwindDataSet
    Dim NorthwindDataSetProductsTableAdapter = _
        New VendorProducts.NorthwindDataSetTableAdapters.ProductsTableAdapter()

    Private Sub Window_Loaded(ByVal sender As System.Object, _
            ByVal e As System.Windows.RoutedEventArgs)
        NorthwindDataSet = _
            CType(Me.FindResource("NorthwindDataSet"), VendorProducts.
NorthwindDataSet)
        NorthwindDataSetProductsTableAdapter.Fill(NorthwindDataSet.Products)
        SyncData()
        Dim ProductsViewSource As System.Windows.Data.CollectionViewSource = _
            CType(Me.FindResource("ProductsViewSource"), _
                System.Windows.Data.CollectionViewSource)
        ProductsViewSource.View.MoveCurrentToFirst()
    End Sub

    Private Sub mnuSave_Click(ByVal sender As System.Object, _
            ByVal e As System.Windows.RoutedEventArgs)
        NorthwindDataSetProductsTableAdapter.Update( _
            NorthwindDataSet.Products)
        MessageBox.Show("Saved")
    End Sub

    Private Sub mnuExit_Click(ByVal sender As System.Object, _
            ByVal e As System.Windows.RoutedEventArgs)
        Application.Current.Shutdown()
    End Sub
```

```
        Private Sub Window_Closing(ByVal sender As System.Object, _
                ByVal e As System.ComponentModel.CancelEventArgs)
            SyncData()
        End Sub

        Private Sub SyncData()
            Try
                Dim syncAgent = New NorthwindLocalDataCacheSyncAgent()
                syncAgent.Products.SyncDirection = SyncDirection.Bidirectional
                Dim syncStats = syncAgent.Synchronize()
                NorthwindDataSet.Products.Merge( _
                    NorthwindDataSetProductsTableAdapter.GetData())
                EventLog.WriteEntry("VendorProducts", "Synchronized Successfully",
                    EventLogEntryType.Information)
            Catch xcp As Exception
                EventLog.WriteEntry("VendorProducts", "SyncError: " + _
                        xcp.Message, EventLogEntryType.Error)
            End Try
        End Sub
    End Class
```

Sample of C# Code

```csharp
using System;
using System.Diagnostics;
using System.Windows;
using Microsoft.Synchronization.Data;

namespace VendorProducts
{
    /// <summary>
    /// Interaction logic for MainWindow.xaml
    /// </summary>
    public partial class MainWindow : Window
    {
        public MainWindow()
        {
            InitializeComponent();
        }

        private VendorProducts.NorthwindDataSet northwindDataSet;
        private VendorProducts.NorthwindDataSetTableAdapters.ProductsTableAdapter
            northwindDataSetProductsTableAdapter =
            new VendorProducts.NorthwindDataSetTableAdapters.ProductsTableAdapter();

        private void Window_Loaded(object sender, RoutedEventArgs e)
        {
            northwindDataSet = ((VendorProducts.NorthwindDataSet)
                (this.FindResource("northwindDataSet")));
            northwindDataSetProductsTableAdapter.Fill(northwindDataSet.Products);
            SyncData();
            var productsViewSource =
                ((System.Windows.Data.CollectionViewSource)
                (this.FindResource("productsViewSource")));
            productsViewSource.View.MoveCurrentToFirst();
        }
```

```
            private void mnuSave_Click(object sender, RoutedEventArgs e)
            {
                northwindDataSetProductsTableAdapter.Update(
                    northwindDataSet.Products);
                MessageBox.Show("Saved");
            }

            private void mnuExit_Click(object sender, RoutedEventArgs e)
            {
                Application.Current.Shutdown();
            }

            private void Window_Closing(object sender,
                System.ComponentModel.CancelEventArgs e)
            {
                SyncData();
            }

            public void SyncData()
            {
                try
                {
                    var syncAgent = new NorthwindLocalDataCacheSyncAgent();
                    syncAgent.Products.SyncDirection = SyncDirection.Bidirectional;
                    var syncStats = syncAgent.Synchronize();
                    northwindDataSet.Products.Merge(
                        northwindDataSetProductsTableAdapter.GetData());
                    EventLog.WriteEntry("VendorProducts", "Synchronized Successfully",
                        EventLogEntryType.Information);
                }
                catch (Exception xcp)
                {
                    EventLog.WriteEntry("VendorProducts", "SyncError: " +
                        xcp.Message, EventLogEntryType.Error);
                }
            }

        }
    }
```

23. Run the application.

At startup, the application will attempt to synchronize with SQL Server. If a connection can be made to SQL Server, you will receive any changes. Modify some of the product names and prices.

24. Be sure to click Save to save to the local cache.

When you exit the application, the application will attempt to synchronize with SQL Server. If a connection can be made to SQL Server, you will receive any changes and send your changes to SQL Server.

25. Try stopping the SQL Server service and perform the previous step. The application should continue to run properly without SQL Server being available.

Lesson Summary

This lesson provided detailed information about synchronizing data by using the Microsoft Sync Framework.

- OCA enables a remote user to continue to access information because the information is stored in a local database on the user's device.
- The Microsoft Sync Framework is for building synchronization logic within your application. It uses SQL Server Compact as its file repository and can use SQL Server 2008 integrated change tracking or custom tracking.

Lesson Review

You can use the following questions to test your knowledge of the information in Lesson 4, "Synchronizing Data." The questions are also available on the companion CD if you prefer to review them in electronic form.

> **NOTE** **ANSWERS**
>
> Answers to these questions and explanations of why each answer choice is correct or incorrect are located in the "Answers" section at the end of the book.

1. You want to synchronize data between your local SQL Server Compact tables and SQL Server 2008. You want the synchronization to send changes to SQL Server 2008, and you want to receive changes from SQL Server 2008. Which setting must you assign to the *SyncDirection* property of your sync agent's tables?

   A. *SyncDirection.Bidirectional*

   B. *SyncDirection.UploadOnly*

   C. *SyncDirection.Snapshot*

   D. *SyncDirection.DownloadOnly*

Case Scenario

In the following case scenario, you apply what you've learned about developing reliable applications, as discussed in this chapter. You can find answers to these questions in the "Answers" section at the end of this book.

Case Scenario: Data Synchronization

You want to create a sales application by which your sales personnel are able to continue using the application when the database server is not accessible. This application will enable the sales personnel to view, add, delete, and modify customers, orders, and order details. In addition, you want the products to be accessible so you can view products and add products to order details of orders. Answer the following questions regarding the implementation of a solution.

1. Can Microsoft Sync Services be a solution for this need?
2. With what types of client applications can you use Microsoft Sync Services 2.1?
3. Will this work with your existing SQL Server 2005 database servers?
4. What can you do if you want to synchronize between a Silverlight application and SQL Azure?

Suggested Practices

To help you successfully master the exam objectives presented in this chapter, complete the following tasks.

You should create at least one OCA that provides the user continuous access to data even when disconnected from the database server. The application should have at least one table. This can be accomplished by completing the practices at the end of Lesson 1 or by completing the following Practice 1.

- **Practice 1**   Create an application that requires the user to have access to data even when the database server is not available and synchronizes the data when the database server is available.
- **Practice 2**   Complete Practice 1 and then add another table to be locally cached.

Take a Practice Test

The practice tests on this book's companion CD offer many options. For example, you can test yourself on just the lesson review content, or you can test yourself on all the 70-516 certification exam content. You can set up the test so that it closely simulates the experience of taking a certification exam, or you can set it up in study mode so that you can look at the correct answers and explanations after you answer each question.

> **MORE INFO**   **PRACTICE TESTS**
>
> For details about all the practice test options available, see the "How to Use the Practice Tests" section in this book's introduction.

CHAPTER 9

Deploying Your Application

When you think of deploying an application, you probably don't think of ADO.NET deployment because it's an integral part of the .NET Framework. Theoretically, if the .NET Framework is installed, ADO.NET is installed. Although this is true, there are still some aspects of ADO.NET you might need to consider when deploying your application, and these are what this chapter focuses on.

Exam objectives in this chapter:

- Deploy ADO.NET components.

Lessons in this chapter:

Before You Begin

You are required to have some understanding of Microsoft C# or Visual Basic 2010. This chapter requires only the hardware and software listed at the beginning of this book. You should also have access to the Northwind database, which is one of the Microsoft "sandbox" databases. The Northwind database can be downloaded from the Microsoft website and is included on the companion disk.

 REAL WORLD

Glenn Johnson

When designing and developing your .NET applications, don't forget to plan your deployment as well. Deployment needs to be well thought out, and you must allocate enough time to ensure that you are able to acquire the necessary equipment and resources.

Lesson 1: Deploying Your Application

Deploying an application that uses ADO.NET is typically not a problem if you're using the core ADO.NET classes, but when you start using LINQ to Entities and Windows Communication Foundation (WCF) Data Services, there are factors you must consider. In this lesson, you learn some of the aspects of ADO.NET deployment.

> **After this lesson, you will be able to:**
> - Package and publish from Microsoft Visual Studio .NET.
> - Install .NET and external providers.
> - Deploy Entity Framework metadata.
> - Deploy WCF Data Services applications.
>
> **Estimated lesson time: 30 minutes**

Packaging and Publishing from Visual Studio .NET

You can use the Visual Studio 2010 packaging and deployment systems to package most types of applications and to add a deployment project to your solution and to configure it to deploy your application. Projects created using the Setup and Deployment Setup Wizard place the deployment files on your local computer for later distribution.

To access the Setup and Deployment Setup Wizard, right-click the *Solution* node in Solution Explorer and then choose Add | New Project. In the Add New Project dialog box, click the *Setup And Deployment Projects* node and then click Setup Wizard.

When running the Setup Wizard, you are prompted to choose a project type. Specify the type of deployment project to be created. You can create a setup project for a Windows or web application, create a merge module to be shared by other applications, or package files in a CAB file.

You are also prompted to choose the project outputs to be added to the deployment project. Select one or more outputs from the list of all outputs available in the solution. When an output is selected, the Description field displays a description of that output.

Another option is to choose files to include, and you can specify the additional files to be included for deployment. Click Add to browse for additional files or click Remove to remove files from the list.

Although you can use the Setup and Deployment Wizard to deploy most applications, the following sections cover items to which you need to pay particular attention.

Deploying WCF Data Services Applications

WCF Data Services provides flexibility in choosing the process that hosts the data service. You can use Visual Studio to deploy a data service to an Internet Information Server (IIS)–hosted web server or to Microsoft Windows Azure.

When WCF Data Services is developed as an ASP.NET project, it can be deployed to an IIS web server by using the standard ASP.NET deployment techniques. Depending on the type of ASP.NET project that hosts the WCF Data Services you are deploying, Visual Studio provides the deployment technologies for ASP.NET.

Deployment for ASP.NET Web Applications

To determine what should be included when the web application is deployed, use the Package/Publish Web tab of the project Properties window, as shown in Figure 9-1, to configure settings that determine what should be included when the web application is deployed.

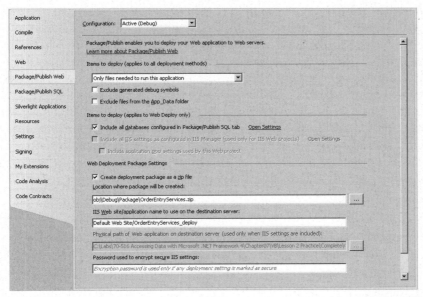

FIGURE 9-1 Use the Package/Publish Web tab to specify what to include in the deployment.

Although the default settings on this tab work for many typical scenarios, the following describes each of the options:

- **Items to Deploy (applies to all deployment methods)**   In this section, specify the settings that apply regardless of which deployment method you choose. (The deployment method is selected in the Publish Web dialog box.) The drop-down list in this section enables you to specify which files you want to copy to the destination server when the project is deployed. Options are Only Files Needed To Run This Application, All Files In This Project, and All Files In This Project Folder.

The Exclude Generated Debug Symbols check box specifies whether generated debug symbols, which are the .pdb files, should be deployed. Debug symbols files are typically generated when you build a web application. Typically, you would not deploy debug symbols to a production server because you would not be debugging it, but you might want to generate the symbols for debugging your test environment.

The Exclude Files From The App_Data Folder check box specifies whether the files in the App_Data folder should be deployed. In many scenarios, the App_Data folder contains test databases during the development cycle, so when moving a site to a production environment, the contents of this folder might not be appropriate for a production environment.

- **Items to Deploy (applies to web deploy only)**   If you select the Web Deploy deployment method in the Publish Web dialog box, these settings apply. They also apply when you create deployment packages. The Include All Databases Configured In Package/Publish SQL Tab check box specifies whether database scripts for the databases that are configured in the Package/Publish SQL tab should be generated. The Include All IIS Settings As Configured In IIS Manager check box, which is used only for IIS web projects, specifies that the IIS settings from the source computer, which is the open IIS web project, should be propagated to the destination computer. Be careful here, because inherited IIS settings are not propagated to the destination server. When the IIS web application you want to deploy is under the default website on the source server, and the default website has Windows authentication set to *true*, if you deploy this site to the default website on a server that has Windows authentication set to *false* for the default website, Windows authentication will be *false* for the deployed website even if you select the Include All IIS Settings As Configured In IIS Manager check box.

    The Include Application Pool Settings Used By This Web Project check box specifies whether the application pool settings from the source server, which is the current IIS web project, should be propagated to the destination server.

- **Web Deployment Package Settings**   This section contains settings that are appropriate for the web deployment package. The Create Deployment Package As A .Zip File check box specifies whether you should create a .zip file or use a folder structure. The Location Where The Package Will Be Created setting specifies where to create the web package when it is created by using Visual Studio.

The IIS Web Site/Application Name To Be Used On The Destination Server setting specifies the name of the website and application in IIS Manager on the destination server. The default value (Default Web Site/WebApplication_deploy) for the website will not work correctly if your operating system uses IIS 6 (Windows Server 2003) and is a language version other than English. In that case, you must enter a value for the website.

The Physical Path Of The Web On The Destination Server setting, which is used only when IIS settings are included for deployment, specifies where to copy the web package files on the destination server.

The Password Used To Encrypt Secure IIS Settings setting specifies an encryption key to use when the deployment process encrypts secure IIS settings. This password is stored in plaintext in the deployment package .cmd file. Don't include characters that have reserved meanings in command files, such as apostrophes (') or percent signs (%), in this string because deployment that uses the .cmd file will fail if the string contains reserved characters.

As a general rule, deploy only the files required to run the site. If the source code files are compiled into assemblies, copy only the assemblies to the destination server.

If the project to deploy is a local IIS web project and you have set up error-handling rules for its IIS application, you don't have to replicate those rules on the destination server. If the project to deploy is a file system web project, there are no IIS settings to replicate. An IIS web project is one in which you have selected Use Local IIS Web Server Or Use Custom Web Server on the Web tab of the project Properties window.

Specifying Database Deployment Options

If the web project you want to deploy uses a database, and if scripts must run during deployment to set up database structures or data in the destination environment, you must enter settings on the Package/Publish SQL tab of the project Properties window, as shown in Figure 9-2. This tab specifies settings for deploying a SQL Server database with a web application project. You can even specify custom scripts that run when the web package is deployed.

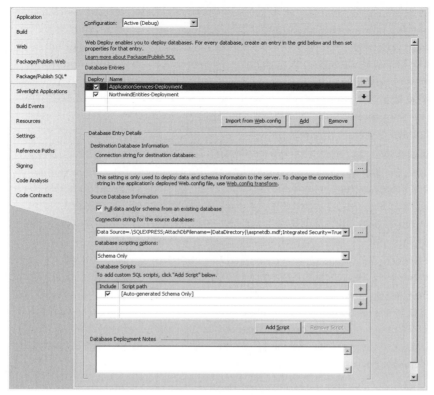

FIGURE 9-2 The Package/Publish SQL screen enables you to publish databases.

This screen is not autopopulated, so you must add the appropriate settings if you need to deploy a database with your web service application. The following list describes the elements of this Package/Publish SQL screen:

- **Database Entries**   This section specifies a list of the databases you need to deploy. The grid contains an entry for each database to deploy.

  The Deploy column of the database entries table specifies whether the selected database should be deployed. This is useful when you want to deploy a database only the first time you deploy a web project. In that case, after you deploy the application the first time, you can clear this check box, and the database is not included when you redeploy the same project.

  The Name column of the database Entries table specifies a name that identifies a database you want to deploy. If the database is represented by a connection string in the Web.config file, this value is typically the name of the connection string with a suffix such as -Deployment or -Web.config. The -Web.config suffix specifies that the connection string value in the Web.config file should be used for deployment.

The up and down arrow buttons enable you to specify the order in which databases are deployed.

You can also click Import From Web.Config to retrieve the connection strings in the Web.config file, which will enter the connections into the database entries grid with -Deployment appended to them. You can change the -Deployment suffix to -Web.config to specify that the connection string value in the Web.config file should be used for deployment.

The *Add* button enables you to add a row to the database entries grid, and the *Remove* button enables you to remove a row from the database entries grid.

- **Database Entry Details**   This section specifies settings for the database selected in the Database Entries section.

  The Destination Database Information section contains a text box in which you can specify the connection string for the destination database. Use this setting if you plan to deploy data and schema information to the destination database. The connection string you specify is used only during deployment; it won't be included in the Web.config file. There is an exception, however: If the *Name* value for this database ends with -Web.config and, if the part of the name that comes before the -Web.config suffix exists as a connection string name in the application Web.config file, the following rules apply:

  - If you leave the text box blank, the connection string value in the Web.config file is used for deployment.

  - If you specify a transform for the connection string, the transformed connection string is used for deployment.

  - If you enter a value in this field, the value you enter is used for deployment, and the destination Web.config file is updated to contain this value.

  - If you specify a database name that ends with -Web.config and you specify a transform for the same connection string, the transform is not used. The value that you enter in this field is used in the destination Web.config file.

  The Source Database Information section contains a check box you can select if you want to pull the schema or data from an existing database. When selected, you can input the connection string for the source database and the scripting options. The scripting options are Schema Only, Schema And Data, and Data Only.

  The Database Scripts section contains scripts that are auto-generated based on your scripting options section. In addition to the auto-generated scripts, you can also add custom scripts. By default, when the auto-generated scripts run during deployment, they run in a transaction, but custom scripts don't run in a transaction.

  The Include column of a database scripts table specifies whether the corresponding script should run when the web project is deployed. You can use this when you want to run some scripts only the first time a project is deployed.

The Script Path column of a database scripts table specifies the path of a script that is to run in the destination database. In the case of automatically generated scripts, a description of the script is displayed instead of the path for the script.

Use the up and down arrow buttons to specify the order in which the scripts run during deployment.

Use the *Add Script* button to add a custom script. Both SQL script and SqlCmd script are supported. Custom scripts are scanned for SqlCmd variables, and these are automatically converted to installation-time parameters in the IIS Web Deployment tool.

Use the *Remove Script* button to remove a script.

■ **Database Deployment Notes**   You can enter free-form notes here about deployment. Your notes are not used for any automated functions.

Specifying Web.config File Transformations

Settings are kept in the Web.config file because you want the ability to edit the settings without being forced to rebuild the application. In addition, your settings typically differ depending on the environment in which the application is running. For example, the database server to which you connect in the production environment is typically different from the database server you use in the development environment. Also, in the development environment, you might want to enable debugging; however, in the production environment, you don't want debugging enabled.

Visual Studio .NET 2010 enables you to create transform files that automate the process of changing Web.config settings during deployment. Use the transform files to specify the changes you want to make at deployment. Each transform file is associated with a build configuration. Visual Studio .NET 2010 creates a transform file for Debug and Release build configurations by default, and you can create custom build configurations.

To create a transform file for a custom build configuration that does not exist, create the build configuration first by using Configuration Manager, which you open by selecting it from the Build menu.

In Solution Explorer, the Web.config file has a plus sign or expansion indicator beside it, which indicates that transform files exist, and you can click the plus sign to see them. The transform file's name indicates the build configuration a transform is for. The transform file for the Debug build configuration is named Web.Debug.config, and the transform file for the Release build configuration is named Web.Release.config.

If you are missing any transform files for any of the build configurations, you can add all missing transform files by right-clicking the Web.config file in Solution Explorer and then clicking Add Config Transforms. All missing transform files will be added.

Open the transform file for the build configuration with which you want to work and edit the file, specifying the changes you want the deployed Web.config file to contain when you deploy by using that build configuration.

The default transform files include comments that show how to code some common transforms. The *configuration* element contains a namespace, aliased as *xdt*, which specifies that this is a transform file. The *xdt* alias has a *Match* locator attribute and the *SetAttributes* transform attribute. The *Match* locator attribute identifies the *add* element in the *connectionStrings* section as the element to change. The *SetAttributes* transform attribute specifies that this element's *connectionString* attribute should be changed to "server=Prod;database =northwind;integrated security=yes."

Sample of Transform File

```
<configuration xmlns:xdt="http://schemas.microsoft.com/XML-Document-Transform">
  <connectionStrings>
    <add name="MyNw"
      connectionString="server=Prod;database=northwind;integrated security=yes "
      xdt:Transform="SetAttributes" xdt:Locator="Match(name)"/>
  </connectionStrings>
</configuration>
```

When you deploy the web application by using the selected build configuration and either a deployment package or one-click publish, the Web.config file is transformed, using the appropriate transform file.

Creating the Deployment Package

You've entered the appropriate settings on the Package/Publish Web and Package /Publish SQL tabs. You've also modified the Web.config transform files to set the database connection string and other options. Now you create the package.

Before creating your deployment package, make sure the active build configuration is set to the one you want to deploy. Select the active build configuration in the Active solution configuration drop-down list in Configuration Manager.

On the Project menu, click Build Deployment Package to create the deployment package. Additional files are provided to help with package installation. These files are locations in the folder you specified on the Package/Publish Web tab. You can view the progress and log in the Output window.

Specifying that the package should be created as a .zip file creates a projectname .deploy-readme.txt file plus the following files in the output location:

- **projectname.deploy.cmd** This is a command-line batch file that invokes Web Deploy to install the web application on the destination server.

- **projectname.SetParameters.xml** This file contains parameters that are passed to Web Deploy on the destination server and contains the values specified during the packaging process, but these values can be changed as needed in order to install the web application on multiple servers by using different settings.

- **projectname.SourceManifest.xml** This file contains settings Visual Studio used to create the web package. This file is required only to create the package; it is not used when the package is installed on the destination server.

- **projectname.zip**   If you specified that the package should be created as a .zip file, this file is the actual deployment package.

If you specified that the package should be created as files in a folder structure, the package is in a folder named Archive, and the name Archive is used for the other files in place of the project name.

Deployment for ASP.NET Websites

When you've completed your ASP.NET website, the next step is to deploy the project to a web server so others can access your application. Deploying a website typically involves more than just copying the application's files from one server to another. Some of the other tasks you typically must perform are:

- Changing Web.config settings as required for the destination environment
- Propagating data and data structures used by the web application
- Configuring IIS settings such as application pool and authentication method on the destination computer
- Installing digital certificates for security such as Secure Sockets Layer (SSL) communications
- Setting values in the registry of the destination computer
- Installing application assemblies in the Global Assembly Cache (GAC) on the destination computer

With most ASP.NET websites, you can simply copy the files by using tools such as Windows Explorer, the Windows *xcopy* command, or an FTP tool. Visual Studio .NET 2010 also provides tools that help automate the process of copying files. In addition, some of these tools can pre-compile a website project as part of the deployment process.

Copy Website Tool

The Copy Website tool automates the process of copying and synchronizing files between the website project you currently have open and a destination site. The Copy Website tool enables you to open a folder on a destination site, which can be on a remote website computer or in a different folder on your computer. You can then copy files between the source website and the destination website. You can copy source code files, including .aspx files and class files, to the target site. Each web page is dynamically compiled when someone requests the page.

The protocols that are supported for copying include local IIS, Remote IIS, and FTP. If you use HTTP protocol, the destination server must have FrontPage Server Extensions installed.

When synchronizing, the files in the source and destination websites are examined, and the synchronization tool tells you which files are more current in each site and enables you to choose the files you want to copy and the direction in which you want to copy them.

The Copy Website tool automatically takes your site offline when copying by placing an App_offline.htm file in the root of the destination website. All requests to the website are redirected to this file, which displays a friendly message that tells clients the website is being updated. When all website files have been copied, the Copy Website tool deletes the App_offline.htm file from the target website.

Publish Website Tool

The Publish Website tool precompiles the content of the website and then copies the output to the destination you specify. By using File Transfer Protocol (FTP) or HTTP, you can publish to any folder you have permissions to access in the local or internal network file system. You can publish directly to a web server as part of the publishing process, or you can precompile to a local folder and then copy the files to a web server yourself.

Using FTP in Visual Studio .NET 2010

In addition to using the Copy Website or Publish Website tools, you can open a website directly on the web server by opening it as a Visual Studio FTP website project. You can work with files directly on the live site, but opening a site by using FTP can be slower than working with files offline. Also, when you update live files on a site, they are live immediately, before you have a chance to test them. This can cause your users to see errors and might lower the perceived reliability and value of your site.

None of the mentioned options copy the Machine.config file or the root Web.config file. Some of the settings in these files are inherited by your website. Therefore, the configuration of your site when it runs on the target web server might differ from its configuration on your computer. This might affect the behavior of the application.

Which Tool Do You Use?

Whether you select the Copy Website tool or the Publish Website tool depends on how you intend to use and maintain your site. Use the Copy Website tool when you make frequent changes to the site and you don't want to compile the site manually every time you make a change. You can also use the Copy Website tool if you want to use the tool's synchronization feature and you want to deploy the site to a remote web server by using FTP or HTTP. The Publish Website tool can copy only to the local computer or to another computer on the local network. Also, if you do not need to precompile the site, the Copy Website tool might be appropriate.

Use the Publish Website tool when you want to precompile the site to avoid putting source code or markup on the web server. This helps protect your intellectual property. You might also want to precompile to avoid the delay caused by dynamic compilation the first time a page is requested from the web server.

Silverlight Considerations

When you deploy a WCF data service to a hosted service provider, changes must be made for the service to work properly with a Silverlight application.

First, you must modify the Web.config of the Silverlight web application because hosted servers typically support many sites. You need to tell your application which site is hosting your application, or you will receive the following error:

"This collection already contains an address with scheme http. There can be at most one address per scheme in this collection."

Correcting this error requires you to add a *<baseAddressPrefixFilters>* element to the *<serviceHostingEnvironment>*, as follows, where the WCF data service is to be hosted on the Northwind website.

Sample Web.config

```
<system.serviceModel>
    <serviceHostingEnvironment aspNetCompatibilityEnabled="true" >
        <baseAddressPrefixFilters>
            <add prefix="http://www.northwind.com"/>
        </baseAddressPrefixFilters>
    </serviceHostingEnvironment>
</system.serviceModel>
```

If you are using the WCF data service with a Silverlight application, you must modify the service reference in the Silverlight code to point to the service with an absolute address, as shown in the following sample code.

Sample of Visual Basic Code

```
Private ctx As New NorthwindEntities(
  New Uri(http://www.northwind.com/NorthwindDataService.svc, UriKind.Absolute))
```

Sample of C# Code

```
private NorthwindEntities ctx = new NorthwindEntities(
  new Uri(http://www.northwind.com/NorthwindDataService.svc, UriKind.Absolute));
```

Another error you might get relates to defining a single authentication scheme. Your site must have only one authentication scheme. If you have defined more than one, you will get an error similar to the following:

"IIS specified authentication schemes 'Basic, Anonymous', but the binding only supports specification exactly one authentication scheme. Valid authentication schemes are Digest, Negotiate, NTLM, Basic, or Anonymous. Change the IIS settings so that only a single authentication scheme is used."

You can reduce your site's authentication to Anonymous, and everything will work as it should.

Deploying Entity Framework Metadata

In Chapter 6, "ADO.NET Entity Framework," you learned that the Entity Framework uses four files. The first file is the Entity Data Model (EDMX extension) the Entity Data Model designer uses. At compile time, the other three files are created from the EDMX file. The first of the three files is a Conceptual Schema Definition Language (CSDL extension) file that contains XML definition of the conceptual model. The second file is the Store Schema Definition Language (SSDL) file that contains XML definition of the storage model. The third file is the Mapping Specification Language (MSL extension) file that contains the mappings between the conceptual and storage models.

Many Entity Framework models will be defined within a stand-alone project that is part of a bigger solution, which preserves modularity and maintainability. The EDMX file contains the CSDL, SSDL, and MSL content as well as data for diagramming support. When you build your application, the EDMX file is processed by the Entity Model Code Generator tool, which extracts corresponding CSDL, SSDL, and MSL files.

The path to the metadata CSDL, SSDL, and MSL files is required as part of your Entity Framework client connection string. The following sample depicts an Entity Framework connection string.

Sample of Connection String

```
<add name="NorthwindEntities"
    connectionString="metadata=res://*/NorthwindModel.csdl|
      res://*/NorthwindModel.ssdl|
      res://*/NorthwindModel.msl;
    provider=System.Data.SqlClient;
    provider connection string=&quot;
    Data Source=.;Initial Catalog=Northwind;
    Integrated Security=True;
    MultipleActiveResultSets=True&quot;"
    providerName="System.Data.EntityClient" />
```

In this connection string, the metadata section references the CSDL, SSDL, and MSL files, which are resources embedded in the compiled assembly. The format for the resource is as follows:

```
Metadata=res://<assemblyFullName>/<resourceName>.
```

The *assemblyFullName* designation is the full name of an assembly with the embedded resource. The name includes the simple name, version name, supported culture, and public key, as follows:

```
ResourceLib, Version=1.0.0.0, Culture=neutral, PublicKeyToken=null
```

Resources can be embedded in any assembly that is accessible by the application. You can also specify a wildcard (*) for *assemblyFullName*, and the Entity Framework run time will search for resources in the following locations, in this order:

1. The calling assembly

2. The referenced assemblies

3. The assemblies in the bin directory of an application

If the files are not in one of these locations, an exception will be thrown.

If your resources are in the current assembly, there is no harm in using the wildcard (*), but when you use the wildcard (*) to locate a resource in a different assembly, the Entity Framework has to look through all the assemblies for resources with the correct name. You can improve performance by specifying the assembly name instead of using the wildcard.

Instead of embedding the metadata files in the compiled assembly as resources, another option is to specify that you want the metadata files to be created in the output directory. This is done by opening the EDMX file in the designer and clicking an empty area of the designer window to view the *Conceptual Entity Model* properties. The *Metadata Artifact Processing* property can be set to *Embed in Output Assembly* (default) or to *Copy to Output Directory*. If you change the setting to *Copy to Output Directory*, the metadata files are included in your output directory, and you can change your connection string to reference the files.

You might run into problems using the *Copy to Output Directory* approach. If you write a physical path, you are constantly changing the physical path for each type of deployment you're performing (QA, Production, and so on). If you write a relative path, it is resolved against the current directory, which can be fragile. If you're working with an ASP.NET website, the current directory is set up by the process hosting the site, and it's usually not what you expect. When you host your site in IIS, most likely it's the system directory, whereas when you are debugging the site inside Visual Studio ASP.NET Development Server, it's the physical location of the files. If you are working with an ASP.NET website, you can use the tilde (~) prefix to denote the path to the website as follows:

Sample of Connection String

```
<add name="NorthwindEntities"
    connectionString="metadata=~/models/NorthwindModel.csdl|
        ~/models/NorthwindModel.ssdl|
        ~/model/NorthwindModel.msl;
        provider=System.Data.SqlClient;
        provider connection string=&quot;
        Data Source=.;Initial Catalog=Northwind;
        Integrated Security=True;
        MultipleActiveResultSets=True&quot;"
        providerName="System.Data.EntityClient" />
```

EXAM TIP

For the exam, remember that the *Metadata Artifact Processing* property is set to *Copy to Output Directory* or to *Embed in the Output Assembly*.

Why would you want the metadata files configured to be external? One reason might be that you can edit them without recompiling your application, but, in most cases, you will be changing code when you tweak these files. Another reason might be that you want to share these files across multiple assemblies, but a better approach is to create an assembly that represents your data model and share the whole assembly to other assemblies. In general, it's best to keep the metadata files embedded in the assembly.

PRACTICE **Deploy a WCF Data Services Application**

In this practice, you deploy the WCF Data Services application you created in Chapter 7 to Internet Information Server (IIS). Currently, when you run the application, the WCF Data Service is hosted by Visual Studio .NET on a virtual web server. After deploying to IIS, you must point your client application to the new location on IIS to verify that the site is functional.

If you encounter a problem completing an exercise, the completed projects can be installed from the Code folder on the companion CD.

EXERCISE Opening the Existing WPF Project

In this exercise, you modify the solution you created in Chapter 7 by adding a deployment project for the WCF Data Services application.

1. In Visual Studio .NET 2010, choose File | Open | Project. The completed project from Chapter 7, Lesson 2, has been copied to the Begin folder of Chapter 9, Lesson 1. Open the solution.

   Be careful. This solution contains two projects: the OrderEntryProject, which is the WCF client GUI, and the OrderEntryServices project, which is the WCF Data Services project you will deploy.

2. From the Configuration Manager drop-down list, change your configuration from Debug to Release before you change any of the following settings.

3. Right-click the *OrderEntryServices* project node and click Properties (usually at the bottom).

4. Choose the Package/Publish Web tab. Select the Exclude The Debug Symbols check box.

5. Be sure the Include All Databases Configured In The Package/Publish SQL tab is selected.

6. Be sure the Create Deployment Package As A Zip File check box is selected.

7. In the text box for Location, where the package will be created, enter the following, based on whether you are using Visual Basic or C#: **C:\PackageVB \OrderEntryServices.zip** or **C:\PackageCS\OrderEntryServices.zip**.

   When you leave this field, Visual Studio .NET replaces the absolute path with a relative path.

8. In the text box for IIS Site/Application Name To Use On The Destination Server, enter the following, based on whether you are using Visual Basic or C#: **Default Web Site/OrderEntryServicesCS** or **Default Web Site/OrderEntryServicesVB**.

9. Click the Package/Publish SQL tab to open the database properties.

10. Click Import From Web.Config to import the existing connection strings into the database grid.

11. In the Database Entries grid, select ApplicationServices-Deployment and click Remove because this application does not use the aspnetdb database.

12. In the Database Entries grid, select NorthwindEntities-Deployment.

13. In the Connection String For Destination Database text box, enter a connection string to create the destination database. The destination database should not exist. Enter the following connection string, which references a database called NW that does not exist.

    Sample of Destination Database Connection String

    ```
    Server=.;Database=NW;Integrated Security=True
    ```

14. In the Database Scripting Options drop-down list, select Schema and Data.

15. Save and close the properties window.

16. Open the Web.Release.config file and add a transform to replace the connection string to reference the new database as follows:

    Sample of Web.Release.config

    ```
    <?xml version="1.0"?>
    <configuration
        xmlns:xdt="http://schemas.microsoft.com/XML-Document-Transform">
        <connectionStrings>
            <add name="NorthwindEntities" connectionString=
    "metadata=res://*/NorthwindModel.csdl|res://*/NorthwindModel.ssdl|
    res://*/NorthwindModel.msl;provider=System.Data.SqlClient;
    provider connection string=&quot;
    Data Source=.;Initial Catalog=NW;Integrated Security=True;
    MultipleActiveResultSets=True&quot;"
    providerName="System.Data.EntityClient"
            xdt:Transform="SetAttributes" xdt:Locator="Match(name)"/>
        </connectionStrings>
    </configuration>
    ```

17. Right-click the OrderEntryServices project and click Build.

18. Right-click the OrderEntryServices project and click Build Deployment Package.

19. Now, to deploy, open a command prompt window as an administrator.

20. Based on whether you are using Visual Basic or C#, change to the appropriate folder by typing either **cd C:\PackageVB** or **cd C:\PackageCS**.

21. Execute the following command, which starts the deployment.

    ```
    OrderEntryServices.deploy.cmd /Y
    ```

22. Watch the messages for errors and correct as necessary.

After the deployment has completed, you should be able to open SQL Management Studio to see the NW database. Also, if you open Internet Information Services (IIS) Manager, you should see the OrderEntryServicesVB or OrderEntryServicesCS web application under Default Website.

23. If you open Internet Explorer and enter the URL to the WCF Data Services application, you should see the metadata, as shown in Figure 9-3.

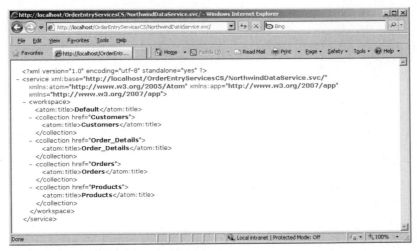

FIGURE 9-3 The WCF Data Services metadata screen.

24. If you add Customers to the end of the URL, you should see the Customers list.

25. In Visual Studio .NET, open the *OrderEntryProject* project node and then open the code-behind file for the MainWindow.xaml page. Replace the URI with the new URI for the deployed OrderEntryServices website as follows

Sample of Visual Basic Code

```
Private ctx As New NorthwindEntities(
    New Uri("http://localhost/OrderEntryServicesVB/NorthwindDataService.svc/",
    UriKind.Absolute))
```

Sample of C# Code

```
private NorthwindEntities ctx = new NorthwindEntities(
    new Uri("http://localhost/OrderEntryServicesCS/NorthwindDataService.svc/"));
```

26. Run the application, which now references the deployed WCF data service.

You should be able to see the customer list and the orders for each customer.

Lesson Summary

This lesson provided information about deploying your ADO.NET application.

- Visual Studio .NET 2010 packaging and deployment systems can package most types of applications.
- When deploying WCF Data Services applications, the deployment approach you take will differ, depending on whether you are working with a web application or a website.
- For WCF Data Services applications, use the project properties to configure the deployment. Most settings are on the Package/Publish Web tab and the Package/Publish SQL tab.
- For WCF Data Services applications, you can also specify Web.Config transformations to replace parts of your Web.config file when deploying.
- For WCF Data Services websites, you can use the Copy Website tool or the Publish Website tool.

Lesson Review

You can use the following questions to test your knowledge of the information in Lesson 1, "Deploying Your Application." The questions are also available on the companion CD if you prefer to review them in electronic form.

> **NOTE ANSWERS**
>
> Answers to these questions and explanations of why each answer choice is correct or incorrect are located in the "Answers" section at the end of the book.

1. You use Visual Studio .NET 2010 to create a WCF Data Services application that uses the ADO.NET Entity Framework to model entities. The WCF Data Services application uses the default model and mapping files that are deployed as application resources. After you deploy the application to the production server, you decide to update the conceptual model. What should you do?

   A. Copy the modified EDMX file to the production server.

   B. Recompile the application and redeploy the modified assembly file.

2. You use Visual Studio .NET 2010 to create a WCF Data Services application that uses the ADO.NET Entity Framework to model entities. You must ensure that the model and mapping files are not deployed as application resources. What should you do?

   A. Modify the connection string in the application's Web.config file to reference the absolute physical path to the EDMX file.

   B. Set the value of the EDMX file's *Metadata Artifact Processing* property to *Copy To Output Directory*.

   C. Modify the connection string in the application's Web.config file to reference the relative path to the model and mapping files.

Case Scenario

In the following case scenario, you will apply what you've learned about deploying your application as discussed in this chapter. You can find answers to these questions in the "Answers" section at the end of this book.

Case Scenario: Data Synchronization

You have written a WCF Data Services application and are ready to deploy it to your production server. You have some concerns about whether you can automate the creation of the database and its tables on the production server. In addition, you want to make sure that the deployed application's connection string will reference the new database. Answer the following questions regarding the implementation of a solution.

1. How can you copy the database schema and data to the production server?
2. How can you modify the connection string as part of the deployment?

Suggested Practices

To help you successfully master the exam objectives presented in this chapter, complete the following task.

Create at least one WCF Data Services application and deploy it by completing the practice at the end of Lesson 1 or by completing the following practice.

- **Practice**   Create a WCF Data Services application that references a SQL Server database and deploy it. This application should reference a SQL Server database by using the Entity Framework.

Take a Practice Test

The practice tests on this book's companion CD offer many options. For example, you can test yourself on just the lesson review content, or you can test yourself on all the 70-516 certification exam content. You can set up the test so that it closely simulates the experience of taking a certification exam, or you can set it up in study mode so that you can look at the correct answers and explanations after you answer each question.

> **MORE INFO**   **PRACTICE TESTS**
>
> For details about all the practice test options available, see the "How to Use the Practice Tests" section in this book's introduction.

Answers

Chapter 1: Lesson Review Answers

Lesson 1

1. **Correct Answer: D**

    A. Incorrect: *DataRow* holds only a single row of tabular data.

    B. Incorrect: The *DataView* object is only a filter index on a data table.

    C. Incorrect: *DataTable* can contain only a single table of rows and columns.

    D. Correct: *DataSet* can contain many *DataTable* and *DataRelation* objects.

2. **Correct Answers: B, C, D**

    A. Incorrect: The *MappingType* property specifies how to output the column when writing to an XML file.

    B. Correct: The *AutoIncrementSeed* property specifies the starting number when auto incrementing.

    C. Correct: The *AutoIncrementStep* property specifies the amount to increment after a number is allocated to a row.

    D. Correct: The *AutoIncrement* property must be set to true to enable automatic incrementing.

Lesson 2

1. **Correct Answer: C**

    A. Incorrect: The *Bindable* attribute is placed on a property to indicate that the property can be data bound.

    B. Incorrect: The *DataObject* object identifies an object as being a data object to GUI data wizards.

    C. Correct: The *Serializable* attribute is needed to enable the data table to be serialized.

    D. Incorrect: The *FileIOPermission* attribute sets file permissions on classes or methods that access the file system.

2. **Correct Answer: A**

    A. Correct: Because your Car is a reference type, changing just a property will not be detected. You must create a new Car with the correct properties and assign that car into the column.

B. Incorrect: The filter detects only a replacement of the *Car* object, not changes to the *Car* object.

3. **Correct Answer: B**

   A. Incorrect: *BatchUpdate* specifies how many rows will be sent to the database server in each batch of updates.

   B. Correct: Setting the *RemotingFormat* property to *SerializationFormat.Binary* will specify that you truly want a binary output file.

   C. Incorrect: The *DefaultView* property specifies a default filter or sort criteria on the table.

   D. Incorrect: The *Constraints* property sets the primary and foreign key constraints.

4. **Correct Answer: C**

   A. Incorrect: The *InferXmlSchema* method infers a schema from a file into the current data set.

   B. Incorrect: The *ReadXmlSchema* method reads a schema into a data set.

   C. Correct: The *WriteXmlSchema* method reads the schema of the current data set and writes the schema to a file.

   D. Incorrect: The *WriteXml* method writes the data to a file. Although this option also enables you to store the schema, it always stores the data.

Chapter 1: Case Scenarios Answers

Case Scenario 1: The Traveling Sales Team

1. Use the *DataSet* class to create a Customers data table and an Orders data table. These tables will be related to enable the user to select a customer and see the orders for that customer.

2. The *DataSet* class has a *WriteXml* method and a *ReadXml* method that can be used to write the *DataSet* object to an XML file, when the application is being closed, and to read the XML file when the application is starting.

3. You can use the provider classes to send changes back to the database server. *SqlConnection* can connect to the database server. The *SqlDataAdapter* class gets the changes in each data table, and *SqlDataAdapter* has *SqlCommand* properties for select, insert, update, and delete.

Case Scenario 2: Sorting and Filtering Data

1. Use the *DataView* class and set the *RowState* property to the desired setting.

2. Use the *DataView* class and set the *Sort* property to the desired criteria.

Chapter 2: Lesson Review Answers

Lesson 1

1. **Correct Answer: C**

   A. **Incorrect:** This is used only to connect to Oracle servers and is deprecated in .NET Framework 4.

   B. **Incorrect:** The *SqlClient* provider can be used on SQL Server 7 and later.

   C. **Correct:** You must use the *Oledb* or *Odbc* provider for SQL Server 6.5 and earlier.

2. **Correct Answer: A**

   A. **Correct:** You must open the connection before you can execute any command over the connection.

   B. **Incorrect:** The *BeginTransaction* method can start a transaction but is not required to execute a single command.

   C. **Incorrect:** *GetSchema* retrieves schema information from the database.

   D. **Incorrect:** The *Close* method can be called only after the command has been executed.

3. **Correct Answer: B**

   A. **Incorrect:** The *BeginTransaction* method does not force encryption.

   B. **Correct:** Adding *Encrypt=true* will force encryption.

   C. **Incorrect:** Encrypting the *CommandText* property will encrypt only the command sent to SQL Server, but it will not encrypt the results of the command.

   D. **Incorrect:** The *Close* method is called after the command has been executed to clean up the connection resources.

4. **Correct Answer: D**

   A. **Incorrect:** The ASPNET_REGSQL tool configures SQL Server.

   B. **Incorrect:** The CASPOL tool configures Code Access Security Policies for the .NET Framework.

   C. **Incorrect:** The INSTALLUTIL tool installs and uninstalls Windows services.

   D. **Correct:** The ASPNET_REGIIS tool configures ASP.NET to work with Internet Information Server (IIS) as well as to encrypt and decrypt sections of your configuration file.

Lesson 2

1. **Correct Answer: C**

   A. **Incorrect:** The *ExecuteScalar* method returns only the first column.

   B. **Incorrect:** The *Close* method is executed after the command has been executed to clean up the connection resources.

C. **Correct:** The *ExecuteReader* method will return a *DbDataReader* object that can be used.

D. **Incorrect:** The *ExecuteNonQuery* method returns only the quantity of rows affected by an insert, update, or delete.

2. **Correct Answer: A, B, D**

   A. **Correct:** *SqlDbType* must be set to *SqlDbType.Udt* for you to receive the output parameter.

   B. **Correct:** *UdtTypeName* must be set to *MyCompanyName*.

   C. **Incorrect:** The *ExecuteXmlReader* method is not needed to access the UDT.

   D. **Correct:** The assembly reference is required if you want to access the UDT as a typed object.

3. **Correct Answer: D**

   A. **Incorrect:** The *ExecuteScalar* method returns only the first column of the first row of a SQL select statement but is not appropriate for a SQL insert statement.

   B. **Incorrect:** The *ExecuteXmlReader* method is appropriate when you want to execute a SQL select command that ends with the FOR XML clause. This returns an XML stream that can be loaded into either an *XmlDocument* or an *XDocument* object.

   C. **Incorrect:** The *ExecuteReader* method is used when a SQL select command is executed and will return a *DbDataReader* object that can enumerate the results.

   D. **Correct:** Use the *ExecuteNonQuery* method when you aren't executing a select statement. This method returns the quantity of rows affected by an insert, update, or delete.

Lesson 3

1. **Correct Answer: B**

   A. **Incorrect:** *SqlCommand* executes the command but does not start a transaction.

   B. **Correct:** The *SqlConnection* class contains the *BeginTransaction* method that can be called to start a transaction.

   C. **Incorrect:** *SqlParameter* passes parameter data to a command.

   D. **Incorrect:** *SqlException* is thrown if SQL Server throws an exception during command execution.

2. **Correct Answer: A**

   A. **Correct:** The *TransactionScope* class starts an explicit promotable transaction.

   B. **Incorrect:** The *SqlConnection* class contains the *BeginTransaction* method that can be called to start a transaction, but it's not in the *System.Transaction* namespace, and it's not promotable.

   C. **Incorrect:** The *SqlTransaction* object is returned when you use the *SqlConnection* object and the *BeginTransaction* method to start a transaction.

3. **Correct Answer: B**
   A. Incorrect: A SOAP file contains a special XML format for use when communicating with Web services.
   B. Correct: The DataGram file contains the full state of the data set, so inserts, updates, and deletes are stored in the file.
   C. Incorrect: A WSDL file identifies the operations a web service exposes.
   D. Incorrect: An XML Schema file specifies the type of data an XML can hold.

Chapter 2: Case Scenarios Answers

Case Scenario 1: Clustered Servers and Connection Pooling

1. To solve the problem, specify a Load Balancing Timeout setting that essentially throws out some of the perfectly good connections on a regular basis so that new connections, when created, can go to a newly added database server.

2. The tradeoff is some loss of performance because perfectly good connections will occasionally be disposed, causing new connections to be created, but this is a minimum performance hit for the benefit of getting the new connections to go to the new server.

Case Scenario 2: The Daily Imports

1. The current application is probably sending one sale to headquarters and deleting that sale from the branch as a transaction, so data is never lost because the sale won't be deleted from the branch until it's been inserted at headquarters and the transaction is committed. The transaction is scoped to the movement of a single sale from the branch office to headquarters.

2. You could modify this application to change the scope of the transaction to encompass the whole import. This ensures that either all sales are imported or none are imported. You could modify the application by placing the import code inside a *TransactionScope* code block, which will start a distributed transaction that will not commit until all sales are imported.

Chapter 3: Lesson Review Answers

Lesson 1

1. **Correct Answers: A, B, D, E, F**
   A. Correct: Classes can have extension methods.
   B. Correct: Structures can have extension methods.

C. Incorrect: Modules (C# static classes) cannot have extension methods because you access an extension method through an instance. Modules (C# static classes) cannot be instantiated.

D. Correct: Enums can have extension methods.

E. Correct: Interfaces can have extension methods.

F. Correct: Delegates can have extension methods.

2. **Correct Answers: A, D**

A. Correct: *Skip* enables you to skip over elements you've already displayed.

B. Incorrect: Use *Except* when you have a sequence of elements and you want to find out which elements don't exist in a second sequence.

C. Incorrect: *SelectMany* projects a single output element into many output elements.

D. Correct: *Take* takes *x* elements from the sequence. Use this in conjunction with the *Skip* method to skip over elements you've already seen.

3. **Correct Answer: C**

A. Incorrect: You can't use *CType* (C# cast) because *IEnumerable* of *Car* is not *List Of Car*.

B. Incorrect: It can be done by using the *ToList()* query extension method.

C. Correct: The *ToList()* query extension method instantiates *List Of Car* and populates it with the *Car* objects.

D. Incorrect: You can't make the assignment because *IEnumerable* of *Car* is not *List Of Car*.

Lesson 2

1. **Correct Answer: D**

A. Incorrect: A cross join is a join of every element in the first sequence to every element in the second sequence to produce a Cartesian product, and no *equals* keyword is required.

B. Incorrect: A left outer join requires you to join all elements from the first (left side) sequence to the second sequence where there is equality, but all items in the first sequence are outputted even if there is no match to the second sequence.

C. Incorrect: A right outer join requires you to join all elements from the first sequence to the second (right) sequence where there is equality, but all items in the second sequence are outputted even if there is no match to the first sequence.

D. Correct: By default, *join/on/equals* performs an inner join.

2. **Correct Answer: A**

A. Correct: The *let* keyword declares a range variable in your LINQ query.

B. Incorrect: The *on* keyword is used with the *join* keyword to specify the join criteria.

C. Incorrect: The *into* keyword references the results of a *join*, *group by*, or *select* keyword.

D. Incorrect: The *by* keyword is used with the *group* keyword to specify the grouping criteria.

Chapter 3: Case Scenario Answers

Case Scenario 1: Fibonacci Sequence

1. Here is a solution using query extension methods that accepts the seed values and the quantity of iterations.

   Sample of Visual Basic Code

   ```
   Dim fib As Func(Of Long, Long, Long, IEnumerable(Of Long)) = Nothing
   fib = Function(prev2, prev1, count) If(count = 0, _
           Enumerable.Empty(Of Long)(), _
           Enumerable.Repeat(prev2 + prev1, 1) _
           .Concat(fib(prev1, prev2 + prev1, count - 1)))
   For Each item In fib(0, 1, 10)
       txtLog.WriteLine(item)
   Next
   ```

   Sample of C# Code

   ```
   Func<long, long, long, IEnumerable<long>> fib = null;
   fib = (prev2, prev1, count) => count == 0 ? Enumerable.Empty<long>()
           : Enumerable.Repeat(prev2 + prev1, 1)
               .Concat(fib(prev1, prev2 + prev1, count - 1));
   foreach (var item in fib(0, 1, 10)) Console.WriteLine(item);
   ```

   This code starts by declaring a variable, *fib*. The next statement assigns a *Func* delegate to *fib* and contains code to capture the previous two numbers, add them together, and decrement the iteration counter. The last part of this expression is a recursive callback into *fib*. This will recursively execute until the iteration count equals zero.

   Note that the variable *fib* could not be declared as part of the same statement that is making the recursive call. Notice how the query extension *Concat* method creates a sequence built by inserting one element-long sequence obtained by using *Enumerable.Repeat*.

2. Here are implementations of the Fibonacci sequence that produce elements until the maximum value of 100 is reached.

   Sample of Visual Basic Code

   ```
   Dim fib As Func(Of Long, Long, Long, IEnumerable(Of Long)) = Nothing
   fib = Function(prev2, prev1, max) If(prev2 + prev1 > max, _
           Enumerable.Empty(Of Long)(), _
           Enumerable.Repeat(prev2 + prev1, 1) _
           .Concat(fib(prev1, prev2 + prev1, max)))
   For Each item In fib(0, 1, 100)
       txtLog.WriteLine(item)
   Next
   ```

   Sample of C# Code

   ```
   Func<long, long, long, IEnumerable<long>> fib = null;
   fib = (prev2, prev1, max) => prev2 + prev1 > max ?
       Enumerable.Empty<long>() :
       Enumerable.Repeat(prev2 + prev1, 1)
   ```

```
            .Concat(fib(prev1, prev2 + prev1, max));
    foreach (var item in fib(0, 1, 100)) txtLog.WriteLine(item);
```

Case Scenario 2: Sorting and Filtering Data

1. Your answer will almost certainly vary, but the following is a LINQ query solution that works.

   Sample of Visual Basic Code

```
Dim result = From c In customers
             Join o In orders
             On c.CustomerID Equals o.CustomerID
             Join oi In orderItems
             On o.OrderID Equals oi.OrderID
             Let totalPrice = oi.Quantity * oi.Price * oi.Discount
             Group New With {totalPrice, oi.Quantity}
             By Key = c Into grouped = Group
             Let OrderAmount = grouped.Sum(Function(g) g.totalPrice)
             Where OrderAmount > 20000
             Order By OrderAmount Descending
             Select New With
             {
                 .CustomerID = Key.CustomerID,
                 .Name = Key.Name,
                 .OrderTotal = grouped.Sum(Function(g) g.totalPrice),
                 .MaxQuantity = grouped.Max(Function(g) g.Quantity)
             }
```

   Sample of C# Code

```
var result = from c in customers
             join o in orders
             on c.CustomerID equals o.CustomerID
             join oi in orderItems
             on o.OrderID equals oi.OrderID
             let totalPrice = oi.Quantity * oi.Price * oi.Discount
             group new { totalPrice, oi.Quantity }
             by c into grouped
             let OrderAmount = grouped.Sum(g => g.totalPrice)
             where OrderAmount > 20000
             orderby OrderAmount descending
             select new
             {
                 grouped.Key.CustomerID,
                 grouped.Key.Name,
                 OrderTotal = grouped.Sum(g => g.totalPrice),
                 MaxQuantity = grouped.Max(g=>g.Quantity)
             };
```

   The solution code starts by joining the customer to the orders and then to the order items. Next, the *let* keyword creates a loop variable, *totalPrice*, that is used several times throughout the rest of the query. Creating the *totalPrice* variable means you don't need to repeat the expression "oi.Quantity * oi.Price * oi.Discount" many times in the query.

Next is the *group* clause in which you specify the items to be aggregated. In this example, *totalPrice* and *oi.Quantity* are aggregated, so an anonymous type is created for these items. The *by* clause specifies the item to be grouped, and the result of the grouping is stored in the *grouped* variable.

The next *let* clause creates another loop variable, *OrderAmount*, which is the sum of the total price of the order items. The *OrderAmount* variable filters and sorts the sequence.

Finally, *select* creates an anonymous type that is populated with the *Customer* information and the aggregated order item information.

2. Here is a solution that uses query extension methods.

Sample of Visual Basic Code

```vb
Dim result = customers _
    .Join(orders, _
            Function(c) c.CustomerID, _
            Function(o) o.CustomerID, _
            Function(c, o) New With {.Customer = c, .Order = o}) _
    .Join(orderItems, _
            Function(temp) temp.Order.OrderID, _
            Function(oi) oi.OrderID, _
            Function(temp, oi) New With _
            { _
                .Customer = temp.Customer, _
                .Order = temp.Order, _
                .OrderItem = oi _
            }) _
    .Select(Function(temp) New With _
            { _
                .Customer = temp.Customer, _
                .Order = temp.Order, _
                .OrderItem = temp.OrderItem, _
                .totalPrice = temp.OrderItem.Quantity _
                            * temp.OrderItem.Price _
                            * temp.OrderItem.Discount _
            }) _
    .GroupBy(Function(temp) temp.Customer, Function(temp) New With _
            { _
                temp.totalPrice, _
                temp.OrderItem.Quantity _
            }) _
    .Select(Function(grouped) New With _
            { _
                .OrderAmount = grouped.Sum(Function(g) g.totalPrice), _
                .MaxQuantity = grouped.Max(Function(g) g.Quantity), _
                .Customer = grouped.Key _
                    }) _
                .Where(Function(temp) temp.OrderAmount > 20000) _
                .OrderByDescending(Function(temp) temp.OrderAmount) _
                .Select(Function(temp) New With _
                    { _
                temp.Customer.CustomerID, _
                temp.Customer.Name, _
                .OrderTotal = temp.OrderAmount, _
```

```
                        temp.MaxQuantity _
            })

    Sample of C# Code

    var result = customers
        .Join(orders,
                c => c.CustomerID,
                o => o.CustomerID,
                (c, o) => new { Customer = c, Order = o })
        .Join(orderItems,
                temp => temp.Order.OrderID,
                oi => oi.OrderID,
                (temp, oi) => new
                {
                    Customer = temp.Customer,
                    Order = temp.Order,
                    OrderItem = oi
                })
        .Select(temp => new
                {
                    Customer = temp.Customer,
                    Order = temp.Order,
                    OrderItem = temp.OrderItem,
                    totalPrice = temp.OrderItem.Quantity
                            * temp.OrderItem.Price
                            * temp.OrderItem.Discount
                })
        .GroupBy(temp => temp.Customer, temp => new
                {
                    temp.totalPrice, temp.OrderItem.Quantity
                })
        .Select(grouped => new
                {
                    OrderAmount = grouped.Sum(g => g.totalPrice),
                    MaxQuantity = grouped.Max(g => g.Quantity),
                    Customer = grouped.Key
                })
        .Where(temp => temp.OrderAmount > 20000)
        .OrderByDescending(temp => temp.OrderAmount)
        .Select(temp => new
                {
                    temp.Customer.CustomerID,
                    temp.Customer.Name,
                    OrderTotal = temp.OrderAmount,
                    temp.MaxQuantity
                });
```

This solution is a good exercise to see the difference between using the LINQ query and the query extension methods. In this lesson, you might have found that in some examples, the LINQ query was more verbose than the query extension methods; however, in this scenario, some query extension methods are much more verbose than the LINQ query. The *join* keyword is much more difficult to implement with the query extension method, and the

LINQ *let* operator translates to a call to the *Select* method. You can also mix and match LINQ operators with query extension methods.

Chapter 4: Lesson Review Answers

Lesson 1

1. **Correct Answer: C**

    A. **Incorrect:** The *DataSet* object is used with traditional ADO.NET.

    B. **Incorrect:** The *SqlDataAdapter* object is used with traditional ADO.NET.

    C. **Correct:** The *DataContext* object is the primary object for moving data when working with LINQ to SQL.

    D. **Incorrect:** *Entity* objects work with the *DataContext* object, but the *DataContext* object is the primary object used with LINQ to SQL.

2. **Correct Answer: B**

    A. **Incorrect:** *Skip* is an extension method that skips over elements you've already displayed.

    B. **Correct:** The *Delay Loaded* property indicates that you want lazy loading of the column.

    C. **Incorrect:** *Take* is an extension method that takes *x* elements from the sequence. It is used in conjunction with the *Skip* method to skip over elements that you've already displayed.

    D. **Incorrect:** The *Auto Generated Value* property indicates that this column automatically gets its value from the database.

Lesson 2

1. **Correct Answer: C**

    A. **Incorrect:** *Contains* checks for existence of an item, and *Intersect* gets items that two collections have in common.

    B. **Incorrect:** *GroupBy* performs group/aggregate operations, and *Last* returns the last item in the collection.

    C. **Correct:** *Skip* skips over previously used items, and *Take* retrieves another page of items.

    D. **Incorrect:** *First* retrieves the first item in the collection, and *Last* retrieves the last item in the collection.

2. **Correct Answer: B**

    A. **Incorrect:** The *let* keyword declares a range variable in your LINQ query.

    B. **Correct:** The *equals* keyword is used with the *join* keyword to specify the join criteria.

    C. **Incorrect:** The *into* keyword references the results of a *join*, *group by*, or *select* clause.

    D. **Incorrect:** The *by* keyword is used with the *group* keyword to specify the grouping criteria.

Lesson 3

1. **Correct Answer: B**

    A. **Incorrect:** The changes are thrown out because the object is delivered from the cache.

    B. **Correct:** The changes are thrown out because the object is delivered from the cache.

    C. **Incorrect:** Although there is a difference in data, no exception is thrown.

    D. **Incorrect:** Although you could create a new *DataContext* object to retrieve the changes, no exception is thrown to indicate that you need a new *DataContext* object.

2. **Correct Answer: D**

    A. **Incorrect:** You will use the *DataContext* object, but it doesn't have an *Update* method.

    B. **Incorrect:** You must call the *SubmitChanges* method on the *DataContext* object to send the changes back to the database.

    C. **Incorrect:** If you call the *Dispose* method on the *DataContext* object, you will lose all your changes.

    D. **Correct:** Calling the *SubmitChanges* method on the *DataContext* object will send inserts, updates, and deletes back to the database.

Chapter 4: Case Scenario Answers

Case Scenario: Object-Oriented Data Access

1. The use of the traditional ADO.NET classes, such as *DataSet* and *SqlDataAdapter*, fulfills the object-oriented requirement because *DataSet* is a class that is instantiated to create a *DataSet* object, and the same is true for the other ADO.NET classes. The LINQ to SQL classes also satisfy the object-oriented requirement because these classes are instantiated to produce objects.

2. The big difference between these techniques is that the traditional ADO.NET classes are data-centric objects, whereas the LINQ to SQL classes are domain-centric. Data-centric objects are created for the sole purpose of providing data access, and these objects have names that reflect the object's usage. Domain-centric means that the classes have names that relate to your domain environment, such as *Customer* and *Vehicle*, and although these classes provide data access, they could also contain business logic.

Chapter 5 Lesson Review Answers

Lesson 1

1. **Correct Answer: A**

   A. **Correct:** The *XmlDocument* class is better suited for single-purpose queries because it supports random access to the XML nodes through XPath queries.

   B. **Incorrect:** The *XmlReader* class is faster but much more difficult to use when running single-purpose queries, and no query language can be used.

2. **Correct Answer: B**

   A. **Incorrect:** The *XmlDocument* class is better suited for single-purpose queries and is much slower than *XmlReader*.

   B. **Correct:** The *XmlReader* class is faster and, when performance is paramount and the query is somewhat fixed, the better choice.

3. **Correct Answer: B**

   A. **Incorrect:** The *XmlDocument* class needs to load the complete XML file into memory before it can be used. Your computer might not have 20GB of memory available for this operation, and even if your computer had enough memory, this operation would be painfully slow.

   B. **Correct:** The *XmlReader* class is stream-based; you can open the file and read until you retrieve the information you need and then close the file. Thus, you didn't need to allocate memory to hold the entire XML file.

Lesson 2

1. **Correct Answer: C**

   A. **Incorrect:** *XmlDocument* does not support LINQ to XML, although it does support XPath queries.

   B. **Incorrect:** *XmlReader* is fastest, but it does not support LINQ to XML, and there is no query language to use.

   C. **Correct:** The *XDocument* class supports LINQ to XML.

2. **Correct Answer: D**

   A. **Incorrect:** The Load method accepts either a string representing the file name from which to load or a *TextReader* class. Although you can load *StringReader* with your string and then pass the stream into the Load method, you can't call *Load* directly with the string.

   B. **Incorrect:** The constructor accepts an XML tree or, if you're using Visual Basic, you can pass a string constant (not a variable) to the constructor.

C. Incorrect: The *WriteTo* method writes the *XDocument* contents to a file.

D. Correct: The *Parse* method converts a string to an *XDocument* class.

Lesson 3

1. Correct Answer: B

    A. Incorrect: C# does not support XML literals.

    B. Correct: Visual Basic supports XML literals.

    C. Incorrect: XML literals are supported by Visual Basic only.

Chapter 5: Case Scenario Answers

Case Scenario: XML Web Service

1. To create the XML web service request, you can use the *XmlSerializer* class to convert your business object to XML. The problem is that the XML created won't match the XML required for the web service request. To convert the XML to the format the XML web service requires, you can use LINQ to XML to perform a transformation.

2. When the response is received from the web service, you can use LINQ to XML to parse and transform the XML into business objects.

Chapter 6: Lesson Review Answers

Lesson 1

1. Correct Answer: B

    A. Incorrect: If you implement the Code First model, you must create the conceptual entities manually.

    B. Correct: Because the database already exists, you can use the Database First model to generate the conceptual entities.

2. Correct Answer: C

    A. Incorrect: LINQ to SQL supports only one-to-one mapping of entities to tables.

    B. Incorrect: LINQ to XML supports only XML, not database tables.

    C. Correct: The Entity Framework supports one-to-many mapping of entities to tables.

3. Correct Answer: C

    A. Incorrect: If you add the method to a new T4 template, it will generate entity classes, but every class will have your new method.

B. Incorrect: The EntityObject Generator provides a T4 text template, and adding the new method to the T4 template will cause the method to be added to all classes.

C. Correct: It's simple to add a new partial class to your project and add the new method to this class.

D. Incorrect: If you modify the entity class that was created by the Entity Framework designer, the next time you generate the entity classes, the Entity Framework designer will overwrite your added method.

4. **Correct Answer: C**

A. Incorrect: This won't provide the functionality you need and would require you to modify the existing classes, which might not be possible.

B. Incorrect: The EDMX-generated entity classes already inherit from *EntityObject*.

C. Correct: You can configure your EMDX to provide a POCO solution, which enables you to use your existing classes.

5. **Correct Answer: A**

A. Correct: In the Entity Framework designer, you can right-click the designer surface and choose Generate Database From Model.

B. Incorrect: You can use the Code First model to create the conceptual model first and then generate the database from it.

6. **Correct Answer: A**

A. Correct: The model-defined functions execute server-side, and you don't need to create any database objects explicitly to implement them.

B. Incorrect: This proposed solution requires you to add the *AsEnumerable* extension method to your LINQ to Entities query, and the method will execute client-side anyway.

C. Incorrect: This is a database object that you need permission to create explicitly to use it.

7. **Correct Answer: A**

A. Correct: *ObjectContext* is the primary object you use when querying and modifying data.

B. Incorrect: The *DataContext* object is used with LINQ to SQL classes.

C. Incorrect: *ObjectStateEntry* holds the state of the instantiated entities but is not the primary object for querying and modifying data.

D. Incorrect: Entity classes that are generated inherit from the *EntityObject* class, but that isn't the primary object for querying and modifying data.

8. **Correct Answer: B**

A. Incorrect: Lazy loading requires you to set the *Lazy Loading Enabled* property on the EDMX file to *true*, and no special calls are required in your query.

B. Correct: Eager loading requires you to use the *Include* extension method to retrieve child rows when you query for the parent rows.

C. **Incorrect:** Explicit loading requires you to use the *Load* method to load child rows explicitly.

Lesson 2

1. **Correct Answer: B**

   A. **Incorrect:** The *SubmitChanges* method is used with the LINQ to SQL *DataContext* object.

   B. **Correct:** The *SaveChanges* method is on the Entity Framework *ObjectContext* object.

2. **Correct Answer: C**

   A. **Incorrect:** The *CREATEREF* function creates a reference to an entity.

   B. **Incorrect:** The *MULTISET* function creates a collection.

   C. **Correct:** The *ROW* function constructs a row.

3. **Correct Answer: A**

   A. **Correct:** If you don't load all dependent objects, an *UpdateException* will be thrown.

   B. **Incorrect:** The Entity Framework cascading delete is a client-side function.

   C. **Incorrect:** Because the Entity Framework cascading delete is a client-side function, you don't need to set up cascading delete at the server.

4. **Correct Answer: C**

   A. **Incorrect:** Saving changes within a single *ObjectContext* object is done within a transaction context, but multiple *ObjectContext* objects require a TransactionScope object.

   B. **Incorrect:** This looks good, but if saving to SQL Server fails, you can roll back the main-frame changes.

   C. **Correct:** The *TransactionScope* implementation provides the best pattern for saving multiple *ObjectContext* objects within a single transaction.

   D. **Incorrect:** This might notify you of success but does not provide any means for rolling back.

Chapter 6: Case Scenario Answers

Case Scenario 1: Choosing an Object-Relational Mapper

1. Possibly; because the application uses inheritance, this could force you to use LINQ to Entities. Also, you might want to use LINQ to Entities to communicate to the Oracle database, but you could still use traditional ADO.NET.

2. LINQ to Entities.

3. You can use LINQ to Entities for the SQL Server data access and for the Oracle data access. The number of tables should not affect your decision. LINQ to Entities also supports inheritance.

Case Scenario 2: Using the Entity Framework

1. The Entity Framework enables you to generate the Entity Data Model from the existing database schema.

2. The Entity Framework enables you to represent an entity across multiple tables. For example, the *Employee* entity name data can be stored in one table, although other information, such as date of birth, might be in a different table. You're not forced into a one entity per table mapping.

3. The Entity Framework supports inheritance mapping scenarios, such as table per type (TPT), that enable you to have a base table that maps to a base class and an additional table per type.

Chapter 7: Lesson Review Answers

1. **Correct Answer: C**
   - **A.** Incorrect: *$skip* is used when paging data to skip over entities.
   - **B.** Incorrect: *$value* simply returns the raw value of a property.
   - **C.** Correct: *$expand* can eager load several tables when executing a query.
   - **D.** Incorrect: *$filter* limits the entities returned from a query.

2. **Correct Answer: A**
   - **A.** Correct: The *ReadSingle* permission allows queries that return only a single row to be executed. Typically, this means that you pass the primary key value to retrieve a single entity.
   - **B.** Incorrect: *ReadMultiple* allows only queries that return many entities.
   - **C.** Incorrect: *AllRead* allows queries that return a single entity but also allows queries that return multiple entities.

3. **Correct Answer: D**
   - **A.** Incorrect: Using *$expand* returns the *Order* entities but also returns the *Customer* entity.
   - **B.** Incorrect: This query returns the *Order* entities but also returns the *Customer* entity.
   - **C.** Incorrect: This might look correct, but you must specify the key of the *Customer* entity by using parentheses, not by using *$filter*.
   - **D.** Correct: This query returns only the *Order* entities for the *Customer* entity whose CustomerID is 'BONAP.'

Lesson 2

1. **Correct Answer: C**
   - **A.** Incorrect: If you modify the *Contacts* entity set in the EDMX file, you potentially break the services that are in the same project.

B. Incorrect: You can add the stored procedure and function import that provides filtering, but that will not filter out employees from requests that are directed to the *Contacts* entity set.

C. Correct: *QueryInterceptorAttribute* can provide filtering when a request is made for the *Contacts* entity set.

D. Incorrect: A lazy loader is not something you can control to the point of providing a custom filter for *Contacts*.

2. Correct Answers: B and D

A. Incorrect: Other types of web services use the SOAP protocol, but it is not available with WCF Data Services.

B. Correct: JSON can be specified in the request header of your AJAX call.

C. Incorrect: WSDL is a format for defining a web service's schema contract and is not a payload format.

D. Correct: AtomPub is the default payload format.

Chapter 7: Case Scenario Answers

Case Scenario: Exposing Data

1. Yes, WCF Data Services can provide access to your data in a simple manner to many client types.

2. The ability to use REST semantics makes your service callable by any application that can create a URI and call it.

3. The ability to return AtomPub or JSON payloads makes WCF Data Services available to any client that can parse XML or JSON.

4. If you needed support for WS* features, WCF Data Services would not be a good choice, but because this is data you are trying to expose to a large audience, WS* features are probably not a constraint.

Chapter 8: Lesson Review Answers

Lesson 1

1. Correct Answer: C

A. Incorrect: If you're working with the LINQ to SQL classes, you can set the *Log* property of a *DataContext* object to a *TextWriter* object, but *ObjectContext* doesn't have a *Log* property.

B. **Incorrect:** The *Connection* property must be set to a database connection object to gain access to the database server.

C. **Correct:** To view the SQL statements that are sent to the database with the Entity Framework, use the *ToTraceString* method on the *QueryObject*.

2. **Correct Answer: B**

A. **Incorrect:** You can view a numeric value only with the *PerformanceCounter* object.

B. **Correct:** A *PerformanceCounter* can only provide a numeric value, not a SQL statement.

Lesson 2

1. **Correct Answer: B**

A. **Incorrect:** A *using* block automatically disposes resources even if an exception occurs, but it does not capture exceptions.

B. **Correct:** The *try/catch* block captures exceptions.

C. **Incorrect:** The *while* statement is used for looping operations.

D. **Incorrect:** You can capture exceptions by using the *try/catch* block.

Lesson 3

1. **Correct Answers: A and D**

A. **Correct:** *DpapiProtectedConfigurationProvider* offers encryption by using the built-in machine key that isn't exportable.

B. **Incorrect:** *RNGCryptoServiceProvider* generates random numbers.

C. **Incorrect:** *SHA256Managed* generates hash values.

D. **Correct:** *RsaProtectedConfigurationProvider* offers encryption by using an exportable pair of keys.

E. **Incorrect:** *RijndaelManaged* provides symmetric encryption but cannot encrypt .config files.

2. **Correct Answer: D**

A. **Incorrect:** *RNGCryptoServiceProvider* is an asymmetric algorithm.

B. **Incorrect:** *RNGCryptoServiceProvider* generates random numbers.

C. **Incorrect:** *SHA256Managed* generates hash values.

D. **Correct:** *RijndaelManaged* is a symmetric algorithm.

Lesson 4

1. **Correct Answer: A**

A. **Correct:** *SyncDirection.Bidirectional* sends changes to the server and receives changes from the server.

B. Incorrect: *SyncDirection.UploadOnly* only sends changes to the server.

C. Incorrect: *SyncDirection.Snapshot* receives a complete copy of the server data and does not send changes to the server.

D. Incorrect: *SyncDirection.DownloadOnly* only receives changes and does not send changes to the server.

Chapter 8: Case Scenario Answers

Case Scenario: Data Synchronization

1. Absolutely, Microsoft Sync Services can provide a local cache by using SQL Server Compact.

2. You can use Microsoft Sync Services on any client application that can host the sync agent. Examples are Console applications, Windows Forms applications, and WPF applications. Although this could also include web applications, remember that the client is the web service, not the browser.

3. Yes, using custom synchronization.

4. For synchronization between Silverlight clients and SQL Azure, you can use Microsoft Sync Services 4.0 or later.

Chapter 9: Lesson Review Answers

Lesson 1

1. **Correct Answer: B**

    A. Incorrect: The application is configured to look for the embedded resource.

    B. Correct: To embed the modified conceptual model into the assembly as a resource, the application must be recompiled after you update the conceptual model.

2. **Correct Answer: B**

    A. Incorrect: You can set the connection string to reference the EDMX file by physical path, but you must set the *Metadata Artifact Processing* property to *Copy To Output Directory* to ensure that the model and mapping files are not deployed as application resources.

    B. Correct: You must set the *Metadata Artifact Processing* property to *Copy To Output Directory* to ensure that the model and mapping files are not deployed as application resources.

    C. Incorrect: You would most likely want to modify the connection string to reference the model and mapping files with a relative path, but this would be performed after you've set the *Metadata Artifact Processing* property to *Copy To Output Directory* to ensure that the model and mapping files are not deployed as application resources.

Chapter 9: Case Scenario Answers

Case Scenario: Data Synchronization

1. You can use the Package/Publish SQL tab in the project properties window to automate the deployment of the database and its tables, including data.

2. You can use Web.config transforms to automate changing a connection string to the destination server's connection string setting.

Index

Symbols and Numbers

A

B

C

T

Y

Z

About the Author

GLENN JOHNSON is a professional trainer, consultant, and developer whose experience spans over 20 years. As a consultant and developer, he has worked on many large projects, most of them in the insurance industry. Glenn's strengths are with Microsoft products, such as ASP.NET, MVC, Silverlight, WPF, WCF, and Microsoft SQL Server, using C#, Visual Basic, and T-SQL. This is yet one more of many .NET books that Glenn has authored; he also develops courseware and teaches classes in many countries on Microsoft ASP.NET, Visual Basic 2010, C#, and the .NET Framework.

Glenn holds the following Microsoft Certifications: MCT, MCPD, MCTS, MCAD, MCSD, MCDBA, MCP + Site Building, MCSE + Internet, MCP + Internet, and MCSE. You can find Glenn's website at http://GJTT.com.

For Visual Basic Developers

Microsoft® Visual Basic® 2010 Step by Step

Michael Halvorson

ISBN 9780735626690

Teach yourself the essential tools and techniques for Visual Basic 2010—one step at a time. No matter what your skill level, you'll find the practical guidance and examples you need to start building applications for Windows and the web.

Coding Faster: Getting More Productive with Microsoft Visual Studio

Zain Naboulsi and Sara Ford

ISBN 9780735649927

Work smarter and increase your productivity with expert tips and tricks using Visual Studio. You'll find practical advice and shortcuts for the code editor, visual designers, search capabilities, debugger, and other features of the IDE.

Inside the Microsoft Build Engine: Using MSBuild and Team Foundation Build, Second Edition

Sayed Ibrahim Hashimi, William Bartholomew

ISBN 9780735645240

Your practical guide to using, customizing, and extending the build engine in Visual Studio 2010.

Parallel Programming with Microsoft Visual Studio 2010

Donis Marshall

ISBN 9780735640603

The roadmap for developers wanting to maximize their applications for multicore architecture using Visual Studio 2010.

Microsoft Visual Basic 2010 Developer's Handbook

Sarika Calla Purohit and Klaus Löffelmann

ISBN 9780735627055

Learn practical, scenario-based approaches for using Visual Basic 2010 for everything from core Window® and web development to building advanced multithreaded applications.

microsoft.com/mspress